Looking in Classrooms

SEVENTH EDITION

Thomas L. Good
University of Arizona

Jere E. Brophy
Michigan State University

 LONGMAN

An imprint of Addison Wesley Longman, Inc.

New York • Reading, Massachusetts • Menlo Park, California • Harlow, England
Don Mills, Ontario • Sydney • Mexico City • Madrid • Amsterdam

Editor-in-Chief: Priscilla McGeehon
Editorial Assistant: Daniel Damkoehler
Supplements Editor: Donna Campion
Project Coordination and Text Design: Ruttle, Shaw & Wetherill, Inc.
Cover Designer: Mary McDonnell
Electronic Production Manager: Christine Pearson
Manufacturing Manager: Helene G. Landers
Electronic Page Makeup: Ruttle, Shaw & Wetherill, Inc.
Printer and Binder: R.R. Donnelley & Sons Company
Cover Printer: The Lehigh Press, Inc.

Library of Congress Cataloging-in-Publication Data
Good, Thomas L., 1943–
    Looking in classrooms   /   Thomas L Good, Jere E. Brophy. — 7th ed.
      p.   cm.
    Includes bibliographical references and indexes.
    ISBN 0–673–99739–1
    1. Teaching.   2. Classroom management.   3. Observation
(Educational method)   I. Brophy, Jere E.   II. Title.
LB1025.3.G66   1997   96-3786
371.1'02—dc20   CIP

0–673–99739–1

6 7 8 9 10—DOC—99 98

Brief Contents

Detailed Contents

Preface

As with previous editions, we have designed the seventh edition of *Looking in Classrooms* to help teachers, principals, and supervisors observe and describe classroom behavior. We also provide strategies teachers can use to enhance the interest, learning, and social development of their students.

One difficulty of teaching is being aware of all of the complex behavior that occurs in classrooms. Teaching in modern classrooms involves information processing, decision making, and the application of knowledge about students and pedagogy in classrooms. Hence, we describe a variety of techniques teachers can use to increase their ability to think and make decisions in the classroom. We believe that when teachers become cognizant of what happens in the classroom and can monitor their own thinking and decision making, they can more easily achieve their instructional and personal goals.

We also present important knowledge, concepts, and research findings that teachers can use to provide instruction. In particular, recent research provides compelling evidence that teachers' decisions about curriculum and instruction significantly affect students' attitudes and achievement. This text focuses on both quantitative and qualitative methods (ways students can observe and reflect on classrooms). We review both types of classroom research, thus providing a useful integration of multiple approaches of classroom learning.

We have updated the text to provide the most comprehensive and current knowledge about teaching. For example, this revised edition describes findings of policy commissions that have urged greater recognition of the student role in learning; emphasizes maintaining the best of traditional classrooms; and at the same time discusses exciting and workable new directions in classroom instruction that can be implemented in modern schools.

In this edition we present up-to-date reviews of research on teacher expectations, classroom organization and management, student motivation, classroom instruction, and several other topics related to successful teaching in contemporary classrooms.

We provide detailed advice about teaching in heterogenous classrooms, including strategies for dealing with student diversity. For example, cooperative learning is considered in detail. Several models are presented and critiqued so that common potential problems with this strategy and means of overcoming them are detailed.

The book contains a chapter integrating social constructivist instructional issues. This chapter stresses that teaching is more than just transmission of knowledge, that it often involves construction of new understandings, and accordingly, the chapter emphasizes the role of socially situated knowledge (i.e., how knowledge is constructed in a social setting) and discusses strategies for transferring responsibility for management of learning from the teacher to students. Also included are an authoritative analysis of traditional instructional methods and helpful strategies for organizing models of effective teaching as traditionally defined (lectures, classroom discussion of recitation, certain forms of inquiry).

We stress the teacher's role in evaluating teaching and argue that staff development programs should recognize the growing authority and competence of classroom teachers in planning their own programs of self-development. The book includes detailed discussions of professional collaboration and ways that schools can support teachers' professional growth.

In Chapters 1 and 2 we emphasize that it is difficult for teachers, observers, or supervisors to monitor accurately and understand what takes place in classrooms because life there is so complex and proceeds at such a rapid pace. To make valid suggestions about how to improve classroom behavior, however, strategies that allow effective classroom observation are necessary. Chapters 1 and 2 discuss general principles for observation and describe quantitative and qualitative procedures that teachers and supervisors can use to record classroom observations that provide a basis for reflective thinking and classroom decision making.

In Chapters 3 through 10 we suggest important dimensions and concepts to consider in analyzing classroom instruction. Chapter 3 provides extensive coverage of the relationship between teacher expectations and student performance. Chapter 4 describes the methods of preventing classroom problems, and Chapter 5 discusses strategies for dealing effectively with misbehavior. Chapter 6 deals with motivation; it suggests how teachers can make assignments more attractive to students. This chapter also introduces project-based learning and discusses school supports necessary for enhancing classroom motivational strategies.

In Chapter 7 we discuss ways in which students can actively engage in dialogue and learning with other students. Here we discuss issues such as peer tutoring, small group learning, and project-based learning. In Chapter 8 we discuss ways in which teachers can deal effectively with issues of teaching in heterogenous classrooms, and the chapter discusses various organizational strategies that are more effective than tracking and other strategies that have been used historically for dealing with diversity. The chapter provides a philosophical argument for an educational system of inclusion rather than exclusion.

Chapter 9 provides an authoritative analysis of traditional instructional methods, and Chapter 10 presents a detailed analysis of teaching for understanding, designing authentic classroom learning activities, and considering the role of socially situated knowledge.

We argue in Chapter 11 that good teachers need continuing opportunities to learn and grow. Teachers can further their professional development through personal reflection and cooperation with their peers to obtain needed feedback. There is growing evidence that school effectiveness can be enhanced when teachers are willing to share knowledge and help one another.

We believe that much of teaching is an art. Successful teachers must be able to observe, comprehend, and respond to the rapid pace of complex classroom behavior. Ultimately, teachers must also develop and continue to refine their own teaching styles. We offer a method of observing, describing, reflecting, and understanding classroom behavior—an important first step in developing a teaching style that is both effective and personally satisfying.

We wish to thank DeWayne Mason at the University of California-Riverside, for his help in preparing the comprehensive and innovative Instructor's Manual that accompanies the text. Further, we wish to thank the following reviewers of the seventh edition: Kay Alderman, University of Akron; Manon D. Charbonneau, College of Santa Fe; Donna J. Merkley, Iowa State University; Mark P. Mostert, Moorhead State University; and Barbara Reider, College of Santa Fe; for helpful suggestions, as well as the reviewers of the sixth edition: Ronald D. Anderson, University of Colorado; Michael Andrew, University of New Hampshire; Walter Doyle, University of Arizona; Carol Goodenow, Tufts University; Laurie Hart, University of Georgia; Leslie McClellan, University of South Florida; Ludwig Mossberg, University of Delaware; and Allen Warner, University of Houston.

Thomas L. Good
Jere E. Brophy

CHAPTER

1

Classroom Life

This book has four major purposes: The first is to help teachers and prospective teachers develop ways of describing what goes on in classrooms. The second is to make teachers aware of the influences of their own previous teaching and life experiences and of how historical and contemporary factors in their lives influence their classroom decisions (Delpit, 1995; Goodson, 1992). The third is to suggest ways in which teachers can have a positive influence on the interests, learning, and social development of their students. The fourth is to help teachers understand current educational research knowledge (e.g., Alkin, 1992; Biddle, Good, & Goodson, 1996; Jackson, 1992; Wittrock, 1986), to use related theories and concepts appropriately, and to combine knowledge of research with knowledge of their own classrooms in ways that lead to new understanding and improved teaching. We want teachers to become reflective about classroom practice and capable of providing instructional leadership (Smylie, 1995).

Teachers are sometimes unaware of what they do or why they engage in a classroom practice, and this lack of perception can result in unproductive behavior. Our intent is to show that teachers need to learn how to observe and describe classroom behavior in order to improve their teaching. If teachers can become aware of what happens in the classroom and can monitor accurately both their own intentions and behaviors and those of their students, they can function as *decision makers*. To the extent that teachers cannot do this, they are controlled by classroom events.

Classroom decision making is not easy, in part because classrooms are complex environments in which teachers often must make quick decisions while using incomplete information. For example, Doyle (1986) cites the following aspects of classrooms that teachers must necessarily accommodate:

1. *Multidimensionality.* Many different tasks and events occur. Records and schedules must be kept, and work must be monitored, collected, and evaluated. A single event can have multiple consequences. Waiting a few seconds for one student to answer a question may increase that student's motivation

but negatively influence the interest of another student who would like to respond, and slow the pace of the lesson for the rest of the class.

2. *Simultaneity.* Many things happen at the same time in classrooms. During a discussion, a teacher not only listens and helps improve students' answers but also monitors unresponsive students for signs of comprehension and tries to keep the lesson moving at a good pace.

3. *Immediacy.* The pace of classroom events is rapid. Teachers must respond to many events as they happen.

4. *Unpredictable and public classroom climate.* Things often happen in ways that are unanticipated. Furthermore, much of what happens to a student is seen by many other students as well. Students make inferences about how the teacher feels toward certain students by the way the teacher interacts with them in class.

5. *History.* After a class has met for several weeks or months, common norms and understandings develop. Events that happen early in the year sometimes influence how classrooms function for the rest of the year.

Teachers do more than manage a class of learners. They also deal with students as social beings and we well know that students learn more than subject matter in school (McCaslin & Good, 1996). They are stimulated by other students and enjoy learning from and with peers as well as teachers. Teachers have to help students cope with the informal as well as the formal curriculum.

Teachers have to recognize students' differences in learning and adjust instruction to individual students. Ladson-Billings (1994) illustrates the need for adjusting and individualizing instruction this way:

> In a classroom of thirty children a teacher has one student who is visually impaired, one who is wheelchair-bound, one who has limited English proficiency, and one who is intellectually gifted. If the teacher presents identical work in identical ways to all of the students, is she dealing equitably or inequitably with the children? The visually impaired student cannot read the small print on an assignment, the wheelchair-bound student cannot do push-ups in gym, the foreign-language student cannot give an oral report in English, and the intellectually gifted student learns nothing by spelling words she mastered several years ago. (p. 33)

ACTION-SYSTEM KNOWLEDGE

Leinhardt, Putnam, Stein, and Baxter (1991) distinguish between subject-matter knowledge and action-system knowledge. *Subject-matter knowledge* includes the specific information needed to present content. *Action-system knowledge* refers to skills for planning lessons, making pacing decisions, explaining material clearly, and responding to individual differences.

In this book we deal with action-system knowledge. Systematic study of such knowledge will help you learn how to manage classrooms and to present information, concepts, and assignments effectively. We hope also to provide knowledge that will help you design engaging learning environments that allow students to be active learners and to develop the capacity for self-regulated learning. This information will complement the subject-matter knowledge you gain in other courses.

Even with both kinds of knowledge, however, some teachers may fail because they do not apply the knowledge they possess. They may have inappropriately low expectations for students' ability to learn or for their own ability to teach. Or they may not be active decision makers. Lacking an integrated set of theories and belief systems to provide a framework for informed decision making, they may not have effective strategies for organizing information gleaned from monitoring and interpreting the rapid succession of events in their classrooms.

We provide useful information to help you consider various issues related to classroom teaching and begin to develop an integrated approach that reflects your teaching style. In addition to knowledge, however, much teaching involves hypothesis testing. For example, a teacher might assume that a student who has been out of his or her seat creating behavior problems needs more structure (e.g., more explicit directions, self-checking devices) to work alone productively. However, other factors may be producing the misbehavior. If the problem is not improved by the correction strategies suggested by the first hypothesis, other strategies will have to be used. Teachers who have a rich fund of action-system knowledge are able to develop better hypotheses and adapt their behavior more appropriately to the needs of their students. Indeed, teachers who learn how to reflect on classroom instruction may even develop insights that challenge traditional views of practice (e.g., Gitlin & Smyth, 1989).

Teaching presents enduring problems. For example, teachers must teach a class or group much of the time but still try to respond to the needs of individuals. Individual students not only differ in how much knowledge they have about a subject but also may vary widely in terms of how they view adults and how they cope with ambiguity. Students' previous experiences and home cultures have important consequences for their beliefs about schooling (Heath, 1982; Hiebert, 1991; McCaslin & Good, 1996; McCaslin & Murdock, 1991; Moll, 1992).

Unless we carefully consider a particular manifestation of teaching practice, we may interpret it in terms of our own history as children and students (for better or worse). For example, many of us have been socialized not to appreciate loud, spontaneous behavior. This socialization pattern may make us more likely to interpret such behavior as aggressive than someone who was socialized differently. Similarly, many of us have learned to expect that genuine interest in something (like a school subject) is accompanied by verbal animation ("Isn't this exciting?" "Look how important this is!"), and we may not realize that others may express interest differently (carefully selecting and organizing materials, etc.). The point we are making here is quite simple: that we are shaped by our history and socialization and, hence, our view of appropriate behavior in a third-grade class is likely to depend heavily on our own experiences in intermediate elementary grades unless we attempt to benefit from research, scholarship, and the experience of others.

Further, it is clear that some students are less active classroom participants than are others. Some teachers see students' lack of overt participation (passivity) as a problem. However, research by Mulryan (1995) has shown that students are passive for various reasons (e.g., boredom, confusion.) Other researchers (Jones & Gerig, 1994) have demonstrated that many high-achieving students are passive participants and feel comfortable in learning by listening and reflection.

Another difficulty for teachers is the ongoing task of covering a broad range of topics, yet doing so in sufficient depth to allow meaningful learning. In Chapter 2 we will discuss more issues that teachers must deal with if they are to be good decision makers and help students individually and collectively to grow socially and academically. However, enough has been said to suggest that teaching is complex. To illustrate teachers' classroom decision making, we begin with simulated dialogue from a classroom.

CLASSROOM NARRATIVE: AN ELEMENTARY SCHOOL EXAMPLE

As you read the following example, try to identify teaching behaviors that you believe are effective or ineffective—and consider why you feel that way. Think about what you would have done differently if you had been the teacher. Jot down your ideas as you read.

Sally Turner is a fifth-grade teacher at Maplewood Elementary School, which is located in a moderate-sized midwestern community. She has 30 students, who come primarily from lower-middle-class and working-class homes. The majority are white (15 students), 8 are black, 6 are Hispanic, and there is 1 Asian student. Sally has taught at Maplewood since graduating from college three years ago.

The following classroom scene takes place in October. The students have been reading about Columbus. The scene begins as Sally passes out copies of a map showing the sea routes that Columbus followed on his four trips to the New World.

BILLY: (*Almost shouting*) I didn't get no map.

TEACHER: (*Calmly and deliberately*) Billy, share Rosie's map. Tim, you can look with either Margaret or Damian.

TIM: Can I look with Jill?

TEACHER: (*Slightly agitated*) Okay, but don't play around. You and Jill always get into trouble. (*Most of the students turn to look at Jill and Tim.*) I don't want you two fooling around today (*smiling but stated with some irritation*). Okay, class. Now, does everybody have a map? I wanted to pass out these maps before we start. You can see that the route of each voyage is traced on the map. It might help you to understand that there were four different trips with different routes. Pay special attention during the discussion because you'll need to know the information for tomorrow's quiz. If the discussion goes well, I have a special treat for you—two filmstrips.

CLASS: (*In a spontaneous, exuberant roar*) Yea!

TEACHER: Who can tell me something about Columbus's background?

EMILY: (*Calling out*) He was born in 1451 in Italy.

TEACHER: Good answer, Emily. I can tell you've been reading. Class, can anyone tell me who influenced Columbus's urge to explore unknown seas? (*She looks around and calls on Roberto, one of several students who have raised their hands.*)

ROBERTO: He'd read about Marco Polo's voyage to Cathay and about the fantastic riches he found there.

TEACHER: Okay. Jan, when did Columbus first land in America?

JAN: In 1492.

TEACHER: Terrific! I know you've been reading. Good girl! Where did Columbus stop for supplies?

MANUEL: (*Laughingly*) But Mrs. Turner, the date was on the map you passed out.

TEACHER: (*With irritation*) Manuel, don't call out without raising your hand!

BILLY: (*Calling out*) The Canary Islands.

TEACHER: Okay, Billy. Now, what were the names of the three ships? (*She looks around the room and calls on Tyler, who has his hand up.*) Tyler, you tell us. (*Tyler's face turns red and he stares at the floor.*) Tyler Taylor! Don't raise your hand unless you know the answer. Okay, class, who can tell me the names of the three ships? (*She calls on Brandon, who has his hand up.*)

BRANDON: (*Hesitantly*) The *Santa Maria,* the *Nina,* and the . . .

TEACHER: (*Supplying the answer*) *Pinta.* Nancy, how long did this first voyage to the New World take?

NANCY: (*Shrugging her shoulders*) I don't know.

TEACHER: Think about it. It took a long time, Nancy. Was it less or more than 100 days? (*Silence*) The answer was on the first page of the reading material. Class, can anyone tell me how long the first voyage took? (*No hands are raised.*) Class, you better learn that because it will be on the exam! Now, who can tell me why Columbus came to the New World? (*Maria and two other students raise their hands.*) Maria?

MARIA: (*Firmly and loudly*) Because they wanted to discover new riches, like the explorers going to the Far East.

TEACHER: (*She pauses and looks at Max and Helen, who are talking, and at Manuel, who is headed for the pencil sharpener. Max and Helen immediately cease their conversation.*) Manuel, sit down this minute. (*Manuel heads for his seat.*) What were you doing, anyway?

MANUEL: (*Smiling sheepishly*) Jan wanted me to sharpen her pencil.

JAN: (*Red-faced and alarmed*) Mrs. Turner, that's not true! (*Class laughs.*)

TEACHER: Quiet, both of you. You don't need a sharp pencil. Sit down. (*Resuming discussion*) Good answer, Maria. You were really alert. Why else, Maria? Can you think of any other reason?

NANCY: (*Calling out*) Because they wanted to find a shortcut to the treasures of the Far East. The only other way was over land, and it was thousands of miles over deserts and mountains.

TEACHER: (*Proudly*) Good, Nancy! Now, who were "they"? Who wanted the riches?

BILLY: (*Calling out*) Queen Isabella and King Ferdinand. She paid for the trip because she thought Columbus would make her rich.

TEACHER: Okay, Billy, but remember to raise your hand before speaking. Why do you think Columbus was interested in making the trip? Just to find money?

CLASS: (*Calling out*) No!

TEACHER: Well, what problems did the sailors have? (*She looks around and calls on Manuel, who has his hand up.*)

MANUEL: Well, they were away from home and couldn't write. Sort of like when I go to summer camp. I don't write. I was lonely the first few days, but . . .

TEACHER: (*Somewhat confused and irritated*) Well, that's not exactly what I had in mind. Did they get sick a lot? Class, does anyone know? (*She looks around the room and sees Claire with a raised hand.*)

CLAIRE: Well, I don't remember reading about sailors getting sick with Columbus, but I know that sailors then got sick with scurvy and they had to be careful. (*Hank approaches the teacher with great embarrassment and asks in hushed tones if he can go to the bathroom. Permission is granted.*)

TEACHER: Yes. Good answer, Claire. Claire, did they try to prevent scurvy?

CLAIRE: They carried lots of fruit. . . . You know, like lemons.

TEACHER: Okay, Claire, but what special kind of fruit was important to eat? (*Claire blushes and Mrs. Turner silently forms the soft "c" sound with her mouth.*)

CLAIRE: Citrus.

TEACHER: Very good! What other problems did the sailors have? (*She calls on Matt, who has his hand up.*)

MATT: Well, they didn't have any maps and they didn't know much about the wind or anything, so they were afraid of the unknown and scared of sailing off the earth. (*Laughter*)

TEACHER: (*Noticing that many students are gazing at the floor or looking out the window, she begins to speak louder and more quickly.*) No, educated people knew that the earth was round. Don't you read very carefully?

ALICE: (*Calling out*) But even though educated people knew the earth was round, Columbus's sailors didn't believe it. They called the Atlantic Ocean the "Sea of Darkness," and Columbus had to keep two diaries. He showed the sailors the log with the fewest miles so they wouldn't get scared. But the men threatened mutiny anyway.

TEACHER: (*With elation*) Excellent answer, Alice. Yes, the men were afraid of the unknown; however, I think most of them knew that the earth was round. Okay, Matt, you made me drift away from my question: Why did Columbus want to go? What were the reasons for his trip other than money? James, what do you think? (*James shrugs his shoulders.*) Well, when you read your lesson, class, look for that answer. It's important and I might test you on it. (*With exasperation*) Tim! Jill! Stop pushing each other this instant! I told you two not to play around. Why didn't you listen to me?

TIM: (*With anger*) Jill threw the map in her desk. I wanted to use it so I could trace my own map.

JILL: But it's my map and . . .

TEACHER: (*Firmly*) That's enough! I don't want to hear anymore. Give me the map and the three of us will discuss it during recess.

PRINCIPAL: (*Talking over the PA system*) Teachers, I'm sorry to break in on your classes, but I have an important announcement to make. The high school band will not be with us this afternoon. So 2:00 to 2:30 classes will not be canceled. Since I have interrupted your class, I would also like to remind you that tonight is PTA. Teachers, be sure that the students remind . . . (*During the announcement many pupils begin private conversations with their neighbors.*)

TEACHER: (*Without much emotion or enthusiasm*) It's not recess time yet. Listen, we still have work to do. Tell you what we're going to do now. I've got two videotapes: one describes the United States astronauts' first trip to the moon; the other describes Columbus's first trip to the New World. Watch closely when we show these films because after we see them, I'm going to ask you to tell me the similarities between the two trips. Ralph, turn off the lights.

HANK: (*Returning from his trip to the restroom*) Hey, Mrs. Turner, why are the lights out? It's spooky in here!

ALICE: (*Impishly*) It's the Sea of Darkness! (*Class breaks out in a spontaneous roar.*)

TEACHER: Quiet down, class! It's time to see the videotape—a long, dangerous, and exciting trip is about to begin.

JUAN: (*Speaking audibly but not loudly*) If I had been there, I'd have said "Buena suerte y buen viaje, Señor Columbus." (*Classmates clap and acknowledge their interest.*)

Teacher and class watch 20-minute videotape of voyage.

HANK: (*Calling out as soon as the program finishes*) My sister told me that Columbus was a mean man!

TEACHER: Hank, what do you mean when you say "mean"?

HANK: My sister told me she had read that Columbus lied to his men to get here, that he brought slaves, and that he brutally killed the Indians.

TEACHER: During the next two days we'll spend time discussing the voyage and its importance. We'll talk about what happened on the trip and what happened once they reached North America. Hank is right; some cruel things happened, and we will talk about "means and ends" issues as we did last week when we discussed the environment and jobs.

We need to discuss various aspects of history—history from everybody's point of view, what we want, and how we get there.

JUAN: (*playfully*) My brother, Ramon, told me that Indians are called Indians only because Columbus was so confused that he thought he was in India.

Our example illustrates many points, such as that teachers are busy, teaching is complex, and the pace of classroom life is hurried. Sally had a constant stream of student behavior to react to, and she had to make a number of decisions instantaneously. We offer this example to illustrate that teaching problems are by no means simple to conceptualize.

What were the teacher's *weaknesses* and *strengths*? If you were to discuss this classroom dialogue with the teacher, what would you tell her? You may want to repeat this exercise when you finish reading the book in order to assess the information you have gained or any changes in your perspective that may occur between now and then. Complete the exercise now; then read some of our reactions to this teaching incident in the following section.

ANALYSIS OF THE CLASS DISCUSSION

Like most teachers, Sally Turner has some strengths and some weaknesses. We have organized our comments around four topics that are basic to most teaching/learning situations: motivation, management, instruction, and expectations. These topics are discussed at length in separate chapters; the discussion here provides an introduction.

Motivation

Sally's attempt to breathe life into history by linking Columbus's explorations to a significant event in the students' lives is notable. In her efforts to help students identify more personally with the content, she has gone to the trouble to order videotapes both of Columbus's voyage (a simulation description) and of the astronauts' trip to the moon. However, even the latter trip occurred before these students were born. It might have been more effective if Sally had attempted to stimulate students' thoughts about the unknown with events that were more personal (e.g., first trip to a camp) or more immediate (soldiers peacekeeping in Bosnia). Or, if several of the students had seen one of the movies or television shows made in connection with the 1992 quincentenary of Columbus's voyages, the discussion of these movies or shows might have stimulated all of the students' interest. Similarly, the teacher might have involved students in a discussion of *Apollo 13* if several students had seen the movie.

Feedback   Sally does a fair job of giving feedback to students about the correctness of their responses. Although this point may seem unimportant, teachers frequently fail to provide students with this information when they should do so (i.e., whenever they are not *deliberately* withholding comments in order to encourage brainstorming or to allow students to discover and correct misconceptions on their own). They do not respond to students' answers, or they respond in a way that makes it difficult for some students to know whether their responses are correct. An example of such ambiguous teacher feedback is, "So, you think it's 1492?" Many students, especially low achievers, will not know whether a response is right or wrong unless the teacher specifically tells them. If students are to learn basic facts and concepts, they must know whether their statements are adequate.

Introducing the Lesson   Some of what Sally communicates to students is likely to harm their motivation. Perhaps most striking is her tendency to emphasize that the discussion is important only because it will prepare students to take a test. Her behavior does not suggest that learning is enjoyable or important for its own sake and does not focus on positive learning goals (see Chapter 6). Note especially Sally's poor introduction to the lesson. She stresses that students will be tested but provides little additional rationale for the discussion of Columbus's voyage. Her introduction should have focused more on positive learning goals and less on tomorrow's quiz.

Although it is probably useful to tell students once that material is important and will be on a quiz, Sally comments several times that listening is important because of future testing. Such behavior may convince students that learning is arbitrary, an irrelevant exercise done only to please adults or to receive high grades (see Chapters 3 and 6).

Sally's attempt to make the history associated with Columbus's discovery of America more personal and meaningful to students is good. Nevertheless, the lesson itself is dry, and students' role in the discussion is relatively passive (see Chapters 9 and 10).

Classroom Management

In the area of classroom management (e.g., creating a learning environment, maintaining student involvement), Sally appears to be an average teacher. Her students are generally attentive, and there are few interruptions to the discussion. Although students do not seem enthusiastically engaged, she has established at least minimal conditions of classroom rapport and management structure.

Sally could improve in several areas. First, she did not have enough maps for all students. Equipment and material shortages inevitably lead to trouble, especially when students are to keep the material. A more careful count of the maps might have prevented both the minor delay at the beginning of the discussion and the major disruption (students fighting over a map) that occurred later. On discovering the shortage and after hearing Tim's request to sit with Jill, Sally might have responded, "Okay, that's fine. Sit with Jill, because I know that you and Jill can share cooperatively. Billy and Tim, I'm sorry you didn't get maps. I didn't make enough copies, but I'll draw each of you a *special* map this afternoon." This way of handling the situation would have accomplished two important things: (1) It would have assured Billy and Tim that they would get maps and made it less likely that they would "take the law into their own hands." (As we point out in Chapter 4, what a teacher does to prevent misbehavior is more important than what is done after misbehavior occurs.) (2) It would have encouraged more appropriate expectations, and perhaps better cooperation, from Jill and Tim. The teacher's original remark ("You and Jill always get into trouble") placed Jill and Tim in the spotlight by implying that misbehavior was expected from them. By subtly condoning misbehavior in this way, the teacher actually made it more likely (see Chapter 3).

Credibility   Sally has developed the bad habit of not following up on what she says. During the discussion, she says on several occasions, "Don't call out answers, raise your hand." However, she repeatedly accepts answers that are called out. Recall this instance:

> TEACHER: (*With irritation*) Manuel, don't call out without raising your hand!
> BILLY: (*Calling out*) The Canary Islands.
> TEACHER: Okay, Billy . . .

Such discrepant teacher behaviors may lead to countless discipline problems if they convince students that teachers do not mean what they say or are not aware of much that happens in the classroom.

Rhetorical Questions   In two situations involving off-task behavior, Sally uses rhetorical questions that cause needless difficulty. For example, Manuel has already started back to his seat when she needlessly asks, "What were you doing, anyway?" This question evokes a more serious disruption. Similarly, in her exchange with Jill and Tim, Sally pointlessly queries, "Why don't you listen to me?" Again, this situation deteriorates and the whole class is distracted. Such rhetorical questions that communicate negative expectations typically lead to clowning or other disruptive student behavior. Consider how you feel when someone says to you, "Why don't you listen?" "Can't you do anything right?" or "Why are you always the difficult one?" These questions irritate most people.

Classroom Instruction

The instructional aspects of the illustrated lesson are limited and in that sense unsatisfactory. It is difficult to understand what Sally wants students to learn and how this lesson fits into the overall unit (how students will use the information later). Effective teaching requires that teachers plan sequences of lessons, not just isolated lessons.

Teacher Questions   The instructional component of the lesson resides in the teacher's questions. For the most part, these appear to be rather mechanical—time-filling rather than thought-provoking. Table 1.1 presents the first ten questions Sally asks. Two things seem apparent from an analysis of these questions. First, most of them are factual (students can answer them by reading the material). Sec-

Table 1.1   PARTIAL LIST OF CONTENT QUESTIONS SALLY ASKED

1. Who can tell me something about Columbus's background?
2. When did Columbus first land in America?
3. Where did Columbus stop for supplies?
4. What were the names of the three ships?
5. How long did this first voyage to the New World take?
6. Was it less or more than 100 days?
7. Why did Columbus come to the New World?
8. Can you think of any other reason?
9. Who wanted the riches?
10. Why do you think Columbus was interested in making the trip? Just to find money?

ond, the questions seem more like an oral quiz than an attempt to initiate a meaningful discussion.

Assessment of students' factual knowledge is important, but if it is overemphasized in discussion, students may believe that the teacher is interested only in finding out who knows the answers. Thus, discussion becomes a fragmented ritual rather than a meaningful, enjoyable process.

A teacher can influence students' answers both through the types of questions asked originally and through follow-up questions posed to students after they respond. Sally Turner's initial questions are primarily factual. Her students might have been more interested in the class discussion if they had been involved more directly in it through questions of value and opinion, such as, "How would you feel if you were isolated from your parents and friends for several days? How would you feel being in a 5 x 7 foot room and unable to leave it? Would you like to be a sailor working on a ship week after week, not knowing where you were going or what you would see? Would you volunteer for such a voyage? Why? Is mutiny ever justified? Would you have felt like mutinying if you had been on Columbus's crew? Was the discovery of the New World important? Why? Would it be important to explore a new planet like Venus? Why?"

Some of these questions (e.g., "Why was the discovery of the New World important?") could be considered factual if the book gives answers to them. How students react to such questions depends on the teacher. Too often teachers' questions implicitly say, "Tell me what the book said." Students should be encouraged to process and respond to what they read, not just memorize it. For example, Sally might ask, "The book states two reasons why the Spaniards sponsored voyages of discovery. What were these reasons, and what beliefs and values underlay them?" Or instead of asking, "When did Columbus discover the New World?" she might ask why the trip was not made before 1492.

Similarly, Sally could ask students to evaluate the social consequences of the events discussed. Was it worth the time and money to send astronauts to the moon? What did we learn (e.g., technological or medical information) as a result of the space program? Alternatively, she could initiate discussion of the risks of explorations, perhaps by noting the numerous ships that have been lost at sea or tragedies in space exploration (e.g., the explosion of the space shuttle *Challenger*). Or, she could comment on the expanding role of women astronauts. In the example, however, Sally asks too many factual questions and too few questions of value and opinion that might have stimulated greater interest in the discussion.

Teacher Questions After Student Responses   Sally seldom encourages students to evaluate their own thinking (e.g., "Well, that's one way; what are some other ways that Columbus could have boosted his crew's morale?" "That's an accurate statement of how the crew members felt, but what about Columbus? Do you think he was fearful?"). Nor does she ask questions to help students evaluate their classmates' answers (e.g., "Juan gave his opinion about sailing with Columbus. Bill, do you agree with him? How do you feel?" "What are some other reasons in addition to the good ones that Tim gave?"). Such opportunities to explore a question in depth make a discussion more enjoyable to students, place less emphasis on just reciting facts, and help teacher and students alike to determine whether they *really* understand the material.

To reiterate, Sally does a good job of giving students feedback about the correctness of answers, and on occasion she does probe for additional information. That is, she seeks an additional response from a student after the first response, for clarification (e.g., "What do you mean?") or elaboration (e.g., "Why do you think that is so?" "How does this relate to . . . ?").

Unfortunately, the word *probe* conjures up a negative image to many teachers. They react to it as though it means "to pick the student's answer apart." No such usage is intended here. Appropriate probing helps students to consider thoughtfully the implications of what they do and say—to think about the material. Probing techniques should be gentle ways to focus students' attention and to help them think. For example, an automatic response to "When did Columbus discover America?" is an unthinking "1492." However, the question "Why not 1400?" forces consideration of what the world was like in 1400 and, more generally, extends understanding and appreciation of Columbus's voyage.

Factual questions should be used with other types of questions so that students also consider the implications of facts or the circumstances that produce them. Probing questions help students think more fully about material. Teachers need to provide conditions that encourage students to engage classroom content thoughtfully. These conditions include questions that press students to reflect and integrate material (Blumenfeld, 1992).

Calling on Students   Sally calls on only one student who does not volunteer. Otherwise, either students call out the answer or Sally calls on a student who has a hand up. However, it is often useful for teachers to call on students who seldom raise their hands, such as shy students or low achievers. Students who avoid public-response situations need to be given opportunities to learn that they can participate successfully. Another consideration is that if students learn that their teacher calls only on those who raise their hands, they may become inattentive. Calling on students who do not have their hands up may increase student attention.

We do not know why Sally fails to call on students who do not raise their hands during this particular lesson, but if this behavior is typical, a clue is provided by one incident. Recall that she scolds Tyler for having the audacity to raise his hand without knowing the answer. This reaction suggests that Sally wants "correct" answers, that she is more interested in establishing a point and moving on with the lesson than in promoting the learning of individual students. If a teacher typically responds this way, students learn not to raise their hands unless they are absolutely sure of their answers.

Some teachers unconsciously call only on students who are likely to know the answer as a strategy to provide self-reinforcement. Teachers need to recognize that no matter how well they plan, students often fail to understand ideas and require reteaching using different procedures and examples. If teachers are to make good decisions about whether students understand material, they need to get feedback from a representative sample of students, including timid students and low achievers (Mulryan, 1995; Rohrkemper & Corno, 1988).

Student Questions   Sally does not encourage students to ask questions or to evaluate responses of classmates. She could have encouraged students in this way: "Today I have several questions that I want to find answers for, and you probably have some questions that weren't answered in the reading material. Maybe the class and I can help you answer these questions. Any questions that we can't answer we'll look up in the encyclopedia or in the school library. I wonder why Queen Isabella picked Columbus to head the voyage? Why not some other sailor? I think that's an interesting question! Now let's have *your* questions. We'll list them on the board and see if we have answered them at the end of the discussion."

Although it is not necessary to solicit questions for every discussion period, it is wise to do so frequently, because this technique tells students that the purpose of discussion is to satisfy their needs and interests as well as the teacher's. Furthermore, in asking for questions the teacher communicates the following messages to students:

1. I have important questions, and I want your viewpoint.
2. You certainly must have important questions too.
3. We'll have an interesting discussion as we address one another's questions.
4. If you need more information, we'll get it.

If used consistently, such an approach will, in time, teach students that discussion is not a quiz but a profitable and enjoyable process of sharing information (see Chapter 9).

Teachers should communicate enthusiasm and respect for students who ask questions. Some teachers call for student questions but then react to them in ways that discourage students from asking about issues that interest them. Comments such as "Well, that is not directly related to our discussion" or "That was answered in the book" may convince a student that the teacher doesn't really want questions or that the student is the only one in class who does not know the answer.

Teacher Expectations

As we see in Chapter 3, teachers hold expectations about individual students, about groups, and about whole classes. Furthermore, teachers sometimes communicate these expectations in their classroom behavior and assignments. The communication of expectations has both positive and negative consequences.

Much research has focused on teachers' interactions with high and low achievers. Since we do not identify students' achievement in the example, it is not possible for us to determine whether Sally acts differently toward students she believes to be high and low performers (e.g., calls on one group more frequently than the other, asks them different types of questions). However, we can assess her behavior toward boys and girls and comment on her gender expectations.

Teacher Behavior Toward Male and Female Students   Sally does not praise boys but frequently praises girls. It is not possible to say unequivocally that she always favors girls, but during this class discussion, she is more responsive and supportive to female students. Also, though Sally makes few attempts to improve poor responses by any of the students, she more often does so with girls than with boys. When a boy gives a poor response, she accepts it and either provides the answer herself or calls on another student. However, on two occasions she prompts a girl who is having difficulty responding. When Nancy fails to answer the question "How long did the voyage take?", Sally first provides a clue ("It took a long time") and then reduces the complexity of the question ("Was it less or more than a hundred days?"). Similarly, when Claire cannot remember the word *citrus,* Sally provides a nonverbal clue.

Sally questions boys and girls with similar frequency (there are no differences in *quantity* of questions), but the *quality* of her feedback to students' responses differs. She is more likely to praise the performance of girls and to work with them when they do not answer correctly, at least during this lesson.

Teacher Sensitivity to Cultural Diversity   When the teacher announces the start of the videotape, Juan, with evident interest, wishes Columbus "Good luck and a pleasant trip" in Spanish, and the class appears to appreciate his good humor. It's not possible to determine Sally's sensitivity to students from different cultural and socioeconomic backgrounds, but she did not take advantage of Juan's heritage and possible personal interest by discussing Spanish culture or even Spain's role in the world at that time. (See Chapter 8 for more discussion of multicultural issues.) After the videotape, however, it is clear that Sally is willing (and perhaps had always planned) to discuss the controversial issues that surround the voyage. When teachers discuss history, it's appropriate to discuss everybody's history (i.e., from the standpoint of the Indians as well as the Spaniards). In this sense, Sally's awareness of cultural issues is evident in her willingness to engage in this type of analysis in the classroom.

Reaction to Students' Spontaneous Comments   Sally also fails to discuss even directly relevant topics that students introduce spontaneously. Part of her plan is to get students to appreciate the sense of adventure and apprehension that explorers face. When two students mention their sense of fear, however, Sally fails to respond. Manuel talks about his loneliness during the first few days of summer camp. Sally could have asked, "Why did you feel this way during the first few days of camp?" "How did you feel on your first day at school?" "Why are we uncomfortable when we do something for the first time?" After such a discussion, the students would likely better appreciate the newness of the situation the explorers faced as well as the related stress and excitement.

A similar opportunity arises when Hank alludes to the spookiness of the room and Alice cleverly labels it the Sea of Darkness. Sally could have profitably paused to point out that Alice's remark was a good one, and perhaps to add in a quiet voice, "Okay, now listen. For one minute, no one will make a noise. Let's pretend that we are on the *Pinta*. We have been at sea for two months. It is now completely dark, and the only noise is the roar of the sea and the creaking of the boat. We are all scared because no one has ever sailed this sea! What will we run into in the darkness? What will our destination be like? Will the people there be hostile?" Teachers often stimulate good discussions when they capitalize on spontaneous student comments or questions. If teachers do not react positively to students' self-initiated questions and concerns, however, the students will stop asking.

LEARNING TO ANALYZE CLASSROOMS

Our brief analysis of Sally's teaching yields some inferences about her classroom behavior and beliefs. Admittedly, one example is enough information on which to base only the most speculative conclusions; however, it should encourage an observer to look for more information to confirm or negate tentative hypotheses (e.g., that Sally does not want students to respond unless they know the answer). Some teachers, especially beginners, unwittingly fall into the trap of discouraging students from responding unless they know the answer perfectly. They find that silence or incorrect answers are difficult to respond to and are often embarrassing or threatening.

The incident with Tyler illustrates two important points: (1) Teachers may encourage students not to listen by falling into ineffective but consistent questioning styles. (2) Often we can get enough evidence from what we observe in classrooms to make decisions and give firm suggestions to teachers, but at other times (e.g., the exchange with Tyler), we may only note clues about a teacher's general behavior patterns or assumptions about students. These speculations need to be checked by talking with the teacher and/or with students (McCaslin & Good, 1996) or by making additional observations (see Chapters 2 and 11).

CLASSROOM NARRATIVE: A SECONDARY SCHOOL EXAMPLE

As you read the following classroom dialogue (Ms. Chavez's class), make notes about effective and ineffective teaching techniques and why you identify them that way. We do not analyze this dialogue, because we want you to form your own impressions and complete your own analysis. After you have read Chapters 3 through 10, return to this narrative to see how your reactions to it have changed.

Ms. Chavez*

Ms. Chavez has rolled the math department computer into her class for the morning and has connected it to her LCD viewer. Her 28 first-year algebra students, seated at round tables in groups of threes and fours, are working on a warm-up problem. The day before they had had a test on functions. For the warm-up to today's class, Ms. Chavez has asked students to set up a table of values and graph the function $y = |x|$.

She has chosen this problem as a way to introduce some ideas for a new unit on linear, absolute value, and quadratic functions. During the warm-up, students can be heard talking quietly to one another about the problem: "Does your graph look like a V-shape?" "Did you get two intersecting lines?" Walking around the room, Ms. Chavez listens to these conversations while she takes attendance. After about five minutes, she signals that it is time to begin the whole-group discussion.

A girl volunteers and carefully draws her graph on a large wipe-off grid board at the front of the room. As she does this, most students are watching closely, glancing down at their own graphs, checking for correspondence. A few students are seen helping others who had some difficulties producing the graph.

Another student suggests that they enter the function into the computer and watch it produce the graph. Several other students chime in, "Yeah!" The first girl does this, and the class watches as the graph appears on the overhead screen. It matches the graph she sketched, and the class cheers, "Way to go, Elena!"

Ms. Chavez then asks the class to sketch the graphs of $y = |x| + 1$, $y = |x| + 2$, and $y = |x| - 3$ on the same set of axes and write a paragraph that compares and contrasts the results with the graph of $y = |x|$. "Feel free to work alone or with the others in your group," she tells them.

After a few minutes, two students exclaim, "All the graphs have the same shape!"

A few other students look up. Another student observes, "They're like angles with different vertex points." "Then they're really congruent angles," adds his partner.

Ms. Chavez circulates through the class, listening to the students' discussions, asking questions, and offering suggestions. She notices one group has produced only one branch of the graphs. "Why don't you choose a few negative values for x and see what happens?" Another group asks, "What would happen if we tried $|x| - 3$?" "Try it!" urges Ms. Chavez.

The students continue working, and the conversation is lowered to murmurs once again. Then the members of one group call out, "Hey, we've got something! All these graphs are just translations of $y = |x|$, just like we learned in the unit on geometry."

"That's an interesting conjecture you have," remarks Ms. Chavez. She looks expectantly at the other students. "Do the rest of you agree?" They are still, many looking hard at their graphs. One student says, slowly, "I'm not sure I get it."

*This narrative is taken from National Council of Teachers of Mathematics (1991). *Professional standards for teaching mathematics* (pp. 47–49). Reston, VA: Author. Reprinted by permission.

A boy in the group that made the conjecture about translations explains, "Like $y = |x| + 2$ is like $y = |x|$ moved up two spaces and $y = |x| - 3$ is moved down three spaces. Its like what Louella said about them being like angles with different vertex points."

Ms. Chavez decides to provoke the class to pursue this. She asks if anyone thinks they can graph $y = |x| + 4$ without first setting up a table of values. Hands shoot up. "Ooooh!!" Scanning the class, Ms. Chavez notices Lionel, who does not volunteer often, has his hand up. He looks pleased when she invites him to give it a try.

Lionel sketches his graph on the dry-erase board. Elena again enters the equation of the graph into the computer and the class watches as the graph is produced. The computer-generated graph verifies Lionel's attempt. Again there are cheers. Lionel gives a sweeping bow and sits down.

Ms. Chavez asks the students to write in their journals, focusing on what they think they understand and what they feel unsure about from today's lesson. They lean over their notebooks, writing. A few stare into space before beginning. She gives them about ten minutes before she begins to return the tests. She will read the journals before tomorrow's class.

At the end of the period, she distributes the homework that she has prepared. The worksheet includes additional practice on the concept of $y = |x| \pm c$ as well as something new, to provoke the next day's discussion: $y = |x \pm c|$.

Over the next couple of weeks, students explore linear, quadratic, and absolute value functions. Nearing the end of this unit, Ms. Chavez decides to engage students in reflecting on and assessing how far they have come.

As she assigns homework for that evening, she announces, "I'd like each of you to write two questions that you think are fair and would demonstrate that you understand the major concepts of this unit. I'll use several of your ideas to create the test. And here's a challenge for the last part of your assignment: you just drew the graph of $f(x) = x^2 - 2x$ as a part of the review. Think about everything we've done so far this semester, and see if you can remember any ideas that will help you draw the graph of $|f(x)|$."

EFFECTIVE TEACHING

Would you prefer to be in Ms. Turner or Ms. Chavez's class? Why? Do you think you would learn more in one class than another? Do you think you would enjoy one more than the other or prefer the climate in one class better? Why? As we think about "effective teaching," we need to become sensitive to the types of "effects" that are considered most desirable. Classrooms are not only about learning academic subject matter. Classroom experiences also involve learning to become self-reliant and self-evaluative, as well as learning how to work cooperatively and productively with others. Classrooms can help us to sharpen our sense of identity, understanding of culture, and explore and internalize general issues of fairness and morality (Jackson et al., 1993). Thus, in part what constitutes effective teaching is dependent on the context of the school and its collective values (Is the development of the capacity for self-management seen as important as, or less important than, subject-matter achievement?). Consider the following exchange between an African American teacher and student in an all African American classroom (Table 1.2). How would you analyze this teaching? How does your analysis compare with those of your classmates? To what extent does this example relate to the issue in Ms. Turner's classroom (history, literature, from what frame of reference)?

Table 1.2   LANGUAGE DIVERSITY AND POWER

TEACHER: What do you think about the book?

JOEY: I think it's nice.

TEACHER: Why?

JOEY: I don't know. It just told about a black family, that's all.

TEACHER: Was it difficult to read?

JOEY: No.

TEACHER: Was the text different from what you have seen in other books?

JOEY: Yeah. The writing was.

TEACHER: How?

JOEY: It use more of a southern-like accent in this book.

TEACHER: Uhm-hmm. Do you think that's good or bad?

JOEY: Well, uh, I don't think it's good for people down this-a-way, cause that's the way they grow up talking anyway. They ought to get the right way to talk.

TEACHER: Oh. So you think it's wrong to talk like that?

JOEY: Well . . . (*Laughs*)

TEACHER: Hard question, huh?

JOEY: Uhm-hmm, that's a hard question. But I think they shouldn't make books like that.

TEACHER: Why?

JOEY: Because they are not using the right way to talk and in school they take off for that, and li'l chirren grow up talking like that and reading like that so they might think that's right, and all the time they are getting bad grades in school, talking like that and writing like that.

TEACHER: Do you think they should be getting bad grades for talking like that?

JOEY: (*Pauses, answers very slowly*) No . . . no.

TEACHER: So you don't think that it matters whether you talk one way or another?

JOEY: No, not long as you understood.

TEACHER: Uhm-hmm. Well, that's a hard question for me to answer, too. It's, ah, that's a question that's come up in a lot of schools now as to whether they should correct children who speak the way we speak all the time. Cause when we're talking to each other we talk like that even though we might not talk like that when we get into other situations, and who's to say whether it's—

JOEY: (*Interrupting*) Right or wrong.

TEACHER: Yeah.

JOEY: Maybe they ought to come up with another kind of . . . maybe black English or something. A course in black English. Maybe black folks would be good in that cause people talk, I mean black people talk like that, so . . . but I guess there's a right way and wrong way to talk, you know, not regarding what race. I don't know.

TEACHER: But who decided what's right or wrong?

JOEY: Well that's true . . . I guess white people did.
(*Laughter. End of tape.*)

Source: Delpit, L. (1995). *Other people's children: cultural conflict in the classroom* (pp. 42–43). New York: The New Press. Reprinted with permission.

Different Types of Observational Procedures

There are many different ways to collect data in classrooms, but they are usually divided into two broad classifications called quantitative and qualitative. In *quantitative* approaches, observers use checklists or coding schemes to record each occurrence of particular categories of events, and then analyze the resulting frequency profiles. Quantitative approaches provide information on how often certain things occurred in the classroom, considered either in their own right or in comparison with other things that might have occurred instead. Thus, quantitative scales allow measurement of particular behaviors or sequences of behavior, and their focus is relatively narrow. The observer may decide what scale to use, or the decision may be based on the teacher's goal or request (e.g., the teacher asks a peer to look for differences in questions posed to male and female students). Further, the decision about what to look for in a classroom is relatively closed—once one or more forms are selected, that decision guides the focus of the observation (examples of quantitative scales are given at the ends of Chapters 3 to 10). Two popular types of quantitative coding are time sampling and event sampling. Examples of these types of coding can be found in Appendix A at the end of Chapter 2.

In *qualitative approaches,* observers do not concentrate on assigning classroom events to categories but instead attempt to collect detailed descriptive information about them. These rich descriptive data are preserved and then analyzed with emphasis on qualitative aspects of the events recorded (i.e., on the specifics of how they unfolded and how they were likely to have been experienced by the teacher and students).

Although there have always been qualitative studies in educational research, the use of qualitative inquiry has become especially popular in the past decade (Erickson, 1986; Goetz & LeCompte, 1984). Qualitative studies generally describe classrooms as richly as possible. These descriptions not only include observation of behavior (as in quantitative studies) but also may include interviews with teachers and students. These studies attempt to understand how individual classroom participants see and interpret behavior. An example of a qualitative study appears at the end of Chapter 2, and in Chapter 2 we provide a brief introduction to case study methods. Further, at the ends of Chapters 3 through 10 we include suggestions about possible qualitative explorations that could be conducted.

We realize that access to classrooms varies widely. Some readers are classroom teachers, whereas others are still preparing to teach. In the questions and activities at the end of the chapters we offer you some opportunity to engage in qualitative, interpretative work. For example, the first question typically asks you to gather data about how you, other teachers or peers, or students react to events. Although you will have to adjust these activities to the circumstances you are in, the purpose of the activities is to emphasize that behavior is only one factor to be considered in analyzing classrooms (one has to understand participants' intentions and interpretations as well). Still, many of the questions focus on examination of behavior per se because the first step in understanding classrooms is to clarify what has occurred. We hope that these questions illustrate both the difficulty as well as the importance of analyzing classrooms.

SUMMARY

In this chapter we suggested that teachers need to be aware of their own formative learning experiences (e.g., how discussions were handled in their family, instructional and management strategies used by their cooperating teacher, preferences of their initial principal, etc.) because these formative experiences may affect their classroom decision making and instruction in subtle but important ways. We argued that, to become active decision makers and to develop their own personal styles, teachers need to understand the knowledge base that supports teaching, including information not only about instructional strategies but also about student development, learning, and motivation. We also noted that teachers need to be reflective (e.g., analyze classroom processes, discuss curriculum and instruction with peers) and to be sensitive to both the context in which they teach and the instructional goals that are most important to them. Thus, teachers who are aware of their own development, who are knowledgeable about research on classroom instruction and student learning, and who frequently reflect on their teaching will be the most active decision makers.

We also noted that there are many methods for observing and analyzing instructional behavior. We introduced two broad types of classroom observational methods—quantitative and qualitative. Other important distinctions will be made in Chapter 2. We emphasize, however, that there is no one correct way to observe and to study classrooms, and that there is critical comment available on both quantitative and qualitative approaches (e.g., Hammersley, 1992; Stodolsky, 1990). The desirability of a particular observational method or research plan depends on the purposes for which one is observing. Different observational methods have different strengths and weaknesses. The desirability of a method resides not in its form but rather in the extent to which it generates useful information and insights.

SUGGESTED ACTIVITIES AND QUESTIONS

1. What were the primary reasons you decided to become a teacher? How will (or how do) these reasons influence how you see your role? Why did your classmates or peers decide to become teachers? What does it mean to become a more effective teacher? How can you tell if you are improving as a teacher? How do your criteria differ from those of others?

2. Consider the grade you teach (or plan to teach) and identify the ten most important skills, attitudes, or behaviors a teacher must possess in order to instruct effectively at this level. Keep this list so you can compare it with a list you make after you have read the entire book.

3. If you could talk with Sally Turner about her lesson, what questions would you ask? Why? How might additional information change your opinion of her teaching?

4. Reread the example of Sally Turner's class and identify four instances in which she could have probed for improved student responses. Write the questions you would have used.

5. We evaluated Sally's teaching. What teaching strengths or weaknesses did you identify that we did not mention? Explain why these behaviors are strengths or weaknesses.

6. We criticized Sally's introduction to the lesson. Improve the introduction by writing your own. In general, what steps should a good introduction include? Why?

7. Reread the questions that Sally asks her class. How could you improve them? Write ten questions of your own. Why are your questions better than hers?

8. If Sally's classroom were composed entirely of inner-city or suburban students, how would you assess her instruction? Does teaching have to be adjusted to the characteristics of students? Explain.

9. After reading the secondary classroom narrative, how would you describe Ms. Chavez's relative strengths and weaknesses?

10. What questions would you have for Ms. Chavez? Why?

11. How might home influences affect how students try to learn in the classroom? For example, how did your parent(s) or guardian react when you asked them a question or they asked you one? How often did your guardian or parent ask about school or particular assignments? How do your experiences vary from those of classmates?

12. Why do teachers have a difficult time being aware of everything that occurs in classrooms?

13. We suggested that before conducting a class discussion, it is often a good idea to solicit questions from students. Why? Under what circumstances might this be a poor approach?

REFERENCES

Alkin, M. (Ed.). (1992). *Encyclopedia of educational research* (6th ed.). New York: Macmillan.

Biddle, B., Good, T., & Goodson, I. (1996). *The international handbook of teachers and teaching.* New York: Kluwer.

Blumenfeld, P. (1992). The task and the teacher: Enhancing student thoughtfulness in science. In J. Brophy (Ed.), *Advances in research on teaching* (Vol. 3, pp. 81–114). Greenwich, CT: JAI Press.

Delpit, L. (1995). *Other people's children: Cultural conflict in the classroom.* New York: The New Press.

Doyle, W. (1986). Classroom organization and management. In M. Wittrock (Ed.), *Handbook of research on teaching* (3rd ed., pp. 392–431). New York: Macmillan.

Erickson, F. (1986). Qualitative methods in research on teaching. In M. Wittrock (Ed.), *Handbook of research on teaching* (3rd ed., pp. 119–161). New York: Macmillan.

Gitlin A., & Smyth, J. (1989). *Teacher evaluation: Educative alternatives.* New York: Falmer Press.

Goetz, J., & LeCompte, M. (1984). *Ethnography and qualitative design in educational research.* New York: Academic Press.

Goodson, I. (1992). Studying teachers' lives: Problems and possibilities. In I. Goodson (Ed.), *Studying teachers' lives* (pp. 234–249). New York: Teachers College Press.

Hammersley, M. (1992). *What's wrong with ethnography?* London: Routledge.

Heath, S. B. (1982). Questioning at home and school: A comparative study. In G. Spindler (Ed.), *Doing the ethnography of schooling* (pp. 102–131). New York: Holt, Rinehart, and Winston.

Hiebert, F. (Ed.). (1991). *Literacy for a diverse society*. New York: Teachers College Press.

Jackson, P. (Ed.). (1992). *Handbook of research on curriculum*. New York: Macmillan.

Jackson, P., Boostrom, R., & Hansen D. (1995). *The moral life of schools*. San Francisco: Jossey-Bass.

Jones, M., & Gerig, T. (1994). Silent sixth-grade students: Characteristics, achievement, and teacher expectations. *Elementary School Journal, 95,* 169–182.

Ladson-Billings, G. (1994). *The dreamkeepers: Successful teachers of African-American children*. San Francisco: Jossey-Bass.

Leinhardt, G., Putnam, R., Stein, M., & Baxter, J. (1991). Where subject knowledge matters. In J. Brophy (Ed.), *Advances in research teaching* (Vol. 2) (pp. 87–113). Greenwich, CT: JAI Press.

McCaslin, M., & Good, T. (1996). *Listening in classrooms*. New York: HarperCollins.

McCaslin, M., & Murdock, T. (1991). The emergent interaction of home and school in the development of students' adaptive learning. In M. Maehr & P. Pintrich (Eds.), *Advances in motivation and achievement* (Vol. 7, pp. 213–260). Greenwich, CT: JAI Press.

Moll, L. (1992). Bilingual classroom studies and community analysis. *Educational Research, 21,* 20–24.

Mulryan, C. (1995). Fifth and sixth graders' involvement and participation in cooperative small groups in mathematics. *Elementary School Journal, 95,* 297–310.

Rohrkemper, M., & Corno, L. (1988). Success and failure on classroom tasks: Adaptive learning and classroom teaching. *Elementary School Journal, 88,* 299–312.

Smylie, M. (1995, September). Special Issue on Teacher Leadership. *Elementary School Journal.*

Stodolsky, S. (1990). Classroom observation. In J. Millman & L. Darling-Hammond (Eds.), *The new handbook of teacher evaluation*. New York: Sage.

Wittrock, M. (Ed.). (1986). *Handbook of research on teaching* (3rd ed.). New York: Macmillan.

Increasing Teacher Awareness Through Classroom Observation

O ur brief glimpse into Sally Turner's classroom in Chapter 1 revealed that it is very busy and that she is probably unaware of much of her behavior and its effects on students. In this chapter, we discuss research indicating that classrooms are complex, that the fast pace in Sally Turner's class is common, and that teachers are unaware of much of their behavior. We argue that teachers do not perceive many classroom events because (1) classroom interaction involves fast and complex communications, (2) different life experiences lead teachers to be more sensitive to some students and certain issues than others, (3) teachers are not trained extensively to monitor and study their instructional behavior, and (4) teachers rarely receive systematic or useful feedback about their behavior. Finally, we emphasize that neither teachers nor observers are likely to understand classroom behavior unless they know what behaviors to look for, know how to collect information accurately, and have a conceptual framework to use in making and analyzing their observations. The final section of the chapter provides detailed information about strategies that can be used to collect reliable and useful information in classrooms.

CLASSROOMS ARE COMPLEX

In a single day, an elementary teacher may engage in more than a thousand interpersonal exchanges with students. Teachers in secondary schools may have interactions with 150 different students a day. Yet teachers must *interpret* and respond to student behavior on the spot. It is not surprising that most teachers are hard pressed to keep track of the number and substance of the contacts they have with each student. It may not be important for teachers to remember all such contacts; however, they must recall certain information (the ten students who did not get a chance to present their class reports; the student who had trouble with vowel sounds during reading, etc.).

Because teachers constantly respond to immediate needs while they teach, they have little time during teaching to consider what they are doing or planning to do. Unless they look for signs of student boredom or difficulty, they may not see them. Teachers are so absorbed in their work that it is difficult for them to get a perspective on what happens in their classrooms.

Those who study teachers often comment on how busy teachers are. For example, according to Maeroff (1988, p. 36):

> Being a schoolteacher is having so much to do and so little time to do it that keeping up with the growth in knowledge is a luxury. Even the most dedicated teacher finds that trying to stay abreast of subject matter is like paddling upstream on a fast-moving river. For the typical high school teacher, meeting with 125 to 175 students a day, marking many of the papers at night, and preparing for the next day's classes—not to mention maintaining a family life and possibly a part-time job—it is a task without beginning or ending.

Teachers not only are busy but they also work alone. Freedman, Jackson, and Boles (1983, p. 270) quote one teacher who described the problem: "We never had any administrative encouragement to work together. There was never any time, there was never any made, there were very few group decisions. It's a very individual thing. If you found someone you wanted to share materials with you did it on your own. No, nobody has ever encouraged that route."

If teachers are to grow as professionals, they have to overcome these problems by learning to monitor their teaching as it occurs, to reflect on it afterward, and to engage in professional development activities with colleagues. Obviously, administrators must allow teachers time to reflect on teaching and to work collaboratively. Fortunately, as we shall see in Chapter 11 some schools have started to emphasize that teachers can work collaboratively (Meier, 1995).

TEACHERS' PERCEPTIONS OF THEIR CLASSROOM BEHAVIOR

A study conducted by Good and Brophy (1974) provided clear evidence that teachers are unaware of some of their behavior. These researchers found that teachers differed widely in the extent to which they stayed with students in failure situations (repeated or rephrased a question, asked a new question) or gave up on them (gave the answer or called on someone else). Interviews with teachers showed that they were largely unaware of the extent to which they generally gave up on or stayed with students, let alone of their behavior toward specific students. Teachers were so preoccupied with running the classroom that awareness of this dimension of classroom life eluded them.

Other researchers have reached similar conclusions. Indeed, even a seemingly simple aspect of teacher-student interaction can be a complex perceptual problem in a fast-moving, complicated social setting such as a classroom. Many teachers cannot accurately recall the extent to which they call on boys versus girls, the frequency with which students approach them, the number of private contacts they initiate with students, or the amount of class time they spend on procedural matters. This lack of awareness is one reason why, in too many classrooms, student gender, race, ethnicity, or culture predict the quality of students' learning opportunity (AAUW, 1992; Delpit, 1995; Sadker & Sadker, 1994).

CLASSROOM PROBLEMS CAUSED BY LACK OF TEACHER AWARENESS

In the following sections, we describe classroom problems that occur in part because of lack of teacher awareness and information. Most of the problems presented here are discussed again later in the book. The material in this chapter is designed to help you begin thinking about factors that affect teacher behavior and student achievement.

Teacher Domination of Classroom Communication

Teachers dominate classroom discussion, even though they sometimes do not want to and are not aware of their behavior. This aspect of classroom life has been known for some time. Adams and Biddle (1970) concluded that teachers are the principal actors in 84 percent of classroom communication episodes. Cuban (1984) found that the basic structure of classrooms (heavy reliance on teacher-student recitation) has remained unaltered for decades. School critics often decry the fact that students are not active enough in school settings (Boyer, 1983; Goodlad, 1984). More recent research continues to confirm that teachers dominate participation in too many classrooms. Further, classrooms also appear, in many cases, to be dominated by a small set of students (Jones, 1990).

We believe that teachers can talk either too much or too little and that both types of teachers may be unaware of their behavior. In any case, the quality of teacher talk is just as important as its quantity. The same is true, of course, for student talk. For example, there is growing agreement among researchers that teachers spend too much time asking (and students answering) isolated factual questions (Goodlad, Soder, & Sirotnik, 1990).

Lack of Emphasis on Meaning

What teachers talk about is important. Durkin (1978–1979) found after 300 hours of observing in reading and social studies classrooms that less than 1 percent of the time was devoted to comprehension instruction. Students were expected to learn by reading, but were not being taught how to do so. Another study indicated that mathematics teachers who actively instructed and emphasized the meaning of concepts obtained higher achievement from students than teachers who used instructional time for other purposes (Good, Grouws, & Ebmeier, 1983). More recent research continues to emphasize the importance of a focus on students' meaningful conceptualization. This is especially the case when students' personal knowledge of the world is used in the instructional setting (Hiebert & Carpenter, 1992).

Few Attempts to Motivate Students

After over 100 hours of observation in six intermediate-grade classrooms, Brophy and Kher (1986) found that only a third of the teachers' task introduction statements included comments judged likely to enhance student motivation. These few comments mostly consisted of predictions that students would enjoy a task or do well on it. There were only nine attempts to explain to students why it was important to learn material, and none to explain how students could derive personal satisfaction from learning relevant skills or knowledge.

Not Cognizant of Effects of Seat Location

For some time it has been known that students' seating location may affect opportunities for participation. Students' assignment to a class location may be affected by various factors. In a study of 70 fifth-grade classrooms drawn from 39 Israeli schools, Babad and Ezer (1993) found that seating location and type of student were correlated. For example, teachers' pets and flatterers were seated closer to the teacher, and rejected students tended to be seated on the sides of the classroom.

Teachers often group students by ability in order to reduce the range of individual differences within each group. Some teachers segregate low- and high-ability students by seating them apart. The top readers sit at the same table, the next best group sits together, and so on. Such seating patterns may create status differences among students and engender an attitude of inferiority in low achievers that removes them from the mainstream of classroom life. Many teachers are probably unaware of how seat assignments and group practices influence student behavior and peer relations.

Overreliance on Repetitive Seatwork

Many students spend considerable time doing seatwork while the teacher instructs other students. During such times some students may engage in off-task behavior that escapes teacher attention. Anderson et al. (1985) conducted one of the few studies that examined in depth what students do during seatwork times and how they attempt to understand and complete their assignments. Results showed that the 32 students studied in first-grade classes spent from 30 to 60 percent of the time allocated to reading instruction doing some type of seatwork. Furthermore, an average of 50 percent of seatwork assignments involved commercial products such as workbooks, dittos, and reading material, often of questionable value (copying sentences with blanks and choosing the correct word from several options). Anderson et al. found that teacher instruction related to seatwork assignments seldom included statements about what would be learned or how the assignment related to other things the students had learned. When teachers observed students who were doing seatwork, they typically monitored students' task engagement but not their understanding of what they were doing. Other researchers have made similar comments about the poor quality of seatwork assignments, especially for low-ability students or students who are placed into low tracks (Allington, 1991; Oakes, 1992; Wells et al., 1995).

DIFFERENTIAL TEACHER-STUDENT INTERACTION

There is evidence that some students receive more opportunity than others to participate in classroom events (Allington, 1991; Jones & Gerig, 1994). These differences are associated with differences in student achievement levels, gender, and race.

Student Achievement

Perhaps the most consistent finding concerning teacher-student interaction is that teachers tend to call more frequently on students they believe to be the most capable. However, qualitative differences in teacher-student interaction patterns also have been observed, even where there were no quantitative differences.

Brophy and Good (1970) studied the classroom behavior of four first-grade teachers toward high- and low-achieving students. They reported only minor differences in the *frequency* of teacher contact with students of different achievement levels but found important variations in the *quality*. Teachers were more likely to praise high-achieving students, even when differences in the correctness of students' answers were taken into account. When high achievers gave a right answer, they were praised 12 percent of the time. Low achievers, however, were praised only 6 percent of the time. Even though they gave fewer correct answers, low achievers received proportionately less praise. Yet low achievers were more likely to be criticized for wrong answers (18 percent of the time compared with only 6 percent for high achievers). Furthermore, teachers were twice as likely to stay with high achievers (repeat the question, provide a clue, ask a new question) when they made no response (or said "I don't know," or answered incorrectly).

Teachers vary widely in the extent to which they are influenced by their expectations and treat low achievers inappropriately. Some teachers show this tendency more than others; many teachers call on high- and low-achieving students equitably, and some even call on low achievers more often than high achievers (see Chapter 3). Many teachers develop appropriate expectations for low achievers and treat them fairly (Brophy & Good, 1974; Cooper & Good, 1983). Many others, however, especially teachers who are unaware of their behavior, favor high achievers (Allington, 1991; Eder, 1981; Good & Weinstein, 1986). Moreover, differences in contact between teachers and certain students may be controlled by students rather than teachers. For example, Jones and Gerig (1994) found that some sixth graders, particularly shy students, avoided classroom participation.

Student Gender

Gender affects the quantity and quality of students' communication with teachers. Studies consistently show that boys have more interactions with teachers than girls (AAUW, 1992; Brophy & Good, 1974; Streitmatter, 1994), with the difference being greatest for disciplinary exchanges and smallest for instructional ones. Some of these differences in interaction patterns are partly due to student behavior. Morse and Handley (1985) studied seventh- and eighth-grade students during science instruction over two consecutive years and found that in the seventh grade, 41 percent of the student-to-teacher academic interactions were initiated by girls; in the eighth grade, these same girls initiated only 30 percent of the interactions. Thus, as they matured, girls initiated fewer interactions in science classes. In contrast, boys' initiation of interactions increased correspondingly over the two years.

A considerable body of literature has examined gender issues in both elementary and secondary schools (e.g., AAUW, 1992; Sadker, Sadker, & Klein, 1991). Unfortunately, although there has been concern with differential interaction in classrooms on the basis of gender for over two decades, there is still evidence that students sometimes receive notably different opportunities in classrooms as a function of their gender.

Subject Matter and Gender

Subject matter can affect teachers' treatment of boys and girls. Leinhardt, Seewald, and Engel (1979) studied teacher-student interactions in 33 second-grade classrooms and found that in reading, girls had a higher percentage of academic contacts with teachers and received somewhat more instructional time than boys. The opposite was true in mathematics, however. In all classrooms, boys had more management contacts with teachers than girls. The authors suggested that differential instructional behavior was linked to student achievement in reading. Although there were no differences in initial abilities, significant gender differences were found in end-of-year reading achievement, presumably because the teachers spent relatively more time with girls in reading.

In related research Jones and Wheatley (1990) examined teacher-student dyadic interactions in 30 physical science classes and 30 chemistry classes. They reported that males receive more teacher contact than females on all types of classroom interaction (both positive and negative). There is some evidence that female students have less access to computers in the classroom than do males; however, in some instances this may be due to female students' disposition rather than to teacher discrimination. Streitmatter (1994) has noted that teachers' beliefs and practices can be notably different. Thus, some teachers engage in discriminatory gender practices because they are unaware of their behavior.

Race

Teacher-student interactions are affected not only by gender but also by other student characteristics such as race (see Grant, 1985). Leacock (1969) found that teachers generally rated black students less favorably than they rated white students, and showed particular hostility and rejection toward the *brightest* black students. The latter result is a reversal of the usual finding in studies involving white students.

However, in some classes black students may be treated differentially on the basis of gender. Ross and Jackson (1991) studied elementary teachers' reactions to questionnaires containing case histories of hypothetical black fourth- and fifth-grade students. Even though the performance abilities of male and female students were constructed in equivalent ways, teachers consistently reported lower expectations for black males and preferred to have black females in their classes.

Classrooms are complex and difficult environments for students as well. Some educators have noted that African American students often place incredible pressures on themselves to perform academically and that these students sometimes feel that their entire academic credibility rests on their ability to answer every question correctly—even trivial ones (Ogbu, 1992; Steele, 1992).

Teachers need to be aware of differences in students that they may overreact to if they are not careful (see Allington, 1991; Brophy & Evertson, 1981; Eisenhart & Cutts-Dougherty, 1991; Grant, 1985; Ogbu, 1992; Wilkinson & Marrett, 1985 for reviews of this literature). The most successful teachers are not merely sensitive to the cultural diversity of the students they teach: They use this diversity to enrich the learning experiences they provide to the class as a whole (Delpit, 1995; Hiebert, 1991; Meier, 1995; Natriello, McDill, & Pallas, 1990).

COOPERATIVE GROUP LEARNING

The research data described above were usually collected when teachers were teaching the class as a whole. There is growing interest in the potential of cooperative small groups for helping students to learn more actively and for ameliorating differences among students in classroom interaction and participation. The effects of grouping, however, are mixed. For example, some students can monopolize small groups just as they dominate whole-class discussions (King, 1993; Mulryan, 1995). Blumenfeld (1992) reported that students found small-group work more motivating and enjoyable but noted that active learning declined during small-group work.

When small-group tasks are poorly designed, students often spend more time carrying out superficial procedures than thinking about the meaning of the task (Good, Mulryan, & McCaslin; 1992; McCaslin & Good, 1992). Moreover, classroom environments become much more complex when the teacher tries to monitor the academic and social progress of seven or eight groups. Hence, unless teachers monitor students carefully as they work in groups, teachers may unintentionally create caste systems in which some groups, or some students within groups, have much more status and power than others. Clearly, shifting the unit of instruction from whole class to small group does not necessarily reduce the complexity of teachers' observing in classrooms. Teachers who make extensive use of small-group strategies will have to develop strategies for listening to and interviewing students as well as skills for meaningful observation (McCaslin & Good, 1996).

FACTORS THAT INFLUENCE ACHIEVEMENT

Use of Time in Classrooms

Allocated Time   Teachers vary widely in *how much* instructional time they allocate to school subjects. For example, Berliner (1979) found that average daily time allocated for second-grade math ranged from a low of 24 minutes to a high of 61 minutes. The range for second-grade reading was from 32 to 131 minutes. Some students received as much as four times more instructional time in a given subject than other students in the same grade. Teachers also vary significantly in how they *use* time. Freeman and Porter (1989) reported that teachers in some math classes focused on conceptual ideas, whereas other teachers emphasized drill and practice of computation skills.

Variations in time use are found in secondary classrooms as well. Some teachers use 40 minutes of a 45-minute period to develop concepts; others use only 20 to 25 minutes for developing subject-matter content. Stallings (1980) studied 87 secondary classrooms and reported that teachers who obtained relatively poor achievement from students used more class time for noninteractive instruction. Most teachers are probably not aware of how their time allocations differ from those of other teachers. National reports like *Prisoners of Time* argue that use of classroom time is often inappropriate (National Education Commission on Time and Learning, 1994).

Teachers' Attitudes   Some research suggests that teachers devote time to subjects partly on the basis of their attitudes toward these subjects. Schmidt and Buchmann (1983) found that teachers who enjoyed teaching reading more than writing tended to stress reading over language arts instruction and that teachers who enjoyed mathematics more than social studies allocated more time to mathematics. Indeed, the teachers who enjoyed teaching mathematics spent over *50 percent* more time teaching math than teachers who did not. Variation among teachers in time allocated to particular subjects was tremendous (e.g., one teacher averaged 2 minutes on science, while another averaged 43.2 minutes). Thus, in addition to becoming aware of how they spend time, teachers may need to alter their knowledge of or attitudes toward certain topics or subjects so that they feel comfortable teaching them.

Opportunity to Learn

Student opportunity to learn also affects achievement. Teachers who are teaching ostensibly the same curriculum present varied information, assignments, and activities to their students, so that even if time allocation is equal, students receive different content and learning opportunities (Porter, 1993). Much of this scheduling occurs as a result of conscious decision making, but some of it also happens without teacher awareness. Brophy (1982) argued that teachers play a key role in determining the curriculum that students actually receive, even if clear curriculum guidelines and adopted materials are in place. The enacted curriculum is further modified by the students themselves when their efforts to make sense of what they are learning cause them to interpret information differently from the way the teacher intended (McCaslin & Good, 1996).

Berliner and Biddle (1995) argued that opportunity to learn is an exceedingly important variable. Indeed, sometimes individual students, their teachers, their schools or school districts, or even their nation's educational systems have been described as inferior simply because students have not had an opportunity to learn material. Berliner and Biddle asserted, "Regardless of what anyone claims about student and school characteristics, *opportunity to learn* is the single most important predictor of student achievement" (p. 55). Reports by various news services frequently contend that the Japanese educational system is performing at a higher level than is the American system. However, recent work by Westbury (1992, 1993) has shown that such contentions are exaggerated. As Figure 2.1 illustrates, when one compares students in the United States with students in Japan who have had equivalent instruction, it is clear that American students are doing reasonably well. Similarly, within this country, statements about students' academic attainments (e.g., high-group versus low-group students) often confuse ability and opportunity to learn.

This distinction is important because there are data to illustrate that when students believed to be less capable academically are given an opportunity to learn, in many cases they do so (e.g., Mason, Schroeter, Combs, & Washington, 1992). Unfortunately, there are writers who continue to underestimate the degree to which students can learn from rich educational experience (e.g., Herrnstein & Murray, 1995) when there is ample evidence to illustrate that opportunity to learn can make a powerful difference in student achievement (Berliner and Biddle, 1995; Porter, 1993).

Curriculum-Test Match

Many school districts use standardized achievement tests that are poorly matched to textbooks or to the instructional approach of particular teachers (Freeman et al., 1983; Good, 1996). Clearly, unless the curriculum and the test are aligned, incorrect conclusions are likely to be drawn about the effects of schooling. In our opinion, curriculum goals should determine the test used and not vice versa.

Related problems occur when curriculum materials are inappropriate for students. Jorgenson (1977) reported that in some classes 85 percent of the students used learning materials that were too difficult for them. Teachers probably were unaware of this mismatch or else did not know what to do about it.

Selection of Classroom Tasks

Doyle (1983) has contended that tasks are a critical aspect of academic work, arguing further that tasks vary widely in the cognitive complexity required (memorize versus analyze) and in the degree of risk taking they require of students. If teachers routinely assign memory work, students will spend their time memorizing isolated facts. In contrast, if tasks require students to integrate and organize information in order to understand concepts, then notably different performance expectations will be communicated. Thus, task structure affects how students think about assigned work in powerful ways.

Doyle (1983) argued that various academic activities or tasks are associated with different levels of ambiguity and risk. Memory tasks (e.g., What happened in 1588? What is the product of 9 x 8?) are low in *ambiguity* because students know in advance what kinds of answers are required. In contrast, students must construct rather than simply reproduce answers for tasks that involve understanding, and they may not have a clear idea about what to do.

Risk refers to the likelihood that students will be unable to produce an acceptable answer or product. Although memory tasks are typically low in ambiguity, they can be high or low in risk, depending on what must be recalled. Academic

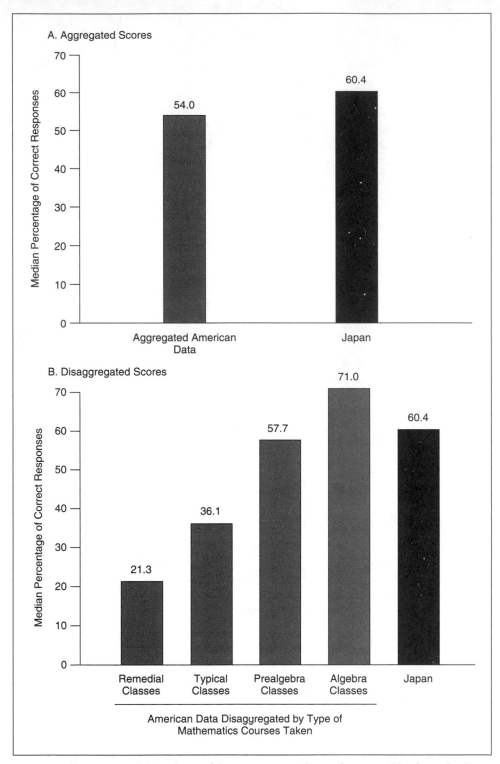

FIGURE 2.1 Japanese and American achievement scores for students age 13—from the Second International Mathematics Study of the IEA.

SOURCE: IAN WESTBURY (1992).

tasks that require understanding are at least moderately high in ambiguity and tend to be high in risk because the precise answer cannot be predicted in advance, so the constructive process is problematic. An accountability system has to be operating for risk to be an important variable: that is, if a teacher accepts any answer, there is no risk.

Many other researchers have examined how task structure influences student learning and curriculum enactment (for comprehensive reviews see Blumenfeld and Meece, 1988; Fisher and Hiebert, 1990; and Mergendoller, 1988). Researchers have not only conducted task research but have moved this conceptualization into particular subject-matter domains including social studies (e.g., Alleman & Brophy, 1992), literacy (e.g., Fisher & Hiebert, 1990), math (e.g., Good, McCaslin, & Reys, 1992), art (e.g., May, 1992), and science (e.g., Blumenfeld, 1992).

Empirical studies suggest that typical tasks assigned to students (laboratory exercises, workbooks, etc.) place only minimal demands for thinking (see, for example, Mergendoller et al., 1988). Further, some teachers design and implement tasks in classrooms that fail to "press" for students' cognitive engagement and understanding of material (Blumenfeld, 1992). It seems clear that some classroom teachers do not attend to the distribution of types of classroom tasks and to the impact of such assignments on students' thinking and performance. Further, the tasks assigned to tracked students in high schools are highly differentiated. Low-track students primarily receive memory tasks, whereas high-track students are more likely to receive tasks that require thinking (Oakes, 1992).

HOW STUDENTS AFFECT TEACHERS

Impression Management

The ways that students present themselves to teachers may make teaching decisions more difficult. Spencer-Hall (1981) described how some students were much better at impression management than others because they had learned to misbehave in ways that escaped the teachers' attention. One such student even was selected by teachers for a good citizenship award, despite the fact that the student had often engaged in disruptive behavior when teachers were nearby. Students who were skilled at misbehaving when the teacher had his or her back turned also were adept at looking appropriately involved when the teacher was monitoring classroom behavior.

There are many examples of the influence of individual students or classes of students on teachers and on classroom procedures. Most students and teachers are aware of students who have successfully manipulated instructors into giving them extra time and help. One of our favorite examples, provided by Professor Myron Dembo (personal communication), concerns successful manipulation by a college student to get extra time to prepare for exams by requesting permission to take exams *early* (due to a supposed conflict). Instructors typically preferred (for purposes of test security) that she take the exam late, however, and often gave her the same exam that was given in class. Hence, she often received extra time and knew the test content. Furthermore, instructors often viewed the student favorably because of her "willingness" to take the exam early.

Students who appear interested in class discussions may be more likely to get a clue or a second chance than students who seem less attentive. More generally, students' self-presentations can lead teachers to make erroneous assumptions about students' knowledge and motivation, especially when teachers have to make rapid decisions in a complex classroom setting. Teachers, for example, may misinterpret the behavior of some students because of cultural reasons (Allington, 1991; Delpit, 1995; Hiebert, 1991; Meier, 1995). Some students prefer not to participate in class discussions and attempt to keep a "low profile" (Jones, 1990; Jones & Gerig, 1994).

Although some researchers have documented a relationship between low participation and student achievement (e.g., Finn, Pannozzo, & Voelkl, 1995), others have noted that some high-achieving and apparently well-adjusted students prefer to learn by listening. Thus, as we noted in Chapter 1, teachers have to do more than observe behavior. Successful teachers are decision makers who come to understand the behaviors.

Individual Differences in Students

Differences in response opportunities often arise in classrooms because of important differences in students. Some students are more active, have more curiosity, and ask more questions than other students. Because of previous experiences, some students are better able than others to use adults as resources. Many differences in classroom participation among students are not attributable to teachers but rather to early socialization or influences outside the classroom (e.g., piano or gymnastics teachers).

Yet, at least some teachers socialize young girls mostly to be responsible and dependable in following conduct rules rather than to use initiative in learning (Grant, 1985). Differential teacher behavior toward male and female students (or high and low achievers) is an individual difference variable. Although some teachers differentiate content and interaction on the basis of student gender, other teachers show little of such behavior (e.g., Eccles & Blumenfeld, 1985). Furthermore, as we have noted, student behavior influences teacher behavior. Brophy and Evertson (1981, p. 118) concluded that most gender differences in teacher-student interactive patterns "are attributable to differences in the behavior of the students themselves and not to significant teacher favoritism of girls or rejection of boys." Bossert (1981) notes that when students work in mixed-gender groups on projects or experiments, boys are likely to manipulate objects and set up equipment, whereas girls are likely to watch and listen or to perform note-taking duties. Bossert found that boys and girls have varied interests and behave differently, so that even if teachers do not assign girls to act as recorders, most girls may assume these duties on their own. He contended that teachers need to be aware of the different interests that students bring to the classroom and be prepared to encourage all students to participate in a variety of classroom work.

Although the above discussion has focused mainly on gender issues, the argument applies largely to any discussion of individual differences. Many differences in student performance are due to home, cultural, and/or societal influences. Although we discuss individual student characteristics such as achievement level or race, we must recognize that students have multiple characteristics and that teachers must respect the complex interconnections of student gender, ethnicity, cultural background, ability, personality, and so on (Ladson-Billings, 1994; McCaslin & Good, 1996; Peshkin, 1991).

Clearly, classrooms are complex for students as well as teachers. Individual differences in how students react to classroom events may make it more or less difficult for teachers to know how to scaffold student learning (more on this in Chapters 3, 9, and 10).

MULTIPLE VIEWS OF CLASSROOM LIFE

There are multiple perspectives from which to view classroom life, and some of these viewpoints are strikingly different. Discrepancy between the viewpoints of a classroom observer and the teacher does not necessarily indicate a weakness on the part of the teacher. Observers can draw inappropriate conclusions about what occurs in classrooms. Similarly, teachers who work together often see or interpret classroom behavior in different ways (Gitlin & Smyth, 1989), and such differences can lead to useful dialogue, insight, and reflection.

Also, students often see things differently from their teacher or observers. Peterson and Swing (1982) studied relationships among students' thought processes, time on-task, and achievement. They reported that students' descriptions of their attending (active listening) to teacher presentations were better predictors of achievement than were observers' ratings of students' time-on-task during teacher presentations. In fact, observers' reports of students' attending behaviors were not good predictors of students' self-reports of attention. Rohrkemper (1985), Weinstein (1982), and Weinstein and Middlestadt (1979) also have demonstrated the value of obtaining students' views of classrooms. As Rohrkemper (1985) argued, information describing how students perceive their classroom experiences is a prerequisite to adequate interpretation of observed classroom interactions (for detailed discussion of how to obtain information about students' perspectives, see McCaslin & Good, 1996).

WHY TEACHERS ARE UNAWARE

We have discussed behaviors that teachers engage in without full awareness and noted that even when teachers are aware of their behavior they may not realize its effects. We believe that teachers' lack of awareness about their behavior or its effects lessens their classroom effectiveness. In this section, we discuss some of the reasons why teachers are unaware.

The most fundamental factor making it difficult for teachers to assess classroom behavior is that so much happens so rapidly. This problem can be solved in part through training. Awareness of everything that occurs is impossible, but with practice teachers can become more aware of their classroom behavior.

A second factor limiting awareness is that, historically, many teacher education programs have failed to equip teachers with specific teaching techniques or with skills for labeling and analyzing classroom behavior. Too often they gave teachers global advice (e.g., teach the whole child, individualize instruction) without linking it to specific behaviors. Recently, teacher education programs have made important strides in helping teachers to enhance their capacity for self-awareness.

Conceptual labels are powerful tools in helping teachers to become aware of what they do. Brophy and Good (1970) found that teachers gave up on low-achieving students who had difficulty responding to questions. However, the teachers did not view their behavior as giving up. Rather, they said that they were embarrassed by the silence, afraid that the students were embarrassed by the silence, or eager to keep the discussion moving. Similarly, teachers in the Rowe (1969) study probably did not realize that they were giving low achievers less time to respond and thereby making a response more difficult, and teachers in the Leinhardt, Seewald, and Engel (1979) study were probably not aware of their differential behavior toward male and female students.

These findings suggest that teacher education programs have not given teachers ways of labeling and monitoring their behavior. We are not saying that teachers should never give up on students in recitation sequences, for there are times when it is appropriate to move on. Teachers should be aware, however, that they are giving up when they do so and should know how often they do it with low achievers. Otherwise, they will teach low achievers that the easiest way to react to a question is to make no response.

Similarly, teachers should know the alternative responses they can make when students make no response or respond incorrectly: providing clues, probing, asking a simpler question, repeating the question, and so forth. Teachers can learn to make such alternative responses if they learn concepts with which to identify and label specific teaching situations and the skills to use in responding to them.

A third obstacle to awareness is that there is no system in place for providing teachers with information about what to do. Teachers are most likely to change when provided with information that shows a discrepancy between what they *want* to do and what they are doing. In-service teachers are unlikely to obtain such information, however, unless they meet with a supervisor several times during the year or have the chance to observe in other classrooms and exchange information frequently with fellow teachers. Yet teachers rarely see supervisors or peers. Many secondary teachers are not observed teaching. Unless they have unusual principals or supervisors, teachers seldom receive direct, useful feedback about their teaching (Rosenholtz, 1989).

IMPROVING TEACHING THROUGH OBSERVATIONAL FEEDBACK

Principals are beginning to visit classrooms more frequently in some school districts; however, visits are typically for purposes of evaluating teaching (Gitlin & Smyth, 1989) rather than for helping teachers to become more aware of their behavior or to improve instruction. Evaluation must occur, but teachers need information about what they are doing and suggestions for improvement as well (see Chapter 11).

Under the supervisory structure used in many schools, teachers may view feedback from supervisors with suspicion or hostility. Teachers know that supervisors' ratings are sometimes unreliable. Also, teachers frequently disagree with supervisors over goals (Gitlin & Smyth, 1989). When teachers believe that supervisors do not spend enough time in the classroom to assess their behaviors adequately, employ vague or irrelevant criteria, or lack the necessary subject-matter knowledge, teachers may reject supervisors' advice (Rosenholtz, 1989). There is reason to believe, however, that teachers want more frequent feedback about their classroom performance, particularly when they help to determine the criteria for evaluation (Rosenholtz, 1989). Indeed, one source of teacher dissatisfaction is *infrequency of evaluation* (Natriello & Dornbusch, 1980–1981; Wise et al., 1985).

Considering the recent interest in making teaching more of a profession by creating more opportunities for professional growth (Griffin, 1985; Smylie, 1992; 1995), we hope that in the next few years there will be a significant increase in opportunities for in-service teachers to obtain useful feedback about their classroom performance (see Chapter 11).

Griffin (1983) found that during supervisory interactions little attention was paid to developing a knowledge base that would help student teachers subsequently when they had their own classrooms. These interactions focused mostly on reacting to immediate, specific problems and a "let's see if this works" style of offering suggestions. Unfortunately, rationales for these suggestions typically were not provided, and there were few references to learning theory, child development, instructional models, and so on. The supervisory interactions were dominated by the cooperating teacher, who selected the topics for conversation and controlled how they were discussed. Conversations usually focused on a particular classroom at a certain time; they seldom involved alternative ways to understand and respond to classroom events.

The ability to describe behavior heightens awareness of it as it unfolds in the classroom. A conceptual system allows teachers to classify what they are doing as they do it, making it possible for them to be aware of what they do and to remember it later. Many school districts now have video equipment so that teachers can see themselves in action. At first glance, videotaping seems like a useful learning aid—what better way for teachers to improve than to see themselves as others do? Unfortunately, studies report that after teachers have viewed videotapes, the changes in their teaching behavior are not impressive.

Seeing a film of oneself teaching is like sitting in a classroom watching another teacher. The behavior on video is still rapid and complex. If teachers do not know what to look for, they do not see much. However, when teachers view videotapes with a consultant who can provide specific feedback or with materials describing what to look for, positive change occurs. Thus, videotapes and audiotapes are likely to help teachers improve their classroom behavior only if specific teaching behaviors are highlighted and discussed. Further, there is some evidence that when teachers are given suggestions about ways to think about teaching (as opposed to directives), teacher conferences are more likely to be productive.

The terms *conceptual and observational tools* refer to a descriptive vocabulary. Every social organization, game, or system has a language of its own. For example, bridge has a unique descriptive vocabulary, as does football. Persons who do not understand such terms as *three no-trump* or *first down* cannot understand the games. Language for describing classrooms is necessarily much more complex, but learnable. We want to make teachers more familiar with this language to enable them to describe and understand what they do in the classroom.

BENEFITS OF CLASSROOM OBSERVATION

We believe that providing you with concepts that describe classroom processes will help you to monitor more of your behavior and how you conceptualize and plan for teaching. For example, knowledge of variables such as *wait time* can help you increase the time you wait for students to respond when it is appropriate to do so. Similarly, awareness of a tendency to *give up* on low achievers can enable you to ask new questions, provide clues, rephrase questions, or otherwise seek to improve the performance of these students more frequently.

Teachers who are trying to understand their behavior can apply observational techniques such as those presented here. Consider the "Sea of Darkness" example in Chapter 1. If the teacher had tape-recorded the lesson, most of the dimensions discussed in our analysis might have become evident to her (high rates of factual questions, lack of a clear pattern to the questions, different reactions toward boys and girls, and so forth). Teachers who tape-record their lessons occasionally (e.g., once every two weeks) could derive many of the same benefits as having an observer in the classroom. However, neither teachers nor observers are likely to understand classroom behavior unless they know how to collect information, know what behaviors to look for, and have a conceptual or theoretical framework to guide their analyses.

PROBLEMS WITH OBSERVATION

Teachers' perceptions of classroom behavior differ in some respects from those of students and observers (McCaslin & Good, 1996; Weinstein, 1983). Part of the reason is that teachers and observers may miss some classroom occurrences because so many things happen so quickly. Further, teachers are intimately involved in running the classroom. Also, teachers and observers can and do *misinterpret* classroom behavior. That is, the problem of observing in classrooms is a bit more complex than we have described so far. Not only is our ability to perceive behavior in the classroom reduced by a fast classroom pace and not knowing what to look for, but on occasion, what we think we see is not congruent with reality. Our beliefs, past experiences, and prejudices can lead us to interpret what we see incorrectly rather than to see, describe, and analyze objectively what really happened.

Personal Biases

Supporters of various theories of teaching may interpret what they see in classrooms differently (Posner, 1985; Jackson, Boostrom, & Hansen, 1993). Those who hold a didactic view believe that teaching is primarily aimed at transmitting knowledge and providing clear explanations or demonstrations that show how the knowledge operates. A discovery view focuses on student experimentation and opportunity to learn inductively from inquiry activities, with a minimum of teacher structure and explanation. An observer who prefers a didactic approach might find it difficult to assess fairly a teacher who uses a discovery approach, and vice versa. Thus, in addition to the problems discussed earlier (speed, complexity, lack of conceptual vocabulary for describing classroom behavior), personal biases (values, preferences) may distort what we see in the classroom.

Those who wish to observe accurately must identify and examine their biases. A classroom observer who is irritated by assertive, highly verbal teachers may see such teachers as punitive and rigid, whereas another observer may view them as well organized and articulate. Similarly, a teacher may see two students exhibit the same behavior yet interpret the students' behavior differently. Imagine the following situation. Mr. Nowicki, who teaches tenth-grade American history, is talking when Derek Jackson calls out, "Why are we talking about this?" Knowing Derek to be a troublemaker and class clown, Mr. Nowicki assumes Derek wants to waste time or provoke an argument, so he responds aggressively, "If you would pay attention, you'd know what we're doing. Pay attention!" Compare this response with Mr. Nowicki's reply to Jim, who calls out in the same tone, "Why are we talking about this?" Because Mr. Nowicki knows that Jim is a good, dependable student, he views Jim's words not as a threat but as a serious question. He reasons that if Jim does not understand the purpose of the discussion, nobody does. He responds, "Jim, I probably haven't made this clear. Last Friday we discussed . . ."

Teachers react according to their *interpretations* of what students say, and their past experiences with a student often influence their response. We do not suggest that teachers should not interpret students' comments, but we argue that teachers should be *aware* of doing so. Some teachers fall into the trap of expecting a student to behave in a certain way and then systematically coloring their interpretations of the student's behavior, so that the behavior appears to fulfill the teacher's expectation. Often the distinction between observed behavior and the teacher's interpretation of that behavior is lost.

Delpit (1995) has asserted that differences in class backgrounds and cultures not only can interfere with teacher-student communication, but also can affect how teachers are rated by supervisors. She notes:

> A further complication is that teachers from some cultures do not expect to have to show competence by *talking* about what they do. They expect that anyone wanting to know what they do in a classroom will watch them teach and then make judgments about their competence. From the perspective of many Native American teachers, the doing of a task should be evidence of competence, whereas Western academic culture views competence as being evidenced only in *talking* about what one has done. Teachers from some cultural groups will likely be reluctant in an interview setting to *talk* about what they may be very good at *doing*—and the assessor may assume, then, that the candidate is incapable of doing what he or she can't explain. (p. 148)

Anyone who tries to observe behavior must guard against this tendency to let personal biases color what is seen. We provide an exercise at the end of the chapter to help you identify some of your classroom biases. After you become more aware of various teacher and student behaviors and your attitudes toward them, you will be able to interpret classroom behavior more objectively. Suggestions are also presented to help you gather classroom data without unduly influencing the behavior of teachers and students.

Teacher Anxiety

Teachers who are insecure and possess a poor teaching self-concept are especially unlikely to seek information about themselves and apt to distort information as threatening when they receive it. Insecure teachers often see instructional difficulties as reflecting factors other than their own lack of competency ("TV and computer games have spoiled students. You can't motivate them anymore.").

How teacher anxiety influences teacher behavior, as well as the anxiety and classroom behavior of students, is complex, but a teacher who is excessively concerned about self is likely to have difficulty monitoring classroom interaction and seeing how others are affected by classroom events. Hence, some teachers may need more peer association than others.

DANGERS OF INTERPRETATION

It is hard to overstate the value of interpreting behavior only after data are collected. Quantitative and qualitative theorists agree on this important point (Evertson & Green, 1986). Quantitative researchers often ask questions before they observe (Is instruction meaningful or rote? Do girls and boys have equally challenging assignments?, etc.) and develop coding systems that are specifically designed to answer these questions. In contrast, qualitative researchers tend to ask questions only after collecting considerable observational data. As Erickson (1986) notes, however, the stereotype of a classroom observer (field worker) arriving with a tabula rasa mind (carrying only a toothbrush and hunting knife), first to find and then to study a question, is romantic and extreme. (See Jacob [1995] for a helpful discussion of how teachers and researchers can effectively use principles from anthropology to explore classroom events more fully.)

Erickson suggests that the observer's task is to become aware of possible frames of interpretation of those who are observed (i.e., How did teachers and students view the behavior?) and to subject observed behaviors to multiple interpretations. According to Erickson, the classroom observer, or field worker, should perform as a progressive problem solver. That is, observers' decisions about whom to talk to and what to observe next are determined as data are collected and analyzed. Thus, whether coders are using categories or field notes, they must be nonjudgmental during data collection. Knowing the question in advance is not likely to prejudice the outcome of research if the question calls for collection of descriptive facts rather than ratings or value judgments and the observer concentrates on collecting these facts before exploring their implications for classroom participants. Indeed, in many ways, formulating questions in advance guarantees that the information collected is relevant to the teacher and classroom being observed.

The teaching incident involving Mr. Nowicki also illustrates that inferences should be made after observers have collected and examined descriptive information. As we have noted, observers' backgrounds, particularly their experiences as students and their views of good teaching, can lead them to draw erroneous conclusions (e.g., Goodson, 1992). If the teacher does something an observer especially likes (e.g., asks questions before calling on students), the observer may rate the teacher high in all areas. Similarly, if the teacher does something an observer particularly dislikes (e.g., humiliates a student who provides a wrong answer), the observer may evaluate the teacher as low on all dimensions of classroom behavior, even if the teacher performs well on some. Thus, observers need to guard against generalizing about behavior. Also, they must not evaluate behavior as positive or negative independent of its effects on students. For example, a teacher whom an observer sees as overly critical may be perceived by students as a person who sets high standards and cares about them (Delpit, 1995; Kleinfeld, 1975; Mitman, 1985).

It is difficult for an observer to record behavior without interpreting it. Observers should concentrate on observing and coding or recording. Looking for specific behaviors is one way to minimize the effects of observers' attitudes and biases on their perceptions. For example, if an observer believes a teacher to be caustic and ineffectual, it is less likely that such an attitude will interfere with the description of classroom life if the observer pays attention to behavior (e.g., how often the teacher calls on low-achieving male students) than it will if the observer tries to describe the teacher in global, inferential terms (warm, friendly, fair, etc.). Behavior can be seen accurately if an observer wants to do so and is willing to practice and to compare his or her observations with those of others.

Common sources of error that can occur during observation appear in Table 2.1. As Everston and Green (1986) note, these issues need attention if we are to observe accurately in classrooms.

CASE STUDY TECHNIQUES

One useful way to improve observational skills is by conducting case studies that focus on one or a few students. Case studies that involve reporting of observed behaviors are particularly helpful. Such assignments facilitate our ability to observe and describe behavior accurately, and these skills are necessary to the generation of effective, concrete plans for dealing with students. Traditional case studies are excellent analytical tools for expanding our ability to see and to interpret student behavior.

Those of you seeking more detailed advice about ways to conduct scientific inquiries using case studies and field notes can profitably consult other sources (e.g., Erickson, 1986). Our focus here is on practical techniques for studying students in one's own classroom.

Discovering Bias

We have noted that observers and teachers often misinterpret behavior because of their backgrounds and biases or because they try to interpret their findings prematurely. The first step in overcoming these problems is to become aware of them.

When we become aware of our attitudes, we can often control our behavior better. For example, the teacher who unhesitatingly says, "I am a fair grader, I am never influenced by the student as a person, and I grade only the paper," may be an unfair grader. The fact is that knowing who wrote a paper does influence most graders. With certain students, especially high achievers, teachers tend to read

Table 2.1   SOURCES OF ERROR IN OBSERVATIONAL RESEARCH

Type of Error	Definition
1. Central tendency	When using rating scales, the observer tends toward the subjective midpoint when judging a series of stimuli.
2. Leniency or generosity	When using rating scales for which a "yes," "sometimes," "rarely," or "no" is required, the observer tends to be lenient or generous.
3. Primacy or recency effects	Observers' initial impressions have a distorting effect on later judgments (primacy). Observers' ratings may be unduly influenced by their most recent observations (recency).
4. Logical errors	Observer makes judgment errors based on theoretical, experiential, or commitment-based assumptions (e.g., the assumption that because a teacher shows warmth to a class, she or he is also instructionally effective).
5. Failure to acknowledge self	The influence of the observer on the setting is overlooked. The investigator's role may lead to the establishment of particular expectations. Judgments can be made in accordance with these expectations.
6. Classification of observations	Construction of macro categories loses fine distinctions. Such categories permit quantification but lose information about the process and fine-grained differences.
7. Generalization of unique behavior	Judgments may be based on evidence from an unrepresentative sample. Can lead to false conclusion or incorrect classifications of people or events.
8. Vested interests and values of observer	Findings become value-laden or otherwise distorted because of unchecked personal bias.
9. Failure to consider perspective of the observed	For investigators interested in a clear picture of everyday life, failure to obtain participants' perspectives may lead to identification of unvalidated factors, processes, or variables.
10. Unrepresentative sampling	Errors may occur based on samples that do not represent the general group of behaviors, that do not occur frequently enough to be observed reliably, or that are inconsistent with the theory guiding the observations.
11. Reactions of the observed	Reactions of participants being observed can distort the process or phenomena being observed (e.g., teachers who are anxious about being observed may behave differently than they would at a calmer time).
12. Failure to account for situation or context	Leads to incorrect conclusions from assumptions of functional equivalents (e.g., reading time 1 = reading time 2). Can lead to overlooking what is being taught, changes in activities, variations in rights and obligations for participation, hence can distort conclusions.
13. Poorly designed observation systems	Lead to problems with reliability and validity.
14. Lack of consideration for the rapid speed of relevant action	Errors may occur based on the omission of crucial features because of the rapidity of actions in the classroom.
15. Lack of consideration for the simultaneity of relevant action	Errors may occur based on failure to account for more than one activity occurring at a time; more than one message being sent at a time (e.g., use of different channels—verbal and nonverbal); and more than one function of a message at a time.

(continued)

Table 2.1   *(continued)*

Type of Error	Definition
16. Lack of consideration of goal-directed or purposive nature of human activity	False conclusion that a behavior lacks stability because of failure to consider the purposes of human behavior.
17. Failure to ensure against observer drift	Errors caused by changes in the way the observer uses a system as time goes on. Can lead to obtaining descriptions that do not match the original categories or that vary from each other.

Source: Adapted from Evertson, C., & Green, J. (1986).Observation as inquiry and method. In M. Wittrock (Ed.), *Handbook of research on teaching* (3rd ed.). New York: Macmillan.

more into an answer than is there. They may demand more proof from other students (e.g., although a student's first paragraph in an essay is excellent, the teacher suspects that this student does not really know the material).

Once teachers realize that they do have biases that interfere with grading fairly, they can take steps to reduce the effects of those biases. For example, teachers can mask the identity of the student who wrote the paper before grading it, grade all papers on the first question before going to the next question, and score only content and not handwriting. In the same way, we can improve other weak spots if we become aware of them.

Difficulties of Self-Study

It is difficult to admit to feelings and reactions that we are afraid are unprofessional or inappropriate. For example, we tend not to accept the fact that we react differently to various students. Greenberg (1969) described some of the myths that frequently produce teacher problems, such as the illusion of liking all students equally. Such magnanimous behavior is impossible. Teachers treat students in equally fair and facilitating ways if and when they are aware of their feelings about the students. This does not mean identical behavior toward all students, however, because some students need more teacher contact, others need more opportunity to work on their own, and so forth. Ladson-Billings (1994) contends that many teachers confuse equality and sameness. She argues the problem this way:

> The notion of equity as sameness only makes sense when all students *are* exactly the same. But even within the nuclear family children born from the same parents are not exactly the same. Different children have different needs and addressing those different needs is the best way to deal with them equitably. The same is true in the classroom. If teachers pretend not to see students' racial and ethnic differences, they really do not see the students at all and are limited in their ability to meet their educational needs. (p. 34)

As human beings, teachers experience the full range of human emotions: they distrust some students, are proud of others, find some delightful, and want to avoid others. Similarly, observers have different reactions toward different teachers.

If we are not careful, these feelings interfere with our ability to perceive classroom events accurately. Once we identify our feelings, it is possible to monitor classroom behavior more objectively.

Using Case Study for Self-Study

The case study assignment described in this section provides you with an opportunity to study your values, preferences, and attitudes. It forces you to consider the types of students (or teachers) whom you find fun and exciting to work with and to identify the types who annoy or bore you.

From the following list, select two contrast groups for study—any two except pairs 1 and 4. If you are not in an observation course, select peers who are in your class or select two college instructors and analyze their behavior. Better yet, arrange to observe in a class similar to the one you teach or will be teaching.

1. Select the two students with whom you would most enjoy working; that is, as a teacher, which two students would you choose first to be in your own room? (Positive feelings)
2. Select the two students whom you dislike the most. (Negative feelings)
3. Select two students for whom you have no strong feeling whatsoever. Use the class roster here so that you do not forget about anyone. (Apathy, indifference, not noticing when they are absent)
4. Select two students (one boy, one girl) who best represent the child you would want your son or daughter to be like at this age. (Identification)
5. Select two students who come from a cultural background that differs from your own. (Need for new knowledge or understanding.)

After selecting the four students, observe them more closely. If you choose to take notes during class, be sure to obtain the teacher's permission and let him or her know that the notes are about students and not the teacher. Some of you will be busy teaching during the day, so your notes will have to be made after class. The notes are for your own use, so their form is completely open. Bear in mind that any information you record in classrooms is confidential; students should never be identified by name. Even notes that you take in class should include no *actual* student names (notes are often lost). For this case study, it is not necessary to collect data from the school files, which might influence the observation anyway. Normal classroom behavior is sufficient.

Analyze the similarities and differences among the four students to get clues regarding the types of student behavior that are likely to elicit positive or negative responses in you. This activity will help you to understand why you behave as you do and help you learn to interact more positively with students who irritate or confuse you. Consider the following questions when you compare and contrast the students:

1. What are they like physically? How do they look? Do they have nice clothes? Are they attractive? Clean? Large or small for their age? Male or female?

2. What are their favorite subjects? What lessons bore them? What are their strong and weak points as students? As persons?

3. What are their most prominent behavioral characteristics? Do they smile a lot? Thank you for your attention? Seek you out in the classroom more or less than the average student? Do they raise their hands to answer often? Can they be depended on to do their own work? How mature are they? Are they awkward or clumsy?

4. What are their social characteristics? What socioeconomic level do they come from? What is their ethnic background?

5. What aspects of classroom life seem most satisfying to them? What is least enjoyable or threatening?

The goal of this exercise is to start you thinking about possible linkages between your feelings about students and the way students treat you and you treat them in the classroom. A valuable parallel exercise would be to list the teacher behaviors that provoke your interest or boredom.

Conducting Case Studies

If you are puzzled about particular students, or merely interested in learning more about them, concentrated and sustained observation usually will reveal new insights and suggest interpretations and explanations. Case studies help teachers overcome the tendency to see students only within the student role. Attention is focused on students as unique individuals, and an attempt is made to empathize with them. This study involves trying to see the classroom environment as students see it and to understand what students are trying to accomplish when they respond to it.

First, who are the students? What are their background characteristics (age, gender, family background)? What are their orientations toward school? Toward the teachers? Toward classmates? What are their hobbies and interests? Their strengths and weaknesses as individuals? As students? Thinking about such questions and jotting down tentative answers can help in developing an open mind toward students and learning to look at them in new ways. These steps may improve your knowledge of a certain student before you spend any time observing that student. For example, if you cannot name several strengths *and* weaknesses, your view of the student is probably biased. In our desire for simplicity and consistency in our perceptions, we tend to emphasize characteristics that fit together and reinforce our biases, and to slight those that do not.

No special preparation or equipment is required to observe a student systematically. An ordinary notebook and pen or pencil will do. You should be near enough to see and hear the student, but not so close as to be inhibiting. Ideally, the student should not know you are observing him or her. If possible, observe the student outside class as well (during recess, at lunch, and between classes), when the student's behavior is likely to be more characteristic than when constricted by the student role.

If the student presents a problem, try to formulate it as specifically as you can, using terms that translate into observable behavior. Include any relevant information about the contexts in which behavior occurs (subject matter, size of group, time of day, type of situation). Patterns in the student's behavior may increase your understanding of it. You also might notice important differences between situations in which the student is and is not a problem (interest in the topic, structure in the activity, active versus quiet activity, type of antecedent experience, presence of peers or other distractors, etc.).

Whatever the activity, focus on the student, including times when he or she is a passive spectator. There is a tendency to observe the teacher or whoever else is the center of attention at times like these, but when you are doing a case study, it is important to concentrate on the student.

Keep a running log of the student's behavior during periods of observation. Observations should be dated and clearly separated from one another in the continuous log, and they should be subdivided into natural units according to what was going on at the time (class periods and breaks between periods, different activities and settings within classes, etc.). The log should contain narrative descriptions of behavior along with interpretations about its possible meanings. It is important to keep objective descriptions of behavior separate from subjective interpretations concerning meaning, because interpretations may change as more information is collected. Probably the easiest way to do this is to use only the left half of the page for keeping the log of behavior. Interpretations can be written on the right half of the page later, when you review your notes and think about what you have observed.

If you interviewed students, you may find that their beliefs about school subjects and other topics differ from what you had concluded on the basis of your observation. Students can be excellent sources of information about how classrooms work. Interview techniques are beyond the scope of this book, but excellent suggestions about the use of student interviews as well as how to conduct them can be found elsewhere (Cazden, 1986; McCaslin & Good, 1996; Meichenbaum et al., 1985; Rohrkemper, 1981, 1985; Spradley, 1979; Weinstein, 1983).

Fact Versus Interpretation

When recording information for a case study, the goal is to include as much pertinent and interpretable information as possible but to stick with the facts and avoid unsupported and perhaps incorrect interpretations. This objective is not difficult to achieve, but it may take some practice to learn to separate vague information from interpretable facts, and interpretable facts from interpretations themselves.

An Example   Suppose an observer were watching Ron, a white student, at a time when he became involved in an incident with Ralph, a black student, and recorded the following information: "Ralph taps Ron, points, and speaks. Ron replies, shaking head. Ralph gestures, speaks. Ron strikes Ralph, and a fight starts." This information is factual, but it is too vague to be much good. Even if the words of the boys are not heard, their gestures and the general nature of their interaction can be described much more clearly. Let's look at another example.

> Ron is working quietly until bothered by Ralph. He listens, then refuses. Ralph becomes angry and abusive. Ron becomes aggressive, triggering a major racial incident.

Assuming that the observer could not hear what was said, this example is not so much an observation as an interpretation. Ron may or may not have "refused" whatever Ralph wanted, Ralph may or may not have "provoked" Ron, and the incident may or may not be "racial." These are interpretations. They fit the facts and may be true, but this also can be said of many other possible interpretations. A competent observer would have recorded the facts as follows:

> Ralph taps Ron on shoulder, shows his assignment, points to something, speaks. Ron looks, shakes head no, says something. Ralph replies with disgusted look, downward gesture of arm. Turns away when finished speaking. Ron says something to Ralph from behind, then slaps Ralph's head. Ralph responds as if attacked, fight begins.

This description contains about as much useful information as could be recorded without becoming interpretive. About all that is missing is a description of Ron's facial expression and general manner when slapping Ralph. This information would be helpful in judging whether the head slap really was meant as an attack (if so, it would be an unusual behavior).

The interpretation of this information would raise questions about its meaning. Who actually started the trouble, and what started it? Is it accurate to call this a racial incident, or is the fact that one boy is black and the other white irrelevant? What really happened?

Ordinarily, the observer would get answers to these and related questions, because interactions as intense as fights usually involve loud talk, which is easy to hear. However, without more information, the interpretation of these facts would have to be confined to speculation. The first fact is that Ralph interrupted Ron by tapping his shoulder, pointing to the assignment, and saying something. The shoulder tap apparently did not bother Ron because he did not show any reaction to it. In fact, he did not appear angry until later. The fact that Ralph showed the assignment and pointed to something suggests that he was seeking help or information about it or was expressing an opinion. However, it is possible that Ralph did these things just to give the appearance of discussing the assignment and that what he had to say to Ron had nothing to do with the assignment. If so, he could have made a provocative statement, but not necessarily.

Ron responded by shaking his head no and saying something. This response could have been a refusal to listen, a refusal of a request, or an answer to Ralph's question, among other things. If Ralph had expressed an opinion, this could have been a disagreement by Ron. In any case, it is clear that Ron responded negatively to whatever Ralph asked or said.

Ralph's gesture and facial expression in his reply suggest disgust and/or anger, although it is not at all clear whether he provoked Ron in some way. He might have, but he might also have been expressing his own frustration with whatever Ron had said. He might even have been giving an opinion. For example, he might have originally pointed out what he considered to be a stupid question and asked Ron if he understood it. Ron might have said that he didn't understand it either, and Ralph might have responded with a gesture and look of disgust while saying something like, "Why do they ask us stuff like this?"

Just as Ralph's behavior may or may not have involved provocation, Ron's behavior may or may not have involved aggression. It could have been an attack on Ralph, perhaps in retaliation for something Ralph said, but it also could have been horseplay. Boys frequently poke or slap one another as a way of teasing (but not attacking), and that could be what happened.

With a little imagination, we can think of several other interpretations of what occurred between Ron and Ralph, but the ones just given are sufficient to indicate the difference between facts and interpretations. Such ambiguous situations are common when classroom observations are collected in case studies, which is why it is important physically to separate facts about observations from interpretations of these observations. The factual record will remain constant even when interpretations change in the light of new evidence. Even when you are not entering observations in a case study record, the distinction between fact and interpretation should be kept in mind. The ability to maintain and be aware of this distinction is an important part of learning to be accurate when observing in classrooms.

Avoiding Bias   Recording and interpreting behavior are two distinct issues. You must determine what behavior to record and how to record it, and then you interpret the behavior. You may have to experiment in order to find the appropriate degree of generality to use in describing behavior. You should not try to record literally everything that you see. Even if this were possible, you would be recording a great deal of information about trivial behaviors and expressions that have no interpretive importance. In contrast, in the interest of objectivity, it is important that you record observable behaviors. Thus, it would be appropriate to note that the student smiled or even smiled at the teacher, but it would be an interpretation to say that the student showed friendly warmth (as opposed to self-satisfaction, for example). Similarly, it would be appropriate to state that the student spent time apparently absorbed in thinking and problem solving, but it would be an interpretation to say that the student *was* thinking and problem solving. Perhaps the student has learned to give this appearance while daydreaming (Peterson & Swing, 1982; Spencer-Hall, 1981).

You want to highlight information relevant to your concerns about the student, but your record should keep everything in proper perspective. For example, if you are watching a student who gets into trouble with peers, you should have detailed descriptions of what happened on two occasions when the student became involved in arguments. It should be clear from the record, however, that these two occasions involved only a few minutes, and the record should provide a running account of what the student was doing during the rest of the period. In fact, when you observe a problem student, it can be helpful to keep in mind the question "What does the student do when not misbehaving?" This question will cue your attention to positive behavior that a teacher should learn about and build on in future interactions with the student. To obtain this information, it is important to fight the tendency to let halo effects structure your perceptions. Just as outstanding students have weaknesses, problem students have strengths.

Behavioral records should be reviewed and checked for completeness and accuracy at the first opportunity. At this time, you can also make initial interpretations, add clarification, and edit your notes. You may or may not be able to interpret everything you see, but your notes should be complete and unambiguous concerning what actually happened. In addition to a description of what transpired, there should be information about the qualitative aspects of the student's behavior (Was it random or purposeful? Was there anything unusual or noteworthy about it?) and explanations for the behavior (What stimulated it? What was its purpose?).

In reviewing behavioral comments, look for correlations and contradictions. Try to identify repeated patterns. Are they well known, or do they suggest new insights? Look for places where a particular pattern might have been expected but did not occur. These could be keys to explaining patterns or to developing ideas about how to get the student to change. If your notes suggest certain hypotheses but do not contain enough information to allow you to evaluate them, try to identify what information you need. Perhaps you can identify specific situations you could observe soon. For example, suppose the student challenged the teacher on two occasions when asked to read aloud. This response could be a defense mechanism used in an attempt to avoid reading, perhaps because the student cannot read. You cannot tell from only two instances, but you could watch for this behavior in the future whenever the class is involved in oral reading, and you could check the student's reading achievement. Such supplementary information then can be added to the log at appropriate places to assist you in interpreting the student's behavior.

SIMPLIFYING THE OBSERVATIONAL TASK

We have emphasized the need to study observer and teacher biases to prevent them from interfering with assessment of classroom events. Another major obstacle to accurate perception of classrooms is their sheer physical complexity. While the teacher instructs a reading group, four students may be at the science table, three listening to tapes at the listening post, four reading at their desks, and three writing at the blackboard. No observer can monitor everything that takes place. Even relatively simple tasks may be impossible to code simultaneously. For instance, if an observer wants to code the number of hands raised when a teacher asks a question and note whether the student called on by the teacher has a hand up, the observer may still be counting hands when the teacher calls on the student and will thus be unable to determine whether the student had a hand up. One excellent way to overcome this complexity, especially when you begin observing in classrooms, is to study the behavior of a few students. You can study these students intensively, and their behavior will probably mirror what is taking place in the entire classroom. An observer can focus on a few students (perhaps two high, two middle, and two low achievers—one female and one male at each level) or on a particular group of students (low achievers). Then a record can be made of certain things these students do. One might record the following information about high, middle, and low achievers:

1. How often do they raise their hands?
2. Do all students approach the teacher to receive help, or do some seldom approach the teacher?

3. How long does each reading group last?

4. Are the students involved in their work? How long do they work independently at their desks?

5. How often are students in different groups praised?

6. What do students do when they finish their experiment, while other students are still completing their lab assignment?

Another useful strategy is to limit the number of behaviors you observe at one time, perhaps restricting attention initially to five to ten behaviors. When we attempt to monitor too many things, we become confused and cannot record objectively. It is better to concentrate on a few behaviors for a while and then to code a new set.

RELIABILITY OF OBSERVATIONS

You should assess your ability to code classroom behavior accurately by comparing your observations with those of others. This method is perhaps the easiest way to determine whether you are observing what happens and not allowing your personal biases to interfere with your observing.

In general, the observation forms presented following Chapters 3 through 10 can be used reliably with little practice. After discussing an observation scale for a short time (5 to 20 minutes, depending on the scale), observers should be able to achieve general agreement (60 to 90 percent) and thus be able to use the scale reliably to code classroom behavior. If observers are watching a videotape and coding the number of academic questions a teacher asks, one observer may have tallied 16 academic questions, whereas another tallied only 10. Agreement between the two observers can be estimated by using this simple formula suggested by Emmer and Millet (1970):

$$\text{Agreement} = 1 - \frac{A - B}{A + B}$$

The formula tells us to subtract the difference between the two observers' counts and to divide by the sum of their counts. The *A* term is always the larger number. Thus, agreement in this example would be:

$$1 - \frac{16 - 10}{16 + 10} = 1 - \frac{6}{26} = 1 - 0.23 = 77\%$$

GENERAL PLAN FOR OBSERVING IN CLASSROOMS

What you observe in a classroom will vary from situation to situation and from individual to individual. Some observers will be able to focus on six behaviors; others may be able to code ten. Some may be in the classroom eight hours a week, some only four. Some may see two or three different teachers; others will remain in the same room. Despite such situational differences, some general principles will apply when observing in classrooms. First, observers often try to reduce the complexity of classroom coding by focusing their attention exclusively on the teacher. This is particularly true for teachers in training, who are still trying to determine what teachers do, but it is misplaced emphasis. *The key to thorough classroom observation is student response.* If students are actively engaged in worthwhile learning activities, it makes little difference whether the teacher is lecturing, using discovery techniques, or using small-group activities for independent study.

Earlier we noted that some observers may see a teacher as punitive and rigid, whereas others see the same teacher as well organized and articulate. A good way to reduce your own bias in viewing teacher behavior is to supplement your observations by examining both teacher and student behaviors. Students influence teachers as much as teachers influence students.

Teachers who want to receive relevant feedback about their behavior and that of their students, and observers who want to see what life in a classroom is like must be careful not to disturb the natural behavior in the classroom. By *natural* we mean the behavior that would take place in the classroom if the observer were not present. Students, especially young ones, adjust quickly to the presence of an observer if teachers prepare them properly and if the observer behaves appropriately. The teacher should explain the observer's presence briefly, so that the students do not have to wonder about the observer or try to question him or her to find out for themselves. For example, a second-grade class might be told, "Mr. Ramon will be with us today and the rest of the week. He is learning about being a teacher. Mr. Ramon will not disturb us because we have many things we want to finish, and he knows how busy we are. Please do not disturb him because he, too, is busy and has his own work to do."

The observer can help the teacher by avoiding eye contact with the students and by refusing to be drawn into long conversations with them or to aid them in their seatwork—unless, of course, the observer is also a participant in classroom life. (Some university courses call for students to serve as teacher aides before they do their student teaching.)

Observers should not initiate contact with students or do anything to draw special attention to themselves (e.g., loudly ripping pages out of a notebook). It is especially important when two observers are in the same room that they not talk with each other, exchange notes, and so forth. Such behavior bothers both the teacher and the students and causes attention to be focused on the observers, so that natural behavior is disturbed.

Before coming into a classroom, observers should talk with the teacher about where they will sit in the room, how they should be introduced to the students, and how they should respond when a student approaches them. Without such preparation, both teachers and observers frequently are paralyzed when students approach the observer. Teachers are embarrassed because students are out of their seats, and they are indecisive about what to do because they do not know whether the observer wants to inspect the students' work or would prefer not to be bothered. Observers are often unskilled at dealing with students. They are not sure how to act when approached, except that they don't want to be a rude guest. The teacher and observers should agree on how to deal with students who are intent on making themselves known to the observer. At such meetings, observers can obtain curriculum materials and information about the students (seating chart, achievement ranking). Such information is necessary if the observer plans to conduct an intensive study of only a few students at different achievement levels. The information needed to use the rating systems at the ends of subsequent chapters is presented in this chapter. If you wish detailed information about more advanced coding systems, consult Appendix A at the ends of this chapter.

In the first two chapters, we have identified many factors that can interfere with your perception of classroom behavior, and we have discussed ways to reduce problems of bias and complexity (students who will conduct research in classrooms can find more detailed discussions about conducting observational research elsewhere). In the following chapters, we develop the theme of looking in classrooms by providing detailed comments about *what* to look for. In these chapters we discuss what could and should be occurring in classrooms. At the ends of most chapters are rating scales that can be used to record the presence or absence of the teaching behaviors discussed in this chapter.

USING RESEARCH AND OBSERVATIONAL FEEDBACK

Research findings and concepts provide a way of thinking about classroom instruction, but they must be used as tools, not rules. Consider Adams and Biddle's (1970) discussion of the action zone, describing their finding that students who sat in the front row and in seats extending directly up the middle aisle received more opportunities to talk than other students. The action zone is a useful concept for identifying *possible* problems in the classroom; it suggests that students in some areas of a classroom may receive more response opportunities than students in other areas. If interpreted too literally, however, the work of Adams and Biddle could be interpreted to mean that action zones are always located in the front row and the middle of the class. A study by Alhajri (1981) showed that only 1 of 32 classrooms had an action zone like the one described by Adams and Biddle, although some kind of action zone was present in many classrooms. This research reaffirmed the value of the action zone concept as a tool for analyzing classroom instruction, even though it showed that action zones can take many forms. If observers or teachers were monitoring classes for only one type of action zone, they would not notice zones that took a different form.

We discuss research findings in terms of concepts that enable teachers to examine classrooms. Research results do not provide answers because they must be applied to particular teachers and students. Research-based concepts can, however, enable educators to observe more behaviors more rapidly. They also can stimulate additional analysis.

Considering the complexity of and variation among instruction-learning settings, research findings—no matter how clear the relevant theory or how robust the findings—must be interpreted in relation to individual teachers and individual schools. Effective use of any concept taken from research on teaching can take many forms, and a teaching behavior may be appropriate in some contexts but not in others. Even behaviors that have wide applicability are not useful in some schools or classrooms. Teachers must analyze and discuss findings and concepts from research on teaching in terms of their own teaching situations. Teachers must learn to reflect carefully, define their classroom problems, and explore research findings and concepts within the dictates of their classroom contexts.

TEACHERS AS DECISION MAKERS

We noted in Chapter 1 that teachers need to be decision makers and to understand that knowledge has to be applied to a particular social and academic setting. Here we want to elaborate on the importance of viewing teaching as decision making. Teachers must *continuously* reflect on their classroom experiences and adapt their teaching to the students in their classes. Teachers also need to obtain new information from research about concepts and ideas they can use to analyze their teaching or improve curriculum and instruction for students.

In a comprehensive review of research on teachers' thought processes, Clark and Peterson (1986) concluded that teaching involves reflective, thoughtful adaptation. They contend that research substantiates the view that teaching is a complex and cognitively demanding process. Adding to this complexity is the fact that teachers hold countless beliefs about students and the learning process, as well as beliefs about the content of various types of subject matter and the ways to teach the content.

A skillful, adaptive teacher may realize that students have not grasped the essential point of a lesson (because the teacher knows to check for understanding and to call on a diverse range of students); still, this knowledge does not predict what action the teacher should take. On a given day, for example, late in the afternoon and with a difficult concept, the teacher may move to a new lesson and not reteach the concept until the next day. Alternatively, the teacher might give the students a reading assignment or ask them to engage in some experimental assignment in order to prepare them for the instruction that will come later. The teacher might make a different decision in other circumstances—to reteach the concept immediately. In this case, the key issue is that the teacher *knows* that the students do not understand the material; hence, the teacher is in a position to take corrective action. Teachers who lack such awareness cannot be decision makers.

Fenstermacher (1983) distinguished the structural elaboration from the personal elaboration of research. Structural elaboration involves using research findings as answers or prescriptions. If, for example, researchers found that ten minutes of homework was effective in a particular program, structural elaboration would advocate that all teachers use ten minutes of homework. In contrast, when research is used for personal elaboration, the decision about how to apply research and about its value resides with the individual teacher, who thinks about the needs of his or her students. It is vital that teachers have access to recent research-based knowledge—knowledge derived from observation of classrooms—but it is important that teachers reflect and form their own ideas about the value of the knowledge and its relevance to their contexts.

Kindsvetter, Wilen, and Ishler (1989) pointed out that many teachers' classroom practice is heavily influenced by their past experience and involves no innovations based on reflection. Some teachers simply teach the way they were taught when they were in school or model more immediate experiences (e.g., teach the way their cooperating teachers did). Some teachers develop a thoughtful approach when they begin teaching but subsequently fail to update curriculum materials or to monitor changes in students' interests that are related to variation in societal expectations, experiences, and so on. Examples that worked fine five years ago may be less compelling to today's students. Instruction in a subject or at a grade level cannot be planned in any final way. Teachers must revise plans and expectations on the basis of new knowledge and new students. Kindsvetter et al. (1989) stress that some teachers fail to avail themselves of new knowledge and hence teach without important information that could improve classroom learning.

The field of teaching has a substantial knowledge base from research (Biddle, Good, & Goodson, 1996; Jackson, 1992) that teachers can use to think about their classrooms and to make decisions. We emphasize the value of personal experience in making teaching decisions. In many respects, teaching involves values (fairness, sensitivity) and is an art at times (spontaneous deviation from intended plans, etc.). However, although intuitive sources of knowledge can be valuable, they are also affected by biases and self-perceptions.

SUMMARY

Teachers are not aware of everything that goes on in the classroom, and this lack of awareness may interfere with their effectiveness. This problem exists for at least two basic reasons. First, classrooms are busy places, and teachers (and students as well) are so busy responding that they have little time to think about what they are doing. Many factors contribute to classroom complexity. The second problem is that teachers are seldom observed systematically, so they rarely receive valuable information about ways to increase their effectiveness. When they are observed, it is typically for purposes of evaluation. Fortunately, this situation is changing in some schools.

Objective recording of behavior provides a way to guard against our biases and gain the most benefit from classroom observations. Personal bias in observing can be reduced by (1) becoming aware of our biases; (2) observing specific behaviors, to alleviate the complexity of the classroom; and (3) checking our observational data against the observations of others. Exercises were suggested to help you observe your own or another's behavior objectively. We also discussed procedures for minimizing the observer's effect on the classroom, along with techniques for observing unobtrusively. These considerations should be borne in mind when you use the observation schedules following Chapters 3 through 10.

Finally, we have suggested that although research and, particularly, observational data about classrooms are important, they should not dictate successful practice. Teachers must integrate rich data with their own beliefs, values, and purposes regarding instruction. Effective classroom teachers function as active decision makers.

SUGGESTED ACTIVITIES AND QUESTIONS

1. Sometimes problems and/or potential are in the eye of the beholder. What one person views as appropriate curiosity or initiative another may believe is unwarranted intrusion or aggression. To explore more fully the ambiguity of behavior (and the need to interpret it), consider what selected behaviors (e.g., cooperation, initiative, leadership) mean to you in a particular instructional context. What student behaviors would imply appropriate initiative in a first-grade versus a seventh-grade classroom? How would you define appropriate cooperative behaviors at these two grades? How do your classmates define these terms at different grade levels? How do first- and seventh-grade students define cooperation? How do teachers at the two grade levels define these terms?

2. After reading the chapter, do you have any questions about the facts or concepts presented? Are there topics that you would like more information about? If so, write two or three questions of your own and turn them in to your instructor for feedback, or trade questions with fellow teachers or students.

3. Most of us find it difficult to monitor our teaching behavior initially, but improvement comes with practice. When you teach (whether micro, simulated, or real), try to monitor your behavior (e.g., the ratio of fact to thought questions) and see how your mental record compares with a record taken by a coder or with what you hear when you play back your tape-recorded lesson. Practice monitoring your behavior, listening to what you say as you teach, and comparing your perceptions with objective records.

4. How can teachers improve their ability to see behavior in classrooms?

5. Why is it important that an observer have a conceptual system for describing classroom behavior and for noticing significant occurrences?

6. Teachers obviously want low achievers to do well, but some low achievers receive less teacher contact and help than high achievers. How can teachers improve their interaction patterns with low achievers without reducing their effectiveness with other students?

7. Why is the use of video equipment (allowing teachers to see themselves teach) relatively ineffective unless it is combined with specific directions concerning what to look for or descriptions of what took place?

8. Visit a classroom or watch a videotape of a discussion and tally the number of times that the teacher: (a) asks a question, (b) responds to a student's answer, and (c) praises a student. Compare your tallies with another observer's by calculating the percentage of agreement between your observations.

9. Think about all your previous teachers and list the major characteristics of your favorite teacher. What was he or she like as a person? What were the chief elements of the teacher's teaching style?

10. Similarly, list the distinguishing factors of your least liked or least effective teacher. Why were you more comfortable or more stimulated in one class than the other? Was it because of the teacher, the subject matter, the students in the class, or a combination of factors?

REFERENCES

Adams, R., & Biddle, B. (1970). *Realities of teaching: Explorations with video tape.* New York: Holt.

Alhajri, A. (1981). *Effect of seat position on school performance of Kuwaiti students.* Unpublished doctoral dissertation, University of Missouri-Columbia.

Alleman, J., & Brophy, J. (1992). Analysis of the activities in a social studies curriculum. In J. Brophy (Ed.), *Advances in research on teaching* (Vol. 3, pp. 47–80). Greenwich, CT: JAI Press.

Allington, R. (1991). Children who find learning to read difficult: School responses to diversity. In E. Hiebert (Ed.), *Literacy for a diverse society* (pp. 237–252). New York: Teachers College Press.

American Association of University Women (AAUW). (1992). *How schools shortchange girls.* Washington, DC: American Association of University Women Educational Foundation.

Anderson, L., Brubaker, N., Alleman-Brooks, J., & Duffy, G. (1985). A qualitative study of seatwork in first-grade classrooms. *Elementary School Journal, 86,* 123–140.

Babad, E., & Ezer, H. (1993). Seating locations of sociometrically measured student types: Methodological and substantive issues. *British Journal of Educational Psychology, 63,* 75–87.

Berliner, D. (1979). Tempus educare. In P. Peterson & H. Walberg (Eds.), *Research on teaching: Concepts, findings, and implications.* Berkeley, CA: McCutchan.

Berliner, D., & Biddle, B. (1995). *The manufactured crisis: Myth, fraud, and the attack on America's public schools.* New York: Addison-Wesley.

Biddle, B., Good, T., & Goodson, I. (1996). *The international handbook of teachers and teaching.* New York: Kluwer.

Blumenfeld, P. (1992). The task and the teacher: Enhancing student thoughtfulness in science. In J. Brophy (Ed.), *Advances in research on teaching* (Vol. 3, pp. 81–114). Greenwich, CT: JAI Press.

Blumenfeld, P., & Meece, J. (1988). Task factors, teacher behavior, and students' involvement and use of learning strategies in science. *Elementary School Journal, 88,* 236–250.

Bossert, S. (1981). Understanding sex differences in children's classroom experiences. *Elementary School Journal, 81,* 255–268.

Boyer, E. (1983). *High school.* New York: Harper & Row.

Brophy, J. (1982). How teachers influence what is taught and learned in classrooms. *Elementary School Journal, 83,* 1–14.

Brophy, J., & Evertson, C. (1981). *Student characteristics and teaching.* New York: Longman.

Brophy, J., & Good, T. (1970). Teachers' communication of differential expectations for children's classroom performance: Some behavioral data. *Journal of Educational Psychology, 61,* 365–374.

Brophy, J., & Good, T. (1974). *Teacher-student relationships: Causes and consequences.* New York: Holt, Rinehart and Winston.

Brophy, J., & Kher, N. (1986). Teacher socialization as a mechanism for developing student motivation to learn. In R. Feldman (Ed.), *Social psychology applied to education.* Cambridge: Cambridge University Press.

Cazden, C. (1986). Classroom discourse. In M. C. Wittrock (Ed.), *Handbook of research on teaching,* (3rd ed. pp. 432–463). New York: Macmillan.

Clark, C., & Peterson, P. (1986). Teachers' thought processes. In M. C. Wittrock (Ed.), *Handbook of research on teaching* (3rd ed., pp. 255–298). New York: Macmillan.

Cuban, L. (1984). *How teachers taught: Constancy and change in American classrooms 1890–1980.* New York: Longman.

Delpit, L. (1995). *Other people's children: Cultural conflict in the classroom.* New York: The New Press.

Doyle, W. (1983). Academic work. *Review of Educational Research, 53,* 159–199.

Doyle, W. (1992). Curriculum and pedagogy. In P. Jackson (Ed.), *Handbook of research on curriculum* (pp. 486–516). New York: Macmillan.

Durkin, D. (1978–1979). What classroom observations reveal about reading comprehension instruction. *Reading Research Quarterly, 14,* 481–533.

Eccles, J., & Blumenfeld, P. (1985). Classroom experiences and student gender: Are there differences and do they matter? In L. Wilkinson & C. Marrett (Eds.), *Gender influences in classroom interaction.* New York: Academic Press.

Eder, D. (1981). Ability grouping as a self-fulfilling prophecy: A microanalysis of teacher-student interaction. *Sociology of Education, 54,* 151–161.

Eisenhart, M., & Cutts-Dougherty, K. (1991). Social and cultural constraints on students' access to school knowledge. In E. Hiebert (Ed.), *Literacy for a diverse society* (pp. 28–43). New York: Teachers College Press.

Emmer, E., & Millett, G. (1970). *Improving teaching through experimentation: A laboratory approach.* Englewood Cliffs, NJ: Prentice-Hall.

Erickson, F. (1986). Qualitative methods in research on teaching. In M. C. Wittrock (Ed.), *Handbook of research on teaching* (3rd ed., pp. 119–161). New York: Macmillan.

Evertson, C., & Green, J. (1986). Observation as inquiry and method. In M. C. Wittrock (Ed.), *Handbook of research on teaching* (3rd ed., pp. 162–213). New York: Macmillan.

Fenstermacher, G. (1983). How should implications of research on teaching be used? *Elementary School Journal, 83,* 496–499.

Finn, J., Pannozzo, G., & Voelkl, K. (1995). Disruptive and inattentive-withdrawn behavior and achievement among fourth graders. *Elementary School Journal, 95,* 421–434.

Fisher, C., & Hiebert, E. (1990). Characteristics of tasks in two approaches to literacy instruction. *Elementary School Journal, 91,* 3–18.

Freedman, S., Jackson, J., & Boles, K. (1983). Teaching: An imperiled "profession." In L. Shulman & G. Sykes (Eds.), *Handbook of teaching and policy.* New York: Longman.

Freeman, D., Kuhs, T., Porter, A., Floden, R., Schmidt, W., & Schwille, J. (1983). Do textbooks and tests define a national curriculum in elementary school mathematics? *Elementary School Journal, 83,* 501–513.

Freeman, D., & Porter, A. (1989). Do textbooks dictate the content of mathematics instruction in elementary schools? *American Educational Research Journal, 26,* 403–421.

Gitlin A., & Smyth, J. (1989). *Teacher evaluation: Educative alternatives.* New York: Falmer Press.

Good, T. (1996). Teacher effectiveness and teacher evaluation. In J. Sikula, T. Buttery, & E. Guiton (Eds.), *Handbook of research on teacher education* (2nd. ed). York, PA: Spectrum Publisher Services.

Good, T., & Brophy, J. (1974). Changing teacher and student behavior: An empirical investigation. *Journal of Educational Psychology, 66,* 390–405.

Good, T., Grouws, D., & Ebmeier, H. (1983). *Active mathematics teaching: Empirical research in elementary and secondary classrooms.* New York: Longman.

Good, T., McCaslin, M., & Reys, B. (1992). Investigating work groups to promote problem solving in mathematics. In J. Brophy (Ed.), *Advances in research on teaching* (Vol. 3, pp. 115–160). Greenwich, CT: JAI Press.

Good, T., Mulryan, C., & McCaslin, M. (1992). Grouping for instruction in mathematics: A call for programmatic research on small-group processes. In D. Grouws (Ed.), *Handbook of research on mathematics teaching and learning* (pp. 165–196). New York: Macmillan.

Good, T., & Weinstein, R. (1986). Schools make a difference: Evidence, criticism, and new directions. *American Psychologist, 41,* 1900–1907.

Goodlad, J. (1984). *A place called school.* New York: McGraw-Hill.

Goodlad, J., Soder, R., & Sirotnik, K. (Eds.). (1990). *Places where teachers are taught.* San Francisco: Jossey Bass.

Goodson, I. (Ed.). (1992). *Studying teachers' lives.* New York: Teachers College Press.

Grant, L. (1985). Race-gender status, classroom interaction, and children's socialization in elementary school. In L. Wilkinson & C. Marrett (Eds.), *Gender influences in classroom interaction.* New York: Academic Press.

Greenberg, H. (1969). *Teaching with feeling.* New York: Macmillan.

Griffin, G. (1983). *Student teaching and the common places of school* (Report No. 9038). Austin: University of Texas, Research and Development Center for Teacher Education.

Griffin, G. (1985). The school as a workplace and the master teacher concept. *Elementary School Journal, 86,* 1–16.

Herrnstein, R., & Murray, C. (1995). *The bell curve: Intelligence and class structure in American life.* New York: The Free Press.

Hiebert, E. (Ed.). (1991). *Literacy for a diverse society.* New York: Teachers College Press.

Hiebert, J., & Carpenter, T. (1992). Learning and teaching with understanding. In D. Grouws (Ed.), *Handbook of research on mathematics teaching and learning* (pp. 65–97). New York: Macmillan.

Jackson, P. (Ed.). (1992). *Handbook of research on curriculum.* New York: Macmillan.

Jackson, P., Boostrom, R., & Hansen, D. (1993). *The moral life of schools.* San Francisco: Jossey-Bass.

Jacob, E. (1995). Reflective practice and anthropology in culturally diverse classrooms. *Elementary School Journal, 95,* 451–463.

Jones, M. (1990). Actions on theory and target students in science classrooms. *Journal of Research in Science Teaching, 27,* 651–660.

Jones, M., & Gerig, T. (1994). Silent sixth-grade students: Characteristics, achievement, and teacher expectations. *Elementary School Journal, 95,* 169–182.

Jones, M., & Wheatley, J. (1990). Gender differences in student-teacher interactions. *Journal of Research in Science Teaching, 27,* 861–874.

Jorgenson, G., (1977). Relationship of classroom behavior to the accuracy of match between material difficulty and student ability. *Journal of Educational Psychology, 69,* 204–232.

Kindsvetter, R., Wilen, W., & Ishler, M. (1989). *Dynamics of effective teaching.* New York: Longman.

King, L. (1993). High and low achievers' perceptions and cooperative learning in two small groups. *Elementary School Journal, 93,* 399–416.

Kleinfeld, J. (1975). Effective teachers of Eskimo and Indian students. *School Review, 83,* 301–344.

Ladson-Billings, G. (1994). *The dreamkeepers: Successful teachers of African-American children.* San Francisco: Jossey-Bass.

Leacock, E. (1969). *Teaching and learning in city schools.* New York: Basic Books.

Leinhardt, G., Seewald, A., & Engel, M. (1979). Learning what's taught: Sex differences in instruction. *Journal of Educational Psychology, 71,* 432–439.

Maeroff, G. (1988). *The empowerment of teachers.* New York: Teachers College Press.

Mason, D., Schroeter, D., Combs, R., & Washington, K. (1992). Assigning average achieving eighth graders to advanced mathematics classes in an urban junior high. *Elementary School Journal, 92,* 587–599.

May, W. (1992). Designing worthwhile activities in elementary art. In J. Brophy (Ed.), *Advances in research on teaching* (Vol. 3, pp. 225–275). Greenwich, CT: JAI Press.

McCaslin, M., & Good, T. (1992). Compliant cognition: The misalliance of management and instruction goals in current school reform. *Educational Researcher, 21,* 4–17.

McCaslin, M., & Good, T. (1996). *Listening in classrooms.* New York: HarperCollins.

Meichenbaum D., Burland, S., Gruson, L., & Cameron, L. (1985). Metacognitive assessment. In S. Yussen (Ed.), *The growth of reflection in children.* New York: Academic Press.

Meier, D. (1995). *The power of their ideas: Lessons for America from a small school in Harlem.* Boston: Beacon Press.

Mergendoller, J. (Ed.). (1988, January). Schoolwork and academic tasks. *Elementary School Journal, 88,* special issue.

Mergendoller, J., Marchman, B., Mitman, A., & Packer, M. (1988). Task demands and accountability in middle-grade science classes. *Elementary School Journal, 88,* 251–265.

Mitman, A. (1985). Teachers' differential behavior toward higher- and lower-achieving students and its relationship with selected teacher characteristics. *Journal of Educational Psychology, 35,* 149–161.

Morse, L., & Handley, H. (1985). Listening to adolescents: Gender differences in science classroom interaction. In L. Wilkinson & C. Marrett (Eds.), *Gender influences in classroom interaction.* New York: Academic Press.

Mulryan, C. (1995). Fifth and sixth graders' involvement and participation in cooperative small groups in mathematics. *Elementary School Journal, 95,* 297–310.

National Education Commission on Time and Learning. (1994, April). *Prisoners of time.* Washington, D.C.: U.S. Government Printing Office.

Natriello, G., & Dornbusch, S. (1980–1981). Pitfalls in the evaluation of teachers by principals. *Administrator's Notebook, 29(6),* 1–4.

Natriello, G., McDill, E., & Pallas, A. (1990). *Schooling disadvantaged children: Racing against catastrophe.* New York: Teachers College Press.

Oakes, J. (1992). Can tracking research inform practice? Technical, normative, and political considerations. *Educational Researcher, 21,* 12–21.

Ogbu, J. (1992). Understanding cultural diversity and learning. *Educational Researcher, 21,* 5–14.

Peshkin, A. (1991). *The color of strangers, the color of friends: The play of ethnicity in school and community.* Chicago: University of Chicago Press.

Peterson, P., Fennema, E., & Carpenter, T. (1992). Teachers' knowledge of students' mathematical problem-solving knowledge. In J. Brophy (Ed.), *Advances in research on teaching* (Vol. 2, pp. 49–86). Greenwich, CT: JAI Press.

Peterson, P., & Swing, S. (1982). Beyond time on task: Students' reports of their thought processes during classroom instruction. *Elementary School Journal, 82,* 481–491.

Porter, A. (1993). School delivery standards. *Educational Researcher, 22,* 24–30.

Posner, G. (1985). *Field experience: A guide to reflective teaching.* New York: Longman.

Rohrkemper, M. (1981). *Classroom perspectives study: An investigation of differential perceptions of classroom events.* Unpublished doctoral dissertation, Michigan State University.

Rohrkemper, M. (1985). The influence of teacher socialization style on students' social cognitions and reported interpersonal classroom behavior. *Elementary School Journal, 85,* 245–275.

Rosenholtz, S. (1989). *Teachers' work place: The social organization of schools.* New York: Longman.

Ross, S., & Jackson, J. (1991). Teachers' expectations for black males' and black females' academic achievement. *Personality and Social Psychology Bulletin, 17,* 78–82.

Rowe, M. (1969). Science, silence, and sanctions. *Science and Children, 6,* 11–13.

Sadker, M., & Sadker, D. (1994). *Failing at fairness: How America's schools cheat girls.* New York: Scribner.

Sadker, M., Sadker, D., & Klein S. (1991). The issues of gender in elementary and secondary education. In G. Grant (Ed.), *Review of research in education* (Vol. 17, pp. 269–334). Washington, DC: American Educational Research Association.

Schmidt, W., & Buchmann, M. (1983). Six teachers' beliefs and attitudes and their curricular time allocations. *Elementary School Journal, 84,* 162–172.

Smylie, M. (1992). Teachers' reports of their interactions with teacher leaders concerning classroom instruction. *Elementary School Journal, 93,* 85–98.

Smylie, M. (1995). New perspectives on teacher leadership. *Elementary School Journal, 96,* 3–7.

Spencer-Hall, D. (1981). Looking behind the teacher's back. *Elementary School Journal, 81,* 281–290.

Spradley, J. (1979). *The ethnographic interview.* New York: Holt.

Stallings, J. (1980). Allocated academic learning time revisited, or beyond time on task. *Educational Researcher, 9,* 11–16.

Steele, C. (1992). Race and the schooling of Black Americans. *The Atlantic, 269,* 68–78.

Streitmatter, J. (1994). *Toward gender equity in the classroom: Everyday teachers' beliefs and practices.* New York: State University of New York Press.

Weinstein, R. (1982, May). Students in classrooms. *Elementary School Journal, 83,* special issue.

Weinstein, R. (1983). Student perceptions of schooling. *Elementary School Journal, 83,* 287–312.

Weinstein, R., & Middlestadt, S. (1979). Student perceptions of teacher interactions with male high and low achievers. *Journal of Educational Psychology, 71,* 421–431.

Wells, A., Hirshberg, D., Lipton, M., & Oakes, J. (1995). Bounding the case within its context: A constructivist approach to studying detracking reform. *Educational Researcher, 24,* 18–24.

Westbury, I. (1992). Comparing American and Japanese achievement: Is the United States really a low achiever? *Educational Researcher, 21,* 18–24.

Westbury, I. (1993). American and Japanese achievement . . . again. *Educational Researcher, 22,* 21–25.

Wilkinson, L., & Marrett, C. (Eds.). (1985). *Gender influences in classroom interaction.* New York: Academic Press.

Wise, A., Darling-Hammond, L., McLaughlin, M., & Bernstein, H. (1985). Teacher evaluation: A study of effective practices. *Elementary School Journal, 86,* 61–121.

Wittrock, M. (Ed.). (1986). *Handbook of research on teaching* (3rd ed.). New York: Macmillan.

APPENDIX A

Coding Vocabulary: Blumenfeld and Miller

There has been rapid growth in the use of observation systems in training and research, and the types of systems used to code classroom behavior have become more varied (Evertson & Green, 1986). The following material was prepared by Phyllis Blumenfeld and Samuel Miller for their students at the University of Michigan. It is an effective device for describing different means of collecting narrative and frequency-count information.

NARRATIVE STRATEGIES

Anecdotal Record

Characteristics:
a. Provides a brief sketch or illustration about a student's behavioral pattern or learning style (e.g., several brief anecdotes might be used to illustrate how a student reacts to a particular situation).

b. Indicates that students have mastered or applied concepts (e.g., brief anecdotes might be used to illustrate that students used knowledge from a subtraction lesson to solve a problem in another subject or outside of class).

Procedure:
a. Write down the incident as soon after it occurs as possible.
b. Identify the basic action of the key person and what was said.
c. Include a statement that identifies the setting, time of day, and basic activity.
d. In describing the central character's actions or verbalizations, include the responses or reactions of other people in the situation.
e. Whenever possible note exact words used, to preserve the precise nature of the conversation.
f. Preserve the sequence of the episode.
g. Be objective, accurate, and complete (i.e., do not interpret).

Running Record

Characteristics:
a. Running records are used to record the situation in a manner that lets someone else read the description later and visualize the scene or event as it occurred.
b. As opposed to anecdotal records, which provide a brief illustrative episode on a student, running records provide a detailed, continuous, or sequential descriptive account of the behavior and its immediate environmental context (eyewitness account par excellence).
c. Running records can be used to help locate the source of the problem or pattern of behavior. (If you wanted to know whether the teacher used effective questioning strategies, you could collect running records of lessons and later go to the records to pinpoint instances of the teacher using effective and ineffective questions.)

Procedure:
a. Describe the scene as it is when the observer begins the description.
b. Focus on the subject's behavior and whatever in the situation affects this behavior.
c. Be as accurate and complete as you can about what the subject says, does, and responds to within the situation.
d. Put brackets around all interpretive material generated by the observer so that the description stands out clearly and completely.
e. Include the "how" for whatever the subject does (e.g., teacher said to be quiet in a high voice while pointing her right hand at the students vs. the teacher said to be quiet).
f. Give the "how" for everything done by anyone interacting with the subject (i.e., emphasis on the details, not on inferences).
g. For every action report all the main steps in their proper order.
h. Describe behavior positively, rather than in terms of what was NOT done.
i. Use observational tools whenever possible (tape recorders, cameras, or videotape).

Comparison of Anecdotal and Running Records

Comparison is related to the following points:
a. *Length of observation.* Anecdotal records require shorter periods of time and are normally completed after the event has occurred, whereas running records are recorded as events occur and usually continue for extended periods of time.

    b. *Amount of detail.* Running records demand a greater number of details than anecdotal records. Additionally, compared to anecdotal records, running records place little emphasis on impressions or interpretations (whenever they occur they are set off by brackets).

    c. *Breadth of focus.* While both records are targeted on a particular student(s) or event(s), the running record includes much more information on the environmental context than does the anecdotal record. Anecdotal records are less sophisticated than running records—they are similar to a diary, whereas the running record is similar to a verbatim report.

    d. *Systematicness.* Anecdotal records do not provide generally systematic evidence. They are brief illustrative sketches of incidents rather than evidence collected across situations and at different times.

FREQUENCY COUNTS

We present two frequency count approaches—time sampling and event sampling. Read the characteristics and procedures for conducting each in order to understand the similarities and differences between the two approaches.

Time Sampling

Characteristics:

    a. In time sampling, behaviors are observed over repeated intervals for different periods of time (e.g., 3 recordings of a behavior per ten minutes for 4 one-hour periods).

    b. Time sampling is appropriate only for behaviors that occur fairly frequently, at least once every 15 minutes on average.

    c. This behavior is then looked on as a "sample" of the person's usual behavior(s).

Procedure:

    a. Identify behaviors that occur regularly and define the behaviors so that others will agree with what the focus of the observation will be (e.g., on-task behavior that may be defined as (1) on-task, engrossed, (2) on-task, at work but not engrossed, (3) off-task, quietly disengaged, or (4) off-task, disruptive).

    b. Decide how long the observation period will be and how many observations are needed within this period (e.g., 3 one-hour observation periods during math where the observer codes on-task behavior of 5 children for 3 minutes, waits 7 minutes, records behavior during another 3-minute period, waits 7 minutes, and so on). If the behavior occurs during an observer wait period, it is not recorded.

Event Sampling

Characteristics:

    a. In event sampling, the observer waits for the selected behavior to occur and records it (i.e., all selected behaviors that occur are recorded).

Procedure:

    a. Clearly identify the kind of behavior you want to study (e.g., how students get the teacher's attention during seatwork).

b. Determine what kind of information you want to record (e.g., call the teacher's name, hold an object in front of his or her face, stand in front of teacher, ask teacher for assistance, cause a disruption).

c. Decide how many times you will observe and how long you will observe during each time (e.g., ten 40-minute seatwork classes).

Comparison of Time Sampling and Event Sampling

a. Both event and time sampling are useful for determining the frequency of behaviors or events, and both allow the collection of a large number of observations in a relatively short time.

b. Time sampling is limited to frequently or regularly occurring behaviors and counts only those behaviors that occur during a recording interval. Event sampling counts all instances of the behavior's occurrence, and the behavior does not have to occur frequently.

c. With both approaches the observer must determine what behaviors are to be observed, when they are to be observed, and for how long they are to be observed to obtain a sample set of behaviors typical of the student(s) in question.

Method	Focus	Advantages/Disadvantages
Case study narratives	Single student	+ Provides a rich, detailed account of an individual's actions + Allows an in-depth examination of a single problem − Descriptions may be affected by the observer's biases − Conclusions may not apply to the same student in other classes or to other students
Frequency counts	Single student Small groups	+ Gives actual number of behaviors per unit of time, which allows comparisons among students or across classes + Allows teacher to receive immediate information on a problem without having to receive extensive training − Actual behaviors recorded may not explain all facets of the problem − Apart from the behavior in question, the teacher will not know what students are doing during the observation time
Classroom observation scale (COS)	Single student Small groups Whole class	+ Gives actual number of behaviors per unit of time, which allows comparisons among students or across classes − Usually involves more observer training than do other methods − Apart from the behavior in question, the teacher will not know what students are doing during the observation time
Questionnaire	Single student Small groups Whole class	+ Allows the collection of information on a variety of topics in a relatively short time + Since students respond to the same set of questions, questionnaires allow comparisons among individuals or across classes − Question construction is more difficult than it may appear (e.g., responses may be affected by how questions are worded) − Responses may not truly represent what students will do in actual situation (validity) − Responses may differ if questionnaire is given at another time (reliability)

(continued)

Method	Focus	Advantages/Disadvantages
Interview	Single student Small groups	+ Yields more student information than do other methods + Allows greater flexibility to probe a student's response more deeply − Since students give more information, comparisons among students may be difficult − Responses given may be affected by student biases − Usually will take longer to conduct than other methods
Ethnography	Whole class	+ Relative to other methods it provides more information on the social context of the classroom − Since the purpose is to interpret behaviors, the analysis may be affected by observer bias − Since the focus is not on a particular set of behaviors for all students, comparisons among students or across classes are difficult − The purpose is not to answer specific questions but to describe the norms governing interactions in social settings—therefore, the information collected may not be appropriate for answering specific questions

APPENDIX B

Brophy-Good Dyadic Interaction System

There are many observational systems we can use to code classroom behavior. All systems are selective and code certain behaviors while ignoring other aspects of the classroom. Hence, the usefulness of a particular observation system depends on your goal. We present one observation system, the Brophy-Good dyadic interaction system, briefly.

In this particular system, the goal is to determine whether individual students receive more or less of certain behaviors than other students (e.g., Are high-achieving female students treated differently from low-achieving male students?). After you read the definitions and examine the coding sheets that follow, go back to Chapter 1 and examine the long classroom scenes. Do the teachers provide equal opportunity for all students? Coding systems like the Brophy-Good system help us to be more systematic in our observations.

BRIEF DEFINITIONS OF VARIABLES CODED IN BROPHY-GOOD DYADIC INTERACTION SYSTEM

The coding sheet (see Figure 2.2) uses the following definitions (presented in the order that they appear on the coding sheet). For an extended discussion of these definitions and coding examples, see Brophy and Good (1970).

Student-initiated question. A student asks the teacher a question in a public setting.

Reading or recitation. Student is called on to read aloud, go through an arithmetic table, and so on.

Discipline question. The discipline question is a unique type of direct question in which the teacher uses the question as a control technique, calling on the student to force him or her to pay better attention rather than merely providing a response opportunity in the usual sense.

1. Class ________ 2. Date ___/___/___ 3. Start ________ 4. Stop ________ 5. Elapsed ________

6. Activity ________ 7. Attendance ________ 8. Observer ________ 9. Page ________ of ________

TIME	RESPONSE OPPORTUNITIES																													CREATED									AFFORDED								
	Child						Question					Answer					Terminal Feedback										Sustaining				Work					Proced.			Work					Beh.			
	Stud	Read	Discip	Direct	Open	Call	PCSS	Prod	Choice	Self	Opinion	+	±	–	DK	NR	+ +	Affirm	SUM	0	Negate	– –	PCSS	Giv S Ans	Ask Oth	Call	Rept	Clue	New Q	Expand	+ +	PCSS	FB	– –	?	+ +	FB	– –	+ +	PCS	FB	– –	?	Proced	+ +	W	– –

EXPECTATION:

REMARKS:

Group Questions

Board Work

FIGURE 2.2
The Brophy-Good dyadic coding sheet.

Direct question. Teacher calls on a student who is not seeking a response opportunity.

Open question. The teacher creates the response opportunity by asking a public question and also indicates who is to respond by calling on an individual student, but the teacher chooses one of the students who has indicated a desire to respond by raising a hand.

Call-outs. Response opportunities created by students who call out answers to teachers' questions without waiting for permission to respond.

Process question. Requires students to explain something in a way that requires them to integrate facts or to show knowledge of their interrelationships. It most frequently is a "why?" or "how?" question.

Product question. Product questions seek to elicit a single correct answer that can be expressed in one word or a short phrase. Product questions usually begin with "who," "what," "when," "where," "how much," and "how many."

Choice question. In the choice question, the student does not have to produce a substantive response but may instead simply choose one of two or more implied or expressed alternatives.

Self-reference question. Asks the student to make some nonacademic contribution to classroom discussion ("show-and-tell"; questions about personal experiences, preferences, or feelings; requests for opinions or predictions, etc.).

Opinion question. Much like a self-reference question (i.e., there is no single correct answer) except that it elicits a student opinion on an academic topic ("Is it worth putting a person on the moon?").

Correct answer. If the student answers the teacher's question in a way that satisfies the teacher, the answer is coded as correct.

Part-correct answer. A part-correct answer is one that is correct but incomplete as far as it goes, or correct from one point of view but not what the teacher is looking for.

Incorrect answer. A response that is treated as simply wrong by the teacher.

Don't know. Student verbally says "I don't know" (or its equivalent) or nonverbally indicates that he or she doesn't know (shakes head).

No response. Student makes no response (verbally or nonverbally) to teacher question.

Praise. Praise refers to the teacher's evaluative reactions that go beyond the level of simple affirmation or positive feedback by verbally complimenting the student.

Affirmation of correct answers. Affirmation is coded when the teacher indicates that the student's response is correct or acceptable.

Summary. Teacher summarizes the student's answer (generally as part of the affirmation process).

No feedback reaction. If the teacher makes no verbal or nonverbal response whatever following the student's answer to the question, the teacher is coded for no feedback reaction.

Negation of incorrect answer. Simple provision of impersonal feedback regarding the incorrectness of the response, without going farther than this by communicating a negative personal reaction to the student. As with affirmation, negation can be communicated both verbally ("No," "That's not right," "Hmm-mm") and nonverbally (shaking the head horizontally).

Criticism. Evaluative reactions that go beyond the level of simple negation by expressing anger or personal criticism of the student in addition to indicating the incorrectness of the response.

Process feedback. Coded when the teacher goes beyond merely providing the right answer and discusses the cognitive or behavioral processes that are to be gone through in arriving at the answer.

Gives answer. This category is used when the teacher gives the student the answer to the question but does not elaborate sufficiently to be coded for process feedback.

Asks other. Whenever the student does not answer a teacher question and the teacher moves to another student in order to get the answer to that same question, the teacher's feedback reaction is coded for *asks other.*

Call-out. The call-out category is used when another student calls out the answer to the question before the teacher has a chance to call on someone.

Repeats question. Teacher asks a question, waits some time without getting the correct answer, and then repeats the question to the same student.

Rephrase or clue. In this feedback reaction, the teacher sustains the response opportunity by rephrasing the question or giving the student a clue as to how to respond to it.

New question. When the first question is not answered or is answered incorrectly, the teacher asks a new question that is different from the original, although it may be closely related. A question requiring a new answer is coded as a new question.

Expansion. Teacher responses to vague or incomplete statements that ask the student to provide more information ("I think I understand, but tell me . . . ").

DYADIC TEACHER-STUDENT CONTACTS

The preceding material has dealt primarily with the coding of response opportunities and reading and recitation turns. Dyadic teacher-student contacts differ from response opportunities and reading and recitation turns in that the teacher is dealing privately with one student about matters idiosyncratic to him or her rather than publicly about material meant for the group or class as a whole.

Dyadic teacher-student contacts are divided into work-related contacts, procedural contacts, and behavioral or disciplinary contacts. They are also separately coded according to whether they are initiated by the teacher (teacher-afforded) or by the student (student-created). The coding also reflects certain aspects of the teacher's behavior in such contacts.

Work-Related Contacts

Work-related contacts include those teacher-student contacts that have to do with the student's completion of seatwork or homework assignments. They include clarification of the directions, soliciting or giving help concerning how to do the work, or soliciting or giving feedback about work already done. Work-related interactions are considered *student-created* if the student brings his or her work up to the teacher to talk about it, raises a hand, or otherwise indicates a desire to discuss it with the teacher. Work-related interactions are coded as *teacher-afforded* if the teacher gives feedback about work when the student has not solicited it (the teacher either calls the student to come up to his or her desk or goes around the room making individual comments to the students). *Created* contacts are not planned by the teacher and occur solely because the student has sought out the teacher; *afforded* contacts are not planned by the student and occur solely because the teacher initiates them. Separate space is provided for coding *created* and *afforded* work-related interactions on the coding sheets, and the coder indicates the nature of an individual dyadic contact by where the interaction is coded.

In addition to noting the interaction as a work interaction and as an interaction that is student-created or teacher-afforded, the coder also indicates the nature of the teacher's feedback to the student during the interactions. He or she indicates this by using one or more of the five columns provided for coding teachers' feedback in work-related interaction: praise (+ +), process feedback (pcss), product feedback (fb), criticism (-), or "don't know" (?). The first four of these categories have the same meaning as they have in other coding of teacher feedback. The additional "don't know" category is added for this coding because frequently the individual teacher-student interaction that occurs in a dyadic contact is carried on in hushed tones or across the room from the coder, where it is not possible to hear the content of the interaction. In such cases, the coder notes the occurrence of the work-related interaction and the fact that it was either teacher-afforded or student-created but enters the student's identification number in the "don't know" column (identified by the question mark on top).

Procedural Contacts

The category of *procedural contacts* includes all dyadic teacher-student interactions that are not coded as work-related contacts or as behavioral contacts. Thus it includes a wide range of types of contacts, most of which are initiated on the basis of the immediate needs of the teacher or student involved. Procedural contacts are *created* by the student for such purposes as seeking permission to do something, requesting needed supplies or equipment, reporting some information to the teacher (tattling on other students, calling attention to a broken desk or pencil, etc.), seeking help in putting on or taking off clothing, getting permission or information about how to take care of idiosyncratic needs (turning in lunch money, delivering a note from the parent to the principal, etc.), as well as a variety of other contacts. In general, any dyadic interaction initiated by the student that does not fit the definition of *work-related contacts* is coded as a *procedural contact.*

Behavioral Contacts

Behavioral contacts are coded whenever the teacher makes some comment on the student's classroom behavior. They are subdivided into *praise, warnings,* and *criticism.* The coder notes the information by entering the student's identification number under the appropriate column. Behavioral evaluation contacts are considered to be *teacher-afforded,* although they usually occur as reactions to the student's immediately preceding behavior. Nevertheless, they are teacher-afforded in the sense that the student usually does not want and does not expect the interaction and that the teacher chooses to single the student out for comment.

APPENDIX C

Emmer Observation System

In Appendix B, we examined parts of the Brophy-Good dyadic interaction system, and we have seen that it allows us to code and/or think more systematically about the two classroom scenes presented in Chapter 1. However, teachers do more than interact with individual students, and we need ways to classify and think about these aspects of classroom interaction as well.

One interesting and useful observational manual has been prepared by Ed Emmer at the University of Texas. We can present only a small part of this system here; if you are interested in more of the observational scales included in the manual and in details of training and reliability, consult Emmer (1971).

Emmer recommends that the scales be used approximately every 15 minutes, because longer periods may reduce reliability by placing too much reliance on the observer's memory, and shorter intervals may fail to provide sufficient information to use the scale. He also suggests that the observer should sit where he or she can observe the teacher and students and be in a position to see the faces of as many students as possible.

What follows are examples of 2 of the 12 scales that appear in the Emmer system.

LEVEL OF ATTENTION

Attention as defined for this scale refers to pupil orientation toward the teacher, the task at hand, or whatever classroom activities are appropriate. If pupils are attending to inappropriate activities or are engaged in self-directed behavior when they are supposed to be engaged in a class activity, this behavior is not considered attentive. Therefore, you should look for behavior that is focused on or engaged in whatever activity is appropriate, whether individual seatwork, group discussion, or listening to the presentation of information. Useful cues in recognizing attentive behavior include eye contact, body orientation, response to questions or other eliciting cues, and participation in class activity. Useful cues in recognizing inattentiveness include inappropriate social interaction, repetitive body movement, visual wandering, and engagement in behavior other than the sanctioned class activity. At times, it will be difficult to determine whether a student is attentive, such as when the teacher presents information and the student sits facing the teacher, with no observable behaviors indicating inattention. In such instances, the pupils are considered attentive until they behave otherwise.

To code behavior on this scale, scan the class on several occasions during each 15-minute observation period. Note how many pupils appear attentive or inattentive at a given time. After some practice you will find it easier to keep in mind your estimate of the number of inattentive students. Average your estimates of attention and record this average using the following scale.

1. Fewer than half of the students are attentive most of the time.
2. One-half to three-fourths of the students appear attentive most of the time; the remainder are attentive only some of the time.
3. Most of the students are attentive, but several (four to six) are attentive only some of the time.
4. Nearly all students are attentive, but a few (one, two, or three) are attentive only some of the time.
5. All of the students are attentive most of the time.

Note—the phrase "most of the time" means at least 75 percent of the time the observer checks the pupils for attentiveness.

Some examples follow from which inattention or attention may be inferred.

Inattention:	Moving around the room at an inappropriate time
	Reading a book during class discussion
	Two students whispering
	Sitting with elbows on desk, fingers holding eyelids open
	Doodling with a pencil
	Laying head on desk
	Asking a question unrelated to the activity of the class
	Staring fixedly at an object not related to class activity
Attention:	Raising hand to volunteer a response
	Maintaining eye contact, following teacher's movements

Turning to watch another student who is contributing to the class activity
Working on assigned activity
If a free-activity period, pupils engaged in some task

TEACHER PRESENTATION

The teacher presentation scale measures only one type of behavior. The observer's task is to estimate the relative amount of class time occupied by teacher presentation of substantive information. *Teacher presentation* means substantive (content-oriented) verbal or nonverbal behavior that provides information and does not imply or require pupil response or evaluate pupil behavior. Thus teacher questions, procedural directions, praise, and criticism are not instances of teacher presentation. Lecturing, reading to the class, answering pupil questions, and any other activity in which the teacher gives information are all instances of teacher presentation.

To use this scale, observe the teacher's behavior and note the amount of teacher presentation as compared to the total of all teacher behavior, pupil behavior, and periods of seatwork or other activities in which there is no verbal interaction.

1. Teacher presentation occurs 0–20 percent of the period.
2. Teacher presentation occurs 21–40 percent of the period.
3. Teacher presentation occurs 41–60 percent of the period.
4. Teacher presentation occurs 61–80 percent of the period.
5. Teacher presentation occurs 81–100 percent of the period.

Note that in order for a 5 to be scored, the observation period must be taken up almost entirely by teacher information-giving. Even a small amount of discussion or other activity is likely to cause the rating to be a 4 or less. On the other hand, a score of 1 occurs only when there is a very small amount of teacher information-giving (less than 20 percent of the time).

Teacher presentation should not be confused with *teacher talk*, since the former may be only a small part of the latter. Although a question-and-answer session might contain 70 percent teacher talk, much of it may be teacher questions and evaluation rather than presentation. Be sure to distinguish teacher presentation from other teacher behaviors.

REFERENCE

Emmer, E. (1971). *Classroom observation scales.* Austin: Research and Development Center for Teacher Education, University of Texas.

APPENDIX D

An Ethnographic Research Study Conducted by Susan Florio

Some qualitative researchers study a single classroom for a long time in order to describe and understand its unique characteristics and functioning. The following article provides one example of how qualitative researchers conduct classroom inquiry. Notice that this research attempts to describe and understand both the social and cognitive tasks of classrooms.

The Problem of Dead Letters:
Social Perspectives on the Teaching of Writing*

SUSAN FLORIO

Institute for Research on Teaching, Michigan State University, East Lansing, Michigan

> *Dead letters! does it not sound like dead men? Conceive a man by nature and misfortune prone to a pallid hopelessness, can any business seem more fitted to heighten it than that of continually handling these dead letters . . . ?*
>
> HERMAN MELVILLE
> Bartleby the Scrivener [1]

Why is it so hard to get students writing in school? Of the language arts, writing is the most troublesome. While the value of literacy is unquestioned by educators and researchers alike, writing, as part of literacy, is typically slighted in the course of a day in school and in research on the basic skills (2).

In attempting to account for this neglect, some have noted that writing—and its pedagogy—require hard work. Thus it could be argued that teachers and students assiduously avoid difficult tasks, and so they avoid writing. Yet, all of us can think of difficulty endured in the pursuit of a valued goal. What is more, from the ranks of the few who have taken a look at the teaching of writing comes a recommendation that is disturbing in its simplicity. We are advised, in a variety of voices, that the best way to teach writing is simply to let students do it! (2, 3, 4).

Why, then, is it so hard to get students writing in school?

When researchers at the Institute for Research on Teaching set out to address this question, they were confronted with much the same finding as the lawyer who set out to discover the roots of Bartleby the Scrivener's "derangement." The problem, in each case, was the lack of meaningfulness. At the heart of a student's successful engagement in the complex and difficult task of writing, experienced teachers told us, was the requirement that the writing task have meaning. Writing requires having something to express, an intended audience, and a chance for some kind of response (4). Apparently the teachers with whom we spoke had shared just about enough of Bartleby's experience to abhor it.

Bartleby's first job involved reading and sorting letters that were undeliverable—dead letters. From that job he went to work as a scribe, or copier of the manuscripts of others, for a lawyer. Is it any wonder that, after years of such meaningless interaction with truncated human communication, his only response when asked by the lawyer to perform written tasks was, "I prefer not to"? Teachers told us that they preferred not to read "dead letters" from their students—exposition going nowhere and written only to fulfill academic requirements. Similarly, the teachers preferred not to ask their students merely to put their own words to someone else's ideas. The teachers knew that the perseverance and the practice needed to master a craft as complex as writing were likely to be present only when school writing tasks had meaningful communicative functions in the lives of their students.

The teachers' insight suggests that writing may be avoided in school not simply because of its inherent difficulty, but also because writing, as one of many tasks in a busy

*From Susan Florio, "The problem of dead letters . . . ," *Elementary School Journal, 80* (1979), 1–7. Reprinted with permission.

school day, typically is not connected to anything or anyone else in the lives of students or teachers. If this is true, then "letting children write" may amount to far more than pedagogical laissez faire. The teaching of writing may require vigilant attention to the learning environments in which writing occurs to insure that written expression is motivated and that it goes somewhere.

Perhaps teachers can best serve the acquisition of writing by structuring both for and with students social occasions in which writing functions meaningfully as communication. The possibility parallels what we know about the acquisition of speaking, another complex communicative skill. Both research and experience tell us that spoken language is acquired literally "in the doing." Children are welcomed as communicators even before their first words are uttered. Early in life, children find that their moves and sounds elicit action from other people. Children, in effect, practice the use of language not as preparation or training for social life, but as social life itself (5).

Research on language acquisition has shown us that requisite grammatical skills are seldom taught directly to children by the adults with whom they communicate. For teachers of writing, an essential lesson from research on language acquisition is that even the most flawed and rudimentary communicative attempts of novices are functional in that they have social meaning. Critical to acquiring language is the social fact that a child's emergent and stumbling efforts are heeded by others. Early talk is meaningful by virtue of the child's membership in the family, the first community.

Classrooms contain the stuff of community, too, and therein lies potential that writing done in them will be meaningful. Classrooms are located in organized social worlds where meanings are shared and values held, and at the same time classrooms individually constitute small communities with cumulative histories, shared beliefs, and rights and responsibilities of membership.

To learn more about the acquisition of writing skills and the ways in which writing in school can be meaningful to students, researchers at the Institute for Research on Teaching have been looking closely at one second-grade classroom in central Michigan. The classroom is notable because children do a great deal of writing there and because a strong sense of community can be found there as well.

To get to Mrs. Frank's second grade you must travel to the small community of Haslett, Michigan. The town of nearly seven thousand is located in the shadow of the state capitol and a large public university. Although some of the residents are farmers, the parents of most of the children in Mrs. Frank's room are employed in one of the area's major activities—state government, education, and manufacturing.

Mrs. Frank's students attend the Ralya School, one of three elementary schools in Haslett. The contemporary school building houses about 170 students and contains one room for each grade from Kindergarten through Grade 5. Approaching Mrs. Frank's room, you already have a sense of why she is well known in and around Haslett and why children look forward to being in her class. The classroom literally spills out into the corridor with bright colors and activity. Upon entering the classroom, you encounter yet another small community, one that the children have dubbed, "Betterburg."

As the map in Figure 2.3 drawn by one of Mrs. Frank's students illustrates, the child-sized, cardboard buildings of Betterburg dominate the physical space of the classroom. We have found that Betterburg dominates as well the social life and the attendant writing that is done in that physical space.

The members of Mrs. Frank's class populate Betterburg, filling its civil offices and making its laws. Betterburg has all the accoutrements of a community—law enforcement, cultural activities, commerce, welfare and, most important for our purposes, a postal system. Of course, the room also has all the other features of standard class-

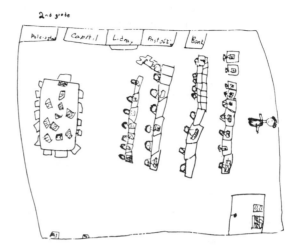

FIGURE 2.3   Map drawn by students on 6/2/78. Instructions were to fill in "important things and places—as many as you can remember."

rooms—blackboards, desks, bookshelves, and the like; but the dominance of the town is clear. One day upon leaving the class the children were asked to draw maps of the important things and places in the room. The children's maps included, often in considerable detail, each aspect of the town. The content of their drawings is summarized in Table 2.2.

During the year that the children in Mrs. Frank's class were observed, they wrote often and produced a wide variety of documents. Table 2.3 displays the written products and the occasions when writing occurred on March 15, 1978, a typical day in the classroom. Activities recorded in Table 2.3 include everything from the practice of motor skills, spelling, and the rules of punctuation to the use of metaphor, simile, and the complex rhetoric of persuasion. Table 2.3 also illustrates the fact that the variety of writing activities done in this classroom involves the practice of a wide range of skills. Sometimes spelling and punctuation are in the foreground for teacher as well as students. At other times, self-expression is most highly valued, and correct spelling is incidental. Such changes in emphasis are accompanied by changes in the behaviors of teacher and students. The teacher's role may vary from that of helper or resource to that of editor or critic. Similarly, what children need to do to complete adequately the various kinds of writing activities changes depending on the particular activity in which they are engaged.

On the day that information for Table 2.3 was compiled, one of the most daring and most sustained writing activities was the writing of letters to manufacturers of the children's favorite games and candies. Betterburg was establishing a store, and the children needed to acquire goods to sell in the store. To turn a profit, it was necessary to buy the goods at the wholesale price. Despite inexperience with the nuances and the intricacies of spelling, punctuation, and sentence structure, the children undertook the sophisticated task of writing persuasively. They needed to interest their readers in the doings of Betterburg. To this end, the children needed to take the perspective of someone who had never heard of the classroom town. Writing from this point

Table 2.2   CLASSROOM AREAS AND OBJECTS AND PERCENTAGE OF STUDENTS NAMING THEM IN CLASSROOM MAPS

Area or Object	Percentage of Children Including Area on Classroom Map
→ Capitol building	83
→ Police station/jail	78
Student desks	78
→ Post office*	74
→Department of Health, Education and Welfare	70
Library	70
Teacher's desk	70
→ Bank	65
→ Mailboxes*	55
Reading table	35
Other tables	35
Chairs	22
Blackboard	13
Plants	13
Coatrack	13
Toys	13
Bulletin board, artwork, books, shelves, cabinets, wastebasket, school bell, wall	10

→Town-related area
*Area related to letter writing

of view, the students had to weave into their letters sufficient information to make subsequent requests for goods sensible. It might be said that the children were out of their depth in such a task but, like young children acquiring speech, they were learning in the doing.

In Betterburg the performance of such complex social and linguistic operations through the medium of the letter was typical. Letter-writing was observed almost daily over months of field work in the classroom, and when the children were interviewed at the end of the year about their activities, the only writing activity on which they commented in detail was letter-writing. Here are excerpts from the interviews.

INTERVIEWER: I want to know about all the things you wrote this year.
STUDENT 1: Yeah, we wrote people to come to our store.
STUDENT 2: Letters.
STUDENT 3: Oh, yeah. We wrote to our moms and dads and wrote to kids in our class.
STUDENT 4: Our post office would get mail.

Additional evidence of the importance of letter-writing in this classroom community can be found in Table 2.3. The post office is among the places most frequently included in the classroom maps. The mailboxes—the one outside the post office as well as those fastened to the children's desks—are included in the maps of more than half

Table 2.3   PRODUCTS AND OCCASIONS FOR WRITING

FIELD NOTES, MARCH 15, 1978

I. Writing Headlines: Teacher as Scribe

It is a typically busy morning in the second-grade classroom. First, the children who have brought in articles from the previous evening's newspaper share them with the class. The teacher acts as scribe, making a headline out of each article.

> N. M. builder recycles tin cans into households. Until recently U.S.'s spendthrifts didn't conserve nation's resources.
>
> We're expecting a blackout because miners haven't obeyed President Carter's demands.
>
> Bicycles and motorcycles aren't safest, insurance company reports. They're larger than children and teen-agers can handle, and we've got record highway injuries.

At the end of the presentation of news, children volunteer to come to the board and circle in the headlines instances of abbreviations, compound words, prefixes, suffixes, contractions, and the like. The noise level rises as children wave their hands in the air, jump up and down, and call "Me! I know it!"

II. Expository Writing and Editorial Work

Later in the morning some of the children work on the manuscript of a book the class is writing. The book is intended for very young children and their parents. It is going to be about becoming a good and happy person. Children have written entries and have drawn pictures to illustrate them. Now the task of layout—the spacing and matching of pictures and words—remains. Some of the entries with which children are working include the following:

> Don't be crool to people because they mite be crool to you because you're teaching them to be crool.
>
> It's like planning how to make a building. You have to think how you want it before you start if you want it to be a beautiful building.
>
> The teacher comments about the manuscript that is taking shape, "It came out real well considering how much they agonized over it."

III. Writing Answers on Worksheets

While the teacher spends the better part of an hour working with reading groups children work quietly at their desks. Some of them catch up on their reading—from primers or from library books. Others work busily on dittoed worksheets, circling, marking with x's and writing an occasional word in answer to a fill in the blank question.

IV. Writing Letters

During seatwork, some of the children are polishing up letters that they have written to companies manufacturing their favorite toys and candies. Because the entire class is planning to have a store this spring, the children have decided to solicit help from the companies. Children have written to makers of Flair pens, Cracker Jacks, Mounds, DC Comics. Here is an example:

> Dear Parker Brothers:
> Hi! My name is Marnie at Ralya School in second grade and we have a town in our classroom. Our town's name is Betterburg because we want to make things better. We'll have a store in our town. We have a police station, Bank, capitol, Library, H.E.W. and a Post Office. My teacher said I could sell anything in the world I wanted to and I

chose you because we have some of your games and we play with them all the time and we like them alot. I always want to buy the games but we don't get enough money. When I'm over to somebody's house I look at the games. If I find a Parker Brothers game I want to play it but if they don't have a Parker Brothers game I don't want to play a game. I have to buy your good games at a good wholesale price or we won't make any money. Please, please give us it at a good wholesale price. We really need it bad. Just send the games and bill. We'll be sure to pay the bill if you send the games with the letter. Thank you for reading my letter.

Your friend,
Marnie

V. "Meta Writing" Spelling Words, Making Concrete Sentences

After the children return from recess, the teacher, standing at the front blackboard, asks them to clear their desks and take out pencils and spelling books. She draws lines on the blackboard. Then she says, "We've been *neglecting* your spelling words." She asks them to pick out the two hardest words from this week's spelling list and write a sentence using each word. "In order to be a sentence, it has to *tell* something. I'm not going to spell any words for you: just sound them out. It isn't a spelling test. The only word I care about your spelling correct is the spelling word."

The children write quietly at their desks. As they finish, a few of them bring their sentences up to the teacher. She tells them, "Sit down." Finally, as the whispering and shifting in seats increases, the teacher says, "Stand up if you are ready." The teacher calls on children standing at their desks to read their sentences. Here is a bit of what follows:

Teacher calls on Christy.

CHRISTY: Do you want to clean your room now?

TEACHER: I should have . . . OK you can either *tell* something or *ask* something. She asked. What did she put at the end of her sentence?

CHILDREN: A question mark!

Another child is called on.

KRISTINA: I clean my room every day.

TEACHER: Oh, you do really? Is she telling or asking?

CHILDREN: Telling.

TEACHER: I'm going to ask your mother about that, Kristina!

JACK: I clean the living room every day.

TEACHER: He *told* you right. Jack, would you like to come over to my house tonight?

CHILDREN: Laughter.

SAM: He is sleeping.

TEACHER: What did Sam do to the word? He put the *ing* on a suffix. Don't do that on the spelling test tomorrow, but it's all right.

VI. Cursive Writing Practice

After many children have shared their sentences, the teacher turns to the lines she has drawn on the blackboard. She says as she does this in brisk, clipped speech, "Up, up! Sit up! Feet on floor. When I say 'ready,' what do you do?" The students reply, "Do we have to write in *cursive?*" The teacher, smiling says, "Yup." What follows is a lesson in cursive writing in which students use the spelling words from their sentences. The teacher coaches in colorful language—each motion of the pen corresponds to a phrase that the children know. Some of them talk along with her: "Rainbow up, straight back. Rocker, come around, straight, rocker." As children finish their words, they are asked to bring them up to show the teacher.

VII. Imaginative Writing

After the children finish their cursive writing, the teacher asks them to sit in a circle at her feet at the front of the room. It is nearing St. Patrick's Day, and the teacher has brought in a story about leprechauns. The children listen quietly. Sometimes the teacher stops to ask questions about the story. The children answer in chorus. After the story there is just time enough before lunch for the children to do one more thing. The teacher, in a soft voice, says, "I want you to think. Shut your eyes. You're a leprechaun now, hiding under your mushroom and you're thinking. 'If I were a leprechaun, what magic would I play?' What magic would you play if you were a leprechaun?"

As the children open their eyes and are sent back to seats, the teacher passes out bright green paper shamrocks. She asks them to write down on lined paper the trick they thought of to play. She says that after writing them, the children will paste them onto the shamrocks and put them in the hall "for everyone to see." She also says they can copy them over into St. Patrick's Day cards to bring home to their mothers.

After the assignment is made, the room is alive with whispering and children leaning over one another's papers. The teacher stands at the board, and as children call out words she spells them for them on the board. As children finish, they bring their tricks up to the teacher. One student reads his aloud to the teacher. "If I were a leprechaun, I'd use my magic finger to turn trash into flowers because I'd like to make the world into a better place." The teacher replies, "He accomplished something with his trick. It wasn't wasted."

---

the students. Finally, when Mrs. Frank and the students recorded the history of Betterburg in a yearbook, the text was made up almost entirely of the letters that had been written during the existence of the town.

The celebration of community in the classroom in the form of Betterburg appears to be related powerfully to the use of letter-writing as an expressive activity. Dewey suggests that education fundamentally involves the child, whose "understandings are primarily personal and concrete," and the transmission of "values incarnate in the mature experience of the adult" (6:4). From this perspective, teaching of writing can be thought of as occurring at the place where the personal world and the wider community meet. Writing is the private struggle of an individual with pen and paper, and writing is the social activity of communication with another. Furthermore, writing occurs within communities. A pedagogy of writing that slights any of these features risks engaging students in the generation of dead letters rather than in communication.

Betterburg enables immediate and explicit sharing of classroom membership, and the town is a powerful organizer of the students' personal experiences. The classroom town also provides the occasion for students to venture outside its borders into the wider adult community. This movement is fundamental to writing. It constitutes, in the words of Elsasser and John-Steiner, a "critical shift in the consciousness of the learner, a shift of attention from an immediate audience that shares the learner's experience and frame of reference to a larger, abstract, and unfamiliar audience" (7:358).

In the classroom community of Betterburg, there is need for discourse across the boundaries. Because Betterburg operates, in microcosm, very much like Haslett, students write to government officials in the town and in the nearby state capital for guidance in the establishment and the enforcement of laws. Similarly, Betterburg, as we have already seen, has a commerce. Haslett and other nearby towns are potential markets for the goods that children sell in their store. Haslett citizens are reached by means of letters to individuals and to the local newspaper.

Because letters are a meaningful medium for Mrs. Frank's class, the postal system of Betterburg is important. In a sense, the postal system epitomizes Betterburg's integrity and links the class to the wider world. The system insures that letters can leave the confines of the classroom, that responses can be distributed, and that letters can be noted officially. Mailboxes serve as a tangible reminder that it is possible to communicate with someone who is not physically present. Perhaps even more dramatically, however, the post office of Betterburg stands for the potential efficacy of the students in the world of communication. An address is not only a place from which to express oneself, it is also a place where one can be reached when someone wants to respond.

Some educators say that one writes if one can realistically expect a response, if one does not feel isolated and powerless. But one does not feel isolated and powerless because one writes and is responded to (7, 8). Bartleby the Scrivener was immobilized by a social order that stymied both the chance for expression and the opportunity for response. Although Mrs. Frank's classroom is perhaps novel in its design, it paints in bold strokes a community spirit that is potentially available in all classrooms. That community spirit stems from recognition both of shared classroom meanings and of access of the class to a world beyond itself by means of the written word. Understanding and using the classroom as a community can rescue children from academic writing activities that are mere copying or expressions falling on deaf ears. As one child in Mrs. Frank's class put it, reflecting on the writing he had done in Betterburg, "I made my own words, and I didn't copy people. The more I learned to write good letters, the better they got."

NOTES

The work reported here is sponsored by the Institute for Research on Teaching, College of Education, Michigan State University. The Institute for Research on Teaching is funded primarily by the Teaching Division of the National Institute of Education, United States Department of Health, Education, and Welfare. The opinions expressed in this article do not necessarily reflect the position, policy, or endorsement of the National Institute of Education. (Contract No. 400–76–0073)

1. HERMAN MELVILLE. "Bartleby the Scrivener," in *Eight Great American Short Novels,* p. 52. Edited by Philip Rahv. New York, New York: Berkeley Publishing Company, 1963.
2. DONALD H. GRAVES. *Balance the Basics: Let Them Write.* New York, New York: The Ford Foundation, 1978.
3. KENNETH KOCH. *Wishes, Lies, and Dreams.* New York, New York: Chelsea House, 1970.
4. JAMES MOFFETT. *Teaching the Universe of Discourse.* New York, New York: Houghton Mifflin, 1968.
5. COURTNEY B. CAZDEN. *Child Language and Education.* New York, New York: Holt, Rinehart and Winston, 1972.
6. JOHN DEWEY. *The Child and the Curriculum* and *The School and Society.* Chicago, Illinois: The University of Chicago Press, 1956.
7. NAN ELSASSER and VERA P. JOHN-STEINER. "An Interactionist Approach to Advancing Literacy," *Harvard Educational Review,* 47 (August, 1977), 355–69.
8. PAULO FREIRE, *Cultural Action for Freedom. Harvard Educational Review* and Center for the Study of Development and Social Change, Monograph Series No. 1. Cambridge, Massachusetts: *Harvard Educational Review* and Center for the Study of Development and Social Change, 1970.

Teacher Expectations

The teachers' behavior is goal directed and thus shaped by their beliefs and expectations about how to accomplish their goals. In planning for and interacting with students, teachers are guided by their beliefs about what students need and by their expectations about how students will respond if treated in particular ways. Also, teachers' beliefs about the academic ability of the class or of individual students may influence their curricular, instructional, or evaluative decisions.

Teachers' expectations are inferences that teachers make about the future behavior or academic achievement of their students, based on what they know about these students now. *Teacher expectation effects* are effects on student outcomes that occur because of the actions that teachers take in response to their expectations.

In this chapter we discuss different types of expectation effects and present models suggesting how sequences of teacher behavior may communicate differential expectations in ways that hinder or enhance student performance. The chapter also presents models of how students may internalize teacher expectations and reciprocally how students' beliefs and behavior may influence teachers. Although much of the chapter deals with how expectations influence classroom interaction, the chapter also explores other areas where expectation effects may be generated (e.g., teachers' knowledge of subject matter; Carlsen, 1991; Stodolsky & Grossman, 1995). Finally, the chapter explores ways that teachers can express realistic and supportive expectations.

AN EXAMPLE

Before we discuss types of expectation effects, read the following example and think about the expectations for performance that the teacher communicates to students. How effective is the communication?

Bill Peeler is a third-year teacher at the Boonville Community High School. The school serves students from a full range of socioeconomic backgrounds. Its student population is 55 percent Anglo, 35 percent African-American, and 10 percent

Asian. Bill teaches two sections of trigonometry, one of calculus, and one of consumer math. As a third-year teacher, he also advises the student yearbook committee and coaches the tennis team. During the first class period he approaches his class this way. "Since fifth grade, your math has been pretty much the same year after year. We're going to do some of the things you've done in the past, but when we do these things, we're going to use them in practical problem-solving situations. The modern world requires all types of mathematics skills, and you need to be able to estimate and to think mathematically as well as to do calculations. Only about one-fourth of the material we study will be review work. I want to introduce new ideas including geometry and algebra principles. These topics are sometimes seen as complex, but they are really only a way of thinking, and I think you'll enjoy these topics and learn a lot. As I hand out the course syllabus, I want you to start thinking about why mathematics is important to today's world. I want each of you to think of five ways you use math now and will use math in the future." What expectations has Mr. Peeler expressed to his students?

TYPES OF EXPECTATION EFFECTS

Researchers have examined two types of teacher expectation effects (Cooper & Good, 1983). The first is the *self-fulfilling prophecy effect,* in which an originally erroneous expectation leads to behavior that causes the expectation to become true. Merton (1948), who coined the term, gave bank failures as an example. He noted that a false rumor that a bank was about to fail could cause depositors to panic and flock to clear out their accounts. If enough depositors acted on this unfounded rumor and demanded their money, the bank's financial position would deteriorate rapidly and failure would occur, even though it would not have occurred if the false rumor had not circulated in the first place. As a classroom example, consider a sixth-grade band teacher who decides that Juana will be one of her best flute players because last year Juana's older sister Rosa was the best flute player in the entire city. Let us assume that Juana is actually a student with average music potential, but that the teacher warms up to her right away, expresses confidence that she will be a good musician, encourages her often in practice, and arranges for her to practice at home with Rosa. Chances are that this treatment will make Juana a top performer before long, even though this probably would not have happened if the teacher had not treated her specially. Juana's rapid progress in musical performance can be seen as a self-fulfilling prophecy effect of her teacher's expectations and related instructional decisions.

The second type of expectation effect is the *sustaining expectation effect.* Here, teachers expect students to sustain previously developed patterns, to the point that teachers take these patterns for granted and fail to see and capitalize on change in students' potential. The findings described in Chapter 2 on teachers' differential treatment of high versus low achievers are examples of sustaining expectation effects. To the extent that teachers wait longer for high achievers to respond to questions, provide them with more second chances following initial failures, and react to their answers with more praise and less criticism, teachers are likely to sustain (and probably increase somewhat) achievement differences between the two groups.

Self-fulfilling prophecy effects are more powerful than sustaining expectation effects because the former introduce significant change in student behavior instead of merely minimizing such change by sustaining established patterns. Self-fulfilling prophecy effects can be powerful when they occur, but the more subtle sustaining expectation effects occur more often. This chapter is organized around the concept of self-fulfilling prophecies, but both types of expectation effects are important and provide useful concepts for examining classroom events.

TEACHERS' EXPECTATIONS AS SELF-FULFILLING PROPHECIES

Robert Rosenthal and Lenore Jacobson's *Pygmalion in the Classroom* (1968) created wide interest in and controversy about self-fulfilling prophecies. In their book they described research in which they manipulated teachers' expectations for student achievement to see whether these expectations would be fulfilled. The study involved several classes in each of the first six grades at Oak School. Expectations were created by claiming that a test (actually a general achievement test) had been developed to identify students who were about to bloom intellectually and therefore could be expected to show unusually large achievement gains during the coming school year. A few students in each class were identified to the teachers as such "bloomers." Actually, the students had been selected randomly rather than on the basis of test scores, so there was no real reason to expect unusual gains from them.

Yet, the "bloomers" did show greater gains than other students on achievement tests given at the end of the year (although primarily in the first two grades). Rosenthal and Jacobson interpreted these results in terms of the self-fulfilling prophecy effects of teachers' expectations. They reasoned that the expectations they created had caused the teachers to treat the "bloomers" differently, so that these students did make unusually high achievement gains that year.

At first, this conclusion was accepted enthusiastically, and secondary sources sometimes even made exaggerated claims that went far beyond those Rosenthal and Jacobson made. For example, an ad in the *Reader's Digest* read: "Actual experiments prove this mysterious force can heighten your intelligence, your competitive ability, and your will to succeed. The secret: Just make a prediction! Read how it works." Soon, however, critics began to attack the study, and a replication attempt failed to produce the same results, leading to debate over the Oak School experiment that has continued for over 25 years (Jones, 1990).

Meanwhile, other investigators did related studies using a variety of approaches, and attention shifted from debates over the original study to attempts to make sense of a growing literature on teacher expectation effects and related topics (Brophy & Good, 1974). This process continues, although it has produced a consensus that teachers' expectations can and sometimes do affect teacher-student interaction and student outcomes, along with a recognition that the processes involved are much more complex than originally believed (Brophy, 1983; Good, 1993; Jones, 1990; Jussim, 1986).

To make sense of the research, one must distinguish between two types of studies. The first, which includes the Rosenthal and Jacobson study, involves experimental attempts to induce teacher expectations by identifying "late bloomers," by using phony IQ scores, or by providing some other fictitious information about students. The second type of study uses the expectations that teachers form naturally on the basis of whatever information they have available (test scores and cumulative folders, information from other teachers, student behavior the first few weeks of class, previous experience with older siblings, etc.).

EFFECTS OF INDUCED EXPECTATIONS

Studies conducted in quite different settings have shown that student achievement can be affected by expectations induced in instructors. Beez (1968), studying adult tutors teaching Headstart children; Eden and Shani (1982), studying Israeli army instructors teaching military skills; and Schrank (1968), working with Air Force mathematics instructors all obtained similar results. In each study, teachers' expectations were manipulated by causing the teachers to believe that certain students or classes they would work with had unusually high learning potential. In fact, the students had been matched or selected randomly. Nevertheless, in each study, the students of instructors who had been led to hold high expectations achieved more than other students.

Some experimental studies failed to produce positive results, apparently because the teachers did not acquire the expectations that the experimenters were trying to induce. In the most obvious case, teachers knew that the expectations were not true, as in Schrank's (1970) adaptation of his earlier study of Air Force mathematics courses. For this second study, Schrank merely simulated the manipulation of teachers' expectations; the teachers knew that their students had been grouped randomly rather than by ability, but were asked to pretend that they were teaching a higher ability group.

Induced expectation experiments have produced clear-cut positive results often enough to demonstrate that teachers' expectations can have self-fulfilling prophecy effects on student achievement (see Jones, 1990). Such demonstrations are necessary because studies of teachers' naturally formed expectations cannot prove cause-and-effect relationships. This is because naturally formed expectations typically are based on real differences in student potential and thus are merely accurate predictions rather than indirect causes of differences in student progress. Studies linking teachers' naturally formed expectations to their classroom interactions with students are also needed, however, because they provide information about *how* teachers' expectations can become self-fulfilling.

STUDIES OF NATURALLY FORMED EXPECTATIONS

In this type of study, teachers' expectations are assessed either prior to their interactions with students (ideally) or early in the term before the teachers have had a chance to obtain much firsthand information about students. Usually, teachers are asked to rank or rate their students on either current achievement or expected improvement over the term. Student outcome data are then examined for differences between groups of students rated low versus high by their teachers.

Palardy (1969) studied the reading achievement produced by two groups of first-grade teachers. Using a questionnaire, he identified 10 teachers who believed that boys in their classes would make just as much progress in reading as girls, and another 14 teachers who expected the girls to do better. Five teachers from each group were selected for further study. All taught in middle-class schools, used the same basal reading series, and worked with three reading groups in heterogeneously grouped, self-contained classrooms.

The two groups did not differ on reading readiness tests given in September. However, on reading achievement tests given in March, boys whose teachers believed that they could achieve as well as girls averaged 96.5, but boys whose teachers did not believe that they could perform as well as girls averaged only 89.2. The girls in these classes averaged 96.2 and 96.7, respectively. Thus, boys did achieve less when taught by teachers who did not think that boys could progress as rapidly as girls.

Most studies of teachers' naturally formed expectations have related such expectations to teacher-student interaction measures rather than to student outcomes. Such studies typically demonstrate that teachers interact differently with high-expectation students than with low-expectation students, and they suggest the mechanisms that mediate sustaining expectation effects.

HOW EXPECTATIONS BECOME SELF-FULFILLING

Teacher expectation effects in classrooms are just special cases of the more general principle that any expectation can become self-fulfilling (Jones, 1990). Although it is not true that "wishing can make it so," our expectations affect the way we behave, and the way we behave affects how other people respond. Sometimes, our expectations about people cause us to treat them in ways that make them respond just as we expected they would.

An Example

For example, look ahead (or back) to your first teaching assignment. Unless they already know the situation, most new teachers want to find out about the school and the principal with whom they will be working. Suppose you spoke to a teacher at the school who said, "Ms. García is wonderful. You'll love working for her. She's warm and pleasant, and she really takes an interest in you. Feel free to come to her with your problems; she's always glad to help." If you heard this about Ms. García how would you respond to her when you met her? Think about this for a few moments, and then consider a different situation. Suppose the teacher had said, "Ms. García? Well, she's hard to describe. I guess she's all right, but I don't feel comfortable around her; she makes me nervous. I get the feeling that she doesn't want to talk to me, that I'm irritating her or wasting her time." How would you act when meeting Ms. García after you heard this?

If you are like most people, your behavior would differ depending on which description you heard. If you had received the positive information, you probably would look forward to meeting Ms. García and approach her with confidence and a friendly smile. You would likely tell her that you had heard good things about her and were looking forward to working with her. Having heard the other description, however, you probably would not look forward to the meeting, and you might be nervous, inhibited, or overly concerned about making a good impression. You might approach her with hesitation, wearing a serious expression or a forced smile, and speak in reserved or formal tones. Even if you said the same words, chances are that they would sound more like a prepared speech than a genuine personal reaction.

Now, put yourself in Ms. García's place. Assume she knows nothing about you. Take time to think about how she might respond to these two disparate approaches. Chances are, Ms. García would respond positively to the first approach. Faced with your warmth, friendliness, and genuine-sounding compliments, she likely would respond in kind. Your behavior would put her at ease and cause her to see you as a likeable, attractive person. When she smiled and said she would be looking forward to working with you, too, she would really mean it.

But what if you took the more nervous, formal approach? Again, Ms. García probably would respond in kind. Your self-presentation would likely make her feel nervous and formal, if she were not already. She would respond in an equally bland and formal manner, and this probably would be followed by an awkward silence that would make you both increasingly nervous.

Brophy and Good's Model

The example shows that it is not just the existence of an expectation that causes self-fulfillment; it is the behavior that the expectation produces. This behavior then affects other people, making them more likely to act in the expected ways. In our early research on teacher expectation effects on individual students (Brophy & Good, 1970), we suggested the following model for how the process might work:

1. Early in the year, the teacher forms differential expectations for student behavior and achievement.
2. Consistent with these differential expectations, the teacher behaves differently toward different students.
3. This treatment tells students something about how they are expected to behave in the classroom and perform on academic tasks.
4. If the teacher's treatment is consistent over time, and if students do not actively resist or change it, it will likely affect their self-concepts, achievement motivation, levels of aspiration, classroom conduct, and interactions with the teacher.
5. These effects generally will complement and reinforce the teacher's expectations, so that students will come to conform to these expectations more than they might have otherwise.
6. Ultimately, this will affect student achievement and other outcome measures. High-expectation students will be led to achieve at or near their potential, but low-expectation students will not gain as much as they could have gained if taught differently.

Self-fulfilling prophecy effects of teachers' expectations can occur only when all elements in the model are present. Often, however, one or more elements is missing. A teacher may not have clear-cut expectations about every student, or those expectations may change continually. Even when expectations are consistent, the teacher may not necessarily communicate them through consistent behavior. In this case, the expectations would not be self-fulfilling even if they turned out to be correct. Finally, students might prevent expectations from becoming self-fulfilling by counteracting their effects or resisting them in a way that makes the teacher change them.

PRACTICE EXAMPLES

In this section we provide some practice examples you can use to improve your understanding of the self-fulfilling prophecy concept. Read each example and determine whether you think a self-fulfilling prophecy is involved. If so, you should be able to identify: (1) the original expectation; (2) behaviors that consistently communicate this expectation in ways that make it more likely to be fulfilled, and (3) evidence that the original expectation has been confirmed. If the example does not contain all three elements, it does not illustrate a self-fulfilling prophecy.

1. Coach Winn knows that Sarah Brown is the daughter of a former professional tennis player. Although he has never seen Sarah play, she predicts, "Sarah will help our team in her sophomore year." In practice sessions, Sarah is treated like all the other team members. She plays the same number of matches and does the same drills, and the coach praises her only when her performance merits it. Sarah is the top-ranked player on the team in her sophomore year and is named to the league's all-star team.

2. Rick Wilson, a tenth-grade social studies teacher, believes that Antonio Navarro and Julia Suárez can be better students. Although they have earned only average grades, he has seen flashes of insight in them that suggest higher potential. Furthermore, their aptitude test scores are higher than their achievement profiles. However, both students have poor work habits. Neither spends much time working on seatwork assignments, and it is not uncommon for Antonio and Julia to fail to hand in homework two or three times a week. Mr. Wilson believes that both students can do better if he can motivate them to work harder, so he begins to call on them more often and to provide more detailed feedback on their seatwork and homework papers. By December, he has seen no progress. Nevertheless, he continues his efforts, and by May, Antonio is performing at a much higher level, but Julia's classroom behavior and test scores have not improved.

3. Jean Rogers is giving directions to John Greene, a second grader who is frequently in trouble. She has no confidence in John's sense of responsibility, so she gives him detailed instructions: "John, take this note to Ms. Turner's room. Remember: Don't make noise in the hall, don't stop to look in other classrooms, and above all, don't go outside." John responds with an obviously pained look, "Ms. Rogers, don't you trust me?"

4. As the school year begins, Tom Bloom is assigned to Dean Smith for academic counseling. The dean knows that Tom will probably flunk out at the end of the term. He has low entrance scores and poor writing skills. He is also shy, making it unlikely that he will get to know his instructors well or

receive much help from them. The dean tells Tom that he is at risk for academic difficulty and urges him to enroll in the study skills clinic and to devote extra time on weekends to his studies. In addition, he has Tom report to his office once a week. Tom realizes that the dean expects him to have trouble unless he works hard, so he works as hard as he can, ultimately earning two Bs and three Cs.

5. Bob Graney knows that Beth Blanton will be a problem. He had her older sister the year before and she was uncontrollable. Trying to keep Beth out of trouble, Bob seats her at a table away from the other third graders in the room. Before long, though, Beth begins to throw things at her peers to attract their attention.

6. Tom Santoro teaches a consumer business course at Mill Tour High School. He believes that students need and want to perform enjoyable drill activities in class but are not interested in tasks that require higher-order thinking. Therefore, in his taxation unit he emphasizes how to fill out tax forms and quick ways to check for computation errors. His other units also emphasize practical exercises involving much drill and practice but comparatively little analysis (Why are taxes collected? How legitimate is the present system? What alternative taxation plans would yield the same revenue but distribute the burden differently?).

7. Judy Jones, a seventh-grade mathematics teacher, uses tests emphasizing speed rather than ability to group students for instruction. At the beginning of the year she teaches new material to her high group (students who did well on the speed test) but requires her low group to review sixth-grade material in order to build up their speed. However, the slower students work only a few of the review problems because they know how to do them and because they want to listen to the teacher work with the high group so that they will be ready to do the work. Their failure to complete the review work during class strengthens the teacher's belief that these students need still more drill. In time the low-group students become bored with the easy, repetitive drill work, do even fewer problems, and even lose interest in listening to the teacher work with the high group (in part because they do not get to work on similar problems). By the end of the year, many slow-group students are engaging in disruptive behavior.

8. Jennifer Ball is concerned about the peer-group adjustment of Dick Ainge, one of her second graders. Dick had participated all year long in the races and games conducted during recess, but he began to withdraw from the group in the spring, when she introduced baseball. Although Dick is coordinated well enough, he had not played much baseball and had difficulty hitting and catching the ball. As a result, he was usually one of the last children chosen when teams were selected. After this happened a few times, Dick began to withdraw, claiming that he did not want to play because he had a headache or sore foot. Jennifer recognized that embarrassment was the real reason.

To help Dick compensate for his deficiencies and maintain peer status, Jennifer began allowing him to serve as umpire for ball games. This gave him an important, active role that she reinforced by praising Dick and calling other children's attention to his umpiring. In private contacts, she reassured Dick that he should not feel bad because he was not playing, because there could not be a ball game without an umpire.

In the last few days of school, Jennifer decided to let Dick play again, now that his confidence was built up. She was gratified to see that he was picked earlier than usual by the team captain. However, his batting and catching were just as bad as before. The next day, he was the last one chosen and he begged off, complaining of a headache.

9. Delpit (1995) reported the following actual event:

> One evening I receive a telephone call from Terrence's mother, who is near tears. A single parent, she has struggled to put her academically talented fourteen-year-old African-American son in a predominantly white private school. As an involved parent, she has spoken to each of his teachers several times during the first few months of school, all of whom assured her that Terrence was doing "just fine." When the first quarter's report cards were issued, she observed with dismay a report filled with Cs and Ds. She immediately went to talk to his teachers. When asked how they could have said he was doing fine when his grades were so low, each of them gave her some version of the same answer: "Why are you so upset? For him, Cs are great. You shouldn't try to push him so much." (p. xiii)

ANALYSIS OF EXAMPLES

Compare your responses with your classmates for examples 5 to 9.

Let us see how well you were able to identify self-fulfilling prophecies. We'll share our reactions to the first four examples.

In Case 1, Coach Winn's original expectation about Sarah is fulfilled. However, there is no evidence that the coach caused this through special behavior toward Sarah. Thus, the coach's prediction did not act as a self-fulfilling prophecy, even though it was accurate.

Case 2 is a self-fulfilling prophecy for Antonio but not for Julia, even though the teacher believed that both students could do better. Rick Wilson's determined teaching apparently was successful in changing Antonio's perceptions and beliefs ("I can do math," "I should do it," "I want to"), thus improving his effort and achievement. However, Mr. Wilson's behavior did not improve Julia's performance (perhaps she viewed his increased questioning as nagging or as a lack of confidence in her ability).

In Case 3, the teacher gives John explicit instructions because she fears that he will misbehave. She subconsciously communicates this expectation through her behavior, and he picks it up. However, there is no evidence that his behavior changes accordingly, so this is not an example of self-fulfilling prophecy. If Jean Rogers were to continue to treat John this way, though, he might begin to behave as she expects. At this point, her expectation would have become self-fulfilling.

Case 4 is especially interesting and instructive. The dean fears that Tom will flunk, and he communicates this expectation. Tom gets the message, but he reacts by working hard to prove himself. He ends up doing well, despite the dean's original expectation. This occurs because the dean communicates serious concern but follows up with attempts to deal with the problem (referring Tom to the study skills clinic, calling for extra study time, scheduling regular counseling appointments). In effect, the dean works against his own expectation by engaging in what might be called "counter-prophetic compensation" behaviors (Brophy, 1985) designed to prevent the feared outcome. If, instead, the dean had communicated hopelessness and had done nothing to change the situation, his expectation probably would have been fulfilled.

Goldenberg (1992) presented two case studies that related to the story of our fictional Tom Bloom. One was remarkably parallel, describing a student whose teacher feared low achievement from her but alleviated it by working hard with her and enlisting special help at home. The other case was the obverse of the first. Here, the teacher had confidence that the student was bright and well-motivated, so she didn't get concerned when the student began to skip assignments and perform less capably. As a result, this student's achievement level kept slipping as the year progressed. By the time the teacher realized what was happening, it was too late to do much about it.

Goldenberg's case studies of actual students illustrate that students sometimes can benefit from initially low teacher expectations if those expectations cause the teacher to take action intended to counteract the feared consequences. Conversely, students can suffer negative consequences from initially high teacher expectations if those expectations cause the teacher to fail to notice changes that call for corrective action.

HOW TEACHERS FORM EXPECTATIONS

We now consider some of the research on teacher expectation effects, along with its implications for teachers. Most of this research has focused on teachers' expectations for students' achievement rather than for other student outcomes (motivation, conduct, social adjustment), and most has focused on expectations about individual students rather than groups or whole classes. Therefore, we emphasize research on teachers' expectations for individual students' achievement, considering the research in terms of the steps in the Brophy and Good model.

The model begins with the statement that teachers form differential achievement expectations for different students at the beginning of the school year. Investigators have studied the nature of the information that teachers use to form these expectations and the degree to which the expectations are accurate.

One body of literature consists of experimental studies of expectation formation in which subjects (not necessarily teachers) are given only carefully controlled information about, and little or no opportunity to interact with, the "students" (usually fictional) about whom they are asked to make predictions. For example, all of the subjects might be given cumulative record forms containing identical test scores, grades, and comments presumably written by previous teachers, but half of the forms would be accompanied by a picture of a white child and the other half by a picture of a black child (to see if knowledge about the fictional student's race would affect predictions about his or her achievement). Such experiments have shown that expectations can be affected significantly by information about performance on tests or assignments, track or group placement, classroom conduct, physical appearance, race, socioeconomic status, ethnicity, gender, speech characteristics, and various diagnostic or special education labels (see Jones, 1990).

These findings are not surprising, given the limited information that experimental subjects had to work with. Unfortunately, however, such results are often cited in discussions about teachers' formation of expectations concerning their actual students, so that teachers sometimes are made to appear to be both gullible (willing to accept whatever phony information someone gives them) and prejudiced (tending to jump to conclusions based on students' race, gender, etc.). However, studies focusing on real teachers' expectations concerning their actual students, conducted under more natural conditions, suggest a much more positive picture. First, teachers will not passively accept phony information if it is contradicted by other information that they have from more credible sources or from their own tests, assignments, or interactions with their students. Furthermore, although evidence of teacher bias based on student gender (Jussim, 1989) or ethnicity (Trujillo, 1986) has been reported occasionally, studies of in-service teachers' achievement expectations for their actual students do not reveal much evidence of grossly biased judgments. For example, most impressions that teachers form from interacting with their students are based primarily on students' participation in academic activities and performance on tests and assignments rather than on physical or other status characteristics.

In summary, in-service teachers usually develop accurate expectations about their students, and they correct inaccurate expectations as more or better information becomes available. This limits the possibilities for self-fulfilling prophecy effects (which are based on false or unjustified expectations), although it still leaves a great deal of room for sustaining expectation effects.

HOW TEACHERS COMMUNICATE EXPECTATIONS TO STUDENTS

Given that teachers have formed differential expectations for different students, the next step of the Brophy and Good model postulates that teachers communicate these differential expectations by treating students differently. Researchers have addressed this issue by documenting differences in the ways teachers interact with students who differ in current or expected achievement.

Rosenthal (1974) reviewed the research on mediators of teacher expectation effects and identified four general factors. Focusing on positive self-fulfilling prophecy effects, he suggested that teachers will maximize student achievement if they

1. Create warm social-emotional relationships with their students (climate)
2. Give them more feedback about their performance (feedback)
3. Teach them more (and more difficult) material (input)
4. Give them more opportunities to respond and to ask questions (output)

This four-factor model is a useful summary, but we prefer a longer list of potential mediating mechanisms, for three reasons. First, teachers and teacher educators can use each of the items in a more detailed list as a basis for observing in classrooms. Second, we want to complement Rosenthal's emphasis on enhancing student achievement through positive expectation effects with an emphasis on ways that teachers might minimize the learning progress of low-expectation students through negative or undesirable expectation effects. Unfortunately, research suggests that teachers are more likely to be affected by information leading to negative expectations than by information leading to positive expectations (Persell, 1977). Third, we want to emphasize that teachers can communicate their expectations in a variety of ways, including some that are much more subtle than the direct ways summarized in Rosenthal's model. Reviews of the literature suggest that the following behaviors sometimes indicate differential teacher treatment of high and low achievers:

1. Waiting less time for lows to answer a question (before giving the answer or calling on someone else)
2. Giving lows answers or calling on someone else rather than trying to improve their responses by giving clues or repeating or rephrasing questions
3. Inappropriate reinforcement: rewarding inappropriate behavior or incorrect answers by lows
4. Criticizing lows more often for failure
5. Praising lows less often for success
6. Failing to give feedback to the public responses of lows
7. Generally paying less attention to lows or interacting with them less frequently
8. Calling on lows less often to respond to questions, or asking them only easier, nonanalytic questions
9. Seating lows farther away from the teacher
10. Demanding less from lows (e.g., teach less, gratuitous praise, excessive offers of help)
11. Interacting with lows more privately than publicly, and monitoring and structuring their activities more closely
12. Differential administration or grading of tests or assignments, in which highs but not lows are given the benefit of the doubt in borderline cases
13. Less friendly interactions with lows, including less smiling and fewer other nonverbal indicators of support
14. Briefer and less informative feedback to questions of lows
15. Less eye contact and other nonverbal communication of attention and responsiveness (forward lean, positive head nodding) in interaction with lows
16. Less use of effective but time-consuming instructional methods with lows when time is limited
17. Less acceptance and use of lows' ideas
18. Exposing lows to an impoverished curriculum (overly limited and repetitive content, emphasis on factual recitation rather than on lesson-extend-

ing discussion, emphasis on drill and practice tasks rather than application and higher-level thinking tasks)

Several points should be made about these forms of differential treatment that have been documented in research. First, they do not occur in all classrooms. Teachers vary considerably in how much they differentiate in their treatment of students toward whom they hold different expectations (more on this later).

Second, there is considerable evidence to suggest that teachers are often unaware of their differential behavior toward students. Babad (1993) has argued that research consistently illustrates that teachers provide low-status students with negative affective messages—that students are often aware of such communication. However, teachers are generally unaware that they are doing this and, rather, believe that they are emotionally supportive of low-achieving students.

Third, sometimes these differences in treatment are due mostly or even entirely to the students rather than to the teacher (e.g., if their contributions to the lesson are of lower quality, it is difficult for the teacher to use their ideas as frequently).

Fourth, some forms of differential treatment are appropriate at times and may even represent appropriate individualizing of instruction rather than inappropriate projection of negative expectations. Lows appear to require more structuring of their activities and closer monitoring of their work, for example, and one could argue that it makes sense at times to interact with them more privately than publicly. It is difficult to distinguish seatwork monitoring that includes just the right degree of extra structuring and assistance from seatwork monitoring that amounts to giving students answers without requiring them to think and learn. Similarly, it may be difficult to determine whether a teacher is challenging a student below, at, or above the optimal level. Thus, one should not assume that the forms of differential treatment described above are necessarily inappropriate whenever they are observed.

These teacher behaviors are danger signals, however, especially if the differentiation is large and occurs on many dimensions rather than one or two. Such a pattern suggests that the teacher is merely going through the motions of instructing low-expectation students, without genuinely trying to encourage their academic progress.

Note also that some of these forms of differential treatment could directly affect students' opportunity to learn. To the extent that lows get less content and feedback, they are almost certain to make less progress than highs, regardless of whether or not lows are aware of this differential treatment and its implications about their teacher's expectations for them. In addition to these expectation effects that occur directly through differences in exposure to content, indirect effects may occur through teacher behavior that affects students' self-concepts, motivation, performance expectations, or attributions for success or failure. This brings us to step 3 of the Brophy and Good model, which postulates that students perceive differential treatment and its implications about what is expected of them.

STUDENTS' PERCEPTIONS OF DIFFERENTIAL TEACHER TREATMENT

Students are aware of differences in teachers' patterns of interaction with different students in the class. Interviews with elementary school students indicate that they see their teachers as projecting higher achievement expectations and offering more opportunity and choice to high achievers, while structuring the activities of low achievers more closely and providing them both with more help and with more negative feedback about their academic work and classroom conduct. Furthermore, students are more aware of such differentiation in classes where more of it occurs (Weinstein et al., 1987).

Cooper and Good (1983) reported similar findings. Compared to low-expectation peers, elementary students for whom their teachers held high expectations reported themselves as engaging more often in teacher-initiated public interactions but less often in teacher-initiated private interactions, supplying correct answers more frequently, and receiving more praise and less criticism from teachers. Observed differences were in the same directions but less extreme, suggesting that students not only perceive differential treatment but exaggerate the differentiation that exists.

Combining their student interview findings with classroom observation of teachers' patterns of interaction with students who differ in expectation or achievement, Good and Weinstein (1986) produced the summary shown in Table 3.1. To the extent that such differentiation exists in a teacher's classroom, expectation effects on student achievement are likely to occur both directly through opportunity to learn (differences in the amount and nature of exposure to content and opportunities to engage in various types of academic activities) and indirectly through differential treatment that is likely to affect students' self-concepts, attributional inferences, or motivation.

Individual differences among students also affect the size of teacher expectation effects. Some students may be more sensitive than others to voice tones or other subtle communication cues, so that they may interpret teachers' communications of expectations more often and accurately. Younger and more teacher-dependent students may also be more susceptible to teacher expectation effects (Persell, 1977).

STUDENTS' RESPONSES TO DIFFERENTIAL LEARNING OPPORTUNITIES

One interesting dilemma that teachers face is that often they need to differentiate instruction because students need different levels of assistance. However, differential treatment by the teacher might be seen, by at least some students, as biased and inappropriate behavior. Fulk and Smith (1995) asked students about strategies that teachers use to adapt instruction and differentiate rules and rewards in order to respond to the diverse needs of students with learning or behavior problems. In general, students reported accepting the need for teachers to differentiate their instruction on the basis of students' needs and interests (including those students identified as having special needs as well as other students). However, most first, fifth, and sixth graders thought that it was unfair for some students to get more dif-

Table 3.1 GENERAL DIMENSIONS OF TEACHERS' COMMUNICATION OF DIFFERENTIAL EXPECTATIONS AND SELECTED EXAMPLES

	Students believed to be MORE capable have:	Students believed to be LESS capable have:

Task environment
  Curriculum, procedures,
  task definition, pacing,
  qualities of environment
	More opportunity to perform publicly on meaningful tasks	Less opportunity to perform publicly, especially on meaningful tasks (supplying alternate endings to a story vs. learning to pronounce a word correctly)

	More opportunity to think	Less opportunity to think, analyze (since much work is aimed at practice)
Grouping practices	More assignments that deal with comprehension, understanding (in higher-ability groups)	Less choice on curriculum assignments—more work on drill-like assignments
Locus of responsibility for learning	More autonomy (more choice in assignments, fewer interruptions)	Less autonomy (frequent teacher monitoring of work, frequent interruptions)
Feedback and evaluation practices	More opportunity for self-evaluation	Less opportunity for self-evaluation
Motivational strategies	More honest/contingent feedback	Less honest/more gratuitous/less contingent feedback
Quality of teacher relationships	More respect for the learner as an individual with unique interests and needs	**Less respect** for the learner as an individual with unique interests and needs

ficult work. Further, first graders suggested that teachers should not provide differential sanctions in response to misbehavior by different students.

Witty and DeBaryshe (1994) examined the extent to which male students and their teachers perceived differences in teacher-student interactions as a function of student achievement level and race. The study indicated that differential treatment was reported, but that teachers and students often disagreed about *where* the differences occurred. For example, male students reported that teachers showed more praise and less negative behavior toward high achieving students and more positive personal regard toward average achieving and African American students.

Given such differential student perceptions, teachers need to consider the extent to which students see such differential behavior as appropriate. If some students appear to resent the differential treatment, teachers will need to develop socialization strategies that help all students understand the rationale for it.

Students not only develop inferences about what teachers think of and expect from them; over time they develop beliefs about their potential and roles as students. Some come to believe that they can learn with relative ease, but others come to believe that they can learn only with great difficulty or perhaps cannot learn at all. Some are willing to try hard to learn, but others conclude that the costs (embarrassment, long hours of effort) are simply not worth the benefits. Some students learn to ask questions when they are confused, but others view such question asking as a form of public humiliation. The latter students learn to hide rather than confront their learning difficulties, and if necessary to turn in incomplete work, affect an air of apathy or disdain, or in other ways project the notion that they are unwilling rather than unable to do the work. This is because they would rather have the teacher or peers question their motivation than their ability.

Students who need the most help often are the least likely to seek assistance, especially once they have been in school long enough to learn that asking questions sometimes yields teacher criticism (for asking at the wrong time, for not having listened carefully, etc.) or causes the teacher or peers to infer that one is not very bright. Good et al. (1987) found that low achievers were just as likely to ask questions as other students in kindergarten classes but that low achievers asked significantly fewer questions than their classmates did in upper-elementary and secondary classes. Similarly, in a study involving grades 2, 4, and 6, Newman and Goldin (1990) found that among sixth graders the lowest achievers had both the greatest perceived need for help and the greatest resistance to asking for it.

Students' ambivalence about asking questions or getting help from teachers becomes especially acute at adolescence, when they have become both more concerned about how they are perceived by peers and more sensitive to the costs as well as the benefits of help seeking. Newman (1990) found that students' attitudes about help seeking were explained by various factors (including intrinsic striving for challenge and dependence on the teacher) at grades 3 and 5, but that by grade 7 students' help-seeking behavior was predicted completely by their beliefs about its probable benefits and costs (e.g., the likelihood that their help seeking would actually yield help that would enable them to learn, balanced against the expected embarrassment that it would entail).

Teachers must recognize and learn to cope effectively with forms of student passivity or resistance that stem from students' attempts to protect themselves from embarrassment. At minimum, teachers should avoid being conditioned by such students to lower expectations for them and thus abandon serious attempts to get them to achieve to their potential. Better yet, teachers should counter these students' fears and pessimistic expectations by convincing them that they can learn if they put forth reasonable effort, and then follow up by teaching students strategies for managing their learning effectively (more on this in subsequent chapters).

Along these lines, Newman and Schwager (1995) have shown the detrimental effects of performance goals on student questioning in laboratory situations. That is, when students were working for learning reasons (trying to understand the material) as opposed to performance reasons (i.e., trying to look good), they were more likely to ask authentic and useful questions. Hence, students' general orientations to learning are as important as particular strategies and skills.

Given that a teacher forms differential expectations and acts on them by treating students differently, and that students perceive this differential treatment and draw inferences about what is expected of them, the stage is set for teacher expectation effects on student achievement that are mediated through effects on students' self-concepts, motivation, expectations, and attributions.

Good's Model of Student Passivity

Good (1981, 1993) suggested that certain forms of teacher treatment induce passivity in low achievers through two mechanisms. First, many teachers call on low achievers less often and wait a shorter time for them to respond than they do for highs. They also give them answers rather than try to improve their poor responses and are less likely to praise their successes but more likely to criticize their failures. Given that low achievers are less likely to be able to answer correctly in the first place and that their mistakes occur in public, they must bear considerably more than the usual levels of ambiguity and risk when they participate actively in lessons. Under the circumstances, a good strategy for them is to remain passive—not to volunteer and not to respond when called on.

A second possible path toward passivity is that low achievers often must adjust to more varied teacher treatment than other students. Their teachers are likely to treat them inconsistently over the course of the school year, trying one approach after another in an attempt to find a strategy that works. Also, they may have more teachers (if they are involved in compensatory or special education), which means exposure to more contrasting strategies. Some teachers call on them frequently in an attempt to get them to participate, but others mostly avoid them. Some rarely praise their successes, but others praise almost everything they do, even responses that are not correct. Student passivity is a likely outcome of such diversity of treatment. Not knowing what to do, low achievers may learn to avoid initiating and wait for the teacher to structure their behavior.

Student Internalization

We have argued that students may receive different types of expectations from different teachers. However, they also may experience inconsistency between their home and school environments. For example, Heath (1983) has noted that lower-class parents generally do not ask their children a question when they, the adults, already know the answer. However, middle-class parents and teachers often engage in this practice. McCaslin and Murdock (1991) have provided detailed case analysis to illustrate how students' home learning may support or conflict with students' understanding and valuing of classroom activities and achievement (e.g., the role of effort may mean notably different things in some homes than what it means to teachers). Much remains to be learned about how students are socialized to accept or to reject the norms that teachers, parents, and other significant adults hold. Sometimes students will react to the same type of teacher behavior in dissimilar ways (some students will hear challenge and appropriate concern; others will hear criticism). If students are consistently exposed to low expectations, however, they will tend to internalize those expectations in time.

Silent Students

Of course, students may be silent for many reasons—some have learned to be silent because of prior experiences in schools; others are silent because of their experiences at home and in their community. Jones and Gerig (1994) studied student-teacher interactions and observed 101 sixth-grade students in one middle school.

Students were observed during 14 classroom periods using the Brophy-Good Teacher-Child Dyadic Observation Instrument (for more information about this instrument, see the appendix at the end of the chapter).

The intent of the study was to identify students who initiated responses infrequently and to explore (through student interviews) the reasons for students' passivity. These students averaged less than one initiated interaction across all of the observations. Jones and Gerig found that silent students were *not* distinguished by gender, race, or achievement. Thus, teachers need to be careful not to equate student-initiated verbal behavior with ability per se—although this may be a factor in some cases (Finn et al., 1995).

Jones and Gerig (1994) found in interviews with students that most of them reported they chose not to initiate verbalization because of personal anxiety or anticipation of possible embarrassment. For these students, low participation was more likely to be due to low self-confidence than low knowledge. Further, they found a few of the students to be shy for cultural reasons (a way to show respect for the teacher and peers). Finally, they found that some students who did not participate (and who described themselves as shy) had adequate social skills, but *preferred* to learn by listening and thinking.

Interestingly, silent students reported two different perceptions of peers who talked frequently in class. Over half of the silent students reported that they found these students irritating and described them in such terms as nerds, etc. They felt that students who talked more were attempting to focus attention on themselves and keeping others from having a turn. Another subset of silent students, however, interpreted their peers' classroom participation in quite different ways. This group of silent students seemed to respect their more talkative peers and indicated that these students were smart and spoke frequently because they knew a lot.

The Jones and Gerig (1994) study provides clear support for Good's passivity model. Some students do appear to internalize classroom messages that reduce their initiative (belief about personal abilities, fear of embarrassment, etc.). However, they also make it clear that some passive students are low participators because they choose to do so (they have both the knowledge and social skills necessary for public responses). Thus, in some contexts low participation ratios may be adaptive for some students. There are various issues that teachers must consider when they intervene with students who do not take the initiative in classroom conversation. One key issue is whether the lack of participation is because of inadequate social knowledge and skills, or because of personal preference. We discuss strategies for helping students to assume more individual initiative (Wade, 1995) and to assume more initiative in working with peers (Mulryan, 1995) in Chapter 7.

FACTORS THAT AFFECT EXPECTATION COMMUNICATION

Context

School contexts vary in the opportunities that they provide for differential teacher-student interaction, and thus for expectation effects to occur. *Grade level* is one such factor. Other things being equal, expectation effects should be greater in the early grades, before students' records of academic achievement and their academic self-concepts and attribution patterns become firmly established. This is what Rauden-bush (1984) found in his review of 18 experiments on induced teacher expecta-tions. Effects were stronger in grades 1 and 2 than in grades 3 through 6. Then ef-fects became strong again at grade 7, the first year of junior high school for most students. This suggests that strong effects might also be seen in the first year of high school, college, or graduate school, or whenever students are new to an institution and their instructors.

Differences between the elementary and secondary grades create variation in the types of differential treatment that occur. Elementary students have the same teacher all day and often interact with that teacher individually. Secondary students see most of their teachers for only an hour or less per day and do not spend much time interacting with them individually. Consequently, in the early grades expecta-tions are likely to be communicated through qualitative aspects of individualized teacher-student interaction (the teacher interacts frequently with all students but may treat highs and lows in quite different ways), but in the secondary grades dif-ferentiation is more likely to occur through the number of individualized teacher-student interactions (the teacher interacts with highs much more often than with lows, because highs contribute to lessons more often).

Time of year is another relevant context factor. Greater expectation effects would be expected early in the year (Brophy & Good, 1974). As the year pro-gresses, teachers may pay relatively less attention to within-class differences be-tween individuals or subgroups and begin to pay more attention to the progress of the class as a whole, adjusting the pace of instruction to suit the potential of the class as they have come to perceive it (Cooper & Good, 1983).

Subject matter is another significant context variable. Smith (1980) reported larger expectation effects on reading achievement than on math achievement. This may be because a greater variety of grouping and instructional practices tends to be used in teaching reading than in teaching math, so that there is more room for teachers to translate differential expectations into differential treatment of stu-dents.

The most important context factor is probably *the nature of the learning environ-ment* that the teacher establishes. The potential for expectation effects (especially for undesirable effects of low expectations) is greatest in classrooms that feature uniform rather than multiple goals, a narrow rather than a broad range of activity structures, norm-referenced achievement standards, a competitive atmosphere, public performance evaluation, emphasis on achievement rather than effort, and frequent publicly perceived differential treatment of high and low achievers.

Teachers' Personal Characteristics

More important than context and setting factors in determining teacher expecta-tion effects are individual differences among teachers, especially in their personal characteristics and their beliefs about teaching and learning. Some teachers are likely to show sizable self-fulfilling prophecy effects, especially negative effects that reduce student achievement gains.

For example, Brattesani, Weinstein, and Marshall (1984) compared class-rooms where the students described the teachers as differentiating considerably in their treatment of high versus low achievers with classrooms where the students reported little such differentiated treatment. They found that including teacher expectation measures added 9 to 18 percent to the predictable variance in year-end achievement beyond what could be predicted from prior achievement in the high-differentiation classes, but added only 1 to 5 percent in the low-differentiation classes. Thus, "high-differentiating" teachers produced sizable expectation effects, but "low-differentiating" teachers did not.

Brophy and Good (1974) suggested that teachers can be ranked on a dimension of expectation formation from proactive through reactive to overreactive. *Proactive* teachers are guided by their own beliefs about what is appropriate in setting goals for the class as a whole and for individual students. If they set realistic goals and have the needed skills, they are likely to move their students systematically toward fulfilling the expectations associated with these goals. Proactive teachers are the most likely to have positive expectation effects on their students.

At the other extreme are *overreactive* teachers who develop rigid, stereotyped perceptions of students based on students' prior records and on first impressions of their behavior. Overreactive teachers tend to treat students as stereotypes rather than as individuals, and they are the most likely teachers to have negative expectation effects.

In between these extremes are *reactive* teachers who hold expectations lightly and adjust them as a result of new feedback. Reactive teachers have minimal expectation effects on their students, tending to maintain existing differences between high and low achievers (although these differences will increase slightly because of different behavior by students themselves that the teachers do not compensate for).

Research has supported these distinctions, but with an important qualification: Unfortunately, most sizable teacher expectation effects on student achievement appear to be negative ones in which low expectations lead to lower achievement than students might have attained otherwise (Brophy, 1983; Simon & Willcocks, 1981). There is little evidence that even proactive teachers significantly augment the achievement of individual students by projecting positive expectations, but much evidence that overreactive teachers minimize student progress by acting on low expectations.

One cluster of traits likely to be found in overreactive or "high-bias" teachers is a tendency toward conventionalism, authoritarianism, or dogmatism (Babad, 1985). Other such personal traits that are less well documented but seem likely are (1) a tendency to maintain expectations rigidly once they are formed; (2) a teacher role definition that minimizes the teacher's personal responsibility for ensuring that students master the curriculum; (3) a tendency to view student ability as unitary and fixed rather than as multiple and open to improvement through instruction and practice; (4) a tendency to notice, think about, and comment on the differences rather than similarities between students, and to take these into account when planning instruction; (5) a tendency to repress or rationalize teaching failures rather than recognize and try to overcome them; and (6) poorly developed classroom management and instructional skills (which give the teacher more to be defensive about and thus more to repress or rationalize).

These personal characteristics of teachers interact with their beliefs about appropriate curriculum and instruction to determine the nature and strength of expectation effects on the achievement of individual students in their classes. Teachers with all of the above-listed characteristics, for example, would tend to have powerful (and mostly negative) expectation effects, including self-fulfilling prophecy effects, on substantial numbers of their students if they were teaching in the primary grades using approaches that maximized the time that they spent with individuals and small groups but minimized the time spent with the class as a whole. In contrast, these same teachers might have relatively minor sustaining expectation effects if they were teaching mathematics to high school students and relying exclusively on a whole-class approach that provided the same instruction, tasks, and requirements to all students and minimized the time spent with individuals.

Students' Personal Characteristics

Students are often inappropriately stereotyped on the basis of their ethnic or cultural background. For example, Hispanic students are often believed to be cooperative students who enjoy learning and sharing together with peers. Although this may be true for some Hispanic students, many such students prefer to learn in large-group settings or to work on individual projects.

Many Asian American students are encouraged to pursue mathematics and science careers because they are believed to be "good" in those subjects. Although some Asian-American students have both the knowledge and dispositions to support a career in mathematics and science, many would much prefer careers in art and/or the social sciences.

African American girls are often stereotyped in ways that are detrimental to their academic achievement. Delpit (1995) notes that because many female African American students are very good at nurturing others (many of them have helped care for younger siblings or cousins), they have become victimized by a "mammy" stereotype. Such perceptions (i.e., good caretakers) lead to situations in which they are often denied the encouragement that white female students receive for academic mastery.

Native American students often suffer the stereotype of "nonverbal Indian child." However, as Delpit (1995) notes, what is most often missing in these perceptions is that these children are verbal and want to share their insights and knowledge, but they need an appropriate context in which to talk. Questions that may be inappropriate to ask Native Americans students in a large-group setting can be appropriately asked in small-group discussions. If students have a history of talking successfully in small groups, they may become (if they choose to do so) more active and successful in large-group settings.

Some students may be subjected to more expectation pressures than others because of their distinctive race or cultural beliefs. Teachers need to develop their beliefs based on the individual student and his or her needs, abilities, and aspirations.

GROUP, CLASS, AND SCHOOL EXPECTATION EFFECTS

So far we have been discussing expectation effects on individual students in the same class. However, expectation effects can operate on groups, classes, or entire schools. Less research is available on such expectation effects, but they appear to be at least as important as effect on individuals. After all, low expectations for an entire class can affect all students in the class.

Group Effects

Weinstein (1976) showed that reading group membership information added 25 percent to the variance in mid-year reading achievement that could be predicted beyond what was predictable from readiness scores taken at the beginning of the year. Placement into high groups accelerated achievement rates, but placement into low groups slowed them down (relative to the rates expected based on initial readiness levels).

Research comparing instruction in different reading groups (reviewed by Allington, 1991) suggests some of the reasons for this. Teachers tend to give longer reading assignments, to provide more time for discussion of the story, to ask more higher-level comprehensive questions, and to be generally more demanding with high groups than with low groups. Teachers are quicker to interrupt low-group students when they make reading mistakes, and more likely to just give them the word or prompt them with graphemic (phonetic) cues rather than to offer semantic or syntactic cues that might help them intuit the word from its context.

The nature and extent of such differential treatment vary across teachers, and at least some of it can be seen as appropriate differential instruction. Even so, widespread and powerful patterns of differential treatment of groups should be cause for concern. Too often, low groups continually get less interesting instruction, less emphasis on meaning and conceptualization, and more rote drill and practice activities (Good & Marshall, 1984). Eder (1981) compared instruction in the high and the low reading groups in a first-grade class in a school serving a relatively homogeneous middle-class population. None of the students could read prior to entering first grade, and given their relative homogeneity of background, it is not clear that ability grouping was needed.

The teacher did use "ability grouping," however, based on kindergarten teachers' recommendations that, in turn, were based on students' maturity in addition to their perceived ability. Consequently, a major reason that the low group progressed slowly was that it contained several immature, inattentive students who frequently disrupted lesson continuity. Compared with those in the high group, low-group students spent almost twice as much time off-task and were more likely to call out words or answers that were supposed to be supplied by other students. Thus, low-group student progress can be slowed not only by low teacher expectations but also by the undesirable social contexts that develop when groups are short on academic peer leaders and long on attention and conduct problems.

A "low-group psychology" often develops when ability grouping is practiced, even in schools whose low-group students would be high-group students somewhere else. Often, low groups are taught at a slower pace and exposed to less inter-esting and varied activities than they are capable of handling. Too often grouping for instruction in subjects like math and reading means that students placed in the low group or low track keep getting a steady diet of "more of the same" curriculum (Ross, et al., 1994).

Class Effects

Brophy and Evertson (1976) found that the most successful teachers believed that their students were capable of mastering curriculum objectives, and that they (the teachers) were capable of meeting students' instructional needs. These expecta-tions were associated with behaviors such as augmenting or even replacing curricu-lum materials or tests if these did not appear to be suited to students' needs.

Ashton and Webb (1986) reported similar findings for teachers who differed in *sense of efficacy*. Teachers who were high in sense of efficacy believed that they were capable of motivating and instructing students successfully. Teachers who were low in sense of efficacy believed either that no teachers could have important effects (because students' motivation and performance depend mostly on their home environments) or that some teachers could have such effects but they per-sonally could not (presumably because they lacked needed knowledge or skills).

Research done in 48 basic-level (i.e., low-achieving) mathematics and com-munication classes in four high schools revealed relationships between teachers' sense of efficacy, patterns of teacher-student interaction, and student achievement gains. Teachers high in sense of efficacy were more confident and at ease in their classrooms, more positive (praising, smiling) and less negative (criticizing, punish-ing) in interactions with their students, more successful in managing their class-rooms as efficient learning environments, less defensive, more accepting of student disagreement and challenges, and more effective in stimulating achievement gains. Midgley, Feldlaufer, and Eccles (1989) found that students' motivational profiles also can be affected by their teachers' efficacy beliefs. In particular, students who were taught mathematics by high-efficacy teachers one year showed notable drops in their self-concepts as mathematics learners if they were taught by low-efficacy teachers the next year.

Teacher expectation effects at the class level are especially likely to appear in schools using tracking systems. Evertson (1982) identified several ways in which stu-dents in low-track classes slowed pacing and shifted teachers' attention from acade-mic to procedural or behavioral matters. However, she also noted differences in how the teachers taught their high- and low-track classes, suggesting that teacher expectation effects were operating in addition to student effects on teachers. Com-pared with their behavior in high-track classes, many teachers of low-track classes were observed to be less clear about objectives, to introduce content less clearly or completely, to make fewer attempts to relate content to students' interests or back-grounds, to be less reasonable in their work standards, to be less consistent in their discipline, and to be less receptive to student input (see also Oakes, 1985; Oakes et al., 1993).

Teachers also tend to assign more independent projects and to introduce more high-level and integrative concepts in high-track classes (Oakes et al., 1993), but to stress more structured assignments dealing with basic facts and skills in low-track classes (Borko, Shavelson, & Stern, 1981). Finally, teachers tend to plan more thoroughly in order to be prepared for the academic challenges that high-track classes present but to be less well prepared for low-track classes and to spend more time allowing students to do activities of their own choosing rather than teaching academic content.

Good and Weinstein (1986) offered the following suggestions for improving classrooms that feature low expectations and boring, unchallenging routines.

1. Broaden goals of lessons and activities. Students need to practice and master basic content and skills, but they also need application opportunities. Something is wrong if students are usually working on phonics exercises but rarely reading, often practicing penmanship or copying spelling words but rarely writing, or regularly working on arithmetic computations but rarely trying to formulate or solve problems.
2. Pay more attention to students' ideas and interests, and encourage them to play a larger role in assessing their own performance. Students are often much more passive and teacher-dependent in their learning efforts than they need to be.
3. Increase opportunities for students to participate actively and use materials in meaningful ways. Teacher-led lessons should require more than just quiet listening, and follow-up assignments should require more than just working through highly structured practice exercises.
4. Besides asking factual questions, ask questions that require students to think, analyze, synthesize, or evaluate ideas. Include questions that can be answered at a variety of levels from a variety of points of view, so that a greater range of students can participate and experience success.
5. Focus on the positive aspects of learning. Encourage, reinforce, and note group progress toward learning goals. Minimize public comparisons of students with one another, criticisms of the class as a whole, or suggestions that material to be learned is overly difficult or unrewarding.

School Effects

High expectations and commitment to bringing about student achievement are part of a pattern of attitudes, beliefs, and behaviors that characterize schools that are successful in maximizing their students' learning gains (Good & Brophy, 1986). Effective school research has consistently found that teachers in effective schools not only held higher expectations but acted on them by setting goals expressed as minimally acceptable levels of achievement (rather than using prior achievement data to establish ceiling levels beyond which students were not expected to progress). These teachers viewed student failure as a challenge and required students to redo failed work (with individualized help as needed) rather than writing them off or referring them to remedial classes. They responded to mistakes and response failures during class with appropriate feedback and reinstruction rather than with lower standards or inappropriate praise. An extensive review by Teddlie and Stringfield (1993) illustrates that actual instructional behaviors and classroom interactions account for additional variation in school-level student achievement. Thus, in addition to the general ethos provided in an effective school, there is also important communication of appropriate expectations from teachers to students.

Rosenholtz (1989) found quite different beliefs about the kinds of professional behavior expected among teachers in more and less effective schools. The teachers in more effective schools looked for ways to share ideas and educational materials and tried to work together to facilitate students' achievement. In contrast, the teachers in less effective schools avoided such professional collaboration with peers and, in particular, avoided discussion of problems. Consequently, they had fewer resources to draw on in trying to solve those problems.

Stevenson and Stigler (1992) compared schooling in China, Japan, and the United States. They noted that in Asian classrooms more emphasis is placed on effort and hard work, but that an emphasis on innate ability in American schools lowers expectations about what can be accomplished through persistent effort. Thus, in terms of international norms, it may be that students perceived to be less talented in American schools receive too little academic demand.

EFFECTS OF EXPECTATIONS ON STUDENTS' PERSONAL AND SOCIAL DEVELOPMENT

In this chapter we have concentrated on teacher expectation effects on student achievement. However, there is reason to believe that teacher expectation effects also play a significant role in shaping students' personal and social development, at least within the school setting.

Experiments on the direct labeling of children by adults (Toner, Moore, & Emmons, 1980) have shown that children labeled as possessing prosocial traits such as patience or charity were more likely to demonstrate these traits in follow-up test situations than control children who were not so labeled. Unfortunately, less desirable outcomes such as learned helplessness can also result from direct labeling effects (Langer & Benevento, 1978). Self-perceptions and behavior also can be affected by expectations communicated indirectly. Hauserman, Miller, and Bond (1983) found that children's self-concepts could be improved by stimulating them to make positive statements about themselves each day. Riggs et al. (1983) showed that even self-perceptions can be induced indirectly (people who were asked questions implying that the experimenter believed them to be introverted later described themselves as more introverted than people who had been asked questions suggesting that they were considered extroverted). Brophy et al. (1983) showed that students were less engaged in activities that teachers introduced in ways suggesting negative expectations (i.e., suggesting that the activities would be very difficult or unenjoyable) than they were in other activities.

Ladson-Billings (1994) notes that teachers' expectations and perceptions may affect students in ways other than achievement on classroom assignments. For example, she theorizes that certain teacher beliefs may help students to develop a

Table 3.2 TEACHERS' COMMUNICATION OF EXPECTATIONS

Culturally Relevant	Assimilationist
Teacher sees herself as an artist, teaching as an art.	Teacher sees herself as technician, teaching as a technical task.
Teacher sees herself as part of the community and teaching as giving something back to the community, encourages students to do the same.	Teacher sees herself as an individual who may or may not be a part of the community; she encourages achievement as a means to escape community.
Teacher believes all students can succeed.	Teacher believes failure is inevitable for some.
Teacher helps students make connections between their community, national, and global identities.	Teacher homogenizes students into an "American" identity.
Teacher sees teaching as "pulling knowledge out"— like "mining."	Teacher sees teaching as "putting knowledge into"— like "banking."

Source: Ladson-Billings, G., (1994). *The Dreamkeepers: Successful Teachers of African American Children* (p. 34). San Francisco: Jossey-Bass. Reprinted with permission.

more culturally relevant perspective, whereas other teacher beliefs (and associated actions) may help students to develop an assimilist position. See, for example, Table 3.2.

Beliefs, attitudes, expectations, and behavior can be socialized, both through deliberate actions and through other behaviors that communicate one's beliefs, attitudes, or expectations. Thus, the success of a teacher's classroom management efforts probably is determined in part by expectations communicated about student conduct; the classroom atmosphere likely depends in part on expectations communicated about student cooperation and interpersonal relationships; and student responsiveness to lessons and assignments is probably affected by expectations communicated about the meaningfulness, interest, or utility of school activities. For example, Fuchs, Fuchs, and Phillips (1994) found that teachers who had the strongest beliefs about the importance of good work habits also appeared to plan with greater responsiveness to student performance.

Carr and Kurtz-Costes (1994) asked teachers to rank students' metacognitive knowledge, self-concept, and attributional beliefs. Carr and Kurtz-Costes found that teachers' general perceptions of students were biased by their perceptions of students' abilities. Students seen as high achieving were ranked higher on the motivational variables; teachers' ratings of students' attributional beliefs or self-concepts were often notably erroneous.

Thus, besides affecting student achievement, teacher expectations can be expected to affect students' attitudes, beliefs, attributions, expectations, motivational patterns, and classroom conduct.

NEW DIRECTIONS FOR EXPECTATION RESEARCH

Expectation research can be expanded in many ways to enhance our understanding of classroom teaching and learning (Good, 1993). In this section we briefly discuss three of many research topics that would yield information about how expectations influence students' performance: teachers' decisions about content, teachers' knowledge of subject matter, and the effects of different teachers' expectations across consecutive years.

Selection of Curriculum Content

Many educators have contended that textbooks define the curriculum. However, recent research challenges this simplistic view and suggests that teachers act as decision makers, modifying the curriculum in relation to factors such as teachers' beliefs about students' aptitude, their instructional intentions, and their subject-matter knowledge. If teachers influence the curriculum, then their decisions about curriculum help to determine performance expectations for students, just as teacher behaviors and activity structures do.

According to Freeman and Porter (1989), teachers make many decisions that influence how much content students receive. For example, teachers decide how much time to spend on mathematics on a certain day, what topics should be taught, how much time should be allocated for each topic, whether all students are taught the same topics, and in what order topics should be presented.

Freeman and Porter (1989) conducted detailed case studies of how four fourth-grade teachers used textbooks to make decisions about what mathematics content to teach. One particularly interesting comparison of two teachers who used the same textbook showed that they presented substantially different content to students. Teacher A allocated her mathematics time in the following ways: conceptions, 23 percent; skills, 59 percent; and applications, 18 percent. In contrast, Teacher B allocated 17 percent to conceptions, 70 percent to skills, and 13 percent to applications. Students in Class A received 13 additional lessons on concepts and 10 additional lessons on applications.

Freeman and Porter (1989) also contrasted time allocation in two classes. In Class A, 7764 minutes of instruction was provided. Class C was divided into two instructional groups, and Teacher C provided only 5830 minutes of instruction for the low group. Using 50 minutes as a class unit, the low group in Class C received 7 1/2 fewer weeks of instruction than did students in Class A. The time spent on instruction and the focus of instruction are two important ways in which expectations might be communicated. Subsequent research could profitably attempt to integrate study of teachers' decisions about how much and what type of content to present with study of teachers' expectations for students (how much students are likely to learn, etc.).

Subject-Matter Knowledge

Teachers' subject-matter knowledge is likely an important factor affecting the performance expectations they communicate to students. Teachers know more about some subjects or concepts than others, and their beliefs about subject matter and how to present it to students can affect their expectations concerning what students should learn and in what way.

Carlsen (1991) documented the effects of four beginning biology teachers' subject-matter knowledge on discourse and activity focus in their classrooms. Teachers taught an equal number of lessons on topics about which they had either high or low knowledge. These teachers were more likely to use lectures and relatively open-ended laboratory activities to teach high-knowledge topics but to use seatwork assignments and non-laboratory projects for topics about which they had low knowledge.

The findings imply that choice of instructional activity affects students' participation in classroom discussion. Teachers used lectures and laboratory activities, which are characterized by high rates of student questioning, with topics they were knowledgeable about. They tended to use classroom activities that involved few student questions when they were unfamiliar with the subject matter.

As Good (1993) has argued, research that examines teachers' performance expectations for individual students along with teachers' subject-matter knowledge would be profitable. When teachers instruct students in topics about which teachers have little knowledge, they may exaggerate differential treatment (i.e., avoid unpredictable questions by low achievers; overdepend on students believed to be more capable). They also may depend heavily on the textbook for their curriculum content, on fill-in-the-blanks worksheets for their activities, and on multiple-choice tests for assessing student learning.

Expectations Across Consecutive Years

As we noted earlier, Midgley et al. (1989) reported that students who moved from high- to low-efficacy math teachers during the transition from elementary to junior high school ended the first junior high year with low performance expectancies (even lower than students who had low-efficacy teachers both years) and high perceptions of task difficulty. The transition had more of an effect on low-achieving than on high-achieving students. In the spring of both years, students with more efficacious teachers had higher expectancies for and perceptions of their performance in math than did students with less efficacious teachers. Moreover, in the spring of their seventh-grade year, students with more efficacious teachers rated math as less difficult than did students with less efficacious teachers.

There is growing evidence that students' views of their potential to understand subject matter and perform in classrooms are not simply a product of the current classroom environment but are also influenced by previous school experiences. Fetterman (1990) found that fifth-grade teachers were unable to implement a process approach to mathematics (teaching students to understand content, explain solution paths) because fourth-grade teachers had encouraged a product approach (quick right answers) and also because of students' expectations about what would happen in the sixth grade. Hence, another important way to think about how expectations affect student performance is through an examination of the match or mismatch of expectations across consecutive school years.

INCREASING EXPECTATIONS

There is growing evidence that the performance of low achievers improves when they are allowed to enroll in more challenging courses or when course content is altered to include more challenging material that traditionally is not available to them. The decision to allow students to engage in more challenging academic work (e.g., move to a higher reading group) can be a powerful strategy for increasing teacher and student performance expectations (see Weinstein, 1976).

A Junior High/Middle School Example

Mason et al. (1992) described a study in which 34 average-achieving eighth-grade math students were assigned to prealgebra classes rather than traditional general mathematics classes. Results showed that students placed in prealgebra classes benefited from advanced placement in comparison to average-achieving eighth graders from the previous year who took general math. Prealgebra students outperformed the comparison cohort group on a concepts subtest while maintaining equivalent performance on the problem-solving and computation subtests. Subsequently, the average-achieving prealgebra students enrolled in more advanced mathematics classes during high school and obtained higher grades in these classes. Moreover, the presence of average achievers in prealgebra classes did not lower the performance of higher-achieving students in these classes.

Comprehensive Intervention in a High School

Efforts to change low expectations for student performance can go beyond altering the practices of one teacher (e.g., how students are assigned to reading groups) or a few teachers (e.g., the criteria math teachers set for entry into prealgebra classes) to include an entire school. For example, Weinstein et al. (1991) reported positive findings from a comprehensive intervention program designed to raise expectations for student achievement. This quasi-experimental field study involved collaboration between university researchers and teachers and administrators at an urban high school. The cooperating teachers attended university classes that focused on ways in which teachers can inadvertently maintain low expectations, and on the special motivational problems of low-achieving students. Teachers and researchers collaborated to develop a program for preventing and remediating low expectations.

This program has had some notable positive effects. For example, teachers were able to implement program procedures designed to increase communication of positive expectations to low achievers. Project teachers' expectations for students, as well as their attitudes toward colleague teachers, became more positive. Project teachers also expanded their roles and worked to change school tracking practices. Positive changes were also evident for the 158 project students. In contrast to 154 comparison students, project students had improved grades, fewer disciplinary referrals postintervention, and increased retention in school a year later.

AVOIDING NEGATIVE EXPECTATION EFFECTS

How can teachers avoid having negative expectation effects, and perhaps have positive expectation effects, on their students? Some authors have suggested that teachers should avoid forming any expectations at all: Refuse to discuss students with their previous teachers and ignore cumulative records and test information. We reject this suggestion, for two reasons.

First, expectations cannot be suppressed or avoided. We remember experiences that make an impression on us. When events occur repeatedly, they become seen as expected and normal. Thus, teachers will form expectations simply from interacting with students, even if they try to avoid other sources of information (Jones, 1990). Second, whether other sources of information are examined is not as important as *how information is used*. Information about students will create expectations, but if the information is accurate it can be useful in planning individualized instruction to meet students' specific needs.

Other authors have suggested that teachers should have only highly positive expectations. This idea is superficially appealing, because confidence and determination are important teacher qualities, and a "can do" attitude helps cut problems down to a workable size. However, positive expectations should not be carried to the point of distorting reality. Students show large individual differences in learning abilities and interests, and these cannot be eliminated through wishful thinking. Teachers will only frustrate both themselves and their students if they set unrealistically high standards that students cannot reach.

Expectations should be *appropriate* given students' current capabilities, and they should be followed by appropriate instructional behavior; that is, planned learning experiences that move students through the curriculum at a pace that fosters continued success and improvement. The pace will necessarily vary for different students. As long as students are working up to their potential and progressing steadily, a teacher has reason to be satisfied.

Regular patterns of student behavior will build up strong expectations in all teachers, including those who try to deny or suppress them. Inevitably, some of these expectations will be pessimistic. However, teachers can avoid undesirable self-fulfilling prophecy effects if they remain alert to the formation of, and changes in, their expectations, and if they monitor their behavior to see that negative expectations are not communicated. To the extent that such expectations do exist, they should take the "Dean Helpful" form in which the teacher combines expressions of concern with behavior designed to remediate difficulties. Thinking that a student needs help is bad only if the teacher does not provide that help in a positive, supportive way.

In Developing Expectations, Consider Students' Full Range of Abilities

Students' scores on intelligence and achievement tests provide useful, but only partial, information about students' abilities. Along with the abilities emphasized in these tests, students possess other forms of intellectual aptitude that they can bring to bear as learning resources if the forms of curriculum and instruction in use in the classroom allow them to do so. For example, Howard Gardner (1983, 1991) argued that people possess at least seven types of intellectual abilities in varying degrees:

Linguistic: Sensitivity to the meaning and order of words and ability to make varied use of language; exhibited by translators and poets.

Logical-mathematical: Ability to handle chains of reasoning and recognize patterns; exhibited by mathematicians and scientists.

Spatial: Ability to perceive the visual world accurately and re-create or transform its aspects based on those perceptions; exhibited by sculptors and architects.

Musical: Sensitivity to pitch, melody, rhythm, and tone; exhibited by composers and singers.

Bodily-kinesthetic: Ability to use the body and handle objects skillfully; exhibited by athletes, dancers, and surgeons.

Interpersonal: Ability to notice and make distinctions among other people; exhibited by politicians, salespeople, and religious leaders.

Intrapersonal: Ability to understand one's own feelings and emotional life; exhibited by therapists and social workers.

Gardner noted that the curriculum content and especially the tests traditionally emphasized in schooling have focused on linguistic and logical-mathematical abilities to the relative neglect of the others. He advocated better-rounded curricula and more use of project learning methods that would allow students to develop their complete range of abilities and bring them to bear as learning resources.

We mention his ideas here because they also serve as a reminder that the traditional emphasis on linguistic and logical-mathematical abilities can condition teachers to restrict themselves to these areas when developing expectations about the performance of their students. A narrow focus on these abilities, especially when they are expressed in a single score such as an IQ score or an achievement-level stanine score, can lead to rigid stereotyping of students. Thus, in getting to know one's students and beginning to develop expectations about them, it is important to pay attention to their full ranges of abilities and to view these abilities not as limiting factors but as resources that students will both develop and use as they participate in classroom activities.

Keeping Expectations Flexible and Current

Expectations based on recurring classroom events can be very compelling. If Susan frequently fails to do homework assignments, her teacher may gradually stop trying to change Susan's work habits and begin to accept her poor performance as "what is to be expected." To avoid falling into this rut, teachers need to keep their expectations flexible and bear in mind their role as instructors. If expectations are allowed to become too strong or too fixed, they can distort perception and behavior. Teachers may notice only those behaviors that fit their expectations and as a result may deviate from good teaching practice.

Once formed, expectations tend to be self-perpetuating because they guide both perceptions and behavior. When we expect to find something, we are much more likely to see it than when we are not looking for it. For example, most people do not notice counterfeit money or slight irregularities in clothing patterns. However, treasury department officials and inspectors for clothing manufacturers do notice them. Hidden abilities and aptitudes also may not be noticed except by those who are on the lookout for them. This is part of the reason why teachers often fail to notice the strengths of students who are frequent discipline problems. When expecting misbehavior, teachers may miss many of these students' academic accomplishments that someone else might have noticed and reinforced. Students' apparent "misbehavior" is subject to multiple interpretations. Segal-Andrews (1994) notes that sometimes a student's misbehavior is not simply lack of respect or boredom, but actually a call for help.

Expectations not only cause us to notice some things and fail to notice others, they also affect the way we *interpret* what we do notice. The optimist, for example, perceives a glass as half full, whereas the pessimist sees it as half empty. Mistaken beliefs about other people can be difficult to correct because of their tendency to influence how we interpret what we see. Consider the teacher who asks a difficult question and then calls on Juan, an intelligent and well-motivated student. Juan remains silent, pursing his lips and knitting his brow. The teacher knows that Juan is working out the problem, so he patiently gives him more time. Finally, Juan responds with a question, "Would you repeat that last part again?" The teacher is happy to do so, because this indicates that Juan has partially solved the problem and may be able to do it by himself with a little more time. The teacher repeats and then waits eagerly, but patiently, for Juan to respond again. If someone interrupted the teacher at this point to ask what he was doing, he might respond that he was "challenging the class to use creativity and logical thinking to solve problems."

Suppose, however, that the teacher had called on Alberto instead. Alberto is a low achiever, and the teacher does not think Alberto is very motivated, either. When called on, Alberto remains silent, although the teacher notes his pursed lips and furrowed brow. This probably means that Alberto is hopelessly lost, although it may mean that he is merely acting, trying to give the impression that he is thinking about the problem. After a few seconds, the teacher says, "Well, Alberto?" Now Alberto responds, but with a question instead of an answer: "Would you repeat that last part again?" This confirms the teacher's suspicions, making it clear that any more time spent with Alberto on this question would be wasted. After admonishing Alberto to listen more carefully, the teacher calls on someone else. If interrupted at this point and asked what he was doing, the teacher might say that he was "making it clear that the class is expected to pay close attention to the discussion, so that they can respond intelligently when questioned."

In this example, the teacher's expectations for the two students caused him to draw inferences from their behavior different from those a more neutral observer would have drawn. Although the behavior of the two boys was the same and they made the same response to the initial question, the teacher interpreted the behavior quite differently by reading initial meaning into it. His interpretations about the two boys may have been correct, but we (and he) cannot tell for certain because he did not verify them. Instead, he acted as if his interpretations were observable facts, so that his treatment of Alberto may have been unjustified.

The fact that a student could not do something yesterday does not mean that he or she cannot do it today, but the teacher will not find out unless the student is given a chance. Expectations stress the stable, unchanging aspects of the world. Teachers, however, are change agents trying to make students different from what they are today. Therefore, teachers must keep their expectations in perspective. To the extent that expectations are negative, they represent problems to be solved, not definitions of reality to which a teacher must adapt.

Emphasizing the Positive

The implication of all this seems to be that teachers should form and project expectations that are as positive as they can be while still remaining realistic. Such expectations should represent genuine beliefs about what can be achieved and therefore should be taken seriously as goals toward which to work in instructing students. The authors of this book have been contending for some time that students who are perceived as having less ability suffer from having a redundant curriculum such that the same topics are presented again and again. Students become bored by the sameness and eventually learn to invest less energy, and thus their teachers perceive the need for even more structure and smaller steps.

Delpit (1995) makes a similar point, noting that because teachers assume deficits in some students, they invariably *teach less* to those students instead of more. She puts it this way:

> We say we believe that all children can learn, but few of us really believe it. Teacher education usually focuses on research that links failure and socioeconomic status, failure and cultural differences, and failure and single-parent households. It is hard to believe that these children can possibly be successful after their teachers have been so thoroughly exposed to so much negative indoctrination. When teachers receive that kind of education, there is a tendency to assume deficits in students rather than to locate and teach to strengths. To counter this tendency, educators must have knowledge of children's lives outside of school so as to recognize their strengths. (p. 172)

Steele (1992), who has written extensively on issues concerning the schooling of African American students, expresses his perception of the problem this way.

> The challenge and the promise of personal fulfillment, not remediation (under whatever guise), should guide the education of these students. Their present skills should be taken into account, and they should be moved along at a pace that is demanding but doesn't defeat them. Their ambition should never be scaled down, but should instead be guided to inspiring goals even when extraordinary dedication is called for. Frustration will be less crippling than alienation. Peer psychology is everything: remediation defeats, challenge strengthens—affirming their potential, crediting them with their achievements, inspiring them. (p. 78)

Thus, he argues that both an academically *challenging* and a *valuing* teacher-student relationship are important. Although students who are at risk (for whatever reason) may need special efforts to feel valued, we believe that students generally need a valuing and challenging school environment.

Brophy (1983) suggested that teachers might accomplish this through several steps, including the following:

1. Keep expectations for individual students current by monitoring their progress closely; stress present performance over past history.
2. Set goals for the class and for individuals in terms of floors (minimally acceptable standards), not ceilings. Let group progress rates, rather than limits adopted arbitrarily in advance, determine how far the class can go within the time available.
3. When individualizing instruction and giving students feedback, stress their continuous progress relative to previous levels of mastery rather than how they compare with other students or with standardized test norms.
4. In responding to student performance, do not evaluate only success or failure. In addition, provide students with feedback or additional instruction they will need to meet the objectives.
5. When students have not understood an explanation or demonstration, diagnose their learning difficulty and follow through by reteaching in a different way rather than merely repeating the same instruction or giving up in frustration.
6. In general, think in terms of stretching the students' minds by stimulating them and encouraging them to achieve as much as they can, not in terms of "protecting" them from failure or embarrassment.

SUMMARY

In this chapter, we have shown how teachers' attitudes and expectations about different students can lead them to treat the students differently, sometimes to the extent of producing self-fulfilling prophecy effects. A particular danger is that low expectations combined with an attitude of futility will be communicated to certain students, leading to erosion of their confidence and motivation for school learning. This will confirm or deepen their sense of hopelessness and cause them to fail when they could have succeeded under different circumstances.

Expectations tend to be self-sustaining. They affect both *perception,* by causing teachers to be alert for what they expect and less likely to notice what they do not expect, and *interpretation,* by causing teachers to interpret (and perhaps distort) what they see so that it is consistent with their expectations. In this way, some expectations can persist even though they are not justified.

Research on teacher expectancies in the classroom has been a rich and exciting area for over 25 years, and many useful constructs have been derived from this work. Although the importance of teacher expectation effects has sometimes been overstated, it is clear that these effects are important, especially when considered with other teaching abilities (Anderson & Burns, 1989; McCaslin & Good, 1992) and other general variables (e.g., home-school correspondence; see McCaslin & Murdock, 1991).

Sometimes teachers give up on certain students and accept failure rather than trying to do anything further with them, and the students are blamed for their failure. This attitude psychologically frees the teacher from continuing to worry about the students' progress and from seeking more successful ways to teach them.

It is natural for teachers to form differential attitudes and expectations, because each student is an individual. To the extent that these expectations are accurate and up to date, they are helpful in planning ways to meet each student's needs. However, expectations must be monitored and evaluated to ensure that they change appropriately in response to changes in students.

Remember, teaching attitudes and expectations can be your allies and tools if properly maintained and used. However, if accepted unquestioningly and allowed to solidify, they can become defense mechanisms that lead you to ignore or explain away problems rather than solve them. Therefore, learn to control your attitudes and expectations—don't let them control you!

SUGGESTED ACTIVITIES AND QUESTIONS

1. How do teachers determine at what pace to teach content and for what level of understanding to hold students accountable? How do teachers make such decisions if they work in a high school that is very different from the high school they attended? How do elementary school teachers develop appropriate expectations for student performance when they do their observational work in a first-grade class, perhaps student teach in a third-grade class, and eventually accept their first job teaching in a sixth-grade class? Try to interview two teachers from the level at which you intend to teach, and determine how they developed expectations for class performance. If teachers are not available, arrange interviews with three or four classmates and discuss for a given academic subject (e.g., third-grade math or American history) and a particular topic how you would decide about what concepts to emphasize and the type of understanding students should demonstrate. What are the major differences in the way individuals approach these important decisions?

2. Which students in your preservice teacher education courses (or teachers at your school) are the brightest? What behavioral evidence and information have you used to form your opinions? How accurate do you think your estimates are?

3. Reread the example that appears at the beginning of the chapter. How appropriate were Mr. Peeler's expectations? Why? Can teachers' expectations be too high as well as too low?

4. Do you think that teachers tend to underestimate or overestimate the learning potential of the following: loud, aggressive males; quiet passive males; loud, aggressive females; quiet, passive females; students who are neat and follow directions carefully; students with speech impediments; and students who complain that schoolwork is uninteresting? Why might teachers overestimate or underestimate the ability of these different types of students?

5. Analyze your own attitudes about classroom learning. As a student, did you find school assignments enjoyable? If so, why? Was it just because you did well, or for

other reasons? What reasons? When learning was unrewarding, was it due to particular teachers or subjects?

6. What are ways in which teachers might inadvertently support the stereotyping of students by projecting classroom messages like "Asian students always do well in math"?

7. Write an original example of a self-fulfilling prophecy, based on something that happened to you, a relative, or a classmate. Include each of these three steps: an original expectation, behaviors that consistently communicated this expectation, and evidence that the expectation was confirmed.

8. Role-play the beginnings and endings of lessons. (You be the teacher and let classmates play students at a specific grade level.) Try to communicate appropriate expectations.

9. How can a teacher's overemphasis on praise of right answers interfere with student learning?

10. How might you as a beginning teacher guard against accepting indiscriminately the expectations of other teachers in your school?

11. How might teachers communicate high or low performance expectations to new teachers in their school?

12. How might the school principal communicate high and low expectations to teachers in a school?

13. Why do the authors stress that expectations should be appropriate rather than necessarily positive and that they must be followed up with appropriate behavior?

14. How do teachers form their expectations about students?

15. Explain in your own words why expectations, once formed, tend to be self-perpetuating.

16. How might a teacher's use of homework and seatwork assignments communicate low expectations to students?

17. Select some of the forms in the Appendix, Measuring Expectations, at the end of the chapter designed to measure behaviors that communicate teacher expectations, and use them to rate actual or videotaped teaching segments.

REFERENCES

Allington, R. (1991). Children who find learning to read difficult: School responses to diversity. In E. Hiebert (Ed.), *Literacy for a diverse society* (pp. 237–252). New York: Teachers College Press.

Anderson, L., & Burns, R. (1989). *Research in classrooms: The study of teachers, teaching, and instruction.* Oxford: Pergamon

Ashton, P., & Webb, R. (1986). *Making a difference: Teachers' sense of efficacy and student achievement.* New York: Longman.

Babad, E. (1985). Some correlates of teachers' expectancy bias. *American Educational Research Journal, 22,* 175–183.

Babad, E. (1993). Teachers' differential behavior. *Educational Psychology Review, 5,* 347–376.

Beez, W. (1968). Influence of biased psychological reports on teacher behavior and pupil performance. *Proceedings of the 76th Annual Convention of the American Psychological Association, 3,* 605–606.

Borko, H., Shavelson, R., & Stern, P. (1981). Teachers' decisions in the planning of reading instruction. *Reading Research Quarterly, 16,* 449–466.

Brattesani, K., Weinstein, R., & Marshall, H. (1984). Student perceptions of differential teacher treatment as moderators of teacher expectation effects. *Journal of Educational Psychology, 76,* 236–247.

Brophy, J. (1983). Research on the self-fulfilling prophecy and teacher expectations. *Journal of Educational Psychology, 75,* 631–661.

Brophy, J. (1985). Teachers' expectations, motives, and goals for working with problem students. In C. Ames & R. Ames (Eds.), *Research on motivation in education, Vol. II: The classroom milieu.* Orlando, FL: Academic Press.

Brophy, J., & Evertson, C. (1976). *Learning from teaching: A developmental perspective.* Boston: Allyn and Bacon.

Brophy, J., & Good, T. (1970). Teachers' communication of differential expectations for childrens' classroom performance: Some behavioral data. *Journal of Educational Psychology, 61,* 365–374.

Brophy, J., & Good, T. (1974). *Teacher-student relationships: Causes and consequences.* New York: Holt, Rinehart and Winston.

Brophy, J., Rohrkemper, M., Rashid, H., & Goldberger, M. (1983). Relationships between teachers' presentations of classroom tasks and students' engagement in those tasks. *Journal of Educational Psychology, 75,* 544–552.

Carlsen, W. (1991). Subject-matter knowledge and science teaching: A pragmatic perspective. In J. Brophy (Ed.)., *Advances in research on teaching* (Vol. 2, pp. 115–144). Greenwich, CT: JAI Press.

Carr, M. , & Kurtz-Costes, B. (1994). Is being smart everything? The influence of student achievement on teachers' perceptions. *British Journal of Educational Pscyhology, 61,* 263–276.

Cooper, H. (1985). Models of teacher expectation communication. In J. Dusek (Ed.), *Teacher expectancies.* Hillsdale, NJ: Erlbaum.

Cooper, H., & Good, T. (1983). *Pygmalion grows up: Studies in the expectation communication process.* New York: Longman.

Delpit, L. (1995). *Other people's children: Cultural conflict in the classroom.* New York: The New Press.

Eccles, J., & Wigfield, A. (1985). Teacher expectations and student motivation. In J. Dusek (Ed.), *Teacher expectancies.* Hillsdale, NJ: Erlbaum.

Eden, D., & Shani, A. (1982). Pygmalion goes to bootcamp: Expectancy, leadership, and trainee performance. *Journal of Applied Psychology, 67,* 194–199.

Eder, D. (1981). Ability grouping as a self-fulfilling prophecy: A micro-analysis of teacher-student interaction. *Sociology of Education, 54,* 151–161.

Evertson, C. (1982). Differences in instructional activities in higher- and lower-achieving junior high English and math classes. *Elementary School Journal, 82,* 329–350.

Fetterman, N. (1990). *The meaning of success and failure: A look at the social instructional environments of four elementary school classrooms.* Unpublished doctoral dissertation, Bryn Mawr College, Bryn Mawr, PA.

Finn, J., Pannozzo, G., & Voelkl, K. (1995). Disruptive and inattentive-withdrawn behavior and achievement among fourth graders. *Elementary School Journal, 95,* 421–434.

Freeman, D., & Porter, A. (1989). Do textbooks dictate the content of mathematics instruction in elementary schools? *American Educational Research Journal, 26,* 403–421.

Fuchs, L., Fuchs, D., & Phillips, N. (1994). The relation between teachers' beliefs about the importance of good student work habits, teaching planning, and student achievement. *Elementary School Journal, 95,* 331–345.

Fulk, C., & Smith, P. (1995). Students' perceptions of teachers' instructional and management adaptations for students with learning or behavior problems. *Elementary School Journal, 95,* 409–420.

Gardner, H. (1983). *Frames of mind: The theory of multiple intelligences.* New York: Basic Books.

Gardner, H. (1991). *The unschooled mind: How children think and how schools should teach.* New York: Basic Books.

Goldenberg, C. (1992). The limits of expectations: A case for case knowledge about teacher expectancy effects. *American Educational Research Journal, 29,* 517–544.

Good, T., (1981). Teacher expectations and student perceptions: A decade of research. *Educational Leadership, 38,* 415–423.

Good, T., (1993). Teacher expectations. In L. Anderson (Ed.), *International encyclopedia of education* (2nd ed.). Oxford: Pergamon.

Good, T., and Brophy, J. (1986). School effects. In M. Wittrock (Ed.), *Handbook of Research on Teaching* (3rd ed.). New York: Macmillan.

Good, T., & Marshall, S. (1984). Do students learn more in heterogeneous or homogeneous achievement groups? In P. Peterson, L. Cherry-Wilkinson, & M. Hallinan (Eds.), *The social context of instruction: Group organization and group processes.* Orlando, FL: Academic Press.

Good, T., Slavings, R., Harel, K., & Emerson, H. (1987). Student passivity: A study of student question-asking in K–12 classrooms. *Sociology of Education, 60,* 181–199.

Good, T., & Weinstein, R. (1986). Teacher expectations: A framework for exploring classrooms. In K. K. Zumwalt (Ed.), *Improving teaching.* (The 1986 ASCD Yearbook.) Alexandria, VA: Association for Supervision and Curriculum Development.

Hauserman, N., Miller, J., & Bond, R. (1983). A behavioral approach to changing self-concept in elementary school children. *Psychological Record, 26,* 111–116.

Heath, S. (1983). *Ways with words.* New York: Cambridge University Press.

Jones, E. (1990). *Interpersonal perception.* New York: W. H. Freeman.

Jones, M., & Gerig, T. (1994). Silent sixth-grade students: Characteristics, achievement, and teacher expectations. *Elementary School Journal, 95,* 169–182.

Jussim, L. (1986). Self-Fulfilling Prophecies: A Theoretical and Integrative Review. *Psychological Review,* Vol. 93, pp. 429–445.

Jussim, L. (1989). Teacher expectations: Self-fulfilling prophecies, perceptual biases, and accuracy. *Journal of Personality and Social Psychology, 57,* 469–480.

Jussim, L. (1990). Social reality and social problems: The role of expectancies. *Journal of Social Issues, 46*(2), 9–34.

Ladson-Billings, G. (1994). *The dreamkeepers: Successful teachers of African-American children.* San Francisco: Jossey-Bass.

Langer, E., & Benevento, A. (1978). Self-induced dependence. *Journal of Personality and Social Psychology, 36,* 886–893.

Mason, D., Schroeter, D., Combs, R., & Washington, K. (1992). Assigning average-achieving eighth graders to advanced mathematics classes in an urban junior high. *Elementary School Journal, 92,* 587–599.

McCaslin, M., & Good, T. (1992). Compliant cognition: The misalliance of management and instructional goals in current school reform. *Educational Research, 21,* 4–17.

McCaslin, M., & Murdock, T. (1991). The emergent interaction of home and school in the development of students' adaptive learning. In M. Maehr & P. Pintrich (Eds.), *Advances in motivation and achievement* (Vol. 7, pp. 213–260). Greenwich, CT: JAI Press.

Meier, D. (1995). *The power of their ideas: Lessons for America from a small school in Harlem.* Boston: Beacon Press.

Merton, R. (1948). The self-fulfilling prophecy. *Antioch Review, 8,* 193–210.

Midgley, C., Feldlaufer, H., & Eccles, J. (1989). Change in teacher efficacy and student self- and task-related beliefs in mathematics during the transition to junior high school. *Journal of Educational Psychology, 81,* 247–258.

Mulryan, C. (1995). Fifth and sixth graders' involvement and participation in cooperative small groups in mathematics. *Elementary School Journal, 95,* 297–310.

Newman, R. (1990). Children's help seeking in the classroom: The role of motivational factors and attitudes. *Journal of Educational Psychology, 82,* 71–80.

Newman, R., & Goldin, L. (1990). Children's reluctance to seek help with school work. *Journal of Educational Psychology, 82,* 92–100.

Newman, R., & Schwager, M. (1995). Students' help seeking during problem solving: Effects of grade, goal, and prior achievement. *American Educational Research Journal, 32,* 352–376.

Oakes, J. (1985). *Keeping track: How schools structure inequality.* New Haven: Yale University Press.

Oakes, J., Quartz, K., Gong, J., Guiton, G., & Lipton, M. (1993). Creating middle schools: Technical, normative, and political considerations. *Elementary School Journal, 93,* 461–480.

Palardy, J. (1969). What teachers believe—what children achieve. *Elementary School Journal, 69,* 370–374.

Persell, C. (1977). *Education and inequality: The roots and results of stratification in American schools.* New York: Free Press.

Raudenbush, S. (1984). Magnitude of teacher expectancy effects on pupil IQ as a function of the credibility of expectancy induction: A synthesis of findings from 18 experiments. *Journal of Educational Psychology, 76,* 85–97.

Riggs, J., Monach, E., Ogburn, T., & Pahides, S. (1983). Inducing self-perceptions: The role of social interaction. *Personality and Social Psychology Bulletin, 9,* 253–260.

Rosenholtz, S. (1989). *Teachers' work place: The social organization of schools.* New York: Longman.

Rosenthal, R. (1974). *On the social psychology of the self-fulfilling prophecy: Further evidence for Pygmalion effects and their mediating mechanisms.* New York: MSS Modular Publications.

Rosenthal, R., & Jacobson, L. (1968). *Pygmalion in the classroom: Teacher expectation and pupils' intellectual development.* New York: Holt, Rinehart and Winston.

Ross, S., Smith, L., Lohr, L., & McNelis, M. (1994). Math and reading instruction in tracked first-grade classes. *Elementary School Journal, 95,* 105–120.

Schrank, W. (1968). The labeling effect of ability grouping. *Journal of Educational Research, 62,* 51–52.

Schrank, W. (1970). A further study of the labeling effect of ability grouping. *Journal of Educational Research, 63,* 358–360.

Segal-Andrews, A. (1994). Understanding student behavior in one fifth-grade classroom as contextually defined. *Elementary School Journal, 95,* 183–197.

Simon, B., & Willcocks, J. (Eds.). (1981). *Research and practice in the primary classroom.* London: Routledge and Kegan Paul.

Smith, M. (1980). Meta-analysis of research on teacher expectation. *Evaluation in Education, 4,* 53–55.

Steele, C. (1992). Race and the schooling of Black Americans. *The Atlantic, 269,* 68–78.

Stevenson, H., & Stigler, J. (1992). *The learning gap.* New York: Summit Books.

Stodolsky, S., & Grossman, P. (1995). The impact of subject matter on curricular activity: An analysis of five academic subjects. *American Educational Research Journal, 32,* 227–249.

Teddlie, C., & Stringfield, S. (1993). *Schools make a difference: Lessons learned from a 10-year study of school effects.* New York: Teachers College Press.

Toner, I., Moore, L., & Emmons, B. (1980). The effect of being labeled on subsequent self-control in children. *Child Development, 51,* 618–621.

Trujillo, C. (1986). A comparative examination of classroom interactions between professors and minority and non-minority college students. *American Educational Research Journal, 23,* 629–642.

Wade, R. (1995). Encouraging student initiative in a fourth-grade classroom. *Elementary School Journal, 95,* 339–354.

Weinstein, R. (1976). Reading group membership in first grade: Teacher behaviors and pupil experience over time. *Journal of Educational Psychology, 68,* 103–116.

Weinstein, R., Marshall, H., Sharp, L., & Botkin, M. (1987). Pygmalion and the student: Age and classroom differences in children's awareness of teacher expectations. *Child Development, 58,* 1079–1093.

Weinstein, R., Soule, C., Collins, F., Cone, J., Mehorn, M., & Simontacchi, K. (1991). Expectations and high school change: Teacher-researcher collaboration to prevent school failure. *American Journal of Community Psychology, 19,* 333–364.

Witty, J., & DeBaryshe, B. (1994). Student and teacher perceptions of teachers' communication of performance expectations in the classroom. *Journal of Classroom Interaction, 29,* 1–8.

APPENDIX

Measuring Expectations

Observation forms are presented here for measuring teacher behavior related to the basic teacher attitudes and expectations discussed in the chapter. Each form has a numbered title, a definition of the classroom situations in which it should be used, and a description of its purpose. Although all the forms possess these common properties, they differ from one another in several ways. Some are confined to strictly behavioral categories and require simple counting of observed events; others require the coder to make inferences or judgments and score the teacher on more global rating scales. Also, some call for only a single coding for a single event; others involve coding several items of information about series of events that occur in sequences.

Skilled coders can use many of the observation forms during a single observation, so long as they do not attempt to code two things at the same time. At the beginning, however, it is best to start with one or two forms while you acquire basic observation and coding skills.

The observation forms define the applicable classroom situation and then list several alternative ways in which the teacher could respond in the situation. The different teacher behaviors listed are most often mutually exclusive, but sometimes more than one could occur in a given situation. To use the observation forms correctly, you must be able to (1) recognize when relevant situations are occurring that call for use of the form, (2) accurately observe the teacher's handling of the situation, and (3) accurately record this information on the form. If the teacher shows more than one codable behavior in the situation, simply number the different behaviors consecutively. This method will preserve not only the information about different techniques that were used but also the sequence in which they were used.

USING CODING SHEETS

See Figure 3.1 for a sample coding sheet. It shows how the coding sheet is used and how the information recorded on it can be recovered later. This sample includes the form used for teacher behavior when introducing lessons or activities or making assignments (Form 3.1). This form is used to measure the teacher's motivation attempt (if any) as opposed to specificity or completeness in presenting the assignment (the latter is covered on a different form).

MOTIVATION ATTEMPT, INTRODUCING ACTIVITIES	EVALUATIONS AFTER ACTIVITIES	INDIVIDUAL PRAISE	INDIVIDUAL CRITICISM
1. Gushy buildup	1. Praises specific progress	1. Perseverance, effort	1. Poor persistence, effort
2. Enjoyment	2. Criticizes specifically	2. Progress	2. Poor progress
3. New information, skills	3. Praises general progress	3. Success	3. Failure
4. No motivation attempt	4. Criticizes general performance	4. Good thinking	4. Faulty thinking, guessing
5. Apologizes	5. Ambiguous praise	5. Imagination, originality	5. Triteness
6. Promises reward	6. Ambiguous criticism	6. Neatness, care	6. Sloppiness, carelessness
7. Warns of test	7. Praises good behavior	7. Obedience, attention	7. Breaks rules, inattentive
8. Threatens to punish	8. Criticizes misbehavior	8. Prosocial behavior	8. Antisocial behavior
9. Gives as punishment	9. No group evaluation	9. Other (specify)	9. Other (specify)
10. Other (specify)	10. Other (specify)		

			STUDENT NUMBERS AND CODES		STUDENT NUMBERS AND CODES	
CODES		*CODES*				
4 1. __26.		5 1. __26.	14 1. 3 __26.		16 1. 3 __26.	
1,3 2. __27.		5 2. __27.	23 2. 3,4 __27.		21 2. 3,4 __27.	
1,3 3. __28.		9 3. __28.	6 3. 3 __28.		5 3. 3 __28.	
__ 4. __29.		__ 4. __29.	18 4. 3 __29.		17 4. 3 __29.	
__ 5. __30.		__ 5. __30.	__ 5. __30.		__ 5. __30.	
__ 6. __31.		__ 6. __31.	__ 6. __31.		__ 6. 31	
__ 7. __32.		__ 7. __32.	__ 7. __32.		__ 7. __32.	
__ 8. __33.		__ 8. __33.	__ 8. __33.		__ 8. __33.	
__ 9. __34.		__ 9. __34.	__ 9. __34.		__ 9. __34.	
__10. __35.		__10. __35.	__10. __35.		__10. __35.	
__11. __36.		__11. __36.	__11. __36.		__11. __36.	
__12. __37.		__12. __37.	__12. __37.		__12. __37.	
__13. __38.		__13. __38.	__13. __38.		__13. __38.	
__14. __39.		__14. __39.	__14. __39.		__14. __39.	
__15. __40.		__15. __40.	__15. __40.		__15. __40.	
__16. __41.		__16. __41.	__16. __41.		__16. __41.	
__17. __42.		__17. __42.	__17. __42.		__17. __42.	
__18. __43.		__18. __43.	__18. __43.		__18. __43.	
__19. __44.		__19. __44.	__19. __44.		__19. __44.	
__20. __45.		__20. __45.	__20. __45.		__20. __45.	
__21. __46.		__21. __46.	__21. __46.		__21. __46.	
__22. __47.		__22. __47.	__22. __47.		__22. __47.	
__23. __48.		__23. __48.	__23. __48.		__23. __48.	
__24. __49.		__24. __49.	__24. __49.		__24. __49.	
__25. __50.		__25. __50.	__25. __50.		__25. __50.	

FIGURE 3.1
Sample coding sheet combining four observation forms.

FORM 3.1. Introducing Lessons, Activities, and Assignments

USE: When the teacher is introducing new activities or making assignments.
PURPOSE: To see whether or not the teacher pictures school work as worthwhile or enjoyable.

Observe teacher behavior when introducing activities and making assignments. For each codable instance observed, record the numbers (consecutively) of each category applicable to the teacher's behavior.

BEHAVIOR CATEGORIES

1. Gushes, gives overdramatic buildup
2. Predicts that group will enjoy the activity
3. Mentions information or skills the group will learn
4. Makes no attempt to motivate; starts right into activity
5. Apologizes or expresses sympathy to group ("Sorry, but you have to . . .")
6. Bribes, promises external reward for good attention or work
7. Warns group, or reminds them, about test to be given later
8. Threatens punishment for poor attention or work
9. Presents the activity itself as a penalty or punishment
10. Other (specify)

NOTES:

CODES

1.	4	26.	___
2.	1,3	27.	___
3.	1,3	28.	___
4.	___	29.	___
5.	___	30.	___
6.	___	31.	___
7.	___	32.	___
8.	___	33.	___
9.	___	34.	___
10.	___	35.	___
11.	___	36.	___
12.	___	37.	___
13.	___	38.	___
14.	___	39.	___
15.	___	40.	___
16.	___	41.	___
17.	___	42.	___
18.	___	43.	___
19.	___	44.	___
20.	___	45.	___
21.	___	46.	___
22.	___	47.	___
23.	___	48.	___
24.	___	49.	___
25.	___	50.	___

On this form, the observer would note carefully what attempt the teacher made to build up interest or *motivate* the students to work carefully on the lesson or assignment; this information is numbered by categories, and these numbers are used to record the behavior in the coding columns.

In the sample (Figure 3.1), the coding sheet shows that three such instances were observed by the coder (the coding sheet has room for 50 instances). Note that the first code entered is a 4, which indicates that the teacher began a lesson or gave an assignment with no attempt at all to motivate or build up interest. Some directions may have been given to get the group started, but no attempt was made to promote the activity ("Yesterday we finished page 53. Open your books to page 54. Mark, begin reading with the first paragraph."). The teacher also did not promise rewards or threaten punishment for good or bad performance in the activity.

The teacher's behavior the second time he or she introduced a lesson or activity is coded in the next row. Here the coder has entered both a 1 and a 3, indicating that the teacher began with a gushy buildup but later also mentioned the information or skills that would be learned in the activity.

The third row also shows a 1 followed by a 3 indicating again that the teacher introduced a lesson or activity with an excessive buildup followed by mention of the information or skills to be learned.

Although not enough instances are recorded to make interpretations with great confidence, a pattern is noticeable in the three instances coded. The teacher appears to be basically positive in the presentation of lessons and activities. No negative motivation attempts (apology, threat of test, or punishment) appear. However, in attempting to provide positive motivation, the teacher may be overdoing it, in that the observer coded two instances of overdramatic buildup.

If this sequence did indeed develop as the teacher's stable pattern, some guidelines for additional questions and observations would emerge. What would be the effects of this overdramatizing on the class? Would it tend to amuse them or cause them to lose respect for the teacher? Would it train them to begin to complain or suspect unenjoyable activities if the teacher failed to give the coming activity a big buildup? If there was evidence that the teacher's overacting was having these kinds of effects on the class, he or she might be advised to tone down the motivation attempts. If there appeared to be no adverse effects on the class, it might be advisable for the teacher to continue the present style of motivating the class and instead work on changing problem behaviors that appear to have negative consequences.

The observation forms here, as well as all of the forms following subsequent chapters, will be partially filled in to show how they look after being used in the classroom. However, we will no longer add our interpretations of the data shown on these sample coding sheets. Studying the partially filled-in coding sheets will help you quickly grasp what is involved in using each observation form. In addition, it will provide a basis for practicing interpretation of coded data. If possible, compare your interpretations of these data with those of a friend or colleague. Discuss any disagreements in detail to discover the reasons for them and to determine what additional information (if any) would be needed to resolve the matter with confidence. Your instructor or in-service leader can help you to resolve coding difficulties.

The observation forms are divided so that each measures just one or a small number of related teacher behaviors. Thus each form is a self-contained observation instrument that can be used independently of the others. Once you have acquired some skill as a coder, however, you will want to observe several aspects of teacher behavior, using several different forms. You may find it convenient to combine several forms onto a single coding sheet. There are many ways to do this, and personal preferences and convenience are the primary criteria for deciding whether a given method is desirable. We have provided a sample coding sheet in Figure 3.1 that combines Forms 3.1, 3.2, 3.3, and 3.4.

The four forms were compressed onto a single coding sheet by using key terms rather than the full behavior category descriptions that appear on the originals. Use and purpose descriptions are omitted entirely, since it is assumed that the coder is already familiar with the four original forms. The result is a sheet with spaces to code up to 50 instances of each of the four teacher behaviors. A coder would use this sheet until all 50 spaces were used for one of the four behaviors and then switch to a new sheet.

Figure 3.1 shows only one of many ways that these four forms could be combined onto a single coding sheet. Feel free to create coding sheets that meet your own preferences and needs. There is no single ideal coding sheet; the one that you like and that does the job is the one you should use.

FORM 3.2. Evaluations After Lessons and Activities

USE: When teacher ends a lesson or group activity.
PURPOSE: To see whether the teacher stresses learning or compliance in making evaluations.
    When the teacher ends a lesson or group activity, code any summary evaluations he or she makes about the group's performance during the activity.

BEHAVIOR CATEGORIES	CODES	
1. Praises progress in specific terms; labels knowledge or skills learned	1. _5_	26. ___
	2. _5_	27. ___
2. Criticizes performance or indicates weaknesses in specific terms	3. _9_	28. ___
	4. ___	29. ___
3. Praises generally poor performance, for doing well or knowing answers	5. ___	30. ___
4. Criticizes generally poor performance (doesn't detail the specifics)	6. ___	31. ___
	7. ___	32. ___
5. Ambiguous general praise ("You were very good today.")	8. ___	33. ___
	9. ___	34. ___
6. Ambiguous general criticism ("You weren't very good today.")	10. ___	35. ___
7. Praises good attention or good behavior	11. ___	36. ___
8. Criticizes poor attention or misbehavior	12. ___	37. ___
9. No general evaluations of performance were made	13. ___	38. ___
10. Other (specify)	14. ___	39. ___
	15. ___	40. ___
NOTES:	16. ___	41. ___
	17. ___	42. ___
Teacher uses stock phrase ("You were really good today; I'm very pleased").	18. ___	43. ___
	19. ___	44. ___
#13 cut off by bell; might have praised otherwise.	20. ___	45. ___
	21. ___	46. ___
1 = Homework Review	22. ___	47. ___
	23. ___	48. ___
2 = Division Facts Drill	24. ___	49. ___
	25. ___	50. ___
3 = Board Work		

Generally, all the information you need to code is on the sheet. For example, in Figure 3.1, column 1, you can see that most of the ways a teacher can motivate students when introducing a lesson have been summarized into nine categories; if the teacher's behavior cannot be described in one of these nine categories, use the tenth category. Occasionally, users will have to supply some information of their own. Notice scales representing Forms 3.3 and 3.4 (individual praise and individual criticism) in Figure 3.1. When individual students must be identified, as in these examples, users will have to supply their own identification codes. In the first instance, under *individual praise,* we see that student 14 received teacher praise for successful accomplishment (category 3).

Thus, depending on their coding goals, users will have to supply appropriate code numbers. For example, if you are interested in how teachers praise male and female students, respectively, then you need only use a 1 when girls are praised and a 2 when boys are

FORM 3.3. Individual Praise

USE: Whenever the teacher praises an individual student.
PURPOSE: To see what behaviors the teacher reinforces through praise, and to see how the teacher's praise is distributed among the students.
      Whenever the teacher praises an individual student, code the student's number and each category of teacher behavior that applies (consecutively).

BEHAVIOR CATEGORIES	STUDENT NUMBER	CODES
1. Perseverance or effort, worked long or hard	14	1. 3
	23	2. 3,4
2. Progress (relative to the past) toward achievement	6	3. 3
	18	4. 3
3. Success (right answer, high score), achievement	8	5. 1
4. Good thinking, good suggestion, good guess or nice try	8	6. 1
	8	7. 1
5. Imagination, creativity, originality		8. __
6. Neatness, careful work		9. __
7. Good or compliant behavior, follows rules, pays attention		10. __
8. Thoughtfulness, courtesy, offering to share; prosocial behavior		11. __
		12. __
9. Other (specify)		13. __
		14. __
NOTES:		15. __
All answers occurred during social studies discussion.		16. __
		17. __
		18. __
		19. __
Was particularly concerned about #8, a low-achieving male		20. __
		21. __
		22. __
		23. __
		24. __
		25. __

praised. Obviously, in Figure 3.1 the coder is coding the entire class, because in the second instance of a teacher praising an individual student, the student's number is 23. If you are interested in coding the behavior of an entire class, simply assign each student a unique number and use this number whenever interactions involving that student are coded.

FORM 3.4. Individual Criticism

USE: Whenever the teacher criticizes an individual student.
PURPOSE: To see what behaviors the teacher singles out for criticism, and to see how the teacher's criticism is distributed among the students.
       Whenever the teacher criticizes an individual student, note the student's name or number and code the behavior that is criticized.

BEHAVIOR CATEGORIES	STUDENT NUMBER	CODES
1. Lack of effort or persistence, doesn't try, gives up easily	16	1. _3_
	21	2. _3_
2. Poor progress (relative to expectations), could do better, falling behind	5	3. _3,4_
	12	4. _3_
3. Failure (can't answer, low score), lack of achievement	5	5. _1_
4. Faulty thinking, wild guess, failure to think before responding		6. ___
		7. ___
5. Trite, stereotyped responses, lack of originality or imagination		8. ___
		9. ___
6. Sloppiness or carelessness		10. ___
7. Misbehaves, breaks rules, inattentive		
8. Selfish, discourteous, won't share; antisocial behavior		11. ___
		12. ___
9. Other (specify)		13. ___
		14. ___
NOTES:		15. ___
		16. ___
All answers during social studies discussion.		17. ___
		18. ___
		19. ___
		20. ___
Teacher sharply critical of student #5; seems irritated with her generally.		21. ___
		22. ___
		23. ___
		24. ___
		25. ___

FORM 3.5. Positive Expectations Communicated to the Class

USE: At any time.
PURPOSE: To document the frequency and nature of the teacher's communication of positive expectations for the class as a whole.

If the teacher's remarks made to the class as a whole include positive expectations or statements about the class, check the type of statement made and record the statement in the space below the checklist.

_____ 1. General goodness of class (they are a fine group of students, the teacher enjoys working with them, etc.)

_____ 2. Intelligence/ability (the students are bright, alert, sharp, etc.)

_____ 3. Careful work (they work carefully on their assignments)

_____ 4. Good ideas/thoughtful (they ask good questions and make good comments about the content; write interesting essays, etc.)

_____ 5. Eager to learn (they are curious, interested in the content, eager to master skills, etc.)

_____ 6. Steady progress (they are making steady progress in mastering material and approaching long-term goals)

_____ 7. Improvement (their work shows notable improvement over earlier levels)

_____ 8. Mature/responsible (they know how to act, use good judgment, can assume responsibility, live up to the teacher's confidence in them, etc.)

_____ 9. Achievement oriented (they work hard because they want to do their best)

_____ 10. Cooperative with teacher (they want to cooperate by following the teacher's and the school's rules, and in general, conducting themselves appropriately)

_____ 11. Prosocial attitudes and behavior (they are, or are striving to be, kind, considerate, and helpful in their dealings with peers and with people generally)

_____ 12. Other (indicate)

NOTES:

Management I: Preventing Problems

INTRODUCTION

Classroom management is important to everyone connected with education. New teachers often fear that students will not respect them. Experienced teachers usually cite establishing management as a major goal in the first few weeks of the year. Principals give low ratings to teachers who lack control of their classes.

Classroom Vignettes

Teachers constantly have to ask questions and make decisions about management (Brophy & McCaslin, 1992; Kauffman et al., 1993). Consider the following four vignettes that illustrate these decisions. As you read each vignette, think about how you would respond as a teacher.

Jan Thorton, who teaches physics at Riverside High School, has become concerned that students are not reading basic assignments before laboratory work. Hence, students are doing the experiments but not really understanding the work they do. She decides to start giving pop quizzes over assigned readings. Is this a good idea? What does this action convey to students?

Bill Reid, a sixth-grade teacher at Truman Middle School, gives students at least 30 minutes of uninterrupted seatwork each day. He expects students to work alone, and he is largely unavailable for assistance because he grades papers during this time. He believes that after a 15- to 20-minute lecture-discussion, students should be able to work independently and that this practice builds self-reliance. What are possible advantages and disadvantages of this "management" of instruction?

José Cruz is a ninth-grade English teacher at St. John High School. He likes to write the names of students on the board when they misbehave. He believes this is a good strategy because as soon as he writes a name on the board, the "named" student settles down and other students in the class seem less disturbed than when he speaks aloud to a misbehaving student. After all, students know the consequences if their name goes on the board twice; thus, Mr. Cruz finds this a very efficient management system. How would you describe the possible advantages and disadvantages of this management technique?

Jim Beam, the art teacher at Bayside High School, doesn't believe in "school detention." However, if students accumulated enough classroom reprimands (written notes), he requires that students either do volunteer work and paint scenery for the theater group or spend a weekend doing community service (e.g., paint over graffiti). Students and parents are told about this consequence at the start of the school. What do you think about this technique?

Management Research

Advice to teachers about classroom management once was based mostly on untested theory or unsystematic individual testimonials about "what works best for me." Much of it was contradictory and very little was based on solid evidence. However, research on classroom management has yielded a knowledge base that offers a coherent set of principles to guide teachers in making decisions about how to manage their classrooms (Brophy & McCaslin, 1992; Emmer & Aussiker, 1990; Evertson & Harris, 1992; Gettinger, 1988; Jones, 1996; McCaslin & Good, 1992). The findings converge on the conclusion that teachers who approach classroom management as a process of establishing and maintaining effective learning environments tend to be more successful than teachers who place more emphasis on their roles as authority figures or disciplinarians. Teachers *are* authority figures and need to require their students to conform to certain rules and procedures. However, these rules and procedures are not ends in themselves but are means for organizing the classroom to support teaching and learning. Thus, classroom management should be designed to support instruction and to help students to gain in capacity for self-control.

It is important to recognize that most classroom management research has been conducted in elementary and junior high school settings (Evertson & Harris, 1992). Little classroom management work has been done in classrooms that are characterized by high levels of gang activity, and it is not clear to what extent research that has been conducted in "regular" classrooms can be applied to classrooms where the problems of order are the most serious. However, with these important qualifications in mind, the research on classroom management is a rich and valuable literature providing general principles and guidelines that teachers can adapt to local conditions.

Student Role

Teachers' expectations about appropriate student activities and behavior can be called the *student role.* Unfortunately, popular notions of the student role usually include elements such as regimentation of activity, restriction of movement, and subordination of individual desires to the personal authority of the teacher and the less personal but often restrictive school and classroom rules. This is a reminder that although rules help provide for orderly and reasonably satisfactory group functioning within the school setting, they do so at a price. Much behavior that is considered natural and appropriate elsewhere, such as boisterous talk or play, is forbidden in the classroom, and certain forms of peer cooperation or helping are considered cheating.

These considerations suggest the value of a cost/benefit approach to classroom management, in which proposed techniques are assessed with an eye toward what side effects they may have. This approach suggests that practices such as requiring students to remain absolutely silent at all times unless addressed by the teacher are inappropriate because they are not essential to any worthwhile goal. Other practices, such as persistently authoritarian and punitive techniques, are inappropriate because their positive effects are outweighed by their negative ones. Our recommendations on classroom management emphasize an approach that has been shown to be effective for establishing good learning environments in classrooms, while at the same time being the least costly to the classroom atmosphere or to teacher-student relationships.

CLASSROOM EXAMPLES

To help you begin thinking about some of the key issues involved, we invite you to consider four common types of classrooms:

1. This class features chaos and uproar. The teacher continually struggles to establish control but never fully succeeds. Directions and even threats are often ignored, and punishment does not seem to be effective for long.
2. This class is also noisy, but the atmosphere is more positive. The teacher tries to make school fun by introducing lots of stories, films, games, and enrichment activities. Still, even though the teacher holds academic activities to a minimum and tries to make them as pleasant as possible, attention to lessons is spotty and seatwork often is not completed or not done carefully.
3. This class is quiet and well disciplined because the teacher has established many rules and makes sure that they are followed. Infractions are noted quickly and cut short with stern warnings or if necessary with punishment. The teacher appears to be a successful disciplinarian because the students usually obey him, although the classroom atmosphere is uneasy. Trouble is always brewing under the surface, and whenever the teacher leaves the room, the class "erupts."
4. This class seems to run by itself. The teacher spends most of her time teaching, not handling discipline problems. When working independently, students follow instructions and complete assignments without close supervision. They often interact with one another as they do so, but the noises they produce are the harmonious sounds of productive involvement in activities, not the disruptive noises of boisterous play or disputes. When noise does become disruptive, a simple reminder from the teacher usually suffices. Observers sense warmth in the atmosphere of this class and go away positively impressed.

These contrasting types of classrooms are found in all kinds of schools, so their differences cannot be attributed entirely to the types of students involved. Furthermore, within any given school, some teachers have chronic control problems, while others regularly gain good cooperation even from students who were problems the year before. We have described four teacher prototypes. The first "can't cope," the second "bribes the students," the third "runs a tight ship," and the fourth "has cooperative students." Before reading on, take time to think about these four teachers. Assume that they each began the year with roughly equivalent groups of students. List three attitudes or behaviors for each teacher that might help explain why the classrooms have evolved along the lines described. What might be their expectations about students and assumptions about the learning process? What might their students learn from observing them as models?

MANAGEMENT AS MOTIVATION AND PROBLEM PREVENTION

The purpose of the previous exercise was to help you focus on the teacher's role in shaping the learning environment. The classroom learning environment develops gradually, in response to the teacher's communication of expectations, modeling of behavior, and approach to classroom management. The same class that is interested and attentive with one teacher can be bored or rebellious with another.

The chapter title refers to *management* rather than to discipline or control. The latter terms have a connotation that we wish to avoid: the idea that managing students is mostly a matter of handling their misbehavior successfully.

Kounin's (1970) Study

Kounin (1970) first found that the key to good management is use of techniques that elicit student cooperation and involvement in activities and thus *prevent* problems from occurring. Kounin observed in classrooms to develop information about relationships between teacher behavior and student behavior. Surprisingly, he found that the teachers' methods of responding to discipline problems were unrelated to the frequency and seriousness of such problems in their classes. That is, the teachers who minimized discipline problems did not differ from those who had frequent and serious discipline problems, *on measures of teacher response to student misbehavior.*

The teachers did differ in other ways, however. In particular, the effective managers minimized the frequency with which students became disruptive in the first place by maximizing the time that students spent profitably involved in academic activities and by resolving incidents of minor inattention before they developed into major disruptions. The following were keys to their success.

"Withitness"   Effective managers monitored their classrooms regularly. They positioned themselves so that they could see all students and they continuously scanned the room to keep track of what was going on, no matter what else they were doing at the time. They also let their students know that they were "with it"— aware of what was happening and likely to detect inappropriate behavior early and accurately. This enabled them to nip problems in the bud before they could escalate into serious disruptions. When they corrected students' misbehavior they did so by correctly naming the students who had started the problem. When teachers were uncertain about the student who started the problem, they simply had the three or four students who were talking to resume their task assignment (i.e., the wrong student was not corrected publicly).

Overlapping   Effective managers could do more than one thing at a time when necessary. When teaching reading groups, for example, they responded to students from outside the group who came to ask questions, but at times and in ways that did not disrupt ongoing group activities. When circulating to check on seatwork progress, they conferred with individuals but still kept an eye on the rest of the class. They met individual students' needs without disrupting the ongoing activities of the class as a whole.

Signal Continuity and Momentum in Lessons   Effective managers were well prepared and thus able to teach smooth lessons that provided students with a continuous "signal" to attend to. They seldom confused the students with false starts or backtracking to present information that should have been presented earlier. They ignored minor, fleeting inattention but dealt with sustained inattention before it escalated into disruption, using methods that were not themselves disruptive (moved near inattentive students, used eye contact when possible, etc.). They realized that when teachers deliver extended reprimands or otherwise overreact to minor inattention, they lose the "momentum" of the lesson and break the "signal continuity" that provides focus for student attention.

Variety and Challenge in Seatwork   Students often worked independently rather than under the direct supervision of the teacher, and effective managers provided the students with tasks that were both (1) familiar and easy enough for them to do successfully and yet (2) challenging and varied enough to sustain motivation.

Other Studies

Subsequent work by other investigators confirms that these teacher behaviors are keys to successful classroom management and also shows that they are associated with student learning gains (Brophy & Good, 1986; Teddlie & Stringfield, 1993). Furthermore, other researchers have elaborated on Kounin's findings by showing how successful managers establish an effective learning environment at the beginning of the year and then maintain it thereafter.

In summary, the key to successful classroom management is a proactive approach that features clarity in communicating expectations. Three characteristics of this proactive approach are (1) it is preventive rather than just reactive; (2) it integrates management methods that encourage appropriate student conduct with instructional methods that encourage student achievement of curricular objectives; and (3) it focuses on managing the class as a group, not just on the behavior of individual students (Gettinger, 1988).

ESSENTIAL TEACHER ATTITUDES

Certain key teacher attitudes must be present if these general principles of classroom management are to succeed. *The attitudes and principles to be described complement one another to form a systematic approach. Attempts to use parts of this system as isolated techniques will not succeed.*

Certain attitudes and personal qualities are basic to successful management because they make the teacher someone whom students will respect and want to please, not merely obey. First, teachers must like their students and respect them as individuals. They need not be demonstratively affectionate; enjoyment of students and concern for their individual welfare will come through in tone of voice, facial expressions, and other everyday behavior.

Teachers should make an effort to get to know students individually (McCaslin & Good, 1996). Students who like and respect their teachers will want to please them and will be more likely to imitate their behavior and adopt their attitudes. They also will be more likely to sympathize when the teachers are challenged or defied, instead of allying with the defiant students.

Teachers must also establish credibility early in the school year and then maintain it thereafter. Because many students have experienced discrepancies between what adults preach and what they practice, such students will doubt or even discount what a new teacher tells them. Credibility is established largely by making sure that words and actions coincide and by pointing this out to the class when necessary. With some students, this may mean discussing the subject directly and pointing to the record: "George, you've got to understand that I mean what I say. I'm not playing games or talking just to hear myself talk. Think—have I misled you or made a promise that I didn't keep? . . . Well, try to remember that. It's frustrating for me to know that you always think I'm trying to put something over on you. Maybe other people have let you down in the past, but I'm not them, and you've got to remember that. I try to give you and everyone else in the class a fair deal, and in return I expect all of you to respect me and trust me. If I ever do anything to let you down, let me know about it right away so that we can straighten it out."

Credibility provides structure that students want and need. If they can depend on what teachers say, they will be less likely to test teachers constantly and more able to accept responsibility for their own behavior. When teachers establish fair rules and enforce them consistently, rule breakers can get angry only at themselves. However, if teachers make empty threats or enforce rules inconsistently, rule breakers who are punished will likely feel picked on.

Appropriate expectations are also involved in establishing credibility. Students tend to conform not so much to what teachers say as to what they actually expect. If students learn that "No talking over there" really means "Keep the noise down to a tolerable level," they will respond to the second message, not the first. This would be all right, except that sometimes the teacher really means "No talking." At these times, the students will react in the usual way, and misunderstanding and resentment may result.

To avoid this, teachers must think through what they really expect from their students and then ensure that their own behavior is consistent with those expectations. Such self-monitoring helps eliminate empty, overgeneralized, or inconsistent statements. Observers can be helpful here, since teachers are often unaware of inappropriate expectations. Teachers who bribe students to learn provide one example. They think of school-related tasks as unrewarding drudgery and do not expect students to enjoy them. Their students soon learn to wince, sigh, or protest at the mention of assignments, which further reinforces the teacher's expectations and bribery behaviors. In general, to establish groundwork for successful classroom management, teachers must (1) earn the respect and affection of the students; (2) be consistent and, therefore, credible and dependable; (3) assume responsibility for seeing that their students learn; and (4) value and enjoy learning and expect the students to do so, too.

GENERAL MANAGEMENT PRINCIPLES

If teachers have these personal qualities, what specific steps can they take to establish good classroom management? We begin with several general principles of classroom organization, all of which are based on the following assumptions:

1. Students are likely to follow rules that they understand and accept.
2. Discipline problems are minimized when students are regularly engaged in meaningful activities geared to their interests and aptitudes.
3. Therefore, management should be approached with an eye toward establishing a productive learning environment, rather than from a negative viewpoint stressing control of misbehavior.
4. The teacher's goal is to develop inner self-control in students, not merely to exert control over them.

Plan Rules and Procedures in Advance

Effective classroom management begins with advanced planning, in which the teacher thinks through the intended curriculum and its implications about the kind of learning environment that will be needed to support it. Advanced planning should attend to both rules and procedures. *Rules* define general expectations or standards for classroom conduct. Useful general rules include "be in your seat and ready to work when the bell rings" and "listen carefully when others speak." Usually, four or five general rules, suited to the grade level and the instructional goals, are sufficient. It is often useful to involve students in these discussions. For example, a teacher could start the discussion by noting, "All of us want a fun and productive atmosphere to allow us to play the best possible music. To do so we have to concentrate. Last year the marching band and I developed these four rules. Let's review them and see if these are okay or if we want to make different rules this year."

Procedures are methods for accomplishing daily routines and other specific activities that recur frequently in classrooms (Emmer, 1987). Teachers need to think about the different *activities* that they plan to use and the procedures that would be appropriate for implementing them: (1) whole-class presentations, recitations, and discussions; (2) teacher-led small groups; (3) independent small-group or project work; (4) individual seatwork; (5) transitions between activities and into and out of the room; and (6) room and equipment use. In addition, procedures need to be planned for *the handling of academic work:* (1) communication of assignments and related work requirements; (2) handling of makeup work and other procedures related to student absences; (3) monitoring of student progress on and completion of assignments, and assisting students who encounter difficulty with these assignments; (4) feedback to students about their progress and procedures for dealing with students who fail to complete work; and (5) grading procedures and related record keeping.

Similarly, Evertson (1987) suggested that procedures are needed for the following *activities:* (1) room use (teacher's desk and storage areas, students' desks and storage areas, wastebasket, lavatories, learning centers or stations); (2) transitions in and out of the room; (3) group work (student movement to the group setting, expected behavior in and out of the group); and (4) teacher-led instruction and seatwork (obtaining help, out-of-seat procedures, talk among students, and what to do after seatwork is completed). Evertson also identified the need for procedures concerning the following aspects of *managing student work:* (1) communicating assignments and work requirements (posting of assignments, accepting incomplete or late work, arranging for makeup work and assistance to absentees, grading procedures); (2) monitoring progress and completion of assignments (what forms of monitoring and checking to use, what records to keep, how to monitor special projects or lengthy assignments); (3) feedback to students (grading procedures that are consistent with the school's policies; what you will do if a student stops doing assignments; how you will communicate with parents; where you might display student work; what work records, if any, students will be expected to keep); and (4) the grading system (what components it will have, the weight or percentage for each component, how to organize the grade book, policies concerning extra credit assignments). The more carefully that teachers have thought out their preferred rules and procedures, the more prepared they will be to explain them clearly to students and to be consistent in ensuring their implementation.

Establish Clear Rules and Procedures Where Needed

Certain aspects of classroom management are part of the daily routine (e.g., use of the toilets and drinking fountains, access to paper and other supplies, use of special equipment, behavior during periods of independent work).

In these or other situations where procedural rules are required, they should be explicit, and the rationales for them should be explained. Explanation is especially important at the beginning of the year and with students in kindergarten or first grade, who are new to school. Some will never have used or even seen pencil sharpeners or certain audiovisual, arts and crafts, or computer equipment, so that verbal explanation alone may not be enough. A *demonstration* followed by the *opportunity to practice* the use and care of such equipment may be needed. Demonstrations and practice are less necessary with older students, but still are important for introducing new responsibilities (such as the use and care of laboratory equipment, critiquing other students' work, etc.). Older students will need thorough discussion of rules and procedures, however. Each new grade adds experiences that students have not been through before. More importantly, last year's teacher may have demanded behavior that differs from what this year's teacher wants, especially on the matter of what things the students must seek permission to do and what may be done without permission.

Behavioral rules should be kept to a minimum and stated clearly with convincing rationales. They should be presented to the class as means, not ends in themselves. For example, the rationale underlying rules about behavior during seatwork times might stress that students should not disrupt concurrent group lessons or work by other students on assignments (because assignments require careful thinking and concentration). The range of activities that students who finish seatwork can engage in without disturbing others needs to be explained. An overgeneralized rule such as "When you finish your seatwork you will remain quiet and not talk to anyone or leave your seats for any reason," would not be justifiable. This is much more restrictive than it should be and will cause more problems than it solves. Instead, the teacher should stress the basic goal of avoiding disturbances to students involved in lessons or seatwork and then list examples of acceptable and unacceptable behavior.

When rules or procedures are no longer needed or no longer do the job they were meant to do, they should be modified or dropped. Teachers should explain the reasons for any such changes, not just announce them. Often, it is worthwhile to explain the problem and invite students to suggest solutions. In summary, good management involves establishing clear rules and procedures where these are needed, reviewing them periodically and changing or dropping them when appropriate, and involving students actively in this process.

Let Students Assume Responsibility

There is no reason for teachers to do what students can do for themselves. With proper planning and instruction, even the youngest students can assume many responsibilities (e.g., pass out supplies). Older students can also work independently or in small groups, check their own work, and edit one another's paragraphs and short essays. Teachers who unnecessarily do these things themselves or control them by calling on students one by one only create delays, lose time that could have been spent teaching, and retard students' development of independent responsibility.

Teachers sometimes say, "I tried to get them to do it themselves, but they couldn't." Often students only need a demonstration lesson or an opportunity to practice the behavior. Time spent giving such explanations and patience in responding to slowness and mistakes early in the year pay great dividends later.

Some teachers adopt overly rigid rules on the grounds that they are needed ("If I put out supplementary books, they'll steal them," "If I allow them to work in groups, they'll just copy from one another or waste time"). This attitude avoids the problem rather than solving it, and it communicates negative expectations by treating students as if they were infants or criminals.

Teacher-Student Cooperation

The application of classroom management research does not imply blind obedience or rigid exercise of teacher authority. Certain types of activities may require a noiseless classroom (when students are reading silently for comprehension or writing essays). However, at other times an orderly classroom may be filled with movement, conversation, and noise that facilitates a productive exchange of information. Most students want a productive learning environment and will apply their talents to school tasks when they feel that teachers are fair and that tasks are appropriate. Teachers can help to develop cooperative relations with students by deleting unneeded rules, encouraging students to take more responsibility, and allowing students to voice concerns.

Minimize Disruptions and Delays

Management problems start and spread more easily when students are idle or distracted. Teachers can do many things to minimize delays, disruptions, and distractions.

One example is to avoid creating situations in which students must idly wait for something, with no clear focus for their attention. Delays frequently result when there is high demand for something that is in short supply, as when the entire class gets laboratory supplies from a single container or uses the same computer. Much time can be saved by storing items in several containers and by breaking the class into subgroups or appointing assistants to help instead of lining up the entire class to do something at one time.

The time needed for distributing supplies can be reduced by having one student from each row or table pass things out. Items should be stored low enough for students to reach them and arranged neatly for easy identification and replacement. They also should be stored as close as possible to where they will be used. The room should be arranged to promote smooth traffic flow. Traffic lanes should be wide enough for students to move freely without bumping into furniture or one another.

In junior high and high school, complicated diagrams, maps, or mathematical computations should be prepared on the chalkboard or overhead before class begins or distributed on mimeographed sheets rather than constructed during class. Similarly, many science experiments and other demonstrations can be partially prepared ahead of time when the preparations themselves do not need to be demonstrated (unless it is important to model the motions involved for students).

When students must wait with nothing to do, four things can happen, and three of them are bad: (1) students may remain interested and attentive; (2) they may become bored or fatigued, losing the ability to concentrate; (3) they may become distracted or start daydreaming; or (4) they may actively misbehave. Therefore, plan room arrangement, equipment storage, preparation of lessons, and transitions between activities to avoid needless delays and confusion.

Plan Independent Activities as Well as Organized Lessons

Disruptions often originate with students who are not working on their assignments or who have finished and have nothing else to do. Teachers who fail to provide worthwhile assignments or to have backup plans prepared for times when seatwork is completed more quickly than anticipated have more management problems than their better-prepared colleagues.

Seatwork is (or should be) a basic part of the curriculum, not merely a time filler. It should provide students with opportunities to practice what they are learning or to apply it in solving problems. Therefore, teachers should plan seatwork as carefully as they plan their lessons, make its importance clear to students when assigning it, and then follow up by monitoring progress and providing additional instruction to students who do not understand. Students must be held accountable for careful work on the assignment if it is to have its desired effects.

In addition to being specific about expected work on assignments, teachers should provide clear expectations about what students should do when they finish. This may involve additional specific assignments, or there may be a range of optional activities to select from. In any case, students should know what options are available if they finish seatwork early. Nor should students have to interrupt their seatwork frequently to get help. Teachers often give students tasks that are too difficult for them (Fisher et al., 1980). This not only impedes their learning progress but also invites management problems, especially when the teacher is trying to teach a small group while the rest of the students work independently. To work independently, students must understand what to do and be able to do it with little or no help. Teachers need to assign seatwork that is appropriate in the first place and make sure that students understand the directions before "turning them loose" to work independently.

Similarly, teachers must not assign students work that is too easy. Work that is too easy not only may lead to boredom or misbehavior by the more talented students, it also fails to provide less talented students with opportunities to overcome initial failure and to develop skills of adaptive problem solving (Rohrkemper & Corno, 1988).

Assignments should be written on the board or available in some other place so that students who are not sure about what to do can check for themselves rather than interrupt the teacher. There should also be clear procedures for students to follow when they know what to do but not how to do it. Different teachers will prefer different procedures, but whatever procedure is adopted should be made clear to the students.

Even when the teacher circulates around the room during seatwork times, disruptions are likely if students must wait for long periods before the teacher gets to them. Sometimes (when everyone seems to need help) the problem is overly difficult work or poor directions. At other times, problems occur because the teacher becomes absorbed with individual students to the point of neglecting the rest of the class. In addition to monitoring continuously and showing "withitness" at these times, teachers need to perfect the art of keeping themselves in circulation and available to give immediate help to students who need it. Interactions with individuals normally should be brief. The teacher should provide them with enough guidance to sustain their work on the assignment but should not necessarily cover everything they eventually will need to know (the teacher can return again after the student does the next set of problems). When many students seem to have the same question or misconception, it is probably worthwhile to briefly clarify the problem to the class as a whole. Otherwise, it is usually best to provide private help to those who need it while allowing the rest of the students to work on the assignment without interruption.

MANAGEMENT OF SMALL-GROUP LEARNING

Although we will say more about the management of small-group instructional settings when we discuss small group instruction and learning in Chapter 7, we want to point out that we believe the general principles of managing small groups are similar to those already described. However, we should acknowledge that managing small groups (e.g., seven groups of 4) is typically more difficult than managing one class of 28 or two groups of 14. A critical difference is that the teacher can interact with only a small portion of the class at a given moment. Thus, the design of curriculum tasks and their appropriateness for given groups of students become critical factors. Tasks must engage group members in ways that are appropriate both for learning (task is meaningful and challenging to all students) and for student self-management (students can handle minor disagreements, students know how to get help when needed).

Obviously teachers can help to make group work more meaningful by explaining the task and allowing students to actively discuss its purpose and related procedures before moving into small groups. Students also may need to role-play or receive direct instruction in various aspects (what cooperation means, how to handle conflict, helping versus giving answers without explaining, etc.).

Monitoring groups is difficult because the teacher can observe only one group at a time. Thus, it is possible that in some groups one or two students will do all the work or that some students will engage in undesirable social behavior. Accordingly, teachers will have to devise monitoring procedures that are appropriate for a small-group context (i.e., the age and ability of the students, instructional goals, etc.). Individual students need to be held accountable for their work in small groups (e.g., through class discussion following group work, performance exams).

When all students are working in small, cooperative groups, groups should know what to do when they finish the task first. Some researchers have found that one of the frequent management problems associated with small groups is finding teacher time for involvement with all groups (Good et al., 1989–1990).

Some groups will finish before others, so teachers need clear procedures for how students can productively turn to other tasks while they wait for their classmates to finish. Teachers also need to socialize students against the norm of quick work (as students see other groups finish, they may hurry their work) (Good et al., 1989–1990). Thus, although the basic management tasks are similar in large-group and small-group settings, there are special issues that teachers will need to address in small groups (Dunne & Bennett, 1990; Weinstein & Mignano, 1993). This issue will vary with the type of small-group format being used, the instructional goal, and the age of students. However, one unique need of the small-group setting is to learn to respect diverse responses and perspectives and use them constructively.

GETTING THE SCHOOL YEAR OFF TO A GOOD START

In a series of studies conducted at both elementary and secondary schools, Evertson, Emmer, and their colleagues developed detailed information about how teachers who varied in classroom management effectiveness handled the first day and the first few weeks of the school year. They took detailed notes about what rules and procedures the teachers introduced, how they did so, and how they followed up when it became necessary to use the procedures or enforce the rules. They also scanned the room every 15 minutes to record the percentage of students who were attentive to lessons or engaged in other teacher-approved activities. They then analyzed the data for relationships between teacher management behaviors and student engagement rates that would provide clues to how the more effective managers accomplished their goals.

Third-Grade Study

The first study (Emmer, Evertson, & Anderson, 1980) was conducted in 28 third-grade classrooms. The study showed that the seemingly automatic, smooth functioning of the classrooms of successful managers resulted from thorough preparation and organization at the beginning of the year. On the first day and throughout the first week, teachers gave special attention to matters of greatest concern to the students (information about the teacher and their classmates, review of the daily schedule, procedures for lunch and recess, where to put personal materials, when and where to get a drink). Procedures and routines were introduced gradually as needed so as not to overload the students with too much information at one time.

Effective managers not only described what they expected, but also modeled correct procedures, took time to answer questions, and, if necessary, arranged for the students to practice the procedures and get feedback. In short, key procedures were formally taught to students, just as academic content is taught.

Although they focused more on instruction than on "control," effective managers were thorough in following up on their expectations. They reminded students about procedures shortly before they were to carry them out, and they scheduled additional instruction and practice when students did not carry out procedures properly. Consequences of appropriate and inappropriate behavior were clear in their classrooms and sanctions were applied consistently. Inappropriate behavior was stopped quickly. In general, the effective managers showed three major clusters of behavior.

Conveying Purposefulness Students were held accountable for completing work on time (after being taught to pace themselves by using the clock, if necessary). Regular times were scheduled each day to review independent work. Completed papers were returned to students promptly, with feedback. In general, effective managers tried to maximize use of the available time for instruction and to see that their students learned the curriculum (not just that they remained quiet).

Teaching Students Appropriate Conduct Effective managers were clear about what they expected and what they would not tolerate. They focused on what students should be doing and taught them how to do it when necessary. This included not only conduct and housekeeping guidelines, but also learning-related behaviors such as how to read and follow directions for assignments. When students failed to follow procedures properly, the teachers stressed specific corrective feedback rather than criticism or threat of punishment.

Maintaining Students' Attention   Effective managers continuously monitored students for signs of confusion or inattention and were sensitive to their concerns. Seating was arranged so students could easily face the point in the room where they most often needed to focus attention. Variations in voice, movement, or pacing were used to refocus attention during lessons. Activities had clear beginnings and endings, with efficient transitions in between. The active attention of all students was required when important information was given.

Effective managers followed up this intensive activity in the early weeks by consistently maintaining their expectations. They no longer needed to devote much time to procedural instruction and practice, but they continued to give reminders and occasional remedial instruction, and they remained consistent in enforcing their rules. The applicability of these general principles continues to be supported by research done in both secondary (Gottfredson, Gottfredson, & Hybl, 1993) and elementary schools (Freiberg, Stein, & Huang, 1995).

Junior High Study

A related study of junior high school teachers (Evertson & Emmer, 1982a) revealed similar findings, as well as a few differences. Junior high teachers did not need to spend as much time teaching their students how to follow rules and procedures, but they did have to communicate expectations concerning student responsibility for engaging in and completing work assignments. Evertson and Emmer (1982b) listed the following as characteristic of effective managers at the junior high school level.

Instructing Students in Rules and Procedures   All teachers had rules and procedures, but the effective managers described their rules more completely and installed their procedures more systematically. They were notably more explicit about desirable behavior (the dos, not just the don'ts).

Monitoring Student Compliance with Rules   The better managers monitored compliance more consistently, intervened to correct inappropriate behavior more consistently, and were more likely to mention the rules or describe desirable behavior when giving feedback at these times.

Communicating Information   The better managers were clearer in presenting information, giving directions, and stating objectives. They broke down complex tasks into step-by-step procedures.

Organizing Instruction   Effective managers wasted little time getting organized or accomplishing transitions between activities, and they maximized student attention and task engagement during activities by maintaining signal continuity and momentum in lessons, overlapping their own activities, and using the other techniques identified by Kounin (1970).

Subsequent Studies

Subsequent work by Evertson, Emmer, and their colleagues involved training teachers in effective classroom management techniques. This work showed that teachers could learn these techniques and thereby decrease classroom disruptions and increase student engagement in academic activities, without undermining classroom climate. Teacher training was accomplished using manuals that summarized research findings about effective classroom management and provided examples, checklists, and step-by-step instructions about how to implement recommended procedures. For reports of the research findings, see Evertson (1985) and Evertson et al. (1983). For classroom management guidelines based on this research, see Emmer et al. (1994) and Evertson et al.(1993). However, the general points already presented above are a good summary of the results that these researchers have obtained.

Others who have studied the factors involved in getting off to a good start on the first day and in the early weeks of the school year have reached conclusions very similar to those of Evertson, Emmer, and their colleagues. The consensus is that although teachers should be friendly and personable rather than austere, they also should be businesslike in visibly taking charge and establishing the desired classroom atmosphere and learning environment (Brooks, 1985; Evertson, 1987; Smith, 1985). It helps to install basic everyday lesson and work routines quickly, but to do so using relatively simple formats and tasks that students are likely to be able to accomplish successfully. Once students become accustomed to everyday routines and begin to follow them habitually without much special direction, the teacher can begin to phase in more challenging work and more complex formats (supplementing whole-class lesson and seatwork activities with small-group activities, special projects, learning centers).

Research sources are a good place for information about useful guidelines. Freiberg, Stein, and Huang (1995) have illustrated the positive effects of a classroom management program on student achievement in inner-city elementary schools. Based on previous work and their own modifications, they developed the Consistency Management Program to reduce disruptive student behavior and increase opportunities for student learning.

Teachers who were taught the Consistency Management Program were subsequently found to have better student attendance, positive attitudes, and enhanced achievement in comparison with control classrooms that had not received the Consistency Management training.

As we have stressed earlier, research has to be adjusted to your context. Also, research guidelines provide only a starting point, since the goal is not to control students but help students over time to develop self-control.

MAINTAINING AN EFFECTIVE LEARNING ENVIRONMENT

In previous sections, we have presented research-based principles for getting the year off to a good start. In the next sections, we describe how teachers can build on this good start by cuing and reinforcing desirable behavior and providing any on-the-spot instructions that may be needed.

Use Positive Language to Cue Desirable Behavior

Learning is easier and more pleasant when we are shown what *to* do rather than told what *not to* do. This is why so many lessons begin with explanation or demonstration. Teachers would not think of teaching addition by naming all the sums that 2 + 2 do not equal, but they (and adults generally) often do not realize that a direct, positive approach is just as important in socializing behavior as it is in teaching school subjects. A string of "don'ts," emphasizing what students should *not* be doing, fails to develop students' understanding and may create anxiety or resentment against the teacher. Teachers should specify desirable behavior in positive terms, as in the following examples.

POSITIVE LANGUAGE

Work as quickly as you can on the computer; other students are waiting.
Close the door quietly.
Try to work these out on your own without help.
Work quietly.
Always dispose of used chemicals like this (demonstration).
Sit up straight.
Raise your hand if you think you know the answer.
When you finish, put the scissors in the box and bits of paper in the wastebasket.
These crayons are for you to share—use one color at a time and then put it back so others can use it too.
Use your own ideas. When you do borrow ideas from the author, be sure to acknowledge them. Even here, try to put them in your own words.
When you make your class presentation speak naturally, as you would when talking to a friend.
Note the caution statements in the instructions. Be sure to check the things mentioned there before proceeding to the next step.
Be ready to explain your answer—why you think it is correct.

NEGATIVE LANGUAGE

Don't "hog" the computer.
Don't slam the door.
Don't cheat by copying from your neighbor.

Don't make so much noise.
That's not how you dispose of chemicals.
Don't yell out the answer.
Don't leave a mess.
Stop fighting over those crayons.
Don't plagiarize.
Don't just read your report to us.
Take your time when doing this experiment or you'll mess it up.
Don't just guess.

Sometimes negative statements are appropriate, as when a student is doing something that must be stopped immediately (fighting, causing a major disruption). Even when used, however, negative remarks should be followed with positive statements about what to do instead. Teachers should phrase instructions in positive, specific language that indicates the desired behavior clearly.

Recognize and Reinforce Desired Behavior

Most sources of advice to teachers urge them to recognize and reinforce students' good conduct, contributions to lessons, or academic work. The idea is that students' accomplishments should be rewarded not only with high grades, but also with verbal praise, public recognition (hanging examples of good work for public display, describing accomplishments in the school newspaper), symbolic rewards (stars, happy faces, stickers), extra privileges or activity choices, or material rewards (snacks, prizes). Social learning theorists and behavior modifiers see reinforcement as essential in providing both motivation and guidance to learners: Behavior that is reinforced is likely to be repeated, but behavior that is not reinforced is likely to be extinguished. Other writers see reinforcement as desirable, if not essential, on the grounds that it helps students to appreciate their successes, develops positive self-concepts, boosts motivation, and develops a sense of accomplishment. Whatever their rationale, most writers state or at least imply that reinforcement is highly desirable and should occur regularly in classrooms.

We accept the validity of the general principle of reinforcement (behaviors that are reinforced will be retained, but those that are not reinforced will be extinguished). However, we question some of the suggestions that have been made for implementing this principle in the classroom. We believe that too much emphasis has been placed on quantity or frequency of reinforcement and not enough on *quality* issues and questions such as whom to reinforce, under what conditions, and with what kinds of reinforcement. We believe that teachers' attempts to reinforce are valuable under certain circumstances, but ineffectual or even counterproductive under other circumstances.

Let us begin by noting that a great deal of reinforcement of student behavior occurs simply as a natural consequence of performing that behavior. Attention to the teacher and effort on assignments typically lead to successful performance, which in turn leads to high grades and feelings of satisfaction. Succeeding in school and gaining the respect of teachers and peers are important goals to most students, so that any behaviors that students recognize as supporting progress toward those goals will be reinforced automatically. Thus the issue is not whether reinforcement should occur in the classroom, but whether (and if so, how much) the teacher should inject additional reinforcement. Our position is that such additional reinforcement is not necessary, although it may be appropriate.

It is not necessary because humans possess thinking and speaking abilities that enable us to learn by observing models and by being instructed, so that, unlike lower animals, we are not dependent on shaping through reinforcement as our primary learning mechanism. Also, we respond to a great many motives (self-actualization, cognitive consistency, curiosity) in addition to, and sometimes instead of, the desire for extrinsic reinforcement. Even when reinforcement is a primary motivator, reinforcement from sources other than the teacher (winning an art or music competition, for example, or gaining peer acceptance) may be more important than anything the teacher does. Thus, reinforcement from the teacher is only one of many factors influencing students' behavior.

Even when reinforcement from the teacher is relevant, there are limits on how much reinforcement is productive. Overly frequent reinforcement is unnecessary to sustain behavior and may become intrusive.

Another complicating factor is individual differences in students' motivational systems (Heckhausen, 1991). Eden (1975) has shown that for a given person and situation, certain motives will be relevant and others will not, so that the success of a motivational effort will depend on how well it fits with the person's present motives. In the classroom, teachers are likely to increase students' motivation to perform a desired behavior only if they deliver some *relevant* motivational consequence following performance of the behavior. If they should deliver a consequence that is irrelevant to the students' currently operating motives, there is likely to be a small *decrease* in overall motivation to continue the behavior. Thus, teachers' motivational efforts may have (slightly) negative effects when they are based on incorrect assumptions about students' motives. Teachers need to monitor their students' responses to consequences intended to be reinforcing, not just assume that all students actually experience these consequences as reinforcing.

Some educational theorists oppose reinforcement even in principle. These writers have urged teachers to capitalize and build on students' intrinsic motivation to learn, without trying to supplement it through extrinsic reinforcement (including praise). Several studies by attribution theorists support this view to some extent (attribution theorists are concerned about what happens when we try to explain our successes or failures to ourselves—when we *attribute* our performance to causes). It has been shown that if you begin to reward people for doing what they already were doing for their own reasons, you decrease their intrinsic motivation to continue the behavior in the future (Deci & Ryan, 1985; Heckhausen, 1991). Furthermore, to the extent that their attention becomes focused on the reward rather than the task itself, their performance tends to deteriorate (Condry & Chambers, 1978). They develop a piecework mentality, doing whatever will garner them the most rewards with the least effort, rather than trying to do the job as well as they can to create a high-quality product.

For a time, it was thought that these undesirable effects were inherent in the use of extrinsic reinforcement, including praise. More recently, it has become clear that the effects of reinforcement depend on the nature of the reinforcement used and especially on how it is presented. Decreases in performance quality and in intrinsic motivation for subsequent repetition of the behavior are most likely when reinforcement has the following characteristics:

High salience (large or highly attractive rewards, or rewards presented in ways that call attention to them)

Noncontingency (rewards are given for mere participation in activities, rather than being contingent on achieving specific performance objectives)

Unnatural/unusual (rewards are artificially tied to behaviors as control devices, rather than being natural outcomes of the behaviors)

In short, reinforcement is likely to undermine students' intrinsic motivation when it implies that their behavior is controlled externally—that they are engaging in an activity only because they must do so in order to earn a reward. Actually, this effect occurs not only with reinforcement, but also with any factor that leads students to attribute their behavior to external pressures rather than their own intrinsic motivation. Other examples include teacher reminders to students that they are under surveillance and student awareness of pressure to meet a time deadline (Lepper, 1982).

In summary, reinforcement of student behavior is likely to be effective only to the extent that the consequences intended to function as reinforcers are actually experienced as reinforcing by the student, are contingent on the achievement of specific performance objectives, and are awarded in ways that complement rather than undermine intrinsic motivation and other natural outcomes of the behavior.

PRAISING EFFECTIVELY

Praise is usually described as a form of reinforcement, although it does not always have this effect (Brophy, 1981). Sometimes teachers do not even intend their praise to be reinforcing, as when they use praise in an attempt to build a social relationship with an alienated student ("I like your new shirt, John"). Even when teachers do intend their praise to be reinforcing, some students will not perceive it that way. In particular, public praise may be more embarrassing than reinforcing to certain students, especially if it calls attention to conformity behavior rather than to some more noteworthy accomplishment. This is especially likely when teachers try to shape the behavior of onlookers by praising peers ("I like the way that Kate is sitting up straight and ready to listen"). Praise has been oversold to teachers as a form of reinforcement, partly because reinforcement in general has been oversold, but also because praise does not always function as reinforcement.

Correlations between teachers' rates of praise and their students' learning gains are not always positive and in any case are usually too low to be of practical importance (Brophy, 1981). For some time we have known that neither teachers nor students see teacher praise as an important or powerful reinforcer (Ware, 1978). In general, teachers' strategies for eliciting desirable student behavior in the first place are much more important than their praising such behavior after it appears. To the extent that praise is important, the key to its effectiveness lies in its quality rather than its frequency.

Effective praise calls attention to students' developing learning progress or skill mastery. It expresses appreciation for students' efforts or admiration for their accomplishments in ways that call attention to the efforts or accomplishments themselves rather than to their role in pleasing the teacher. This helps students to learn to attribute their *efforts* to their own intrinsic motivation rather than to external manipulation by the teacher, and to attribute their *successes* to their own abilities and efforts rather than to dependency on the teacher, lack of challenge in the task, or sheer luck.

Unfortunately, much teacher praise is directed more toward controlling students than toward expressing admiration for their efforts or accomplishments. Also, much teacher praise functions less as reinforcement than as an indication of teachers' expectations or attitudes. Brophy and Evertson (1981) found that teachers were credible and spontaneous when praising students whom they liked, often smiling as they spoke and praising genuine accomplishments. They praised students whom they disliked just as often, but usually without accompanying spontaneity and warmth and often with reference to appearance or behavior rather than to academic accomplishments. Dweck et al. (1978) found that teachers tended to praise boys only for objectively successful performance but sometimes praised girls for neatness, for following instructions to the letter, or for answering in proper form. Teachers sometimes even praise poor responses, especially when interacting with low achievers (Nafpaktitis, Mayer, & Butterworth, 1985).

Such praise is part of a well-intentioned attempt to encourage low achievers, but it often backfires because it undermines credibility and confuses or depresses the students, especially if they realize that they are being treated differently from their classmates. Research by Blumenfeld et al. (1982) suggests there is little point in teachers' trying to shield students from classroom realities. Younger students (in the early elementary grades) tend to think of themselves as successful as long as they complete their work successfully (regardless of what other students are doing), and older students are aware of how their performance compares to that of others, even when their teachers try to hide this. Students (especially those who are struggling) need encouragement, but they also need accurate feedback about their performance.

Praise is most likely to be effective when delivered as spontaneous, genuine reaction to student accomplishment rather than as part of a calculated attempt to manipulate the student. Other guidelines for effective praise are given below and in Table 4.1.

1. Praise simply and directly, in a natural voice, without gushing or dramatizing.
2. Praise in straightforward, declarative sentences ("I never thought of that before") instead of gushy explanations ("Wow!") or rhetorical questions. The latter are condescending and more likely to embarrass than reward.

Table 4.1   GUIDELINES FOR EFFECTIVE PRAISE

Effective Praise	Ineffective praise
1. Is delivered contingently	1. Is delivered randomly or unsystematically
2. Specifies the particulars of the accomplishment	2. Is restricted to global positive reactions
3. Shows spontaneity, variety, and other signs of credibility; suggests clear attention to the student's accomplishment	3. Shows a bland uniformity that suggests a conditioned response made with minimal attention
4. Rewards attainment of specified performance criteria (which can include effort criteria, however)	4. Rewards mere participation, without consideration of performance processes or outcomes
5. Provides information to students about their competence or the value of their accomplishments	5. Provides no information at all or gives students information about their status
6. Orients students toward better appreciation of their own task-related behavior and thinking about problem solving	6. Orients students toward comparing themselves with others and thinking about competing
7. Uses student's own prior accomplishments as the context for describing present accomplishments	7. Uses the accomplishments of peers as the context for describing student's present accomplishments
8. Is given in recognition of noteworthy effort or success at difficult (for this student) tasks	8. Is given without regard to the effort expended or the meaning of the accomplishment
9. Attributes success to effort and ability, implying that similar success can be expected in the future	9. Attributes success to ability alone or to external factors such as luck or (easy) task difficulty
10. Fosters endogenous attributions (students believe that they expend effort on the task because they enjoy the task and/or want to develop task-relevant skills)	10. Fosters exogenous attributions (students believe that they expend effort on the task for external reasons—to please the teacher, win a competition or reward, etc.)
11. Focuses students' attention on their own task-relevant behavior	11. Focuses students' attention on the teacher as an external authority figure who is manipulating them
12. Fosters appreciation of, and desirable attributions about, task-relevant behavior after the process is completed	12. Intrudes into the ongoing process, distracting attention from task-relevant behavior

Source: Brophy, J. (1981). Teacher praise: A functional analysis. *Review of Educational Research, 51,* 5–32.

3. Specify the particular accomplishment being praised and recognize any noteworthy effort, care, or perseverance ("Good! You figured it out all by yourself. I like the way you stuck with it without giving up" instead of "Good"). Call attention to new skills or evidence of progress ("I notice you've learned to use different kinds of metaphors in your compositions. They're more interesting to read now. Keep up the good work").

4. Use a variety of phrases for praising students. Overused stock phrases soon begin to sound insincere and give the impression that the teacher has not really paid much attention to the accomplishments.

5. Back verbal praise with nonverbal communication of approval. "That's good" is rewarding only when delivered with a smile and a tone that communicates appreciation or warmth.

6. Avoid ambiguous statements (e.g., "You were really good today") that students may take as praise for compliance rather than for learning. Instead, be specific in praising learning efforts: "I'm very pleased with your reading this morning, especially the way you read with so much expression. You made the conversation between Billy and Mr. Taylor sound very real. Keep up the good work."

7. Ordinarily, individual students should be praised privately. Public praise will embarrass some students and may even cause them problems with peers. Delivering praise during private interactions helps show the student that the praise is genuine and avoids the problem of sounding as though you are holding the student up as an example to the rest of the class.

When used appropriately, teacher attention and praise can reinforce desired behavior by helping students to know that their efforts are seen and appreciated. This is especially likely if praise is delivered in natural, genuine language that includes a description of the specific behavior being commended.

GETTING AND HOLDING ATTENTION

In this section we suggest techniques for dealing with everyday problems of minor inattention and disruption caused by boredom, fatigue, or situational distractions. This is accomplished mostly with "low profile" techniques that minimize disruptions to ongoing activities.

Focus Attention When Beginning Lessons

Teachers should establish that they expect each student's full attention to lessons. First, they should have everyone's attention before beginning lessons. Some teachers fail to do this, or even deliberately start the lesson in a loud voice in an attempt to get students to pay attention. This involves talking *at* rather than *to* students, and it causes many of them to miss the beginnings of lessons. Teachers should use a standard signal that tells the class "We are now ready to begin a lesson."

After giving the signal, teachers should pause briefly to allow it to take effect. Then, when they have attention, they should begin briskly, ideally by describing what will be done in an overview that provides motivation and an attention set for learning. The pause between giving the signal and beginning the lesson should be brief, just long enough for students to focus their attention. If the pause is too long, some students will lose this sharp focus. Therefore, the teacher should act quickly if a few students do not respond. If they are looking at the teacher, expressions and gestures can be used to indicate that they should pay attention. If not, the teacher should call their names. Usually this will be enough by itself; if not, a brief focusing statement can be added ("Look here").

Keep Lessons Moving at a Good Pace

Teachers often begin with good attention but lose it by spending too much time on minor points or by causing everyone to wait while students respond repetitively or when something they clearly understand is being rehashed needlessly. Review lessons are often abused in this way. If only a few students need further review, work with them individually or in a small group.

Monitor Attention During Lessons

Teachers should regularly scan the class or group throughout the lesson. Students are much more likely to maintain attention if they know that the teacher regularly watches everyone for signs of attention and confusion or difficulty). Teachers who bury their nose in paperwork, rivet their eyes on the board, or look only at the student who is speaking are asking for trouble.

Stimulate Attention Periodically

When things become too predictable and repetitive, the mind tends to wander. There are several things teachers can do to help ensure continual attention as a lesson or activity progresses. One is to provide variation. There is no need for theatrics, but lectures delivered in a dull monotone with few facial expressions or gestures soon produce yawns. Teachers should speak loudly enough for everyone to hear and should modulate their tone and volume to break monotony. It also helps to use a variety of techniques. Lectures should be mixed with questions or activities; group responses with individual responses; and reading or factual questions with thought-provoking discussion questions.

Extended presentations usually can be broken into several parts. By changing voice inflections or using transitional signals ("In summary," "The second reason . . . "), teachers can stimulate attention by cuing students that they are moving into a new phase.

Attention also can be stimulated more directly. For example, the teacher can challenge the class. "Here's a tricky question—let's see if you can figure it out," or create suspense, "So, what do you think happened next?" When the type of question changes, this can be noted in a statement that not only calls attention to the change, but also stimulates interest: "All right, you seem to know the theory, let's see if you can apply it to a practical problem."

Maintain Accountability

All students should be accountable for attending to lessons continuously, not just when they respond to questions or demonstrate. Several techniques are useful with students whose attention tends to wander. One is to develop variety and unpredictability in asking questions so that students learn that they may be called on at any time, regardless of what has gone on before. Teachers should occasionally question students again after they have answered an earlier question or ask them to comment about an answer just given by another student ("Paul, do you agree with Ted's answer?"). Note that these techniques are intended to challenge the class, stimulate interest, and avoid predictability, not to catch inattentive students in order to embarrass or punish them. If misused this way, they will cause resentment and probably not have the desired positive effects. Thus, teachers ordinarily should not say, "Remember, I might call on you at any time to tell me what's happening, so pay attention." It is better just to use this technique without calling attention to it, meanwhile stimulating interest in the topic and communicating expectations for attention in more positive ways as well.

Also, note the emphasis on *occasional* use of these accountability devices; they may be counterproductive if used too often or in the wrong situations. Teachers who use accountability devices moderately are more successful than those who use them either too often or not often enough. Accountability devices are essentially methods of recapturing lost attention, so that frequent use implies that the teacher is not doing enough of the fundamental things that establish and maintain good attention in the first place.

In the early grades, such accountability devices are not as important as careful monitoring, because the main problem facing teachers in these grades is helping students to be *able* to follow lessons, not making sure that they *choose* to follow them. This is accomplished through such techniques as teaching the children in small groups, having them follow with their finger or a marker, or monitoring them regularly to see that they have their place. Here, predictability is probably helpful. Brophy and Evertson (1976) and Anderson, Evertson, and Brophy (1979) found that teachers who had students read in a predictable order during reading groups got better results than those who called on students to read "randomly." This may have been because the predictable pattern provided structure that helped students follow the lesson. When students become able to keep track without help, and especially when they learn to anticipate what they will be held accountable for and practice it ahead of time, teachers will have to call on them in less predictable patterns.

Because brighter and more assertive students tend to seek response opportunities and get called on more often than reticent students, teachers should keep track of who has responded and who has not. Teachers can monitor this by tallying response opportunities in a log book (in fact, using a simple coding system, they also can keep track of students' rates of success in handling questions of varying difficulty levels).

Continuing accountability for attention also can be fostered by putting questions to the class as a whole and allowing time for thinking before calling on a student to respond. Students who know they may be called on to answer are likely to think about the question and try to form an answer if given time to do so. If the teacher names a student to answer a question before asking it, however, the rest of the class will know they are not going to be called on. This may cause some of them to turn their attention elsewhere.

Terminate Lessons That Have Gone On Too Long

When the group is having difficulty maintaining attention, it is better to end the lesson early than to continue doggedly. When lessons continue beyond the point where they should have been terminated, more of the teacher's time is spent compelling attention and less of the students' time is spent thinking about the material.

Teachers usually know this but sometimes pursue lessons anyway because they do not want to get off schedule. This attitude is self-defeating, because students do not learn efficiently under these conditions and the material will probably have to be retaught.

Teachers sometimes prolong an activity needlessly because they want to give each student a chance to participate individually. This intention is usually laudable, but when recitation becomes boringly repetitive it is time to move on to something else. Some teachers deliberately prolong repetitive activities in order to use them as time fillers or to create opportunities for them to do paperwork. Students know that if activities are really important, teachers will participate actively and pay careful attention to what is happening. They also know an uninterested babysitter when they see one.

INDEPENDENT WORK

Typical elementary school teachers instruct small reading groups for about 20 minutes each. To create time for sustained interaction with these small groups, they must organize the class so that students not in the group being taught at the time can work productively on their own. Students in most secondary classes also spend much time working independently (writing essays, solving proofs, etc.). In this section we discuss some of the special management problems that are associated with seatwork supervision. We focus on elementary reading, although the problems are similar (conceptually) in other grades and subjects.

One study (L. Anderson et al., 1985) found that in most classrooms the assigned seatwork was low-level and repetitive, the directions seldom included statements about what would be learned or how the assignment related to other learning, and teachers' monitoring of progress focused on students' behavior rather than their levels of understanding or performance. When providing feedback, teachers' explanations were usually procedural (e.g., "Read the sentence and then pick the word that completes it"), with little attention to the cognitive demands of the task (i.e., strategies for selecting the appropriate word). Likewise, much teacher feedback focused on correctness of answers or neatness of work.

Low Achievers' Assignments

The same study (L. Anderson et al., 1985) noted that low achievers often received inappropriate assignments, did poorly on them, and derived answers by using strategies that allowed them to complete the assignments without understanding what they were supposed to be learning. One student commented as he finished his seatwork, "There! I didn't understand that, but I got it done."

In these classrooms, the teachers generally emphasized keeping busy and finishing work rather than understanding what was being taught. L. Anderson et al. (1985) suggested that low achievers who often work on assignments they do not understand may come to believe that schoolwork does not have to make sense, and that consequently, they do not need to obtain assistance when they do not understand it (see also the discussions of Good's passivity model in Chapter 3).

Criteria for Worthwhile Assignments

Osborn (1984) noted that much of what appears in workbooks is confusing or trivial. Teachers who are effective instructional managers can prevent much wasted time by carefully reviewing seatwork assignments and assuring that seatwork activities have the following characteristics: (1) they allow students to work successfully and independently, (2) they are interesting and reflect variety in type of assignment and in how it is to be completed, (3) they frequently allow students to read for comprehension and pleasure, and (4) they relate the content to students' personal lives.

From time to time it is necessary for teachers to work in a concentrated, sustained manner with small groups. During these times, the rest of the students will need seatwork that they can complete successfully without needing to interrupt the teacher to get help. Such seatwork does not have to be dull or mechanical, but too often it is. Many of the activities included in workbooks require only a limited level of reading and do not ask students to draw conclusions or reason about the material they read. Few workbook activities foster fluency or strategic reading (R. Anderson et al., 1985). Almost none require extended writing. Rather, responses usually involve filling a blank, circling or underlining a word, or selecting one of several choices. The exercises often have difficult-to-understand directions, yet drill students on skills that have little value in learning to read. Furthermore, workbook activities are often unrelated to the current reading lesson.

Classroom research consistently shows that the amount of time devoted to worksheets is unrelated to students' year-to-year gains in reading proficiency. This is not surprising, given the typically low level of these assignments. For these reasons, teachers need to either improve their worksheets and supplement them with more meaningful activities or use such materials less frequently.

Instead of always filling in worksheets, students could be assigned to read and answer questions, write an alternative ending to a story, write a story, write an ending for a story that another student started, or engage in any of a great many different language arts tasks. Similarly, instead of always working alone, students could work together on some assignments (two or more students may debate issues in a story or compare and contrast endings that they have written independently).

Assignments that students are interested in may also encourage sustained effort over a long period of time. For example, one of the authors observed a small group of fifth-grade students write and rewrite with great enthusiasm and intensity their descriptions of a baseball card during several free time periods over two weeks. Students displayed considerable imagination in their writing (e.g., detailing records of players' accomplishments with various baseball clubs) and had a chance to practice several skills (organizing and editing information) during an enjoyable activity.

At least occasionally, assignments should allow students to influence other persons or future classroom events. Third graders and fourth graders could prepare and share stories with kindergarten students and first graders in order to provide the older students with a real audience for their writing. Similarly, third graders and fourth graders will benefit from seeing or reading plays written by sixth graders and from the chance to write letters in response (expressing thanks, seeking more information, or providing critiques). Even kindergarten students can learn from communicating with others (e.g., preparing valentines for parents or senior citizens) and gain satisfaction from doing so. Students also enjoy and become involved in activities that allow them to influence classroom events (e.g., respond to themes like, "If I could be the teacher for the day, . . .").

We have discussed elementary reading and language arts as a special instance, but it is clear that seatwork management is important at all levels of schooling and in all subjects. For example, in a study of junior high English classes, Doyle (1984) found that successful managers established an activity system early in the year and then supervised it closely to protect it from intrusion or disruption. For the first three weeks, contacts with individual students during seatwork were brief as the teachers circulated the room and maintained a whole-group perspective. In response to disruptions, they tended to talk about completing the assignment successfully rather than about misbehavior. Less successful managers focused attention on misbehavior by their frequent public reprimands, so that eventually all work ceased. Observations indicated that if a work system was established effectively by November, the teacher then could spend less time supervising the class and more time with individual students. By this point, the work system itself seemed to keep students productively engaged in work on assignments and the teacher was free to attend to other classroom events. Assignments are means to instructional ends, not ends in themselves. Thus, assignments are not appropriate just because they are easy for the teacher to manage. If they are to be productive, they need to be meaningful for the students as well as functional in moving them toward instructional goals.

SELF-REGULATED MANAGEMENT

Students should assume as much responsibility for self-management as they can handle. Opportunities for self-evaluation should be provided for both academic areas (e.g., students should be encouraged to compare a composition written in September with one written in May and to make their own assessment of growth) and social areas (e.g., the chance to work collaboratively with peers in increasingly complex ways). Rules that are no longer needed should be deleted or revised in ways that recognize and value students' increasing capacity for self-evaluation (no more than one student out of the room at a time; no more than six students at the library at the same time). In many school situations, the modern curriculum emphasizing adaptive problem solving and meaningful learning is "sabotaged" by a management system that encourages student passivity and obedience (McCaslin & Good, 1992).

Students must come to take responsibility for the management system as they progress through school. They cannot learn self-regulation and self-control if the teacher does all of the alerting, accountability, and so on (McCaslin & Good, 1992). Students need to be taught to manage time (we have 15 minutes to finish a task) and to define their own work and procedures (what is the critical problem—

how else might the problem be approached?). Thus, appropriate management necessitates that rules and structures—the scaffolding—be progressively altered to encourage more responsibility for self-control.

What constitutes student self-regulation will vary markedly in terms of students' ages and background experiences and teachers' instructional intentions and expectations. We believe that students should be able to regulate both their instruction and their behavior to the maximum extent possible. Although younger students need much more structuring, support, and teacher guidance than do older students, the goal of classroom socialization should be to help all students become as autonomous and as adaptive as possible (McCaslin & Good, 1992).

Students should be able to maintain both a focus on learning and the intention to understand and to master material (Corno, 1992, 1993) without constant teacher monitoring or encouragement. In time, students need to learn to transform information and to make it their own rather than simply accepting someone else's words or definitions. Students must develop the capacity for integrating current instruction with previous instruction and their own life experiences (Lave & Wenger, 1992).

In the areas of classroom management and personal behavior, students should be encouraged to develop numerous dispositions and skills over time. For example, they should learn how to set goals and to delay gratification (e.g., "I'll do two drafts of the paper before seeking feedback"). Students should know how to seek resources appropriately in the classroom (when to get information and how to get it) from teachers, peers, the library, and computers.

Students need to develop rudimentary self-control of learning situations (judge the amount of time it will take to complete an assignment, decide whether it is useful to do something at home or to wait for a study period the next day, etc.) and to set guidelines that help them to organize their time ("I will do at least three problems before class ends so that I can get help if I need it"). Students must also develop the capacity for self-assessment (knowing when they understand an assignment and the topic they are dealing with and when they are confused) and should be able to engage in self-reward as appropriate (recognizing when something is finished or relatively complete).

Over time, students need to learn more sophisticated strategies for intervening in their environment. Rohrkemper and Corno (1988) argued persuasively that students should be able to change themselves, change the task, or change the environment when it is appropriate to do so. For example, students should recognize inappropriate self-affect that promotes passivity (undue thoughts about how hard the task is, how long it will take, what will happen if they do not complete the task). These researchers indicated that students should be able to change tasks to make them more interesting ("I'll see if I can do the first two in five minutes"; "I'll see if I can come up with a general rule that explains the relationship across these problem sets") or change the environment (move away from a noisy friend who is interfering with task completion).

As students become more sophisticated they should become adept at allocating their personal resources adaptively (realizing how much time to spend on a biology homework assignment and how much time to spend studying for a Spanish quiz). Students must recognize that an adaptive aspect of self-regulation is changing goals as well as maintaining them. That is, sometimes students have to decide to cut their losses and recognize when they have reached the point of diminishing returns (McCaslin & Good, 1996). For example, after reviewing material three times, a fourth review is unlikely to help. Instead, getting new information or a new perspective or simply moving to a different area might be more productive.

Johnson and Johnson (1989–1990) suggest that teachers construct a T-chart on which the skill being developed is listed and then add two columns of information solicited from students indicating what the skill (e.g., participation, active listening) should look and sound like. If the teacher is developing the concept of encouraging participation, descriptors in the "looks like" column might include eye contact and smiles. The "sounds like" column would include comments such as "good idea, I never thought of that before."

SUMMARY

The key to successful classroom management is prevention—teachers do not have to deal with misbehavior that never occurs. Many problems originate when students are crowded together or forced to wait.

Classroom management and equipment storage can be planned so that traffic is minimized and needed items are accessible. Problems that occur when everyone needs the same item can be reduced by stocking several items rather than just one. Waiting can be minimized by allowing students to handle most management tasks on their own, by eliminating needless rituals and formalities, and by assigning various jobs to be done simultaneously by different subgroups. Confusion and idleness can be minimized by preparing appropriate independent work assignments in sufficient quantity and variety and by seeing that students know what to do if they finish or if they need help.

Teachers need to specify desired behavior in positive terms, provide instruction and opportunities to practice routines, offer cues or reminders when particular procedures are to be followed, and monitor students for compliance with expectations. Teaching strategies should maximize student involvement in productive activities. Teachers should establish clear signals to gain students' attention and alert them when an activity is beginning, provide a brief overview or advance organizer to help them prepare for it, and then keep the activity moving at a brisk pace, avoiding unnecessary delays. If an activity has gone on too long, it should be terminated. When it is necessary to hold students accountable for material and to stimulate their continuing attention, teachers should vary their questioning patterns and avoid falling into predictable patterns that tempt certain students to try to "beat the system." The more directive aspects of classroom management can be faded to minimal levels as students acquire the ability to manage their own learning with increasing degrees of autonomy and responsibility.

Teachers who consistently apply the strategies presented in this chapter will maximize productive student activity and minimize the time students spend "in neutral" or misbehaving. To be most effective, however, all aspects of good management must occur in combination as a system. Attempts to use certain techniques in isolation are unlikely to succeed for long.

SUGGESTED ACTIVITIES AND QUESTIONS

1. Students constantly mediate teachers' instructional statements. That is, students interpret the meaning behind the teacher's message, just as people interpret the meaning of even ordinary, everyday events (e.g., is the honking of a car horn a friendly hello or a threat?). Think about some of the instructional behaviors mentioned in this chapter (accountability, alerting, etc.). Is it possible that some students might interpret teachers' alerting behaviors as nagging while other students see them as helpful hints? If you have access to a classroom, try to interview three or four different types of students and determine what they think about a particular teacher behavior (do they like reminders—why, what type?).

   If you do not have access to students, arrange to interview or form a discussion group with three or four classmates to see how you may view the Kounin variables discussed in the chapter differently. The interview or discussion might focus on the appropriateness of these variables in a college setting (e.g., is a predetermined set of dates for quizzes appropriate organization and good alerting or needless control?).

2. Reread the four vignettes that appear at the start of the chapter. Which of the strategies do you agree with? Why?

3. What routines and procedures might you want to establish early in the school year?

4. In one section of this chapter, we advise that requests be phrased in positive language. The examples given on page 141–142 are primarily elementary school examples. Write five examples of positive language that would be appropriate at the high school level.

5. Teachers sometimes conduct meaningful and worthwhile learning activities only to undermine students' intrinsic motivation by telling them such things as "You've done so well today that I am going to give you a free hour after lunch so you can do the things you really want to do." What guidelines should teachers follow when they summarize learning activities? Apply your ideas to the case study of Mrs. Turner in Chapter 1. What would be an effective way to end the lesson she presented? Write out your ending in a few sentences and compare it with the endings written by others.

6. Describe in your own words how teachers can praise appropriately. What type of student will be most difficult for *you* to praise? Why?

7. Why is it suggested that teachers show variety and unpredictability in asking questions?

8. Specify the minimum set of rules that will be observed in your classroom. Be sure to state them in positive terms. Are your rules essential for establishing a good learning climate? Why?

9. Why is it important to prevent classroom disruptions before they occur? What preventive steps can teachers take to reduce the number of disruptions they will face?

10. Using the criteria given in this chapter for praising effectively, describe how you should respond to these situations:

    a. The class as a whole, except for two students, does very well on a test.

b. One of your slowest students struggles but eventually succeeds in doing a relatively easy math problem at the board, in front of the class.

c. One of your alienated underachievers does very well on a test, but you suspect cheating or lucky guessing.

d. Mary and Joe turn in perfect papers again this week, as they have all term long.

e. Randy asks a question that is relevant to the topic and indicates interest and good thinking on his part, although he would have known the answer to his question if he had read the assignment.

f. Your lowest reading group finally finishes a reader that the other groups finished weeks ago.

g. Dull, methodical Bernie turns in a composition that is trite but neat and error free. Creative but erratic Linda turns in one that contains exciting content written sloppily with many spelling errors.

11. Think about the seatwork assignments you will make. What kinds are appropriate for the subject/grade you will teach? Why?

12. In what ways can you as a teacher establish credibility with your students? Be explicit.

REFERENCES

Anderson, L., Brubaker, N., Alleman-Brooks, J., & Duffy, G. (1985). A qualitative study of seatwork in first-grade classrooms. *Elementary School Journal, 86,* 123–140.

Anderson, L., Evertson, C., & Brophy, J. (1979). An experimental study of effective teaching in first-grade reading groups. *Elementary School Journal, 79,* 193–223.

Anderson, R., Hiebert, E., Scott, J., & Wilkinson, I. (1985). *Becoming a nation of readers: The report of the Commission on Reading.* Washington, DC: National Institute of Education.

Blumenfeld, P., Pintrich, P., Meece, J., & Wessels, K. (1982). The formation and role of self-perceptions of ability in elementary classrooms. *Elementary School Journal, 82,* 401–420.

Brooks, D. (1985). The teacher's communicative competence: The first day of school. *Theory Into Practice, 24,* 63–70.

Brophy, J. (1981). Teacher praise: A functional analysis. *Review of Educational Research, 51,* 5–32.

Brophy, J., & Evertson, C. (1976). *Learning from teaching: A developmental perspective.* Boston: Allyn & Bacon.

Brophy, J., & Evertson, C. (1981). *Student characteristics and teaching.* New York: Longman.

Brophy, J., & Good, T. (1986). Teacher behavior and student achievement. In M. Wittrock (Ed.), *Handbook of research on teaching* (3rd ed.). New York: MacMillan.

Brophy, J., & McCaslin, M. (1992). Teachers' reports of how they perceive and cope with problem students. *Elementary School Journal, 93,* 3–68.

Condry, J., & Chambers, J. (1978). Intrinsic motivation and the process of learning. In M. Lepper & D. Greene (Eds.), *The hidden costs of reward: New perspectives on the psychology of human motivation.* Hillsdale, NJ: Erlbaum.

Corno, L. (1992). Encouraging students to take responsibility for learning and performance. *Elementary School Journal, 93* (1), 69–84.

Corno, L. (1993). The best-laid plans: Modern conceptions of volition and educational research. *Educational Researcher, 22,* 14–22.

Deci, E., & Ryan, R. (1985). *Intrinsic motivation and self-determination in human behavior.* New York: Plenum.

Delpit, L. (1995). *Other people's children: Cultural conflict in the classroom.* New York: The New Press.

Doyle, W. (1984). How order is achieved in classrooms: An interim report. *Journal of Curriculum Studies, 16,* 259–277.

Dunne, E., & Bennett, N. (1990). *Talking and learning in groups.* London: Macmillan Education.

Dweck, C., Davidson, W., Nelson, S., & Enna, B. (1978). Sex differences in learned helplessness: II. The contingencies of evaluative feedback in the classroom, and III. An experimental analysis. *Developmental Psychology, 14,* 268–276.

Eden, D. (1975). Intrinsic and extrinsic rewards and motives: Replication and extension with Kibbutz workers. *Journal of Applied Social Psychology, 5,* 348–361.

Emmer, E. (1987). Classroom management and discipline. In V. Richardson-Koehler (Ed.), *Educators' handbook* (pp. 233–256). New York: Longman.

Emmer, E., & Aussiker, A. (1990). School and classroom discipline programs: How well do they work? In O. C. Moles (Ed.), *Student discipline strategies: Research and practice.* Albany: State University of New York Press.

Emmer, E., Evertson, C., & Anderson, L. (1980). Effective classroom management at the beginning of the school year. *Elementary School Journal, 80,* 219–231.

Emmer, E., Evertson, C., Sanford, J., Clements, B., & Worsham, M. (1994). *Classroom management for secondary teachers* (3rd ed.). Boston: Allyn & Bacon.

Evertson, C. (1985). Training teachers in classroom management: An experimental study in secondary school classrooms. *Journal of Educational Research, 79,* 51–58.

Evertson, C. (1987). Managing classrooms: A framework for teachers. In D. Berliner & B. Rosenshine (Eds.), *Talks to teachers* (pp. 54–74). New York: Random House.

Evertson, C., & Emmer, E. (1982a). Effective management at the beginning of the school year in junior high classes. *Journal of Educational Psychology, 74,* 485–498.

Evertson, C., & Emmer, E., (1982b). Preventive classroom management. In D. Duke (Ed.), *Helping teachers manage classrooms.* Alexandria, VA: Association for Supervision and Curriculum Development.

Evertson, C., Emmer, E., Clements, B., Sanford, J., & Worsham, M. (1993). *Classroom management for elementary teachers* (3rd ed.). Englewood Cliffs, NJ: Prentice-Hall.

Evertson, C., Emmer, E., Sanford, J., & Clements, B. (1983). Improving classroom management: An experiment in elementary classrooms. *Elementary School Journal, 84,* 173–188.

Evertson, C., & Harris, A. (1992). What we know about managing classrooms. *Educational Leadership, 49,* 74–78.

Fisher, C., Berliner, D., Filby, N., Marliave, R., Cahen, L., & Dishaw, M. (1980). Teaching behaviors, academic learning time, and student achievement: An overview. In C. Denham & A. Lieberman (Eds.), *Time to learn.* Washington, DC: National Institute of Education, U.S. Department of Education.

Freiberg, H., Stein, T., & Huang, S. (1995). Effects of a classroom management intervention on student achievement in inner-city elementary schools. *Educational Research and Evaluation: An International Journal on Theory and Practice, 1,* 36–66.

Gettinger, M. (1988). Methods of proactive classroom management. *School Psychology Review, 17,* 227–242.

Good, T., Reys, B., Grouws, D., & Mulryan, C. (1989–1990). Using work groups in mathematics instruction. *Educational Leadership, 47,* 56–62.

Gottfredson, D., Gottfredson, G., & Hybl, L. (1993). Managing adolescent behavior: A multiyear, multischool study. *American Educational Research Journal, 30,* 179–215.

Heckhausen, H. (1991). *Motivation and action.* (P. Leppman, Trans.). Berlin, Germany: Springer-Verlag.

Johnson, D., & Johnson, R. (1989–1990). Social skills for successful group work. *Educational Leadership, 47,* 30–32.

Jones, V. (1996). Classroom management. In J. Sikula, T. Buttery, & E. Guyton (Eds.), *Handbook of research on teacher education* (Vol. 2). New York: Macmillan.

Kauffman, J., Hallahan D., Mostert, M., Trent, S., & Nuttycombe, D. (1993). *Managing classroom behavior: A reflective case-based approach.* Boston: Allyn & Bacon.

Kounin, J. (1970). *Discipline and group management in classrooms.* New York: Holt, Rinehart and Winston.

Lave, J., & Wenger, E. (1992). *Situated learning: Legitimate peripheral participation.* New York: Cambridge University Press.

Lepper, M. (1982). Extrinsic reward and intrinsic motivation: Implications for the classroom. In J. Levine & M. Wang (Eds.), *Teacher and student perceptions: Implications for learning.* Hillsdale, NJ: Erlbaum.

McCaslin, M., & Good, T. (1992). Compliant cognition: The misalliance of management and instructional goals in current school reform. *Educational Researcher, 21,* 4–17.

McCaslin, M., & Good, T. (1996). *Listening in classrooms.* New York: HarperCollins.

Nafpaktitis, M., Mayer, G., & Butterworth, T. (1985). Natural rates of teacher approval and disapproval and their relation to student behavior in intermediate school classrooms. *Journal of Educational Psychology, 77,* 362–367.

Osborn, J. (1984). Workbooks that accompany basal reading programs. In G. Duffy, L. Roehler, & J. Mason (Eds.), *Comprehension instruction: Perspectives and suggestions.* New York: Longman.

Rohrkemper, M., & Corno, L. (1988). Success and failure on classroom tasks: Adaptive learning and classroom teaching. *Elementary School Journal, 88,* 299–312.

Smith, H. (1985). The marking of transitions by more and less effective teachers. *Theory Into Practice, 24,* 57–62.

Teddlie, C., & Stringfield, S. (1993). *Schools make a difference: Lessons learned from a 10-year study of school effects.* New York: Teachers College Press.

Ware, B. (1978). What rewards do students want? *Phi Delta Kappan, 59,* 355–356.

Weinstein, C., & Mignano, A., Jr. (1993). *Elementary classroom management: Lessons from research and practice.* New York: McGraw-Hill.

FORM 4.1. Transitions and Group Management

USE: During organizational and transition periods before, between, and after lessons and organized activities.
PURPOSE: To see if teacher manages these periods efficiently and avoids needless delays and regimentation.
How does the teacher handle early morning routines, transitions between activities, and clean-up and preparation time?

Record any information relevant to the following questions:

1. Does the teacher do things that students could do for themselves?

2. Are there delays caused because everyone must line up or wait his or her turn? Can these be reduced with a more efficient procedure?

3. Does the teacher give clear instructions about what to do next before breaking a group or entering a transition? *Students often aren't clear about assignment so they question her during transitions and while she is starting to teach next group.*

4. Does the teacher circulate during transitions, to handle individual needs? Does he or she take care of these before attempting to begin a new activity? *Mostly, problem is poor directions __before__ transition, rather than failure to circulate here.*

5. Does the teacher signal the end of a transition and the beginning of a structured activity properly, and quickly gain everyone's attention? *Good signal but sometimes loses attention by failing to start briskly. Sometimes has 2 or 3 false starts.*

Check If applicable:

_____ 1. Transitions come too abruptly for students because teacher fails to give advance warning or finish up reminders when needed

_____ 2. The teacher insists on unnecessary rituals or formalisms that cause delays or disruptions (describe)

___✓___ 3. Teacher is often interrupted by individuals with the same problem or request; this could be handled by establishing a general rule or procedure (describe) *See #3 above.*

___✓___ 4. Delays occur because frequently used materials are stored in hard to reach places *Pencil sharpener too close to reading group area, causing frequent distractions.*

_____ 5. Poor traffic patterns result in pushing, bumping, or needless noise

_____ 6. Poor seating patterns screen some students from teacher's view or cause students needless distraction

_____ 7. Delays occur while teacher prepares equipment or illustrations that should have been prepared earlier

FORM 4.2. Classroom Rules and Routine

USE: Whenever sufficient information is available.
PURPOSE: To assess the adequacy of the teacher's system of classroom rules and routines.

Students should be clear about each of the following issues. Check each issue that is handled adequately through classroom rules and routines, and explain the problem when the issue is not handled adequately.

_____ 1. What books and supplies are to be brought to class routinely
_____ 2. Where to sit and store personal belongings
_____ 3. Precisely when class begins and what is expected at that time (in terms of attention to the teacher and advance preparation of materials)
_____ 4. When and for what purposes students may leave their seats
_____ 5. When and for what purposes students may converse with one another
_____ 6. Rules for participation in whole-class or small group lessons (when, if at all, it is allowable to call out responses without first raising one's hand and being recognized)
_____ 7. When it is permissible to approach the teacher with personal concerns and when the teacher should not be interrupted except for emergencies
_____ 8. What to do if you enter the class late or leave it early
_____ 9. Rules regarding use of equipment and learning centers
_____ 10. Procedures for distributing and collecting work or supplies
_____ 11. What forms of student cooperation in working on assignments are allowed or encouraged
_____ 12. Due dates for assignments and penalties for unexcused late, incomplete, or missing work
_____ 13. What will be taken into account in assigning grades
_____ 14. Other (sources of student confusion or managerial difficulty that could be eliminated by clarifying rules or procedures)

NOTES:

CHAPTER

5

Management II: Coping with Problems Effectively

onsistent application of the principles discussed in the previous chapter will minimize problems of inattention and misbehavior. Some such problems will occur, however, and teachers must be prepared to cope with them. The present chapter contains suggestions on how to interpret such problems, identify their causes accurately, and respond effectively. As a way to begin to think about management issues, read the vignettes that follow and consider how you would respond to each of the issues.

CLASSROOM VIGNETTES

Elementary School Example

Mr. Brandon is a fifth-grade teacher at Willow Heights Elementary School, which is located in a rich suburban school district about 10 miles from a major urban city. Students at the school are all from upper-class families, predominantly European Americans but with a significant (12 percent) Asian-American representation and a sprinkling of Hispanic Americans and African Americans as well. Mr. Brandon has been using small cooperative groups to teach social studies twice a week for 30 minutes after lunch. He divides his students into seven groups of four or five, and students are assigned to groups primarily on the basis of achievement.

During the small-group work period when students are discussing social studies issues, Mr. Brandon typically prepares for the science class that follows. He occasionally walks around the room to assure himself that students are still on task, and after the students have worked for about 25 minutes, he takes 5 minutes for a whole-class discussion of the issues students have been talking about in small groups.

Today, while working with a group that has a procedural problem, he inadvertently overhears the discussion taking place at a nearby table. Kristin (apparently holding back tears) says, "Carly, that's a cruel thing to say! I am too mature! I've grown up a lot this year!" Carly shrugs her shoulders, and Adam says, "That's right, you have grown up a lot this year." Then Mark, Carly, and Adam exchange glances, laugh and say together, "Not!" Now Kristin begins to sniffle. If you were the teacher, what would you say or do now, if anything? What would you do or say later? How can teachers monitor discussions that take place during academic group work?

Middle School Example

Nick Rawlings is an eighth grader at Pattonville Middle School. Pattonville is a small town of about 8000 located in an agricultural area in a midwestern state. Nick is sitting in the principal's office awaiting the principal's decision about an out-of-school suspension.

The problem started three weeks ago when Nick and five other students created a disturbance during study hall. All of the students received a three-day after-school detention for their misbehavior. A week after that, a student who disliked Nick shoved him in the locker room after football practice. Nick shoved the player back, and when the coach entered the locker room, Nick and Jason Benedict were fighting. The football coach reported the players to the principal (as required by school rules), and the principal gave Nick a three-day in-school suspension (Nick comes to school but has to stay in the study hall).

After this episode, Nick became "fair game." Nick is not popular, in part because he comes from a poor family. Further, he has limited academic ability; he was retained twice—in the first and third grades. Many of his peers like to poke fun at him because of his poor academic record and his family. One area in which Nick excels is sports. He won the local Punt, Pass, and Kick Contest and represented his city in the state competition. Nick has been looking forward to playing basketball after the football season ends, but the school has a rule that a student who receives an out-of-school suspension is automatically banned from sports for the rest of the year.

For several consecutive days Nick has been needled relentlessly by three football team members who dislike him. To his credit, Nick has refrained from reacting to their comments. Finally, they go too far, and he shoves one of them, knocking him over a bench. The coach reports the episode to the principal, who, according to school rules, should give Nick an out-of-school suspension because this is Nick's fourth infraction.

Nick tries to tell his side of the story, but the principal does not want to listen. He says, "Nick, there are always reasons why one loses self-control, but there is no acceptable reason. You'll have to live with the consequences of your behavior. I don't like doing this, it probably hurts me more than it hurts you, but rules have to be enforced. I have no alternative but to give you an out-of-school suspension."

Do you agree with the principal's decision? Can school rules create unintended consequences? Can teachers and administrators enforce rules without understanding why students misbehaved? Why or why not?

Junior High School Example

Carolyn Reid is a first-year teacher at Southern Junior High, which is one of three junior highs in a city of about 50,000 located in the Southeast. The school enrolls a wide mixture of students from various socioeconomic levels, races, and ethnic backgrounds. Carolyn teaches ninth-grade science and physics. Her third-period physical science class is one of those "fated" classes in which everything that can go wrong does.

Today, there are too few lab sheets available for students, and while Ms. Reid is rummaging through her desk to find extra lab sheets, a pair of students (students are working with lab partners) begin the experiment and inadvertently mix the wrong chemicals, causing a small fire that Ms. Reid hurriedly puts out. In the haste of putting out the fire, the bunsen burner is knocked off the table and damaged so that the two students cannot use it and must be reassigned to work with other pairs.

Five minutes later, the class is finally working productively on their assigned experiments, when Chris Vaughn throws a spitball at Tasha Wood, who is sitting at an adjoining table. Tasha watches the object land in front of her and smiles to herself. Chris, not satisfied with her response, says in a subdued voice, "Hey, Tasha, look here and give me a smile." Tasha beams, and as she turns, gesturing in Chris's direction, she knocks the test tube from her lab table.

How might the teacher have prevented this situation? What should she do at this point, if anything? What should she do later?

High School Example

Judy Burden teaches an honors English course for seniors at Owensboro High School, the only high school in a town of about 20,000 located in a western state. Judy is worried about one of her students, Allen Thorton, who has been late about half the time for her first-period class and has missed six classes during the first month of school. When Allen is in class, he is cooperative but lethargic and appears haggard. His late arrivals are becoming a joke (and very disruptive). However, Allen has turned in two acceptable papers. Ms. Burden is meeting with him after class to discuss his excessive tardiness and absences. She confronts him directly: "Allen, I'm concerned about your excessive tardiness and absences. In fact, I examined school records and found that last year you were almost always in class and on time. What's going on?"

Allen (looking embarrassed and staring at the floor) says, "Everything's falling apart this semester! But your class is the only one that I've been tardy for. The only other class I've missed a lot is second period. Some mornings I just can't get out of bed and get going, but I always get here by mid-morning so I don't miss my third-period class."

Ms. Burden: "But what's the problem? Why can't you get up in the morning?"
Allen: "I took a job last May at a fast-food chain, and the manager really liked me. In August I was promoted to manager. Now I'm in charge of the 9 to midnight shift. After midnight, I have to clean up, so I don't get home until 1 A.M. Also, if anything goes wrong, like some equipment is dirty or inventories aren't complete,

the manager calls me at 6 A.M. complaining or asking questions. I'm trying to get it under control so it won't interfere with my schoolwork, but I really need the job. My family. . . . "

If you were Judy Burden, what would you say or do? Should the teacher talk to Allen's parents? Should schools work with businesses that employ students to develop policies that minimize conflicts between students' work and school? Should consequences be imposed for Allen's excessive absences and tardiness?

DEALING WITH MINOR INATTENTION AND MISBEHAVIOR

Techniques for dealing with minor inattention or misbehavior are designed to achieve a single goal: *eliminate the problem quickly and with minimal distraction of other students.* These techniques should be used whenever students are engaged in minor mischief and the teacher wants to refocus their attention on the lesson or activity.

Monitor the Entire Classroom Regularly

Successful classroom managers display "withitness"—their students know that they always "know what is going on" in the room (Evertson et al., 1994; Kounin, 1970). Teachers who regularly scan the room can respond to problems effectively and nip most of them in the bud. Those who fail to notice what is going on are prone to such errors as failing to intervene until a problem becomes disruptive or spreads to other students, attending to a minor problem while failing to notice a more serious one, or rebuking a student who was drawn into a dispute instead of the one who started it. Teachers who regularly make such errors convince students that the teachers do not know what is happening. This will make the students more likely to misbehave and also to test teachers by talking back or trying to confuse them.

Most disruptions begin when one student "starts something" while the teacher's back is turned. Once one student becomes inattentive, it is likely that at least some of the others will too (Felmlee, Eder, & Tsui, 1985). Thus, it is important for teachers to monitor their classrooms regularly, even while conducting small-group lessons, writing on the board, or talking with individual students.

Ignore Minor, Fleeting Misbehavior

Teachers should not intervene every time they notice a problem, because such intervention may be more disruptive than the problem itself. For minor misbehavior, it is better to delay action or simply ignore the problem. For example, suppose a student has dropped a pencil or neglected to put away some equipment. Such incidents rarely require immediate action, so teachers should wait until they can deal with them without disrupting the continuity of ongoing activities.

Much minor misbehavior can be ignored, especially when it is fleeting. If the group is distracted momentarily because someone snaps a pencil, or if two students briefly whisper and then return attention to the lesson, it is usually best to take no action at all since students' attention is already back on the lesson.

Stop Sustained Minor Misbehavior

When minor misbehavior is repeated or intensified, or when it threatens to spread or become disruptive, teachers cannot simply ignore it; they must take action to stop it. Unless the misbehavior is serious enough to call for investigation (and it seldom is), teachers should try to eliminate it quickly and without disrupting the flow of classroom activity, using the following techniques to redirect inattentive students.

1. *Eye contact.* When it can be established, teachers can compel attention with simple eye contact, perhaps adding head nods or gestures such as looking at the book the student is supposed to be reading. Eye contact is doubly effective for "with-it" teachers who monitor regularly. When students know that a teacher continuously scans the room, they tend to look at the teacher when they misbehave (to see if the teacher is watching). This makes it easier for the teacher to intervene through eye contact.

2. *Touch and gesture.* When the students are close by, as in small groups, teachers can use touch to gain attention. A light tap, perhaps followed by a gesture toward the book, delivers the message without need for verbalization. Such touching is most useful in the early grades, when much teaching is done in small groups and distraction is a frequent problem. Also, some adolescents resent any touching by teachers. Gestures are helpful for dealing with events going on elsewhere in the room. Teachers may be able to communicate by shaking their heads, and so forth.

3. *Physical proximity.* When checking seatwork or moving about the room, teachers often can eliminate minor misbehavior simply by moving close to the offending students. If students know what they are supposed to do, the teacher's presence will motivate them to get busy.

4. *Asking for responses.* During lessons, the simplest method of capturing students' attention may be to ask them questions or otherwise call for responses. Such requests compel attention automatically, without requiring mention of the misbehavior.

   This technique should be used with care, however, because it can backfire. If teachers use it too often, students may perceive this method as an attempt to "catch" them. Also, the questions must be ones that students can answer, so that they will not feel embarrassed and end up disrupting the lesson by admitting that they were not paying attention or responding with an aggressive remark. Thus, it would be appropriate to ask a clearly inattentive student a question that she or he can respond to even if the student did not hear the previous question (e.g., "Rachel, Shane says that the villain was motivated by jealousy. What do you think?").

5. *Name dropping.* When giving information or instructions rather than asking questions, a teacher can call for the attention of a particular student by inserting his or her name into the middle of an instructional statement ("The next step, Rachel, is to . . . ").

These "low-profile" techniques enable teachers to eliminate minor problems without disrupting ongoing activity by calling attention to the misbehavior (McDaniel, 1986).

DEALING WITH PROLONGED OR DISRUPTIVE MISBEHAVIOR

When misbehavior is prolonged, dangerous, or seriously disruptive, teachers will have to stop it directly by calling out the students' names and correcting them. *Because such direct correction is itself disruptive, it should be used only when necessary.*

Also, like the techniques described in the previous section, *direct correction should be used only when no information is needed*—when the disruptive students know what they are supposed to be doing and the nature of the misbehavior is obvious and does not require investigation (e.g., loud socializing, shooting of rubber bands, or horseplay). Here, teachers need to get the students back on task. In more ambiguous situations where students may not know what they are supposed to be doing or where the teacher is not sure what is going on (e.g., two students are talking but may or may not be discussing the assignment), the teacher may need to get more information and make some decisions before acting.

Appropriate Direct Correction

There are two ways for teachers to intervene directly. First, they can *demand appropriate behavior*. Such demands should be short and direct, naming the students and indicating what they should be doing. The teacher should speak firmly but not shout or nag. Commands such as "Leon! Get back to your seat and get to work" and "Gail, Laura! Stop talking and pay attention to me" unnecessarily call attention to the misbehavior. Instead, a brief direction telling the students what to do is sufficient: "Leon, finish your work" and "Gail and Laura, look here."

A second direct correction technique is to *remind students of rules and expectations*. If clear rules have been established, with thorough discussion of the reasons for them, teachers can use brief reminders of these rules to correct misbehavior without sermonizing or embarrassing students unnecessarily. During independent work periods, rule reminders are often the best responses when the class becomes noisy. Rather than naming offenders, the teacher can say, "Class, you're getting too loud. Remember, talk only about the assignment, and speak softly."

As with other forms of direct intervention, rule reminders should be brief and firm. Usually they are preferable to demanding appropriate behavior because they help students internalize behavioral control. When students are clear about rules and the reasons for them, rule reminders help them to accept responsibility for their own misbehavior and help keep down conflict.

Inappropriate Direct Correction

There are several things that teachers should *not* do in response to easily interpretable misbehavior. First, *teachers should not ask questions about obvious misbehavior*. If the situation is clear and the goal is simply to return students to productive work, there is no need to conduct an investigation. Also, the questions asked in such situations tend to be counterproductive and rhetorical. The meaninglessness of these questions and the tone in which they are asked show that they are not really questions at all but attacks on the student: "What's the matter with you?" "How many times do I have to tell you to get busy?" Such questions do no good and may cause embarrassment, fear, or resentment.

Teachers should also *avoid unnecessary threats and displays of authority.* By simply stating how they want the student to behave, teachers communicate the expectation that they will be obeyed. However, if they add a threat ("Do it or else . . . "), they not only invite power struggles with students but also suggest indirectly that they are not sure students will obey.

If students ask why they are being told to do something, teachers should give reasons. Teachers who become defensive and appeal to authority ("You do it because I say so!") will produce resentment. Also, because such authoritarian comments directly challenge students and can cause them to lose face before their peers, they may even produce an outburst against the teacher. Furthermore, if onlookers believe the teacher is acting unfairly, the teacher's relationship with them will suffer too.

Finally, teachers must *avoid dwelling on misbehavior (nagging).* In a direct correction situation, there is no reason to describe the present problem in detail or to catalog the student's past misbehavior. Attacks on students place the teacher in conflict with the students and endanger credibility and respect. If a teacher attacks students regularly, students may come to see it as funny. Some may even begin to provoke the teacher deliberately.

Teachers sometimes forget to stress desired behavior and instead just *describe* misbehavior instead of *changing* it. In effect, they tell students that they have given up hope of change ("Phyllis, every day I have to speak to you for fooling around instead of doing your work. It's the same again today. How many times do I have to tell you? You never learn."). Chances are that it will be the same story tomorrow and the day after too unless the teacher attempts to effect change. Instead of merely nagging Phyllis, the teacher should try to identify the cause of her misbehavior and develop a solution. Perhaps the seatwork is too easy, too difficult, or otherwise inappropriate for her. Perhaps Phyllis is "fooling around" with a classmate, so that a conference, and possibly a new seating arrangement, is required. In any case, rather than let the situation continue, the teacher should discuss it with Phyllis and come to an agreement with her about the future.

In summary, teachers should avoid the following behaviors when intervening to correct misbehavior: (1) rhetorical or meaningless questions, (2) unnecessary threats or displays of authority, and (3) dwelling on misbehavior (nagging). These reactions do no good and may cause needless anxiety or resentment.

Conducting Investigations

When situations are not clear enough to allow teachers to act without additional information, they will need to question one or more students. Such questions should be genuine attempts to get information, not rhetorical questions. They should be direct and addressed primarily to matters of *fact.* Some questions about students' *intentions* may also be needed to establish what the student was doing and why ("Why did you leave the room?" "Why haven't you turned in your homework?").

However, any questions about intentions should not berate students, impugn their motives ("Did you think you could get away with it?"), or confuse them by raising issues that they cannot answer ("Why didn't you remember to be more careful?").

When questioning to establish the facts in a dispute, it usually is best to talk in private. This avoids putting individuals on the spot in front of the group, where they may be tempted to try to save face with lies or confrontations. When questioning two or more students together, teachers should insist that each individual be allowed to respond without interruption (otherwise students are likely to argue over who did what to whom first).

When responses conflict, teachers must guard against making premature judgments or accusations of lying. They should point out the discrepancies and perhaps indicate that they find certain statements hard to believe. This avoids rejecting anyone's statement out of hand and leaves the door open for someone to change his or her story.

Teachers should make it clear that they expect the truth and should back their words with credible actions that cast them as helpers who want the best for all concerned and not as authority figures interested only in assessing guilt. There must be no reward for lying and no punishment for telling the truth.

The facts need not always be established in detail. If the goal is to promote long-term development of integrity and self-control, not merely to settle a single incident, it may be desirable to leave contradictions unresolved or even to accept a lie or exaggeration without labeling it as such. This is especially true when teachers suspect that students are not telling the truth but are unable to prove it. Even when such students are guilty, they will respond poorly to a teacher who insists that they are lying (conclude that the teacher is picking on them, etc.). Thus, teachers confronted with unresolvable discrepancies should remind the students that they try to treat them fairly and honestly and expect them to reciprocate; state that they "just don't know what to think," in view of the discrepancies and contradictions; state that there is no point in further discussion without new information; and restate expectations. Compared with the alternatives (punishing everyone or affixing blame without proof), this procedure promotes progress toward long-run goals by increasing the probability that the students who lied will admit this to themselves and feel remorseful about it.

CONFLICT RESOLUTION

Most misbehavior can be either prevented or handled on the spot with techniques described so far. However, students with chronic personality or behavioral problems will require more intensive treatment. Two approaches to such treatment are Gordon's "Teacher Effectiveness Training" and Glasser's "Ten Steps to Good Discipline."

Gordon

Gordon (1974) advocates what he calls the "no lose" approach to resolving conflicts. He begins by analyzing the degree to which each party "owns" the problem. The teacher owns the problem when the teacher's needs are being frustrated (as when a student persistently disrupts class by clowning). Students own the problem when their needs are frustrated (as when a student is rejected by the peer group). Finally, teachers and students share problem ownership whenever each is frustrating the needs of the other.

Gordon believes that student-owned problems call for the teacher to provide sympathy and help, especially in the form of *active listening*. Active listening involves not only listening to students describe the problem and trying to understand it from their point of view but also reflecting their statements back to them to show them that they have been understood accurately. It also involves listening for the personal feelings and reactions that students express to the events being described and reflecting these as well.

When the teacher owns the problem, Gordon recommends explaining it to the student using *"I" messages*. "I" messages have three major parts. The first part indicates the specific behavior that leads to the problem ("When I get interrupted . . . "). The second specifies the effect on the teacher (" . . . I have to start over and repeat things unnecessarily . . . "). The third part specifies feelings generated within the teacher (". . . and I become frustrated."). Taken together, the three parts link specific student behavior as the cause of a specific effect on the teacher, which in turn produces undesirable feelings in the teacher. The idea is to get the student to recognize both the problem behavior and its effects on the teacher (but without blaming or rejecting the student).

Gordon believes that active listening and "I" messages will help teachers and students to achieve shared rational views of problems and to assume a cooperative, problem-solving attitude. Research by Peterson et al. (1979) showed that "I" messages reduced disruptive behavior in most students, and other studies (reviewed by Emmer & Aussiker, 1987) have shown mixed but mostly positive results.

When conflicts are involved (i.e., when problem ownership is shared), Gordon advocates the following six-step "no lose" method for finding the solution that best satisfies all concerned:

1. Define the problem.
2. Generate possible solutions.
3. Evaluate those solutions.
4. Decide which is best.
5. Determine how to implement the best solution.
6. Assess the effectiveness of this solution after it is implemented. If it is not working satisfactorily to all concerned, begin again and negotiate a new agreement.

Glasser

Glasser's (1977) ten-step approach is intended for use with students who persistently violate rules that are reasonable and are administered fairly by teachers who maintain a positive, problem-solving stance in dealing with those students. It emphasizes showing students that they will be held responsible for their in-school behavior. The ten steps are as follows. Starting with step 4, each new step escalates reaction to the problem, so new steps are not taken unless previous steps have not solved the problem.

1. List your typical reactions to the student's disruptive behavior.
2. Analyze the list to see what techniques do or do not work and resolve not to repeat the ones that do not work.
3. Improve your relationship with the student by providing extra encouragement, asking the student to perform special errands, showing concern, or implying that things will improve.
4. Focus the student's attention on the disruptive behavior by requiring the student to describe what he or she has been doing. Continue until the student describes the behavior accurately and then request that it be stopped.
5. Call a short conference and again have the student describe the behavior. Then have the student state whether or not the behavior is against the rules or recognized expectations and ask the student what he or she should be doing instead.
6. Repeat step 5, but this time add that the student will have to formulate a plan to solve the problem. The plan must be more than a simple agreement to stop misbehaving. The plan must include commitment to positive actions designed to eliminate the problem.
7. Isolate the student from the class until he or she has devised a plan for ensuring that the rules will be followed in the future, gotten the plan approved, and made a commitment to follow it.
8. If this does not work, the next step is in-school suspension. Now the student must deal with the principal or someone other than the teacher, but this person will repeat earlier steps in the sequence and press the student to devise a plan that is acceptable. The student will either follow the reasonable rules in effect in the classroom or continue to be isolated outside of class.
9. If students remain out of control or do not comply with in-school suspension rules, their parents are called to take them home for the day, and they resume in-school suspension the next day.
10. Students who do not respond to the previous steps are removed from school and referred to another agency.

Thompson and Rudolph (1992) elaborated on Glasser's ten-step method and reviewed research on its implementation in schools. Also, Glasser himself has continued to develop his ideas. His intervention model was originally developed as an application of a treatment approach called reality therapy. More recently, Glasser incorporated these and other notions into what he called control theory. He emphasized that people are responsible for their own goals, decisions, and general degree of happiness in their lives, and he described methods for taking control of one's life. In his book *Control Theory in the Classroom* (1986), he urged teachers to function as managers who motivate students by empowering them with the responsibility for learning. Drawing parallels to management practices that have been used successfully in business and industry, he suggested an emphasis on cooperative learning, in which students work in pairs and small groups to collaborate in the learning process.

More recently, in *The Quality School: Managing Students Without Coercion*, Glasser (1990) contrasted boss managers and lead managers. Boss managers motivate by punishing rather than reinforcing, telling rather than showing, overpowering rather than empowering, and emphasizing rule enforcement rather than cooperation. Lead managers do the reverse. Glasser emphasized that the lead manager approach is more compatible with the goal of empowering students to take control of their lives at school, and more likely to be successful in eliciting their cooperation.

Complementary ideas about school and classroom management have been advanced by Carl Rogers and H. Jerome Freiberg (1994) in the book *Freedom to Learn.* They put forth a model of person-centered classrooms in which students are taught to develop self-discipline by making choices, organizing their time, setting priorities, helping and caring about one another, listening, constructing a social fabric, being peacemakers when others engage in disputes, trusting one another, and engaging collaboratively in the learning process. They emphasized that creating a person-centered classroom is not merely a method but a philosophy: Unless teachers believe that their students can be trusted with the responsibilities involved, they won't be successful in granting them the freedom they need if they are to make their own choices (and mistakes). Moving from external discipline to self-discipline may take time, so teachers and students may need to move toward it in small steps. Such movement may be well worth the effort, however. Classroom management interventions in inner-city schools that were derived from the person-centered classroom notion have produced remarkable improvements in both school climate and student achievement (Freiberg, Stein, & Huang, 1995).

Comer

The same has been true of interventions based on the school development model described by James Comer (1980) in his book *School Power.* Developed as a way to improve the educational experiences of poor minority youth, Comer's program emphasizes building supportive bonds among students, their parents, and the school staff in order to promote a positive school climate. It is designed to create a school environment where students feel comfortable, valued, and secure. In such an environment, they form positive emotional bonds with teachers and parents and a positive attitude toward school, which in turn facilitates their academic learning. Three principles underlie the process: (1) schools review their problems in open discussion and a no-fault atmosphere; (2) collaborative working relationships are developed among the principal, teachers, parents, community leaders, and mental and physical health-care workers; and (3) all decisions are reached by consensus rather than issued by decree (Haynes & Comer, 1993).

Each Comer school is governed by three teams: (1) The school planning and management team. Headed by the principal but comprised of teachers, administrators, parents, support staff, and a child development specialist, this team is responsible for identifying targets for social and academic improvement, establishing policy guidelines, developing systematic school plans, responding to problems, and monitoring program activities. (2) The mental health team. Also headed by the principal, this team includes teachers, administrators, psychologists, social workers, and nurses. It analyzes social and behavioral patterns within the school and determines how to solve chronic problems by applying principles of child development.

(3) The parents' group. The goal of this group is to involve parents in all levels of school activity, from volunteering in the classroom to school governance.

Application of the Comer model involves communicating something like the following to a persistently troublesome student: "We know that you are unhappy and that that is a big part of the reason that you are having trouble in school. We want you in our school, we like you, we know that you can learn and get along, and we want to help you do so. But we cannot tolerate your attacking other children and showing disrespect for your teacher. We know that you don't want to do these things either. We are going to go a step at a time in helping you make it at school. When you are doing OK at a given step, you can move to the next. You let us know when you think you need more help. When you are not getting along well, we will hold you back. It's up to you. Do you have any ideas about how we can handle this whole thing better? . . . "

This beginning is followed by attempts to ignore minor misbehavior and encourage activities that bring the student positive feedback and success. When this is unsuccessful and the student increases misbehavior or begins to lose inner control, additional interventions are required. These are attempts to prevent the student from hurting someone, engendering more disapproval, causing self-embarrassment, or increasing a general sense of personal failure. To prevent these outcomes, the student is helped to leave the room gracefully, by communicating messages such as the following: "I can see that you are having a tough time today. Before we have a big problem, I want you to go and sit in the principal's office for awhile until you can pull yourself together. It's one o'clock now, and you ought to be able to do that by 1:30." If necessary, the teacher or another staff person trained for this task speaks to the student while he or she is out of the room—to talk about the problem, help to cool down emotions, and help him or her begin to think about better ways to handle the situation. Throughout the process, the emphasis is on helping the student avoid embarrassment or loss of control, not on punishing misbehavior. On a "bad day," it is assumed that something is bothering the student, so he or she is invited to talk about it and is encouraged and helped to reestablish self-control and productive behavior.

Peer Counseling

An increasingly popular component of programs for crisis intervention in schools (especially secondary schools) is peer counseling. In these programs, selected students are trained to act as mediators or provide support or assistance to troubled peers. Peer mediators, for example, are trained to help disputing peers to generate and evaluate options for reaching a mutually acceptable solution. When implemented by students well trained in confidentiality, impartiality, focusing disputants on problem solving rather than blaming, finding mutually agreeable solutions, and other conflict resolution skills, peer mediation programs can help reduce violence in the school and community. They can be especially useful for resolving conflicts involving issues that the disputants may be willing to discuss with certain peers but not with teachers or other authority figures. For information about peer counseling, see Byers (1994), D'Andrea (1983), Morgan (1994), or Tindall (1995).

PUNISHMENT

Use of punishment signifies that a teacher has not been able to cope with a problem. It also communicates lack of confidence in students, indicating that the teacher thinks that their misbehavior is deliberate and that they are not trying to improve. Even if these perceptions are accurate, communicating them can damage students' self-concepts and further reduce their willingness to cooperate.

Teachers who rely heavily on punishment can achieve only limited and temporary success. They may achieve grudging compliance, but at the cost of chronic group tension and conflict. Their students may obey them out of fear when they are present but then go out of control when the teacher is not in the room. Thus, teachers are well advised not to use punishment if other methods will suffice. Punishment sometimes is necessary, however, and teachers should use it appropriately when circumstances call for it.

Effective Punishment

Generally, punishment is used only in response to *repeated* misbehavior. It is a treatment of last resort for students who persist in misbehaving despite continued teacher expressions of concern and assistance. It is a way to exert control over students who will not control themselves. Thus, punishment is not appropriate for dealing with isolated incidents, even severe ones, if there is no reason to believe that the student will repeat the action. Even with repeated misbehavior, punishment should be minimized when students are trying to improve. Teachers should give students the benefit of the doubt by assuming their good will, and should use punishment only when students repeatedly fail to respond to more positive treatment.

A great body of evidence (reviewed in Bandura, 1986, 1989) shows that *punishment can control misbehavior, but by itself it will not teach desirable behavior or even reduce the desire to misbehave.* Thus, punishment is never a solution by itself; it can only be part of a solution.

When used, punishment should be employed deliberately as part of a planned response to repeated misbehavior. It should not be applied unthinkingly or vengefully. When teachers punish in response to their own anger, the punishment is usually accompanied by statements or thoughts like "We'll fix your wagon" or "We'll see who's boss." Such statements do not indicate use of punishment as a deliberate control technique; they are emotional outbursts indicating poor self-control and emotional immaturity.

The effectiveness of a punishment depends in part on the way the teacher presents it to students. Punishment should be threatened before actually being used, so that students have fair warning. They should see that their own behavior has made punishment necessary because they have left the teacher no other choice.

Tone and manner are important. The teacher should avoid dramatizing ("All right, that's the last straw!" "Now you've done it!") or implying a power struggle ("I'll show you who's boss"). The need for punishment should be stated in a quiet, almost sorrowful voice, in a manner that communicates a combination of deep concern, puzzlement, and regret over the student's behavior. Whether or not it is stated overtly, the implied message should be, "You have misbehaved continually. I have tried to help with reminders and explanations, but your misbehavior has persisted. I cannot allow this to continue. If it does, I will have to punish you. I don't want to, but I must if you leave me no choice."

If punishment becomes necessary, it should be related to the offense. If a student misuses materials, for example, it may be most appropriate to restrict or suspend his or her use of them for awhile. If students continually get into fights during recess, they can lose recess privileges or be required to stay by themselves. If they are continually disruptive, they can be excluded from the group.

The teacher should explain why students are being punished and what they must do to restore normal status. Students should know that they are being punished solely because of their unacceptable behavior and that they can regain normal status by changing the behavior.

This is in contrast to the "prison sentence" approach ("You have to stay here for ten minutes." "No recess for three days") and the "I am the boss" approach ("You stay here until I come and get you"). These statements include no explicit improvement demands, and they make it easy for the student to get angry or feel picked on. Even worse are overreactive inflexible statements ("You'll stay after school for a week, . . . get an 'F' in conduct, . . . have to get special permission to leave your seat from now on") that leave teachers stuck with either enforcing them or taking them back.

Exclusion from the Group   If not handled properly, exclusion from the group may actually function as a reward rather than a punishment. Excluded students should be placed where they cannot easily attract peer attention, perhaps behind the other students and facing a corner or wall. The idea is to make them *feel* excluded, psychologically as well as physically.

Withdrawal of privileges and exclusion from the group should be tied closely to remedial behavior whenever possible. This means telling students not only why they are being punished, but also what they may do to regain their privileges or rejoin the group. ("When you share with the others without fighting." "When you pay attention to the lesson."). Students should have only themselves to blame for their punishment, but they should also be given a way to redeem themselves, to focus their attention on positive behavior and provide an incentive for changing.

Exclusion should be terminated when excluded students indicate that they are ready to behave properly. Stated intentions to behave should be accepted without "grilling" the students to extract specific promises ("You'll stop calling out answers without raising your hand?" "You'll stop making fun of other students during small-group lessons?").

Also, when students request readmittance, the teacher should respond in ways that clearly accept them back into the group. Avoiding vague phrases like "Well, we'll see," teachers should show excluded students that they have accepted their intention to reform and then should instruct them to rejoin the class ("Well, John, I'm glad to hear that. I hate to have to exclude you from the class. Go back to your seat and get ready for math.").

Sometimes, excluded students may offer only halfhearted pledges to reform, and the teacher may wish to hold out for a more credible commitment, especially if there has been a previous history of failure to take exclusion seriously. This should be done with caution, since it is usually better to give students the benefit of the doubt than to risk undermining reform efforts. When a pledge is rejected, the reasons must be made clear. The students must see that the teacher is acting on the basis of observed behavior ("I'm sorry, John, but I can't accept that. Several times recently you promised to behave and then broke that promise as soon as you rejoined the group. I don't think you realize how serious this problem has become. Go back to the corner and stay there until I get a chance to come and talk to you about this some more").

Inappropriate Punishment

Abusive Verbal Attacks   These are never appropriate. Severe personal criticism cannot be justified on the grounds that the student needs it. It has no corrective function and will only cause resentment, both in the victim and in the rest of the class.

Physical Punishment   We do not recommend physical punishment, even where it is legal, for several reasons. First, by its very nature, it places the teacher in the position of attacking students, physically if not personally. This can cause injury, and in any case, it will undermine the teacher's chances of dealing with the students effectively in the future.

Although physical punishment still exists in many schools and often is defended by principals and teachers, research reveals that it typically is used ineffectively and counterproductively, mostly by inexperienced or poorly trained personnel who have not learned effective alternatives; most often against younger students from lower-class and minority groups, who are unlikely to defend themselves physically or legally; and for such offenses as tardiness, unfinished homework, or forgotten gym clothing rather than for physical aggression or insubordination (Hyman & Wise, 1979). In short, it is used by the ineffective to take out their frustrations on the weak and vulnerable.

Also, physical punishment is intense and focuses attention on itself rather than on the misbehavior that led to it. Yet, it is over quickly and has an air of finality about it, so that it usually fails to induce guilt or acceptance of personal responsibility for misbehavior. The offenders are more likely to be sorry for having gotten caught than for having misbehaved. Finally, physical punishment's long-term costs outweigh its short-term benefits. The least controlled, most hostile students usually come from homes where their parents beat them regularly. Criminals convicted of assault and other violent crimes almost always have home backgrounds in which physical punishment was common. In general, physical punishment teaches people to attack others when angry. It does not teach them appropriate behavior, which is the purpose of discipline.

Extra Work   We do not recommend assigning extra schoolwork as punishment because this may cause students to view schoolwork as drudgery. Both teachers and students should see work assignments as useful learning devices, not as punishments.

Requiring students to copy rules or write compositions about them may or may not be effective punishment, depending on how it is handled. Writing "I must not disrupt the class" five or ten times might help students remember the rule. However, requiring them to write it 50 or 100 times calls attention more to the punishment than the rule.

Ordinarily, it is more effective to ask older students to write a composition about how they should behave. This will force them to think about the rationales underlying the rules rather than just copy rules by rote. The teacher should follow up by discussing the composition with the student. The punishment itself is only part of the treatment.

Lowering Academic Grades   Punishment that is closely related to the offense is more easily seen as fair. Students can blame only themselves if they lose a privilege because they have abused it, but they can easily feel picked on if the teacher punishes by imposing restrictions in an entirely unrelated area. An especially bad practice of this type is to lower the students' academic grades as punishment for misbehavior or to deny students the chance to play sports or be in the band because of school tardiness, and so forth. Students who misbehave frequently are often low achievers as well, and lowering their grades as punishment for misbehavior is likely to further alienate or discourage them from academic efforts. Except when the punishment is *directly related* and *proportional* to the offense, as when a student who cheats on a test is given a failing grade for that test (and only that test), students should *not* be punished by having their grades lowered.

Punishment as a Last Resort

We cannot stress too strongly that punishment is a measure of last resort, appropriate only as a way to curb misbehavior in students who know what to do but refuse to do it. It should not be used when misbehavior is not disruptive or when problems exist because students do not know what to do or how to do it.

This does not mean that all nondisruptive problems should be ignored. Withdrawal, daydreaming, or sleepiness can be serious problems if they are characteristic and continuing (especially if they are related to drug use). However, punishment is not an appropriate response to such behavior, nor is it helpful for problems such as failure to answer questions or to do assigned work. Students who fail to turn in work should not be punished beyond imposition of standard penalties for late or missing work. More importantly, they should be made to complete the work during free periods or after school (this is not punishment, but simply insistence that students meet their responsibilities). Finally, when students do not know what to do or how to do it, they need instruction, not punishment.

Bear in mind that punishment focuses attention on undesirable behavior, and it tends to reduce work involvement and increase the tension in the room (Kounin, 1970). Using it in response to one problem may cause several others. This is one reason why teachers who rely on punishment have more, not fewer, control problems.

CHOOSING YOUR ROLE

Different grade levels offer different opportunities and challenges to teachers in their roles as managers of classrooms and socializers of students. As students progress through school, their personal and social development affects the role of the teacher and the goals and techniques of classroom management. Brophy and Evertson (1978) identified four developmental stages:

1. *Kindergarten and the early elementary grades.* Here students are socialized into the student role and instructed in basic skills. The emphasis is on teaching students what to do rather than on getting them to comply with familiar rules. Most still are predisposed to do what they are told and are likely to feel gratified when they please teachers and upset when they do not. They turn to teachers for directions, encouragement, solace, and personal attention. Teachers spend considerable time teaching students how to carry out basic routines and procedures.

2. *The middle elementary grades.* This stage starts when basic socialization to the student role is completed and continues as long as most students remain adult-oriented and relatively compliant. Students are familiar with most school routines and the serious disturbances seen frequently in later years are not yet common. Creating and maintaining an appropriate learning environment remain central to teaching success, but these tasks consume less time and teachers are able to concentrate on instructing students in the formal curriculum.

3. *The upper elementary or junior high school grades.* As more and more students change their orientation from pleasing teachers to pleasing peers, they begin to resent teachers who act as authority figures. Certain students become more disturbed and harder to control than they used to be. As a result, classroom management again becomes a prominent part of the teacher role. Now, however, the teacher's primary problem is motivating students to behave as they know they are supposed to, not instructing them in how to behave, as in the first stage.

4. *The upper high school grades.* As many of the most alienated students drop out of school and the rest become more mature, classrooms once again assume an academic focus. Classroom management requires even less time than it did during the second stage, because students handle most student role responsibilities on their own. Teaching at this level is mostly a matter of instructing students in the formal curriculum, although socialization occurs during informal, out-of-class contacts with individual students.

These developmental aspects of classroom management should be considered when thinking about the grade level one is preparing to teach. Teachers who like to provide nurturant socialization as well as instruction, who enjoy working with young children, and who have the patience and skills needed to socialize them into the student role would be especially effective in the primary grades. Elementary teachers who want to concentrate mostly on instruction would be best placed in the middle grades. Grades 7 to 10 would be best for teachers who enjoy or at least are not bothered by "adolescent" behavior and who see themselves as socialization agents and models at least as much as instructors. The upper high school grades are best for teachers who want to function mostly as subject-matter specialists.

THE TEACHER AS A SOCIALIZATION AGENT

At all four of the levels of schooling, there are problem students who require more intensive management and socialization than most of their classmates do. Many of these students will have social-emotional needs that interfere with their attempts to meet the challenges of schooling. Teachers need to develop knowledge and strategies for meeting these needs, not just to foster these students' social-emotional adjustment, but also to enable them to make satisfactory academic progress. Some teachers may be expected to address these needs primarily on their own, especially if they work in an elementary school where they teach the same students all day long and have only limited access to social workers, counselors, or other professional specialists. Teachers are not expected to assume as much of the student socialization burden in high schools, where they usually see students for only one period each day. In fact, at most urban and suburban high schools, dealing with problem students has become more of a school-level function performed by administrators and professional specialists than a classroom-level function performed by teachers.

In between these two extremes of the elementary teacher/socializer expected to take full charge of the whole child and the secondary subject-matter specialist expected to concentrate on academics, there is a range of teaching situations and associated role expectations. Teachers at middle, junior high, or even high schools may be expected to assume considerable socialization responsibilities if they work within a small team or a "school within a school" arrangement designed to ensure that they get to know their students as individuals (Little, 1995; Sizer, 1992). Or, they may be expected to work closely with a school counselor or social worker in seeking to resocialize problem students. On the other hand, if they teach in a large, impersonal, and bureaucratic school, they may be expected only to refer "troublemakers" to the office for "discipline."

Teachers have to decide which problems they are prepared to handle on their own; which require consultation with a school administrator, counselor, psychologist, social worker, or educational specialist; and which require involvement of community agencies or resources beyond those available at the school. They also need to work with parents, usually just to share information and perspectives on the problem and develop mutually acceptable plans for addressing it, although in some cases to solicit their cooperation in arranging for assessment and potential specialized treatment by professionals who work at the school district (if available) or in the larger community.

There has been much debate, but little research and certainly no conclusive evidence, about how to handle the most serious behavioral problems: racial and other group tensions; severe withdrawal and refusal to communicate; hostile, antisocial acting out; truancy; drug abuse; refusal to work or obey; vandalism; and severe behavior disorders or criminality. Psychotherapists have not achieved much success in dealing with behavior disorders, and neither they nor correctional institutions have dealt effectively with severe delinquency and criminality. Yet, teachers must cope with such problems while at the same time instructing all their students in the curriculum.

Some teachers accept this challenge by addressing the full spectrum of responsibilities with determination to solve whatever problems come along. However, other teachers are philosophically opposed to this level of emphasis on student socialization, are not interested in it, believe that they are temperamentally unsuited to it, or are hesitant to engage in much of it without specialized training. These positions are understandable, and to an extent, justified. Teachers who recognize their limitations and work within them probably will have more positive effects in the long run than they would have if they tried to do everything and ended up doing nothing very well.

However, there are limits to how much teachers can minimize their roles as authority figures and socializers of students. Research on school-wide approaches to managing disruptive behavior has shown that administrators and teachers work together in schools that respond effectively to problem students (Anderson, 1985; Gottfredson & Gottfredson, 1986; Jones, 1996; Metz, 1978). In contrast, there are more student misbehavior problems in schools where teachers place most discipline issues immediately into the hands of administrators and emphasize control and punishment over helping students to develop more productive behavior (Hawkins, Doueck, & Lishner, 1988; Wu et al., 1982). Jones (1988), after reviewing these studies, argued that teachers should assume responsibility at least for initial efforts at corrective intervention. We also encourage teachers to take a proactive role in guiding and socializing at least some of their troubled students, especially the ones who appear to have no other positive influences in their lives.

Difficulties of Socialization

Teachers who do want to socialize students can accomplish this goal by making a commitment to deal with student problems in addition to providing academic instruction. However, teachers who do so must be prepared to

1. Cultivate personal relationships with students that go far beyond those necessary for purely instructional purposes.
2. Spend time outside of school hours dealing with students and their families without receiving extra financial compensation for their efforts.
3. Deal with complex problems that have developed over a period of years, without benefit of special training as a mental health professional.
4. Perhaps encounter some opposition from school administrators.
5. Perhaps encounter expressions of frustration or resentment from students, their parents, or others involved in the situation.

Teachers typically do not have the luxury of interacting with students in a friendly, nonauthoritarian therapist's role. Indeed, they must find ways to reach disturbed students while still playing the role of authority figure and dealing with them every day in class. Rewarding experiences occur, but so do frustrations. Some students do not respond despite continued attempts to reach them. Others make initial progress only to regress and end up worse than when they started. Furthermore, not all "success cases" respond with overt gratitude or other direct reinforcement of the teacher. Finally, teachers can work intensively with only so many students at one time, so they have to be selective about their "caseloads," holding them within a manageable limit.

Teachers do have certain advantages over mental health professionals in helping students with their problems. For one thing, they see their students every day and under a variety of conditions, so they have more and better information about them than most therapists (who usually must rely on what their clients choose to tell them). Also, teachers are sometimes in a position to take direct action to help students cope with their problems, rather than just coaching them from afar. Even the authority-figure role has its advantages. Teachers can provide consequences (both rewards and punishments) to selected student behavior, and in the process, attempt to resocialize the students' beliefs and attitudes. Finally, teachers' interactions with their students are viewed by all concerned as normal forms of adult-child contact, so there is no reason for students to feel ashamed or identified as abnormal when their teachers talk with them about their problems. If you think that you can try to reach students persistently despite a steady diet of frustrations, you probably have a good chance to be a successful socialization agent. In fact, if you find the prospect challenging rather than daunting, you might consider teaching in grades 6 to 10, where student socialization needs are most frequent and intense.

Coping with Serious Adjustment Problems

Most classrooms have students whose serious and continuing problems require individualized treatment beyond that suggested so far. This section presents suggestions for dealing with them. Although different problems require different treatment, certain general considerations apply to all of them.

Do Not Isolate Students or Label Them as Unique Cases   Because labels call undue attention to misbehavior and suggest that more of the same is expected, it is important that problem students not be labeled or treated as qualitatively different from their peers. This is doubly important for students with continuing behavior problems, because problems are harder to eliminate once they become labeled as characteristic of a student.

Stress Desired Behavior   Teachers should stress desired behavior, not the misbehavior the student is showing. Teachers must not only talk, but also think and act in a manner consistent with the intention of moving the student toward desired behavior. This even applies to such behaviors as stealing or destroying property. If destruction is due to impulsiveness or carelessness, the teacher can instruct the student about how to handle property carefully. If stealing results from real need (poverty), teachers can plan with students ways they can borrow the stolen items or earn the right to keep them. Meanwhile, students can be praised for progress in acting responsibly or respecting the property rights of others. If students have been stealing or destroying property to seek attention or express anger, teachers can help them recognize this and develop better ways to meet their needs. Here again, the teacher should label and praise any positive progress students show.

By defining problems positively, teachers give students a goal and suggestions about how to work toward it. This helps both teachers and students feel that they are making progress. When the problem is defined negatively ("You've got to stop . . . "), both teachers and students are left where they started, and the cycle is likely to repeat itself over and over again.

Focus on Students' School-Related Behavior   Seriously disturbed behavior in school is usually part of a larger pattern of disturbance caused by many factors, including some that the teacher can do little or nothing about (parental conflict, inadequate or sadistic parent, poor living conditions). Even so, all students can learn to play the student role by behaving in ways that teachers expect. Factors in the home or out-of-school environments may need to be taken into account, but teachers should not use them as excuses for failing to deal with school-related misbehavior.

Generally, teachers are advised to confine their treatment efforts to school behavior and to aspects of the home environment that are closely related to school behavior (such as asking parents to see that students get to bed early enough on nights before school or that they do their homework). Going beyond such appropriate and expected teacher concerns is risky unless the teacher has both therapeutic expertise and a good relationship with the student and the family.

Build a Personal Relationship with the Student   It is important for the teacher to build close relationships with problem students as individuals, both to develop better understanding of their behavior and to earn the respect and affection that will make the students want to respond to change efforts. To do this, teachers need to take time to talk with such students individually, either after school or at conferences during school hours, making clear their concern about the students' welfare (not merely about their misbehavior) and willingness to help them improve. They should encourage students to talk about their problems in their own words, listening carefully and asking questions when they do not understand.

Ideally, the student will say something that suggests treatment procedures. If teacher behavior has been part of the problem, the teacher should admit this and promise to change. Reasonable student suggestions should be accepted. For example, a seventh grader may request that he not be asked to read aloud from the history book, since he reads at the second-grade level. This request could be granted, provided that a plan is devised to see that the student learns to read better. When a student's suggestions cannot be accepted, the reasons should be explained. The teacher may also wish to offer suggestions and elicit the student's opinions about whether the suggestions would help. Serious, deep-rooted problems will not be solved in one day with one conference. It is sufficient as a first step if both parties communicate honestly during the conference and come away from it feeling that progress has been made. Discussions should continue until mutual understanding is reached and both parties agree to try a particular suggested solution.

Most of these suggestions reflect the findings of the Classroom Strategy Study, which focused on teachers' reported strategies for coping with students who present chronic personality or behavior problems (Brophy, 1996; Brophy & McCaslin, 1992). Across problem types, two factors were consistently associated with principals' and observers' ratings of teachers' effectiveness in dealing with difficult students. The first was a willingness to assume responsibility for solving the problem. Higher-rated teachers would try to address problems personally, whereas lower-rated teachers often would disclaim responsibility or competence to deal with the problem or try to refer it to the principal. Second, higher-rated teachers emphasized long-term, solution-oriented approaches to problem solving, whereas lower-rated teachers emphasized controlling misbehavior in the immediate situation, often by relying on threat or punishment. The higher-rated teachers spoke of helping their students to understand and cope with the conflicts or problems that cause their misbehavior. These teachers usually did not find it necessary to punish students, although they sometimes included punishment as part of a larger solution strategy. The guidelines suggested in the following sections reflect the views of these higher-rated teachers, as well as the findings of other research studies cited. More specific suggestions about treatment of several common behavior problems are given in the following sections.

Showing Off   Some students continually seek attention by trying to impress or entertain teachers or peers. They can be enjoyable if they have the talent for the role and confine their showing off to appropriate times. Often, though, they are exasperating or disruptive. The way to deal with show-offs is to give them the attention and approval they seek, but only for appropriate behavior. Ignore inappropriate behavior, or when it is too disruptive to be ignored, do not call attention to it or make the student feel rejected. Thus, a comment like "We're having our lesson now" is better than "Stop acting silly." Students who seek attention at an awkward time should be delayed (i.e., told that the teacher will see them later at a specified time) rather than refused.

Show-offs need constant reassurance that they are liked, and teachers should try to fill this need. However, their inappropriate behavior should go unrewarded and, as much as possible, unacknowledged.

Defiance   Most teachers find defiance threatening, even frightening. What is the teacher to do with students who vehemently talk back or refuse to do what they are asked to do? To begin with, the teacher must remain calm so as not to get drawn into a power struggle. The natural tendency of most adults is to get angry and strike back with a show of force designed to show such students that they "can't get away with it." This may suppress the immediate defiance, but it will probably be harmful in the long run, especially if it involves loss of temper by the teacher or public humiliation of the student.

Teachers who overcome the tendency to react with immediate anger will gain two advantages by pausing a moment before responding to defiance: (1) they gain time to control their tempers and think about what to do before acting, and (2) the mood of the defiant student is likely to change from anger and bravado to fear and contrition during this time. When teachers do act, they must do so decisively, although in a calm and quiet manner. If possible, they should give an assignment to the class and then remove the defiant student for a private conference. If this is not possible or if the defiant student refuses to leave for a conference, he or she should be told that the matter will be discussed after school. The teacher's tone and manner should communicate serious concern, but no threats should be made. The defiant student and the rest of the class should know that action will be taken but should not be told exactly what it will be. The following response would be appropriate: "Daryl, I can see that something is very wrong here and that we'd better do something about it before it gets worse. Please step into the hall and wait for me—I'll join you in a minute." Stating that the matter will be dealt with in a private conference tells the class that the teacher will handle the situation yet does not humiliate the defiant student or incite further defiance. The teacher can even afford to let the student "get in the last word," because the matter will be taken up again later.

Students are unlikely to defy their teachers unless they resent them for some reason. Therefore, teachers must be prepared to hear defiant students out. When students claim unfair treatment, teachers must entertain the possibility that this is true. When mistakes have been made, teachers should admit them and promise to change.

It is usually best to encourage angry students to say everything they have on their minds *before* responding to the points they raise. This helps teachers to get the full picture and allows them some time to think about what they are hearing. If they try to respond separately to each point as it is raised, the discussion may turn into a series of accusations and rebuttals. Such exchanges usually leave students feeling that their objections have been "answered" but that they still are right in accusing the teacher of general unfairness.

With some defiant students, it may be important to review the teacher's role. Students should understand that teachers are interested primarily in teaching them, not in ordering them around or playing police officer, but this requires the students' cooperation. Regardless of the points students raise, teachers should express concern for these students and a desire to treat them fairly. This reassurance (backed, of course, by appropriate behavior) will be more important to the students than responses to specific accusations.

Even serious defiance can usually be handled with one or two sessions like these, if teachers are honest in dealing with students and if they follow up the discussion with appropriate behavior. Although unpleasant, incidents of defiance can be blessings in disguise. They bring out into the open problems that have been smoldering for a long time. Defiant acts usually have cathartic effects on students, releasing built-up tensions and leaving students more receptive to developing a constructive relationship with the teacher.

Both the higher-rated teachers from the Classroom Strategy Study and the research literature agreed that defiant students need consistent application of authoritative socialization principles for managing the classroom (so as to minimize the frequency with which they become defiant in the first place), along with consistent use of "no lose" strategies for resolving conflict when responding to the incidents of defiance that do develop. It also helps to establish positive or at least functional working relationships with these students, to ignore or at least avoid overresponding to their less serious provocations, and to supply them with support, instruction, or counseling to help them to achieve better insights into their behavior and its consequences and to learn to handle frustration and conflicts with authority figures more productively.

Aggression Against Peers   Aggressive students must not be allowed to hurt classmates or damage property. When such behavior appears, teachers should demand an end to it immediately. If the student fails to respond, the teacher should send another student for help and, if necessary and feasible, should physically restrain the student who is out of control. Most teachers rarely will be required to intervene in this way, but all should be prepared to do so. Such preparation should include training in techniques of restraining students and breaking up fights effectively, as well as development of clear procedures for emergency situations with the principal, other teachers, and support staff who may be available. A good rule of thumb is that teachers' responsibilities in these situations are first to the safety of themselves and the other students, then to the aggressive student, and then to property.

While being restrained, students may respond by straining to get away, making threats, or staging temper tantrums. If so, they should be held until they regain self-control. The teacher should speak firmly but quietly, telling them to calm down and get control of themselves. The students should be reassured that the problem will be dealt with, but not until they calm down. If they insist that the teacher let go, they should be told firmly that this will happen as soon as they stop yelling and squirming. Such verbal assurance can be reinforced nonverbally by relaxing the grip as the student gradually tones down resistance.

Restraint may be required if two students are fighting and do not respond to demands that they stop. Do not try to stop a fight by getting between the participants and trying to deal with both at the same time. This will result in delay, confusion, or even the teacher getting hit. Instead, restrain one of the participants, preferably the more belligerent, or the one with whom you have less rapport, by pulling him back and away from his opponent so that he is not hit while being held (pull at the belt or waistband, leaving the arms free for self-defense). This will stop the fight, although it may be necessary to order the other participant to stay away. It is helpful if the teacher does a lot of talking at this point, calming the students down and explaining that the matter will be dealt with when they comply.

Humor is helpful if the teacher has the presence of mind to use it. Threats or face-saving actions are effective only when taken seriously. If teachers respond to them with smiles or little remarks to show that they are considered funny or ridiculous ("All right, let's stop blowing off steam"), they are likely to stop quickly.

Once aggressive students calm down, teachers should talk with them individually. It is important to help them see the distinction between feelings and behavior. Feelings should be accepted as legitimate or at least understandable. Students who state that they are angry or claim unfair treatment should be asked to state their reasons for feeling this way. The feeling itself should not be denied or attacked. If the student has been treated unfairly, the teacher should express understanding and sympathy.

If angry feelings are not justified, the teacher should explain in a way that recognizes the reality of the feelings but does not legitimate them ("I know you want to be first, but others do too. They have the same rights as you. So there's no point in getting angry because they went first. You'll have to wait your turn. If you try to be first all the time, everyone will think you are selfish."). Although teachers should accept and sometimes expressly encourage legitimate *feelings,* they should not accept *misbehavior.*

Habitually aggressive students must learn that frustration and anger do not justify aggressive behavior. They should be given suggestions about how to express feelings verbally rather than physically. For example, students who "hit first and ask questions later" need instruction about how to resolve conflict through discussion and negotiation. In response to classmates who cause them problems, they should ask what the classmates are doing and why (instead of assuming that the classmates are provoking them deliberately) and should express their feelings verbally when others cause them to become angry (because peers may not even realize that they have made them angry or why).

Teachers should also appeal to the Golden Rule to try to help aggressive students see the consequences of their behavior. Students usually can see that if they dislike and avoid others who bully, cheat, or destroy property, others will dislike and avoid them for the same reasons. It is helpful to show by examples the value of verbalizing feelings and seeking solutions to problems instead of striking out at others. Aggressive students must learn that others will know why they are angry only if they tell them and that hitting will only make the others angry too.

Attacks on others for no apparent reason are more serious. Students who do this regularly may require professional treatment. Even so, a teacher can provide assistance in many ways. For example, suppose that a student has developed a self-image as a "tough guy" and actually wants others to fear and dislike him. As with any serious problem, the teacher should deal with aggressive acting out as it occurs and talk with the student to develop understanding and to explain behavioral expectations. In addition, the teacher can cope with the problem indirectly, to help both the student and others in the class to see him in a more positive light.

First, the teacher should avoid labeling the student or reinforcing any negative label he may apply to himself. Instead, the teacher can express confidence that the student will achieve better self-control and arrange for him to play a more positive role toward his classmates. It might be helpful for this student to be used as a tutor to teach academic content or other skills that he may know (tying shoes, operating equipment, arts and crafts, music, or other talents). In reading and role-playing situations, he should be assigned parts that feature kindness, friendship, and helpfulness toward others. He would be ideal for the part of an ogre who everyone feared and disliked until they found out how good he was underneath.

Potentially serious conflicts can be nipped in the bud if teachers spot them early enough and turn them into cooperative situations by suggesting how students can resolve the problem. For good measure, teachers can add that they are pleased to see the students cooperating.

So far, we have noted what teachers *should* do with aggressive students. Before leaving this topic, it is worth discussing one frequently advocated technique that we do *not* recommend. This is the practice of providing substitute methods for expressing aggression, such as telling the student to hit a punching bag instead of another student. By encouraging students to act out hostility against substitute objects, teachers merely prolong and reinforce immature emotional control. If kept up long enough, this will produce adults who are prone to temper tantrums at the slightest frustration and who spend much of their time building up and then releasing hostile feelings. This sort of person is neither happy nor likeable. Instead of trying to get students to act out all emotions, teachers should help students to distinguish between emotions and behavior and between appropriate and inappropriate emotions. Inappropriate emotions (unjustified anger or other emotional overreactions) should be labeled as such, and the reasons why they are inappropriate should be explained.

The higher-rated teachers from the Classroom Strategy Study reported responding to aggression as a serious behavioral problem calling for resocialization of aggressive students' responses to situations in which they tended to act out, not as a neurotic symptom or a relatively minor problem that could be handled through brief management responses. These teachers placed firm limits on aggressive students, demanded that they curb their aggressive behavior, and were prepared to back their demands with punishment if necessary. However, high-rated teachers also reported that they would try to encourage change by providing aggressive students with counseling or instruction in more effective ways of handling frustration, controlling their tempers, solving conflicts through communication and negotiation rather than aggression, and expressing anger verbally rather than physically.

The research literature also favors firm refusal to allow aggression combined with social skills training. Aggressive students often are unaware of their own behavior, how it is perceived by others, or the negative effects that it has on their social acceptance. Also, many do not know how to implement more effective methods of responding to conflict situations, so that they often resort to aggression for lack of better alternatives (Coie, Underwood, & Lochman, 1991; Furlong & Smith, 1994; Goldstein, 1988; Hughes, 1988; McGinnis & Goldstein, 1984; Pepler & Rubin, 1991).

Unresponsiveness   Some students lack the self-confidence to participate normally in classroom activities. They do not raise their hands to answer questions and they copy, guess, or leave an item blank rather than ask the teacher about their seatwork. When they are called on and do not know an answer, they stare at the floor silently or perhaps mumble incoherently. Sometimes this "strategy" is successful, because many teachers become uneasy and give the answer or call on someone else rather than keep such students "on the spot."

The key to success in working with shy or inhibited students appears to be application of steady but indirect and patient pressure for change. Higher-rated teachers from the Classroom Strategy Study reported that they would take problems of shyness or inhibition seriously and work to change students' behavior but would do so in indirect and supportive ways (private talks and special activities or assignments to draw students out, minimizing stress or embarrassment, praising accomplishments and encouraging efforts, and where necessary, building up students' academic self-concepts).

Teachers should generally treat inhibitions about classroom participation indirectly. Attacking the problem directly by labeling it and urging the students to overcome it can backfire by making students more self-conscious and inhibited (much research on stuttering, for example, shows this). The teacher should stress what the students should be doing rather than what they are not doing. Questions should be asked directly rather than prefaced with stems such as, "Do you think you could . . . ", which suggest uncertainty and make it easy for students to remain silent. Also, the teacher should pose questions in a conversational tone. More formally stated questions may sound like test items and thus produce anxiety.

Questions should be accompanied by appropriate gestures and expressions to communicate that the teacher is talking to the student and expects an answer. If the student answers, the teacher can respond with praise or relevant feedback. If the answer is too soft, the teacher might say, "Good! Say it louder so everyone can hear." When students appear to be about to answer, but hesitant, teachers can help by nodding their heads or encouraging verbally, "Say it!" When students do not respond at all, teachers can give the answer and then repeat the question or ask students to repeat the answer. Make it clear to students that they are expected to speak up, give them practice in doing so, and reassure and reward them when they do.

Interactions with reticent students should be deliberately extended at times, both to give them practice at extended discussions and to combat the idea that students can keep interactions short by offering brief responses. Once they begin to respond correctly, move to more demanding questions as their confidence grows.

Inhibited students need careful treatment when they do not respond. As long as they appear to be trying to answer the question, teachers should wait them out. If they begin to look anxious, teachers should intervene by repeating the question or giving a clue. They should not call on another student or allow others to call out the answer.

Teachers should not allow students to "practice" resistance or nonresponsiveness. Anxiety or resistance should be cut off before it builds. Students who do not respond to questions requiring a verbal answer can be asked to make nonverbal responses such as shaking their heads or pointing. It is important to get some form of positive response before leaving the student. Students at all levels should be instructed to say "I don't know" rather than remain silent when they cannot respond. Many students hesitate to say "I don't know," because previous teachers reinforced the idea that such responses are shameful through such comments as "What do you mean you don't know?" By legitimating "I don't know," the teacher makes it possible for students to respond verbally even when they do not know the answer.

These methods are difficult to apply in large-group situations with extremely unresponsive students who often do not say anything at all. Such students may have to be brought along slowly in individual and small-group situations first. A smaller setting does not necessarily make communication easier, however. The teacher will need to be careful to monitor the behavior of shy students when using small-group cooperative methods because research suggests that these students are encouraged by other students to remain passive (Mulryan, 1992).

Getting rid of strong inhibitions or fears takes time, and much progress can be undone by trying to push too far too fast.

Failure to Complete Assignments   Certain students fail to complete seatwork or homework assignments. Methods for dealing with this depend on why assignments are not turned in. Some students do not turn in work because they have not been able to figure out how to do it. This is not a motivational problem; it is a teaching problem calling for remedial work to help the students learn what they do not understand. This may seem obvious, but students report that teachers often not only fail to provide this help to slow learners but also routinely collect seatwork assignments before students have had a chance to finish (Weinstein & Middlestadt, 1979).

Patience and determination are needed in working with slow students because they need support and encouragement just to keep trying. If the teacher shows impatience, they will likely begin to copy from neighbors rather than continue to try to do the work themselves. Teachers can encourage these students by pointing out their progress and by making time for remedial teaching with them (or arranging for some other form of assistance).

A different problem is presented by students who can do the work but do not finish it or turn it in. The best way to deal with this problem is to stop it early, before it becomes entrenched. From the beginning of the year, teachers should be clear about expectations for seatwork and homework. Their purpose and importance should be explained, and the assignments should be collected, checked, and followed up with feedback and, when necessary, remedial work.

Although the teacher may wish to make open-ended assignments (such as identifying problems to do for extra credit or "to see if you can figure them out"), all students should have a clear-cut minimum amount of work for which they are accountable. There should be a clear understanding about what to turn in, when it is due, and the consequences for missing the deadline.

Teachers should also make clear that students are expected to finish assignments before doing anything else during seatwork time. Students involved in seatwork should be monitored to see that they are working productively. The established policy must be enforced consistently so that everyone forms the habit of doing the seatwork.

Failure to turn in homework is a more difficult problem, because teachers cannot monitor and intervene if students are not working properly. They can keep track of whether homework is being turned in, however, and can assign students who did not complete it to do so during free periods. Students who do not complete the job during free periods should be kept after school. Here again, the policy that assignments are to be completed and turned in on time must be established from the beginning of the year. If failure to turn in homework is common, teachers should review and if necessary adjust the nature or difficulty level of the homework or the way it is monitored and corrected.

Students with Attention Deficit or Hyperactivity Problems   Most students have at least occasional problems maintaining concentration on lessons and assignments, but for certain students inattentiveness is a chronic problem. In the primary grades it typically takes the form of short attention span or distractibility. In later grades it may be manifested more as daydreaming or difficulty in sustaining concentration on work.

Another common problem is behavioral hyperactivity. Certain students show excessive and almost constant movement, even when sitting. They are easily excitable, tend to blurt out answers and comments, are often out of their seats, and even when in their seats are likely to be squirming, jiggling, or bothering other students with noises or movements.

Attentional distractibility and behavioral hyperactivity often go together, but opinions about the nature of their relationship have waxed and waned. Prior to the 1970s, attention focused on the more obvious and immediately troublesome hyperactivity problem, with distractibility treated as secondary. During the 1970s, however, evidence was developed to suggest that distractibility not only was part of the larger hyperactivity syndrome, but was the key to it. More recent research suggests that this view overemphasizes the role of attention deficits in leading to hyperactivity problems, and that hyperactivity is linked more closely with oppositional and aggressive conduct disorders. In this view, attention deficit problems without accompanying hyperactivity are very different from hyperactivity problems, especially if the latter are accompanied by aggression or other conduct problems.

Laub and Braswell (1991) collected suggestions from teachers concerning ways to keep distractible students involved in lessons. The teachers suggested seating these students away from both the hallway and the windows, near the teacher, and facing the teacher during lessons, as well as creating study carrels or other distraction-reduced environments for them to use when working on assignments. They also recommended standing near these students when presenting lessons or giving instructions, actively involving them by asking them to hold up props or write ideas on the board, using their names or calling on them frequently during lessons, and frequently using computerized learning, cooperative learning, or other formats that allow for more active participation.

Similarly, the higher-rated teachers from the Classroom Strategy Study recommended a combination of environmental engineering and instructional support designed to reduce the frequencies with which these students become distracted, reduce the demands on them for sustained concentration (at least at first), and help them learn to monitor and control their attention more successfully. If organization is a problem, teachers can help distractible students learn to keep track of their things better by making schedules, keeping assignment notes and checklists, and periodically taking stock of their accomplishments and reorganizing their folders and work areas.

Despite the diversity in points of view about the nature and causes of behavioral hyperactivity, recent reviews show a great deal of agreement in summarizing the research on treatment approaches (Barkley, 1990; Fiore, Becker, & Nero, 1993; Friedman & Doyal, 1992; Gomez & Cole, 1991). Three main approaches are commonly recommended: medication, behavioral treatments, and cognitive-behavioral treatments.

The most prevalent therapy, and also the most efficacious and carefully studied, is stimulant medication—typically methylphenidate (Ritalin). In about 75 percent of cases, stimulant medication produces immediate and dramatic reductions in hyperactive behavior and improved performance on tasks requiring concentrated attention. These effects may be enhanced by changed expectations in the students themselves, their parents, and their teachers, but they are not explained by expectation effects. Careful double-blind studies have shown that teachers notice much more improvement in and respond much more positively to hyperactive students taking stimulant medication than to hyperactive students taking placebos.

Despite producing dramatic reductions in short-term hyperactive behavior in the classroom, however, stimulant medication has only negligible effects on long-term academic achievement and social behavior (Swanson et al., 1993). Thus, even for students formally diagnosed with attention deficit/hyperactivity disorder (ADHD), stimulant medication is only a partial treatment. A comprehensive approach also includes components designed to improve these students' academic skills, motivation to learn, or general intellectual or moral functioning. Behavioral treatments, particularly contracting and other reinforcement-based methods, are commonly recommended for this purpose. Because hyperactive students often have attention deficits as well, it is important to be unusually clear and specific in stating behavioral goals to these students, specifying the contingencies between behaviors and consequences, and reminding them of these contingencies when following through on them.

Cognitive-behavioral treatments appear to be ideally suited to the needs of hyperactive students because they involve training them in skills such as coming to attention and settling into a task, concentrating on task-relevant stimuli, keeping aware of goals and strategies, budgeting time, delaying gratification, and inhibiting inappropriate responses. Unfortunately, however, applications of cognitive strategy training with hyperactive students so far have produced mostly unsatisfactory or mixed results. Perhaps these students' attentional deficits do not enable them to master cognitive strategies well enough to be able to use them effectively, or perhaps effective instructional approaches have not been developed yet. Braswell and Bloomquist (1991) have published a manual for planning and carrying out cognitive-behavioral interventions with hyperactive students.

Popular books and articles on hyperactivity often recommend a fourth treatment: avoiding or limiting the child's exposure to food additives, fluorescent lighting, bright colors, sugars, or other substances described as toxic to children in general or hyperactive children in particular. Unfortunately (because it would be nice to see a complex problem have a simple solution for a change), research does *not* support these ideas.

Several common themes appear in suggestions to teachers about instructing hyperactive students. One is "Don't let these kids turn you off so that you begin to treat them inappropriately." The disruptions caused by hyperactive students can be exasperating, making it difficult for teachers to be welcoming and supportive with them. When interviewed as adults, hyperactive students typically report feeling misunderstood and rejected by their teachers and often their classmates, constantly being criticized for doing things that they were not even aware of doing, let alone doing deliberately (Weiss & Hechtman, 1986).

A related point is that just because hyperactive students often display normal attention and self-regulation for short periods of time, this does not mean that they could do it all the time "if they really wanted to."

Kirby and Kirby (1994) suggested that teachers help these students to understand their condition by telling them that they are just as capable as other students but they sometimes miss things because their attention wanders, so that what they retain may resemble memories of a television program that was interrupted several times by transmission interference. Also, without blaming them, teachers might make these students realize that classroom disruptions take time away from instruction and that hyperactive behavior (especially if aggressive) turns off peers and impedes the formation of friendships. Having called attention to these problems, teachers then can follow up by reassuring the hyperactive student that they will work on the problems together.

Higher-rated teachers from the Classroom Strategy Study emphasized the need to increase hyperactive students' awareness of their behavior and its effects on the teacher and their classmates, to impress on them the need to develop better self-control, and to help them do so by giving them cues and reminders, shaping improvements through successive approximations, praising and rewarding such improvements, reducing distractions during work times, allowing these students more frequent opportunities to move about, and providing other forms of assistance or support. To the extent that hyperactive students are also aggressive or defiant, they will need special treatment designed to reduce these problems as well.

ANALYZING PROBLEM BEHAVIOR

Many forms of problem behavior have not been discussed in this chapter: student habits that irritate or disgust the teacher, students who bait the teacher with provocative remarks, and various signs of child abuse or mental or emotional disorder. When faced with such symptomatic behaviors, teachers need to try to find out why the students are behaving as they are, and in the process, develop clues to successful treatment.

Finding Out What Problem Behavior Means

To the extent that behavior problems occur in the classroom, teachers should question students and systematically observe them. What is the meaning of the behavior? Why does the student act this way? *Remember, surface misbehavior may be just a symptom of an underlying problem, and the symptomatic behavior may not be as important as the reasons that are producing it.*

If the behavior is just a habit, not part of a larger complex of problems, the teacher should insist that the student drop it. This demand should be supported by an appropriate rationale. Where objectionable habits are not fundamentally immoral but merely violate school rules, social convention, tact, good taste, or the teacher's personal preferences, this distinction should be noted. Students should not be made to feel guilty or to believe that their habits indicate that something is seriously wrong with them. Teachers are justified in forbidding habits that are disruptive or irritating but should not describe such habits as worse than they really are.

If the problem behavior is more serious or complex than a simple habit and the student has not given an adequate explanation for it, careful observation is needed. Observations should begin by describing the behavior more precisely. Is it a ritual that is repeated pretty much the same way over and over (masturbating, spitting, nose picking), or is it a more general tendency (aggression, suspiciousness, sadistic sense of humor) that is manifested in many different ways? Perhaps the description can be narrowed. Is there a recognizable pattern? For example, do students' suspicions center around a belief that others are talking about them behind their backs, or do they think they are being picked on or cheated? If they think others are talking about them, what do they think is being said? If students laugh inappropriately, what makes them laugh? Such information provides clues to what the behavior means.

Besides enabling the teacher to describe the behavior more specifically, observations should establish the conditions under which it occurs. Is it a chronic problem or something that started recently? Does it happen at a particular time of the day or week? Does it occur when tests are given, for example, or when a student has lost a competition? Such common elements might point to events that trigger the reaction. In addition, discussing these observations with the student may produce insights that increase both the teacher's and the student's understanding of the behavior and lead to useful suggestions for problem solving.

Teachers should also note what they themselves were doing immediately before the students acted out. Perhaps they triggered the behavior by treating students in ways that the students think are unfair. Analyses of this sort help teachers place students' problem behaviors in context and begin to see them as symptoms that may help identify underlying causes. This will move teachers away from essentially negative, describe-the-problem-but-don't-do-anything-about-it approaches ("How can I get Lynn to stop sulking?") and toward diagnosis and treatment ("How can I help Lynn see that I am not rejecting her personally when I refuse her requests?").

Arranging a Conference

The simplest and often best way to understand students' behavior is to talk to them about it in a conference during a free period or after school. Teachers should note what they have observed, express concern about the behavior, and ask for an explanation. Students usually lack the insight to explain fully why they act as they do, and teachers should not expect them to. Instead, the hope is that helpful information will emerge from the discussion. If it does produce a breakthrough, fine. If not, something is still accomplished if students learn that the teacher is concerned about them and wishes to help.

Conferences should be concluded in ways that give students a feeling of closure. If the problem behavior has been disruptive, teachers should clarify expectations and limits as well as reach agreements with students about any special actions to be taken. If the problem requires no special action or if it is not yet clear what action to take, teachers can conclude by telling students that they are glad to have had a chance to discuss the problem and that they will help in any way they can if students will let them know how.

Bringing in Parents and Other Adults

If students simply refuse to cooperate in seeking acceptable solutions, or if they persistently fail to follow through on their commitments, teachers may need to involve the parents or seek help from a social worker, counselor, school psychologist, school administrator, or fellow teacher. Discussing the problem with a good resource person, preferably one who is familiar with the situation and has observed in the classroom several times, may help produce new insights or specific suggestions.

Teachers can set the stage for effective problem solving with parents by developing collaborative relationships with them right from the beginning of the school year. Family involvement in children's education is associated with better attendance, more positive attitudes toward school, and higher academic achievement.

When involving parents, the goal is to find solutions for the problem, not to find someone to blame for it. The parents are likely to be embarrassed about their child's problems and fearful of interacting with the teacher because they believe that the problems are their fault. Whether or not this is true, teachers need to focus on problem solving rather than blaming if they want the parents to play a constructive role.

For example, they might contact the parents, arrange for a meeting at the school (or by phone if necessary), and begin by saying something like, "I'm seeing some concerns with Sarah in the classroom that I'd like to share with you. I think that if we work together, we can help Sarah deal with these problems successfully." Then, the teacher might express concerns in a nonjudgmental way and ask the parents if they are seeing any of these problems in Sarah's behavior at home or in the neighborhood.

Sometimes these inquiries will yield information about stress factors in the child's life (an impending divorce, a death or serious illness in the family, etc.). Such information might help put the child's classroom behavior into perspective (e.g., seeing it as preoccupation with or defense against fears, and indirectly, a cry for help). This knowledge would make the teacher more informed and more able to express concern directly in private interactions with the student ("Sarah, I understand that your brother is sick. I wonder if sometimes you think about this instead of working on your assignments.").

Merely informing parents about problems is not helpful. If they get the impression that they are expected to "do something" they might just threaten or punish their child and let it go at that. Therefore, teachers should make suggestions about how the parents might help their child, and if necessary, try to resocialize the parents' attitudes or beliefs about effective child rearing. In particular, the need to think of punishment as a last resort and the need for confidence and positive expectations are two principles that many parents violate when their children have problems.

Teachers who call parents mostly just to get information should make this clear to them, then communicate observations about their child and ask if they can add anything that might increase understanding (e.g., how much they know about the problem and what their explanation for it is). If some plan of action emerges, the teacher and parents should discuss and agree on its details.

If no parental action seems appropriate, the teacher should bring the conference to some form of closure ("I'm glad we've had a chance to talk about Jason today. You've given me a better understanding of him. I'll keep working with him in the classroom and let you know about his progress. Meanwhile, if anything comes up that I ought to know, please give me a call."). The parents should emerge from the conference knowing what to tell their child about it and what, if anything, the teacher is requesting them to do.

There are many advantages to having close collaborative relationships between school and family. Collaboration enables the teacher to have more information to use in understanding students' classroom behavior. Reciprocally, families who are better informed about teachers' and schools' intentions can provide more support. It is beyond the scope of this chapter to provide detailed information about strategies for creating, maintaining, and improving home-school relationships. Fortunately, several excellent sources are available (e.g., Hoffman, 1991; Kauffman et al., 1993; McCaslin & Good, 1996; Weinstein & Mignano, 1993).

OTHER APPROACHES TO CLASSROOM MANAGEMENT

Our approach to classroom management is eclectic, stressing principles gathered from many theories. A few systematic approaches stress principles developed within one theory or point of view. Three of the most prominent are assertive discipline, contingency contracting, and cognitive behavior modification.

Assertive Discipline

Assertive discipline is an approach developed by Lee and Marlene Canter (1992) and promoted through in-service training workshops sponsored by their corporation. It stresses the rights of teachers to define and enforce standards for student behavior that allow the teachers to instruct successfully. Teachers who do this are described as assertive teachers and are contrasted both with submissive teachers who fail to enforce standards and hostile teachers who do so but in ways that violate the best interests of students. Recommended methods focus on developing clearly specified expectations for student behavior, translating these into a set of rules that specify acceptable and unacceptable behavior, and linking these to a system of rewards and punishments. The most widely used punishment is a penalty system in which the names of misbehaving students are written on the board and check marks are added following their names for repeated offenses. These students are subject to detention or to progressively more serious punishments including notes sent home to parents, time out from the classroom, or referral to the principal.

Assertive discipline is controversial. Lee Canter (1988) claims that the approach is supported by research, and supporters (e.g., McCormack, 1989) cite testimonials and survey data to suggest that it is popular among practitioners who are convinced that it works. However, independent reviewers have concluded that the Canters have failed to conduct systematic research on the effectiveness of the approach they have been promoting for 20 years, and that the limited research available on the approach simply does not support claims for its effectiveness (Emmer & Aussiker, 1987; Render, Padilla, & Krank, 1989). Only one study (involving 15 elementary teachers in Australia) has involved systematic introduction of assertive discipline and monitoring of its effects (Nicholls & Houghton, 1995). It yielded significant increases in on-task behaviors and decreases in disruptions, although the investigators noted that improvements were observed only in a subset of the classes studied.

Several authors have also voiced philosophical objections to the assertive discipline model. Curwin and Mendler (1988) characterized it as an example of an *obedience model,* in which power-based methods are used to compel students to conform to rules. They consider such obedience models less desirable than *responsibility models,* in which the goal is to develop responsibility for inner self-guidance in students, using methods that emphasize rationale explanations and natural consequences of behavior rather than threats and punishment. Similarly, McDaniel (1989, p. 82) criticized assertive discipline as being "not much more than applied behavior modification and take-charge teacher firmness with rules and consequences." The designers of the assertive discipline program have recently expanded its initial focus on controlling student behavior by adding materials on beginning the school year, working with parents, and helping students with homework. Even so, the program retains its primarily behavioral character and thus in our view is less helpful than more eclectically derived programs.

We see value in several aspects of the assertive discipline approach (especially its emphasis on developing and communicating clear expectations for student behavior). This can be helpful for teachers who are notably lacking in both confidence and viable strategies for dealing with problem students. However, we share the concerns voiced by its critics. We believe that the approach places too much emphasis on threat and punishment, so that it is a much less desirable alternative than the approach outlined here, which is based on replicated findings obtained by several research teams working independently in different parts of the country. Further, we believe that any management system is incomplete if it relies on teachers to regulate student behavior but lacks a concomitant emphasis on student self-control. As McCaslin and Good (1992) noted, it is foolish to try to teach a problem-solving curriculum while undermining it by using rigid behavior control management systems.

Contingency Contracting

Teachers can provide reinforcement when students pay attention, do their work, or keep the rules, and can withhold it when they do not. Students can be given a more active role in this process through *contingency contracting,* which involves conferring with the student about possible alternatives and then jointly drawing up a contract that specifies what the student will be expected to do in order to earn contingent rewards. The contract can be purely oral, although it helps to formalize it by having the student write down the details of the agreement. Contracts might call for students to complete a certain amount of work at a certain level of proficiency, or to improve their classroom behavior in specified ways, in order to earn specified rewards. For example, a level of performance that will require sustained effort (for a particular student) can be required for a grade of "A," with lesser requirements for lower grades.

Contracts for behavioral improvement can be developed using the same principles. Conduct that represents the best that can be expected from *this* student at *this* time can be required for maximum reinforcement, with less acceptable levels producing less reinforcement. As students become able to control themselves more successfully, new contracts requiring better behavior can be introduced.

Contingency contracting usually works best when students are presented with a variety of attractive reinforcements. These "reinforcement menus" might include opportunities to spend time in learning centers or other enrichment activities, to go to the library, to play games, or even just to converse with friends. Specified good behavior or acceptable completion of assignments is rewarded with so many points, and these points can be "spent" on reinforcements. The "prices" of reinforcements may vary according to their attractiveness and the demand for them. The most popular ones are the most expensive. Occasional changes in reinforcement menus or prices provide variety and help avoid satiation with the reinforcers.

It is harder than it might seem to arrange contingencies so that desired behaviors are reinforced. Sometimes proper contingencies are not established; at other times, the problem is in the presumed reward that is supposed to function as a reinforcer. Analyze the behavior modification attempts presented in the examples below. Are they likely to be successful? Why or why not?

1. Ms. Bussey has set up a contingency-contracting system. Students who complete assignments get tokens they can spend on reinforcers. However, the work must be correct. If students come with incomplete or incorrect work, they must return to their desks and finish it correctly.

2. Mr. Skinner gives out goodies every Friday afternoon as a way to motivate students to apply themselves. He sees that everyone gets something but makes sure to give the more desirable items to students who appear to have worked hard during the week. He refers to this as "payday," and says "Good work" to each student when passing out the goodies.

3. Ms. Calvin announces that from now on, the student who finishes the afternoon math assignment first will be allowed to dust the erasers.

4. Mr. Caries is frustrated because his students do not keep orderly desks. To encourage better habits, he occasionally (and unpredictably) announces that today students who do a good job of cleaning their desks will get candy. After allowing enough time, he goes around to check and gives candy to those who have neat desks.

Superficially, all four examples are similar: the teacher offers rewards to improve some performance. However, subtle differences make it likely that only Ms. Bussey will succeed. She has attractive reinforcers available, and students can get them only by turning in complete and correct work. Assuming that all students can do the work assigned to them, the contingencies are such that rewards will function as reinforcement for sustained and careful work on assignments.

Mr. Skinner will not succeed because there is no clear contingency between performance of the behaviors he is trying to reinforce and delivery of the reinforcements. All students get some kind of reward whether they apply themselves or not, and differences in the attractiveness of the rewards given to individuals depend on his unsystematic perceptions and fallible memory rather than on objective evidence of effort. Some students get more than they deserve, and others get less than they deserve because Mr. Skinner does not realize how deserving they are. His students will learn that there is no clear contingency between reward and performance, so that few of them will be motivated to work harder by this gimmick, even though they will enjoy the goodies.

Ms. Calvin's scheme is almost certain to fail, for three reasons. First, she should reward effort and accomplishment, not speed. Second, the possibility for reinforcement exists for only those few students who can work fast enough to finish first. Finally, it is unlikely that many students will be motivated by the opportunity to dust erasers. Ms. Calvin is offering a weak reinforcer, susceptible to early satiation.

Mr. Caries will also fail. His reinforcements are contingent on performance of the desired behavior, but they are offered only occasionally and always announced beforehand. Thus, the contingency here is not "Students who have neat desks every day will get rewarded," but "Students who clean their desks whenever Mr. Caries promises rewards will get rewarded." By always announcing the availability of rewards ahead of time, Mr. Caries eliminates their power to reinforce clean-up efforts even when they are not available.

These examples illustrate some of the problems involved in using contingency contracting in schools. The proper contingencies are hard to establish, and satiation with the available rewards is a continuing problem. When used effectively, however, contingency contracting helps students to see the relationship between their behavior and its consequences. Also, when they draw up the contracts themselves, they are more likely to make personal commitments that are real and meaningful to them because they express them in their own words. Contracts are especially useful for situations in which students know what they are supposed to do and are capable of doing it if they put their minds to it, but currently are not conscientious or motivated enough to do so consistently.

Contracting provides built-in opportunities for teacher-student collaboration in negotiating expectations and rewards. If perfect performance is currently an unreasonable expectation, the negotiation process might yield specifications calling for reinforcement of a level of improvement that the student views as reasonable and the teacher is willing to accept (at least for now). Contracting also provides opportunities to offer students choices of rewards, thus ensuring that the intended reinforcement is experienced as such.

Cognitive Behavior Modification

Experience with goal setting, self-monitoring, and other cognitive elements of contingency contracting led to the realization that they have important positive effects of their own, independent of the effects of reinforcement. For example, inducing students to set work output goals for themselves can improve performance, especially if the goals are specific and difficult rather than vague or too easy (Rosswork, 1977). Even more powerful than inducing students to set goals is inducing them to monitor and maintain daily records of their own study behavior. If taught properly, students can learn to monitor their behavior more closely and control it more effectively (Hughes, 1988).

Self-control skills are taught using procedures that Meichenbaum (1977) has called cognitive behavior modification. One particularly powerful technique combines modeling with verbalized self-instructions. Rather than just tell students what to do, the teacher demonstrates the process, not only by going through the physical motions involved but also by verbalizing the thoughts and other self-talk (self-instructions, self-monitoring, self-reinforcement) that direct the activity.

Meichenbaum and Goodman (1971) originally used the technique with cognitively impulsive students who made frequent errors on matching tasks because they responded too quickly, settling on the first response alternative that looked correct rather than taking time to examine all of the alternatives before selecting the best one. As the models "thought out loud" while demonstrating the task, they made a point of carefully observing each alternative, resisting the temptation to settle on the first one that looked correct, reminding themselves that one can be fooled by small differences in detail that are not noticed at first, and so on. Variations of this approach have been used not only to teach cognitively impulsive students to approach tasks more reflectively, but also to teach all students to be more creative in problem solving, to help social isolates learn to initiate activities with peers, to help aggressive students to control their anger and respond more effectively to frustration, and to help defeated students learn to cope with failure and respond to mistakes with problem-solving efforts rather than resignation. Various approaches have in common the attempt to teach students that they can exert control over their own behavior and handle frustrating situations effectively through rational planning and decision making (Durlak, Fuhrman, & Lampman, 1991; Forman, 1993).

A simple example is the "turtle" technique of Robin, Schneider, and Dolnick (1976), in which teachers teach aggressive students to assume a turtle position when upset. The students learn to place their heads on their desks, close their eyes, and clench their fists. This gives them an immediate response to use in anger-provoking situations and enables them to delay inappropriate behavior and to think about constructive solutions. Actually, the turtle position itself is mostly a gimmick; the key is training students to postpone impulsive responding while they gradually relax and consider constructive alternatives.

Douglas et al. (1976) trained hyperactive students to approach seatwork tasks carefully. They used modeling and verbalized self-instruction designed to enable the students to think before acting ("What plans can I try?" "How would it work if I did that?"), to monitor their performances during the task ("What shall I try next?" "Have I got it right so far?"), to check and correct mistakes ("See, I made a mistake there—I'll correct it." "Let's see, have I tried everything I can think of?"), and finally, to reinforce themselves ("I've done a pretty good job").

The "Think Aloud" program of Camp and Bash (1981) is a structured curriculum designed to teach students to use their cognitive skills to cope with social problems. It teaches the students to pose and develop answers to four basic questions: "What is my problem?" "How can I do it?" "Am I using my plan?" and "How did I do?" Think Aloud activities can be used with the class as a whole, although they are probably of most value with impulsive and aggressive students taught in small groups.

Other approaches to what is becoming known as strategy training have been developed by theorists working outside of the cognitive behavior modification tradition. Much strategy training involves teaching social skills. Students are given modeling and instruction, then engaged in role play and other practical application exercises, to teach them better ways of interacting with peers and solving social problems. Social skills training programs have been used to teach strategies for initiating and maintaining social conversations, joining ongoing games or group activities, playing or learning cooperatively, and resolving conflicts through negotiation without resorting to aggression. Research indicates that social skills training can be effective for improving a wide range of student behaviors (DuPaul & Eckert, 1994; Gesten et al., 1987; Sabornie, 1991; Zaragoza, Vaughn & McIntosh, 1991). For examples of classroom applications, see Adalbjarnardottir (1994), Cartledge and Milburn (1995), Elias and Clabby (1989), King and Kirshenbaum (1992), Matson and Ollendick (1988), or Walker (1987).

Whenever problem behavior appears because students lack strategies for coping effectively with particular situations, teachers will need to *teach* them how to handle those situations better—not just *urge* them to do so. The most effective form of strategy teaching is likely to be modeling combined with verbalized self-instructions, because this demonstrates the processes directly for students. If teachers just provide an explanation, students will have to translate the teacher's directions into forms of self-talk that they can use to guide their behavior.

BEARING THE UNBEARABLE

Teachers often must cope with problems that cannot be solved. If enough seriously disturbed students are in the room, the teacher cannot deal with all of them successfully and teach the curriculum too. When things get unbearable, something has to give; either the problem has to be reduced or the teacher needs help from professionals outside the school. Unfortunately, outside resources adequate to do the job usually are not available, and available resources often are not successful. Genuinely therapeutic treatment is available, but unless the family is able and willing to pay high professional fees, students will likely have to go on waiting lists. They may get treated some months later, but not immediately. Removing the student from the school is rarely an effective strategy. Suspension from school merely deepens students' alienation and makes it harder for them to cope when they come back (*if* they come back). Placement in a class for the retarded, disturbed, or delinquent, although well meant and often considered "treatment," generally is another step toward total failure.

Thus, the only effective treatment that most disturbed students get must come from their classroom teachers, with the assistance of counselors, social workers, psychologists, and administrators. For students who are almost old enough to drop out of school or are in danger of being thrown out, this may be the last real chance to head off a lifelong pattern of failure and misery.

SUMMARY

Consistent use of the preventive techniques described in the previous chapter will avert most problems, and the rest can be handled with techniques described in the present chapter. Many major disruptions start as minor misbehavior, so teachers should monitor the classroom continuously and know how to stop minor problems quickly and nondisruptively.

Much misbehavior can be ignored. When it is fleeting and not disruptive, there is no point in interrupting activities to call attention to it. If misbehavior is prolonged or begins to become disruptive, direct intervention is needed. When students know what they are supposed to be doing and when the nature of their misbehavior is obvious, there is no need to question them. Return them to productive activity as quickly and nondisruptively as possible. When it is not possible to use nondisruptive techniques, call the students' names and correct their behavior by telling them what they are supposed to be doing or reminding them of the rules. Such interventions should be brief, direct, and focused on desirable behavior. Questions, threats, and nagging should be avoided.

It is necessary to question students when misbehavior has been serious or disruptive and the teacher is unclear about the facts. Such investigations should be conducted privately so that students will have less reason to engage in face-saving behavior. Teachers should not make decisions until they have heard everyone out. After gathering the facts, teachers should take action aimed at both resolving the present problem and preventing its return. This will mean clarification of expected behavior and perhaps a new rule or agreement. Ordinarily, there will be no need for punishment.

Because punishment is a stopgap measure rather than a solution and because it involves many undesirable side effects, it should be used only as a last resort. When it is used, everyone should understand that punished students brought on the punishment through repeated misbehavior, leaving the teacher no other choice. Appropriate forms of punishment include restriction of privileges, exclusion from the group, and assignments that force students to reflect on the rules and their rationales. Punishment should be related to the offense, as brief and mild as possible, and flexible enough to allow students to redeem themselves by correcting their behavior.

A few students with long-standing and severe disturbances will require extra-ordinary corrective measures. Suggestions for dealing with several common types of disruptive behavior are given in this chapter. Such serious problems require careful observation and diagnosis, followed by individualized treatment.

This chapter and the last have been eclectic, drawing ideas about classroom management from many sources. Readers wanting more information can consult sources that describe methods based on particular points of view, such as contingency contracting, cognitive behavior modification, social skills instruction, or the approaches recommended by Comer, Glasser, or Gordon.

SUGGESTED ACTIVITIES AND QUESTIONS

1. Part of dealing with problems effectively is the ability to recognize and conceptualize problems and potential solution strategies. However, behavior one teacher views as a problem and reacts to quickly and strongly may not seem noteworthy to another teacher. Think about the teaching situation you envision yourself in and identify behaviors that, although relatively minor, you would want to eliminate—behaviors that you would deal with overtly and publicly. How do your perceptions of minor problems correspond with those of your classmates? If you have not student-taught, try to find two or three friends who have done so to see if their lists are different from yours. Would teachers with more experience be more or less likely to react to minor problems? To what extent do you think students would agree with your examples of minor problems that you would not tolerate? Would students be more or less lenient than you would be? Why?

2. Reread the cases presented in Chapter 1, pinpoint any management errors the teacher made, and describe which of the teachers is the best manager. Why? How could even this teacher have behaved more profitably?

3. Reread the four cases that appear at the beginning of this chapter. Analyze each case and indicate ways in which the situation could be improved on.

4. Summarize in seven brief paragraphs the guidelines for dealing with showing off, defiance, aggression, unresponsiveness, failure to complete assignments, attention deficits, and hyperactivity. Practice your ability to deal with these problems in role-playing situations. Specify a hypothetical problem, assign some participants to the student and teacher roles, and allow the rest to observe and provide feedback.

5. Review or construct a list of student behaviors or characteristics that are most likely to embarrass you or to make you anxious. Practice how you will deal with these. For example, if you dislike threats to your authority, list student behaviors likely to anger you and practice how you would respond. Then role-play your response with other participants. For example, how would you respond (or would you respond) in this situation?

TEACHER: You're right, Frank. What I told you yesterday was incorrect.

HERB: (Gleefully bellowing from the back of the room) You're always wrong! We never know when to believe you!

6. Why do the authors not recommend the use of physical punishment?

7. What steps can teachers follow to make exclusion from the group effective punishment? In particular, how should teachers behave when excluding or readmitting students to group activities?

8. A ninth-grade teacher sees Bill Thomas (without apparent provocation) grab Tim Grant's comb and throw it on the floor. Bill and Tim begin to push each other. What should the teacher do? Be specific. Write out or role-play the actual words you would use. Would you behave differently if you had not seen what preceded the pushing?

9. Compare how you responded to the vignettes about contingency contracting on page 196 with the responses of a few classmates.

REFERENCES

Adalbjarnardottir, S. (1994). Understanding children and ourselves: Teachers' reflections on social development in the classroom. *Teaching and Teacher Education, 20,* 409–421.

Anderson, C. (1985). The investigation of school climate. In G. Austin & H. Garber (Eds.), *Research on exemplary schools.* New York: Academic Press.

Bandura, A. (1986). *Social foundations of thought and action: A social cognitive theory.* Englewood Cliffs, NJ: Prentice-Hall.

Bandura, A. (1989). Human agency in social cognitive theory. *American Psychologist, 44,* 1175–1184.

Barkley, R. (1990). *Attention-deficit hyperactivity disorder: A handbook for diagnosis and treatment.* New York: Guilford.

Braswell, L., & Bloomquist, M. (1991). *Cognitive-behavioral therapy with ADHD children: Child, family, and school interventions.* New York: Guilford.

Brophy, J. (1996). *Teaching problem students.* New York: Guilford.

Brophy, J., & Evertson, C. (1978). Context variables in teaching. *Educational Psychologist, 12,* 310–316.

Brophy, J., & McCaslin, M. (1992). Teachers' reports of how they perceive and cope with problem students. *Elementary School Journal, 93,* 3–68.

Byers, G. H. (1994). *Collaborative discipline for at-risk students: A complete step-by-step activities program for grades 7–12.* West Nyack, NY: Center for Applied Research in Education.

Camp, B., & Bash, M. (1981). *Think aloud: Increasing social and cognitive skills—a problem-solving program for children, primary level.* Champaign, IL: Research Press.

Canter, L. (1988). Let the educator beware: A response to Curwin and Mendler. *Educational Leadership, 46*(2), 71–73.

Canter, L., & Canter, M. (1992). *Assertive discipline: Positive behavior management for today's classroom* (2nd ed.). Santa Monica, CA: Lee Canter & Associates.

Cartledge, G. and Milburn J. (1995). *Teaching social skills to children and youth: Innovative approaches* (3rd ed.). New York: Pergamon.

Coie, J., Underwood, M., & Lochman, J. (1991). Programmatic intervention with aggressive children in the school setting. In D. Pepler & K. Rubin (Eds.), *The development and treatment of childhood aggression* (pp. 389–410). Hillsdale, NJ: Erlbaum.

Comer, J. (1980). *School power: Implications of an intervention project.* New York: The Free Press.

Curwin, R., & Mendler, A. (1988). Packaged discipline programs: Let the buyer beware. *Educational Leadership, 46*(2), 68–71.

D'Andrea, V. J. (1983). *Peer counseling: Skills and perspectives.* Palo Alto: Science and Behavior Books.

Douglas, V., Perry, P., Marton, P., & Garson, C. (1976). Assessment of a cognitive training program for hyperactive children. *Journal of Abnormal Child Psychology, 4,* 389–410.

DuPaul, G., & Eckert, T. (1994). The effects of social skills curricula: Now you see them, now you don't. *School Psychology Quarterly, 9,* 113–132.

Durlak, J., Fuhrman, T., & Lampman, C. (1991). Effectiveness of cognitive-behavior therapy for maladapting children: A meta-analysis. *Psychological Bulletin, 110,* 202–214.

Elias, M., & Clabby, J. (1989). *Social decision-making skills: A curriculum guide for the elementary grades.* Rockville, MD: Aspen.

Emmer, E., & Aussiker, A. (1990). School and classroom discipline programs: How well do they work? In O. C. Moles (Ed.), *Student discipline strategies: Research and practice.* Albany: State University of New York Press.

Evertson, C., Emmer, E., Clements, B., & Worsham, M. (1994). *Classroom management for elementary teachers* (3rd ed.). Englewood Cliffs, NJ: Prentice-Hall.

Felmlee, D., Eder, D., & Tsui, W. (1985). Peer influence on classroom attention. *Social Psychology Quarterly, 48,* 215–226.

Fiore, T., Becker, E., & Nero, R. (1993). Educational interventions for students with Attention Deficit Disorder. *Exceptional Children, 60,* 163–173.

Forman, S. (1993). *Coping skills interventions for children and adolescents.* San Francisco: Jossey-Bass.

Freiberg, H. J., Stein, T., & Huang, S. (1995). The effects of a classroom management intervention on student achievement in inner-city elementary schools. *Education Research and Evaluation, 1,* 36–66.

Friedman, R., & Doyal, G. (1992). *Management of children and adolescents with Attention Deficit-Hyperactivity Disorder* (3rd ed.). Austin, TX: Pro-Ed.

Furlong, M., & Smith, D. (Eds.). (1994). *Anger, hostility, and aggression: Assessment, prevention, and intervention strategies for youth.* Brandon, VT: Clinical Psychology Publishing.

Gesten, E., Weissberg, R., Amish, P., & Smith, J. (1987). Social problem-solving training: A skills-based approach to prevention and treatment. In C. Maher & J. Zins (Eds.), *Psychoeducational interventions in the schools* (pp. 26–45). New York: Pergamon.

Glasser, W. (1977). Ten steps to good discipline. *Today's Education, 66,* 61–63.

Glasser, W. (1986). *Control theory in the classroom.* New York: Harper & Row.

Glasser, W. (1990). *The quality school: Managing students without coercion.* New York: Harper & Row.

Goldstein, A. (1988). *The prepare curriculum.* Champaign, IL: Research Press.

Gomez, K., & Cole, C. (1991). Attention Deficit Hyperactivity Disorder: A review of treatment alternatives. *Elementary School Guidance and Counseling, 26,* 106–114.

Gordon, T. (1974). *T.E.T. Teacher effectiveness training.* New York: McKay.

Gottfredson, G., & Gottfredson, D. (1986). *Victimization in six hundred schools: An analysis of the roots of disorder.* New York: Plenum.

Hawkins, D., Doueck, H., & Lishner, D. (1988). Changing teaching practices in mainstream classrooms to improve bonding and behavior of low achievers. *American Educational Research Journal, 25,* 31–50.

Haynes, N., & Comer, J. (1993). The Yale School Development Program: Process, outcomes, and policy implications. *Urban Education, 28,* 166–199.

Hoffman, S. (Ed.). (1991). Educational partnerships: Home and school community. *Elementary School Journal, 91*(3). Special Issue.

Hughes, J. (1988). *Cognitive behavior therapy with children in schools.* Elmsford, NY: Pergamon.

Hyman, I., & Wise, J. (Eds.). (1979). *Corporal punishment in American education: Readings in history, practice and alternatives.* Philadelphia: Temple University Press.

Jones, V. (1988). *A systematic approach for responsibly managing the disruptive and irresponsible behavior of at-risk students.* Paper presented at the annual meeting of the American Educational Research Association, New Orleans.

Jones, V. (1996). Classroom management. In J. Sikula, T. Buttery, & E. Guyton (Eds.), *Handbook of research on teacher education* (2nd ed.,). New York: Macmillan.

Kauffman, J., Hallahan, D., Mostert, M., Trent, S., & Nuttycombe, D. (1993). *Managing classroom behavior: A reflective case approach.* Boston: Allyn & Bacon.

King, C. and Kirschenbaum, D. (1992). *Helping young children develop social skills: The social growth program.* Pacific Grove, CA: Brooks-Cole.

Kirby, E., & Kirby, S. (1994). Classroom discipline with Attention Deficit Hyperactivity Disorder children. *Contemporary Education, 65,* 142–144.

Kounin, J. (1970). *Discipline and group management in classrooms.* New York: Holt, Rinehart and Winston.

Laub, L., & Braswell, L. (1991). Appendix C: Suggestions for classroom teachers of ADHD elementary school students. In L. Braswell & M. Bloomquist (Eds.), *Cognitive behavioral therapy with ADHD children: Child, family, and school interventions* (pp. 349–354). New York: Guilford.

Little, J. (1995). Contested ground: The basis of teacher leadership in two restructuring high schools. *Elementary School Journal, 96,* 47-64.

Macmillan, A., & Kolvin, I., (1977). Behavior modification in teaching strategy: Some emergent problems and suggested solutions. *Educational Researcher, 20,* 10–21.

Matson, J., & Ollendick, T. (1988). *Enhancing children's social skills: Assessment and training.* Oxford: Pergamon.

McCaslin, M., & Good, T. (1992). Compliant cognition: The misalliance of management and instructional goals in current school reform. *Educational Researcher, 21,* 4–17.

McCaslin, M., & Good, T. (1996). *Listening in classrooms.* New York: HarperCollins.

McCormack, S. (1989). Response to Render, Padilla, and Krank: But practitioners say it works! *Educational Leadership, 47*(7), 77–79.

McDaniel, T. (1986). A primer on classroom discipline: Principles old and new. *Phi Delta Kappan, 68,* 63–67.

McDaniel, T. (1989). The discipline debate: A road through the thicket. *Educational Leadership, 47*(7), 81–82.

McGinnis, E., & Goldstein, A. (1984). *Skillstreaming the elementary school child.* Champaign, IL: Research Press.

Meichenbaum, D. (1977). *Cognitive-behavior modification: An integrated approach.* New York: Plenum.

Meichenbaum, D., & Goodman, J. (1971). Training impulsive children to talk to themselves. *Journal of Abnormal Psychology, 77,* 115–126.

Metz, M. (1978). *Classrooms and corridors.* Berkeley: University of California Press.

Morgan, S. R. (1994). *At-risk youth in crises: A team approach in the schools* (2nd ed.). Austin, TX: Pro-Ed.

Mulryan, C. (1992). Student passivity during cooperative small groups in mathematics. *Journal of Educational Research, 85,* 261–273.

Nicholls, D., & Houghton, S. (1995). The effects of Canter's Assertive Discipline Program on teacher and student behavior. *British Journal of Educational Psychology, 65,* 197–210.

Pepler, D., & Rubin, K. (Eds.). (1991). *The development and treatment of childhood aggression.* Hillsdale, NJ: Erlbaum.

Peterson, R., Loveless, S., Knapp, T., Loveless, B., Basta, S., & Anderson, S. (1979). The effects of teacher use of I-messages on student disruptive and study behavior. *Psychological Record, 29,* 187–199.

Render, G., Padilla, J., & Krank, H. (1989). What research really shows about assertive discipline. *Educational Leadership, 47*(7), 72–75.

Robin, A., Schneider, M., & Dolnick, M. (1976). The turtle technique: An extended case study of self-control in the classroom. *Psychology in the Schools, 13,* 449–453.

Rogers, C., & Freiberg, H. J. (1994). *Freedom to learn* (3rd ed.). New York: Merrill.

Rohrkemper, M. (1982). Teacher self-assessment. In D. Duke (Ed.), *Helping teachers manage classrooms.* Alexandria, VA: Association for Supervision and Curriculum Development.

Rosswork, S. (1977). Goal-setting: The effects of an academic task with varying magnitudes of incentive. *Journal of Educational Psychology, 69,* 710–715.

Sabornie, E. (1991). Measuring and teaching social skills in the mainstream. In G. Stoner, M. Shinn, & H. Walker (Eds.), *Interventions for achievement and behavior problems* (pp. 161–177). Silver Spring, MD: National Association of School Psychologists.

Sizer, T. (1992). *Horace's school: Redesigning the American high school.* Boston: Houghton Mifflin.

Swanson, J., et al. (1993). Effect of stimulant medication on children with Attention Deficit Disorder: A "review of reviews." *Exceptional Children, 60,* 154–162.

Thompson, C., & Rudolph, L. (1992). *Counseling children* (3rd ed.). Pacific Grove, CA: Brooks/Cole.

Tindall, J.A. (1995). *Peer programs: An in-depth look at peer helping: Planning, implementation, and administration.* Bristol, PA: Accelerated Development.

Walker, H. (1987). *The ACCESS Program (Adolescent Curriculum for Communication and Effective Social Skills).* Austin, TX: Pro-Ed.

Weinstein, C., & Mignano, A., Jr. (1993). *Elementary classroom management: Lessons from research and practice.* New York: McGraw-Hill.

Weinstein, R., & Middlestadt, S. (1979). Student perceptions of teacher interactions with male high and low achievers. *Journal of Educational Psychology, 71,* 421–431.

Weiss, G., & Hechtman, L. (1986). *Hyperactive children grown up: Empirical findings and theoretical considerations.* New York: Guilford.

Wu, S., Pink, W., Crain, R., & Moles, O. (1982). Student suspension: A critical reappraisal. *Urban Review, 14,* 245–303.

Zaragoza, N., Vaughn, S., & McIntosh, R. (1991). Social skills interventions and children with behavior problems: A review. *Behavioral Disorders, 16,* 260–275.

FORM 5.1. Teacher's Reaction to Inattention and Misbehavior

USE: *When the teacher is faced with problems of inattention or misbehavior.*
PURPOSE: *To see if teacher handles these situations appropriately.*
        Code the following information concerning teacher's response to misbehavior or to inattentiveness. Code only when teacher seems to be aware of the problem; do not code minor problems that teacher doesn't even notice.

BEHAVIOR CATEGORIES   CODES

A. TYPE OF SITUATION   *A*   *B*   *C*
    1. Total class, lesson or discussion   1.   _3_ _3_ _4_
    2. Small group activity—problem in group   2.   _3_ _3_ _4,6_
    3. Small group activity—problem out of group   3.   _1_ _2_ _2_
    4. Seatwork checking or study period   4.   _1_ _3_ _4_
    5. Other (specify)   5.   _4_ _3_ _2_

B. TYPE OF MISBEHAVIOR   6.   ___ ___ ___
    1. Brief, nondisruptive, should be ignored   7.   ___ ___ ___
    2. Minor, but extended or repeated. Should   8.   ___ ___ ___
       be stopped nondisruptively   9.   ___ ___ ___
    3. Disruptive, should be stopped quickly. No   10.   ___ ___ ___
       questions needed
    4. Disruptive, questions needed or advisable   11.   ___ ___ ___
    5. Other (specify)   12.   ___ ___ ___
                                                     13.   ___ ___ ___
C. TEACHER'S RESPONSE(S)   14.   ___ ___ ___
    1. Ignores (deliberately)   15.   ___ ___ ___
    2. Nonverbal; uses eye contact, gestures or
       touch, or moves near offender   16.   ___ ___ ___
    3. Praises someone else's good behavior   17.   ___ ___ ___
    4. Calls offender's name; calls for attention or 18.   ___ ___ ___
       work; gives rule reminder. No overdwelling   19.   ___ ___ ___
    5. Overdwells on misbehavior, nags   20.   ___ ___ ___
    6. Asks rhetorical or meaningless questions
    7. Asks appropriate questions–investigates publicly 21.   ___ ___ ___
    8. Investigates privately, now or later   22.   ___ ___ ___
    9. Threatens punishment if behavior is repeated 23.   ___ ___ ___
    10. Punishes (note type)   24.   ___ ___ ___
    11. Other (specify)   25.   ___ ___ ___

CHECK IF APPLICABLE

_____ 1. Teacher delays too long before acting, so problems escalate
_____ 2. Teacher identifies wrong student or fails to include all involved
_____ 3. Teacher fails to specify appropriate behavior (when this is not
             clear)
_____ 4. Teacher fails to specify rationale behind demands (when this is
             not clear)
_____ 5. Teacher attributes misbehavior to ill will, evil motives
_____ 6. Teacher describes misbehavior as a typical or unchangeable trait;
             labels student

NOTES:
        #1, 2, and 4 were all for student #12 (he seems to be the only consistent problem as far as management goes).

FORM 5.2. Teacher's Response to Problem Students

USE: When the class contains one or more students who present chronic, severe problems in personal adjustment or classroom behavior.
PURPOSE: To inventory the teacher s coping strategies.
Pick a particular student and check the strategies that the teacher uses for coping with this student.

A. GENERAL STRATEGIES

_____ 1. Control undesirable behavior through demands or threats of punishment
_____ 2. Offer incentives or rewards for improved behavior
_____ 3. Provide modeling, training, or other instruction designed to teach the student more effective ways of coping (either in general or in particular situations in which problem behavior is frequent for this student)
_____ 4. Identify and treat underlying causes believed to be responsible for the student's symptomatic behavior (home pressures, self-concept problems, etc.)
_____ 5. Provide counseling designed to increase the student's insight into the problem behavior and its causes or meanings
_____ 6. Attempt to change the student's troublesome attitudes or beliefs through logical appeal or persuasion
_____ 7. Attempt to provide encouragement, reassurance, or support to the student's self-concept through creating a supportive environment
_____ 8. Attempt to develop a close personal relationship with the student
_____ 9. Other (describe)

B. SPECIFIC STRATEGIES

_____ 1. Minimize conflict by intervening as seldom and as indirectly as possible
_____ 2. Use humor or other face-saving or tension reduction techniques when direct intervention is necessary
_____ 3. Maintain close physical proximity or monitor the student's behavior closely
_____ 4. Use time-out procedures to extinguish disruptive behavior by removing the opportunity for the student to misbehave and be reinforced for it
_____ 5. Use time-out procedures to allow the student an opportunity to calm down and reflect after an outburst
_____ 6. Use behavior contracts to formalize offers of reward for improved behavior
_____ 7. Use modeling or role play procedures to help student learn the self talk that controls adaptive responses to frustrating or threatening situations
_____ 8. Adjust work expectations or assignments if these seem inappropriate and appear to be contributing to the problem
_____ 9. Adjust seat assignment, group assignment, or other social environment/peer relationship factors
_____ 10. Attempt to develop peer support for the problem student

Form 5.2 (continued on next page)

FORM 5.2. (Continued)

_____ 11. Attempt to develop peer pressure on the problem student (to stop behaving inappropriately)

_____ 12. Active listening. "I" statements, or attempts to negotiate "no-lose" solutions (Gordon's techniques)

_____ 13. Attempt to get the student to recognize problem behavior, accept responsibility, and commit to a plan for improvement (Glasser's techniques)

_____ 14. Contact with family members

_____ 15. Involvement of mental health professionals

_____ 16. Other (describe)

C. ASSESSMENT

Which of these strategies appear to be helpful, and which do not? Which might be more helpful if they were implemented more often, more systematically, or in a different way? Are there strategies that the teacher doesn't use that might be helpful?

6

Motivation

INTRODUCTION

"You can lead a horse to water, but you can't make it drink." Teachers face the problem summed up in this familiar saying. Appropriate curricula and good teaching are necessary but not sufficient for ensuring that students accomplish instructional goals. If students minimize their investment of attention and effort, they won't learn much. The degree to which they invest attention and effort depends on their *motivation*—their willingness to engage in classroom activities and their reasons for doing so.

Motivation is subjective experience that cannot be observed directly. Instead, it must be inferred from students' self-reports and classroom behavior. For example, Sherry is staring in the direction of the clock. Is she thinking about the assignment or something else? If she is thinking about the assignment, is she focused on the task and thinking productively, or might she be upset because she is "lost"? If she is not thinking about the task, is this because she has completed it successfully, or might she be bored or preoccupied with some personal matter?

Seemingly similar behavior patterns can result from quite different underlying motivational patterns, although the dynamics involved might remain hidden unless teachers get to know their students as individuals. For example, McCaslin (1990) interviewed sixth graders about how they handle the "hard stuff" in mathematics. The following excerpts are from interviews with two girls who both were viewed by their teacher as persistent and effortful in working on assignments. Nevertheless, the girls were quite different in their approach to difficult math problems. Both girls persistently tried to solve the problems, but one did so mostly in order to get the assignment finished so that she could interact with her friends. She made strategic use of fantasies connected with this goal as a way to help her get through the rough spots:

A lot of times I get sick of things so I just want to stop. And I do . . . whenever I'm working and I just get sick of working, I just stop because I can't stand it anymore. I think of things that I like to do. Like in school, I'm going to play with my friends, I think of all the things that are fun that we do, and stuff. But I have to get this done and *right* before I can go to do that.

The other girl was more focused on learning with understanding (not just getting correct answers). Yet, she was less successful in avoiding the frustration and worry that accompanied failure to solve difficult problems easily. Not having developed the ability to use fantasy strategically, she had to distract herself by engaging in alternative activities:

> Well, I think I'm going to get them all wrong. And I kind of feel like I have to get up and walk around and think about it. I feel like I have to stop and work on something else for a little bit. I might get up and work on spelling for a minute 'cause that's pretty easy and I don't have to think about it, 'cause spelling I just know the answers and they're right there. I can't think about the math and what I'm going to do. . . . When I get pretty frustrated, I think to myself "You can't do this," and I start tearing, I start biting my pencil. Then I know I have to get up and do something else. I just get so frustrated with it, I can't think. . . . I start to fiddle with my hands, go like that. I know I have to do something else. 'Cause I really get mad. I don't take a real long (break) time, maybe just 10 minutes. Then I come back to work again. Just to get it out of my mind for a minute.

Students differ dramatically in motivational patterns and in the related strategies that they employ for setting goals, addressing task demands, and making "repairs" when their initial efforts do not succeed. Their motives and coping strategies are affected by what they learn at home, by interaction with peers, and by the expectations that prevail in the classroom and the larger school environment, in addition to what their teacher says and does (Eccles, 1993; Ryan, Connell, & Grolnick, 1992). Even so, teachers need to do what they can to encourage students to engage in activities with the intention of developing the intended knowledge and skills.

In this chapter we focus on conditions that teachers can create and strategies they can use to increase the likelihood that their students will be motivated to learn with understanding. We begin with two brief vignettes depicting teachers starting instruction on the *Declaration of Independence* and the *U.S. Constitution*. Read each vignette and then record your answers to the questions.

Frank Thomas's Class

Teacher Frank Thomas begins the week with the following statement:

> Read Chapter 17 carefully because it is a key chapter; in fact, questions on it will represent about 50 percent of the next unit test. I'm going to ask a lot of questions about the facts in Chapter 17 because it covers an important part of American history. In particular, the *Declaration of Independence* is a key document that you should know "cold." You should also understand the Preamble to the United States *Constitution* and be able to discuss it at length. Let's begin by considering the important facts. First, who was the most important person involved in drafting the *Declaration of Independence?*

Jane Strong's Class

Jane Strong is teaching the same material to similar students. She begins in the following way:

> Before beginning our discussion of important ideas associated with the *Declaration of Independence* and the United States *Constitution* and their roles in American history, I want to raise four questions to provide some structure. Write down these four questions now. Later, I'll give you time to talk about them in small-group discussions: (1) What is protest? (2) Under what circumstances is it appropriate? (3) Think about the rights and privileges that you have in school and the constraints that apply here. If you were going to write a constitution for this school, what are three important points you would include? (4) To what extent do you think that your view of a good government for this school is shared by other students?
>
> We need to consider these questions before we begin formal discussion so that you can see the problems of consensus that the framers of our *Constitution* faced. To what extent do different individuals see government in the same way? Do they have common expectations for services that facilitate their needs and regulations that inhibit their freedom? Tomorrow we are going to draft a constitution for the class.
>
> Toward the end of the week we will consider the *Declaration of Independence* more formally as we attempt to organize our understanding of the document in the following ways: (1) the historical background of its development; (2) the philosophical ideas that influenced its framers; (3) its continuing effects on life in American society.

Questions

Given these brief glimpses into the two classrooms, would you rather have Frank Thomas or Jane Strong as your history teacher? Why? Which teacher's students are likely to be more motivated to learn about the *Declaration of Independence* and the *U.S. Constitution*? To be more concerned about passing the test and getting a good grade? How might the two classes differ in (1) how they would describe the nature and purposes of history classes, (2) how they would approach the content when studying, and (3) what they would learn from the unit?

Skill in Motivating Students

Until motivation began to receive attention from classroom researchers, teachers were forced to rely on advice stemming from questionable theorizing. Much of this advice was based on one or the other of two frequently expressed views that are both incorrect (at least in their extreme form). The first view is that learning should be fun and that motivation problems appear because the teacher somehow has converted an inherently enjoyable activity into drudgery. We believe that students should find academic activities meaningful and worthwhile, but not fun in the same sense that recreational games and pastimes are fun. The second view is that school activities are necessarily boring, unrewarding, and even aversive, so that we must rely on extrinsic rewards and punishments in order to force students to engage in these unpleasant tasks.

Recent theory and research on motivation have led to rejection of both of these extreme views in favor of a more balanced and sophisticated approach that includes a rich range of motivational strategies. We summarize this theory and research here. For more information see Ames (1992a & b); Dweck (1991); Good and Brophy (1995); Heckhausen (1991); McCombs and Pope (1994); Raffini (1993); Spaulding (1992); and Stipek (1993).

BASIC MOTIVATIONAL CONCEPTS

Psychologists traditionally use motivational concepts to account for the initiation, direction, intensity, and persistence of behavior. *Motives* are hypothetical constructs explaining why people are doing what they are doing. Motives are distinguished from related constructs such as *goals* (the immediate objectives of particular sequences of behavior) and *strategies* (the methods used to achieve goals and thus to satisfy or at least respond to motives). For example, a person responds to hunger (motive) by going to a restaurant (strategy) to get food (goal). Motives, goals, and strategies are less easily distinguished in analyses of classroom situations that call for intentional learning of cognitive content, because optimal forms of motivation to learn and optimal strategies for accomplishing the learning tend to occur together (Lehtinen et al., 1995; Meece, Blumenfeld, & Hoyle, 1988; Pintrich & DeGroot, 1990; Schiefele, 1991). We can make conceptual distinctions for purposes of analysis, but it can be difficult to separate motives, goals, and strategies or even to separate motivation from cognition.

Consider the vignettes presented earlier. If the two classes responded solely to what their respective teachers emphasized in introducing the *Declaration of Independence* and *U.S. Constitution,* they would develop contrasting motives, goals, and strategies. Frank Thomas's students would be motivated primarily by a desire to do well on the unit test. Furthermore, given what Frank said about the test, their primary study goal would be to memorize the *Declaration of Independence,* the *Preamble to the U. S. Constitution,* and various facts (names, dates, etc.). Consequently, their study efforts would emphasize rote memorizing strategies (repeating the material until they could regurgitate it "by heart").

In contrast, Jane Strong's students more likely would *want* to learn about the *Declaration of Independence* and the *U.S. Constitution* because they found the information interesting and important, not just because they needed it to pass a test. Given Jane's introduction, they probably would adopt goals and strategies that involve concentrating on the meanings and implications of the material, placing it in historical context, relating it to personal ideas and experiences, and thinking about its applications to the modern world. This is a much more personalized and meaningful way of processing the information than merely committing facts to memory. It involves a broader range of goals and more diverse strategies for accomplishing those goals (posing and answering questions about the material, discussing it with peers, putting oneself in the place of the framers and considering the documents as vehicles constructed to accomplish political purposes rather than merely as text to be learned).

The motives, goals, and strategies that students develop in response to classroom activities depend both on the nature of the activities themselves and on how the teacher presents them. If students are motivated solely by grades or other extrinsic rewards, they are likely to adopt goals and strategies that concentrate on meeting minimum requirements that entitle them to acceptable reward levels. They will do what they must to prepare for tests, then forget most of what they learned. It is better when students find academic activities intrinsically rewarding. However, they still may not learn what their teacher would like them to learn if the basis for their intrinsic motivation is primarily affective (they enjoy the activity) rather than cognitive (they find it interesting, meaningful, or worthwhile to learn what the activity is designed to teach). Consequently, it is important that teachers use strategies designed to *motivate their students to learn* from academic activities—to seek to gain the intended knowledge and skill benefits from these activities and to set goals and use cognitive strategies that will enable them to do so.

MOTIVATION AS EXPECTANCY $\times$ VALUE

Most approaches to motivation fit within *expectancy $\times$ value theory* (Feather, 1982). This theory holds that the effort people are willing to expend on a task is a product of (1) the degree to which they *expect* to be able to perform the task successfully if they apply themselves (and thus to get whatever rewards successful task performance will bring), and (2) the degree to which they *value* those rewards. Effort investment is viewed as the product rather than the sum of the expectancy and value factors because it is assumed that no effort at all will be invested in a task if one factor is missing entirely. People do not invest effort in tasks that do not lead to valued outcomes even if they know that they can perform the tasks successfully, nor do they invest in even highly valued tasks if they believe that they cannot succeed on these tasks no matter how hard they try. Thus, *expectancy $\times$ value theories of motivation imply that teachers need to both help their students appreciate the value of school activities and make sure that the students can achieve success in these activities if they apply reasonable effort.*

The rest of the chapter is organized according to these expectancy $\times$ value theory ideas. We begin with basic preconditions that must be in place if teachers are to be successful in motivating their students, then discuss approaches to motivation that involve establishing and maintaining success *expectations* in students. Next we describe three sets of motivational strategies designed to enhance the subjective *value* that students place on school tasks: extrinsic motivational strategies, intrinsic motivational strategies, and strategies for stimulating motivation to learn.

ESSENTIAL PRECONDITIONS FOR SUCCESSFUL USE OF MOTIVATIONAL STRATEGIES

Supportive Environment

To be motivated to learn, students need both ample opportunities to learn and steady encouragement and support. Such motivation is unlikely to develop in a chaotic atmosphere, so it is important to organize and manage the classroom as an effective learning environment (see Chapters 4 and 5).

Furthermore, because anxious or alienated students are unlikely to develop motivation to learn, it is important that learning occurs within a supportive atmosphere. *The teacher should be a patient, encouraging person who supports students' learning efforts.* Students should feel comfortable taking intellectual risks because they know that they will not be embarrassed or criticized if they make a mistake. The instructional emphasis should be on helping students to achieve mastery rather than on displaying their current abilities to perform, and the evaluation emphasis should be on assessing their progress toward instructional goals rather than on comparing them with one another (Ames, 1992a & b; Anderman & Maehr, 1994; Marshall, 1990; Meece, 1994; Midgley, 1993).

Appropriate Level of Challenge or Difficulty

Activities should be at an appropriate level of difficulty. If tasks are so familiar or easy that they constitute nothing but busywork, and especially if they are so difficult that even persistent students cannot handle them, no strategies for inducing motivation are likely to succeed. *Tasks are of appropriate difficulty when students are clear enough about what to do and how to do it so that they can achieve high levels of success if they persistently employ appropriate strategies.* When students encounter such tasks routinely, they can concentrate on learning without worrying about failure (Blumenfeld, Puro, & Mergendoller, 1992).

Meaningful Learning Objectives

Activities should teach things that are worth learning. Students are not motivated to learn when engaged in pointless or meaningless activities such as the following: continuing to practice skills that they already have mastered thoroughly; memorizing lists for no good reason; looking up and copying definitions of terms that are never used in activities or assignments; reading material that is written in such sketchy, technical, or abstract language as to make it essentially meaningless; and working on tasks assigned merely to fill time rather than to fulfill worthwhile instructional objectives. Where skills must be practiced until they become smooth and automatic, most such practice should be embedded within whole-task application activities rather than confined to isolated practice of part skills. Elementary students should be given opportunities to read for information or pleasure in addition to practicing word attack skills, to solve problems and apply mathematics in addition to practicing number facts and computations, and to write prose or poetry compositions or actual correspondence in addition to practicing spelling and penmanship. Secondary students should learn how and why knowledge was developed in addition to acquiring the knowledge itself and should have opportunities to apply what they are learning to their own lives or to current social, political, or scientific issues.

Moderation and Variation in Strategy Use

Motivational strategies can be overused in two respects. First, the need for such strategies varies with the situation. When content is unfamiliar and its value is not obvious to students, several motivational strategies may be needed. In contrast, little or no special motivational effort may be needed when the activity involves things that students are already eager to learn. Motivational strategies can be counterproductive if they are used when they are not needed or are carried on too long. Second, any particular strategy may lose its effectiveness if used too often or too routinely. Thus, teachers should use a variety of motivational strategies.

With these four preconditions in mind, let us consider the motivational strategies that various writers have suggested.

MOTIVATING BY MAINTAINING SUCCESS EXPECTATIONS

Much of the best-known research on motivation has focused on students' success expectations. Research on *achievement motivation* (Dweck & Elliott, 1983) has established that effort and persistence are greater in individuals who set goals of moderate difficulty (neither too hard nor too easy), seriously commit themselves to pursuing these goals rather than treat them as mere "pie-in-the-sky" hopes, and concentrate on trying to achieve success rather than on trying to avoid failure. Research on *efficacy perceptions* (Bandura, 1989; Bandura & Schunk, 1981) has shown that effort and persistence are greater in individuals who view themselves as competent or efficacious—who believe that they are capable of performing a task successfully and thus earning the rewards that such success will bring. Research on *causal attributions* for performance suggests that effort and persistence are greater in individuals who attribute their performance to internal and controllable causes rather than to external or uncontrollable causes (Weiner, 1992).

These and related approaches suggest that teachers need to encourage their students to develop the following perceptions and attributional inferences concerning their performance at school:

> *Effort-outcome covariation.* Recognition that there is a predictable relationship between the level of effort invested in a task and the level of success or mastery that can be expected (Cooper, 1979).
>
> *Internal locus of control.* Recognition that the potential to control outcomes (the degree of success achieved) lies within themselves rather than in external factors that they cannot control (Stipek & Weisz, 1981; Thomas, 1980).
>
> *Concept of self as origin rather than pawn.* Recognition that they can bring about desired outcomes through their own actions (act as origins) rather than feeling that they are pawns whose fate is determined by factors beyond their control (deCharms, 1976).
>
> *Sense of efficacy/competence.* Confidence that they have the ability (including the specific strategies needed) to succeed on a task if they choose to invest the necessary effort (Bandura, 1989; Schunk, 1991).
>
> *Attribution to internal, controllable causes.* Tendency to attribute successes to a combination of sufficient ability and reasonable effort. Also, tendency to attribute failures to insufficient effort, confusion about what to do, or reliance on inappropriate strategies for trying to do it (but not to lack of ability or to uncontrollable factors such as bad luck) (Weiner, 1992; Whitley & Frieze, 1985).

Incremental concept of ability. Perception of academic ability as potential that is developed continually through learning activities rather than as a fixed capacity that determines and limits what can be accomplished (Dweck & Elliott, 1983).

Several strategies can help students to maintain success expectations and these associated perceptions and attributions. All assume that students are given tasks of appropriate difficulty and receive timely and informative feedback about the correctness of their responses and about the progress they are making toward ultimate goals. Thus, these strategies involve helping students to make and recognize genuine progress rather than misleading them or offering them only empty reassurances.

Programming for Success

The simplest way to ensure that students expect success is to make sure that they achieve it consistently so that they can adjust to each new step without much confusion or frustration. However, two points need to be made about this strategy so that it is not understood as suggesting that teachers should mostly assign underchallenging busywork.

First, we speak here of *success that leads to gradual mastery of appropriately challenging objectives,* not to quick, easy success achieved through "automatic" application of overlearned skills to overly familiar tasks. Students should be paced through the curriculum as briskly as they can progress without undue frustration. Thus, programming for success is a means toward the end of maximizing ultimate achievement, not an end in itself.

Second, keep in mind *the role of the teacher.* Potential levels of success depend not only on the difficulty of the task itself, but also on the degree to which the teacher prepares the students through advance instruction and assists their learning efforts through guidance and feedback. A task that would be too difficult for students left to their own devices might be just right when learned with assistance. In fact, learning theorists believe that instruction should focus on the *zone of proximal development,* which refers to the range of knowledge and skills that students are not yet ready to learn on their own but could learn with help from teachers (see Chapter 10).

Programming for success means continually challenging students within their zones of proximal development, yet making it possible for them to meet these challenges by providing sufficient instruction, guidance, and feedback. It may be necessary to provide extra instruction to slower students, to monitor their progress more closely, and to give them briefer or easier assignments if they cannot handle the regular ones even with extra help. Nevertheless, teachers should continue to expect these students to put forth reasonable effort and progress as far as their abilities allow. Effective teachers do not give up on low achievers or allow them to give up on themselves.

Teaching Goal Setting, Performance Appraisal, and Self-Reinforcement

Students' reactions to their own performance depend not just on the absolute level of success they achieve but also on their perceptions of what this means. Some may not fully appreciate their accomplishments unless helped to identify and use appropriate evaluation standards.

This process begins with *goal setting.* Research indicates that setting goals and making a commitment to trying to reach these goals increase performance (Bandura & Schunk, 1981; Locke & Latham, 1990). Goal setting is especially effective when the goals are (1) *proximal* rather than distal (they refer to a task to be attempted here and now rather than to some ultimate goal for the distant future), (2) *specific* (complete a page of math problems with no more than one error) rather than global (do a good job), and (3) *challenging* (difficult but reachable rather than too easy or too hard). For example, a struggling mathematics student faced with 20 problems of varying difficulty might be asked to adopt the goals of making a serious attempt to solve each problem and persisting until confident that at least 15 of the problems have been solved correctly. This is likely to lead to more persistent and higher quality problem-solving efforts than suggestions such as "Do the best you can," or "Do as many as you can." The latter suggestions are too vague to function as specific challenges toward which students can work as goals.

For a brief assignment, meeting the instructional objective is the appropriate goal. However, perfect performance on more comprehensive assignments or tests is not a realistic goal for many students, and these students may need help in formulating challenging but reachable goals. In the case of a long series of activities that ultimately leads to some distal goal, it is important to establish proximal goals for each activity and make students aware of the linkages between these activities and achievement of the ultimate goal (Bandura & Schunk, 1981; Morgan, 1985).

Goal setting must be accompanied by *goal commitment.* Students must take the goals seriously and commit themselves to trying to reach them. It may be necessary to negotiate goal setting with some students, or at least to provide them with guidance and stimulate them to think about their performance potential. One way is to list potential goals and ask students to commit themselves to a particular subset (and associated levels of effort). Another is performance contracting, in which students formally contract for a certain level of effort or performance in exchange for specified grades or rewards (Tollefson et al., 1984). This method is time consuming and may call more attention to rewards than is desirable, but it does ensure active teacher-student negotiation about goal setting and it formalizes student commitment to goals.

Finally, students may need help in using *appropriate standards for judging levels of success.* In particular, they may need to learn to compare their work with absolute standards or with their own previous performance rather than with the performance of others. Feedback about specific responses must be accurate (errors must be labeled as such if they are to be recognized and corrected), but more general evaluative comments should provide encouragement. The teacher might note levels of success achieved in meeting established goals or describe accomplishments with reference to what is reasonable to expect rather than to absolute perfection. Some students need *specific, detailed feedback* concerning both the strengths and weaknesses of their performance (Butler, 1987; Elawar & Corno, 1985; Krampen, 1987). They may have only a vague appreciation of when and why they have done well or poorly, so that they need not only general evaluative feedback but concepts and language that they can use to describe their performance with precision. This is especially true for compositions, research projects, laboratory experiments, and other complex activities that are evaluated qualitatively. Concerning compositions, for example, teachers can comment on the relevance, accuracy, and completeness of the content; the organization and sequencing of the content into a coherent beginning, middle, and end; the structuring of paragraphs to feature main ideas; the appropriateness of the style and vocabulary; and the mechanics of grammar, spelling, and punctuation.

Zuckerman (1994) found that even first graders can learn to apply individual reference norms and self-evaluation processes when assessing their learning. In this study, students were taught to pay attention to the match between teacher evaluation and self-evaluation. If these two evaluations coincided (regardless of the level of success achieved), a child was praised for accurate self-evaluation. Clear overestimations or underestimations were confronted. Evaluative responses that were not related to objective criteria were treated as opinions (individual points of view that cannot be characterized as either correct or incorrect). Over time, the students became more accurate and evidence-based in assessing their work against objective criteria.

Students who have been working toward specific proximal goals and who have the concepts and language needed to evaluate their performance accurately are in a position to *reinforce themselves* for their successes. Many do this habitually, but others need encouragement to check their work and take credit for their successes (that is, to attribute such successes to the fact that they had the ability and were willing to make the required effort). If necessary, teachers can compare students' current accomplishments with performance samples from earlier times or have them keep portfolios, graphs, or other records to document their progress.

Helping Students Recognize Effort-Outcome Linkages

Modeling   Teachers can model beliefs about effort-outcome linkages when talking to students about the teachers' own learning and when demonstrating tasks by thinking out loud as they work through them. It is especially useful if, when teachers encounter frustration or temporary failure, they model confidence that they will succeed if they persist and search for a better strategy or for some error in their application of the strategies already tried.

Socialization and Feedback   Teachers can also stress effort-outcome linkages when socializing students or giving them feedback. They can explain that curriculum goals and instructional practices have been established to make it possible for students to succeed if they apply themselves. When necessary, teachers can reassure students that persistence (perhaps augmented by extra help) eventually pays off. Some students may need repeated statements of the teacher's confidence in their abilities to do the work or willingness to accept slow progress so long as they consistently put forth reasonable effort.

Extra socialization is needed with low achievers when grades must be assigned according to fixed common standards or comparisons with peers or norms rather than according to degree of effort expended or degree of success achieved in meeting individually prescribed goals. Low achievers may need to be socialized to take satisfaction in receiving Bs or Cs when such grades represent, for them, significant accomplishment. When this is the case, teachers should express to these students (*and* their parents) recognition of the accomplishment and appreciation of the effort it represents.

Portray Effort as Investment Rather Than Risk   Students need to be made aware that learning may take time and involve confusion or mistakes, but that persistence and careful work eventually should yield knowledge or skill mastery. Furthermore, they need to realize that such mastery not only represents success on the task involved but also provides them with knowledge or skills that will make them more capable of handling higher-level tasks in the future. If they give up on a task because of frustration or fear of failure, they cheat themselves out of this growth potential.

Portray Skill Development as Incremental and Domain-Specific   Students need to know that their intellectual abilities are open to improvement rather than fixed and that they possess a great many such abilities rather than just a few. Difficulties in learning usually occur not because students lack ability or do not make an effort but because they lack *experience* with the type of task involved. With patience, persistence, and help from the teacher, students can acquire knowledge and skills specific to the domain that the task represents, and such *domain-specific knowledge and skills* will enable them to succeed on this task and others like it. Difficulty in learning mathematics need not imply difficulty in learning other subjects, and within mathematics, difficulty in learning to graph coordinates need not mean difficulty in learning to solve differential equations or to understand geometric relationships. Even within a particular problem area, students can expect to build up knowledge and skills gradually if they persistently apply themselves, accept teacher help, and do not lose patience or give up whenever success is not achieved easily.

Focus on Mastery   In monitoring performance and giving feedback, teachers should stress the quality of students' task engagement and the degree to which they are making continuous progress toward mastery, not make comparisons with how other students are doing (Ames, 1992a & b; Krampen, 1987; McColskey & Leary, 1985). Errors should be treated as learning opportunities, not test failures, and should lead to additional instruction and practice opportunities. Makeup exams or extra-credit assignments should be used to provide struggling students with opportunities to overcome initial failures through persistent efforts.

Encouraging Effort: An Example

If students appear convinced that they cannot do the work, teachers must pursue a fine line between two extremes. First, they must repeatedly encourage the students and express the belief that they will be able to succeed with continued effort. The students' expressions of inability should not be accepted or even legitimatized indirectly through such comments as "Well, at least try." Students should know that they learn the most by doing as much as they can for as long as they can, and therefore that they should not seek help at the first sign of difficulty. On the other hand, teachers should make it clear that they are available and willing to help if help is really needed (Brophy, 1996). Here is how the situation might be handled appropriately:

STUDENT: I can't do number 4.

TEACHER: What part don't you understand?

STUDENT: I just can't do it, it's too hard!

TEACHER: I know you can do part of it because you've done the first three problems correctly. The fourth one is similar, but just a little harder. You start out the same way, but there's one extra step. Review the first three; then see if you can figure out number 4. I'll come back in a few minutes to see how you're doing.

Compare this with the following inappropriate scenario.

STUDENT: I can't do number 4.

TEACHER: You can't! Why not?

STUDENT: I just can't do it, it's too hard!

TEACHER: Don't say you can't do it—we never say we can't do it. Did you try hard?

STUDENT: Yes, but I can't do it.

TEACHER: You did the first three. Maybe if you work a little longer you could do the fourth. Why don't you do that and see what happens?

In the first example, the teacher communicated positive expectations and provided a specific suggestion about how to proceed, yet did not give the answer or do the work. Also, in providing feedback about performance on the first three problems, this teacher was more specific in noting that the answers were correct and in attributing this success to the student's knowledge and abilities, thus supporting the student's self-efficacy beliefs. In the second example, the teacher communicated halfhearted and somewhat contradictory expectations, leaving the student with no reason to believe that further effort would succeed. Students need to be socialized to recognize and rely on their own capabilities and to respond to frustration with coping strategies rather than withdrawal or dependency.

Remedial Work with Discouraged Students

Some students become discouraged to the point of "failure syndrome" or "learned helplessness." They tend to give up at the first sign of difficulty or frustration and need more intensive and individualized encouragement.

A few of these are bright students who have become accustomed to consistent, easy success that they attribute to high ability (rather than to the combination of ability and effort). When they finally encounter challenges that they cannot meet with ease, they may overreact to their difficulties and conclude that they lack ability for that content or task. Such students need to be helped to see that abilities can be developed, but the process requires active learning efforts rather than mere activation of already available knowledge and skills. Also, the process may take some time and involve some confusion or frustration. These students need to view academic activities as opportunities to learn, not just to display already developed skills.

Teachers may also encounter a few "committed underachievers" who set low goals and resist "accepting responsibility for their successes" because they do not want to be expected to maintain a high level of performance. These students need reassurance that they can attain consistent success with reasonable effort (that is, that it will not take superhuman effort). They also may benefit from counseling designed to show them that their deliberate underachievement is contrary to their own long-run best interests (McIntyre, 1989; Thompson & Rudolph, 1992).

Most students who need remedial work on their expectations are low achievers of limited ability who have become accustomed to failure. These students may benefit from the strategies used in *mastery learning* approaches: Make success likely by giving them tasks that they should be able to handle, provide them with individualized tutoring as needed, and allow them to contract for a particular level of performance and to continue to study, practice, and take tests until that level is achieved (see Chapter 8 for more on mastery learning). By virtually guaranteeing success, this approach builds confidence and increases discouraged students' willingness to take the risks involved in seriously committing themselves to challenging goals (Grabe, 1985).

Discouraged students may also benefit from "attribution retraining" approaches (Craske, 1988; Dweck & Elliott, 1983) in which they are given modeling, socialization, practice, and feedback designed to teach them to (1) concentrate on the task rather than worry about failure; (2) cope with failure by retracing their steps to find their mistake or by trying another approach rather than giving up; and (3) attribute their failures to insufficient effort, lack of information, or reliance on ineffective strategies rather than to lack of ability. Discouraged students are especially likely to benefit from exposure to programs that combine attribution retraining with training in strategies for accomplishing tasks (Van Overwalle, Segebarth, & Goldschstein, 1989), and from exposure to "coping models" who maintain their composure and focus on developing solutions when confronted with failure (as opposed to "success models" who sail through problems without making mistakes) (Borkowski, Weyhing, & Carr, 1988). Thus with discouraged students it is important to model not only initial problem-solving strategies but also *repair strategies*— how to diagnose and make corrections when they discover that they made an error in executing an appropriate strategy or that they were using the wrong strategy in the first place.

Findings from the Classroom Strategy Study (Brophy, 1996) indicated that higher-rated teachers suggested a combination of support, encouragement, and task assistance to shape gradual improvement in failure syndrome students' work habits. They would make it clear that these students were expected to work conscientiously and persistently so as to turn in assignments done completely and correctly. However, these teachers also would reassure failure syndrome students that they would not be given work that they could not do, monitor their progress and provide any needed assistance, and reinforce them by praising their successes, calling attention to their progress, and providing them with opportunities to display their accomplishments publicly. Special treatment would be faded gradually as students gained confidence and began to work more persistently and independently.

These teachers would be more demanding and less willing to make allowances with students who underachieved because they were unmotivated rather than because they believed that the work was too difficult for them. Most recommended performance contracting and related approaches that call for rewarding unmotivated students if they meet imposed or negotiated performance expectations but punishing them if they do not. However, they also spoke of building positive relationships with these students and resocializing their attitudes by helping them to appreciate the connections between schoolwork and their current or future needs or stressing the work's potential for enriching their lives. The research literature supports this general approach, especially if it is extended to include cooperation with the parents in developing and following through on performance contracts (McCall, Evahn, & Kratzer, 1992).

Finally, some students may need extra help because they suffer from severe *test anxiety*. They may learn smoothly in informal, pressure-free situations but become highly anxious and perform considerably below their potential on tests or during any testlike situation in which they are aware of being monitored and evaluated (e.g., public "solo" performance situations in music or physical education classes). Teachers can minimize such problems by

> Avoiding time pressures unless they are truly central to the skill being taught
>
> Stressing the feedback functions rather than the evaluation or grading functions of tests when discussing tests with the students
>
> Portraying tests as opportunities to assess progress rather than as measures of ability
>
> Where appropriate, telling students that some problems are beyond their present achievement level so that they should not be concerned about missing them
>
> Giving pretests to accustom the students to "failure" and to provide baselines for comparison when posttests are administered later
>
> Teaching stress management skills and effective test-taking skills and attitudes
>
> (See Naveh-Benjamin, 1991; Wigfield & Eccles, 1989; Zeidner, 1995).

Concluding Comments About Success Expectations

The expectancy aspects of student motivation depend less on the degree of objective success that students achieve than on how they view their performance: what they see as possible for them to achieve with reasonable effort, whether they define this achievement as success or not, and whether they attribute their performance to controllable factors (effort, choice of strategies) or to uncontrollable factors (fixed general abilities, luck). Therefore, the motivation of all students, even the most extreme cases of learned helplessness, is open to reshaping. Empty reassurances or a few words of encouragement will not do the job, but a combination of appropriately challenging demands, socialization designed to make the students see that success can be achieved with reasonable effort, and coaching in needed cognitive strategies should be effective.

Teachers and students need to learn to view academic frustrations and failures realistically and to respond to them adaptively. As Rohrkemper and Corno (1988) pointed out, not only is some student failure inevitable, but a manageable degree of student failure is desirable. When students are challenged at optimal levels of difficulty, they make mistakes. The important thing is to arrange learning conditions so that the students get useful feedback that will enable them to respond to their mistakes with renewed motivation rather than discouragement.

INDUCING STUDENTS TO VALUE ACADEMIC ACTIVITIES

Following a period of concentration on expectancy issues (Berndt & Miller, 1990), motivation researchers have begun to focus on task value issues. Eccles and Wigfield (1985) suggested that subjective task value has three major components: (1) *attainment value* (the importance of attaining success on the task in order to affirm our self-concept or fulfill our needs for achievement, power, or prestige); (2) *intrinsic or interest value* (the enjoyment that we get from engaging in the task); and (3) *utility value* (the role that engaging in the task may play in advancing our career or helping us to reach other larger goals). We believe that this is a useful classification scheme, although we place more emphasis on the cognitive aspects of student motivation to learn academic content. Thus we include *the pleasure of achieving understanding or skill mastery* under attainment value; *aesthetic appreciation of the content or skill* under intrinsic value; and *awareness of the role of learning in improving the quality of one's life or making one a better person* under utility value.

The expectancy × value model stresses that student motivation is affected not only by expectations and attributions concerning performance (Can I succeed on this task? Why did I achieve the level of success that I did?) but also by attributions concerning the reasons for engaging in the tasks in the first place (What am I trying to accomplish here? What benefits can I expect to obtain from my efforts?). Traditionally, teachers have been advised to supply answers to the latter questions either by offering incentives for good performance (extrinsic motivation approach) or by teaching content and designing activities that students find enjoyable (intrinsic motivation approach). We discuss each of these approaches and then turn to a third approach: stimulating students' motivation to learn.

STRATEGIES FOR SUPPLYING EXTRINSIC MOTIVATION

Extrinsic motivation strategies are in some ways the simplest, most direct, and most adaptable of the methods for dealing with the value aspects of motivation. These strategies do not attempt to increase the value that students place on the task itself, but instead link task performance to delivery of consequences that students do value.

Offer Rewards as Incentives for Good Performance

Rewards are one proven way to motivate students to put forth effort. They have come under attack recently, notably in a popular book claiming that the effectiveness of rewards has been exaggerated and that rewarding students for learning undermines their intrinsic interest in the material (Kohn, 1993). However, undermining of intrinsic motivation is not likely except when students are rewarded merely for participating in activities (as in some programs that "pay" students for reading library books). Rewards are likely to have more desirable effects when they are offered as incentives for striving to reach specified levels of performance (Cameron

& Pierce, 1994; Chance, 1993). Commonly used types include (1) material rewards (money, prizes, trinkets, consumables); (2) activity rewards and special privileges (opportunity to play games, use special equipment, or engage in self-selected activities); (3) grades, awards, and recognition (honor rolls, displaying good papers); (4) praise and social rewards; and (5) teacher rewards (special attention, personalized interaction, opportunities to go places or do things with the teacher).

Rewards are more effective for increasing effort than for improving quality of performance. They guide behavior more effectively when there is a clear goal and a clear strategy to follow than when goals are more ambiguous or when students must discover or invent new strategies rather than merely activate familiar ones. Thus, rewards are better used with routine tasks than with novel ones, better with specific intentional learning tasks than with incidental learning or discovery tasks, and better with tasks where speed of performance or quantity of output is of more concern than creativity, artistry, or craftsmanship. It is better to offer rewards as incentives for meeting performance standards (or performance *improvement* standards) on skills that require a great deal of drill and practice (arithmetic computation, musical scales, typing, spelling) than it is for work on a major research or demonstration project.

Rewards are effective as motivators only for those students who believe that they have a chance to get the rewards if they put forth reasonable effort. Therefore, to create incentives for the whole class and not just the high-ability students, it is necessary to ensure that everyone has equal (or at least reasonable) access to the rewards. This may require performance contracting or some less formal method of individualizing criteria for success.

The comments in Chapter 4 about using rewards and praise to motivate students to conform to classroom expectations also apply to the use of these incentives to motivate students' learning efforts. In particular, it is important to offer and deliver incentives in ways that encourage students to appreciate their developing knowledge and skills rather than just to think about getting rewards. Teachers can do this by following the guidelines in Table 4.1.

Call Attention to the Instrumental Value of Academic Activities

Some knowledge and skills taught in school can be applied immediately in the students' lives or will be needed as "life skills" later. These natural consequences of task mastery are likely to be more effective for motivating learning efforts than arbitrary extrinsic rewards. When possible, teachers should note that the knowledge or skills developed by a task are useful in enabling students to meet their own current needs, in providing them with a "ticket" to social advancement, or in preparing them for occupational or other success in life. Better yet, teachers can cite examples by relating personal experiences or telling anecdotes about individuals with whom the students can identify (famous people they look up to or former students from the same school).

This strategy probably is not employed as often as it could be, and when it is, it is often used in self-defeating ways. Rather than stress the present or future application value of what is being learned, many teachers stress personal embarrassment ("You don't want people to think you are ignorant") or future educational or occupational disasters ("You'll never get through the sixth grade"; "How are you going to get a job if you can't do basic math?"). Other teachers use variations that cast the student in a more positive light but portray society as a hostile environment (urging the students to learn to count so that merchants don't cheat them or to learn to read so that they don't get taken when signing contacts).

We suggest that teachers be more positive in their efforts to help students appreciate specific applications of what they are learning. Basic language arts and mathematics skills are used daily when shopping, banking, driving, reading instructions for using some product, paying bills, carrying on business correspondence, and planning home maintenance projects or family vacations. Scientific knowledge is useful for everything from coping effectively with minor everyday challenges to making good decisions in emergency situations. Knowledge of history and related social studies topics is useful for everything from voting on local issues to determining national policy. In general, a good working knowledge of the information, principles, and skills taught in school prepares people to make well-informed decisions that can save time, trouble, expense, or even lives, and it empowers people by preparing them to recognize and take advantage of the opportunities that society offers. Teachers should help their students to appreciate this and to see academic activities as enabling opportunities to be valued rather than as unwelcome impositions. More generally, they should help their students to appreciate that schools are established by society for their benefit. (We have come to take for granted educational opportunities that are available only to the privileged few in many countries.)

Structure Appropriate Competition

The opportunity to compete can add excitement to classroom activities, whether the competition is for prizes or merely for the satisfaction of winning. Competition may be either individual (students compete against everyone else) or group (students are divided into teams that compete with one another). Traditionally, competitions have been structured around test scores or other performance measures, but it also is possible to build competitive elements into ordinary instruction by including activities such as argumentative essays, debates, or simulation games that involve competition (Keller, 1983).

Several important qualifications concerning competition should be noted, however. First, participating in classroom activities involves risking public failure and a great deal of competition is already built into the grading system. Therefore, it may be counterproductive to introduce additional competitive elements.

Second, competition is even more salient and distracting than rewards for most students, so it is important to depersonalize the competition and to emphasize the content being learned rather than who won or lost. For example, a teacher might divide the class into six teams and require each team to develop a campaign speech based on specified criteria. Next, the teams would use the criteria to rate the speeches produced by the other teams. Then, each team would take the best features from all six of the initial versions and produce an improved speech that represents the class's best thinking. Such a task involves competitive elements, but it focuses on the content rather than the competition.

Third, the qualifications that apply to use of rewards as incentives also apply to competition. In particular, competition is more appropriate for use with routine practice tasks than with tasks calling for discovery or creativity, and it can be effective only if everyone has a good (or at least an equal) chance of winning. To ensure the latter, it is necessary to use team competition in which the teams are balanced by ability profiles or to use individual competition in which a handicapping system enables each student to compete with his or her own previous performance rather than with classmates. Combined approaches that feature both a handicapping system to supply individual criteria for scoring each student's work and an incentive system involving group rewards for winners of competitions between teams provide the most desirable forms of competition—they can be structured so that students cooperate in addition to competing (see Chapter 7).

Finally, a root problem with competition is that it creates losers as well as winners (usually many more losers than winners). Even when there is no rational reason for it, a loser's psychology tends to develop whenever individuals or teams lose competitions. Individuals may suffer at least temporary embarrassment, and those who lose consistently may suffer more permanent losses in confidence, self-concept, and enjoyment of school. Losing team members may devalue one another and scapegoat individuals they hold responsible for the team's loss (Ames, 1984; Johnson & Johnson, 1985).

Concluding Comments About Extrinsic Motivational Strategies

Extrinsic strategies can be effective in certain circumstances, but teachers should not rely on them too heavily. If students are preoccupied with rewards or competition, they may not pay much attention to what they are supposed to be learning or appreciate its value. The quality of task engagement and of ultimate achievement is higher when students perceive themselves to be engaged in a task for their own reasons rather than in order to please an authority figure, obtain a reward, or escape punishment (Deci & Ryan, 1985; Flink et al., 1992; Lepper, 1988). If students perceive themselves as performing a task solely to obtain a reward, they tend to concentrate on meeting minimum standards for performance rather than on doing a high-quality job. As a result, they may write 300-word essays containing exactly 300 words or read only those parts of the text that they need to read in order to answer the questions on an assignment. In view of these dangers, teachers should use extrinsic approaches sparingly, keeping in mind the qualifications just described and the guidelines in Table 4.1.

STRATEGIES FOR CAPITALIZING ON STUDENTS' INTRINSIC MOTIVATION

The intrinsic motivation approach is based on the idea that teachers should emphasize academic tasks that students find inherently interesting and enjoyable so that they engage in these tasks willingly without need for extrinsic incentives. This is an appealing idea, although research on characteristics of tasks that people tend to find intrinsically rewarding suggests that it is difficult for teachers to accomplish in typical classroom settings (Deci & Ryan, 1985; Malone & Lepper, 1987; Ryan & Stiller, 1991).

For one thing, the simplest way to ensure that people value what they are doing is to maximize their free choice and autonomy—let them decide what to do and when and how to do it. However, schools are not recreational settings designed primarily to provide entertainment; they are educational settings that students are required to come to for instruction in a prescribed curriculum. Some opportunities exist for teachers to take advantage of existing intrinsic motivation by allowing students to select activities according to their own interests, but most of the time teachers must require students to engage in activities that they would not have selected on their own.

Also, intrinsically rewarding activities are usually free of pressures or risks (beyond those that people assume voluntarily when they choose to engage in the activities). However, teachers' motivational attempts in the school setting are complicated by the grading system and the public nature of most teacher-student interaction. Anxiety about public embarrassment or low grades is a significant impediment to the learning efforts of many students (Covington, 1992). Even when this is not a problem, students usually want to predict, and if possible control, the relationship between their academic performance and their grades. They may try to avoid tasks that involve ambiguity (about what will be needed to earn high grades) or risk (due to high difficulty or strict grading standards) and to avoid asking questions or seeking to probe deeper into the content because they want to stick with safe, familiar routines (Hughes, Sullivan, & Mosley, 1985). Thus, even if students enjoy particular school activities, their potential for intrinsic motivation may be negated by concerns about embarrassment or failure. Finally, teachers act as authority figures and not just as instructors. They evaluate and grade student performance, and they enforce classroom rules. In the process, they sometimes engender resentment that may interfere with their attempts to motivate.

These considerations underscore the importance of establishing the classroom as a supportive learning environment. To create conditions that protect and encourage the extension of students' existing intrinsic motivation for learning what is taught in school, teachers need to act as inviting and encouraging resource persons and deemphasize their roles as authority figures and evaluators (Deci & Ryan, 1994; Valas & Sovik, 1993). This will position them to take advantage of students' existing intrinsic motivation by selecting or designing classroom activities that contain elements that students are likely to find enjoyable or intrinsically rewarding. No single element will be rewarding to *all* students, but there do appear to be elements that *most* students find rewarding. We describe some of these in the following sections.

Opportunities for Active Response

Students prefer activities that allow them to respond actively—to interact with the teacher or one another, manipulate materials, or do something other than just listen or read. This is one function of drill, recitation, board work, and seatwork activities. However, students also should get opportunities to go beyond the simple question-answer formats seen in typical recitation and seatwork activities in order to do projects, experiments, discussions, role play, simulations, computerized learning activities, educational games, or creative applications. Language arts instruction should include dramatic readings and prose and poetry composition; mathematics instruction should include problem-solving exercises and realistic application opportunities; science instruction should include experiments and other laboratory work; social studies instruction should include debates, research projects, and simulation exercises; and art, music, and physical education instruction should include opportunities to use developing skills in authentic application activities, not just to practice the skills in isolation. Such activities allow students to feel that school learning involves *doing* something.

Inclusion of Higher-Level Objectives and Divergent Questions

Even within traditional lesson formats, teachers can create more active student involvement by going beyond factual questions to stimulate their students to discuss or debate issues, offer opinions about cause-and-effect relationships, speculate about hypothetical situations, or think creatively about problems. Students need to learn basic facts, concepts, and definitions, but a steady diet of lower-level content soon becomes boring. Therefore, there should be frequent activities or parts of activities devoted to higher-level objectives (application, analysis, synthesis, or evaluation of what has been learned at the knowledge and comprehension level).

Students often complain about problems in this area ("We never get to *do* anything"). So do curriculum experts ("Schools were established to promote higher-level objectives—to get students to think about and use what they learn—but you wouldn't know this from visiting classrooms. Most 'discussions' are really just recitations or oral quizzes on basic facts, and seatwork usually means workbooks, dittos, or pages of computation problems"). Yet curriculum developers usually do not provide much help to teachers in this regard. Curriculum packages (including software for computerized learning) seldom include many higher-level questions or activities, let alone systematic plans for structuring thoughtful discussion and engaging application of the content. Part of the problem is that higher-level activities designed to elicit opinions, predictions, suggested courses of action, solutions to problems, or other divergent thinking can be time-consuming to implement and difficult to evaluate. Yet it is important to include such activities, not only for motivational reasons but to ensure that school learning is meaningful and applicable.

The same principles apply to skills instruction. Students need to learn basic skills and often must practice them to the point of smooth, rapid, and "automatic" correct performance. However, most of this practice should be embedded within application opportunities. Students should not be spending most of their time practicing penmanship without getting opportunities to compose essays or other meaningful communications, and they should not continually practice mathematical computations without solving problems or applying what they are learning.

Feedback Features

Students enjoy tasks that allow them not only to respond actively but to get immediate feedback that they can use to guide subsequent responses. Such feedback features are among the reasons for the popularity of computer games and other pastimes featured in arcades (Malone & Lepper, 1987). Automatic feedback features are also built into many educational games and computerized learning systems.

Teachers can provide such feedback themselves when leading the class or a small group through a lesson or when circulating to supervise progress during independent seatwork times. When teachers are less available for immediate response (such as when they are teaching a small group), they still can arrange for students to get feedback by consulting answer keys, following instructions about how to check their work, consulting with an adult volunteer or appointed student helper, or reviewing and discussing the work in pairs or small groups.

Feedback provides immediacy and impact to an activity. Psychologically, most students find it much more difficult and less rewarding to go back and try to relearn something that "we did already" than to respond to immediate feedback when learning something for the first time.

Incorporation of Gamelike Features into Activities

Practice and application activities can be structured to include features typically associated with games or recreational pastimes (Keller, 1983; Lepper & Cordova, 1992; Malone & Lepper, 1987). With a bit of imagination, ordinary seatwork assignments can be transformed into "test-yourself" challenges, puzzles, or brainteasers. Some such activities involve clear goals but require the student to solve problems, avoid traps, or overcome obstacles in order to reach the goals (such as exercises calling for students to suggest possible solutions to science or engineering problems or to find a shortcut that will substitute for a tedious mathematical procedure). Other activities challenge students to "find the problem" by identifying the goal itself in addition to developing a method for reaching the goal (many "explore and discover" activities follow this model). Some gamelike activities involve elements of suspense or hidden information that emerges as the activity is completed (puzzles that convey some message or provide the answer to some question once they are filled in). Other such activities involve a degree of randomness or uncertainty about what the outcome of one's performance is likely to be on any given trial (knowledge games that cover a variety of topics at several difficulty levels and are assigned according to card draws or dice rolls—Trivial Pursuit is an example).

Note that most of these gamelike features involve presenting intellectual challenges appropriate for use with either individuals or cooperative groups. We mention this to call attention to the fact that *gamelike features* has a much broader meaning than *games,* a term that most teachers associate specifically with team *competitions.* The gamelike features described above are likely to be both less distracting from curriculum objectives and more effective in promoting student motivation to learn than are competitive games, especially games that emphasize speed in supplying memorized facts rather than integration or application of knowledge.

Opportunities for Students to Create Finished Products

Industrial psychologists have shown that workers enjoy jobs that allow them to create products that provide tangible evidence of the fruits of their labor. Similarly, students are likely to prefer academic tasks that have meaning or integrity in their own right over tasks that are mere subparts of some larger entity, and to experience a satisfying sense of accomplishment when they finish such tasks. Ideally, task completion will yield a finished product that the students can use or display (a map, diagram, or other illustration; an essay or report; a scale model).

Inclusion of Fantasy or Simulation Elements

If more direct applications are not feasible, teachers can introduce fantasy or imagination elements that will engage students' emotions or allow them to experience events vicariously (Lepper & Hodell, 1989). In studying poems or stories, teachers can encourage their students to debate the authors' motives in writing the work or to learn about formative experiences in the authors' lives. In studying scientific or mathematical principles and methods, teachers can help students to appreciate the practical problems that needed to be solved or the personal motives of the discoverers that led to development of the knowledge or skills being taught. Alternatively, teachers can set up role-play or simulation activities that allow students to identify with real or fictional characters or to deal with academic content in direct, personalized ways. Rather than just assign their students to read history, for example, elementary teachers can make it come alive by arranging for students to role-play Columbus and his crew debating what to do after 30 days at sea, and secondary teachers can do so by arranging for students to take the roles of the American, British, and Russian leaders meeting at Yalta.

Simulation activities need not be confined to full-scale drama, role play, simulation games, and other "major productions." More modest simulation exercises can be incorporated into everyday instruction. In teaching a mathematical procedure, for example, teachers might ask students to name problems in everyday living that the procedure might be useful in solving (and then list these on the board). Secondary social studies teachers might "bring home" material on totalitarian societies by asking students to imagine and talk about what it would be like to seek housing in a country where the government owned all of the property or to get accurate information about world events in a country where the government controlled all the media.

Opportunities for Students to Interact with Peers

Students usually enjoy activities that allow them to interact with peers. Teachers can build peer interaction into whole-class activities such as discussion, debate, role play, or simulation. In addition, they can plan follow-up activities that allow students to work together in pairs or small groups to tutor one another, discuss issues, develop solutions to problems, or work as a team preparing for a competition, participating in a simulation game, or producing some group product (a report, display, etc.).

Peer-interactive activities are likely to be most effective if (1) they are worthwhile learning experiences and not merely occasions for socializing, and (2) every student has a substantive role to play in carrying out the group's mission (see Chapter 7).

An Example: Project-Based Learning

Blumenfeld et al. (1991) described *project-based learning,* a comprehensive approach to classroom teaching and learning that incorporates most of these principles for capitalizing on students' intrinsic motivation. The approach calls for involving students in *projects:* relatively long-term, problem-focused, and meaningful units of instruction that integrate concepts from a number of disciplines or fields of study. Within this framework, students pursue solutions to authentic problems by asking and refining questions, debating ideas, making predictions, designing plans or experiments, collecting and analyzing data, drawing conclusions, communicating their ideas and findings to others, asking new questions, and creating products.

There are two essential components to projects: (1) a question or problem organizes and drives the activities, and (2) the activities result in a series of products that culminates in a final product that represents the students' problem solutions in a form (e.g., a model, report, videotape, or computer program) that can be shared with others and critiqued. Feedback from others permits the learners to reflect on and extend their emergent knowledge and to revise their products if necessary. Motivational elements of project work include: tasks are varied and involve novel elements, problems are authentic and challenging, the work leads to closure in the form of the final product, students exercise choice in deciding what to do and how to do it, and they collaborate with peers in carrying out the work.

These motivational elements do not automatically ensure that students engage in project work by investing the effort necessary to acquire information, generate and test solutions, and evaluate their findings carefully. Projects need to be planned and implemented with attention to the student motivation and knowledge needed to engage in cognitively difficult work. Novel, dramatic, or unique elements should support learning goals and not be distracting "bells and whistles." Projects should be interesting and authentic to the students, not just to subject-matter experts. Students should view the products they create as worthwhile, not just as artificial school exercises, and creating the products should require the students to integrate information and use complex thought. In addition, students need to possess sufficient knowledge of the content and specific skills to explore information pertinent to the problem (skills for using cognitive tools like computers and accompanying software programs, and proficiency in using cognitive and metacognitive skills to generate plans, systematically make and test predictions, interpret evidence in the light of these predictions, and determine solutions). They also need to view errors as natural consequences of attempts to solve problems, so that they can sustain their learning efforts and avoid becoming overly frustrated.

Projects can be developed for any subject, although they are especially well suited to science and social studies. Blumenfeld et al. (1991) suggested ways in which projects can be designed to maximize their motivational impact. They also described some of the ways in which emerging technology is making project-based learning more interesting and challenging (by enabling students to work with computerized databases in conducting their research and to use computerized design, video technology, and other innovations in developing their products). Gardner (1991) proposed a radical restructuring of K–12 schooling in which students would spend most of their time engaged in project-based learning, in and out of classroom settings.

Concluding Comments About Intrinsic Motivational Strategies

Schooling should be as enjoyable as it can be for both teachers and students. Therefore, whenever curriculum objectives can be met through a variety of activities, wise teachers will emphasize activities that students find rewarding and avoid ones that they find boring or aversive. However, there are two important limitations on what can be accomplished through intrinsic motivational strategies.

First, opportunities to use intrinsic motivational strategies in the classroom are limited. Teachers must teach the whole curriculum, not just the parts that appeal to students, and content coverage pressures limit opportunities to use choice, autonomy, gamelike features, etc. Learning often is enjoyable, but it still requires concentration and effort.

Second, although intrinsic motivational strategies should increase students' enjoyment of classroom activities, they do not directly stimulate an intention to accomplish the activities' learning goals. Therefore, even when intrinsic strategies are used, they will need to be supplemented with strategies for stimulating student motivation to learn (described in the next section). Otherwise, students may enjoy classroom activities but fail to derive the intended knowledge or skills from them.

Our colloquial language for discussing intrinsic motivation is misleading. We commonly describe certain topics or tasks as "intrinsically interesting" and speak of engaging in activities "for their own sake." Such language implies that motivation resides in activities rather than in people. In reality, *people generate intrinsic motivation;* it is not somehow built into topics or tasks. We study or do something not for *its* sake but for *our* sake—because it provides enjoyable stimulation or satisfaction. Each of us has a unique motivational system, developed in response to our experiences and to socialization from significant persons in our lives. In the case of motivation to learn academic knowledge and skills, teachers are important "significant persons." Therefore, rather than just accommodating classroom activities to students' existing motivational patterns, teachers can think in terms of *shaping* those patterns through socialization designed to stimulate student motivation to learn.

STRATEGIES FOR STIMULATING STUDENT MOTIVATION TO LEARN

By *motivation to learn,* we mean a student's tendency to find academic activities meaningful and worthwhile and to try to get the intended learning benefits from them. In contrast to intrinsic motivation, which is primarily an affective response to an activity, motivation to learn is primarily a cognitive response involving attempts to make sense of the activity, understand the knowledge it develops and relate it to prior knowledge, and master the skills that it promotes (Brophy, 1983; Brophy & Kher, 1986).

This definition of motivation to learn implies a distinction between learning and performance: *Learning* refers to the information processing, sense making, and advances in comprehension or mastery that occur while one is acquiring knowledge or skill; *performance* refers to the demonstration of such knowledge or skill after it has been acquired. Strategies for stimulating student motivation to learn apply not only to performance (work on tests or assignments) but also to the information-processing activities that are involved in learning content or skills in the first place (attending to lessons, reading for understanding, comprehending instructions, putting things into one's own words). Thus, these strategies emphasize encouraging students to use thoughtful information-processing and skill-building strategies when they are learning. This is quite different from merely offering them incentives for good performance later.

Student motivation to learn can be thought of both as a *general trait* and as a *situation-specific state* (Brophy, 1983; Gottfried, 1985). As a general *trait,* it is an enduring disposition to value learning—to approach the process of learning with effort and thought and to value acquiring knowledge and skill. In specific situations, a *state* of motivation to learn exists when students engage purposefully in an activity by adopting its goal and trying to learn the concepts or master the skills involved. Even students who do not have much motivation to learn as a general trait may display it in specific situations because the teacher has sparked their interest or made them see the importance of the content (Deci et al., 1991).

The learning taught in schools is mostly cognitive learning—abstract concepts and verbally coded information. In order to make good progress in such academic learning, students need to develop and use *generative learning strategies* (Weinstein & Mayer, 1986). That is, they need to process information actively, relate it to their existing knowledge, put it into their own words, make sure that they understand it, and so on. Therefore, motivating students to learn means not only stimulating them to take an interest in and see the value of what they are learning, but also providing them with guidance about how to go about learning it. We recommend the following strategies for teachers who want to stimulate students' motivation to learn the content or skills that instructional activities were designed to develop.

The first three strategies are general ones that describe pervasive features of the learning environment that should be established in every classroom. These strategies help develop student motivation to learn as a general trait. They involve socializing students to understand that the classroom is primarily a place for learning and that acquiring and applying knowledge and skills are important contributors to quality of life (not just to report card grades).

Model Your Own Motivation to Learn

Teachers should routinely model interest in learning throughout all of their interactions with their students. This modeling should encourage the students to value learning as a rewarding, self-actualizing activity that produces personal satisfaction and enriches one's life. Therefore, in addition to teaching what is in the textbooks, teachers should share their interests in current events and items of general knowledge (especially as they relate to aspects of the subject matter being taught). Teachers can call attention to current books, articles, television programs, or movies on the subject and to examples or applications in everyday living, in the local environment, or in current events.

By "modeling," we mean more than just calling students' attention to examples or applications of concepts taught in school. We mean that *teachers should act as models by sharing their thinking about such examples or applications so that the students can* *see how educated people use information and concepts learned in school* to understand and respond to everyday experiences in their lives and to news about current events occurring elsewhere. Without being preachy about it, teachers can relate personal experiences illustrating how language arts knowledge enables them to communicate or express themselves effectively in important life situations, how mathematical or scientific knowledge enables them to solve everyday household-engineering or repair problems, or how social studies knowledge helps them to appreciate things they see in their travels or to understand the significance of events in the news. Through teacher modeling, students should come to see how it is both stimulating and satisfying to understand (or even just to think, wonder, or make predictions about) what is happening in the world around us.

Teachers' modeling of ways of thinking about subjects can affect their students' interest in subjects (Woolfolk, Rosoff, & Hoy, 1990) and self-concepts of ability to learn the subjects (Midgley, Feldlaufer, & Eccles, 1989). Often teachers are unaware of the attitudes they communicate to students. Consider the following dialogue:

MRS. CHEN: We started out with 18 links and divided them into groups of 3; so how many groups are we going to get?

JONATHAN: Six.

MRS. CHEN: Six groups. You're right. We could say 6 groups of 3 make 18, right? Okay, this time, let's say I'm going to take away 1. How many would I have then? Seventeen. I want someone to come up and put these 17 into groups of 2. How many do you end up with?

LYDIA: Eight groups plus 1 left over.

MRS. CHEN: Can't you put it in with one of the others? Well, okay, we counted 8 groups of 2, but what else have we got?

LYDIA: One left over.

MRS. CHEN: One left over. Okay, in math what do we call a leftover?

LYDIA: A remainder.

MRS. CHEN: Right. So this problem is a little more interesting—we have a remainder.

While instructing third graders in division with remainders, this teacher is teaching attitudes about mathematics as well. She presents the concept of remainders in a positive and problem-solving fashion that encourages students to view mathematics with interest and a "can do" attitude. Another teacher might have made the mistake of introducing the new level of complexity with a sense of futility or irritation ("You don't know what to do now, do you?" "This problem has a remainder, so it's more difficult"). If made consistently, such comments might teach students to view division as complicated and frustrating.

One important place for teachers to model curiosity and interest in learning is when responding to students' questions, especially questions that are not covered in the textbook. Questions from the class indicate that students are interested in the topic and thinking actively about it rather than just listening passively. Consequently, teachers should respond in ways that show that such questions are valued. First, acknowledge or praise the question itself: "That's a good question, LaTonya. It does seem strange that the people of Boston would throw the tea into the water, doesn't it?" Then, answer the question or refer it to the class: "How about it, class? Why would they throw the tea in the water instead of taking it home with them?"

If the question is one that no one is prepared to answer, some strategy should be adopted to address it. The teacher might promise to get the answer, or better yet, invite the student who asked the question to go to the library (or another resource) to find the answer and then report back to the class. Teachers also can model curiosity in responding to questions for which they do not have ready answers: "I never thought about that before. Why didn't they take the tea home with them? They must have decided not to steal it but throw it into the water instead. How come?" The teacher could continue in this vein or invite suggestions at this point.

Curiosity and interest in learning can be modeled in information that teachers give about their lives outside of school. Without belaboring the point, they can communicate that they regularly read the newspaper ("I read in the paper that . . . "), watch the news ("Last night on the news they showed . . ."), and participate in various educational and cultural pursuits. Also, they can announce television programs, museum exhibits, or other special events of educational or cultural value. Students should be aware that their teacher thinks carefully about and participates in elections, keeps abreast of current events, and otherwise shows evidence of an active, inquiring mind.

Communicate Desirable Expectations and Attributions

Teachers should routinely project attitudes, beliefs, expectations, and attributions (statements about the reasons for students' behavior) implying that students share the teachers' enthusiasm for learning. To the extent that teachers *treat students as if they already are eager learners,* the students are more likely to become eager learners. Teachers should let their students know that they are expected to be curious, to want to learn with understanding, and to want to apply what they are learning to their everyday lives (Marshall, 1987).

Minimally, this means avoiding suggestions that students will dislike academic activities or work on them only to get good grades. Preferably, it means treating students as active, motivated learners who care about their learning and are trying to learn with understanding (Blumenfeld & Meece, 1988). One teacher we observed communicated positive expectations by announcing at the beginning of the year that she intended to make her students into "social scientists." She referred to this idea frequently throughout the year in comments such as, "Since you are social scientists, you will recognize that the description of this area as a tropical rain forest has implications about what kinds of crops will grow there," or "Thinking as social scientists, what conclusions might we draw from this information?"

Minimize Performance Anxiety

Motivation to learn is likely to develop most fully when students are goal oriented but relaxed enough to be able to concentrate on the task at hand without worrying about whether they can meet performance expectations. Teachers can accomplish this by making clear distinctions between instruction or practice activities designed to promote learning and tests designed to evaluate performance. *Most classroom activities should be structured as learning experiences rather than as tests.*

If instruction or practice activities include testlike events (recitation questions, practice exercises), these should be treated as opportunities for the students to work with and apply the material rather than as opportunities for the teacher to test students' mastery. If teachers expect students to engage in academic activities with motivation to learn (which implies a willingness to take intellectual risks and make mistakes), they will need to protect the students from anxiety or premature concern about performance adequacy.

Eventually, of course, teachers will have to evaluate student performance and assign grades using tests or other assessment devices. Until that point, however, the emphasis should be on teaching and learning rather than on performance evaluation, and students should be encouraged to respond to performance demands in terms of "Let's assess our progress and learn from our mistakes," rather than "Let's see who knows it and who doesn't." If necessary, teachers may also want to make statements such as "We're here to learn, and you can't do that without making mistakes," or to caution students against laughing at the mistakes made by peers.

The three *general strategies* described in the previous sections should be pervasive aspects of the learning environments that teachers establish in their classrooms. If used consistently, they should subtly encourage students to develop motivation to learn as a general personal trait. In particular learning situations, teachers can supplement these general strategies with one or more of the following *specific strategies* for motivating students to learn what an activity is designed to teach.

Project Intensity

Teachers can use timing, nonverbal expressions and gestures, and cueing and other verbal techniques to project a level of intensity that tells students that the material is important and deserves close attention. Often, an intense presentation will begin with a direct statement of the importance of the message ("I am going to show you how to invert fractions—now pay close attention and make sure that you understand these procedures"). Then, the message itself is presented using verbal and nonverbal public speaking techniques that convey intensity and cue attention: a slow-paced, step-by-step presentation during which key words are emphasized; unusual voice modulations or exaggerated gestures that focus attention on key terms or procedural steps; and intense scanning of the group following each step to look for signs of understanding or confusion (and to allow anyone with a question to ask it immediately). In addition to the words being spoken, *everything about the teacher's tone and manner communicates to the students that what is being said is important* and that they should give it full attention and ask questions about anything that they do not understand.

Teachers will have to "pick their spots" for using an intense communication style. They cannot be intense all the time, and even if they could, students would adjust to it so it would lose much of its effectiveness. Therefore, teachers should reserve intensity for the times when they want to communicate "This is important; pay especially close attention." Likely occasions include introduction of important new terms or definitions, especially those that may be confusing to students; demonstration of procedures (such as preparing paint in an art class or serving a volleyball skillfully); modeling problem-solving techniques, including instructions for assignments; and instruction that is intended to eliminate misconceptions (and thus requires making students aware that even though they think they already understand the point at issue, their "knowledge" is incorrect).

Project Enthusiasm

Students take cues from their teachers about how to respond to school activities. If teachers present a topic or assignment with enthusiasm, suggesting that it is interesting, important, or worthwhile, students are likely to adopt this same attitude (Bettencourt et al., 1983).

In suggesting that teachers project enthusiasm we do not mean pep talks or unnecessary theatrics. Instead, we mean that *teachers identify their own reasons for viewing a topic as interesting, meaningful, or important and project these reasons to the students* when teaching about the topic. Teachers can use dramatics or forceful salesmanship if they are comfortable with these techniques, but if not, low-key but sincere statements of the value that they place on a topic or activity will be just as effective (Cabello & Terrell, 1994). Thus, a brief comment showing that the topic is food for thought or illustrating how it is interesting, unique, or different from previously studied topics may be sufficient. The primary objective of projecting enthusiasm is to induce students to value the topic or activity, not to amuse, entertain, or excite them.

We observed a history teacher generate a great deal of interest (and also pull together a great many concepts) by enthusiastically explaining to his students that during the Middle Ages, the Mediterranean was the center of the world. Mediterranean seaports were major trade centers and places like England were outposts of civilization, but this changed drastically with the discovery of the New World and the emergence of new centers of trade and culture. His presentation included references to maps, reminders about the primary modes of transportation at the time, and characterizations of the attitudes of the people and their knowledge about other countries and trade possibilities. He was able to parlay personal interest and detailed knowledge about the topic into an effective presentation that sparked interest and elicited many questions and comments.

Induce Task Interest or Appreciation

Teachers can induce appreciation for a topic or activity by verbalizing reasons why the students should value it (Newby, 1991). They also can mention new or challenging aspects of activities that the students can anticipate. We observed a history teacher motivate students to read about the ancient Greek legal system by noting that it was similar to our own system in many ways but that it called for 501 jurors. A geography teacher motivated his students to study a map of Greece with interest and appreciation by explaining that no place in Greece was more than 40 miles from the sea and that the country's jagged contours gave it far more coastline than most larger countries.

Induce Curiosity or Suspense

Teachers can stimulate curiosity or suspense by posing questions or doing "setups" that make students feel the need to resolve some ambiguity or obtain more information about a topic. To prepare their students to read material on Russia, for example, teachers could ask the students if they knew how many time zones there are in Russia or how the United States acquired Alaska. Such questions help transform "just another reading assignment" into an interesting learning experience and make new information food for thought rather than merely more material to be memorized. It is mind-boggling for most students to discover that one country encompasses 11 time zones or that the United States purchased Alaska from Russia. These are just two basic facts found in most treatments of the history or geography of Russia. Whether students will find them (or a great many others that could have been mentioned) interesting and will think about them rather than merely attempt to memorize them will depend largely on the degree to which their teachers stimulate curiosity about them and provide a context for thinking about their associations with existing knowledge or beliefs. This is another illustration of points made earlier: Interest resides in people rather than in topics or activities, and motivation that develops in particular situations does so as a result of interactions among persons, tasks, and the larger environmental context.

Teachers can encourage their students to generate such interest by (1) asking them to speculate or make predictions about what they will be learning; (2) raising questions that successful completion of the activity will enable them to answer; and (3) where relevant, showing them that their existing knowledge is not sufficient to enable them to accomplish some valued objective, is inconsistent with the new information, or is currently scattered but can be organized around certain powerful ideas (Malone & Lepper, 1987). More generally, teachers can put their students into an active information-processing or problem-solving mode by posing interesting questions or problems that the activity will address (Keller, 1983).

Make Abstract Content More Personal, Concrete, or Familiar

Definitions, principles, and other abstract information may have little meaning for students unless made more concrete. One way to accomplish this is to relate experiences or anecdotes illustrating how the content applies to the lives of individuals. We observed a history teacher read aloud a brief selection about Spartacus in order to personalize students' learning about slavery in ancient times. When covering the Crusades, this teacher gave particular emphasis to the Children's Crusade, noting that the children involved were "your age and younger" and that most of them died before the Crusade ultimately ended in failure. He also made poignant connections to contemporary Iran, where religion-based zeal led preadolescents to volunteer to go to war. Another teacher brought the medieval guilds alive for her students by describing them in detail and soliciting the students' reactions to the fact that if they had lived during the Middle Ages, to become a journeyman they would have had to leave their homes as children and spend seven years apprenticed to a master craftsman.

Teachers can make abstractions concrete by showing objects or pictures or by conducting demonstrations. They also can help students to relate new or strange content to their existing knowledge by using examples or analogies that refer to familiar concepts, objects, or events. We have observed teachers make the following connections: (1) the Nile River flooding and its effects on Egyptian customs compared to the spring flooding in Michigan rivers and its effects on local customs; (2) the Washington Monument as a modern example of an obelisk; (3) three times the size of the Pontiac Silverdome as an example of the size of the largest Roman circus colosseums; (4) identification of students in the class (or failing that, famous personalities) descended from the ancient peoples or the geographical areas being studied; (5) linking of students' family names to the guilds (Smith, Tanner, Miller, Baker); (6) similarities in climate and potential for flower raising and dairy farming as reasons why the Dutch were drawn to the Holland, Michigan, area; (7) similarities in the customs associated with the Roman Saturn Festival compared to those associated with modern Christmas festivities; and (8) explanation of how the medieval social and political systems worked by describing the local (rural central Michigan) area as part of the outlying lands surrounding a manor based in Lansing, which in turn would be under the protection of and would pay taxes to "the King of Detroit."

Finally, teachers may need to adapt their curriculum to make sure that it features gender equity and suitable adaptation to the ethnic and cultural backgrounds of their students. Even when content is selected and taught effectively in other respects, certain students may feel excluded and lose interest if they come to believe that a school subject is about "them" rather than "us" (Alton-Lee, Nuthall, & Patrick, 1993). Consequently, treatment of history should include sufficient attention to social history, women's roles, and the lives of everyday people along with political and military events, and should include multiple perspectives on their meanings and implications. Similarly, study of literature, biography, and contributions to society and culture should include sufficient attention to contributions by women and members of minority groups, especially groups represented in the class. Research assignments connected with this content should include opportunities for students to choose biographical subjects, literature selections, or historical events on which to focus. In this way, students who wish to do so can pursue their interests in content with which they identify in part because of its relevance to gender or cultural identity issues that are important to them.

Induce Dissonance or Cognitive Conflict

If the topic of a text is already familiar, students may think that they already know all about it and thus may read the material with little attention or thought. Teachers can counter this tendency by pointing out unexpected, incongruous, or paradoxical aspects of the content; by calling attention to unusual or exotic elements; by noting exceptions to general rules; or by challenging students to solve the "mystery" that underlies a paradox.

One teacher introduced a unit on the Middle Ages by telling students that they would learn about "our ancestors" who chose to remain illiterate and ignorant and who persecuted people who did not share their religion. Later he contrasted the Moslem advances in mathematics, medicine, and the construction of libraries with the illiteracy of most Christian kings and lords during the Middle Ages. Another teacher stimulated curiosity about the Persian Empire by noting that Darius was popular with the people he conquered and asking students to anticipate reasons why this might be so. Another introduced a selection on the Trojan War by telling the students that they would read about "how just one horse enabled the Greeks to win a major battle against the Trojans."

The school curriculum includes a great many "strange but true" phenomena, especially in mathematics and science. By calling attention to such phenomena, teachers can get their students to begin asking themselves "How can that be?" Otherwise, students may treat new material as just more information to be absorbed without giving it much thought or even noticing that it seems to contradict previously learned information.

Induce Students to Generate Their Own Motivation to Learn

Teachers can induce students to generate their own motivation to learn by asking them to think about topics or activities in relation to their own interests and preconceptions. For example, they can ask the students to identify questions about the topic that they would like to get answered or to note things that they find to be surprising as they read. One way to accomplish this is through the K-W-L technique (Ogle, 1986). Developed originally as a way to facilitate reading comprehension, K-W-L promotes learning by helping students to retrieve relevant background knowledge and learn with awareness of purpose and accomplishment. Students complete the K-W-L exercise in two steps. As they are about to begin study of a topic, they write down what they already *K*now (or think they know) about the topic and what they *W*ant to learn about it (alternatively, this can be done as a teacher-led group activity, in which students' responses are listed on the board or the overhead projector). During study of the topic, the teacher follows up by addressing any misconceptions that emerged and by providing answers (or arranging for the students themselves to get answers) to the questions they raised. As a culmination to the study of the topic, the students describe what they *L*earned about it. They may wish to change some of the statements they made earlier, if they have discovered that some of what they thought they knew was incorrect.

State Learning Objectives and Provide Advance Organizers

Instructional theorists have shown that learners retain more information when their learning is goal directed and structured around key concepts. They commonly advise teachers to introduce activities by stating learning objectives and by providing advance organizers characterizing what will be learned in general terms that enable the learners to know what to expect and help them prepare to learn efficiently. This is good advice for motivational reasons as well (Lane, Newman, & Bull, 1988; Marshall, 1987). Learning objectives and advance organizers call students' attention to the benefits that they should receive from engaging in a task, and this helps them establish a learning set to use in guiding their responses.

Provide Informative Feedback

Feedback is another factor that is important from a motivational as well as a purely instructional point of view. If students are to function as self-regulated learners, they will need opportunities to assess their progress. As soon as possible after being exposed to information through reading or teacher presentation, students should be given questions or assignments that will require them to restate the information in their own words; to show that they can apply it successfully; or to summarize, integrate, or evaluate what they have learned.

Model Task-Related Thinking and Problem Solving

The information-processing and problem-solving strategies needed for thinking about particular content or responding to particular tasks will be unknown to many students unless teachers make them overt and observable by modeling them. This includes artistic, athletic, and musical performances as well as academic activities. Therefore, teachers should model the processes involved by showing students what to do and thinking out loud as they demonstrate. Such modeling should include the thinking that goes into selecting the general approach to use, deciding on what options to take at choice points that arise during the process, checking on progress as one goes along, and making certain that one is on the right track. It also should include recovery from false starts and from use of inappropriate strategies, so that students can see how one develops a successful strategy even when one was not sure about what to do at first (Schunk & Hanson, 1985).

This kind of cognitive modeling is powerful not just as an instructional device but as a way to *show students what it means to approach a task with motivation to learn.* That is, it allows the teacher to model the beliefs and attitudes that are associated with such motivation (patience, confidence, persistence in seeking solutions through information processing and rational decision making, benefiting from the information supplied by mistakes rather than giving up in frustration, concentrating on the task and how to respond to it rather than focusing on oneself and worrying about one's limitations).

Induce Metacognitive Awareness of Learning Strategies

When motivated to learn, students do not merely let information "wash over them" and hope that some of it will stick. Instead, they process the information actively by concentrating their attention, making sure that they understand, integrating new information with existing knowledge, and encoding and storing this information in a form that will allow them to remember it and use it later. Many students will need instruction in cognitive and metacognitive skills for learning and studying effectively. Therefore, teachers should train their students to be aware of their goals during task engagement, to monitor the strategies they use in pursuing these goals, to note the effects of these strategies as they are employed, and to monitor subjective responses to these unfolding events (Pressley & Beard El-Dinary, 1993).

Actively Preparing to Learn   Teachers can train their students to prepare to learn actively by mobilizing their resources and approaching tasks in thoughtful ways:

getting ready to concentrate, previewing tasks by noting their nature and objectives, and developing plans before trying to respond to complex tasks.

Committing Material to Memory   If material must be memorized, teachers can help by teaching their students techniques for memorizing efficiently. Such techniques include active rehearsal; repeating, copying, or underlining key words; making notes; or using imagery or other mnemonic strategies.

Encoding or Elaborating on the Information Presented   Usually it is not appropriate (or even possible) to expect students to rely on rote memory to retain information verbatim. More typically, students must retain the gist of the information and be able to apply it later. It helps if they learn strategies for identifying and retaining the gist: paraphrasing and summarizing the information to put it into their own words, relating it to what they already know, and assessing their understanding by asking themselves questions.

Organizing and Structuring the Content   Students also need to learn to structure extensive content by dividing it into sequences or clusters. Teachers can train their students to note the main ideas of paragraphs, outline the material, and notice and use the structuring devices that have been built into it. Students will also benefit from instruction in effective note-taking (Devine, 1987; Kiewra et al., 1991).

Monitoring Comprehension   In giving instructions for assignments, teachers can remind their students to remain aware of the instructional objectives, the strategies that they use to pursue these objectives, and the corrective efforts they undertake if the strategies have not been effective. They also can teach strategies for coping with confusion or mistakes: backing up and rereading, looking up definitions, identifying previous places in the text where the confusing point is discussed, searching the recent progression of topics for information that has been missed or misunderstood, retracing steps to see whether the strategy has been applied correctly, and generating possible alternative strategies.

Maintaining Appropriate Affect   Finally, teachers can model and instruct their students in ways of approaching academic activities with desirable affect (relaxed but alert and prepared to concentrate, ready to enjoy or at least take satisfaction in engaging in the task) and ways of avoiding undesirable affect (anger, anxiety, etc.).

Such instruction should include modeling of self-reinforcement for success and of coping skills for responding to frustration or failure (reassuring self-talk, refocusing of attention on the task at hand, using strategies listed at the end of the previous paragraph).

BUILDING MOTIVATION INTO THE SCHOOL ENVIRONMENT

Researchers studying motivation in education have begun to develop programs that integrate various motivational strategies and connect them with strategies for accomplishing related goals such as establishing productive school-wide learning environments and helping students to assume more responsibility for managing their own learning.

An example is the TARGET program for managing classrooms in ways that promote student motivation to learn (Ames, 1992a). The TARGET acronym stands for the program's six major facets: task, authority, recognition, grouping, evaluation, and time. Teachers learn to manage these facets in ways that encourage students to engage in activities with a focus on task mastery rather than on their public performance and how it reflects on their abilities. *Tasks* are selected to provide an optimal level of challenge and to emphasize activities that students find interesting. *Authority* is shared with students and exercised with consideration of their needs and feelings. *Recognition* is provided to all students who make noteworthy progress, not just the highest achievers. *Grouping* is managed in ways that promote cooperative learning and minimize interpersonal competition and social comparison. *Evaluation* is accomplished using multiple criteria and methods, focusing on individualized assessment of progress rather than comparisons of individuals or groups. Finally, *time* is used in creative ways that ease the constraints of rigid scheduling and allow for more use of activities that are hard to fit into 45- to 60-minute periods.

Maehr and Midgley (1991) have extended Ames's TARGET model from the classroom level to the school level, reasoning that the motivational efforts of individual teachers will have much more powerful cumulative effects on students if they reinforce one another and if the environment in the school as a whole supports students' motivation to learn. Key principles of their approach are summarized in Table 6.1. They represent ways in which motivational principles can be integrated with classroom management principles and applied at the school level in addition to the classroom level (Midgley, 1993).

BUILDING MOTIVATIONAL STRATEGIES INTO INSTRUCTIONAL PLANS

Teachers who are planning courses from scratch can apply these strategies for motivating students to learn by building them directly into their plans. Teachers who are already working with given curricula and materials can use the strategies by adjusting their instructional plans as needed.

For All Activities

The following questions should be considered in planning for any academic activity. First, what are its *goals*? Why will the students be learning this information or skill? When and how might they use it after they learn it? Answers to these questions suggest information that should be conveyed when introducing the activity to the students.

Before getting into the activity itself, is there a way to characterize it using familiar, general terms that indicate its nature and provide students with organizing concepts? If so, such advance organizers should be communicated to the students.

What elements of the activity could be focused on to create interest, identify practical applications, or create curiosity, suspense, or dissonance? Does the activity include information that the students are likely to find interesting, or build skills that they are eager to develop? Does it contain unusual or surprising information? Can the content be related to current events or events in the students' lives? Is there information that the students are likely to find surprising or difficult to believe? Are there ways to stimulate curiosity or create suspense by posing interesting questions?

Table 6.1   GENERAL FRAMEWORK EMPLOYED IN DEVELOPMENT OF A SCHOOL-WIDE STRESS ON TASK GOALS IN LEARNING

TARGET Area	Focus	Goals	Strategies
Task	Intrinsic value of learning	Reduce the reliance on extrinsic incentives Design programs that challenge all students Stress goals and purposes in learning Stress the fun of learning	Encourage programs that take advantage of students' backgrounds and experience Avoid payment (monetary or other) for attendance, grades, or achievement Foster programs that stress goal setting and self-regulation/management Foster programs that make use of school learning in a variety of nonschool settings (e.g., internships, field experiences, and cocurricular activities)
Authority	Student participation in learning/school decisions	Provide opportunities to develop responsibility, independence, and leadership skills Develop skills in self-regulation	Give optimal choice in instructional settings Foster participation in cocurricular and extracurricular settings Foster opportunities to learn metacognitive strategies for self-regulation
Recognition	The nature and use of recognition and reward in the school setting	Provide opportunities for all students to be recognized Recognize progress in goal attainment Recognize efforts in a broad array of learning activities	Foster "personal best" awards Foster policy in which all students and their achievements can be recognized Recognize and publicize a wide range of school-related activities for students
Grouping	Student interaction, social skills, and values	Build an environment of acceptance and appreciation of all students Broaden range of social interaction, particularly of at-risk students Enhance social skill development Encourage humane values Build an environment in which all can see themselves as capable of making significant contributions	Provide opportunities for group learning, problem solving, and decision making Allow time and opportunity for peer interaction to occur Foster the development of subgroups (teams, schools within schools, etc.) within which significant interaction can occur Encourage multiple group membership to increase range of peer interaction

(continued)

Table 6.1 GENERAL FRAMEWORK EMPLOYED IN DEVELOPMENT OF A SCHOOL-WIDE STRESS ON TASK GOALS IN LEARNING *(continued)*

TARGET Area	Focus	Goals	Strategies
Evaluation	The nature and use of evaluation and assessment procedures	Increase students' sense of competence and self-efficacy Increase students' awareness of progress in developing skills and understanding Increase students' appreciation of their unique set of talents Increase students' acceptance of failure as a natural part of learning and life	Reduce emphasis on social comparisons of achievement by minimizing public reference to normative evaluation standards (e.g., grades and test scores) Establish policies and procedures which give students opportunities to improve their performance (e.g., study skills and classes) Create opportunities for students to assess progress toward goals they have set
Time	The management of time to carry out plans and reach goals	Improve rate of work completion Improve skills in planning and organization Improve self-management ability Allow the learning task and student needs to dictate scheduling	Provide experience in personal goal setting and in monitoring progress in carrying out plans for goal achievement Foster opportunities to develop time-management skills Allow students to progress at their own rate whenever possible Encourage flexibility in the scheduling of learning experiences

Source: Maehr, M., & Midgley, C. (1991). Enhancing student motivation: A schoolwide approach. *Educational Psychologist, 26,* 399–427.

For Listening and Reading Activities

Teachers might consider the following questions when planning activities that require students to attend to an oral presentation, watch a visual presentation, or learn by reading. First, what aspects of the content are interesting, noteworthy, or important, and why? Answers to these questions will help teachers identify reasons for enthusiasm about the topic, and these reasons should be communicated to the students.

Can personal experiences be related or artifacts be displayed in relation to the content? Are there content-related anecdotes about the experiences of others or about how the knowledge was discovered that could add spice to the presentation? Will the lesson contain sufficient variety in the cognitive levels of information communicated and the types of responses demanded? If it appears that there will be too much uninterrupted lecture or reading, the teacher can plan to ask questions, initiate a discussion, or allow time for students to take notes or do a brief assignment.

How should the students respond to the presentation or text? Should they take notes or underline key ideas? Keep particular issues or questions in mind as they listen or read? Outline the material or respond to a study guide? Identify organizational structures embedded in the material? If students are to do something more specific than just pay attention, teachers should tell them what to do, and if necessary, help by supplying questions, outlines, study guides, or information about how the material is organized.

Is there some key point that the students might easily miss if not forewarned? Are there abstractions that will not be meaningful without additional explanation or concrete examples? Are there concepts that may be troublesome because they are subtle or difficult, because they are not well explained in the text, or because they conflict with the students' experiences? If so, teachers may want to call attention to these trouble spots to prepare students for viewing or reading.

For Activities Requiring Active Response

Teachers might consider the following questions when planning activities that require students to do something more than just listen or read (answer questions, prepare a report, work on a project, etc.). Is the activity presented as an opportunity to apply knowledge or develop skills rather than as a test (unless it *is* a test)? When and how might the students be encouraged to ask questions or seek help?

Does the activity demand new or complex responses that should be modeled? If so, what steps should be modeled at what level of detail? Are there important hypothesis-testing strategies (considering alternatives at a choice point and then selecting the correct one after reasoning or brief experimentation) or troubleshooting or repair strategies (responding to confusion or errors with diagnosis of the problem or generation of alternative strategies) that should be modeled?

When, how, and from whom will the students get feedback on their performance? What should they do if they do not understand a question or are not sure about how to begin a response? What should they do when they think they are finished? How might they be encouraged to check their work, to generate and respond to their own questions about it, or to engage in follow-up discourse with peers?

SUMMARY

The effort that students are likely to invest in an academic task will be determined by how much they value the rewards associated with completing it successfully and the degree to which they expect to be able to succeed on the task and thus reap the rewards. A complete motivational program will attend to both the expectancy aspects and the value aspects of student motivation.

The following four essential preconditions set the stage for use of recommended motivational strategies: (1) The teacher organizes and manages the classroom as an efficient learning environment and creates an atmosphere that supports students' learning efforts, (2) students are given tasks of appropriate difficulty, (3) activities have been selected with worthwhile academic objectives in mind, and (4) the teacher shows moderation and variation in using motivational strategies.

Four sets of motivational strategies were reviewed in the chapter. *The first set is designed to motivate by maintaining students' success expectations and related perceptions and beliefs* (perception of covariation between effort and outcome, internal locus of control, concept of self as origin rather than pawn, sense of efficacy or competence, attribution of outcomes to internal and controllable causes, incremental concept of ability). The most basic strategy is programming for success by assigning tasks on which students can succeed if they apply reasonable effort and by instructing them thoroughly so that they know what to do and how to do it. Other strategies include helping students to set appropriate (proximal, specific, challenging) goals, to commit themselves to these goals, to use appropriate standards for appraising their levels of success, and to reinforce themselves for the success that they do achieve; helping students to recognize the linkages between effort and outcome through modeling, socialization, and feedback; portraying effort as an investment rather than a risk; portraying skill development as incremental and domain specific; focusing on mastery; and doing remedial work with discouraged students.

The other three sets of strategies address the *value aspects* of student motivation. *Extrinsic motivation strategies* do not attempt to increase the value that students place on academic activities themselves but instead link task performance to delivery of consequences that the students do value. They include offering rewards as incentives for good performance, calling attention to the instrumental value of academic activities (their potential for developing "life skills" or providing "tickets" to social advancement), and using individual or team competition to enhance interest in an activity. Teachers who use rewards or competition should keep in mind the undesirable side effects that these approaches can have (undermining intrinsic motivation to engage in academic activities, distracting attention from the academic goals that the activities were intended to accomplish). In this regard, the comments made about use of rewards in Chapter 4 and the guidelines summarized in Table 4.1 should be kept in mind.

The next set of motivational strategies calls for *taking advantage of students' existing intrinsic motivation* by designing or selecting activities containing elements that students enjoy: opportunities to respond more actively than by merely listening or reading; opportunities to pursue higher-level objectives and respond to divergent questions that call for creative or challenging application of the content (rather than just memorizing facts or practicing basic skills); tasks that provide immediate feedback to students' responses and thus allow them to experiment and improve with practice; activities that include gamelike features such as "test-yourself" challenges, puzzles, or brain teasers; activities that allow students to create a finished product; activities that include fantasy or simulation elements; and activities that provide opportunities to interact with peers. Opportunities to use intrinsic motivational strategies are limited by the teacher's responsibility to teach the established curriculum within time constraints. Even when such strategies can be used, they merely increase the likelihood that students will enjoy an activity; they do not directly stimulate the students' motivation to learn what the activity was designed to teach.

To accomplish the latter goal, *strategies for stimulating student motivation to learn* are needed. Viewed either as a general personal trait or as a situation-specific state, motivation to learn is a tendency to find learning activities meaningful and worthwhile and to try to get the intended academic benefits from them. The concept emphasizes learning (acquiring information or skills in the first place) and not merely performing (activating the knowledge or skills later in an attempt to meet performance standards), and it carries cognitive implications (goal-oriented information processing, sense making, and use of generative learning strategies) in addition to more purely motivational implications. Three general strategies describe pervasive features of the classroom learning environment that support development of student motivation to learn as a general trait: modeling the thinking and actions associated with motivation to learn, communicating expectations and attributions implying motivation to learn in the students, and creating a supportive environment for learning.

Other strategies for inducing student motivation to learn are more situation-specific and would be included in the planning for particular academic activities: projecting intensity that communicates the importance of an activity; projecting enthusiasm for the topic; inducing task interest or appreciation by pointing out aspects that the students should find interesting or important; inducing curiosity or suspense by raising interesting questions that the students will get a chance to answer in the process of carrying out the activity; elaborating on vague or abstract content to make it more personal, concrete, or familiar; inducing dissonance or cognitive conflict by mentioning strange but true aspects of the content; inducing students to generate their own motivation to learn by identifying their own interests and the questions that they would like to get answers to; stating learning objectives and providing advance organizers; providing informative feedback to students' responses; modeling the information-processing and problem-solving strategies that would be used when approaching the activity with motivation to learn; and inducing students' metacognitive awareness of their own learning efforts by teaching them strategies for actively preparing to learn, committing material to memory, encoding or elaborating on the information presented, organizing and structuring the content, monitoring their comprehension or mastery, and maintaining appropriate affect.

The chapter concludes with suggestions on ways that teachers can build these motivational strategies into their instructional plans by asking themselves questions about the content or skills involved in an academic activity and then using the answers to these questions as guidelines for planning motivational elements.

SUGGESTED ACTIVITIES AND QUESTIONS

1. What does it mean to say that a student "is motivated" or "has no motivation?" What evidence would lead you to make such judgments? How does your answer to these questions compare with those of your peers?
2. Think back to when you were a student similar (in grade level, subject matter, etc.) to the students you plan to teach. What were your *favorite* learning activi-

ties? What were your *most valuable* learning experiences? Compare your answers with those of peers who plan to teach similar students. What do your answers imply about effective motivation strategies?

3. How does motivation to learn differ from intrinsic motivation to engage in classroom activities?

4. To what extent do you think it necessary or advisable to use extrinsic motivation approaches (rewards, competition) in the classroom? If you intend to use extrinsic approaches, how do you plan to minimize their undesirable side effects?

5. As a person who chose to go into teaching, you probably were a well-adjusted student who felt comfortable in classrooms and enjoyed academic activities. Yet, teachers have to cope with students who have histories of failure and find schooling to be boring or aversive. How will you cope with such students? With a friend or colleague, role-play your interaction with a student who is alienated to the point of persistent inattention to lessons and failure to complete assignments.

6. Sometimes the toughest part of motivating students is meeting the essential preconditions for developing student motivation to learn, especially those calling for worthwhile learning objectives and appropriate difficulty levels. What should you do if you find that several activities in the workbooks that come with your adopted curriculum appear to be pointless? Discuss this issue with friends or colleagues.

7. What should you do if certain students cannot handle the same material and move at the same pace as the rest of the class? What might you begin to do differently with these students and how might you explain it to them in ways that would support rather than erode their motivation to learn?

8. Why do the authors make a point of distinguishing between learning and performance when talking about motivating students to *learn*?

9. The authors note that intrinsic motivation resides in persons rather than in topics or activities, but they talk about capitalizing on students' existing intrinsic motivation by emphasizing topics or activities that students find interesting or enjoyable. Explain this seeming contradiction.

10. Similarly, the authors speak of motivation to learn as generated by learners themselves, but suggest that teachers can stimulate their students to develop such motivation to learn through general modeling and socialization and various more specific strategies. Again, explain this seeming contradiction. How can teachers stimulate the development of something that students must develop themselves?

11. Explain the implications of the following statement for motivating students in the classroom: We don't do something for *its* sake, we do it for *our* sake.

12. How would you respond to unmotivated students who genuinely want to know why they are asked to study Shakespeare's sonnets or the history of ancient Greece?

13. Take any three topics in English, science, or mathematics and write a one-page introduction to each topic. In planning your introduction, consider the following questions. What are some elements that could be focused on as a means to create interest, identify application potential, or create curiosity? Is there information that the students are likely to find surprising or difficult to believe? Can the content be related to current events or events in the students' lives?

14. Obtain students' textbooks in English, science, or mathematics and examine the exercises presented there. Given the considerations discussed in this chapter, how satisfactory are the questions and exercises? Find three or four examples that need to be improved, and write out your strategy for improving them or write different questions that have more motivational (and presumably instructional) value.

15. How can teachers model curiosity and interest in learning?

REFERENCES

Alton-Lee, A., Nuthall, G., & Patrick, J. (1993). Reframing classroom research: A lesson from the private world of children. *Harvard Educational Review, 63,* 50–84.

Ames, C. (1984). Competitive, cooperative, and individualistic goal structures: A cognitive-motivational analysis. In R. Ames & C. Ames (Eds.), *Research on motivation in education. Vol. 1: Student motivation.* New York: Academic Press.

Ames, C. (1992a). Achievement goals and the classroom motivational climate. In D. Schunk & J. Meece (Eds.), *Student perceptions in the classroom* (pp. 327–348). Hillsdale, NJ: Erlbaum.

Ames, C. (1992b). Classrooms: Goals, structures, and student motivation. *Journal of Educational Psychology, 84,* 261–271.

Anderman, E., & Maehr, M. (1994). Motivation and schooling in the middle grades. *Review of Educational Research, 64,* 287–309.

Bandura, A. (1989). Human agency in social cognitive theory. *American Psychologist, 44,* 1175–1184.

Bandura, A., & Schunk, D. (1981). Cultivating competence, self-efficacy, and intrinsic interest through proximal self-motivation. *Journal of Personality and Social Psychology, 41,* 586–598.

Berndt, T., & Miller, K. (1990). Expectancies, values, and achievement in junior high school. *Journal of Educational Psychology, 82,* 319–326.

Bettencourt, E., Gillett, M., Gall, M., & Hull, R. (1983). Effects of teacher enthusiasm training on student on-task behavior and achievement. *American Educational Research Journal, 20,* 435–450.

Blumenfeld, P., & Meece, J. (1988). Task factors, teacher behavior, and students' involvement and use of learning strategies in science. *Elementary School Journal, 88,* 235–250.

Blumenfeld, P. C., Mergendoller, J. R., & Swarthout, D. W. (1987). Task as a heuristic for understanding student learning and motivation. *Journal of Curriculum Studies, 19,* 135–148.

Blumenfeld, P., Puro, P., & Mergendoller, J. (1992). Translating motivation into thoughtfulness. In H. Marshall (Ed.), *Redefining student learning: Roots of educational change* (pp. 207–239). Norwood, NJ: Ablex.

Blumenfeld, P., Soloway E., Marx, R., Krajcik, J., Guzdial, M., & Palcinsar, A. (1991). Motivating project-based learning: Sustaining the doing, supporting the learning. *Educational Psychologist, 26,* 369–398.

Borkowski, J., Weyhing, R., & Carr, M. (1988). Effects of attributional retraining on strategy-based reading comprehension in learning-disabled students. *Journal of Educational Psychology, 80,* 46–53.

Brophy, J. (1983). Conceptualizing student motivation. *Educational Psychologist, 18,* 200–215.

Brophy, J. (1996). *Teaching problem students.* New York: Guilford.

Brophy, J., & Kher, N. (1986). Teacher socialization as a mechanism for developing student motivation to learn. In R. Feldman (Ed.), *Social psychology applied to education.* New York: Cambridge University Press.

Butler, R. (1987). Task-involving and ego-involving properties of evaluation: Effects of different feedback conditions on motivational perceptions, interest, and performance. *Journal of Educational Psychology, 79,* 474–482.

Cabello, B., & Terrell, R. (1994). Making students feel like family: How teachers create warm and caring classroom climates. *Journal of Classroom Interaction, 29,* 17–23.

Cameron, J., & Pierce, W.D. (1994). Reinforcement, reward, and intrinsic motivation: A meta-analysis. *Review of Educational Research, 64,* 363–423.

Chance, P. (1993). Sticking up for rewards. *Phi Delta Kappan, 74,* 787–790.

Cooper, H. (1979). Pygmalion grows up: A model for teacher expectation communication and performance influence. *Review of Educational Research, 49,* 389–410.

Covington, M. (1992). *Making the grade: A self-worth perspective on motivation and school reform.* Cambridge: Cambridge University Press.

Craske, M. (1988). Learned helplessness, self-worth motivation and attribution retraining for primary school children. *British Journal of Educational Psychology,* 58, 152–164.

deCharms, R. (1976). *Enhancing motivation: Change in the classroom.* New York: Irvington.

Deci, E., & Ryan, R. (1985). *Intrinsic motivation and self-determination in human behavior.* New York: Plenum.

Deci, E., & Ryan, R. (1994). Promoting self-determined education. *Scandinavian Journal of Educational Research, 38,* 3–14.

Deci, E., Vallerand, R., Pelletier, L., & Ryan, R. (1991). Motivation and education: The self-determination perspective. *Educational Psychologist, 26,* 325–346.

Devine, T. (1987). *Teaching study skills: A guide for teaching* (2nd cd.), Boston: Allyn and Bacon.

Dweck, C. (1991). Self-theories and goals: Their role in motivation, personality, and devel opment. In R. Dienstbier (Ed.), *Perspectives on motivation: Nebraska Symposium on Motivation, 1990* (Vol. 38, pp. 199–235). Lincoln: University of Nebraska Press.

Dweck, C., & Elliott, E. (1983). Achievement motivation. In P. Mussen (Ed.), *Handbook of child psychology* (4th ed.), Vol. IV: *Socialization, personality, and social development.* New York: Wiley.

Eccles, J. (1993). School and family effects on the ontogeny of children's interests, self-perceptions, and activity choices. In J. Jacobs (Ed.), *Nebraska Symposium on Motivation, 1992: Developmental perspectives on motivation* (pp. 145–208). Lincoln: University of Nebraska Press.

Eccles, J., & Wigfield, A. (1985). Teacher expectations and student motivation. In J. B. Dusek (Ed.), *Teacher expectancies.* Hillsdale, NJ: Erlbaum.

Elawar, M. C., & Corno, L. (1985). A factorial experiment in teachers' written feedback on student homework: Changing teacher behavior a little rather than a lot. *Journal of Educational Psychology, 77,* 162–173.

Feather, N. (Ed.). (1982). *Expectations and actions.* Hillsdale, NJ: Erlbaum.

Flink, C., Boggiano, A., Main, D., Barrett, M., & Katz, P. (1992). Children's achievement-related behaviors: The role of extrinsic and intrinsic motivational orientations. In A. Boggiano & T. Pittman (Eds.), *Achievement and motivation: A social-developmental perspective* (pp. 189–214). Cambridge: Cambridge University Press.

Gardner, H. (1991). *The unschooled mind: How children think and how schools should teach.* New York: Basic Books.

Good, T., & Brophy, J. (1995). *Contemporary educational psychology* (5th ed.). New York: Longman.

Gottfried, A. (1985). Academic intrinsic motivation in elementary and junior high school students. *Journal of Educational Psychology, 77,* 631–645.

Grabe, M. (1985). Attributions in a mastery instructional system: Is an emphasis on effort harmful? *Contemporary Educational Psychology, 10,* 113–126.

Heckhausen, H. (1991). *Motivation and action* (2nd ed.). New York: Springer-Verlag.

Hughes, B., Sullivan, H., & Mosley, M. (1985). External evaluation, task difficulty, and continuing motivation. *Journal of Educational Research, 78,* 210–215.

Johnson, D., & Johnson, R. (1985). Motivational processes in cooperative, competitive, and individualistic learning situations. In C. Ames & R. Ames (Eds.), *Research on motivation in education.* Vol. 2: *The classroom milieu.* Orlando, FL: Academic Press.

Keller, J. (1983). Motivational design of instruction. In C. Reigeluth (Ed.), *Instructional-design theories and models: An overview of their current status.* Hillsdale, NJ: Erlbaum.

Kiewra, K., Dubois, N., Christian, D., McShane, A., Meyerhoffer, M., & Roskelley, D. (1991). Note-taking functions and techniques. *Journal of Educational Psychology, 83,* 240–245.

Kohn, A. (1993). *Punished by rewards: The trouble with gold stars, incentive plans, A's, praise, and other bribes.* Boston: Houghton Mifflin.

Krampen, G. (1987). Differential effects of teacher comments. *Journal of Educational Psychology, 79,* 137–146.

Lane, D., Newman, D., & Bull, K. (1988). The relationship of student interest and advance organizer effectiveness. *Contemporary Educational Psychology, 13,* 15–25.

Lehtinen, E., Vauras, M., Salonen, P., Olkinuora, E., & Kinnunen, R. (1995). Long-term development of learning activity: Motivational, cognitive, and social interaction. *Educational Psychologist, 30,* 21–35.

Lepper, M. (1988). Motivational considerations in the study of instruction. *Cognition and Instruction, 5,* 289–309.

Lepper, M., & Cordova, D. (1992). A desire to be taught: Instructional consequences of intrinsic motivation. *Motivation and Emotion, 16,* 187–208.

Lepper, M., & Hodell, M. (1989). Intrinsic motivation in the classroom. In C. Ames & R. Ames (Eds.), *Research on motivation in education* (Vol. 3, pp. 75–105). New York: Academic Press.

Locke, E., & Latham, G. (1990). A *theory of goal setting and task performance.* Englewood Cliffs, NJ: Prentice-Hall.

Maehr, M., & Midgley, C. (1991). Enhancing student motivation: A schoolwide approach. *Educational Psychologist, 26,* 399–427.

Malone, T., & Lepper, M. (1987). Making learning fun: A taxonomy of intrinsic motivation for learning. In R. Snow & M. Farr (Eds.), *Aptitude, learning, and instruction: III. Conative and affective process analysis.* Hillsdale, NJ: Erlbaum.

Marshall, H. (1987). Motivational strategies of three fifth-grade teachers. *Elementary School Journal, 88,* 135–150.

Marshall, H. (1990). Beyond the workplace metaphor: The classroom as a learning setting. *Theory Into Practice, 29,* 94–101.

McCall, R., Evahn, C., Kratzer, L. (1992). *High school underachievers: What do they achieve as adults?* Newbury Park, Ca.: Sage.

McCaslin, M. (1990). Motivated literacy. In J. Zutell & S. McCormick (Eds.), *Literacy theory and research: Analyses for multiple paradigms* (39th Yearbook, pp. 35–50). Rochester, NY: National Reading Conference, Inc.

McColskey, W., & Leary, M. R. (1985). Differential effects of norm-referenced and self-referenced feedback on performance expectancies, attributions, and motivation. *Contemporary Educational Psychology, 10,* 275–284.

McCombs, B., & Pope, J. (1994). *Motivating hard to reach students.* Washington, DC: American Psychological Association.

McIntyre, T. (1989). *A resource book for remediating common behavior and learning problems.* Boston: Allyn & Bacon.

Meece, J. (1994). The role of motivation in self-regulated learning. In D. Schunk & B. Zimmerman (Eds.), *Self-regulation of learning and performance: Issues and educational applications* (pp. 25–44). Hillsdale, NJ: Erlbaum.

Meece, J., Blumenfeld, P., & Hoyle, R. (1988). Students' goal orientations and cognitive engagement in classroom activities. *Journal of Educational Psychology, 80,* 514–523.

Midgley, C. (1993). Motivation and middle level schools. In P. Pintrich & M. Maehr (Eds.), *Advances in motivation and achievement* (Vol. 8, pp. 217–274). Greenwich, CT: JAI Press.

Midgley, C., Feldlaufer, H., & Eccles, J. (1989). Change in teacher efficacy and student self- and task-related beliefs in mathematics during the transition to junior high school. *Journal of Educational Psychology, 81,* 247–258.

Morgan, M. (1985). Self-monitoring and attained subgoals in private study. *Journal of Educational Psychology, 77,* 623–630.

Naveh-Benjamin, M. (1991). A comparison of training programs intended for different types of test-anxious students: Further support for an information-processing model. *Journal of Educational Psychology, 83,* 134–139.

Newby, T. (1991). Classroom motivation: Strategies of first-year teachers. *Journal of Educational Psychology, 83,* 195–200.

Ogle, D. (1986). K-W-L: A teaching model that develops active reading of expository text. *Reading Teacher, 39,* 564–570.

Pintrich, P., & DeGroot, E. (1990). Motivational and self-regulated learning components of classroom academic performance. *Journal of Educational Psychology, 82,* 33–40.

Pressley, M., & Beard El-Dinary, P. (Guest editors). (1993). Special issue on strategies instruction. *Elementary School Journal, 94,* 105–284.

Raffini, J. (1993). *Winners without losers: Structures and strategies for increasing student motivation to learn.* Boston: Allyn & Bacon.

Rohrkemper, M., & Corno, L. (1988). Success and failure on classroom tasks: Adaptive learning and classroom teaching. *Elementary School Journal, 88,* 297–312.

Ryan, R., Connell, J., & Grolnick, W. (1992). When achievement is *not* intrinsically motivated: A theory of internalization and self-regulation in school. In A. Boggiano & T. Pittman (Eds.), *Achievement and motivation: A social-developmental perspective* (pp. 167–188). Cambridge: Cambridge University Press.

Ryan, R., & Stiller, J. (1991). The social contexts of internalization: Parent and teacher influences on autonomy, motivation and learning. In P. Pintrich & M. Maehr (Eds.), *Advances in motivation and achievement* (Vol. 7, pp. 115–149). Greenwich, CT: JAI Press.

Schiefele, U. (1991). Interest, learning, and motivation. *Educational Psychologist, 26,* 299–323.

Schunk, D. (1991). Self-efficacy and academic motivation. *Educational Psychologist, 26,* 207–231.

Schunk, D. H., & Hanson, A. R. (1985). Peer models: Influence on children's self-efficacy and achievement. *Journal of Educational Psychology, 77,* 313–322.

Spaulding, C. (1992). *Motivation in the classroom.* New York: McGraw-Hill.

Stipek, D. (1993). *Motivation to learn: From theory to practice* (2nd ed.). Englewood Cliffs, NJ: Prentice-Hall.

Stipek, D., & Weisz, J. (1981). Perceived personal control and academic achievement. *Review of Educational Research, 51,* 101–137.

Thomas, J. W. (1980). Agency and achievement: Self-management and self-reward. *Review of Educational Research, 30,* 213–240.

Thompson, C., & Rudolph, L. (1992). *Counseling children* (3rd ed.). Pacific Grove, CA: Brooks/Cole.

Tollefson, N., Tracy, D., Johnsen, E., Farmer, W., & Buenning, M. (1984). Goal setting and personal responsibility for LD adolescents. *Psychology in the Schools, 21,* 224–233.

Valas, H., & Sovik, N. (1993). Variables affecting students' intrinsic motivation for school mathematics: Two empirical studies based on Deci and Ryan's theory of motivation. *Learning and Instruction, 3,* 281–298.

Van Overwalle, F., Segebarth, K., & Goldschstein, M. (1989). Improving performance of freshmen through attributional testimonies from fellow students. *British Journal of Educational Psychology, 59,* 79–85.

Weiner, B. (1992). *Human motivation: Metaphors, theories and research.* Newbury Park, CA: Sage.

Weinstein, C., & Mayer, R. (1986). The teaching of learning strategies. In M. C. Wittrock (Ed.), *Handbook of research on teaching* (3rd. ed.). New York: Macmillan.

Whitley, B. E., & Frieze, I. H. (1985). Children's causal attributions for success and failure in achievement settings: A meta-analysis. *Journal of Educational Psychology, 77,* 608–616.

Wigfield, A., & Eccles, J. (1989). Test anxiety in elementary and secondary school students. *Educational Psychologist, 24,* 159–183.

Woolfolk, A., Rosoff, B., & Hoy, W. (1990). Teachers' sense of efficacy and their beliefs about managing students. *Teaching and Teacher Education, 6,* 137–148.

Zeidner, M. (1995). Adaptive coping with test situations: A review of the literature. *Educational Psychologist, 30,* 123–133.

Zuckerman, G. (1994). A pilot study of a ten-day course in cooperative learning for beginning Russian first graders. *Elementary School Journal, 94,* 405–420.

FORM 6.1. Attributing Success to Causes

USE: Whenever teacher makes a comment to explain a student's success.
PURPOSE: To see whether the teacher's statements support student
confidence and motivation to learn.
        For each codable instance, code each causal attribution category that
applies. How does the teacher explain good performance by students?

CAUSAL ATTRIBUTION CATEGORIES   CODES

  1. Effort or perseverance ("You worked hard, stuck to   1. ___   26. ___
     it")   2. ___   27. ___
  2. Accurate problem representation and solution ("You   3. ___   28. ___
     developed a good plan, followed the right process")   4. ___   29. ___
  3. Good progress in learning the domain ("You've really   5. ___   30. ___
     learned how to _____")
  4. Native intelligence or ability ("You're smart")   6. ___   31. ___
  5. Compliance ("You listened carefully, did as you were   7. ___   32. ___
     told")   8. ___   33. ___
  6. Irrelevant attributes ("You're a big boy")   9. ___   34. ___
  7. Cheating ("You copied." "Did someone tell you the   10. ___   35. ___
     answer?")
  8. Other (specify)   11. ___   36. ___
                                                             12. ___   37. ___
NOTES: 13. ___   38. ___
                                                             14. ___   39. ___
                                                             15. ___   40. ___

                                                             16. ___   41. ___
                                                             17. ___   42. ___
                                                             18. ___   43. ___
                                                             19. ___   44. ___
                                                             20. ___   45. ___

                                                             21. ___   46. ___
                                                             22. ___   47. ___
                                                             23. ___   48. ___
                                                             24. ___   49. ___
                                                             25. ___   50. ___

FORM 6.2. General Motivational Strategies

USE: When the teacher has been observed frequently enough so that reliable information is available.
PURPOSE: To assess the degree to which the teacher's general approach to instruction supports students' self-confidence and motivation to learn.
How regularly does the teacher follow the motivational guidelines listed below? Rate according to the following scale:

    5 = always
    4 = most of the time
    3 = sometimes
    2 = occasionally
    1 = never

A. ESSENTIAL PRECONDITIONS

_____ 1. Maintains a supportive learning environment (classroom atmosphere is businesslike but relaxed, teacher supports and encourages students' learning efforts)
_____ 2. Assigns tasks at an appropriate level of difficulty (students can achieve success with reasonable effort)
_____ 3. Assigns tasks with meaningful learning objectives (the tasks teach some knowledge or skill that is worth learning)
_____ 4. Demonstrates moderation and variation in use of motivational strategies (does not overuse particular strategies to the point that they become counterproductive)

B. MAINTAINING STUDENTS' SUCCESS EXPECTATIONS

_____ 1. Programs for success
_____ 2. Helps students to develop their skills for goal setting, performance appraisal, and self-reinforcement
_____ 3. Helps students to recognize effort-outcome linkages
_____ 4. Portrays effort as investment rather than risk
_____ 5. Portrays skill development as incremental and domain-specific (rather than as determined by fixed general abilities)
_____ 6. Focuses on mastery in monitoring performance and giving feedback (stresses student's continuous progress toward mastery rather than comparisons with other students)
_____ 7. If necessary, does remedial motivational work with discouraged students (to help them see that they have ability and can reach goals if they put forth reasonable effort)

C. STIMULATING STUDENTS' MOTIVATION TO LEARN

_____ 1. Models own motivation to learn (portrays learning as a self-actualizing activity that produces personal satisfaction and enriches one's life)
_____ 2. Communicates desirable expectations and attributions (implying that students see classroom activities as worthwhile and are eager to acquire knowledge and master skills)
_____ 3. Minimizes performance anxiety (treats mistakes as understandable and expected; minimizes the threat of tests)

NOTES:

FORM 6.3. Teacher's Response to Students' Questions

USE: *When a student asks the teacher a reasonable question during a discussion or question–answer period.*
PURPOSE: *To see if teacher models commitment to learning and concern for students' interests.*
    Code each category that applies to the teacher's response to a reasonable student question. Do not code if student wasn't really asking a question of if he or she was baiting the teacher.

BEHAVIOR CATEGORIES
  1. Compliments the question ("Good question")
  2. Criticizes the question (unjustly) as irrelevant, dumb, out of place, etc.
  3. Ignores the question, or brushes it aside quickly without answering it
  4. Answers the question or redirects it to the class
  5. If no one can answer, teacher arranges to get the answer or assigns a student to do so
  6. If no one can answer, teacher leaves it unanswered and moves on
  7. Other (specify)

NOTES.

   #7 Explained that question would be
      covered in tomorrow's lesson.

CODES			
1.	4	26.	
2.	4	27.	
3.	14	28.	
4.	4	29.	
5.	4	30.	
6.	3	31.	
7.	4	32.	
8.	4	33.	
9.	7	34.	
10.	4	35.	
11.	4	36.	
12.		37.	
13.		38.	
14.		39.	
15.		40.	
16.		41.	
17.		42.	
18.		43.	
19.		44.	
20.		45.	
21.		46.	
22.		47.	
23.		48.	
24.		49.	
25.		50.	

Students' Interactions with One Another

In previous chapters, we have discussed the roles of teachers' expectations, class-room management, and motivational strategies in establishing productive learning environments. Here, we shift focus from the teacher to the students, considering the makeup of the class and the ways in which students might interact with one another within productive learning environments.

Thinking about issues of who should be in the regular classroom and how these students should interact with one another has evolved considerably in recent decades. At one time, there was heavy emphasis on excluding certain students from regular classrooms and on dividing the remaining students into more homogeneous groups through tracking at the school level and ability grouping at the classroom level. Definitions of effective teaching emphasized efficiency in moving students through progressive sequences of instructional objectives, and it was thought that this process would unfold with maximum efficiency if the students were as similar to one another as possible.

Thinking has moved away from these notions in recent years, in several respects. Many educators object on philosophical grounds to policies of exclusion and homogeneous grouping, arguing that educational approaches should be assessed not only in terms of their efficiency but also in terms of equity. They value diversity, policies of inclusion, and practices that meet the needs of all students rather than favoring some over others. These educators argue that heterogeneous classes are just as effective as homogeneous classes for accomplishing achievement and other cognitive outcomes, but in addition are more effective for accomplishing affective and social outcomes such as promoting cultural understandings and prosocial behaviors across racial and ethnic groups. To accomplish important social and affective goals, these educators argue, schools need to shift from homogeneous to heterogeneous grouping and from classroom discourse patterns that are mostly limited to teacher-student interaction to patterns that include a great deal of student-student interaction.

Recently developed social constructivist theories of teaching and learning (described in Chapter 10) reinforce these arguments by suggesting that increased emphasis on student-student interaction is important for achieving cognitive outcomes as well. In these views, learning should not be viewed as transmission of knowledge from a teacher to students who imitate or memorize it, but instead as social construction of new understandings accomplished primarily through sustained discussion. Besides learning through interacting with teachers, students learn by collaborating with peers in pairs and small groups and by interacting with them during class discussion. Assuming that everyone participates, diversity in students' backgrounds and points of view would be considered an asset, not a liability, so heterogeneous classes (and small groups) would be preferable to homogeneous ones.

In this chapter, we discuss and consider the implications of theory and research on issues relating to the composition of the class and to students' interactions with one another. We begin with the goals of excellence and equity and their implications concerning student diversity and inclusion. Then we consider tracking and ability grouping. Finally, we address cooperative learning, peer tutoring, and other formats that allow students to learn by collaborating with one another.

EDUCATIONAL EXCELLENCE AND EQUITY

School quality (*educational excellence* as it has come to be called) is a continuing concern of the general public. By many criteria (including literacy rates and the percentage of the population who earn high school diplomas and college degrees) education in the United States has been quite successful both in absolute terms and in comparison with other countries (Berliner & Biddle, 1995). Historically, the general public has shown continuing commitment to the public schools and a perception that most of them are adequate, if not outstanding.

However, disenchantment sets in periodically, either in response to the writings of popular educational critics and would-be reformers or as a reaction to events perceived as indications of slippage in the nation's competitive position. For example, recently, the economic successes achieved by the Japanese at the expense of American electronics and automobile manufacturers have produced a great deal of public debate about the schools and spurred a variety of reform movements (e.g., see [National Education Commission on Time and Learning, *Prisoners of Time*, 1994]).

When fueled by concern about educational excellence, reforms tend to concentrate on cognitive rather than affective or social objectives, and in particular on achievement test scores. Calls for upgrading schools commonly include recommitment to academic objectives and standards, mandated performance objectives and associated testing programs, increases in course requirements and reductions in course options, more rigorous grading, more challenging curricula, and more homework. Often there are calls for special programs to accommodate the perceived needs of "the best and the brightest": special tracks or courses for gifted elementary students and honors or advanced placement courses for qualifying secondary students.

In short, the "educational excellence" approach tends to identify school quality with success in maximizing achievement test scores. This is rejected as overly narrow by educators who wish to define school quality at least in part in terms of *educational equity:* fair and effective treatment of all students regardless of gender, race, ethnicity, socioeconomic status, or handicapping conditions. Equity concerns were the primary motives behind two of the most widespread changes introduced into the schools during the 1960s and 1970s: desegregation and mainstreaming.

Desegregation

Following the *Brown v. Board of Education* Supreme Court decision in 1954, separate schools for black students were abolished and district lines were redrawn so as to bring more black and white students together. Since then, attention has shifted from the legal and structural aspects of accomplishing desegregation to methods of addressing the equity issues it introduces: the need for multicultural awareness and fair treatment of different groups, the desire to elicit active participation of all students in classroom activities, and the attempt to get beyond mere tolerance by promoting positive, prosocial interactions among students of different backgrounds.

At the school level, this goal requires minimizing between-class achievement grouping. In most school populations, there are substantial correlations among race, socioeconomic status, and achievement, so that creating homogeneous classes in desegregated schools resegregates students and thus minimizes cross-racial contact.

At the classroom level, the degree to which the ultimate goals of desegregation are likely to be accomplished depends on the activities and organizational structures that the teacher introduces. Within-class grouping tends to resegregate students, and a heavy reliance on the traditional whole-class instruction/recitation/seatwork approach to teaching minimizes students' opportunities to interact with their peers. Positive attitudes and frequent cross-race interaction are more likely in classrooms in which teachers frequently use small-group projects and other peer interaction formats (Nickerson & Prawat, 1981). The cooperative learning approaches that we describe later in the chapter have proven especially effective for improving cross-racial attitudes and behavior (Slavin, 1983).

Inclusion of Special Needs Students

In the past, schooling was treated as a privilege for students who fulfilled certain criteria rather than as a right guaranteed to all. Schools often denied enrollment to students whom they viewed as potential threats to smooth classroom functioning because of mental or physical handicaps, poor health, flagrant misbehavior, pregnancy, or even unconventional clothing or personal appearance. A series of court decisions in the 1960s and 1970s, however, established public education as a universal right rather than a privilege that schools could revoke capriciously. Also, resistance began to develop against the practice of placing students into special classes. There was concern about undesirable expectation and labeling effects on students diagnosed as handicapped and about special classes being dumping grounds for problems rather than improved educational settings that provide students with needed treatment.

Pressures for change culminated in Public Law 94–142, which became effective in 1977. This law directs public schools to search out and enroll all handicapped children and to educate them in the *least restrictive environment* in which they are able to function and still have their special needs met. The idea is to minimize the degree to which special students are labeled and treated as "different" and to maximize the degree to which they function as ordinary students participating in regular classes in usual ways. Teachers and administrators are expected to utilize all reasonable possibilities before seeking special programs (Schloss, 1992). In essence, the concept of a least restrictive environment suggests that a special education student should not be classified as a disability and given permanent special placement on the basis of such classifications. Students are to be moved to special settings only if necessary and only for as long as necessary.

The following continuum of educational environments proceeds from most to least restrictive (Reynolds, 1978):

Full-time residential school
Full-time special day school
Full-time special class
Regular class plus part-time special class
Regular class plus resource room help
Regular class with assistance by itinerant specialists
Regular class with consultive assistance
Regular class only

The passage of the Education for All Handicapped Children Act of 1975 (now referred to as the Individuals with Disabilities Education Act or IDEA) resulted in the identification of many more students as learning disabled. However, as Bateman (1992) noted, there are still gaps in the field's knowledge of curriculum materials and teaching strategies for students with disabilities. Increasingly, educators have encouraged educating students with mild disabilities within the regular educational setting. Such orientations are commonly called the regular education initiative, or REI (Ainscow, 1991). The law calls for an individualized educational program (IEP) to be developed for each student who is recommended for special educational services. The IEP is developed by a committee that is likely to include the principal, teachers who instruct the student, a school psychologist or social worker who evaluates the student, and when feasible, a parent and the student. The IEP describes the student's present educational performance, identifies short-term and longer-term goals, and specifies a plan for achieving these goals through a combination of regular classroom teaching and whatever specialized instruction might be needed.

As a classroom teacher, you should be aware that both professional sentiment and the law of the land suggest that students should be in the least restrictive environment. However, there is considerable disagreement among professionals about when students are ready for reintegration. Teachers often have to make difficult decisions about when students should be removed from a classroom to a special setting or about the curriculum students should receive when they are reintegrated. It is the case that parents and other specialists will be involved in making such decisions; however, a key component of the decision-making process is your judgment based on careful observation and reflection on student performance (both academic and social). The goal is to place students in the least restrictive environment (Schloss, 1992); however, for some students that environment is a special setting.

Research on regular versus special classroom placement suggests that the achievement progress of special education students depends not so much on what kind of classroom they are assigned to as on the amount and quality of the instruction they receive there. In general, the classroom management and instructional approaches that are effective with special students tend to be the same ones that are effective with other students (Crawford, 1983; Larrivee, 1985), although students with learning disabilities or handicaps may need individualized curricula and more one-to-one instruction (Leinhardt & Pallay, 1982; Madden & Slavin, 1983), and students with behavior disorders may need closer supervision (Thompson, White, & Morgan, 1982). Special students may be assigned to resource rooms where they receive instruction in basic skills from special education teachers who work with only 5 to 10 students at a time. These students spend the rest of their time in regular classrooms for instruction in other subjects.

"Mainstreamed" or "inclusion" students are likely to adjust well to regular classrooms if they receive acceptance and support from their teachers and peers. Teachers' attitudes and expectations are critical. It is important for teachers to think of these students as "their own" and as bona fide members of the class, not as visitors on loan from the special education teachers. These students should participate as fully and equally in classroom activities as possible and should be treated primarily in terms of what they can accomplish (or learn to accomplish with help) rather than with emphasis on what they cannot do because of their handicapping conditions. Detailed suggestions about teaching students with special disability conditions (e.g., visual impairment, hearing impairment, stuttering, behavior disorders, learning disabilities, etc.), can be found elsewhere (Good & Brophy, 1995; Hallahan & Kauffman, 1991; Smith & Luckasson, 1992).

BETWEEN-CLASS GROUPING (TRACKING)

Between-class grouping involves assigning students to classes that are as homogeneous as possible. Two subtypes are grouping by ability or achievement and grouping by curriculum (Rosenbaum, 1980). *Grouping by ability or achievement* is more common in elementary and middle schools, where it is often called *homogeneous grouping*. To group 69 third graders homogeneously, for example, school staff would examine standardized achievement test scores and assign the highest 23 scorers to the top class, the next 23 to the middle class, and the last 23 to the bottom class. There might be some minor variations to the procedure, such as making the top class a little larger and the bottom class a little smaller. However, the result would be three classes, each much more homogeneous in achievement than if the students had been assigned randomly or in some other fashion that yielded heterogeneous grouping. Homogeneously grouped classes are usually taught essentially the same curriculum, but higher-ranking classes are taught in greater depth and breadth.

Grouping by curriculum is more frequently used in junior and especially senior high schools. It is commonly called *tracking*. Instead of merely introducing differences in the depth and breadth of instruction in the same curriculum, tracking creates separate curricula for students in the different tracks. College preparatory students take one curriculum, business-secretarial students another, vocational students another, and general education students another. Some ninth graders take algebra, some prealgebra, some business math, and some general math.

American educators have always been ambivalent about between-class ability grouping (Rosenbaum, 1980). It is a sensible idea in theory because reducing heterogeneity should make it easier for teachers to meet more of their students' needs more consistently. In practice, however, it is less appealing. Its effects on achievement are weak and mixed rather than reliably positive, and it appears to have undesirable affective and social effects that conflict with the nation's egalitarian traditions. Consequently, opposition to tracking has been building and has culminated recently in policy statements by various blue ribbon panels and professional educational organizations calling for elimination or at least minimization of tracking (Oakes & Lipton, 1992).

Teachers' attitudes toward tracking tend to vary according to the subject they teach (Dar, 1985; Evans, 1985). Teachers who favor tracking tend to teach subjects such as mathematics or foreign languages in which the content is largely abstract and arranged hierarchically. In contrast, teachers of literature, history, and other humanities and social studies subjects see the least need for tracking, apparently because they can relate their subjects to everyday experience and develop them using commonsense explanations. Thus, it is easier for them to keep a heterogeneous class of students meaningfully focused on a common topic. Teachers whose subject matter lies in between these extremes of abstraction and hierarchical organization of content (science teachers, for example) tend to have mixed views of tracking.

Effects on Achievement

In theory, between-class ability grouping should improve achievement and be equally beneficial for both low and high achievers. In fact, however, reviews suggest only weak and mixed effects on achievement (Gamoran, 1993; Kulik & Kulik, 1989; Oakes, 1992; Slavin, 1990a & b). Research cannot indicate why tracking has not lived up to its theoretical potential, because most investigators have used a black box approach—looking only at outcomes without collecting information about curriculum and instruction in classrooms that might provide a basis for explaining conflicting results. If teachers provide essentially the same curriculum and instruction to both tracked and untracked classes, there is little reason to expect either benefits or detriments to student achievement. Such effects can be expected only when teachers differentiate their instruction to different classes (Gamoran, 1993; Good & Marshall, 1984). Gamoran (1993) reports some examples in Catholic schools where it appears that effective teaching has occurred in low-track class-rooms. He found that these schools (1) did not assign weak or less experienced teachers to lower tracks, (2) communicated high-performance expectations to low-track students, (3) focused their curriculum on academics, (4) stressed interactive exchange between teachers and students, and (5) reflected considerable effort on the part of teachers.

Studies of tracking do not usually yield such positive findings, probably because low tracks often become dumping grounds for low achievers instead of mechanisms for meeting their needs more effectively. In addition, there is concern that any potential positive effects of tracking may be undercut by its negative effects.

Affective and Social Effects

Critics have identified four types of negative effects that tracking is likely to have on students (Gamoran, 1993; Oakes, 1992; Page, 1992). First are the social labeling and teacher attitude and expectation effects we reviewed in Chapter 3. Investigators have found that teachers dislike teaching low-ability classes, spend less time preparing for them, and schedule less varied, interesting, and challenging activities in them (Evertson, 1982; Oakes, 1985). This is true even in elite schools where most students in low-track classes would be in higher tracks elsewhere (Page, 1992). Instead of being taught by means of curricula and methods suited to their needs, students in low-track classes may not be taught much at all. Often they are merely kept quiet with busywork rather than being challenged with effective instruction.

Even where the situation has not deteriorated to this extent, teachers tend to teach high- and low-track classes differently. Compared with their behavior in high-track classes, many teachers in low-track classes are less clear about objectives, introduce content less clearly or completely, make fewer attempts to relate content to students' interests or backgrounds, and are less receptive to student views. Instruction tends to be conceptually simplified and to proceed slowly in lower-track classes, with emphasis on rote memory, oral recitation, and use of low-level worksheets. In contrast, high-track classes study more interesting, complex material, taught at a faster pace and with more enthusiasm. Classroom discourse features discussion or debate rather than just recitation, and applications feature authentic activities calling for critical thinking and decision making, not just filling in blanks on worksheets. Much of what high-track students learn is likely to be applicable to their lives outside of school and to function as "cultural capital" that they can draw on in coping with modern society's complex demands.

The second problem with tracking is the undesirable peer structures it creates in low-track classes. In heterogeneously grouped classes, the brighter and better socially adjusted students tend to assume academic peer leadership, so that each class tends to function primarily as a learning environment and most time is spent engaged in academic activities. However, tracking systems place most of these academic peer leaders in upper-track classes, so that lower-track classes can become leaderless aggregations of discouraged and alienated students. These students may respond to their low status defensively by refusing to commit themselves seriously to academic achievement goals and by deriding classmates who do (Gamoran & Berends, 1987). Even if teachers approach these low-track classes with desirable attitudes and expectations, they may find it difficult to establish effective learning environments if they encounter defeatism, alienation, or flat-out resistance. Similarly, low-track students who want to accomplish as much as they can may have a difficult time doing so if classmates deride their efforts or if instructional continuity is often disrupted. Experimental data indicate that students assigned to higher groups achieve more than comparable students assigned to lower groups (Douglas, 1964; Mason et al., 1992; Tuckman & Bierman, 1971). Also, students in classes with primarily higher-achieving classmates tend to achieve more than students in classes with primarily lower-achieving classmates (Beckerman & Good, 1981; Veldman & Sanford, 1984; see also Leiter, 1983, for mixed results).

Another related issue associated with tracking is the general normative climate associated with a school track. Damico and Roth (1993) interviewed 178 adolescents who were general track students in three Florida school districts selected to represent varying graduation rates. Students in low-graduation rate schools saw them as highly punitive in orientation, with such tight controls on student behaviors that students thought that they were always being watched and distrusted. In contrast, students in high-graduation rate schools reported a facilitative orientation in the school and an attempt by teachers to direct student behavior in positive ways. Further, in these schools high expectations for performance were communicated and teachers expressed interest in working with students, and thus, assuming joint responsibility with students for learning. These differences may be further exaggerated in high- and low-track classrooms.

A third criticism of between-class ability grouping is that assignment to tracks tends to be permanent: There is little movement from one track to another once initial assignments have been made, and the movement that does occur tends to be downward. Thus, initial placement into a low track may categorize a student permanently and close off academic and career advancement options. For example, if students in low-track classes get general math instead of algebra, they will be prevented from enrolling in all future mathematics courses for which algebra is a prerequisite (and perhaps from enrolling in certain science and computer courses as well). Ultimately, even if they graduate from high school they will do so with a diploma but without many of the prerequisites demanded by high-quality college programs. Thus, tracking decisions made even as early as first grade might affect students' academic progress from that point on, for good or ill. This might be of less concern if students were always grouped accurately, but there is reason to believe that many students are misclassified due to imperfection of tests as predictors of future performance. This problem is especially acute when test data are used to group young students or students with limited facility in the language in which the test is administered.

The lack of movement from lower to higher tracks is another indication that tracking typically does not lead to adaptive instruction of low achievers. If it did, many of these students would show improved achievement and move up to higher tracks.

The fourth problem with tracking is that it minimizes contact between students of differing achievement. As a result, it also minimizes contact between students who differ in social class, race, or ethnicity.

Taken together, the data on tracking suggest that it offers little or no advantage as a way to increase student achievement and has some important negative effects on affective and social outcomes. Consequently, we agree with the developing consensus that tracking should be minimized.

Where tracking is considered unavoidable, we recommend that it be delayed as long as possible and be confined to grouping by curriculum rather than grouping by ability or achievement. We do not see justification for grouping classes by ability or achievement when all students are going to be taught essentially the same curriculum.

Where conditions appear to compel homogeneous grouping, we recommend partial or compromise arrangements over arrangements that segregate different groups completely. One such compromise is the Joplin plan and its many variations. In the original Joplin plan, students were assigned to heterogeneous classes for most of the day but were regrouped for reading instruction across grades (teachers all taught reading at the same time to make such regrouping possible). For example, a fourth-grade, first-semester reading class might include high-achieving third graders. The class would be taught as a whole or perhaps divided into just two groups, but no more. Students would be assigned strictly according to reading achievement level (not IQ or some less direct measure) and would be reassigned when their performance warranted it.

The Joplin plan requires coordinated scheduling and cooperation among teams of teachers, but it simplifies reading instruction by making it possible for each teacher to instruct the entire class as a group or to divide the class into only two subgroups instead of three or more. This simplifies management and increases the time that students receive instruction from the teacher rather than work independently on assignments. Slavin (1987) reported that the Joplin plan showed significant positive effects on achievement compared with traditional homogeneous or heterogeneous grouping within grades, although Kulik and Kulik (1989) reported more modest effects.

Variations on the Joplin plan call for grouping students for reading instruction within rather than across grades or for regrouping in subjects other than reading. Regrouping is more likely to be used for reading and mathematics than for science or social studies.

Three first-grade teachers we know devised a plan for regrouping students within grades for both reading and mathematics. Originally, students had been assigned randomly to each class. The teachers taught and carefully observed them for six weeks, then divided them into high, middle, and low groups for mathematics and reading instruction (the groups were not the same for each subject). The teacher who taught the low readers taught the high mathematics students, and vice versa, so that students did not come to view one classroom as the "dummy room" and another as the "brain trust room." Also, the teachers were careful to treat students as individuals even though they had been assigned together because of similar aptitudes.

The students remained with their regular teacher for all other activities (science, social studies, art, music, lunch, and recess), where they were taught in mixed-ability groups. They worked with two or even three teachers and yet spent most of the day with the same teacher (an arrangement we think facilitates young students' affective growth). When a student experienced academic difficulty, all three teachers frequently had pertinent knowledge to contribute to a group planning session to develop new strategies.

The Controversy Continues

Consensus is growing around the ideas that tracking should be minimized, should be delayed as long as possible, and when used, should be confined to grouping by curriculum rather than by ability or achievement. Controversy continues, however. Some reformers favor restructuring schools so as to eliminate tracking entirely and have begun to identify strategies for changing the culture of schools in ways that would make this possible (Oakes & Lipton, 1992; Wheelock, 1992). Other reformers have concentrated on methods of delaying the inception of tracking and modifying the forms that it takes (Braddock & McPartland, 1990).

Suggestions include postponing tracking by deferring it as late in the grade span as possible; limiting it to basic academic subjects where differences in skills are clear detriments to whole-class instruction; using multiple placement criteria rather than a single test score to determine the track placement; experimenting with ideas such as offering students incentives for taking challenging courses; minimizing separate offerings for gifted and special needs students; rotating teachers among track levels; and encouraging students to move up to higher tracks and providing them with extra help if they need it.

Opposition to tracking is not unanimous, however. Proponents of tracking claim that many of the arguments against it are based more on ideology and theoretical commitments than on empirical findings demonstrating negative effects on students. In addition, advocates of acceleration programs and special courses for gifted students claim that the existing literature supports this particular form of tracking and that additional support would be forthcoming if a broader range of outcome criteria was used to judge its effectiveness (Allan, 1991). Opponents of tracking respond that the seeming advantages to tracking suggested by certain studies result from the enriched curriculum enjoyed by high-track students rather than from the homogeneity of their classes. They argue for an enriched curriculum for all students and maintain that there are no advantages but many disadvantages to grouping students homogeneously.

WITHIN-CLASS ABILITY GROUPING

Whether or not their schools employ tracking systems, teachers can arrange to instruct their students in homogeneous small groups rather than as whole classes. This system is used routinely for beginning reading instruction and often for elementary mathematics instruction as well.

Ability grouping within classes offers certain advantages over ability grouping between classes. First, only one teacher is involved, so that there is no need for cooperative planning and scheduling. Within-class ability grouping is also more flexible in that it is easier for the teacher to vary the number and size of groups and to move students from group to group. Whenever the teacher is instructing a small group, however, provisions must be made to keep the rest of the students profitably occupied. Consequently, instructional planning and classroom management are considerably more complicated than they are when the teacher uses whole-class methods. The result is that the potential advantages that within-class ability grouping offers to students (the opportunity to receive intensive small-group instruction in content and skills that are closely matched to current achievement) are offset by certain disadvantages (reduction in time taught directly by the teacher, increase in time spent in independent seatwork).

Even in districts that assign students with comparable achievement profiles to classrooms, some teachers regroup the students again to further reduce variations in achievement levels, at least in certain subjects. Mason and Good (1993) tested the effects of two models of active teaching on the mathematics learning of over 1700 fourth-, fifth-, and sixth-grade students drawn from 81 classrooms in a district that assigned students to classes on the basis of achievement (i.e., used regrouping in mathematics). Both models attempted to deal with student diversity by reducing the range of achievement levels that a teacher would deal with at a given time. One approach was a *structural approach* in which students' diversity was reduced before instruction. Students in these classrooms were divided into two groups on the basis of their previous year's performance, and teachers taught mathematics to these two groups separately. The second approach, the *situational approach,* involved changing student groups *after* instruction. That is, the teacher initially taught the class as a whole and then provided ad hoc instruction (review, enrichment, etc.) to a subset of students as needed. The situational approach is more consistent with the view that students' abilities are varied and that even within a subject, student learning may be more insightful in some topics than in others.

Mason and Good found that the situational model proved to be more effective than the structural model. In the situational model, teachers taught the whole class first and placed more emphasis on development (trying to explore and "connect" mathematical ideas) and on assessing student understanding (encouraging students to explain their thinking) than did teachers in the structural model. Importantly, the whole-class teachers also found more time to individualize instruction, in part because they spent less time on management issues associated with managing two groups.

More research is needed to consider the range of diversity that a teacher can handle at a given time; however, the situational model would appear to be a more adaptive model in many contexts. Thus, within-class ability grouping may be needed only when student populations are very diverse. This view is consistent with Kulik and Kulik's (1989) review reporting trivial-to-small positive effects of within-class grouping on student achievement.

Remarkably, in view of the near-universal use of reading groups, there are no clear research data comparing small-group versus whole-class instruction in beginning reading. However, within-class ability grouping for beginning reading is often criticized on logical grounds. First, ability grouping tends to exaggerate preexisting differences in achievement by accelerating the progress of students in the top groups but slowing the progress of students in the bottom groups (Rowan & Miracle, 1983; Weinstein, 1976). This effect is especially pronounced when the groups are notably different from one another and the teacher treats them very differently. Second, high groups seem to benefit not only from faster pacing but from better instruction from the teacher, a more desirable work orientation, and greater attention to the lesson (Eder & Felmlee, 1984). Third, group membership tends to remain highly stable once groups are formed, so group assignments affect peer contact and friendship patterns in addition to achievement, more so as time goes on (Hallinan & Sorensen, 1985). In classrooms where race is correlated with achievement, ability grouping results in de facto resegregation of students, even though race as such may not be taken into account in making group assignments (Haller, 1985). Finally, ability grouping can result in the labeling effects, "low-group psychology" effects, and related undesirable expectation effects that we reviewed in Chapter 3.

Enough problems with within-class ability grouping have been reported to cause educators to begin to question this practice and seek alternatives to it, even educators concerned with beginning reading instruction, where such grouping has been standard practice. The report *Becoming a Nation of Readers* (Anderson et al., 1985), for example, calls for reduced emphasis on oral reading in small homogeneous groups and suggests that teachers experiment with alternatives as settings for reading practice. Some programs have accomplished this through whole-class instruction followed by silent reading and comprehension assignments. As students work on their assignments, the teacher circulates to listen to individuals read orally. Other programs assign students to work in pairs, alternately taking the reader and the listener role.

It is too early to say whether such alternatives will prove more effective than teaching reading to homogeneous small groups. It is clear, however, that within-class ability grouping can have a great range of effects on students, depending on the decisions made when forming these groups and the nature of the instruction provided to the groups. We have several suggestions for those considering within-class ability grouping.

First, the number and composition of the groups should depend on the variation in achievement and instructional needs among students in the class. In other words, if you believe that within-class grouping is necessary to achieve homogeneity among students assigned to the same group, then make sure that such homogeneity is achieved—don't just arbitrarily divide the class into three equal-sized groups.

Second, grouping should lead to more effective meeting of instructional needs, not merely to differentiated pacing through the curriculum. Teaching will still have to be individualized within groups, and students who continue to have trouble will need additional instruction. This may mean simply repeating the material, but often it means reteaching a concept in a different way with new examples. Students who did not learn something the first time are unlikely to learn it the second time unless the teacher presents it in a new or more thorough way.

Third, group assignments should be flexible. Assignments should be reviewed regularly with an eye toward disbanding groups that have outlived their usefulness and forming new groups to respond to current needs.

Fourth, group scheduling and instructional practices should also be flexible. When there are good instructional reasons for it, a particular group might best meet for 40 minutes on one day and 20 minutes the next day, but this will not happen if the teacher rigidly adheres to a schedule calling for each group to meet daily for 30 minutes. Also, there is no need for the teacher to continue to work with the entire group throughout the time allotted. One way to meet the needs of individuals within the group is to release students who have mastered the day's objectives and let them get started on seatwork assignments while keeping the remaining students for more concentrated and individualized instruction.

Fifth, because of the potential dangers of labeling effects and because grouping affects peer contacts, teachers should limit the degree to which group membership determines students' other school experiences. Members of the same reading group should not be seated together or otherwise dealt with as a group outside of reading instruction, and if ability grouping is used for mathematics or other subjects, group assignments should be based on achievement in these subjects rather than in reading.

Finally, groups should be organized and taught in ways that provide low achievers with the extra instruction they need. For example, teachers can assign more students to high groups and fewer students to low groups, thus arranging for more intensive instruction of low achievers within the group setting (Dreeben, 1984). Or, teachers can spend more of their time providing direct instruction and supervision to low groups while high groups spend more time working cooperatively or independently (Anderson & Pigford, 1988).

Planned Heterogeneous Grouping

Small groups do not have to be formed based on student ability, especially if the object is merely to reduce the number of students to be taught together at one time and not necessarily to homogenize the group. For example, beginning reading instruction may be best conducted in small groups when it involves slow-paced oral reading, so even in classrooms composed of students of similar ability, teachers may want to use small groups for oral reading practice. If so, teachers do not necessarily have to group students by ability. Often, in fact, it may make more sense to group students randomly or on the basis of managerial considerations (e.g., separating students who tend to become disruptive when assigned to the same group).

Under some circumstances, you may want group assignments to achieve some kind of planned heterogeneity. For example, in activities designed to promote social awareness and acceptance, you might want to make sure that each group includes both genders and members of whatever racial or ethnic groups are represented in the class. We will consider such grouping in more detail in discussing cooperative group activities.

COOPERATIVE LEARNING

The traditional approach to schooling calls for whole-class lessons followed by independent seatwork. Cooperative learning approaches replace independent seatwork with small groups of students (typically four to six students) who work together on practice or application exercises. Thus, under cooperative learning arrangements students receive information and feedback from peers in addition to the teacher and the curriculum materials. Cooperative learning methods differ according to the task structures and incentive structures that are in effect (Slavin, 1990a & b).

Small-group learning has become popular because of its potential for engaging students in meaningful learning with authentic tasks in a social setting. Educators are increasingly calling for environments that allow students to construct knowledge actively (Chapter 10 provides details of this perspective), and, under appropriate conditions, small-group methods can support such social construction of knowledge (i.e., students learning from and with one another). However, small-group instruction varies widely in terms of tasks, group composition, and goals. Small groups can be used for drill, practice, learning facts and concepts, discussion, and problem solving. Even when the purpose of small-group instruction is inquiry or problem solving, those results are not automatic (Blumenfeld, 1992). Educators have much to learn about how to design small-group instruction in order to stimulate comprehension and higher-order thinking.

In the rest of this chapter we explore the possible uses and misuses of small groups. We want readers to consider both the potential payoff and inherent problems associated with small-group instruction. As we shall see, much more is known about the effects of small-group instruction than about how or why such effects occur, and more is known about its effects on skill and fact acquisition than about its effects on problem solving and conceptual understanding.

Task Structure

The term *task structure* refers to the nature of the task (its goal, the kinds of responses it requires, etc.) and the working conditions that accompany it. Task structures may be individual, cooperative, or competitive. *Individual task structures* require students to work on the task alone (except for help from the teacher if necessary). Traditional independent seatwork employs an individual task structure. *Cooperative task structures* require students to work cooperatively in order to meet task requirements. Assignments that call for students to assist one another in learning or to work together to produce a group product involve cooperative task structures. Finally, *competitive task structures,* such as contests, debates, and various competitive games, require students to compete (either as individuals or as teams) in order to fulfill task requirements.

Within groups, members may cooperate in working toward either group or individual goals. When pursuing *group goals,* the members work together to produce a single product that results from the pooled resources and shared labor of the group. For example, the group might paint a mural, assemble a collage, or prepare a skit or report to be presented to the rest of the class. When working cooperatively to reach *individual goals,* group members assist one another by discussing how to respond to questions or assignments, checking work, or providing feedback or tutorial assistance. Cooperative work toward individual goals occurs when individual students are responsible for turning in assignments but are allowed to consult with one another as they work on those assignments.

Cooperative task structures also differ according to whether or not there is task specialization. When there is no task specialization, each member works on the same task. *Task specialization* is in effect when the larger task to be accomplished is divided into several subtasks on which different group members work. In preparing a report on a foreign country, for example, task specialization would be operative if one group member was assigned to do the introduction, another to cover geography and climate, another to cover natural resources and the economy, and so on.

Incentive Structure

Besides differing in task structure, group activities differ in incentive structure. *Incentive structure* (also called *reward structure* or *goal structure*) refers to methods used for motivating students to perform the task. These include the nature of incentives themselves (grades, concrete rewards, symbolic rewards) as well as rules specifying what must be done to earn rewards and how they will be delivered. Like task structures, incentive structures can be individual, cooperative, or competitive. Under *individual incentive structures,* any particular student's performance has no consequences for other students' chances of earning available rewards. That is, individuals are rewarded (or not) depending on whether they meet specified performance criteria, regardless of how the rest of the class performs. Under *cooperative incentive structures,* individuals' chances of earning rewards depend not only on their own efforts but on those of other members of their group. Thus, instead of or in addition to rewarding students as individuals, the teacher rewards groups of students according to the performance that results from their combined efforts. Finally, under *competitive incentive structures,* groups or individuals must compete for whatever rewards are available. The winners get the most desirable rewards, and the losers get less desirable rewards or no rewards at all. Classes in which grades are assigned according to preset curves explicitly involve competitive incentive structures, and any classes in which grades are assigned at least partly on the basis of comparative performance implicitly involve competitive incentive structures.

Cooperative and competitive incentive structures can also be differentiated according to whether they involve group or individual rewards. *Group rewards* are distributed equally to all members of the group. These may involve a single reward to be shared by the group (such as a prize or a treat) or assigning the same reward to each group member (if the group's product receives a grade of A, each group member receives a grade of A, regardless of that member's contribution to the group product). *Individual rewards* are assigned differentially to individual students depending on effort or performance. For example, students may be encouraged to cooperate with peers in discussing assignments and preparing for a test but be required to take the test individually and be graded according to their own performance.

Task and incentive structures are independent; cooperative task structure does not necessarily imply a cooperative incentive structure, and so on. In fact, any incentive structure could be imposed on any task structure, although some such arrangements would be highly artificial and unusual. For example, a teacher could require students to work on assignments alone (e.g., to use an individual task structure) but impose a competitive reward structure by dividing students into teams that never work together but are rewarded partly on the basis of how well team members do as a group on unit tests. Table 7.1 shows the combinations of task and reward structures that are typically used.

Well-Known Cooperative Learning Programs

We describe some of the best-known and widely researched cooperative learning programs here.

Learning Together

The Learning Together model of cooperative learning was developed by David and Roger Johnson (Johnson & Johnson, 1975; Johnson et al., 1984). Early versions called for students to work together in four- or five-member heterogeneous groups on assignment sheets. The major interest was in getting students who differed in achievement, gender, race, or ethnicity working together. The groups handed in a single sheet and were praised as a group for working well together and for their performance on the task.

Experimentation with this approach revealed that some variations worked better than others, and eventually the Johnsons identified four elements that should be included in any cooperative learning activity (Johnson & Johnson, 1985b; Johnson et al., 1984).

1. *Positive interdependence.* Students should recognize that they are interdependent with other members of their group in achieving a successful group product. Positive interdependence can be structured through mutual goals (goal interdependence); division of labor (task interdependence); dividing materials, resources, or information among group members (resource interdependence); assigning students unique roles (role interdependence); or giving group rewards (reward interdependence).
2. *Face-to-face interaction among students.* Tasks that call for significant interaction among group members are preferred over tasks that can be accomplished by having group members work on their own.
3. *Individual accountability.* Mechanisms are needed to ensure that each group member has clear objectives for which he or she will be held accountable and receives any needed assessment, feedback, or instructional assistance.
4. *Instructing students in appropriate interpersonal and small-group skills.* Students cannot merely be placed together and told to cooperate. They need instruction in skills such as asking and answering questions, ensuring that everyone participates actively and is treated with respect, and assigning tasks and organizing cooperative efforts (see Johnson & Johnson, 1982).

Group Investigation

Shlomo Sharan and his colleagues (Sharan & Sharan, 1976; Sharan et al., 1984) developed what they call Group Investigation models in Israel. Group Investigation students form their own two- to six-member groups to work together using cooperative inquiry, group discussion, and cooperative planning and projects. Each group

Table 7.1   POSSIBLE COMBINATIONS OF TASK AND REWARD STRUCTURES
(all combinations are possible, but some are more typically used than others)

		Incentive Structures				
	I. Individual*	**II. Cooperative†**		**III. Competitive†**	
Task structures		**A. Individual rewards**	**B. Group reward**	**A. Individual rewards**	**B. Group reward**
I. *Individual.* Each student works alone.	Typical	Possible	Possible	Typical	Possible
II. *Cooperative.* Students work together or help one another.					
A. *Group goals.* Individuals cooperate to create a group product.					
1. *Undifferentiated roles.* Each student has the same task.	Possible	Possible	Typical	Possible	Typical
2. *Differentiated roles.* Different students perform different tasks.	Possible	Possible	Typical	Possible	Typical
B. *Individual goals.* Individuals help one another to fulfill their respective individual responsibilities.					
1. *Undifferentiated roles.* Each student has the same task.	Typical	Typical	Possible	Typical	Possible
2. *Differentiated roles.* Different students perform different tasks.	Typical	Typical	Possible	Typical	Possible
III. *Competitive.* The task requires students to compete.					
A. *Individual competition.*	Typical	Typical	Possible	Typical	Possible
B. *Team competition.*	Possible	Possible	Typical	Possible	Typical

*Reward depends strictly on one's own performance.
†Reward depends, at least in part, on group performance.
†Reward depends, at least in part, on the outcome of a competition.

chooses a subtopic from a unit studied by the whole class, breaks this subtopic into individual tasks, and carries out the activities necessary to prepare a group report. Eventually, the group makes a presentation or display to communicate its findings to the class and is evaluated based on the quality of this report.

Jigsaw

The Jigsaw approach (Aronson et al., 1978) ensures active individual participation and group cooperation by arranging tasks so that each group member possesses unique information and has a special role to play. The group product cannot be completed unless each member does his or her part, just as a jigsaw puzzle cannot be completed unless each piece is included. For example, information needed to compose a biography might be broken into early life, first accomplishments, major setbacks, later life, and world events occurring during the person's lifetime. One member of each group would be given the relevant information and assigned responsibility for one of the five sections of the biography, and other group members would be assigned to other sections. Members of different groups who were working on the same section would meet together in "expert groups" to discuss their sections. Then they would return to their regular groups and take turns teaching their groupmates about their sections. Since the only way that students can learn about sections other than their own is to listen carefully to their groupmates, they are motivated to support and show interest in one another's work. The students then prepare biographies or take quizzes on the material individually.

Several cooperative learning methods have been developed by Robert Slavin and others at Johns Hopkins University. Collectively, these methods are known as *Student Team Learning*. We will discuss four variations.

Teams-Games-Tournament (TGT)

The Teams-Games-Tournament approach (DeVries & Slavin, 1978; DeVries et al., 1980) calls for students to work together in four- to five-member heterogeneously grouped teams to help one another master content and prepare for competitions against other teams. After the teacher presents the material to be learned, team members work together, studying from worksheets. Typically they discuss the material, tutor one another, and quiz one another to assess mastery. Cooperative practice in this form continues throughout the week in preparation for tournaments held on Fridays.

For the tournaments, students are assigned to three-person tables composed of students from different teams who are similar in achievement. The three students compete at academic games covering the content taught that week and practiced during team meetings. Most of these games are simply numbered questions on a handout. A student picks a number card and attempts to answer the question corresponding to that number. Students can earn points by responding to questions correctly or by successfully challenging and correcting the answers of the other two students at the table. These points are later summed to determine each team's score, and the teacher prepares a newsletter that recognizes successful teams and unusually high scores attained by individuals. The newsletter may also contain cumulative team scores if tournaments last longer than a week. Prior to the next tournament, the teacher may reassign certain students to different tournament tables in order to keep the competition as even as possible at each table. This ensures that even though the teams are heterogeneous in composition and team membership remains the same, all students begin each tournament with an equal chance to earn points for their teams because they are competing against peers whose achievement is similar to theirs. This incentive structure motivates students not only to master the material on their own but also to help their teammates master the material.

Student Teams-Achievement Divisions (STAD)

Student Teams-Achievement Divisions is a simplification of TGT (Slavin, 1986). It follows the same heterogeneous grouping and cooperative learning procedures as TGT but replaces the games and tournaments with a quiz. Quiz scores are translated into team competition points based on how much students have improved their performance over past averages.

Both TGT and STAD combine cooperative learning task structures with team competition and group rewards for cumulative individual performance. However, STAD depersonalizes the competition. Rather than compete face-to-face against classmates at tournament tables, students in STAD classrooms try to do their best on quizzes they take individually. Over time, Slavin and his colleagues have emphasized STAD more and TGT less, because STAD is simpler to implement and reduces the salience of competition.

Jigsaw II

Jigsaw II is an adaptation of the original Jigsaw (Slavin, 1980b). In the new version, the teacher does not need to provide each student with unique materials. Instead, all students begin by reading a common narrative and then each group member is given a separate topic on which to become an expert. Next, as in the original Jigsaw, students who have the same topic assignments meet in expert groups to discuss topics and then return to their teams to teach what they have learned to their teammates. Then the students take the quiz and their individual scores are summed to compute team scores, and team accomplishments are recognized through a class newsletter.

Team-Assisted Individualization (TAI)

Team-assisted individualization (TAI) is an adaptation of individualized mathematics instruction that introduces cooperative learning methods and team competition with group reward, as in STAD (Slavin, 1985). TAI combines direct instruction (to small, homogeneously formed groups) by the teacher, follow-up practice using programmed curriculum materials, and a student-team learning approach to seatwork management (see Slavin, 1985 for details).

Controlled Conflict and Controversy in Small Groups

David and Roger Johnson and their colleagues developed an interesting variation on small-group cooperative learning methods in which controlled conflict or controversy is introduced into the group. We refer here to intellectual controversy involving conflict of opinion about academic issues, not physical aggression or other forms of personal conflict. In a review of these issues, Johnson and Johnson (1979) found that constructively managed controversy in the classroom promotes a healthy uncertainty about the correctness of one's views, curiosity for more information, and better achievement. Studies conducted since then have supported this interpretation.

Smith, Johnson, and Johnson (1981) studied the learning of sixth graders about controversial issues such as whether or not strip mining should be allowed. Students were presented with material offering pro and con views on the issues and directed to study the material either individually or in small groups. Controversy groups were subdivided to represent the two sides and encouraged to debate the issues, but concurrence-seeking groups were directed to study the material together and avoid arguing. The results indicated that the controversy group condition promoted higher achievement, more accurate understanding of both positions on each issue, interest in getting more information, and better attitudes toward classmates and the value of constructive controversy. Similarly positive results have been obtained in two subsequent studies (Johnson & Johnson, 1985a; Johnson, et al., 1985). Teachers whose subjects lend themselves to controversy and debate (policy issues in social studies and science classes; interpretation issues in humanities and literature courses) should consider including controversy groups among their instructional activities.

RESEARCH ON COOPERATIVE LEARNING METHODS

There has been a great deal of research on cooperative learning methods, and several summaries are available (Johnson, Johnson & Maruyama, 1983; Sharan, 1980; Slavin, 1980a, 1983, 1990a & b). The results are generally positive, although some studies are misleading because they begged the questions they were supposed to be studying by using learning tasks that are accomplished more effectively by groups than by individuals, or by allowing groups to work together on tests and then assigning a group's test score to each group member (many of whom would not have scored so highly if they had been required to take the test on their own). Even with such studies eliminated, however, the research indicates that cooperative learning methods are feasible in many classroom situations and that they are likely to have positive effects both on achievement and on other outcome variables. However, we reiterate, positive results have primarily focused on low-level achievement outcomes (facts, simple computations, etc.).

Cooperative Versus Traditional Methods

The effects on *achievement* are positive, although they appear to be related to the use of specific group rewards based on members' individual performance rather than to the cooperative task structures used (Slavin, 1983). That is, the student team learning methods that include team rewards (TGT, STAD, Jigsaw II, TAI) tend to have consistently positive effects on student achievement, whereas the more purely cooperative methods (Learning Together, Group Investigation, and the original Jigsaw) are less likely to produce a significant achievement advantage over traditional techniques (Lew et al., 1986; Moskowitz et al., 1985; Okebukola, 1985; Slavin, 1983). It may be the case that truly cooperative methods require much more "up-front" time than simple tutoring models. It may require extensive work with students before they can truly cooperate.

Also, methods ensuring the accountability of individual group members to their groupmates produce higher achievement than methods in which it is possible for one or two students to do the work while others take more passive roles. The most effective methods combine group goals with individual accountability (Slavin, 1988).

The findings on task specialization are mixed, probably because its appropriateness varies with subject matter and the instructional objectives pursued. Task specialization seems most useful in social studies and with assignments emphasizing higher-level cognitive skills (Graybeal & Stodolsky, 1985). It is difficult to use task specialization for mathematics or other linearly sequenced curricula.

There is no evidence that group competition offers advantages over other cooperative learning methods so long as arrangements are made to provide group rewards based on the cumulative performance of individual group members. Besides direct group competitions as in TGT and STAD, good results have been obtained by giving teams certificates for meeting preset standards independently of the performance of other teams and by using task specialization to motivate students to encourage their groupmates. Thus, although the effects of cooperative learning on achievement appear to be primarily motivational, the key is not motivation to win competitions against other teams but motivation to assist one's teammates to meet their individual goals and thus ensure that the team will do well.

Effects on outcomes other than achievement are more impressive. Cooperative learning arrangements promote friendships and prosocial interaction among students who differ in achievement, sex, race, or ethnicity, and they promote the acceptance of mainstreamed handicapped students by their nonhandicapped classmates. Cooperative methods also frequently have positive effects, and rarely have negative effects, on affective outcomes such as self-esteem, academic self-confidence, liking for the class, liking and feeling liked by classmates, and various measures of empathy and social cooperation.

Group Composition and Processes

In addition to the research just summarized comparing cooperative with traditional learning methods, there have been studies of the effects on students' achievement of group composition and the nature of students' interaction during group meetings (Bennett & Cass, 1988; Peterson et al., 1984; Swing & Peterson, 1982; Webb, 1982, 1989; Webb & Cullian, 1983). These studies typically involved groups of four students whose interactions were tape-recorded for later analysis. Three main conclusions have emerged from this research.

First, whether students master the content to be learned depends not only on their entry-level achievement but on their experiences in the group. Giving explanations to other group members is positively correlated with achievement, even when entry-level ability is controlled. This confirms the findings from peer-tutoring studies (e.g., Graesser & Person, 1994) and other research indicating that explaining material to others is an effective learning experience for the explainer as well as the person receiving the explanation. Receiving explanations usually also correlates positively with later achievement scores, indicating that students who know what to ask about and succeed in getting their questions answered are likely to master the material. In contrast, negative correlations with achievement have been noted for asking questions without getting a response or receiving only a direct answer to a question without an explanation of how to arrive at the answer (Nattiv, 1994).

A second, related finding is that quality of interaction in small groups can be enhanced through training. Compared with those in untrained control groups, students given training in how to interact during small-group activities have been shown to spend more time on-task (asking questions, giving feedback, checking answers) and to go beyond just giving answers by giving more detailed explanations designed to make sure that the listener understands the concept or process.

A third finding is that certain combinations of students seem to work better with one another than other combinations do. In mixed groups containing one high achiever, two average achievers, and one low achiever, most of the interaction involved tutoring of the low achiever by the high achiever, with the average achievers remaining relatively passive. Thus, heterogeneous small groups seemed to be relatively less effective with average achievers, at least when the students had not been trained in how to interact during small-group activities.

Homogeneous groupings produced mixed results. Groups of average students worked well together, helping one another and interacting actively. However, groups in which the students either were all high achievers or all low achievers did not work well together or interact much about the academic content. Members of homogeneous high-achieving groups apparently assumed that no one needed help, and members of homogeneous low-achieving groups often became frustrated because they were unable to explain material effectively to one another.

Bennett and Cass (1988) conducted a study in Britain to explore the effects of three types of groups on student performance. Groups studied included ability groups (high, average, low); mixed ability groups containing a high, an average, and a low student; and mixed groups that contained only high and low achievers. Two comparisons were built in. One group was composed of two high students and one low student (2HL), and the other included two low students and one high student (2LH).

The researchers found the 2LH performed much better than 2HL groups. When the low-achieving student worked with two high achievers, the low student was ignored or chose to withdraw from active participation. Lack of involvement led the low student to misunderstand the basis on which decisions were made and lowered performance. High achievers performed well in all group settings. These students provided more suggestions, had more suggestions accepted by group members, and provided both more explanations and more appropriate explanations. Thus, within the context of this study, high-achieving students' performance was not affected by working with low achievers.

LIMITATIONS OF FINDINGS ON SMALL-GROUP LEARNING

Although research illustrates that students can learn cooperatively under certain conditions, many issues about small-group instruction have not been resolved. Davidson (1985) notes that achievement comparisons have been made in reference to computational skills, simple concepts, and simple application problems.

Thus, a relatively narrow range of dependent measures has been explored. Davidson argues that more information is needed about how higher-order skills are influenced by small-group mathematics learning, especially since educators increasingly advocate that instruction emphasize understanding rather than the learning of isolated skills.

Cooperative learning research has also been questioned on theoretical grounds. For example, many educators question the value of competition if cooperative learning is the goal. Research by Stipek (1986) and others who have explored intrinsic motivation concepts shows that teachers need to pay careful attention to what happens to students when cooperative behavior is maintained by the use of external incentives over an extended period.

Pepitone (1985) contends that the concept of group goals has largely been neglected in cooperative learning research, although distinctions between task goals and group goals have long been made. Some theorists contend that if a group is to work cooperatively, it must work on goals that are important to group members, not just on assigned work.

Yet another weakness of the research base on cooperative learning is that few observational data describe how students interact in groups and how achievement and affective gains actually occur. This deficiency is especially important for teachers and researchers who are interested in student development and not simply outcomes on an achievement test. Theorists such as Noddings (1989) would be interested in a broad range of outcomes (meaningful learning of subject matter, learning prosocial skills, developing alternative approaches to problem solving, exploring conjecturing, and growing in social intelligence).

Researchers have been encouraging more study of group processes in order to determine whether or not some of the putative goals of small-group instruction are being attained (Bossert, 1988–1989; Good & Biddle, 1988; Good, Mulryan, & McCaslin, 1992). Bossert noted that researchers have often failed to verify whether students have even engaged in cooperative interactions, and that when they have observed instructional processes, their results have not always supported theories of cooperative learning.

As a case in point, Mulryan (1989, 1995) studied students' behavior during whole-class and small-group mathematics instruction. She found that students manifested more attending behavior in the cooperative mathematics small-group context than the whole-class context. However, high achievers exhibited significantly more quality attending behavior in cooperative small groups than did low achievers. Further, high achievers spent 5 percent of their time in cooperative small groups in off-task behavior, whereas low achievers were off-task 13 percent of the time. Low achievers asked more questions and high achievers did more information giving. Mulryan (1995) also reported that male students initiated more interactions in small-groups than did females.

Mulryan argued that the roles of helping that emerged in these small groups may not have been useful, especially when the same students played these roles consistently. Such circumstances create a "caste" system that discourages the active involvement of some students. Mulryan (1995) found that low-achieving female students appear to be losing out the most during cooperative small-group settings. She concluded that without careful teacher structuring and monitoring, those same students who benefit the most from whole-class instruction are also the most likely to learn best in small-group learning situations.

During interviews some students indicated that they perceived low achievers as a burden to other members of cooperative groups. Building on Good's (1981) passivity model, Mulryan (1992) identified six types of passive students: the discouraged student; the unrecognized student; the despondent student; the unmotivated student; the bored student; and the intellectual snob. The discouraged students were mainly low achievers who became passive because they perceived the group task as too difficult and thought it better to leave the work to peers who knew more content. The unrecognized students became passive because their initial efforts to participate were ignored or not recognized by other group members. Most unrecognized students were low achievers. Despondent students included both high and low achievers. They tended to be passive because they disliked or felt uncomfortable with one or more persons in their group. Some of their passivity appeared due to their perception of the cooperative learning task as unimportant or "only a game." Bored students also included both low and high achievers, although there were more high achievers than lows. They perceived the task as boring because it was too easy. Finally, intellectual snobs were passive in cooperative work because they thought their peers were less competent at math and they did not want to explain constantly to them.

Mulryan noted that some students were uninvolved in the official learning task but showed other active behaviors in their group. She identified social opportunists (students who wanted to talk with peers about social issues) and intentional loafers (students who allowed other students to do the work). Most social opportunists and intentional loafers were low achievers.

Other researchers have also observed problems of group interaction. King (1993) found that high-achieving students dominated group discussions and task initiation and generally played leadership roles. Even though low achievers were relatively passive during group work, they reported that they enjoyed working in small groups (especially the social aspects) and looked forward to more opportunities for group work.

As Good, McCaslin, and Reys (1992) have noted, students' affective reports of satisfaction on questionnaires or in interviews may mask important problems in group functioning. Thus, teachers who use small-group work as a method for engaging students in problem solving and higher-order thinking must be careful to monitor group processes in order to assess the quality of student interactions. Teachers need to develop strategies for monitoring group processes (occasionally tape-recording a group, sitting in on a group, etc.) in order to assess the quality of the discussions that take place (McCaslin & Good, 1996).

POTENTIAL ADVANTAGES AND DISADVANTAGES OF COOPERATIVE GROUPS

We have seen that students report liking small-group work better than whole-room classwork. However, some of this positive attitude may be due to novelty and in some cases, students' misconceptions. For example, Paulus et al., (1993) have argued that research evidence illustrates that individuals produce fewer ideas in interactive brainstorming groups than when brainstorming alone. However, many individuals believe that they are more productive in the group brainstorming situation. The authors refer to the illusion of group productivity. There is ample literature to illustrate that cooperative learning structures can be extremely useful in facilitating student motivation (e.g., working faster and more accurately when doing simple activities). That is, working in the presence of others can improve motivation and performance as students can share information as necessary. However, what is more problematic is the extent to which, generally, small-group environments can facilitate and sustain *cooperative interactions* that involve true problem solving and negotiation (e.g., where correct answers are not obvious).

Building on the research of Johnson and Johnson (1985a & b), Bossert (1988–1989) noted that four major explanations could account for the success of cooperative methods: (1) reasoning strategies—cooperative groups may stimulate more higher-order thinking; (2) constructive controversy—heterogeneous cooperative groups force the accommodation of the opinions of various members, and students must engage in problem solving and take another's perspective; (3) cognitive processing—cooperative methods increase opportunities for students to rehearse information orally and to integrate it; and (4) peer encouragement and involvement in learning. Positive interactions increase friendship, acceptance, and cognitive information processing.

There are at least eight additional reasons why cooperative groups may enhance students' achievement and social relations (Good, Mulryan, & McCaslin, 1992; McCaslin & Good, 1996).

1. Subject-matter knowledge is increased. The knowledge of procedures and content that the group possesses is almost always greater than the knowledge of any individual student. Thus, with more knowledge, group problem-solving strategies can be more varied, fine-tuned, and powerful.
2. Students value shared academic work. It is likely that students will understand mathematics better in small groups because proportionately more group time is spent on conceptual understanding, in comparison to individual time, which tends to be spent on products. Thus, students may value shared academic work more because of the increased emphasis on understanding during small-group instruction.
3. Students can regulate their own resources. An individual's work pace can be more flexible in a group setting.
4. Students learn to manage others' resources. Students learn how to coordinate work with others, how to obtain information from peers, which peers to ask for what type of help, etc.
5. Students develop appropriate dispositions toward challenging work on shared tasks. Because academic work is done with others, challenging tasks are more malleable, approachable, or more do-able because of shared expertise.
6. School tasks are similar to those outside school. Tasks done in small work groups tend to be more like work done at home (and in many jobs), where everyone pitches in (or does his or her part) to get a job done.

7. Group members serve as models for one another. Students have the chance to learn important learning-to-learn skills from other students—for example, how to ask questions and how to self-regulate.
8. Students develop an expanded understanding of self and others. The opportunity to work with others helps students to identify and to appreciate individual differences in performance and motivation. Students learn that peers are not just "smart" or "dumb"; they develop a sense that everyone possesses both weaknesses and strengths. This awareness of variability in social and cognitive aptitude may allow students to be more creative, to view errors as acceptable, and to learn from failure.

Despite these ways in which small groups can provide useful learning experiences for students, problems that develop in some group situations may prevent or minimize constructive learning. Good, Mulryan, and McCaslin (1992) and McCaslin and Good (1996) identify several potential problems:

1. Students' misconceptions are reinforced. Students often have misconceptions about academic content and these may be reinforced during small-group interactions.
2. Students shift dependency from teacher to peers. The shift from whole-class to small-group instruction may be a superficial change (i.e., student as teacher) rather than an actual structural change (i.e., collaborative learning).
3. Students value the product more than the process. If group members focus too narrowly on the group product, speed may take precedence over the problem-solving process, and groups may pay more attention to product rate than to the process of problem solution.
4. Students value group processes more than the academic product. In some classrooms, attention to group processes and "learning to learn with others" may take precedence over subject-matter learning so that much time is spent teaching students elaborate and potentially artificial procedures for dealing with controversy, and so forth.
5. Students receive differential attention and status. Some group situations may present little more than an opportunity for high-achieving students to perform for other students. In other groups, high achievers may feel excessive pressure to do the work for the group.
6. Some students believe they are not able to contribute. Some students will perceive themselves as having little to contribute to their peers during group learning. These students may become indebted to group members who consistently help them do most of the work.
7. Some students may learn that they do not need to contribute. Social comparison may exacerbate social loafing. Some students may consistently receive feedback suggesting that their skills are not valued as much as those of some of their peers. Both high- and low-ability students may recognize that their group makes progress whether or not they contribute actively.

These students may learn to engage in social loafing—they do relatively little thinking or participating during group work either because they do not value the work or the group, or because they do not excel and, thus, are trying to protect their self-esteem.

8. Group accountability may mediate failure-avoiding and success-enhancing behavior. For example, students who have reputations as "know-it-alls" may withhold information so as not to enhance their (unwanted) reputations. Other students may withhold information in an attempt to be fair and to let other students contribute more. Such altruistic behavior may come at the expense of learning.

CONCLUSIONS FROM RESEARCH ON COOPERATIVE LEARNING

We recommend cooperative learning methods to teachers, although with certain qualifications. First, it is important to view the cooperative learning approach not as a wholesale replacement of traditional whole-class instruction but as an adaptation of this approach in which active whole-class instruction by the teacher is retained but many follow-up practice and application activities are accomplished through small-group cooperation rather than through individual seatwork. Peers are not an acceptable substitute for active instruction by the teacher as the basic method for conveying content to students. Peers can deliver effective explanations about how to respond to specific questions or assignments, but they cannot be expected to have the subject matter and pedagogical knowledge needed to provide effective advance organization and structuring of content, systematic development of key concepts, or sophisticated remedial instruction. Nor can students be expected to tutor one another effectively on tasks that focus on higher-order objectives (Ross, 1988).

Second, cooperative learning approaches may be more feasible and valuable in certain classes than in others. So far, these methods have been used most frequently in (and most of the research supporting them comes from) classes in grades 4 through 9. They may be less relevant or more difficult to implement for teachers working with primary-grade students or upper secondary-school students. Also, methods that emphasize group rewards and individual accountability to other group members for one's own effort and performance (TGT, STAD, Jigsaw II, TAI) appear to be more appropriate for work in mathematics and other subjects that emphasize individual practice of sequenced skills. Methods that emphasize group discussion and investigation, structured controversy, differentiated roles and responsibilities, or cooperative development of a group product may be more appropriate for social studies and for assignments that focus on higher-level cognitive objectives (application, problem solving, analysis, synthesis, evaluation).

Third, it is not yet clear what the effects would be if cooperative learning methods were used in most courses year after year. Students who are social and those who receive considerable help from their peers would likely respond very positively, but other students might not. The latter include all students who enjoy working alone much of the time, as well as students who are academic leaders within teams and assume much of the responsibility for tutoring their teammates. Even students who enjoy learning cooperatively in moderation might tire of it if called upon to do so too often. Thus, there is probably some optimal level of use of cooperative learning methods, both within any course and across the school day or school year.

Fourth, although it may often be important to use methods that involve group rewards and individual accountability to the group for one's effort, we advise emphasizing cooperation but deemphasizing competition. Thus, STAD is preferable to TGT, for example. Competition is a form of extrinsic motivation that may distract students from basic learning goals unless it is handled carefully. Another problem is that competition creates losers as well as winners, and the bad feelings that result from losing competitions may undermine some of the potential contributions of small-group cooperative learning arrangements to improved personal and social outcomes (Ames & Felker, 1979).

Fifth, students need to be trained to work cooperatively, especially if they are not familiar with cooperative learning approaches. Some students may not know how to act in small-group situations or may even be hostile in responding to the contributions of their peers. Consequently, teachers may need to show students how to share, listen, integrate the ideas of others, and handle disagreements. In the early grades, most group assignments probably should be short, highly structured, enjoyable, and unlikely to produce conflict. Students can be moved gradually into longer and more demanding tasks as their skills develop. When structured effectively, cooperative small-group activities not only produce peer support and encouragement for learning but may result in the development of higher-quality strategies for understanding and responding to tasks than students develop when working alone (Johnson, Skon, & Johnson, 1980). In the process of discussing tasks and helping one another to learn, students can discover a great deal about how to search efficiently and identify key information, recognize what is given and what is called for in a problem, and formulate problem-solving strategies that feature systematic hypothesis testing rather than random guessing and allow for checking of answers and identification of errors. This increases the likelihood that students will get the intended cognitive benefits, and not merely the right answers, from problem-solving exercises.

However, problem-solving approaches may be high risk, especially if students are not prepared for cooperative work and if student work is not supervised. Problems that call for cognitive flexibility and interpersonal negotiation can generate considerable frustration and anger among students.

In discussing strategies for training students in group work skills, Bennett and Dunne (1992) suggest that cooperative skills need to be taught directly. Initially, if students have had limited experience in cooperative group work, they should receive a series of relatively simple tasks. This allows teachers to emphasize how to work cooperatively and to supervise students closely so that relevant feedback can be given about their cooperative and social skills. Students need to develop an awareness of what it means to work cooperatively in social settings and to learn the skills needed to do so. Some cooperative models may require considerable instructional time to help students develop needed social skills.

What is critical in helping students learn to work cooperatively is to prepare them for both the social and cognitive demands of cooperation. Some models of cooperation require more ability to negotiate, compromise, and handle discontinuity and ambiguity. Teachers need to be aware of the need to help students understand both types of responsibilities more fully.

Finally, teachers who wish to use cooperative learning effectively need to assign tasks and activities that are well suited to it. This often means adapting or substituting for traditional assignments meant for individuals. Good et al. (1989–1990), for example, found that small-group cooperative learning did not work well in many mathematics classes because most assigned tasks involved routine computation practice, an activity that students are accustomed to working on alone and that does not lend itself to cooperative interaction. If students are actually meant to cooperate rather than just compare answers, they need to be assigned to work on problems that admit to a range of formulation and solution strategies that can be discussed and debated, or else be assigned more complicated tasks that must be done in stages requiring cooperative planning and perhaps differentiation of roles for students in the group. Also, the activities assigned for cooperative learning must be continuous with the curriculum if cooperative learning is to be an integral part of subject-matter teaching rather than an isolated add-on. Thus, cooperative learning activities should engage students in exploring or applying the content currently being taught, with the scope of the task and the degree of autonomous cooperative work expected from students depending on their familiarity with both the academic content and the cooperative learning format.

IMPLEMENTATION GUIDELINES

Johnson et al. (1984) suggest the following steps for teachers interested in implementing small-group cooperative learning:

OBJECTIVES
1. Specify academic and collaborative skills objectives.

DECISIONS
2. Decide the size of the group (typically from two to six, depending on the nature of the task, the time available, and the experience of the teacher in using small-group methods).
3. Assign students to groups (preferably by ensuring heterogeneity rather than grouping by ability or allowing students to form their own groups).
4. Arrange the room so that the teacher has access to each group and group members can meet in a circle and sit close enough to each other to communicate effectively without disrupting other groups.
5. Plan instructional materials to promote interdependence (if necessary, give only one copy of the materials to each group or give each group member different materials so as to force task differentiation).
6. Assign roles to ensure interdependence (assign different members complementary and interconnected roles such as summarizer-checker, researcher-runner, recorder, encourager, and observer).
7. Explain the academic task.

8. Structure positive goal interdependence, peer encouragement, and support for learning (ask the group to produce a single product or use an assessment system in which individuals' rewards are based both on their own scores and on the average for the group as a whole).
9. Structure individual accountability (by using quizzes or randomly selecting group members to explain answers or present the group's conclusions).
10. Structure intergroup cooperation.
11. Explain success criteria.
12. Specify desired behaviors (define cooperative learning operationally by requesting that students take turns, use personal names, listen carefully to one another, encourage everyone to participate, etc.).

MONITORING AND INTERVENING

13. Monitor student behavior (circulate to listen and observe groups in action; note problems in completing assignments or working cooperatively).
14. Provide task assistance.
15. Intervene to teach collaborative skills (where groups are experiencing major problems in collaborating successfully).
16. Provide closure to the lesson.

EVALUATION AND PROCESSING

17. Evaluate quality and quantity of students' learning.
18. Assess how well the group functions (give feedback about how well the members worked with one another and accomplished assigned tasks and how they could improve).

USING EXTANT CURRICULUM AND TRAINING MATERIAL

A number of valuable sources provide ideas for helping students understand and respond to cooperative learning situations (e.g., Bennett & Dunne, 1992; Cohen, 1994; Jenkins, 1989; Kagan, 1988). Such sources provide activities that teachers can adapt to their own classrooms. Teachers who are making decisions about group work must understand the long-term reasons why they are using cooperative learning and design activities that help students to work successfully under a specific model. Sometimes activities (even valuable activities) can become ends in themselves and lead to counterproductive behavior, beliefs, and norms.

Cohen (1986) provides a strategy that can be useful in getting students to monitor and to pay attention to group processes. The strategy, amended from Epstein (1972), has been labeled the four-stage rocket. Students are divided into groups and presented with a short discussion task. The teacher observes various groups and notes appropriate and inappropriate discussion techniques. Then the teacher conducts a whole-class discussion of these observations. Students are told that they will have the opportunity to practice four skills that are necessary if the discussion is to "take off like a rocket." The four skills are conciseness, listening, reflecting, and everyone contributing. Students practice each skill.

Assuming that an appropriate discussion task has been selected, such an activity can provide an interesting orientation to small-group work. However, to reiterate, teachers must help students to see the broad purposes of small-group work. Conciseness of expression may be a virtue initially, but as they explore open-ended problems, students should be expected to deal with the ambiguities of going beyond the information given and explore problems. Further, an emphasis on time (only 15 seconds) may inadvertently suggest to students that *speed* is important. Hence, if teachers intend to develop a proactive and thoughtful approach to group problem solving, then they must establish these expectations with these students.

MEANINGFUL IMPLEMENTATION

The guidelines just presented appear deceptively simple. However, some of the steps may require much time to develop. Also, techniques that may be useful at certain stages (e.g., the assignment of roles) may become unnecessary or even counterproductive (role assignments may interfere with authentic communication when students work as a group). For example, Good et al. (1989–1990) found that role assignment was often artificial and in some cases students spent more time discussing role boundaries than thinking about the task. Thus, it may make sense to use roles for a limited time for young students or when cooperative techniques are first being introduced and then to discard them and allow students to develop their own communication styles.

PROVIDING OPPORTUNITY FOR SELF-EVALUATION

Opportunities for self-evaluation are critical if students are to improve at monitoring and cooperative interactions. Clearly, students at different ages will need different kinds of evaluation activities, and students who have had more or less experience in cooperative settings will need different types of evaluation questions. For example, Figure 7.1 provides a straightforward method for helping young children reflect on group processes. One could have students fill out the sheet individually or in groups. In time, the teacher might allow individual students to explain why they disagree with other group members. However, again, it is important to stress the evolutionary nature of questions and activities that encourage students to become more sophisticated participants over time. For example, item 6 in Figure 7.1 might be appropriate when students are beginning to practice group skills, but in time, this question might be counterproductive (students spend time clarifying when there is no point to the activity) and more mature issues should be addressed. Teachers must use student self-evaluation activities that are appropriate to the age and experience of students.

In evaluating the success of small-group work, it is useful to consider the needs of individual students as well as their responsibilities. For example, Samples (1992) argued that one fundamental obligation of teachers is to ensure that the cooperation and autonomy that they attempt to develop in the classroom are authentic. If there is authenticity in cooperation, some of the following characteristics should be present: students have a large voice in defining the task, real problem

Group evaluation	Always	Sometimes	Never
1 We checked to make sure everyone understood what we did	....	....	....
2 We answered any questions that were asked	....	....	....
3 We gave explanations wherever we could	....	....	....
4 We asked specific questions about what we didn't understand	....	....	....
5 Anyone who had difficulty got extra practice and help	....	....	....
6 We paraphrased what others said to be sure we understood	....	....	....

Group signatures

X ....   X ....

X ....   X ....

FIGURE 7.1
Evaluation of group processes.

solving is required (outcomes are not known in advance); a primary source of satisfaction has to come from the experience itself; there are shifts of authority and responsibility within the group; students provide different types of leadership at different times; and the teacher serves as resource and guide rather than as the dominant figure.

According to Samples, authenticity and autonomy are needed in an era that is encouraging cooperative education. Thus, teachers must be aware of the integrity of individual student autonomy while encouraging cooperation. He noted that consensus and fitting in can be overdetermined and that teachers must foster the integrity of both the solitary self and the social self in the process of cooperative learning. Some appropriate indicators for assessing authenticity and autonomy include: students are comfortable when they choose to be alone; students occasionally choose to withdraw from a group for temporary exploration; students respect what they know and what they do not know.

Another example of a self-evaluation or group evaluation form appears in Figure 7.2. This example is from Kagan (1988), who suggested that the first three questions should be addressed frequently and that the other questions on the scale would help students to focus on specific issues from time to time as appropriate.

A small-group format can take a variety of forms depending on whether more or less teacher direction and/or direct involvement is desired. Mason, Reys, and

1 What one word would you use to describe how the group was today?

....

2 What one word would describe the way you would like the group to be?

....

3 Is everyone participating?
Yes, always .... Usually .... Occasionally........................
Rarely .... No, never ....

4 Are you (everyone in group) trying to make each other feel good? If not, what are you doing?
Yes, always .... Usually .... Occasionally........................
Rarely .... No, never ....

5 Are you trying to help each other feel able to talk and say what you think?
Yes, always .... Usually .... Occasionally........................
Rarely .... No, never ....

6 Are you listening to each other?
Yes, always .... Usually .... Occasionally........................
Rarely .... No, never ....

7 Are you showing you are listening by nodding at each other?
Yes, always .... Usually .... Occasionally........................
Rarely .... No, never ....

8 Are you saying 'That's good' to each other when you like something?
Yes, always .... Usually .... Occasionally........................
Rarely .... No, never ....

9 Are you asking each other questions?
Yes, always .... Usually .... Occasionally........................
Rarely .... No, never ....

10 Are you listening and really trying to answer these questions?
Yes, always .... Usually .... Occasionally........................
Rarely .... No, never ....

11 Are you paying attention to each other?
Yes, always .... Usually .... Occasionally........................
Rarely .... No, never ....

12 Is any one person talking most of the time? Yes .... No................

13 Is there a way to have a group where everyone talks about equally?
Yes .... No ....

FIGURE 7.2
Evaluation of group processes.

Good (1990) described three instructional models that could be used for small-group work. These models illustrate how small-group instruction might be organized. Although each model is teacher-directed to some extent, teacher direction and student group work vary (the role of teacher as director of learning decreases, and the role of students as directors or orchestrators of learning increases).

Approximate Time	Activity	Locus of Control
30-40 min.		Teacher

> **Develop New Concepts and Skills with Stress on Meaning**
> • Explanation
> • Demonstration
> • Illustration
> • Discussion
> **Describe Work-Group Task**
> • Exploration
> • Investigation
> • Generalization
> • Application

5-10 min.		Group

> **Work-Group Task**
> Inquiry, reinforcement, or extension of concepts using work-group task
> • Exploration
> • Investigation
> • Application

5-10 min.		Teacher

> **Review/Summarization of Task**
> • Brief Review of Objectives
> • Review of Work-Group Task
> • Review of Findings
> • Connections to Future/Past Study

Notes: Time lines are suggested; particular lessons call for different time distributions, and lesson elements may vary substantially in length.
Review of seatwork, homework, and reteaching should be used as appropriate prior to beginning the active teaching and active learning component.
Establish routines to eliminate lengthy transitions, explanations, and directions.
Assure accountability on seatwork and homework through direct method of monitoring.

FIGURE 7.3
A model of active teaching and active learning in mathematics using work groups as an extension of teacher development of a concept.

Model 1 (Figure 7.3) is highly teacher-directed; the lesson begins with a 30- to 40-minute teacher-led active teaching and learning component on a new concept. One student group-work session follows and varies from 5 to 10 minutes. Model 2 (Figure 7.4) employs a recursive pattern in which teacher direction and facilitation components are alternated three or more times with student work in groups. Time allocated for work groups is increased to as much as 40 minutes (although this includes some time for teacher assessment, clarification, and new task assignment).

Approximate Time	Activity	Locus of Control
10 min.		Teacher

Introduce, Explore, Investigate Apply, or Reinforce Concept
- *Explore* New Concepts and Skills with Stress on *Understanding*
- Provide Problematic Situations and Modeling of Strategies
- Guide Meaningful Discussion
- Clarify Outcomes to Be Attained

| 5-10 min. | | Group |

Work-Group: Task 1
Inquiry, reinforcement, or extension of concept using task
- Exploration   • Application
- Investigation   • Reinforcement

| 5 min. | | Teacher |

Assess Progress/Process and Clarify
- Active Q/A Interactions
- Discuss Problem Situation
- Discuss Strategies/Process/Findings
- Provide New Development
- Provide New Tasks

| 10-15 min. | | Group |

Work-Group: Task 2

| 5 min. | | Teacher |

Assess Progress/Process and Clarify

| 10-15 min. | | Group |

Work-Group: Task 3

| 5 min. | | Teacher |

Review/Summarization of Task
- Brief Review of Objectives
- Review of Tasks
- Review of Findings
- Connections of Future/Past Study

Notes: Time lines are suggested; particular lessons call for different time distributions, and lesson elements may vary substantially in length.
Review of seatwork, homework, and reteaching should be used as appropriate prior to beginning the active teaching and active learning component.
Establish routines to eliminate lengthy transitions, explanations, and directions.

FIGURE 7.4
A model of active teaching and active learning in mathematics using groups of four and teacher development in a recursive pattern.

In Model 3 (Figure 7.5), the teacher's role changes from director to facilitator. Although the teacher fosters an appropriate environment for group work by creating interest and outlining pertinent questions, students in groups are the primary orchestrators of learning as they formulate and carry out the plan for addressing the question under study.

Model 1 is similar to traditional whole-class teaching except that students work together extending the ideas presented by the teacher rather than working individually on seatwork designed to reinforce the ideas. In Model 1 students see teacher demonstrations and explanations but also explore and discuss mathematical ideas and problem-solving strategies in both whole-class and small-group settings.

In Model 2, teachers engage students (through work groups) in a series of connected explorations, each building on the preceding one, and link those explorations with summarization of ideas and stimulation of new ideas. Teachers are asked not only to introduce students to each new task but to model strategies for solving the higher-level thinking problems.

In using Model 3, teachers simply introduce a problem by explaining to students that they have an opportunity to apply previously learned concepts or skills, seek multiple solutions, brainstorm with work-group teammates, and cooperate to develop strategies for solving the problem. Although teachers using Model 3 are asked not to model strategies for solving the problem, they should still review procedural rules as necessary and clarify the outcomes to be attained.

Each model encourages active student learning through teacher development and/or work-group activity. As appropriate, teachers are encouraged to organize activities involving exploration, discovery, problem solving, or application that enable students to construct or extend their understandings of mathematics with peers. For an illustration of how each model might be used with specific mathematics content, see Good, McCaslin, and Reys (1992).

Since research has not been conducted on these models, no sequence or value should be assumed. For example, some students may need considerable experience with Models 1 and 2 before they can function well in Model 3. However, extended participation in Models 1 and 2 could create misconceptions about Model 3 learning that would be difficult to correct.

Model 3 presents a way to provide students with more control and power over subject-matter knowledge and learning. The extent to which Models 1 and 2 are necessary instructional scaffolding is an interesting issue that will require considerable theory and research. Furthermore, we do not contend at this point that one model is better than the others. Experience in Model 2 with both frequent peer and teacher interaction may help students to develop mathematical power more effectively than will Model 3, which may place too much responsibility on students too soon. In contrast, Model 3 may be most productive for students who have the capacity for self-evaluation and autonomous mathematical reasoning. Model 1 may be optimal for other mathematical outcomes or types of students because it combines teacher modeling and whole-class discussion (with both teacher-student and student-student dialogue) with small-group exploratory work. Issues of authority and control (control of subject matter; control of discussion; control of evaluation) are important. The three models provide a theoretical basis on which to plan instructional sequences and research that will inform our understanding of these issues.

Approximate Time	Activity	Locus of Control
10 min.		Teacher

Introduce Problematic Situation
- Guide Meaningful Discussion
- Application/Transfer
- Solutions
- Brainstorming
- Teamwork/Cooperation
- Stress Sharing Strategies
- Assign Task
- Clarify Outcomes to be Attained

25-40 min.		Group

Work-Group Task
Problem formulation/clarification, solution strategy formulation, data collection, etc., depending on task.
- Exploration
- Investigation
- Application

5-10 min.		Teacher

Summarization of Group Progress
- Active Q/A Interactions
- Discussion of Problematic Situation and Findings
- Discussion of Strategies/Process
- Justification of Answers/Process
- Provision of New Alternatives
- Summary of Activity
- Direction for Continuing Exploration Out of Class

60 min.

Notes: Time lines are suggested; particular lessons call for different time distributions, and lesson elements may vary substantially in length.

Review of seatwork, homework, and reteaching should be used as appropriate prior to beginning the active teaching and active learning component.

Establish routines to eliminate lengthy transitions, explanations, and directions.

FIGURE 7.5

A model of active teaching and active learning in mathematics using groups of four in a highly independent pattern.

ARRANGING TUTORIAL ASSISTANCE FOR STUDENTS

Individualized tutoring would be the optimal means of achieving most academic objectives, but classroom management responsibilities severely limit teachers' opportunities to provide such tutoring. We recommend that you tutor struggling students as often as you can, both by making time to help them individually during class and by arranging to tutor them outside class if possible (before or after school or between class periods). Even here, though, there are limits to what can be accomplished by even the most dedicated teacher.

One way to supplement instruction is to arrange for students to be tutored by someone other than the teacher. If teacher aides are available, this is one important function they could perform. The same is true of adult volunteers in the classroom and parents or older siblings at home. If you structure the tutoring by providing appropriate materials and exercises and by training the tutors in how to fulfill their roles effectively, you can significantly increase the amount of instruction that slower students receive, perhaps enough to make the difference between keeping up with the class or falling increasingly behind.

Students can also tutor one another, which we noted earlier as one benefit of student teams and other cooperative learning arrangements. The models that require individual products from students who work in small groups are essentially group tutorial models where students can receive help as needed. Options include cross-age tutoring (older students work with younger students) and peer tutoring (students are tutored by classmates).

Cross-Age Tutoring

Cross-age tutoring is commonly used in elementary schools, where, for example, teachers may arrange for fifth- and sixth-grade students to tutor first- and second-grade students at designated times. Cross-age tutoring generally improves both the attitudes and achievement of students involved (Cohen, Kulik, & Kulik, 1982; Devin-Sheehan, Feldman, & Allen, 1976; Paolitto, 1976; Sharpley, Irvine, & Sharpley, 1983). Furthermore, these desirable outcomes are likely to occur not only for the tutees who receive instruction but also for the tutors who provide it. In part, this arrangement exemplifies the truism that we master material more thoroughly when we teach it to someone else than when we merely respond to it as learners.

The tutors' achievement gains may also be attributed to improved attitudes or self-concepts rather than to deeper exposure to academic content (because they are tutoring younger students on material several grades below their present status). Tutors often respond very positively to their responsibilities. The role involves serious concern about learning academic content, and it appears to stimulate many tutors to identify more closely with the teacher and to become more concerned about their own learning. The tutoring experience may cause underachievers to take their own work more seriously, or lead antisocial students to become more appreciative of their potential for prosocial interaction with others.

Thus, tutors should not be seen merely as performing a service for the teacher. If structured properly, cross-age tutoring presents opportunities for the tutors, and not just the tutees, to derive a variety of cognitive and affective benefits.

Tutoring should not be overused, however, and students (especially high achievers) should not be asked to do so much of it that they lose opportunities to do challenging or interesting work at their own level. If anything, the potential benefits of assuming the tutor role are greatest for low achievers, who rarely get the opportunity to act as the competent expert giving instruction rather than receiving it. Yet, low achievers often can play this role effectively when tutoring younger students (Bar-Eli & Raviv, 1982).

The role of tutee also presents many potential benefits. Interactions with tutors are typically friendly and experienced as enjoyable and helpful (Fogarty & Wang, 1982), and they provide a change of pace from more typical learning situations. They also provide opportunities for tutees to take a more active role in structuring their learning experiences to meet their needs by asking questions or calling for particular forms of help. This may be especially important for discouraged or alienated students accustomed to feigning competency rather than seeking help, all the more so if the new behavior generalizes to their interactions with the teacher.

Under some circumstances, students may learn more readily from student tutors than from teachers. In the case of an unresolved personality clash or communication problem between a teacher and a student, for example, the student might not only be more comfortable but also learn more during individualized instruction from an older student. Also, student tutors may use language or examples that are more easily understood than those of the teacher, or may identify learning problems more accurately because they have experienced the same problems recently.

Thomas (1970) showed the value of student tutors in his study of the relative effectiveness of fifth and sixth graders versus college students as tutors of second graders in reading. He found that, in general, the elementary school tutors were just as effective as the college students (seniors enrolled in a reading methods course, who had almost completed undergraduate teacher education programs).

Although they lacked both the general intellectual development and the specialized knowledge about reading instruction that the college students had, the fifth and sixth graders were more comfortable and spontaneous in assuming the role of tutor. Thomas (1970) stated it this way:

> In analyzing the different groups of tutors, one is struck by the differences in their approach to the tutees. The college-aged tutors seemed to be attempting to coax the tutees into liking them, into enjoying the reading materials, and into practicing the reading skills. The elementary-aged tutors, for the most part, were more direct and businesslike. They seemed to accept the fact that the tutees had problems in their schoolwork, and seemed to feel that the tutoring sessions were for teaching those materials in front of them, not for going off in tangents and discussing matters outside the lesson.

Thomas's observations suggest that elementary-grade tutors can be as successful as adolescents or adults and that under some circumstances, they may even have certain advantages: (1) successful tutoring may demand direct instruction, and adults may tend to be too indirect; (2) the adults' vocabulary and examples may be too complex for young children to follow easily; and (3) tutors who are close in age to tutees may remember their own difficulties with materials and thus may be able to identify and respond to learning problems more effectively or maintain a patient, lesson-focused orientation longer than adults.

In general, though, adults are more effective tutors than children, especially in supplementing nonverbal demonstrations with verbal explanations of related concepts and in helping tutees learn the general principles that specific examples are designed to teach (Ellis & Rogoff, 1982). Fuchs et al., (1994) showed that even after training, the nature of student explanations in tutoring situations tended to be algorithmic, not conceptual.

Thus, student tutoring is more likely to be successful when used to provide supervised practice and other follow-up to instruction originally presented by the teacher than when it is expected to stand on its own.

Peer Tutoring by Classmates

Teachers also can use peer-tutoring arrangements calling for one classmate to tutor another under specified conditions. Simmons et al., (1995) have illustrated that elementary school learning-disabled students may benefit when explicit teaching is supplemented with peer tutoring. Their data illustrate the potential of peer tutoring as a supplement to reading instruction in regular general education classrooms. Graesser and Person (1994) have illustrated the potentially positive effects of peer tutoring as a vehicle for allowing students to become more active learners. Their study documented the questioning processes that occurred during tutoring using two different samples (college students discussing research methods and seventh graders discussing algebra). They noted in tutoring sessions that questions from tutors were only slightly more frequent than teacher questions (in whole-class settings); however, the students were found to ask many more questions in the tutorial situation. Further, Graesser and Person report that student achievement was correlated positively with the *quality* of student questions—but not the *frequency* of student questions.

Such peer tutoring must be handled carefully, however, because it "officially" identifies the tutee as needing help on the material being tutored. Some students may resist this role because they do not believe they need the help (Fogarty & Wang, 1982), because they are afraid of losing face before their peers, or because they believe they know more about the material than the students who are supposed to tutor them (Rosen et al., 1978). Problems of this sort are less likely to occur with cross-age tutoring or with tutoring that occurs within small-group cooperative learning arrangements, although they can occur even here if the same students are always tutored or if the teacher presents the tutoring as a remediation requirement rather than as an individualized learning opportunity.

LEARNING IN DYADS

Students can also learn new material together in pairs. Although one member of the pair may have a higher achievement profile, students of unequal ability can work together to explore new problems. For example, Kutnick and Thomas (1990) found that 11- to 12-year-old students did better on the cognitively based Science

Reasoning Task than did students working individually. These results reflected improvement in both partners' individual performances, not just a simple sharing of abilities.

However, such gains are not automatic. Stacey (1992) explored mathematical problem solving by junior secondary students and found that in a written test of problem solving, randomly assigned students working alone did better than did students working as a group (mostly pairs with some triads). The test contained six items and required students to solve nonroutine mathematical problems. In exploring why group performance was not better than individual performance, Stacey found that during group discussions students consistently ignored right ideas in favor of simpler but incorrect ideas. The group was capable of generating many ideas; however, the choices they made between possible ideas were not considered carefully.

Thus, teachers who use peer tutoring or peer learning need to monitor the process of student exchange regularly to assure both the value of content and the sensitivity of communication. As in all aspects of classroom life, teachers need to make decisions about when and how to use peer tutoring and peer learning dyads. If teachers use dyads, they should consider the guidelines we presented earlier in the chapter. We give guidelines for peer tutoring (where one student explicitly helps another) in the section that follows.

We suggest the following guidelines for teachers considering peer tutoring (for additional suggestions see Goodlad & Hirst, 1989, or Jenkins & Jenkins, 1987).

Learning Outlook   Create the mental set that *we learn from one another*. This is more readily achieved when you consistently model and point out to students how you learn from them. Also, you can help reduce unnecessary competition by stressing that the goal is for all students to learn as much as they can and that the measure of success is how we compare with our own past performance rather than how we compare with others in the class.

Procedural Details   Decisions need to be made about the following procedural matters:

1. Definite times of the day should be set aside for tutoring, so that students quickly learn that only certain class times are for helping one another (to avoid continuous disruption of the class).
2. Specific assignments need to be outlined. The teacher should mimeograph the directions each tutor is to follow each week. For example, "Johnny, this week from 8:00 to 9:00 you will work with Jill and Terry. On Monday you will use flash cards to review the 7, 8, and 9 multiplication tables. Go through each table twice with them and then get individual responses from each. The last time, write down the mistakes that each makes and return the sheet to me. On Tuesday, play audiotape Number 16 for Jill and Terry and listen with them to the rhyming words. Then go to the word

box and find the rhyming words and sheet. Read the material sentence by sentence and have Jill and Terry identify the rhyming words."

3. Allow a tutor to work with one or two tutees long enough (one or two weeks) so that you can make sequential assignments, and learning exercises are not constantly starting anew. However, switch tutoring assignments every couple of weeks to prevent attitudes such as "I'm your teacher" from developing.

4. Tutors should not be asked to administer real tests to tutees. One purpose of peer tutoring is to encourage cooperation between students. Asking tutors to quiz their tutees often defeats this purpose.

5. All students in the class should at times be tutors, and all should be tutees. In this way, students learn that they all can help and can benefit from one another. For example, if they are given the necessary answer keys, slower students can help faster ones by listening to their spelling words or administering and scoring flash card drills in math.

6. Teachers need not adhere to the tutor model (one student flashes cards, the other responds) but can expand, when appropriate, to small work-team assignments (from two to eight students on a team). Shy students can be assigned to work with friendly extroverts. Students with artistic talents can be paired with bright but unartistic students in teams to gather facts and then represent them graphically. These combinations allow students to work together and gain interpersonal skills as well as to master content.

7. Both learning teams and peer tutoring take considerable teacher time to get off to a good start, especially if students have not participated in these activities before. Take your time at first and be sure that all students understand what to do. The first week you ask students to tutor, model the behaviors you want. For example, pass out instructions and have all students read them. Then tutor one or more students in accordance with the directions. Do not just describe what to do; actually do it, modeling the appropriate behaviors. After this demonstration, select another two students to model the next set of directions. Then break the group into pairs and go around listening and answering questions. After a couple of such practice sessions, most students are able to assist others effectively, at least in repetitious drill-like activities. The first week you implement a peer-tutoring program you may have a loud, somewhat disorganized room as students argue over where to go or what to do. Remember that learning does not necessarily require passive, quiet students and that any teacher trying new activities has minor adjustment problems as students learn new roles.

8. Pairing of best friends is often unwise, for several reasons: Friends tend to drift away from learning exercises; the number of classmates that a given student interacts with is reduced; and friends, in moments of anger, are more likely to become excessively critical or indulge in ridicule. Although many friends can work well together, many others cannot, and you should use caution in such groupings.

9. Communicate to parents that all students will both tutor and be tutored by classmates. This is especially important in high-socioeconomic-status areas where some parents may become upset on learning that their child is being tutored by a neighbor's child, fearing that the neighbors will see them as inadequate parents. Needless concern can be eliminated if you communicate to parents the purpose of the tutor program in a letter or visit and point out that tutoring occurs at particular times during the day. List these times and invite the parents to visit whenever they want to do so.

SUMMARY

As we have noted, educators' thinking has progressively moved away from policies of exclusion and homogeneous grouping toward an emphasis on the value of diversity, policies of inclusion, and practices that meet the needs of all students. More and more educators are arguing that heterogeneous classes are just as effective as homogeneous classes for obtaining achievement and other cognitive outcomes as well as affective and social goals such as cultural understanding and prosocial behavior across racial and ethnic groups.

In this chapter, following social constructivist theories of teaching and learning, we have argued for an increased emphasis on student-student interaction. We have noted that learning should not be viewed as transmission of knowledge from a teacher to students who imitate or memorize it, but instead as social construction of new understandings accomplished primarily through sustained discussion. Besides learning through interacting with teachers, students learn by collaborating with peers in pairs and small groups and by interacting with them during classroom discussion. Assuming that everyone participates, diversity in students' backgrounds and points of view should be considered an asset, not a liability.

Under certain conditions and for limited periods of time, it may be useful to accommodate student heterogeneity by grouping students on the basis of achievement profiles. Some educators advocate between-class ability grouping, and in theory such grouping should enable teachers to instruct all students more effectively. However, in practice, the effects of such grouping are weak and mixed. Further, critics have identified problems associated with between-class ability grouping including negative social labeling effects, removing academic peer leaders from low-ability classes, and countering progress toward desegregation and mainstreaming by minimizing contact between peers who differ in achievement. For these reasons, we recommend that between-class ability grouping be confined to grouping by curriculum in high school and that grouping by ability or achievement in earlier grades be avoided except in extreme circumstances.

A second strategy for coping with student heterogeneity is *within-class ability grouping*, especially for beginning reading instruction. We recommend that teachers minimize within-class ability grouping (using it only when necessary to achieve homogeneity, for example, and not merely to reduce the number of students to be taught at the same time). If within-class grouping is used, we recommend that it be used to meet particular needs rather than merely to pace students differentially through the same curriculum using the same instructional methods. Thus, we recommend that group assignments be flexible and reviewed frequently, and that teachers arrange to provide low-group students with extra and more individualized instruction.

Students should frequently be taught in heterogeneous groups in order to maximize the time for students to be active learners and to learn in a social context. Our focus is on valuing diversity and allowing students to respect differences in backgrounds and interests (more on this in Chapter 8). We think it important for different types of students to interact frequently for purposes of promoting both affective and cognitive gains.

Cooperative learning approaches involve assigning students to small groups for cooperative work on group tasks (group members cooperate to produce a single group product) or individual tasks (group members help one another complete individual assignments). Successful cooperative learning programs typically feature positive interdependence of group members, face-to-face interaction of group members, individual accountability for mastering assigned material, and instruction of students in how to interact effectively during small-group activities. Incentive structures involving group rewards appear to be responsible for the achievement benefits of cooperative learning (by motivating students within groups to help one another do as well as they can and thus ensure that the group does as well as it can). This feature is most characteristic of the Student Team Learning approaches (TGT, STAD, Jigsaw II, TAI) that have been used mostly with practice in mathematics and other basic skills.

The affective benefits of cooperative learning appear to occur either when there is an incentive structure featuring group rewards (even if students work on their own on individual tasks rather than on cooperative tasks) or when the task structure is cooperative and students work together to produce a common product (often under task differentiation conditions calling for each group member to take a unique role or fulfill a unique function). Such cooperative task structures are featured in the Learning Together, Group Investigation, and original Jigsaw methods commonly used in social studies classes or in activities designed to accomplish higher-level cognitive objectives.

In contrast to most other proposed adaptations of traditional classroom teaching, cooperative learning approaches have proven to be relatively easy to implement and likely to yield significant advantages (in both cognitive and affective outcomes). Consequently, we recommend that most teachers make at least some use of these methods as alternatives to traditional independent seatwork to provide students with opportunities to practice and apply what they are learning. However, most of our knowledge of small groups is based on research in which students worked on relatively simple content. Even when the purpose of small-group instruction is inquiry or problem solving, those results are not automatic (Blumenfeld, 1992). Educators have much to learn about how to design small-group instruction in order to stimulate higher-order thinking and comprehension.

Tutoring by teacher aides or other adult volunteers can be an important supplement to instruction from the teacher and a valuable means of providing extra assistance to slower students. So can cross-age tutoring, in which older students tutor younger students. Research has shown that cross-age tutoring benefits tutors as well as tutees. Peer-tutoring arrangements in which classmates work with one another can also be effective, but careful planning, training, and supervision are necessary so that the program is not more trouble than it is worth by upsetting parents or engendering resentment among students.

SUGGESTED ACTIVITIES AND QUESTIONS

1. Try to observe two small groups (three to five group members) working on the same topic. In what ways is group process the same and how does it differ? Is one group more cohesive than another? What accounts for the difference?

2. Try to interview the students you observed. What are their beliefs about the group process? Do those students who talked a lot feel differently from those who talked less? Do students who participated less see more talkative students as helpful or bossy?

3. If there is variation in the use of between-class ability grouping at the grade or subject you teach, arrange to observe in local schools that use heterogeneous grouping and others that use homogeneous grouping. What are the trade-offs involved, and what opportunities and constraints do they create for teachers? Which types of students (high or low achievers, phantom students versus social students) benefit more from homogeneously grouped classes? Why?

4. In which setting do you prefer to teach, and why? Given that you may not have this choice, what adjustments in your role as teacher will you have to make if you are assigned to a school that does not use the grouping arrangement you prefer?

5. If you plan to use within-class ability grouping, state the criteria you will use to assign students to groups initially. After these initial assignments, when and how will you schedule reassessments and arrange for regrouping?

6. What classes (in terms of grade, subject, and student composition) are most and least appropriate for within-class ability grouping? Why?

7. Why does placing students in a higher group than their achievement suggests tend to enhance their subsequent achievement?

8. In this chapter we have stressed the need for students occasionally to work in small heterogeneous groups; however, we have discussed both the advantages and disadvantages of small-group work. Given your intended (or present) teaching level and your goals, what reasons do you believe are most important for using small-group instruction?

9. What are the relative advantages and disadvantages of cross-age tutoring? Peer tutoring? Which types of students are most or least likely to benefit from peer tutoring (alienated, phantom, dependent)? Why?

10. How would you organize a cross-age student tutoring program at your school? What provisions could be made for evaluating and making adjustments in the program?

11. What can teachers do in advance to make peer-tutoring programs effective?

12. Given your preferred grade level and subject matter, are cooperative learning approaches likely to be worthwhile components of instruction? Why or why not?

13. Considering the differences among the cooperative learning methods described in the chapter, which would be the most appropriate for use in your preferred grade level or subject matter? Why?

14. If teachers group on the basis of one student characteristic (e.g., reading level), how might this affect other characteristics (dependency, sociability)? Does it make more sense to group on the basis of achievement than according to personal or social traits?

15. Some research suggests that the quality of questions asked during tutoring exchanges is more related to achievement than the frequency of questions asked. Why would this be? How can you assess the quality of a question?

REFERENCES

Ainscow, M. (Ed.). (1991). *Effective schools for all.* London: David Fulton.

Allan, S. (1991). Ability-grouping research reviews: What do they say about grouping and the gifted? *Educational Leadership, 48*(6), 60–65.

Ames, C., & Felker, D. (1979). An examination of children's attributions and achievement-related evaluations in competitive, cooperative, and individualistic reward structures. *Journal of Educational Psychology, 71,* 413–420.

Anderson, L., & Pigford, A. (1988). Teaching within-classroom groups: Examining the role of the teacher. *Journal of Classroom Interaction, 23*(2), 8–13.

Anderson, R., Hiebert, E., Scott, J., & Wilkinson, I. (1985). *Becoming a nation of readers: The report of the Commission on Reading.* Washington, DC: National Institute of Education.

Aronson, E., Blaney, N., Stephan, C., Sikes, J., & Snapp, M. (1978). *The jigsaw classroom.* Beverly Hills, CA: Sage.

Bar-Eli, N., & Raviv, A. (1982). Underachievers as tutors. *Journal of Educational Research, 75,* 139–143.

Bateman, B. (1992). Learning disabilities: The changing landscape. *Journal of Learning and Disabilities, 25,* 29–36.

Beckerman, T., & Good, T. (1981). The classroom ratio of high- and low-aptitude students and its effect on achievement. *American Educational Research Journal, 18,* 317–327.

Bennett, N., & Cass, A. (1988). The effects of group composition on group interactive processes and pupil understanding. *British Educational Research Journal, 15,* 19–32.

Bennett, N., & Dunne, E. (1992). *Managing small groups.* New York: Simon & Schuster.

Berliner, D., & Biddle, B. (1995). *The manufactured crisis: Myth, fraud, and the attack on America's public schools.* New York: Addison-Wesley.

Blumenfeld, P. (1992). The task and the teacher: Enhancing student thoughtfulness in science. In J. Brophy (Ed.), *Advances in research on teaching* (Vol. 3, pp. 81–114). Greenwich, CT: JAI Press.

Bossert, S. (1988–1989). Cooperative activities in the classroom. In E. Rothkopf (Ed.), *Review of research in education* (Vol. 15, pp. 225–250). Washington, DC: American Educational Research Association.

Braddock, J., & McPartland, J. (1990). Alternatives to tracking. *Educational Leadership, 47*(7), 76–78.

Cohen, E. (1986). *Designing group work: Strategies for the heterogeneous classroom.* New York: Teachers College Press.

Cohen, E. (1994). *Designing group work: Strategies for heterogeneous classrooms (2nd ed.).* New York: Teachers College Press.

Cohen, P., Kulik, J., & Kulik, C. (1982). Educational outcomes of tutoring: A meta-analysis of findings. *American Educational Research Journal, 19,* 237–248.

Crawford, J. (1983). A study of instructional processes in Title I classes: 1981–82. *Journal of Research and Evaluation of the Oklahoma City Public Schools, 13*(1).

Damico, S., & Roth, J. (1993). General track students' perceptions of school policies and practices. *Journal of Research and Development in Education, 27,* 1–8.

Dar, Y. (1985). Teachers' attitudes toward ability grouping: Educational considerations and social organizational influences. *Interchange, 16*(2), 17–38.

Davidson, N. (1985). Small-group learning and teaching in mathematics: A selective review of the literature. In R. Slavin, S. Sharan, S. Kagan, R. Lazarowitz, C. Webb, & R. Schmuck (Eds.), *Learning to cooperate, cooperating to learn* (pp. 211–230). New York: Plenum.

Devin-Sheehan, L., Feldman, R., & Allen, V. (1976). Research on children tutoring children: A critical review. *Review of Educational Research, 46,* 355–385.

DeVries, D. L., & Slavin, R. E. (1978). Teams-Games-Tournament (TGT): Review of ten classroom experiments. *Journal of Research and Development in Education, 12,* 28–38.

DeVries, D. L., Slavin, R. E., Fennessey, G. M., Edwards, K. J., & Lombardo, M. M. (1980). *Teams-Games-Tournament: The team learning approach.* Englewood Cliffs, NJ: Educational Technology Publications.

Douglas, J. (1964). *The home and the school: A study of ability and attainment in the primary school.* London: McGibbon and Kee.

Dreeben, R. (1984). First-grade reading groups: Their formation and change. In P. Peterson, L. Wilkinson, & J. Hallinan (Eds.), *The social context of instruction: Group organization and group processes.* Orlando, FL: Academic Press.

Eder, D. (1981). Ability grouping as a self-fulfilling prophecy: A microanalysis of teacher-student interaction. *Sociology of Education, 54,* 151–161.

Eder, D., & Felmlee, D. (1984). Development of attention norms in ability groups. In P. Peterson, L. Wilkinson, & M. Hallinan (Eds.), *The social context of instruction: Group organization and group processes.* Orlando, FL: Academic Press.

Ellis, S., & Rogoff, B. (1982). The strategies and efficacy of child versus adult teachers. *Child Development, 53,* 730–735.

Epstein, C. (1972). *Affective subjects in the classroom: Exploring race, sex and drugs.* Scranton, PA: Intext Educational Publishers.

Evans, J. (1985). *Teaching in transition: The challenge of mixed ability grouping.* Philadelphia: Open University Press.

Evertson, C. (1982). Differences in instructional activities in higher- and lower-achieving junior high English and math classes. *Elementary School Journal, 82,* 329–350.

Fantuzzo, J., King, J., & Heller, L. (1992). Effects of reciprocal peer tutoring on mathematics in school adjustment: A component analysis. *Journal of Educational Psychology, 84,* 331–339.

Fogarty, J., & Wang, M. (1982). An investigation of the cross-age peer tutoring process: Some implications for instructional design and motivation. *Elementary School Journal, 82,* 451–469.

Fuchs, L., Fuchs, D., Bentz, J., Phillips, N., & Hamlett, C. (1994). The nature of student interactions during peer tutoring with and without practice, training, and experience. *American Educational Research Journal, 31,* 75–103.

Gamoran, A. (1993). Alternative uses of ability grouping in secondary schools: Can we bring high-quality instruction to low-ability classes? *American Journal of Education, 102,* 1–22.

Gamoran, A., & Berends, M. (1987). The effects of stratification in secondary schools: Synthesis of survey and ethnographic research. *Review of Educational Research, 57,* 415–435.

Good, T. (1981). Teacher expectations and student perceptions: A decade of research. *Educational Leadership, 38,* 415–423.

Good, T., & Biddle, B. (1988). Research and the improvement of mathematics instruction: The need for observational resources. In D. A. Grouws & T. J. Cooney (Eds.), *Perspectives on research on effective mathematics teaching* (Vol. 1, pp. 112–114). Hillsdale, NJ: Erlbaum.

Good, T., & Brophy, J. (1995). *Contemporary educational psychology* (5th ed.). White Plains, NY: Longman.

Good, T., & Marshall, S. (1984). Do students learn more in heterogeneous or homogeneous groups? In P. Peterson, L. Wilkinson, & M. Hallinan (Eds.), *The social context of instruction: Group organization and group processes.* New York: Academic Press.

Good, T., McCaslin, M., & Reys, B. (1992). Investigating work groups to promote problem solving in mathematics. In J. Brophy (Ed.), *Advances in research on teaching* (Vol. 3, pp. 115–160). Greenwich, CT: JAI Press.

Good, T., Mulryan, C., & McCaslin, M. (1992). Grouping for instruction in mathematics: A call for programmatic research on small-group processes. In D. Grouws (Ed.), *Handbook of research on mathematics teaching and learning* (pp. 165–196). New York: Macmillan.

Good, T., Reys, B., Grouws, D., & Mulryan C. (1989–1990). Using work groups in mathematics instruction. *Educational Leadership, 47*(4), 56–62.

Goodlad, S., & Hirst, B. (1989). *Peer tutoring: A guide to learning by teaching.* New York: Nichols.

Graybeal, S. S., & Stodolsky, S. S. (1985). Peer work groups in elementary schools. *American Journal of Education, 93,* 409–428.

Graesser, A., & Person, N. (1994). Question asking during tutoring. *American Educational Research Journal, 31,* 104–137.

Hallahan, D., & Kauffman, J. (1991). *Exceptional children: Introduction to special education.* Englewood Cliffs, NJ: Prentice-Hall.

Haller, E. J. (1985). Pupil race and elementary school ability grouping: Are teachers biased against black children? *American Educational Research Journal, 22,* 465–483.

Hallinan, M. T., & Sorensen, A. B. (1985). Ability grouping and student friendships. *American Educational Research Journal, 22,* 485–499.

Jenkins, J., & Jenkins, L. (1987). Making peer tutoring work. *Educational Leadership, 44*(6), 64–68.

Jenkins, L. (1989). *Making small groups work.* Oxford: Penguin Educational.

Johnson, D., & Johnson, R. (1975). *Learning together and alone.* Englewood Cliffs, NJ: Prentice-Hall.

Johnson, D., & Johnson, R. (1979). Conflict in the classroom: Controversy and learning. *Review of Educational Research, 49,* 51–70.

Johnson, D., & Johnson, R. (1982). *Joining together: Group therapy and group skills.* Englewood Cliffs, NJ: Prentice-Hall.

Johnson, D., & Johnson, R. (1985a). Classroom conflict: Controversy versus debate in learning groups. *American Educational Research Journal, 22,* 237–256.

Johnson, D., & Johnson, R. (1985b). Cooperative learning and adaptive education. In M. C. Wang & H. J. Walberg (Eds.), *Adapting instruction to individual differences.* Berkeley, CA: McCutchan.

Johnson, D., Johnson, R., Holubec, E. J., & Roy, P. (1984). *Circles of learning: Cooperation in the classroom.* Alexandria, VA: Association for Supervision and Curriculum Development.

Johnson, D., Johnson, R., & Maruyama, G. (1983). Interdependence and interpersonal attraction among heterogeneous and homogeneous individuals: A theoretical formulation and a meta-analysis of the research. *Review of Educational Research, 53,* 5–54.

Johnson, D., Skon, L., & Johnson, R. (1980). Effects of cooperative, competitive, and individualistic conditions on children's problem-solving performance. *American Educational Research Journal, 17,* 83–93.

Johnson, R., Brooker, C., Stutzman, J., Hultman, D., & Johnson, D. (1985). The effects of controversy, concurrence seeking, and individualistic learning on achievement and attitude change. *Journal of Research in Science Teaching, 22,* 141–152.

Kagan, S. (1988). *Cooperative learning: Resources for teachers.* Riverside: University of California.

King, L. (1993). High and low achievers' perceptions and cooperative learning in two small groups. *Elementary School Journal, 93,* 399–416.

Kulik, J., & Kulik, C. (1989). Meta-analysis in education. *International Journal of Educational Research, 13,* 221–340.

Kutnick and Thomas. (1990) "Dyadic pairings for the enhancement of cognitive development in the school curriculum: some preliminary results on science tasks, *British Educational Research Journal, 16,* 399–406.

Larrivee, B. (1985). *Effective teaching for successful mainstreaming.* New York: Longman.

Leinhardt, G., & Pallay, A. (1982). Restrictive educational settings: Exile or haven? *Review of Educational Research, 52,* 557–578.

Leiter, J. (1983). Classroom composition and achievement gains. *Sociology of Education, 56,* 126–132.

Lew, M., Mesch, D., Johnson, D., & Johnson, R. (1986). Components of cooperative learning: Effects of collaborative skills and academic group contingencies on achievement and mainstreaming. *Contemporary Educational Psychology, 11,* 229–239.

Madden, N., & Slavin, R. (1983). Mainstreaming students with mild handicaps: Academic and social outcomes. *Review of Educational Research, 53,* 519–569.

Mason, D., & Good, T. (1993). Effects of two-group and whole-class teaching on regrouped elementary students' mathematics achievement. *American Educational Research Journal,* 328–360.

Mason, D., Reys, B., & Good, T. (1990). *Three models of active teaching and learning in mathematics using work groups* (Technical Report No. 492). Columbia: University of Missouri, Center for Research in Social Behavior.

Mason, D., Schroeter, D., Combs, R., & Washington, K. (1992). Assigning average-achieving eighth graders to advanced mathematics classes in an urban junior high. *Elementary School Journal, 92,* 587–599.

McCaslin, M., & Good, T. (1996). *Listening to students.* New York: HarperCollins.

Moskowitz, J. M., Malvin, J. H., Shaeffer, G. A., & Schaps, E. (1985). Evaluation of Jigsaw, a cooperative learning technique. *Contemporary Educational Psychology, 10,* 104–112.

Mulryan, C. (1989). *A study of intermediate-grade students' involvement and participation in cooperative small groups in mathematics.* Unpublished doctoral dissertation, University of Missouri-Columbia.

Mulryan, C. (1992). Student passivity during cooperative small groups in mathematics. *Journal of Educational Research, 85,* 261–273.

Mulryan, C. (1995). Fifth and sixth graders' involvement and participation in cooperative small groups in mathematics. *Elementary School Journal, 95,* 297–310.

National Education Commission on Time and Learning. (1994, April). *Prisoners of time.* Washington, DC: U.S. Government Printing Office.

Nattiv, A. (1994). Helping behaviors and math achievement gain of students using cooperative learning. *Elementary School Journal, 94,* 285–298.

Nickerson, J. R., & Prawat, R. S. (1981). Affective interaction in racially diverse classrooms: A case study. *Elementary School Journal, 81,* 291–303.

Noddings, N. (1989). Theoretical and practical concerns about small groups in mathematics. *Elementary School Journal, 89*(5), 607–624.

Oakes, J. (1985). *Keeping track: How schools structure inequality.* New Haven: Yale University Press.

Oakes, J. (1992). Can tracking research inform practice? Technical, normative, and political considerations. *Educational Researcher, 21*(4), 12–21.

Oakes, J., & Lipton, M. (1992). Detracking schools: Early lessons from the field. *Phi Delta Kappan, 73,* 448–454.

Okebukola, P. A. (1985). The relative effectiveness of cooperative and competitive interaction techniques in strengthening students' performance in science classes. *Science Education, 69,* 501–509.

Page, R. (1992). *Lower track classrooms: A curricular and cultural perspective.* New York: Teachers College Press.

Paolitto, D. (1976). The effect of cross-age tutoring on adolescence: An inquiry into theoretical assumptions. *Review of Educational Research, 46,* 215–238.

Paulus, P., Dzindolet, M., Poletes, G., & Camacho, L. (1993). Perception of performance in group brainstorming: The illusion of group productivity. *Personality and Social Psychology Bulletin, 19,* 78–89.

Pepitone, E. (1985). Children in cooperation and competition: Antecedents and consequences of self-orientation. In R. Slavin, S. Sharan, S. Kagan, R. Lazarowitz, C. Webb, & R. Schmuck (Eds.), *Learning to cooperate, cooperating to learn* (pp. 17–67). New York: Plenum.

Peterson, P. L., Wilkinson, L. C., Spinelli, F., & Swing, S. R. (1984). Merging the process-product and the sociolinguistic paradigms: Research on small-group processes. In P. Peterson, L. Wilkinson, & M. Hallinan (Eds.), *Instructional groups in the classroom: Organization and processes.* New York: Academic Press.

Reynolds, M. (1978). Some final notes. In J. Grosenick & M. Reynolds (Eds.), *Teacher education: Renegotiating roles for mainstreaming.* Reston, VA: Council for Exceptional Children.

Rosen, S., Powell, E., Schubot, D., & Rollins, P. (1978). Competence and tutorial role as status variables affecting peer-tutoring outcomes in public school settings. *Journal of Educational Psychology, 70,* 602–612.

Rosenbaum, J. E. (1980). Social implications of educational grouping. In D. C. Berliner (Ed.), *Review of research in education* (Vol. 8). Itasca, IL: Peacock.

Ross, J. (1988). Improving social-environment studies problem solving through cooperative learning. *American Educational Research Journal, 25,* 573–591.

Rowan, S., & Miracle, A. (1983). Systems of ability grouping and the stratification of achievement in elementary schools. *Sociology of Education, 56,* 133–144.

Samples, R. (1992). Using learning modalities to celebrate intelligence. *Educational Leadership, 50,* 62–66.

Schloss, P. (Ed.). (1992, January). Integrating learners with disabilities in regular education programs (special issue). *Elementary School Journal, 84.*

Schmuck, R., & Schmuck, P. (1988). *Group processes in the classroom* (5th ed.). Dubuque: William C. Brown.

Sharan, S. (1980). Cooperative learning in small groups: Recent methods and effects on achievement, attitudes, and ethnic relations. *Review of Educational Research, 50,* 241–271.

Sharan, S., & Sharan, Y. (1976). *Small-group teaching.* Englewood Cliffs, NJ: Educational Technology Publications.

Sharan, S., et al. (1984). *Cooperative learning in the classroom: Research in desegregated schools.* Hillsdale, NJ: Erlbaum.

Sharpley, A. M., Irvine, J. W., & Sharpley, C. F. (1983). An examination of the effectiveness of a cross-age tutoring program in mathematics for elementary school children. *American Educational Research Journal, 20,* 103–111.

Simmons, D., Fuchs, L., Fuchs, D., Mathes, P., & Hodge, J. (1995). Effects of explicit teaching and peer tutoring on the reading achievement of learning-disabled and low-performing students in regular classrooms. *Elementary School Journal, 95,* 387–408.

Slavin, R. (1983). *Cooperative learning.* New York: Longman.

Slavin, R. (1986). *Using Student Team Learning* (3rd ed.). Baltimore: Johns Hopkins University, Center for Research on Elementary and Middle Schools.

Slavin, R. (1987). Ability grouping and student achievement in elementary schools: Best evidence synthesis. *Review of Educational Research, 57,* 293–336.

Slavin, R. E. (1980a). Cooperative learning. *Review of Educational Research, 50,* 315–342.

Slavin, R. E. (1980b). *Using Student Team Learning* (rev. ed.). Baltimore: Johns Hopkins University, Center for Social Organization of Schools.

Slavin, R. E. (1985). Team-Assisted Individualization: A cooperative learning solution for adaptive instruction in mathematics. In M. C. Wang & H. J. Walberg (Eds.), *Adapting instruction to individual differences.* Berkeley, CA: McCutchan.

Slavin, R. E. (1988). Cooperative learning and student achievement. *Educational Leadership, 46*(2), 31–33.

Slavin, R. E. (1990a). Ability grouping and student achievement in secondary schools. *Review of Educational Research, 60,* 417–499.

Slavin, R. E. (1990b). *Cooperative learning: Theory, research, and practice.* Englewood Cliffs, NJ: Prentice-Hall.

Slavin, R. E., Sharan, S., Kagan, S., Hertz-Lazarowitz, R., Webb, C., & Schmuck, R. (Eds.). (1985). *Learning to cooperate, cooperating to learn.* New York: Plenum.

Smith, D., & Luckasson, R. (1992). *Introduction to special education: Teaching in an age of challenge.* Needham Heights, MA: Allyn & Bacon.

Smith, K., Johnson, D., & Johnson, R. (1981). Can conflict be constructive? Controversy versus concurrence seeking in learning groups. *Journal of Educational Psychology, 73,* 651–663.

Stipek, D. (1986). Children's motivation to learn. In T. Tomlinson & H. Walberg (Eds.), *Academic work and educational excellence* (pp. 197–221). Berkeley, CA: McCutchan.

Swing, S. R., & Peterson, P. L. (1982). The relationship of student ability and small-group instruction to student achievement. *American Educational Research Journal, 19,* 259–274.

Thomas, J. (1970). *Tutoring strategies and effectiveness: A comparison of elementary age tutors and college tutors.* Unpublished doctoral dissertation. Austin: University of Texas.

Thompson, R. H., White, K. R., & Morgan, D. P. (1982). Teacher-student interaction patterns in classrooms with mainstreamed mildly handicapped students. *American Educational Research Journal, 19,* 220–236.

Tuckman, B., & Bierman, M. (1971). *Beyond Pygmalion: Galatea in the schools.* Paper presented at the annual meeting of the American Educational Research Association, New York.

Veldman, D. J., & Sanford, J. P. (1984). The influence of class ability level on student achievement and classroom behavior. *American Educational Research Journal, 21,* 629–644.

Webb, N. M. (1982). Student interaction and learning in small groups. *Review of Educational Research, 52,* 421–445.

Webb, N. M. (1989). Peer interaction and learning in small groups. *International Journal of Educational Research, 13,* 21–29.

Webb, N. M., & Cullian, L. K. (1983). Group interaction and achievement in small groups: Stability over time. *American Educational Research Journal, 20,* 411–423.

Weinstein, R. (1976). Reading group membership in first grade: Teacher behaviors and pupil experience over time. *Journal of Educational Psychology, 68,* 103–116.

Wheelock, A. (1992). *Crossing the tracks: How "untracking" can save schools.* New York: New Press.

FORM 7.1. Small-Group Interaction

USE: Whenever a small group of students is working and the teacher is not a formal part of the group.
PURPOSE: To determine how the group spends its time.
Make a code every 15 seconds to describe what the group is doing at that moment.

Frequency   Type Contact

_____   1. Reading (finding information, etc.)
_____   2. Manipulating equipment
_____   3. Task discussion: general participation
_____   4. Task discussion: one or two students dominate
_____   5. Procedural discussion
_____   6. Observing
_____   7. Nontask discussion
_____   8. Procedural dispute
_____   9. Substantive (task relevant) dispute
_____ 10. Silence or confusion

FORM 7.2. Individual Participation in Small-Group Work

USE. When a small group is operating and the teacher is not part of the group.
PURPOSE: To assess the involvement and participation of individual students during small-group work.
Observe the target student for 15 seconds and make a code. Repeat the cycle for the duration of small-group activity. *

_____   1. Reading (finding information)
_____   2. Manipulating equipment (filmstrip, slide rule)
_____   3. Participating in general discussion (telling and listening to others)
_____   4. Listening to general discussion
_____   5. Presenting idea to group (others are listening to the target student)
_____   6. Talking to individual (an aside: the conversation is not part of the group discussion)
_____   7. Listening to individual (an aside: the conversation is not part of the group discussion)
_____   8. Passive (can't tell if student is involved)
_____   9. Misbehaving
_____ 10. Leaves group

*Note that it would be possible to use the form to code different individual students in the group (code one student for a minute, then switch to another student). Furthermore, the scale could be altered to provide information about the group. For example, the percentage of the group that falls into each category could be noted.

8

Teaching Heterogeneous Classes and Differentiating Instruction

THE SCHOOL-AGE POPULATION IS BECOMING MORE DIVERSE

The term *educationally disadvantaged* is defined differently by various educators. However, the number of disadvantaged students in U.S. schools seems certain to increase in the coming years. According to Natriello, McDill, and Pallas (1990, p. 13), "Some students will have suffered from a lack of appropriate formal educational experiences, others will have suffered from the lack of intellectual experiences in the family, and still others will have suffered from the lack of educational experiences in the community."

These authors reported that the U.S. population under 18 years will increase by about 4 percent between 1988 and 2020. The number of white students is expected to decline by about 27 percent (12.2 million students) during this period, whereas the number of Hispanic children will triple, from 6.8 million in 1988 to 18.6 million in 2020. The population of black youth under age 18 is predicted to increase 9 percent (from 9.6 million to 10.5 million), and the population of other groups is projected to double (increase by 2.3 million children).

These projected changes suggest that there will be a substantial rise in the percentage of students at risk for school failure. Unfortunately, racial and ethnic group status are correlated with poverty and other indicators of educational disadvantage (Miller, 1995). Assuming that these relationships continue, there will be more children living in poverty as the proportion of black and Hispanic children increases. Indeed, the number of U.S. children living with mothers who have not completed high school and having a primary language other than English is projected to increase notably in the next decades.

Hiebert (1991) noted that diversity (differences among learners) traditionally has been conceptualized as a problem to be overcome through programs designed to reduce or remove differences. Many educators, however, are beginning to view diversity as a resource rather than a liability. For example, students with different backgrounds can interact with one another and learn how the same text material or concept can be interpreted differently by persons from different backgrounds. Thus, teachers can use unique student experiences to make classroom learning richer and more sensitive to differences among students.

We also view diversity as an opportunity to enrich classroom learning. Although widely diverse groups of learners complicate teaching in some respects, most instruction should occur in heterogeneous settings. Dealing with diversity has become progressively more important as educational settings have become more inclusive at all levels. In this chapter we discuss common strategies for responding to student diversity.

DEALING WITH DIVERSITY

At one time, only the children of the rich received formal education, typically in the form of private individualized tutoring. Such tutoring is the method of choice for most educational purposes, because the curriculum can be individualized and the teacher can provide the student with sustained personalized attention (Bloom, 1984). Unfortunately, private tutoring is too expensive for most families. Consequently, as systems for mass education developed, one constant feature was an arrangement whereby each teacher worked with many students (Kliebard, 1986).

Colonial times featured the one-room schoolhouse, in which students of all ages were instructed in all subjects by a single teacher who had few if any commercially prepared texts or curriculum materials to work with (Grinder & Nelsen, 1985). Except for so-called primers for reading instruction (containing the alphabet and short sections such as proverbs, catechisms, or passages from the Bible), teachers made do with slates, chalkboards, and materials that they had purchased themselves or induced their students to bring from home (maps, books published for use by the general public). Recitations and rote memory exercises were used when texts or other curriculum materials were not available.

With the industrial revolution and the population shift to the cities, schools became larger and education became more standardized and formalized. Age grouping became the basis for assigning students to classes, curriculum guidelines were established for each grade level, and teachers began using commercial textbooks and tests. Certain practices for organizing and managing instruction became well established and have continued as the traditional model of classroom teaching: the *lock-step curriculum* with its grade-level sequencing, division of the school day into periods for teaching different subjects, and division of instruction in each subject into units and lessons; *group pacing*, in which the whole class is moved through the same curriculum at roughly the same pace using largely the same materials and methods; and *whole-class instructional methods*, in which the teacher typically begins a lesson by reviewing prerequisite material, introduces and develops new concepts or skills, leads the group in a recitation or supervised practice or application activity, and then assigns seatwork or homework for students to do on their own. The teacher may occasionally teach small groups rather than the whole class (especially for beginning reading instruction) and may provide a degree of individualized instruction when "making the rounds" during seatwork times. However, despite these and other minor variations, the basic whole-class instruction/recitation/seatwork model has persisted as the dominant approach to teaching since public schools first became established, despite frequent criticism and calls for reform (Goodlad, Soder, & Sirotnik, 1990).

The persistence of the traditional approach suggests that it has certain enduring strengths. Indeed, it works reasonably well for students whose rates of learning and responses to commonly used instructional materials and methods are similar to those of the mythical "average student" at the grade level. Furthermore, given that teachers must work with classes of 20 to 40 students, the traditional method may be the best compromise available, allowing teachers to meet more of the needs of more of their students than they could meet using any other feasible method. However, the traditional approach also has weaknesses. Two major ones are that the majority of students must work without close supervision whenever teachers work with small groups or individuals, and teachers cannot get around to each student often enough to provide effective individualized instruction.

Due to these and other limitations, the traditional approach periodically becomes the focus of calls for reform (e.g., Goodlad, 1984). Some critics describe it as unduly teacher dominant, rigidly structured, fostering passive and repetitive learning, or unimaginative and boring. Others acknowledge that it is adequate for average students but believe that brighter students should get more enrichment or accelerated pacing, slower students should get extra instruction or more time to master material, and students with special instructional needs should be taught using materials or methods different from those suitable for the majority.

Critics commonly call for more variety in educational curricula and methods and for more attempts to adapt schooling to the needs and interests of students (Hiebert, 1991; Natriello et al., 1990). Recent reform documents published by organizations concerned with teaching in the subject areas have called for more active involvement of students (through discussion groups, project work, etc.) and more student responsibility for learning. We will discuss these instructional methods and the constructivist theories of learning that underlie them in Chapter 10. Here we discuss broad strategies that teachers can use to organize instruction for diverse learners in the same classroom.

MASTERY LEARNING

One way to adjust traditional whole-class pacing is to allow slower students more time to master curriculum objectives. The traditional model allocates a fixed amount of learning time for each unit and accepts individual differences in mastery. An alternative is the Mastery Learning model (Bloom, 1980), which calls for all learners to master a common set of objectives but allows for individual differences in learning time. The mastery approach assumes that the major difference between learners is the time it takes them to learn. It seeks to enable all students to master all basic objectives by providing the slower ones with more time (and usually additional tutoring or other assistance) to learn material that classmates have mastered more quickly. The original mastery model emphasized individualized tutoring, but it was later adapted for use within the context of group-based instruction (Block & Anderson, 1975). Principles of mastery learning have been integrated into diverse instructional methods (Gagné, Briggs, & Wager, 1992; Stallings & Stipek 1986), and they comprise a major part of the rationale for the curriculum reform approach known as Outcome-Based Education (Guskey, 1994; Schwarz & Cavener, 1994). Most current programs feature group-based rather than individualized instruction (Levine, 1985).

Anderson (1985) suggested that the following features are found in any true mastery learning program:

1. Clearly specified learning objectives
2. Short, highly valid assessment procedures
3. Preset mastery performance standards
4. A sequence of learning units, each composed of an integral set of facts, concepts, principles, and skills
5. Provision of feedback about learning progress to students
6. Provision of additional time and help to correct specified errors and misunderstandings of students who have not yet mastered the objectives

The heart of mastery learning is the cycle of teaching, testing, reteaching, and retesting. Students are informed of the unit's objectives and then receive instruction. Upon completion of instruction and related practice activities, students take formative evaluation tests designed to assess their mastery. Those who achieve preset performance standards (usually, passing at least 80 percent of the items) are certified as having mastered the unit. Certified students then move on to the next unit, or more typically, work on enrichment activities until the entire class is ready to move on. Meanwhile, students who have not met mastery criteria receive corrective instruction and additional practice before their mastery levels are assessed again. Theoretically, these cycles of assessment and reteaching continue until all students reach mastery, but in practice, attempts to bring students to mastery usually cease after the second test, and the class then moves to the next unit. Thus, group-based mastery learning programs are a compromise between traditional programs that allow little if any extra time for slow learners and ideal mastery programs that would allow all learners as much time as they needed.

Mastery approaches increase (often dramatically) the percentages of students who master basic objectives (Guskey & Pigott, 1988; Kulik, Kulik, & Bangert-Drowns, 1990). They provide extra time and instruction to enable low achievers to master more content than they would master otherwise, and this additional mastery is likely to bring motivational benefits as well. In particular, mastery approaches are likely to convince chronic low achievers that the old academic "game" has been replaced by a new one that gives them a chance to "win" consistently if they have appropriate learning strategies and apply reasonable effort. Thus, at least some attempt to implement the mastery learning philosophy appears desirable.

It seems to us, however, that teachers should concentrate on maximizing each student's achievement progress even if this means maintaining or even increasing the range of individual differences in achievement levels in a class. The mastery approach will not reduce the time that slow learners need to learn (relative to the time that fast learners need), so teachers can reduce individual differences in achievement progress only by deliberately holding back fast learners. This is not to say that teachers should continually push fast learners to master more of the curriculum instead of allowing them to engage in enrichment activities or alternative tasks. However, the activities planned for fast learners should be selected for sound pedagogical reasons and not as mere time fillers designed to slow their progress through the curriculum in order to reduce individual differences. A sensible compromise to this dilemma may be to identify the most essential learning objectives and see that all students master these, while tolerating more variable performance on other objectives. Teachers can supplement the basic curriculum with enrichment opportunities that students work on individually or in groups when the teachers are busy helping slower students to catch up.

INDIVIDUALIZED INSTRUCTION

Mastery learning adjusts for student differences in time needed to learn, but it calls for using essentially the same methods and materials to move all students toward mastery of the same achievement goals. A more complete accommodation is to retain the same achievement goals but introduce variation not only in time to learn but in the methods and materials used to accomplish the learning. The most complete accommodation, however, is to use individualized instruction (also called adaptive education) methods that allow students to pursue different achievement goals and to exercise a great deal of autonomy in deciding what to learn and how to learn it.

Some individualized approaches allow students to learn using different materials or methods but require them to show mastery in the same way. Others allow demonstration of mastery in different ways (written report, written exam, oral exam, etc.). Savage and Armstrong (1992) noted that four major variables can be altered to individualize instruction: rate of learning, content of learning, method of learning, and goals of learning. These variables can take many forms and can be combined in multiple ways, however, so there is a range of individualized instructional concepts and programs. Teachers can create their own programs, for example, by adapting an individualized mathematics program to their classes but using whole-class methods to teach other subjects.

Wang and Lindvall (1984) listed the following distinguishing features of *adaptive education* approaches:

1. Instruction is based on the assessed capabilities of each student.
2. Materials and procedures permit each student to progress at a pace suited to his or her abilities and interests.
3. Periodic evaluations inform the student concerning mastery.
4. Students assume responsibility for identifying needs and abilities, planning learning activities, and evaluating mastery.

5. Alternative activities and materials aid student acquisition of essential academic skills and content.
6. Students exercise choice in selecting educational goals, outcomes, and activities.
7. Students assist one another in pursuing individual goals and cooperate in achieving group goals.

Few individualized instruction or adaptive education programs have all seven of these features, but most have several of them.

Reformers calling for individualization or adaptation of the traditional model of schooling have been active in every educational era. At any given time, at least some of their suggestions are adopted by about one-third of the elementary teachers but less than one-fifth of secondary teachers (Cuban, 1984). Usually these innovations call for shifting responsibility for planning and accomplishing learning from the teacher to the student and for shifting responsibility for communicating content from the teacher to the instructional materials, because it is not possible for one teacher to meet the needs of all students in a class simultaneously (Jackson, 1985). The innovations are popularized by committed advocates (usually without data to back up their claims), thrive briefly, and then wane. Certain elements of the innovations sometimes are assimilated into traditional schooling, but the innovations are not retained as complete packages that supplant traditional methods. Typically, this is because reformers make unwarranted assumptions about students' capabilities for independent goal setting and learning, produce materials that are focused on low-level isolated skills, or require too much testing or other managerial complexities (Grinder & Nelsen, 1985). Similar problems have been observed in computer software designed to assist in individualizing instruction (Beynon & MacKay, 1993).

Individualization has become easier in recent years with the development of materials and methods designed to allow teachers to differentiate instruction for different students. Many specialized materials are augmented with audiovisual components (audiotaped or videotaped instruction, computer software, CD-ROMs) and provide instruction and practice opportunities for students without involving the teacher. There is also advice about how to select appropriate media (see Gagné, Briggs, & Wager, 1992). Usually there is some initial assessment to determine where students should begin, and then they work on their own. In heavily individualized programs, students receive more instruction from the curriculum materials than from the teacher, who acts mostly as a materials manager, tester, and progress monitor. Productive use of individualized instructional materials requires thoughtful teacher decision making. For example, teachers might adapt individualized programs for use in some subjects (in part to develop students' skills for time management, etc.) but not others. Those who intend to do so will need to critically assess the content of the programs and supplement it if necessary (e.g., adding higher-order questions and application exercises).

Most individualized instructional materials use principles of *programmed instruction* in which students move in small steps from "entry-level" performance toward ultimate objectives. Programs are divided into self-contained modules ready for independent use by individual students. Each module reviews prerequisite knowledge or skills and introduces new information and opportunities to practice by having students answer questions or carry out tasks. Students receive immediate feedback after they respond, and some programs have diagnostic and remediation features that allow students to skip segments they have mastered or to get extra instruction on material that they have not mastered by working through the regular program.

Research on Individualized Instruction

Information about student achievement in individualized programs often is hard to evaluate because it is confined to scores on criterion-referenced tests that come with the programs. Such data usually show success in meeting the objectives of the program as formulated by its developers, at least in classes where the program is considered to be well implemented. However, such data do not allow conclusions about either the absolute effectiveness or the cost-effectiveness of these programs in comparison with traditional approaches. Comparisons typically report no differences or minor differences, with more variation within than between the two types of programs (Bangert, Kulik, & Kulik, 1983; Horak, 1981). The best results appear to be associated with frequent assessment, student self-management and choice, and peer cooperation rather than with reliance on individualized progress through programmed materials.

Another problem in evaluating individualized programs is that most models offer teachers flexibility. Thus, two teachers ostensibly using the same program may implement it very differently. Also teachers using a presumably individualized program may do just as much group-based instruction and no more individualized instruction than most other teachers. Many evaluation attempts did not include classroom observation to verify whether a program was implemented as the designers intended, so it is not always clear what comparisons of "individualized" and "traditional" programs mean.

Slavin (1984) suggested that for any kind of instruction to be effective, four conditions must be satisfied: (1) The instruction must be high in quality, (2) the instruction must be appropriate to students' levels, (3) students must be motivated to work on tasks, and (4) students must have adequate time to learn. Slavin argued that individualized instructional programs have not lived up to expectations because they have concentrated on increasing the appropriateness of instruction but have not addressed the other three essential conditions. Quality of instruction is reduced because students are not taught directly by the teacher but instead required to learn on their own. They are not adequately motivated because working through individualized programs often is boring and seldom offers incentives for moving through the curriculum rapidly. Finally, much classroom time is spent on procedural matters (passing out material, waiting for the teacher to check work, taking tests), to the point that time for learning is actually reduced in many cases.

Arlin (1982), Carlson (1982), Everhart (1983), and Jones et al. (1985) also highlighted the difficulties teachers have had implementing individualized instructional programs and described how students' actual experience in the classroom fell far short of what the programs' developers had envisioned. Some of these problems are remediable: Developers can supply more and better materials to teachers, offer a more balanced and integrative curriculum rather than focus on low-level isolated skills, and supply multimedia components that reduce students' need to learn exclusively through reading. The basic problem, however, seems to be the student-teacher ratio. No individualized or adaptive education program is likely to work effectively if it depends on the teacher to provide individualized instruction simultaneously to all students in a class, especially if the teacher is expected to develop curriculum materials for the program as well. So, unless such programs are implemented in very small classes, or with significant help from aides or other adults, they will have to rely on other strategies.

Computerized Instruction

Assuming comparable instructional content, computerized instruction offers several advantages over conventional textbooks and programmed learning materials. It brings novelty or at least variety to students' school experiences and thus is likely to be more enjoyable than conventional seatwork. Through linkage with other developing technologies such as videodiscs, CD-ROM, and hypermedia, computer-based education now can incorporate animation, time-lapsed photography, and other audiovisual techniques for communicating information and demonstrating processes in ways that are not possible through conventional print materials. Also, some programs allow students to respond more actively and in more varied ways than they can respond to conventional instructional materials. Along with electronic workbooks for drill and practice, there are tutorial programs that provide not only feedback but tutorial instruction and friendly encouragement similar to what the student might receive from a tutor (Lepper & Chabay, 1985). Some programs provide opportunities for higher-level problem solving, work with complex databases, or simulation activities of a kind seldom seen in conventional seatwork or programmed instruction.

For example, computer technology could allow students in Ann Arbor, Michigan; Tucson, Arizona; and Perth, Australia to work cooperatively to create networks of information in order to test hypotheses about environmental issues (Soloway, 1991). To the extent that these potential advantages of computerized instruction can be achieved at reasonable cost, transferring significant instructional functions from the teacher to the computer might be a feasible way of implementing individualized instruction or adaptive education principles in typical classrooms (Lipson & Fisher, 1983; Taylor, 1980).

As computer-based tutorial programs have grown in sophistication, their potential benefits have multiplied (Lepper & Gurtner, 1989). Many programs now pose quite complex problems for students, provide further instruction or assistance at their request, and then present them with immediate and graphic feedback. Some use Socratic tutoring methods to call students' attention to inconsistencies in their understanding of the topic. Some programs even incorporate complex "intelligent tutoring systems" that are based on detailed models of expected lines of progress from novice to expert status in the domain of knowledge involved. These programs can provide students with precise analyses and corrective instruction concerning their misconceptions (Psotka, Massey, & Mutter, 1988).

Microcomputers serve as multipurpose tools and resources. Their *text editing* capabilities can help students develop writing and communication skills. Word-processing programs reduce the drudgery of writing and make it easier for students to edit and revise their work. Programs that check spelling or grammar may help students to improve those skills and programs that aid in outlining a paper may help students learn to organize their thoughts before beginning to write. The *graphics* capabilities of microcomputers have considerable potential for application in courses in design, art, and architecture. Through the *simulation* capacity of computers, students can conduct inquiry and experimentation that would be too time consuming, costly, or dangerous for them to undertake in reality. Microcomputers can provide access to dictionaries, encyclopedias, map collections, statistical abstracts, and other *databases* that students can use when preparing a research report or engaging in other forms of inquiry learning (Scardamalia et al., 1992). Videodisc technology has dramatically enhanced the potential for use of computers as sources of *visual input* to students, and material on videodiscs can be accessed much more quickly and easily than material on film or videotape.

Language arts instruction is being enhanced through programs such as *Write to Read, Bank Street Writer,* and programs designed to teach students to plan, write, and edit stories or poetry (Cochran-Smith, Paris, & Kahn, 1991; Grejda & Hannafin, 1992). Mathematics education is being supplemented with applications of *LOGO* (Papert, 1980), *Turtle Geometry* (Abelson & diSessa, 1981) and other imaginative forms of computerized instruction (Davis, 1984). Interesting tutorial programs and simulation activities have been developed for science as well (Arons, 1984; Stewart et al., 1992). Social studies instruction can be enhanced with programs such as *Oregon Trail,* a simulation of a pioneer family's journey to the West in a covered wagon, or *Community Search,* a game in which student teams act as leaders of a primitive agricultural society trying to decide where and how to relocate their community to a better natural environment. Recently, there has been a proliferation of simulation programs and videodisc databases for use in social studies (Ehman et al., 1992; Laughlin, Hartoonian, & Sanders, 1989; Martorella, 1994; Savage & Armstrong, 1992). The databases are used for developing reports on nations, regions, or cultures, and the simulation programs offer opportunities to engage in critical thinking and decision making about social and civic issues.

Research on Computerized Instruction

Research on the relative effectiveness of computerized instruction has yielded mixed findings concerning both its absolute effectiveness and its cost-effectiveness. However, the general pattern of findings has become more positive recently as costs have dropped and educational software has increased in variety and advanced in sophistication (Fletcher, Hawley, & Piele, 1990). Evaluations of some of the more highly touted programs have been disappointing. The *Write To Read* program does not appear to offer any particular advantages to alternative programs as a method of fostering early achievement in reading and language arts (Freyd & Lytle, 1990; Slavin, 1991). Applications of *LOGO* programming in elementary schools have produced gains on skills developed directly in the programs but not the advances in general thinking and problem-solving abilities that were anticipated by its creators (Lehrer, Guckenberg, & Lee, 1988; Miller, Kelly, & Kelly, 1988; Pea, Kurland, & Hawkins, 1985; Salomon & Perkins, 1987). On the whole, however, computerized instruction has moderately positive effects on achievement (Lepper & Gurtner, 1989). Effects are stronger with programs that involve tutorials rather than simple drill and practice, with younger rather than older students, and with lower-ability or remedial students rather than other students. There has been less research on the effects of some of the newer programs designed to stimulate inductive learning through complex and interactive problem solving. However, several promising applications have been reported (Clements, 1986; Lehrer & Randle, 1987; Miller & Emihovich, 1986), and there appears to be a trend for more positive results developing over time (Lepper & Gurtner, 1989). Finally, students usually express enthusiasm about working with computers (Becker, 1988).

Several qualifications on these positive findings should be noted, however. First, there was no control for the amount of instructional time in about half of the studies, so that much of the reported achievement advantage to computerized instruction may have been due to greater opportunity to learn the material rather than to use of the computer. Also, computerized instruction was just being introduced when many of these studies were conducted, so that achievement and especially attitude findings might have been inflated by the effects of novelty, additional adult attention, and other situational effects. Finally, several reviewers have cautioned that there is great variability in the findings and that more positive results are to be expected when the quality of the program's instruction is good, its content is aligned with the rest of the curriculum, the activities and responses required of the students are well suited to the grade level and the computer environment, and the students receive sufficient advance instruction and subsequent coaching to enable them to participate in the computer-based learning experience successfully (Bangert-Drowns, 1993; Cochran-Smith, 1991; Lepper & Gurtner, 1989; Means et al. 1993). We would add that we hope to see the development of more programs suited to students from diverse cultural backgrounds.

Limited access to computers can create feasibility problems. Even in classrooms containing eight computers, students spend as much as three-fourths of their time waiting for a turn at the computer (Center for Social Organization of Schools, 1984). However, this problem can be alleviated by having students work together in small groups on a single computer (Clements & Nastasi, 1988; Fish & Feldman, 1987). In fact, if used with software designed for group rather than individual use, computers can provide learning environments conducive to good group thinking and problem solving (Chernick, 1990).

Hadley and Sheingold (1993) surveyed teachers in grades 4 to 12 who were enthusiastic about computers and had made significant progress in integrating computerized instruction into their teaching. These teachers reported that using computers had changed their classrooms in three important ways: (1) They had come to expect more of their students and had begun presenting more complex material to them, (2) computerized instruction helped them to provide more individualized instruction than they had been providing before, and (3) their classrooms had become less teacher-centered and more student-centered, with their students doing more collaborative learning in pairs and small groups and the teachers acting more as coaches than as information dispensers. As they developed experience in using computers across periods of five years or more, these teachers reported making greater use of word processing (students creating their own compositions or other products) and databases (students doing research), but less use of drill and practice programs, *LOGO*, or computerized games that lacked connection to curricular goals. Given these developments in patterns of computer use, it is not surprising that these teachers also reported that computerized instruction had helped them to make academic subjects more interesting and had increased their students' enthusiasm for learning.

Schofield, Eurich-Fulcer, and Britt (1994) reported similarly encouraging findings in a study of the use of computer-based tutoring programs in high school geometry classes. They found that, rather than replacing the teacher, the programs provided an additional resource for students and allowed the teachers to provide for more individualized help. Students were pleased because the programs allowed them more control over the kind and amount of help that they received from the teacher and because helping interactions were more private and less potentially embarrassing than the more public interactions that take place when more traditional methods are used.

Like other technological innovations, computers can improve schooling, but as tools that enhance the effectiveness of teachers rather than as replacements for them. Computers have already proven valuable for several purposes, and new ones are likely to be established as the state of the art advances. Resources and interactive participation programs for both teachers and students are proliferating daily on the Internet. Consequently, if you have not done so already, you will need to acquaint yourself with the use of microcomputers, both as tools for assisting with some of the general tasks of teaching (planning, record keeping, reporting progress to parents) and as a vehicle for providing useful learning experiences to your students. For information about using computers in the classroom, see Bitter, Camuse, and Durbin (1993) and Harris (1994).

Conclusions About Individualized Instruction

It is difficult to generalize about programs for individualized instruction or adaptive education, including computerized programs. There is great variety in these programs and they are often implemented differently from their developers' guidelines. Programs that are confined to repetitive drill of low-level isolated skills seem clearly inadequate. So do programs that actually reduce instructional time by requiring students to spend a great deal of time handling procedural matters or simply waiting for attention from the teacher.

Good and Stipek (1983) concluded that no dimension of individual differences has unambiguous implications for instruction. It seems more appropriate to develop high-quality instructional materials and methods intended for all students than to set out from the beginning to develop different materials and methods for various students. Still, some students need extra instruction or learning time, and some need to be retaught in a different way rather than exposed to more of the same instruction. Teachers can include a degree of individualization within a whole-class approach by drawing on their knowledge of students' individual needs, interests, and learning styles.

Another criticism of individualized instruction is that although it is well suited to drill and practice in basic facts, concepts, and skills, it is not well suited to instruction in higher cognitive processes (problem solving, thinking, creativity) or to developing general dispositional states such as interests, attitudes, or values (Jackson, 1985). This is one reason why we recommend that individualized instruction requiring students to learn from curriculum materials be used in combination with, rather than instead of, whole-class or small-group instruction from the teacher.

Active instruction from the teacher has its own motivational and instructional advantages. It often saves both teachers and students a great deal of time, and teacher presentation underscores the importance of the content and provides the teacher with an opportunity to make it come alive for students. Also, research on factors associated with student achievement suggests that teachers who spend considerable time actively instructing students obtain better achievement gains than teachers who rely on curriculum materials to carry the content. Active instruction from the teacher is especially important for younger students, slower students, and students who come from less advantaged home backgrounds.

Even older, brighter students who seem to be progressing well through individualized learning programs can run into trouble if left on their own too long. Often, they do not even realize the problem. Erlwanger (1975) interviewed bright students who were consistently meeting mastery criteria on unit tests from their individualized mathematics curriculum. He found that many of them had misunderstood the material and developed mathematical conceptions that were at least partly incorrect, even though they were able to supply correct answers to application exercises and test items. The students had invented their own rules of thumb, which were useful for solving particular problems but would not work (and would leave the students badly confused) later on when they had to apply concepts to new situations.

Such findings illustrate a complaint that many teachers have voiced about individualized programs: Their students "can pass the tests but don't understand the concept." This is likely to happen if mastery criteria are set too low (70 to 80 percent instead of 90 to 100 percent) or if students continually retake the same test so that they eventually memorize the answers. Even with stiffer mastery criteria and several forms of each test, however, student confusion can go undetected unless teachers monitor progress closely and require students to explain concepts in their own words or show their work in detail (not just supply answers to highly structured questions).

In conclusion, we do not recommend individualized instruction if it means that students spend most of their time working on their own trying to learn from curriculum materials. However, we do favor individualization when it accommodates individuals' needs within the group context and achieves an appropriate balance of instructional activities (whole-class instruction, small-group instruction, cooperative learning activities, individual work). Even within the traditional whole-class approach, teachers can individualize instruction to a degree by taking students' interests into account in presenting content and making assignments, by asking different kinds of questions or giving varied assignments to different students, by allowing student choice and autonomy when the objectives can be met in different ways, by providing enrichment for faster learners and extra instruction in basic skills for slower learners, and by using some of the specialized small-group and individualized learning approaches we discuss here and in Chapter 7.

SUPPLEMENTAL INSTRUCTION FOR AT-RISK STUDENTS

Attempts to provide supplemental instruction for low achievers have not been very successful, usually because they paid too much attention to deficits and too little attention to making instruction meaningful (Knapp, 1995).

Shepard (1991) argued that most strategies for dealing with diversity have not improved the educational lives of students. In particular, tracking, special education through pull-out instruction, grade retention, kindergarten retention, and programs for at-risk kindergartners all have tried to individualize learning by placing children in homogeneous groups where they could receive more "appropriate" instruction. Shepard and other researchers have concluded that, ironically, students in any of these arrangements are likely to receive poorer instruction than if they had remained in regular classrooms. Further compounding inequality is the more frequent assignment of students from culturally and linguistically disadvantaged backgrounds to these remediation programs.

Shepard articulated four principles that provide a theoretical perspective for planning appropriate instruction for diverse student populations. First, recognize that intelligence and reasoning are developed abilities. Students who have difficulty with rote learning and who are retained in first grade (and who receive similar instruction the following year) are unlikely to learn to read for meaning. Students need opportunities to plan and evaluate their own learning and to develop strategies for self-checking and problem solving, so a steady diet of work focused on structure and drill is ineffective.

Second, recognize that developed ability and learning-to-learn strategies are largely context specific. For example, students who have a great deal of practical knowledge about mathematics (e.g., they frequently go to the store with parents, plan a budget, and so forth) will have developed the language and social interaction patterns necessary to appear capable during mathematics instruction. However, this does not necessarily mean that these students will be proficient at social studies or playing chess. Shepard contended: "The children who have developed the language and social interaction patterns appropriate in one context will look ignorant and deficient to teachers who are unaware of the arbitrary language and learning conventions they impose on the basis of their own cultural norms" (p.

294). Teachers need to be aware of and to use the learning strategies students have developed and need to show students how to use their knowledge in new ways.

Third, learning is a constructive process. Students do not learn effectively when they are presented with many discrete pieces of information, especially when these pieces seem unconnected. Students need the opportunity to think about and apply material, not just to memorize and rehearse it.

Finally, *meaning is socially constructed.* How and what children learn are highly dependent on their histories as learners and the social arrangements that support their learning at home and school.

According to Shepard, these four principles provide a framework for considering appropriate instruction in diverse settings:

> It follows from these principles that effective instruction should engage children in meaningful, contextually situated tasks where the goal is to practice and develop strategic thinking about important subject matter. The progress of instruction should be designed to help students use what they already know to arrive at new understandings. Prior knowledge is defined not just as vocabulary and information mastery, but includes all of the images, language patterns, social relations, and personal experiences that a student relies on to make sense of something new. [p. 295]

Allington (1991) noted that although individualization is frequently mentioned as a strategy for dealing with students who have difficulty learning, there is actually little evidence that individualization occurs—that is, that the amount or type of instruction these children receive differs from what other students receive. Few reliable effects of individualized instruction can be documented in studies of schools (Leinhardt, Zigmund, & Cooley, 1981), primarily because students who receive individualized instruction typically do not receive adjustments in instruction that are appropriate or of high quality.

McGill-Franzen and Allington (1990) conducted an observational study to determine what individualized instruction actually meant for remedial and special education students. They found that at-risk learners usually worked alone on tasks involving low-level skills. Ironically, when learners were assigned to a remedial resource room, the "individualized" instruction was often identical for all students in the room, despite the fact that their "learning problems" often varied considerably. This finding is similar to the paradox that Fraatz (1987) found: schools attempt to teach all students in a similar way in order to guarantee equity, but it is necessary to teach them differently in order to provide for individualization.

Theoretically, individualized instruction can be effective. In practice, however, attempts to individualize instruction by removing students from the regular classroom or placing them in a separate program are usually fraught with difficulties. We agree with Allington (1991, p. 246):

> Little of what is done in the name of individualization in schools seems to address an individual child's instructional needs. When decisions about individual needs lead to smaller amounts of instruction, to reduced curriculum

coverage, to the neglect of comprehension development, and to perpetuation of low-achievement status for some children, one must question whether those children are well served.

RESEARCH ON DIFFERENTIAL CLASSROOM INSTRUCTION

There is some research on the topic of differential instruction. Much of it has been conducted in secondary classes.

Instruction in Secondary English Classes

Some form of differentiated instruction to groups or individuals may be necessary when classroom composition is extremely heterogeneous. Research by Evertson, Sanford, and Emmer (1981) illustrates methods teachers have used to cope with these difficult situations. The study focused on ways junior high English teachers adapted instruction in heterogeneous classrooms compared with the ways they taught more homogeneous classes. The heterogeneous classes had 8- to 10-year spreads in grade-level-equivalent units between low and high achievers.

Observations revealed that all of the heterogeneous classes got off to a bad start because the methods and materials used seemed poorly adapted to students' interests and abilities. Success rates in terms of completeness and correctness of assignments were low. This pattern continued or deteriorated further in classes in which the teachers lacked the managerial skills to respond effectively to the problem. However, after about three weeks, the more effective teachers were able to overcome these problems to some extent by using the following strategies: (1) special attention and help for lower-ability students; (2) limited use of within-class grouping and differentiated materials or assignments; (3) limited differential grading based on individualized effort and continuous-progress criteria; (4) limited use of peer tutoring; and (5) frequent monitoring and provision of academic feedback to all students, coupled with mechanisms to ensure student accountability for participating in lessons and completing assignments.

Because of these teachers' managerial and instructional skills, not to mention their sheer energy and determination, there was no difference in achievement gain between the heterogeneous and the homogeneous classes. Still, there were limits on what could be accomplished. The pressures of meeting the greater range of instructional needs in the heterogeneous classes left the teachers with little time for personalized interactions with students, especially interactions concerning nonacademic topics. In the poorly managed heterogeneous classes, there also were yearlong problems of frequent student boredom or frustration due to inappropriate assignments. Probably because of these problems, ratings of student task engagement and cooperation remained lower in the heterogeneous classes throughout the year. Thus, this study illustrates that heterogeneous classes present difficulties, but that teachers can respond effectively to them by using appropriate techniques for managing the classroom and providing differentiated instruction. Teachers need to be sure that they use a variety of formats and consider both affective and cognitive goals when teaching heterogeneous groups. With careful planning, teachers can allow for new learning and appropriate practice and review for all students in the same lesson.

Response to Heterogeneity in a British School

Evans (1985) presented an interesting ethnographic study of what happened when a comprehensive secondary school (grades 7 through 9) in England switched from the traditional streamed (i.e., tracked) arrangement to mixed-ability grouping. Many teachers persisted with whole-class methods directed toward students with high or medium achievement within the class, just as they had done previously when students had been tracked. Most of them reduced teacher-led class instruction and increased individualized seatwork assignments, but essentially still taught the heterogeneous groups as whole classes.

Consequently, these teachers were forced to slow the pace of instruction and concentrate even more than before on lower-level facts and skills rather than higher-level cognitive objectives. As a result, many of the brightest students were bored and many of the slowest students still had difficulty keeping up. Lacking the time to teach the latter students to the level of true mastery, teachers "piloted" them through the curriculum. They often gave answers when students did not supply them, responded to weak answers as if they indicated full understanding, and "summarized" answers in ways that actually elaborated on them considerably. Similarly, the teachers guided slower students through individualized seatwork assignments by simplifying directions and giving feedback in ways that converted cognitive tasks into mere procedural tasks. They often allowed students to copy answers from peers or to look them up in the back of the book without truly understanding how to arrive at these answers or why they were correct. Thus, teachers who persisted with whole class methods in highly heterogeneous classes accepted the appearance of progress from slower students in the place of actual progress in mastering the curriculum.

STUDENT ENGAGEMENT AND ACHIEVEMENT IN AMERICAN SECONDARY SCHOOLS

As part of a series of studies on student engagement and achievement in American secondary schools, Newmann (1992) and his colleagues studied methods that schools developed for responding to student diversity. They found that the most important factor contributing to schools' success with students in general and at-risk students in particular was development of a "culture of inclusion" that featured a welcoming attitude toward all students, communication of positive expectations, and support for their learning efforts. Within the classroom, the most successful efforts involved curriculum and instruction that featured thoughtful classroom discourse and work on authentic learning activities (these aspects of Newmann's work are described in detail in Chapter 10).

Newmann noted that attempts to respond to student diversity required attempts to negotiate some form of synthesis between recommendations stemming from those concerned with high academic standards and teaching of subject matter for understanding and those concerned with improving student engagement by making instruction more student-centered and allowing students more opportunities for autonomy and choice in their learning. Thus, traditional classrooms were restructured by connecting students to computers and electronic media, emphasizing cooperative small-group work and individually paced study, and replacing worksheets with projects. However, Newmann identified a problem with these new techniques and processes: They do not define what should be taught or the degree of depth desired. Nor do they communicate a sense of what outstanding teachers do or how they talk with students about the subjects of study in these new circumstances.

Unfortunately, in observing how these attempts to innovate worked out in practice, Newmann reported problems similar to those previously reported by Evans (1985) in England:

> In their effort to reach out to low-achieving students and to incorporate student interests in the curriculum, many teachers have virtually abandoned the teaching of complex content in the main subjects of mathematics, science, English, and social studies. To feel included, students need support, success, caring, and incorporation of their ideas into academic study. But students' prior experiences and viewpoints must not be confused with the formal knowledge that educators are obligated to provide. The point is not to build curriculum on student personal experience instead of disciplined knowledge, but to show how disciplined knowledge can empower students by expanding and offering new tools with which to interpret personal experience. (Newman, 1992, p. 185)

Newmann went on to call for attention to curricular as well as instructional aspects of teaching in heterogeneous classrooms. In particular, he called for studies that would document in detail the nature of the curriculum and instructional methods used by teachers who are notably successful in these settings.

Clearly, teachers in heterogeneous classrooms are faced with the challenge of learning to deal with student diversity productively. Many educators find this challenge daunting and abandon the effort, relying instead on tracking and pull-out instruction methods. However, the latter methods entail social costs that tend to cancel out their potential advantages in instructional efficiency.

Research by Brantlinger (1993) provided stark reminders of this in its quotations from interviews with high school students. Brantlinger found that students from low-income and high-income families had very different school experiences, even when they attended the same schools. Low-income students felt shunned by high-income students, whom they simultaneously envied and resented. They complained about divisive, differentiating, and humiliating school practices such as receiving low grades, placement in low tracks or special education classes, and harsh or humiliating discipline. They were frustrated by their unsuccessful school careers and inequitable relationships with teachers. Those who were involved in special education tended to have positive attitudes toward their teachers but very negative experiences to report about being labeled as different (i.e., inferior), being removed from regular classes for pull-out instruction, and then finding that much of what they were asked to do in the pull-out settings involved repetitive low-level work that was not as interesting or useful to them as the activities they were missing in the regular classrooms.

GENERAL PRINCIPLES FOR DIFFERENTIATING INSTRUCTION

Although they underscore its difficulty, studies of teachers working with heterogeneous classes suggest certain general principles. First, as the range of student ability increases, the role of whole-class teaching will need to decrease. However, students in mixed-ability classes can still benefit from exchanging ideas in a large-group setting (speaking before a group, etc.). Furthermore, managerial issues, unit introductions and reviews, demonstration of experiments and use of equipment, and certain other types of information exchange still lend themselves to whole-class presentations in mixed-ability classes. In general, though, the frequency and duration of whole-class teaching will be reduced, and teachers' use of individual assignments and small-group work will increase.

Matching Assignments to Student Ability

Some students can read well and do so enthusiastically; others have limited skills and interest in reading. To enable students of mixed ability to work on similar projects, teachers must solve the reading problem. One strategy for doing this is to instruct students in independent reading and study skills. Another is to gather a wide assortment of materials written at varying levels of difficulty on a few core topics (it is unrealistic to try to acquire and store several books on every curriculum topic).

Books are available that differ in detail or vocabulary but allow diverse students to read materials with a common focus on historical events (the Civil War) or famous persons (Booker T. Washington, Marie Curie, César Chávez, Babe Ruth). Furthermore, many stories of literary significance are written with a low vocabulary demand. Students reading at different grade levels could benefit from reading these books, even though the teacher may eventually ask them to respond to the books in different ways.

Use of Multiple Reading Sources

Memory and Uhlhorn (1991) reviewed research indicating that weak readers do not benefit from materials originally written for more able readers but modified to present the same concepts in language that yields lower readability scores. Focusing on science, they offered suggestions for teachers who want to use textbooks (or other materials) written at different readability levels. First, teachers need to consider whether the easier books contain brief chapters with helpful comprehension questions at the ends. Poor readers, at least initially, are unlikely to read for extended periods, and follow-up questions encourage them to consider content and integrate it with their previous knowledge. However, the questions should foster comprehension and higher-order processing of main ideas, not just call for regurgitation of miscellaneous facts or unimportant information. Memory and Uhlhorn also suggested scheduling comparable time for all students to work on reading assignments. Even if students realize they are reading at different levels, there will be less social stigma if all of them are expected to spend the same amount of time completing assignments. Also, teachers should outline key concepts that all students are expected to learn, regardless of the difficulty of the texts they use. Finally, brief study guides presenting open-ended questions can alert students to significant content and help them to prepare for class discussions and unit tests. Study guide questions should be prepared using the vocabulary of the text at the lowest level of reading difficulty.

Ciborowski (1992) provided additional information about making textbooks suitable for work with low-achieving students. She argued that good readers and poor readers differ notably in how they think before, during, and after reading activities (these differences are presented in Table 8.1). For example, good readers are more likely than poor readers to think about what they already know about a subject when they begin reading. Hence, teachers must help poor readers develop

Table 8.1   A COMPARISON OF GOOD AND POOR READERS

Good Readers	Poor Readers
Before Reading	
Think about what they already know about a subject	Begin to read without thinking about the topic
Know the purpose for which they read	Do not know why they are reading
Are motivated or interested to begin reading	Lack interest and motivation to begin reading
Have a general sense of how the BIG ideas will fit together	Have little sense of how the BIG ideas will fit together
During Reading	
Pay simultaneous attention to words and meaning	Overattend to individual words; miss salience
Read fluently	Read slower and at the same rate of speed
Concentrate well while reading	Have difficulty concentrating, particularly during silent reading
Willing to "risk" encountering difficult words and able to grapple with text ambiguities	Unwilling to "risk"; easily defeated by difficult words and text
Construct efficient strategies to monitor comprehension	Unable to construct efficient strategies to monitor comprehension
Stop to use a "fix-it" strategy when confused	Seldom use a "fix-it" strategy; plod on ahead, eager to finish
Reading skills improve	Reading progress is painfully slow
After Reading	
Understand how the pieces of information fit together	Do not understand how the pieces of information fit together
Able to identify what's salient	May focus on the extraneous, peripheral
Interested in reading more	See reading as distasteful

Adapted from the Orange County Public Schools, Department of Secondary Reading, Orlando Florida.

the skills and strategies that good readers already possess—comprehension strategies that will enable them to understand what they read and take a more strategic, active role in reading and studying. (For a review of research on strategy instruction see Pressley & Beard El-Dinary, 1993). Poor readers need to be taught to predict what they think they will learn, monitor what they are learning as they read, and eventually summarize the learning and compare their conclusions with those of peers.

Preparing Assignments

Even individualized assignments that do not demand a great deal of reading must be carefully prepared with low achievers in mind. If slow students are to comprehend written instructions and function independently, the instructions must be stated in clear and explicit terms. Otherwise, teachers spend too much time clarifying directions and responding to the managerial problems that occur when students do not know what to do. As students gain confidence in their independent learning skills, they can be challenged with progressively more complex tasks. Teachers must also be sensitive to the different backgrounds of students and ensure that students see the connection between tasks and their own experience.

Cooke (1976) suggested ways to develop individual seatwork cards for students of varying ability who are working on similar historical topics:

1. Develop a core program card for each topic and require all students to complete these activities at their own pace.
2. Develop option cards that provide guidelines for more intensive subject work, special activities, and so on, and allow students to choose from these.
3. Do not try to develop option cards for each individual (this is unnecessary and impractical) but do produce separate option (or even core) cards for *three or four ability levels.*

Figures 8.1, 8.2, and 8.3 illustrate work cards prepared for students at three ability levels. The figures show how the same historical topic could be pursued in different ways. Figure 8.1 shows the assignment for slow 12-year-olds. Notice that it focuses on concrete details (helping the student to search parts of a passage in order to find material to make comparatively simple judgments).

Figures 8.2 and 8.3 illustrate assignments for middle- and high-level students. Progressively, instructions are written in less specific terms, students are directed to search different books, page references are omitted in favor of references to general sources or indexes, more deduction is demanded, and the use of supporting evidence for ideas is encouraged. For the most capable students, considerable initiative is required and more problem-solving questions are raised (dealing with conflicting accounts of history, etc.).

Students at all levels can benefit from problem-solving activities as well as from searching for facts and performing simple verification tasks. The work cards in Figures 8.1, 8.2, and 8.3 illustrate the relative emphasis that students of varying achievement levels need in seatwork assignments. To the extent that students who need

Roman Britain   Work card 1

HADRIAN'S WALL

       This is a picture of a part of Hadrian's Wall as it is now. You can also see the ruins of the Roman fort at Housesteads.
       Have a copy of *A Soldier on Hadrian's Wall* by D. Taylor on your table.

Things To Do

1. Write down these sentences and fill in the missing words. Pages 14 and 16 of *A Soldier on Hadrian's Wall* will help you.

    a. Hadrian's Wall was built from . . . . .in the east to . . . . .in the west. It is . . . . miles long.

    b. It was made of . . . .

    c. It measures . . . . feet high and. . . . . feet thick.

    d. In front of the wall was a. . . . . and behind it was a. . . . .

2. Imagine that you are the Roman officer in charge of building the wall. Write a letter to a friend in Rome telling him or her what the various buildings on the wall are and what they are used for. You can find out about these buildings in your book, pp. 16-20.

3. Draw a diagram of one of the buildings in your letter. Label all the parts and sizes of it. If you prefer, make a model of it to scale.

4. Draw and color a picture showing a scene from Hadrian's Wall, perhaps an enemy attack or soldiers marching along it. From the picture on this card, imagine what it must have been like on the wall.

FIGURE 8.1
An example of a work card for low-achieving students.

Roman Britain   Work card 2
HADRIAN'S WALL

This is a picture of Hadrian's Wall today.

Read

     A Soldier on Hadrian's Wall by D. Taylor

     Roman Britain by R. Mitchell

     Roman Britain by J. Liversidge, pp. 16-33

     The Romans in Scotland by O. Thomson, Chapter 3

Things To Do

1. Answer these questions as fully as you can:

    a. Why did Hadrian build a wall across Britain?

    b. If you were an enemy of the Romans trying to break through the wall
        from the north, where do you think its weakest points would be? You
        will need to find information about the various forts and defenses
        along the wall.

    c. Another wall was built 20 years later by the Romans in Scotland.
        Which Emperor built it? Why was it built? How different was it from
        Hadrian's Wall?

2. Imagine that you are the Roman officer in charge of building Hadrian's
    Wall. Write a report to the Emperor telling him why you have decided to
    change the wall from turf to stone and to alter the size.

3. Draw a diagram of a cross-section of the wall, or of a fort, and label it care-
    fully. If you prefer, make a scale model of it.

4. *Either*, as the Roman officer, write an entry for your diary describing an
    incident on the wall.
    Or, draw and color a picture of the incident.
    Do both of these if you wish.

FIGURE 8.2
An example of a work card for average students.

Roman Britain

Work card 3

HADRIAN'S WALL

Consult the books in the class history library on Roman Britain, in particular *The Roman Frontiers of Britain* by D. R. Wilson; *The Roman Imperial Army of the First and Second Centuries* by G. Webster; *The Romans in Scotland* by O. Thomson; *Handbook to the Roman Wall* by I. A. Richmond.

1. Why did Hadrian build a wall across Britain between the Solway and the Tyne? Why were no other routes suitable?

2. Find a picture of a British hill fort (e.g., Maiden Castle or Hod Hill) and compare it with Housesteads as a fortification. Illustrate your answer.

3. If you were an enemy of the Romans trying to break through the wall from the north, where do you think its weakest points would be? Why?

4. The Emperor Antoninus Pius decided to build a wall in Scotland in about A.D. 142. Imagine and write a conversation between Antoninus and his senior advisor about building the wall in Scotland in which they discuss why Hadrian's Wall is no longer suitable, and in what ways the new wall should be different.

5. *Either*, make a scale model *or draw* a picture of part of Hadrian's Wall. Do both if you wish.

FIGURE 8.3
An example of a work card for high-achieving students.

"structure" receive and learn to handle appropriate learning assignments as depicted in Figure 8.1, they need more assignments like those in Figures 8.2 and 8.3.

Teachers have to decide when it is possible to keep students of mixed ability working on the same topic. Perhaps the best strategy in a subject like history is to identify core topics that all students can learn and separate topics that more capable students can pursue at more complex and challenging levels. For example, all students might learn about the major causes of the Civil War, but only more capable students would be assigned to do research on the details of the leadership decisions that shaped them. For more about teaching mixed-ability students in a variety of subjects, see Evans (1985), Sands and Kerry (1982), or Wragg (1976).

Accommodating Students' Personal Characteristics

We have emphasized the need to build different assignments around common themes to allow students who differ in ability and achievement to address the same content at varying levels of sophistication. Students also differ, however, in personal and social traits such as energy, assertiveness, sociability, and patience. As teachers become more proficient at matching curriculum and instruction to students' achievement, they may wish to introduce additional individualization by accommodating differences in students' personalities, learning styles, or preferences.

The number of student factors that could be listed for consideration by teachers is endless, so there is no point in trying to construct an exhaustive list. However, we can present guidelines for differentiated instruction of a few common student types that teachers can expect to find in most classrooms. Good and Power (1976) identified the following five types of students:

1. **Successful students** are task oriented, academically successful, and cooperative. They typically participate actively in lessons, turn in complete and correct assignments, and create few if any discipline problems. They tend to like school and to be well liked by both teachers and peers.
2. **Social students** are more person oriented than task oriented. They have the ability to achieve but value socializing with friends more than working on assignments. They tend to have many friends and to be popular with peers but are usually not well liked by teachers because their frequent socializing creates management problems.
3. **Dependent students** frequently look to the teacher for support and encouragement and often ask for additional directions and help. Teachers generally are concerned about the academic progress of these students and do what they can to assist them. Peers may reject dependent students because they tend to be socially immature.
4. **Alienated students** are reluctant learners and potential dropouts. Extremely alienated students reject school and everything it stands for. Some are openly hostile and create disruptions through aggression and defiance. Others withdraw, sitting at the fringes of the classroom and refusing to participate. Teachers tend to reject students who express alienation openly and to be indifferent toward those who express it passively.

5. Phantom students seem to fade into the background because they are rarely noticed or heard from. Some are shy, nervous students; others are quiet, independent workers of average ability. They work steadily on assignments but rarely participate actively in group activities because they do not volunteer, and are rarely involved in managerial exchanges because they do not create disruptions. If asked to name all of their students from memory, teachers are most likely to forget phantom students.

Good and Power (1976) suggested ways that teachers might differentiate instruction to accommodate these students' preferences and needs (see Table 8.2). Although based partly on research, these suggestions are speculative rather than proven guidelines, for two reasons. First, accommodating students' preferences is not the same as meeting their needs. Several studies have shown that allowing students to choose their own learning methods or arranging to teach them in the ways that they prefer to be taught may produce *less* achievement than teaching them in some other way, even if it improves their attitudes toward learning (Clark, 1982; Schofield, 1981; Solomon & Kendall, 1979). Second, accommodating students' personal characteristics may reinforce these characteristics, including ones that ought to be changed if possible. For example, it would be easy to respond reciprocally to the behavior of phantom, passive-withdrawn, or alienated students by minimizing interaction with them—never calling on them unless they raise their hand or indicate a need for help. This behavior might even maximize the comfort of both the teacher and the students involved. However, it probably would not be in these students' best interests.

Even though such complexities must be kept in mind, Table 8.2 offers suggestions for introducing a degree of individualization into your instruction while primarily teaching the class as a group. Some of these suggestions can be incorporated easily (e.g., interacting more often or more affectively with certain students). Others would be more difficult or time-consuming to implement (e.g., preparing different activities or assignments for different groups of students). It may not be possible to vary the activities and assignments planned for each day, but these guidelines are useful for judging the appropriateness of longer-range plans. Each week or unit should provide enough balance to deliver something for everyone rather than be limited to activities and assignments that are well matched to the needs of one or two subgroups but poorly matched to the needs of others.

A single teacher cannot provide optimal curriculum and instruction to all students in a class simultaneously, because different subgroups present conflicting needs and because classroom management considerations take first priority. For example, dependent students (at least until they are taught self-regulation skills and gain the confidence to use them) need close supervision and frequent teacher feedback during independent seatwork. However, wise teachers reserve the first few minutes of seatwork to make sure that students in general and alienated students in particular get started on their assignments. Furthermore, teachers learn to keep their interactions with individuals brief so that they can circulate and be available to students who need immediate help. All students, even the most successful, need monitoring and feedback.

Table 8.2 SUGGESTIONS FOR MEETING THE NEEDS OF FIVE DIFFERENT TYPES OF STUDENTS

	Success	Social	Dependent	Alienated	Phantom
1. Type of information needed from teacher					
a. Substantive explanation of content	Very high	Very high	High	High	High
b. Procedural directions	Low	Low	High	Moderate-high	Moderate-low
c. Socializing, emotional support, humor	Very low	Low-moderate	Moderate	Moderate (establish private rapport)	Low
2. Type of task needed					
a. Reading skills required	High	High	Low	Low	Moderate
b. Task difficulty level	Very high	High	Low-moderate	Low-moderate	Moderate
c. Abstractness level	High	Moderate	Low initially	Low initially	Moderate
d. Cognitive level	High	Moderate	Low-moderate	Low-moderate	Moderate
e. Degree of structure (specificity about what to do and how to do it)	Low	Moderate	High	High	Moderate
f. Opportunity to make active, overt responses	Not important	High	High	High	Moderate
g. Opportunity to make choices	Moderate (stress on enrichment)	Moderate (stress on choices to work with others)	Low	Moderate (stress on relevance)	Low
h. Interest value of task to student	Not important	Moderate	Low	High	Low
i. Length of task	Long	Short	Moderate	Moderate	Long
3. Type of response demanded					
a. Written	High	Low	High	Moderate	High
b. Oral	Low	High	Low	Low	Low
c. Physical	Low	Moderate	Moderate	High	Low
4. Individual versus group settings					
a. Individual	High	Low	High	High	High
b. Group	Low	Moderate	Low	Low-moderate	Low
5. Emphasis on competition	High	Moderate	Low initially	Low	Moderate
6. Type of feedback from teacher					
a. Personal praise	Low	Low	Moderate	Moderate (private)	Low
b. Personal criticism	Low	Low	Low	Very low	Low
c. Praise of good work	Low	Moderate	Moderate	Moderate (private)	Low-moderate
d. Criticism of poor work	Moderate	Moderate	Low	Low (but communicate demand)	Low-moderate

Source: Adapted from Good, T., and Power, C. (1976). Designing successful classroom environments for different types of students. Journal of Curriculum Studies, 8, 45–60.

Teachers who have developed a workable system for instructing the whole class can then use this system as a base from which to introduce differentiated instruction. It helps if a variety of work settings or assignment formats is available and if the number of students working individually at a given time is limited so that the teacher does not have to try to provide individualized feedback to the entire class. For example, an elementary-grade teacher might assign dependent, alienated, and social students to work on individualized seatwork during the early morning when these students are not involved in reading-group activities. These relatively brief times (typically two 20-minute periods) for individual work could be used profitably by these students (who may react less favorably to longer individual seatwork assignments), especially if the teacher supplies answer sheets or other self-checking devices that they can use to monitor their progress. Success students and phantom students might be engaged in brief small-group projects during these same periods. Then, after recess, the students might all be engaged in whole-class work in mathematics. In the afternoon, success students and phantom students could be assigned to individual work while the teacher actively supervises the small-group work of other students.

However, there is only so much that can be accomplished even by experienced teachers who have developed sophisticated systems for organizing and managing instruction. Consequently, even the combination of methods we have discussed so far (ability grouping, differentiated curriculum materials and assignments, and differentiated teacher instruction) may not be enough to accommodate the diverse needs of students in heterogeneous classes. You may want to take the additional step of sharing instructional responsibilities with the students themselves by using cooperative learning approaches or by arranging for students to receive tutorial assistance (see Chapter 7). At least for certain purposes and for some types of students, such sharing may present a useful alternative or supplement to traditional methods.

INDEPENDENT WORK AND LEARNING CENTERS

Teachers can use well-chosen independent-work and learning center activities to enrich instruction and adapt it to individual differences. One way to create time for working with small groups and individuals is to structure time for students to engage in interesting, creative tasks of their own choosing. Some students, especially high achievers, are indirectly punished (given more of the same work to do, etc.) for finishing their work quickly. Instead, teachers should allow them to engage in enrichment activities. Students who work slowly are usually denied the opportunity to reflect on what they have done, because they need all of the allotted time just to finish their assignments. To give slower students time to reflect and improve, teachers might direct them to reread their work and reflect on it as an appropriate homework assignment.

Older elementary students might develop an open-ended personal yearbook in which they write and illustrate stories or record their reactions after they finish assignments. What students put in these yearbooks is left completely up to them. Other possibilities include allowing students to read and review books on some curriculum topic (e.g., American Indians) or to act as resource specialists or tutors for other students. However, book reports, if overly structured, may do little to encourage reading for enjoyment and interest. Often it is useful for the teacher and the student to discuss the book, including not only the plot but also why the student liked or disliked it. Occasionally, teachers should carefully structure long periods of independent work for all students (not just those who finish quickly) and thereby create time for remediation, enrichment, and informal conversations with individuals.

The classroom can be arranged to facilitate independent study. Figure 8.4 shows how one teacher arranged her first-grade classroom. This diagram was made as the teacher instructed a reading group. Note how the room arrangement allows for both group work and independent activities. Six students are in the reading group with the teacher, and two are reading at the independent-reading table. The reading center, separated by bookcases from the rest of the room, provides a place where students can read their favorite books in comfortable privacy when they finish their work. The teacher may, at times, use the reading center for an independent but structured learning activity. For example, students may be asked to write reports on chosen or assigned books.

Eight students are working at the listening center, which is a tape recorder with eight earphones that can be wheeled from table to table. One student has passed out pencils and accompanying exercise sheets; another is in charge of turning the tape recorder on and off. All students have been taught how to operate the recorder, and student helpers are assigned and rotated regularly. Similarly, four students are viewing filmstrips without teacher supervision. The student in charge today runs the machine and calls on students in turn to read the story that accompanies the pictures. When the students finish watching the filmstrip and complete written exercises, they move to another activity at their seats.

When the arrangement shown in Figure 8.4 was recorded, nine students were working independently at their seats and three were at the social studies center. Two of the latter were "buddy reading" stories about the social studies unit that had been printed by their fellow classmates, while the third was painting a picture. When the teacher terminated the reading group, all students rotated to a new activity.

Below we present one student's schedule for an entire day. Although a few other students would have the same schedule, there would be many different schedules within the room and the room would be divided to allow for various learning centers (see Figure 8.5). For example, another student might begin the day reading with the teacher in a reading group and end it at the listening post.

JOHNNY'S SCHEDULE

8:30–9:15	**Math corner**
9:15–9:30	**Math with his group**
9:30–10:00	**Reading with his group**
10:00–10:30	**Morning recess**
10:15–10:30	**Social studies with entire class**

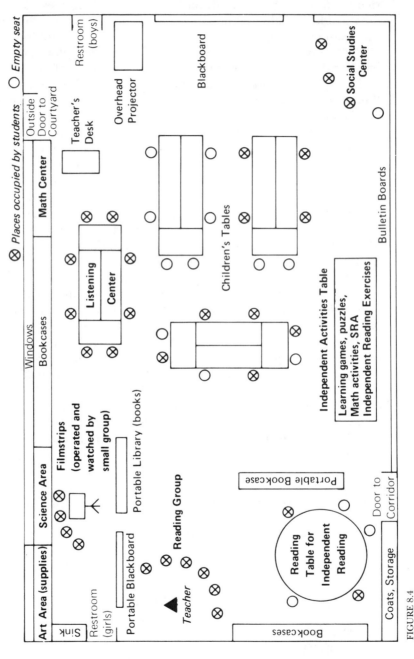

FIGURE 8.4
Physical arrangement of a first-grade classroom.

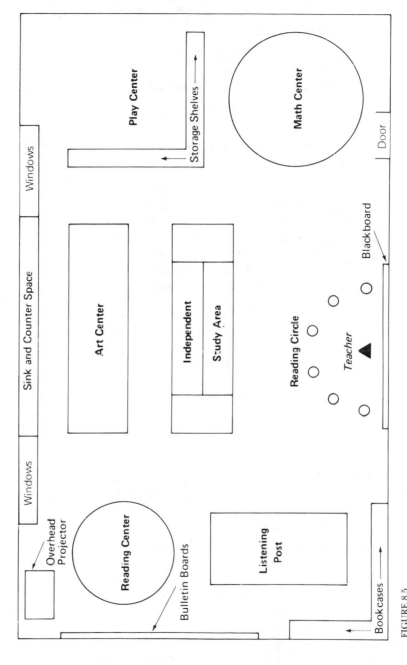

FIGURE 8.5
A classroom divided into learning centers.

10:15–11:10	Social studies in small-project group
11:15–11:45	Lunch
11:45–12:15	Story center (on alternative day or week the science center)
12:15–1:00	Free selection
1:10–1:30	Math instruction with entire class
1:30–2:00	Art center
2:00–2:15	Recess
2:15–2:30	Listening post (on alternative day or week at the writing center)
2:30–3:00	Reading instruction—independent work at the study area

Such scheduling allows students to work at different learning centers or in different project groups; the teacher then has free time for instruction of small groups or remedial work with individuals. Although many teachers may prefer not to use centers this heavily, such centers do provide excellent independent study areas and add flexibility by increasing the variety of assignments available.

Where there is room for only one or two centers at any one time, teachers can provide variety by setting up science and mystery reading centers for a few weeks, then creative writing and exploratory centers, and then art and historical centers. If such centers are more lesson oriented than project oriented they can be altered daily or weekly. The possibilities are limited only by a teacher's imagination.

Students need to learn how to use learning centers. As with all classroom assignments, tasks at learning centers need to be clearly specified so that students can work on their own with minimal teacher guidance. Rules for using equipment and handing in assignments must be established, appropriate to the ages and aptitudes of students.

Self-Regulation

It may be useful to have rules posted at each learning center to help the students function quasi-independently. Young students, for example, might be asked to do independent work by listening to a story and then responding to questions about it. The questions can be simple, "How many bears were there in the story?" or complex, "Listen to the story and then write your own ending." Teachers are free to use their own imaginations and to create material when setting up learning centers. Although companies make filmstrips, tapes, and other materials that can be used for independent work, some of the best assignments come from spontaneous events that occur in the classroom.

For example, one day during a seventh-grade English class, the principal makes one of his frequent PA announcements. At the end of it, Joe Jordan says, loudly enough to be heard by half the class, including the teacher, "Wouldn't it be great if just one day he kept his mouth shut?" After the snickering dies down, the teacher, Mr. Thornton, appeals to logic: "But what would happen if he made no announcements?" The class concludes that nothing significant would be lost if the principal never spoke over the PA again, because teachers could make announcements. The teacher then gives the following assignment for independent work. "Assume there was no television, radio, or newspaper communication for two weeks. Write a theme on one of the following topics: (1) how your life would be affected; (2) how attendance at sports events would be affected; (3) how someone wanting to buy a house would be affected; (4) how supermarkets could advertise their specials; or (5) think of your own topic and have me approve it."

Let us look at a few other assignments that teachers can use.

Examples of Elementary Learning Center Assignments

The listening post is a popular learning place in first- and second-grade classrooms. It is a table equipped with a stack of answer sheets, a can of pencils, six to eight earphones, a tape recorder, and taped stories. The stories are taken from supplementary information in the teachers' editions of textbooks, Science Research Associates' commercially produced products, or the *Weekly Reader,* or are recorded by the teacher based on special interests or incidents that have emerged in the classroom.

To avoid confusion, one student is designated as leader. After the others sit down and put on the earphones, the leader starts the tape recorder, stops it at the signal given on the tape, passes out paper and pencils for the questions, starts the tape recorder again, stops it at the end, collects the paper and pencils, rewinds the

April, 1996

Ƨ	M	T	W	T	ꟻ	S
	1	2	Ɛ	ᔭ	5	6
8	7	9	10	11	21	1Ɛ
14	15	1ᘐ	17	18	19	20
12	22	23	2ᔭ	26	27	28
2P	30	31				

FIGURE 8.6
An independent worksheet.

tape, and sees that the table is ready for use by the next group. To make the learning activity more autonomous and to provide students with quicker feedback, teachers can put the correct answers at the end of the tape. After a few drills on procedure, even first graders are able to function independently at the listening post. Similarly, students can be taught necessary skills for using the computer, video players, and various other types of media.

In addition to tapes and filmstrips, learning centers can be equipped with a greater variety of photocopied learning sheets. The complexity of the tasks, of course, varies with the ages and aptitudes of the learners. For example, in the math corner on April Fool's Day, a second-grade teacher might give students the sheet in Figure 8.6 and ask them to circle all errors that appear in the calendar (or students could be asked to make their own calendars and see if their classmates can find the errors they included).

Many teachers have found special-feature learning centers to be useful. For example, the teacher may write an introduction to a mystery story (3 to 15 pages, the length varying with reader age and aptitude). Younger students are requested to tape-record their own endings to the story; older ones may be requested to write their own endings and compare them with those of others. Young children, if properly prepared, can prove helpful giving feedback about peers' writing (Beachy, 1992). At other times in the special-feature corner, the teacher may have students respond to interesting questions: "On one page respond to this question: How would you spend a million dollars? Think! Tell *why,* as well as *what* you would buy." "Relate in 200 words or fewer how you would feel if you (dropped, caught) the winning pass in a championship football game." "Assume that you woke up today in the year 2025. Describe what you will actually be doing in the year 2025. How old will you be then? What job do you expect to hold?" The ideas presented here are only a few of the many activities that teachers can use in learning centers. The really good activities will probably be exercises you prepare especially for a class or a smaller group based on special interests you have observed.

Teachers at the same grade level can share ideas for independent learning centers. In fact, one teacher could put together several weeks of math work while another makes multiple copies of listening tapes and assignment sheets and a third works on language arts units. Such cooperation enables teachers to produce high-quality units in less time, and once created, the units can be used year after year with only minor modifications (most changes involve the addition of new units based on the spontaneous interests of students).

Similarly, a good project for preservice teachers in a college course would be to form work teams (e.g., math, social studies, reading, or science), with each group preparing from five to ten projects. In this way, students could swap ideas and learn how to implement the learning-center concept by actually planning and writing sequential units. In addition, students could keep copies of all class materials and thus would be able to begin teaching with a number of units they could use in their own classrooms.

For more suggestions about learning centers in elementary classrooms, including the design of accountability and evaluation systems and the use of individualized contracting approaches in connection with learning centers, see McCarthy (1977), Gagné, Briggs, & Wager (1992), or Savage and Armstrong, (1992).

Independent Work for Secondary Students

The learning center notion as discussed so far has more relevance for the elementary school teacher than for the secondary teacher who teaches one subject and sees students for only about one hour each day. However, certain subjects at the secondary level are well suited to independent study or independent group projects.

In addition to allowing students to learn from one another, independent group projects give secondary teachers time to meet with individual students or to pass from group to group, sharing ideas and talking informally. The guidelines here are similar to those suggested for younger students working in project teams, except that secondary students are able to work for longer periods without assistance. Students may be assigned to one- or two-week projects. Again, the assignments should involve interesting, enjoyable activities that encourage students to think about topics of interest and to discuss ideas or solve problems cooperatively.

Topics can be traditional assignments, such as having all groups first do basic research on four candidates seeking the presidential nomination (e.g., summarize their positions on selected issues), then having each group decide how one candidate would respond to a list of questions asked at press conferences in the South, North, East, and West, and then role playing these press conferences.

The key points to note in such assignments are (1) students begin with a common reading assignment, so that they share a base of information and have knowledge that they can use to solve problems; (2) students are then required to summarize their information and apply it to a particular situation (typically, they are given a choice regarding which specialty group they want to work in); and (3) they share information with other groups by presenting the views of their candidate in a general classroom discussion; where (4) they receive evaluative feedback (correcting factual errors or contradictions in their position) from the teacher and fellow students.

Most students enjoy working independently to gather facts on a problem and using the information in simulated situations. Again, organization is the key. Teachers need to structure the learning task, identify pertinent resources, and let students know how they will be held accountable. Of course, teachers need not structure all assignments. After students have been through the process, the teacher can solicit and use their ideas in creating new tasks. The important elements of group work are that the assignment has a clear focus (whether teacher defined or group defined), that each student is held accountable for at least part of the discussion, and that group tasks are enjoyable and involve authentic learning.

Topics need not always be traditional, content-centered assignments. Attitudes and awareness may be stimulated by combining factual knowledge with students' impressions and values. For example, the exercise just described involves mostly describing and reciting what journalists have written. Other assignments might begin with content and end with expression of feelings. For example, tenth graders in a world history class might be divided into four independent groups. Each group would be presented with summary descriptions of desirable physical and personality characteristics of women in four different countries in the 1850s. One group might then be asked to speculate about the cultural factors that led to these notions. Another might be asked to respond to such questions as "What were the roles of women in each of these countries and to what extent were women satisfied with these roles?"

Later, group discussion could center on the frustrations that led to women's rights movements in the United States and on why some countries allowed women to assume more responsibility than others. When and under what circumstances did women become activists? How did men respond to the emerging independence of women? What is male chauvinism? How has this definition changed across various periods—1920–1940; 1975–1995? Can a woman become president? What is women's role in contemporary American life?

Teachers who prefer not to devote much time to independent group work can still use brief assignments. Those who lecture daily or involve the entire class in daily discussion will be surprised at how effectively group assignments can enhance such a discussion. The basic procedure is as follows: (1) The previous night, the class is assigned certain pages to read; (2) at the beginning of the period, the class is broken into five small groups, each with two or three different questions to answer; (3) each group is allowed 10 to 15 minutes to discuss its answers, look up information, and so forth; (4) the class is brought back together, and the teacher calls on an individual to answer one of his or her group's questions. The teacher then encourages students from other groups to evaluate the answer and allows students who were in the original group to embellish the answer, defend it with logical argument, and so on.

Several good things can occur when teachers use small groups. First, students interact regularly with many of their peers, and, in discussing interesting questions about course material, have the chance to learn from one another. Students in small groups also have more chances to talk than they do in large groups, and shy students are likely to feel more comfortable expressing ideas in safer surroundings (when these students learn that they can express themselves and that others are interested in what they have to say, they will be more able to speak freely in front of the whole class). Students will be task oriented in these sessions when they know that any one of them may be called on to answer any one of the group's questions and that the teacher or a student in another group may ask for a clearer answer or more information. Perhaps most importantly, this procedure mobilizes students' attention, forces them to focus their thinking on relevant questions, and promotes learning. Finally, after listening and practicing their own responses, students will be interested in discussing their ideas and getting comments from others. If the teacher models interest in students' answers and responds to their comments constructively, students will learn that the teacher is genuinely interested in their learning, not just quizzing them about the reading assignment.

CURRICULUM AND STUDENT DIVERSITY

As student groups become culturally more diverse, teachers will need to consider all students' history, language, and culture. Balancing the curriculum to achieve both academic goals and fair representation of various groups is no easy task, especially if teachers are narrowing the content covered in order to deal more effectively with a smaller number of concepts in order to promote understanding and application.

Applebee (1991) reviewed the historical role of literature in the American curriculum and concluded that early educators selected literature that would reduce diversity and promote a core set of values and a common culture. Even in recent studies of secondary schools with reputations for excellent English programs, literature was dominated by traditional British and American selections, with only token attention to world literature, contemporary literature, and works by women or minorities.

Similarly, a 1988 national survey of representative secondary schools revealed that their required reading lists looked remarkably like those of secondary schools at the turn of the century. However, other studies have shown that the secondary curriculum provides more diversity in areas such as short stories, poems, and nonfiction. Still, book-length works (epics, novels, and plays) receive the most attention and often are the core around which other selections are organized. According to Applebee, until this imbalance is changed, minority authors and women will continue to be placed at the margin of the culture, and in a dramatic way that is sanctioned by schools.

Consistent with the hypothesis that learning is socially situated and that students are more likely to be knowledgeable about topics that are more central to their own racial and ethnic groups, Applebee reports on recent national assessment data showing that students' knowledge of literature is linked to the diversity of their own backgrounds. Although African American students did less well overall than white pupils, they did better than whites on questions dealing with literature by or about African Americans. "To take a typical example, 53% of African American students answered a question about Langston Hughes correctly compared with only 35% of white students and 27% of Hispanics" (p. 234).

Applebee argued that the issue is not one of simply guaranteeing that all students read works from their own heritage but rather of finding the proper balance among the many traditions, providing an appropriate mixture that represents the complex and changing fabric of American society, and striking a balance between a curriculum that is too standardized and one that is too particularized.

It is beyond the scope of this chapter to discuss in detail issues of multicultural education. There are many excellent chapters and book-length manuscripts that focus exclusively on this topic (Agger, 1992; Appleton, 1983; Baker, 1983; Banks & Banks, 1995; Casanova, 1987; Grant, 1992; Lynch, Modgil, & Modgil, 1992; Nieto, 1992; Sleeter, 1992). However, we do want to assert that teachers, especially if they have not had coursework in this area, need to explore the ethnic and cultural differences of their students. It is important to understand values and behaviors that make people similar as well as to appreciate differences that make them distinctive. Casanova (1987) noted that all students will react differently to instruction because of unique experiences each student brings to the classroom. Although many of these experiences do not interfere with learning, some do, and it is the teacher's responsibility to recognize such problems. Research findings illustrate that certain types of conflict can pose significant problems.

Heath (1983) illustrated how differences in communication patterns can lead erroneously to the perception of lack of ability. African American children in Heath's study were much more adept at illustrating their comprehension of a story when they were invited to retell a story rather than to respond to isolated recall

Strategies for Favorable Intergroup Relations

A study of family life patterns. This strategy requires that students study each other's families. The study, if handled maturely, should provide insight into the backgrounds and experiences of students from nontraditional families, extended families, and single-parent families. The study should include, but would not be limited to, an analysis of family roles, family livelihood, family problems and concerns, and family recreation patterns.

A study of minority and majority group communities. This strategy includes a study of minority and majority group communities. The study would include, but not be limited to, an analysis of organizing generalizations:

1. Communities have similarities and differences.
2. Communities require interlocking relationships, i.e., human interdependence.
3. Community conditions are results of current forces as well as the community's history.

A study of intergroup experiences. This strategy gets at the crux of the intergroup relations approach because all students are taught to analyze objectively the intergroup relations process. The strategy answers this question: What happens when a minority group and a majority group come into contact?

1. Students study in-group/out-group processes, stereotyping, ethnocentrism, elitism, racism, sexism, discrimination.
2. Students study attitudes, values, and beliefs of peers through surveys, personal interviews, and panel discussions.
3. Students study their own attitudes, values, and beliefs as well as their ancestral ties through genealogies, historical lifelines, and "roots" family study.

A study of sexism, gender-role stereotyping, and gender bias. This strategy emphasizes the idea that each person can develop a unique self-concept and that gender-role attitudes are learned rather than innate characteristics.

1. Students study the sociocultural concepts of self-concept, social roles, gender roles, and gender-role stereotyping.
2. Students study how different societies teach their conception of gender roles through toys, games, and play activities.
3. Students study the autobiographies/biographies of men and women who have defied the gender-role stereotypes of their generation, e.g., Marie Curie, scientist, or Robert Frost, poet.
4. More mature students study existing biological differences between men and women and how they are interpreted differently in different societies. (This refers to the nurture/nature issue regarding sex differences; students would need to be able to read and evaluate studies conducted by adults for other adults.)

A study of social stratification in industrial and nonindustrial societies. This strategy emphasizes the universal nature of social stratification and the division of labor. By comparing stratification systems in industrial, hunting and gathering, and agricultural societies, students can gain insight into the economic and political reasons for social classes and social roles.

1. Students should study how families "make a living" in a hunting-gathering society, in an agricultural society, and in an industrial society.

2. Students should study the specific characteristics of the stratification systems of industrial societies.
3. Students should study how social classes are like ethnic groups which have distinct values, beliefs, behavioral patterns (customs, traditions, folkways), and dialects.
4. Students should study how social class membership is initially a matter of luck but that in dynamic societies some upward mobility is possible.

A study of handicapping conditions. This strategy requires accurate, timely information at the factual as well as the emotional levels regarding handicapping conditions. The strategy requires a candid examination of handicapping conditions and the social difficulties faced by handicapped individuals.

1. By reading and discussing biographies or autobiographies of handicapped individuals, e.g., Helen Keller or Louis Braille, students can learn about the social and personal impact of handicapping conditions.
2. By researching and group reporting, students can get accurate information about specific handicapping conditions, e.g., Down syndrome, dyslexia, hearing impaired.
3. By role playing and assuming a handicapping condition, students can gain an awareness of the condition's impact on the individual, e.g., ear plugs for hearing impaired or blindfold for visually impaired.
4. By practicing signing, students can learn how specific handicapping conditions require compensatory use of other senses to overcome the specific handicap.

A study of racism, prejudice, stereotyping in ethnically and racially homogeneous classrooms. This strategy is intended for classrooms where no visible ethnic or racial mixture of students exists.

1. Students experience in-group/out-group processes vicariously through open-ended stories, role playing, simulations.
2. Students visit and study ethnic minority community action agencies.
3. Students visit and study schools with high concentrations of ethnic minority students.
4. Resource speakers from ethnic minority groups are incorporated into courses of study.

A study of intergroup relations with emphasis on the nature of racism between in- and out-groups. Such a study requires a serious study of the following characteristics of racist and prejudiced thinking.

Emotional racism. This kind of racism ranges from slight distaste to extreme hate of ethnically and racially different out-groups.

Cognitive racism. This kind of racism focuses on perceptions of meanings and understandings of what out-group people are like. Whatever the facts may be about the out-group people, the racist person has his or her stereotypes as "facts" about out-group peoples.

Action racism. This kind of racism is observable; avoidance, discourtesy, exclusion, exploitation, and violence against out-group peoples are evident behaviors of this kind of racism. This is what is considered racial and ethnic discrimination.

Value racism. This kind of racism focuses on the values a racist person wishes to maintain or preserve. Preservation of racist values ensures material gain; it becomes necessary to maintain racist values to ensure material gain and economic security.

questions. Au and Mason (1981) found that allowing Hawaiian students to use conversational forms used in their homes (talking through a story) enabled them to achieve better in school.

Garcia (1991) discussed issues associated with teaching in a pluralistic society. He recommended the strategies presented in the box on pages 346 to 347 for helping students to become more sensitive to individual differences between cultures.

A large study by Knapp (1995) that focused on teaching for meaning in high-poverty classrooms included analysis of the ways in which teachers working in ethnically heterogeneous classrooms responded to the cultural diversity of their students. Nonconstructive teachers held negative stereotypes of students from certain ethnic or socioeconomic backgrounds. Overreacting to these stereotypes, they treated these students in ways that limited their learning opportunities and communicated low expectations (see Chapter 3). In contrast, constructive teachers held more positive expectations of their students and possessed a basic knowledge of their cultures. The most effective ones explicitly accommodated the students' cultural heritages by communicating to them that their cultural backgrounds were not problems to be overcome but rather strengths to be acknowledged and exploited in schooling. For example, here is a description of a bilingual teacher of a combined first- and second-grade class composed of a mixed population of Hispanic, African American, and white students:

> Mr. Callio holds high expectations for his students and demands strict accountability for the work assigned to them. He recognizes that his students do not arrive at school with all the skills he would like them to have and plans his instruction accordingly. At the same time, his approach builds in a respect for the strengths and backgrounds of the students in his class. For example, Mr. Callio's classroom is alive with pictures from different parts of the world, showing the different ethnic, racial, and cultural groups represented in his students. One display reads "Yo soy Latino y orgulloso" ("I am Latin and proud of it") in big letters surrounded by pictures of pyramids, indigenous Mesoamericans, and other Latino faces. Another reads "I am African American and proud" and displays pictures of African people, places, and artifacts. Mr. Callio argues that it is imperative to provide positive self-images and role models if a teacher expects students to be driven to succeed. Mr. Callio uses his Spanish extensively in the classroom—and not simply to help those students with limited English proficiency. Rather, he argues that Spanish is an important language to know and encourages his monolingual English speakers to try to learn it. One of the top students in the class, an African-American male, regularly tries to piece together Spanish sentences. (Knapp, 1995, p. 39)

It is difficult to write about cultural differences because the research base is very underdeveloped, and superficial discussions tend to solidify features of cultural groups in ways that lead to stereotyping. Casanova (1987) argued that differences between cultural groups mask considerable individual differences within groups:

> In our discussion, culture and ethnicity will be considered as part of everyone's personal being rather than special characteristics of people who differ

from the dominant culture. At no time will the word *culture* be used to suggest artistic or intellectual achievement, nor will it be used to refer to surface differences such as style of dress or music. Culture includes all the ways in which people think, feel, and act as they try to solve their particular problems. Because these things are not static, we view culture as dynamic. Part of our humanity is the ability to learn and grow. Some changes, like learning that one buys fruit at the store, come easy; some, like acquiring different rules of politeness, are more difficult; and some behaviors, like looking away from or looking directly at a person to whom one is speaking, are almost impossible to change because they are unconscious. (p. 373)

We echo the conclusions of Lynch, Modgil, and Modgil (1992) that teachers must be sensitive when they make judgments about students who come from cultural groups that differ substantially from their own. They argue that teachers " . . . need to be trained to be more circumspect in their judgments, more aware of the limits of reliability and validity of their assessment, not least in the use of so-called objective tests, and more able to recognize their own limitations to make judgments and to allocate life chances. Their judgments need, therefore, to be more easily reversible and the culture of teaching and learning needs to endorse that reversibility as a norm" (p. 451). Fortunately there is a growing body of knowledge that can help teachers be more sensitive to the issues of cultural diversity and more adequate to respond to these issues (Garcia, 1991, Grant, 1992; Harry, 1992).

To reiterate, a comprehensive discussion of issues like cultural influences on thought, culture, and communication, sociolinguistic differences, nonverbal communication, and school culture versus home culture is beyond the scope of this chapter. However, to teach heterogeneous classes, teachers need to value diversity and to encourage students to learn from one another and to appreciate different languages and traditions. For the most part, differences among students are to be respected and understood, not altered.

SUMMARY

The United States and hence U.S. schools are becoming more racially and ethnically diverse. The school population will change dramatically in the next few decades. Many have seen diversity as a problem that must be overcome, and most strategies for dealing with diversity have not improved the educational lives of students. Programs like pull-out instruction, tracking, and grade retention (all designed to accommodate diversity by placing children in homogeneous groups where they can receive more "appropriate" instruction) have largely been unsuccessful. Indeed, most researchers have concluded that these arrangements are more likely to lead to poorer instruction for students than if they had remained in regular classrooms. Unfortunately, students from culturally and linguistically disadvantaged backgrounds are assigned to such remediation programs more frequently, further compounding educational inequality.

Students with different backgrounds can interact with one another profitably if their teachers use the students' diverse, unique experiences to make classroom learning richer and treat individual and cultural differences among students with sensitivity. Diversity creates opportunities for enriching classroom learning, although dealing with widely diverse groups of learners can make teaching difficult.

We reviewed several ways that teachers can respond to student differences (including individualized instruction, computer-based instruction, and supplemental instruction for low achievers). We discussed general principles for planning appropriate instruction for diverse student populations and presented many practical ideas for implementing these principles in elementary and secondary classrooms (e.g., learning stations, etc.).

We advocated more research on strategies for individualizing and making instruction more responsive to diverse student populations. Finally, we noted that if teachers are to teach heterogeneous classes successfully, they need to value diversity and to encourage students to respect differences in languages, traditions, and cultural beliefs.

SUGGESTED ACTIVITIES AND QUESTIONS

1. Observe or at least interview teachers who teach diverse learners. How do these settings compare with the classrooms in which you were instructed? How might your beliefs, norms, and preferences about teaching be influenced by diverse settings? What do teachers think is most rewarding and most difficult about teaching diverse classes? In what ways do their responses differ?

2. Visit a school that uses computers for activities other than drill and practice. Observe at least two students as they work on the computer and then interview them about their experiences. What were the students thinking about and attempting to accomplish while working? Many contend that students' thinking and intentions mediate instruction and thus affect instructional outcomes. To what extent do your interviews support or challenge this position?

3. Visit local schools or classes that purport to implement mastery learning. How do teachers' roles and responsibilities and students' opportunities in these settings compare with those in traditional classrooms? What is expected of students, and how do they respond to these expectations? Arrange a few interviews with students in both settings and ask them about their experiences. For example, do students in mastery learning classes think that speed is more important than do students in traditional classes? Do students in the two types of classes view mistakes differently (e.g., helpful, embarrassing)? What other questions should you ask students about their experiences in these two settings?

4. Consider your own expectations as a college student. How much structure do you want, and how much freedom, in deciding what courses to take (given your goals)? Talk to others to get their views, and then design a system to manage college courses that will satisfy all students' needs. Is it possible to do so?

5. Often, pressure on schools to change comes from public sources (such as information in newspapers that achievement scores are declining) and from parents. Changes seldom take into account students' opinions. Should students, as consumers, be given more of a say about day-to-day school procedures and routines?

6. Outline a plan that allows students to spend parts of each day at learning centers. Specify the room arrangement required, the nature and location of learning centers, and typical schedules for groups or individual students.

7. In this chapter, we suggested that some teachers might want to organize courses around different textbooks that cover the same material but vary in amounts of material provided and reading difficulty. To what extent is it reasonable to match content to students' reading level? We also noted that materials of varying reading difficulty are available for secondary science instruction. Consider the subject you are going to teach and assess the extent to which reading materials could be adjusted for individual differences among students.

8. As a teacher, how much time would you want to spend in whole-class, individualized, and small-group instruction? Why? Would time allocations vary with particular units? What criteria would you use to make such decisions?

9. As a way to illustrate some of the differences in students, the chapter presented five types of students (successful, social, dependent, alienated, and phantom). Which types are most likely to benefit from computer-based instruction? The least? Why? Would your answers differ if you interpreted "benefit" to mean learning versus interest?

REFERENCES

Abelson, H., & diSessa, A. (1981). *Turtle geometry: The computer as a medium for exploring mathematics.* Cambridge, MA: MIT Press.

Agger, B. (1992). *Cultural studies as critical theory.* London: Falmer Press.

Allington, R. (1991). Children who find learning to read difficult: School responses to diversity. In E. Hiebert (Ed.), *Literacy for a diverse society: Perspectives, practices, and policies* (pp. 237–252). New York: Teachers College Press.

Anderson, L. W. (1985). A retrospective and prospective view of Bloom's "Learning for mastery." In M. C. Wang & H. J. Walberg (Eds.), *Adapting instruction to individual differences.* Berkeley, CA: McCutchan.

Applebee, A. (1991). Literature: Whose heritage? In E. Hiebert (Ed.), *Literacy for a diverse society: Perspectives, practices, and policies* (pp. 237–252). New York: Teachers College Press.

Appleton, N. (1983). *Cultural pluralism in education: Theoretical foundation.* White Plains, NY: Longman.

Arlin, M. N. (1982). Teacher responses to student time differences in mastery learning. *American Journal of Education, 90,* 334–352.

Arons, A. (1984). Computer-based instructional dialogs in science courses. *Science, 224,* 1051–1056.

Au, K., & Mason, J. (1981). Social organizational factors in learning to read: The balance of rights hypothesis. *Reading Research Quarterly, 17,* 115–152.

Baker, G. (1983). *Planning and organizing multicultural instruction.* Reading, MA: Addison-Wesley.

Bangert, R. L., Kulik, J. A., & Kulik, C. C. (1983). Individualized systems of instruction in secondary schools. *Review of Educational Research, 53,* 13–158.

Bangert-Drowns, R. (1993). The word processor as an instructional tool: A meta-analysis of word processing in writing instruction. *Review of Educational Research, 63,* 69–93.

Banks, J., & Banks, C. (Eds.). (1995). *Handbook of research on multicultural education.* New York: Macmillan.

Barth, J., Craycraft, K., Marker, P., Stitt, J., Willis, L., & Wineman, S. (1984). *Principles of social studies.* Lanham, MD: University Press of America.

Beynon, J., & MacKay, H. (Eds.). (1993). *Computers into classrooms: More questions than answers.* London: Falmer Press.

Biehler, R. (1971). *Psychology applied to teaching.* Boston: Houghton-Mifflin.

Bitter, G., Camuse, R., & Durbin, V. (1993). *Using a microcomputer in the classroom* (3rd ed.). Boston: Allyn & Bacon.

Block, J., & Anderson, L. (1975). *Mastery learning in classroom instruction.* NY: Macmillan.

Bloom, B. (1980). *All our children learning.* Hightstown, NJ: McGraw-Hill.

Bloom, B. (1984). The search for methods of group instruction as effective as one-to-one tutoring. *Educational Leadership, 41*(8), 4–17.

Brantlinger, E. (1993). *The politics of social class in secondary school: Views of affluent and impoverished youth.* New York: Teachers College Press.

Carlson, D. (1982). "Updating" individualism and the work ethic: Corporate logic in the classroom. *Curriculum Inquiry, 12,* 125–160.

Casanova, U. (1987). Ethnic and cultural differences. In V. Richardson-Koehler (Ed.), *Educators' handbook: A research perspective* (pp. 370–393). White Plains, NY: Longman.

Center for Social Organization of Schools. (1984, November). *School uses of microcomputers: Reports from a national survey* (Issue No. 6). Baltimore: Johns Hopkins University.

Chernick, R. (1990). Effects of interdependent, coactive, and individualized working conditions on pupils' educational computer program performance. *Journal of Educational Psychology, 82,* 691–695.

Ciborowski, J. (1992). *Textbooks and the students who can't read them.* NY: Brookline Books.

Clark, R. (1982). Antagonism between achievement and enjoyment in ATI studies. *Educational Psychologist, 17,* 92–101.

Clements, D. (1986). Effects of *LOGO* and CAI environments on cognition and creativity. *Journal of Educational Psychology, 78,* 309–318.

Clements, D., & Nastasi, B. (1988). Social and cognitive interactions in educational computer environments. *American Educational Research Journal, 25,* 87–106.

Cochran-Smith, M. (1991). Word processing and writing in elementary classrooms: A critical review of related literature. *Review of Educational Research, 61,* 107–155.

Cochran-Smith, M., Paris, C., & Kahn, J. (1991). *Learning to write differently: Beginning writers and word processing.* Norwood, NJ: Ablex.

Cooke, B. (1976). Teaching history in mixed-ability groups. In E. Wragg (Ed.), *Teaching in mixed-ability groups.* London: David and Charles Ltd.

Cuban, L. (1984). *How teachers taught: Constancy and change in American classrooms, 1890–1980.* New York: Longman.

Davis, R. (1984). *Learning mathematics: A cognitive science approach to mathematics education.* London: Croom Helm

Dollar, B. (1972). *Humanizing classroom discipline.* New York: Harper & Row.

Ehman, L., Glenn, A., Johnson, V., & White, C. (1992). Using computer databases in student problem solving: A study of eight social studies teachers' classrooms. *Theory and Research in Social Education, 20,* 179–206.

Erlwanger, S. (1975). Case studies of children's conceptions of mathematics (Pt. I). *Journal of Children's Mathematical Behavior, 1,* 157–283.

Evans, J. (1985). *Teaching in transition: The challenge of mixed ability grouping.* Philadelphia: Open University Press.

Everhart, R. B. (1983). *Reading, writing, and resistance: Adolescence and labor in a junior high school.* Boston: Routledge and Kegan Paul.

Evertson, C., Sanford, J., & Emmer, E. (1981). Effects of class heterogeneity in junior high school. *American Educational Research Journal, 18,* 219–232.

Fish, M., & Feldman, S. (1987). Teacher and student verbal behavior in microcomputer classes: An observational study. *Journal of Classroom Interaction, 23,* 15–21.

Fletcher, J., Hawley, D., & Piele, P. (1990). Costs, effects, and utility of microcomputer assisted instruction in the classroom. *American Educational Research Journal, 27,* 783–806.

Fraatz, J. (1987). *The politics of reading: Power, opportunity, and prospect for change in America's public schools.* New York: Teachers College Press.

Freyd, P., & Lytle, J. (1990). A corporate approach to the 2R's: A critique of IBM's Writing To Read program. *Educational Leadership, 47,* 83–89.

Gagné, R., Briggs, L., and Wager, W. (1992). *Principles of instructional design,* (4th ed.) New York: Holt, Rhinehart and Winston.

Good, T., & Power, C. (1976). Designing successful classroom environments for different types of students. *Journal of Curriculum Studies, 8,* 1–16.

Good, T., & Stipek, D. (1983). Individual difference in the classroom: A psychological perspective. In G. Fenstermacher & J. Goodlad (Eds.), *Individual differences and the common curriculum* (82nd yearbook of the National Society for the Study of Education, Part I). Chicago: University of Chicago Press.

Goodlad, J. (1984). *A place called school.* New York: McGraw-Hill.

Goodlad, J., Soder, R., & Sirotnik, K. (Eds.). (1990). *Places where children are taught.* San Francisco: Jossey-Bass.

Grant, C. (1992). *Research in multicultural education: From the margins to the mainstream.* London: Falmer Press.

Grejda, G., & Hannafin, M. (1992). Effects of word processing on sixth-graders' holistic writing and revisions. *Journal of Educational Research, 85,* 144–149.

Grinder, R., & Nelsen, E. A. (1985). Individualized instruction in American pedagogy: The saga of an educational ideology and a practice in the making. In M. C. Wang & H. J. Walberg (Eds.), *Adapting instruction to individual differences.* Berkeley, CA: McCutchan.

Guskey, T. (1994). Defining the differences between Outcome-Based Education and Mastery Learning. *School Administrator, 51*(8), 34–37.

Guskey, T., & Pigott, T. (1988). Research on group-based mastery learning programs: A meta-analysis. *Journal of Educational Research, 81,* 197–216.

Hadley, M., & Sheingold, K. (1993). Commonalities and distinctive patterns in teachers' integration of computers. *American Journal of Education, 101,* 261–315.

Harris, J. (1994). *Way of the ferret: Finding educational resources on the internet.* Eugene, OR: International Society for Technology in Education.

Heath, S. (1983). *Ways with words.* New York: Cambridge University Press.

Hiebert, E. (1991). Introduction. In E. Hiebert (Ed.), *Literacy for a diverse society: Perspectives, practices, and policies* (pp. 1–6). New York: Teachers College Press.

Horak, B. (1981). A meta-analysis of research findings on individualized instruction in mathematics. *Journal of Educational Research, 74,* 249–253.

Jackson, P. W. (1985). Private lessons in public schools: Remarks on the limits of adaptive instruction. In M. C. Wang & H. J. Walberg (Eds.), *Adapting instruction to individual differences.* Berkeley, CA: McCutchan.

Jones, B. F., Friedman, L. B., Tinzmann, M., & Cox, B. E. (1985). Guidelines for instruction-enriched mastery learning to improve comprehension. In D, Levine (Ed.), *Improving student achievement through mastery learning programs.* San Francisco: Jossey-Bass.

Kliebard, H. (1986). *The struggle for the American curriculum, 1893–1958.* New York: Routledge.

Knapp, M. (1995). *Teaching for meaning in high-poverty classrooms.* New York: Teachers College Press.

Kulik, C., Kulik, J., & Bangert-Drowns, R. (1990). Effectiveness of mastery learning programs: A meta-analysis. *Review of Educational Research, 60,* 265–299.

Laughlin, M., Hartoonian, H., & Sanders, N. (Eds.). (1989). *From information to decision making: New challenges for effective citizenship* (Bulletin No. 83). Washington, DC: National Council for the Social Studies.

Lehrer, R., Guckenberg, T., & Lee, O. (1988). Comparative study of the cognitive consequences of inquiry-based *LOGO* instruction. *Journal of Educational Psychology, 80,* 543–553.

Lehrer, R., & Randle, L. (1987). Problem solving, metacognition and composition: The effects of interactive software for first-grade children. *Journal of Educational Computing Research, 3*, 409–427.

Leinhardt, G., Zigmond, N., & Cooley, W. (1981). Reading instruction and its effects. *American Educational Research Journal, 18*, 343–361.

Lepper, M., & Chabay, R. (1985). Intrinsic motivation and instruction: Conflicting views on the role of motivational processes in computer-based education. *Educational Psychologist, 20*, 217–230.

Lepper, M., & Gurtner, J. (1989). Children and computers: Approaching the twenty-first century. *American Psychologist, 44*, 170–178.

Levine, D. (1985). *Improving student achievement through mastery learning programs.* San Francisco: Jossey-Bass.

Lipson, J. (1974). IPI math—an example of what's right and wrong with individual modular programs. *Learning* (March), 60–61.

Lipson, J., & Fisher, K. (1983). Technology and the classroom: Promise or threat? *Theory into Practice, 22*, 253–259.

Lynch, J., Modgil, C., & Modgil, S. (Eds.). (1992). *Education for cultural diversity convergence and divergence* (vol. 1). London: Falmer Press.

Martorella, P. (1994). *Social studies for elementary school children: Developing young citizens.* New York: Merrill.

McCarthy, M. (1977). The how and why of learning centers, *Elementary School Journal, 77*, 292–299.

McGill-Franzen, A., & Allington, R. (1990). Comprehension and coherence: Neglected elements of literacy instruction in remedial and resource room services. *Journal of Reading, Writing, and Learning Disability, 6*, 149–180.

Means, B. et al. (1993). *Using technology to support education reform.* Washington, DC: U.S. Department of Education.

Memory, D., & Uhlhorn, K. (1991). Multiple textbooks at different readability levels in the science classroom. *School Science and Mathematics, 91*, 64–72.

Miller, G., & Emihovich, C. (1986). The effects of mediated programming instruction on preschool children's self-monitoring. *Journal of Educational Computing Research, 2*, 283–297.

Miller, L.S. (1995). *An American imperative: Accelerating minority educational advancement.* New Haven: Yale University Press.

Miller, R., Kelly, G., & Kelly, J. (1988). Effects of *LOGO* computer programming experience on problem solving and spatial relations ability. *Contemporary Educational Psychology, 13*, 348–357.

Natriello, G., McDill, E., & Pallas, A. (1990). *Schooling disadvantaged children: Racing against catastrophe.* New York: Teachers College Press.

Newmann, F. (Ed.). (1992). *Student engagement and achievement in American secondary schools.* New York: Teachers College Press.

Nieto, S. (1992). *Affirming diversity: The sociopolitical context of multicultural education.* White Plains, NY: Longman.

Papert, S. (1980). *Mindstorms: children, computers, and powerful ideas.* New York: Basic Books.

Pea, R., Kurland, D., & Hawkins, J. (1985). *LOGO* and the development of thinking skills. In M. Chen & W. Paisley (Eds.), *Children and microcomputers* (pp. 193–212). Beverly Hills, CA: Sage.

Pressley, M., & Beard El-Dinary, P. (Guest editors). (1993). Special issue on strategies instruction. *Elementary School Journal, 94*, 105–284.

Pstoka, J., Massey, L., & Mutter, S. (Eds.). (1988). *Intelligent tutoring systems: Lessons learned.* Hillside, NJ: Erlbaum.

Salomon, G., & Perkins, D. (1987). Transfer of cognitive skills from programming: When and how? *Journal of Educational Computing Research 3*, 149–169.

Sands, M., & Kerry, T. (Eds.). (1982). *Mixed ability teaching*. London: Croom Helm.

Savage, T., & Armstrong, D. (1992). *Effective teaching in elementary social studies* (2nd ed.). New York: Macmillan.

Scardamalia, M., Bereiter, C., Brett, C., Burtis, P., Calhoun, C., & Lea, N. (1992). Educational applications of a networked communal database. *Interactive Learning Environments, 2*, 45–71.

Schofield, H. (1981). Teacher effects on cognitive and affective pupil outcomes in elementary school mathematics. *Journal of Educational Psychology, 73*, 462–471.

Schofield, J., Eurich-Fulcer, R., & Britt, C. (1994). Teachers, computer tutors, and teaching: The artificially intelligent tutor as an agent for classroom change. *American Educational Research Journal, 31*, 579–607.

Schwarz, G., & Cavener, L. (1994). Outcome-based education and curriculum change: Advocacy, practice, and critique. *Journal of Curriculum and Supervision, 9*, 326–338.

Shepard, L. (1991). Negative policies for dealing with diversity: When does assessment and diagnosis turn into sorting and segregation? In E. Hiebert (Ed.), *Literacy for a diverse society: Perspectives, practices, and policies* (pp. 279–298). New York: Teachers College Press.

Slavin, R. (1991). Reading effects of IBM's "Writing to Read" program: A review of evaluations. *Educational Evaluation and Policy Analysis, 13*, 1–11.

Slavin, R. E. (1984). Component building: A strategy for research-based instructional improvement. *Elementary School Journal, 84*, 255–269.

Sleeter, C. (1992). *Keepers of the American dream: A study of staff development and multi-cultural education*. London: Falmer Press.

Solomon, D., & Kendall, A. (1979). *Children in classrooms: An investigation of person-environment interaction*. New York: Praeger.

Soloway, E. (1991). *The promise of technology for promoting change*. Paper presented at the annual meeting of the American Educational Research Association.

Stallings, J. & Stipek, D. (1986). Research on Early Childhood and Elementary School Teaching Programs. In N.M. Whitrock (Ed.), *Handbook of research on teaching* (3rd Ed., pp. 727–753). New York, MacMillan.

Taylor, R. P. (Ed.). (1980). *The computer in the school: Tutor, tool, tutee*. New York: Teachers College Press.

Wang, M. C., & Lindvall, C. M. (1984). Individual differences in school learning environments: Theory, research, and design. In E. W. Gordon (Ed.), *Review of research in education* (Vol. 11). Washington, DC: American Educational Research Association.

Wragg, E. (Ed.). (1976). *Teaching in mixed ability groups*. London: David and Charles Limited.

FORM 8.1. Student Independence in Individual Work

USE: When students interact with teacher during periods of individual work assignment and/or in open settings.
PURPOSE: To see if individual students or students generally, over time, are becoming more autonomous learners.
Below is a list of student behaviors that could occur during seatwork assignments. Check each behavior as it happens.

Frequency*   Type of Contact

_____ 1. After beginning task, student seeks additional instructions
              about what to do.
_____ 2. Student seeks confirmation about being on the right track
              ("Is this okay?").
_____ 3. Student seeks substantive advice from teacher ("Is there
              another source that could be consulted?").
_____ 4. Student seeks evaluative feedback ("What do you think
              about this conclusion?").
_____ 5. Student tells teacher what was done and why (showing,
              justifying).
_____ 6. Student asks teacher what to do next after completing the
              initial assignment (seeks direction).

*In this particular example, the scale will yield information describing the frequency of different types of contact that occur with the teacher during a given amount of time. However, codes could be entered for individual students or for types of students by assigning them a number (high achievers = 1, middle achievers = 2, and so forth).

FORM 8.2. Learning Centers

USE: In classrooms containing one or more learning centers.
PURPOSE: To describe the content and management of learning center activities.

> *Enter a check mark (to indicate presence) or a 0 (to indicate absence) for each of the following questions:*

CHECKLIST

_____ 1. Has the center been created with clear curricular objectives in mind (that is, is it designed to ensure that the students learn something rather merely to entertain them)?

_____ 2. Given the curricular goals, are the activities appropriate in difficulty level and otherwise likely to succeed in enabling the students to meet the objectives?

_____ 3. Are the activities interesting or otherwise appealing to the students?

_____ 4. Is there an appropriate amount and variety of materials and tasks (if necessary to accommodate a range of student ability levels)?

_____ 5. Have the students been prepared (via demonstration and practice) in how to use the center?

_____ 6. Has the center been equipped with appropriate furnishings and materials?

_____ 7. Has the design and location of the center taken into account equipment storage and traffic patterns?

_____ 8. Has the teacher posted a schedule or articulated clear guidelines to enable students to know when they can or should use the center?

_____ 9. Are there clear management rules (concerning how many students may use the center at once, who should take charge of the group activities, cleanup and restoration of equipment, etc.)?

_____ 10. Do students know what to do when they get to the center (or can they consult clear guidelines posted at the center when they get there)?

_____ 11. Have provisions been made so that students can get feedback and check their work when they finish center activities?

_____ 12. Do the students know when and how to get help with center activities if they need it?

_____ 13. Is there a clear accountability system for center assignments (students know what they are supposed to do, know when and where to turn in completed work, and know that the work will be checked and followed up)?

_____ 14. Does the center emphasize hands-on activities that allow the students to explore or manipulate (rather than just provide more seatwork but in a different location)?

_____ 15. Have the activities been planned to allow students to work cooperatively or assist one another?

_____ 16. Does the teacher phase new activities into the center as the objectives of earlier activities are met?

COMMENTS:

Active Teaching

*I*n previous chapters we addressed important factors involved in setting the stage for productive instruction: teacher expectations, classroom management, student motivation, and cooperative learning environments. We also noted that the task of teaching 20 or more students forces most teachers to rely on whole-class instructional methods as their basic approach, but that this approach can be modified in various ways to adapt to students' individual differences. We now turn to the core topic of instruction itself. Here in Chapter 9 we discuss research relating teacher behavior to student achievement and its implications about the role of the teacher in actively presenting information to students, involving them in discussions, and engaging them in learning activities and assignments. In Chapter 10 we will discuss recent research and scholarship indicating that learning with understanding involves not only receiving information from a teacher or text but actively constructing understandings through social interaction. These ideas imply a need to modify traditional teaching methods so as to create more and better opportunities for students to construct understandings through productive interactions with the teacher and with their classmates. Once again we see that teacher decision making, guided by clear goals, is the key to effective instruction.

INSTRUCTIONAL METHODS AS MEANS TO ACCOMPLISH CURRICULAR GOALS

There are many different approaches to instruction. Some are mutually exclusive, but most are merely different. For example, Joyce and Weil (1986) described over 20 approaches to teaching, classified into four types—information processing, social interaction, focus on the individual person, and behavior modification. *Information-processing approaches* organize instruction to present material so that learners can process and retain it most easily. They also attempt to foster students' information-processing skills. *Social interaction approaches* stress the group-living aspects of schooling. Instruction is arranged so that students learn from one another as well as the teacher, who focuses on fostering group relations as well as on instruction. *Personal approaches* draw on humanistic psychology to promote intellectual and emotional development (self-actualization, mental health, creativity). Finally, *behavior modification approaches* sequence activities to promote efficient learning and shape behavior through reinforcement.

Specific teaching methods are useful for accomplishing certain purposes in certain situations. No one method is optimal for all purposes in all situations. Thus, one cannot teach effectively by using a single method all the time. Doing this would treat instructional method as an end in itself rather than as a means of accomplishing one's instructional goals.

A method is most effective when used as part of a coherent instructional program that is *goals driven*—designed to accomplish clear goals that are phrased in terms of student capabilities to be developed. A goals-driven program features *alignment* among the goals themselves and each of the program's components: the content selected for focus; the organization, sequencing, and representation of this content; its elaboration and application during lessons, activities, and assignments; and the methods selected for evaluating learning.

This notion of alignment among the elements in a goals-driven instructional plan implies the need for teacher decision making about goals and methods. Only certain methods are suited to particular goals, so that other methods will be irrelevant or even counterproductive. Given formulation of appropriate goals and identification of appropriate content, the primary planning task is to identify the combination of methods that is most likely to accomplish the goals. If several methods seem equally appropriate, the teacher might make the choice on the basis of secondary criteria such as personal preference, student responsiveness, availability of materials, or cost in time and trouble.

It may seem obvious that curriculum planning should be goals-driven and should feature alignment among its elements, but this ideal model is not often implemented in classrooms. Teachers typically plan by concentrating on the content they will teach and the activities their students will do, without giving much consideration to the goals that provide the rationale for the content and activities in the first place (Clark & Peterson, 1986). In effect, most teachers leave crucially important decisions about goals to the publishing companies who supply them with instructional materials. This would not be so bad if materials were clearly goals-driven and featured alignment among their elements. However, analyses indicate that they tend to treat content coverage as an end in itself, so that too many topics are covered in not enough depth; that content exposition often lacks coherence and is cluttered with insertions and illustrations that have little to do with the key ideas that should be stressed; that skills are taught separately from knowledge content rather than integrated with it; and that, in general, there is little evidence of planning for development of key ideas and use of these ideas in ways that would help students to accomplish major instructional goals (Beck & McKeown, 1988; Brophy, 1992b; Dreher & Singer, 1989; Elliott & Woodward, 1990; Tyson-Bernstein, 1988).

Teachers cannot simply follow the suggestions that come with their textbooks and expect to achieve coherent programs of curriculum and instruction. They will have to be prepared to elaborate on or even substitute for much of the content in the texts and many of the activities suggested in the accompanying manuals. This implies that teachers will need not only sufficient content knowledge, but also familiarity with a variety of instructional methods and awareness of when and why these methods are used. Unfortunately, debates about methods are often framed unproductively. In particular, these arguments frequently are reduced to false dichotomies (phonics method versus whole-word method, didactic instruction versus discovery learning), as if there were only two choices available. Worse, such arguments often imply that there is one best way to teach, when we know that different situations and goals call for different methods, that a given method may have different effects on different students, and that the effectiveness of a method depends not just on its form but on how skillfully it is used. Once again, instructional methods are means to ends, not ends in themselves.

RESEARCH RELATING TEACHER BEHAVIOR TO STUDENT LEARNING

Teachers' decisions about instructional methods need to be informed by research. So far, there exists only a limited and for the most part recently developed knowledge base to inform such decisions. Many important findings come from studies designed to assess the relationships between *processes* (what the teacher and students do in the classroom) and *outcomes* (changes in students' knowledge, skills, values, or dispositions). Two forms of *process-outcome research* are school effects research and teacher effects research. Each of these has emphasized identifying process variables that are associated with student gains on standardized achievement tests.

School Effects Research

School effects research has been done by creating process and outcome measures for entire schools and looking for correlations (Creemers & Scheerens, 1989; Good & Brophy, 1986; Teddlie & Stringfield, 1993). The outcome measures are usually adjusted gain scores on standardized achievement tests. The process measures usually include school-level measures (administrative leadership, school climate) and classroom-level measures (teachers' attitudes and practices). The latter are averaged across teachers to produce a score for the school as a whole. Most school effects studies have focused on basic skills instruction, especially in schools serving socioeconomically disadvantaged populations. Also, most have been correlational rather than experimental, so their findings are subject to multiple interpretations.

Still, it is useful to know that school effects research has identified several characteristics that are observed consistently in schools that elicit good achievement gains: (1) strong academic leadership that produces consensus on goal priorities and commitment to excellence; (2) a safe, orderly school climate; (3) positive teacher attitudes toward students and expectations regarding their abilities to master the curriculum; (4) an emphasis on instruction (not just on filling time or on nonacademic activities) in using time and assigning tasks to students; (5) careful monitoring of progress toward goals through student testing and staff evaluation programs; (6) strong parent involvement programs; and (7) consistent emphasis on the importance of academic achievement, including praise and public recognition for students' accomplishments. Some school improvement programs based on these findings have yielded significant gains in student achievement (Freiberg et al., 1990).

Teacher Effects Research

Process-outcome research at the classroom level (Brophy & Good, 1986; Good, 1996; Reynolds, 1992; Waxman & Walberg, 1991) has been done in more grades, in more subjects, and with a broader range of students than school effects research, although it also has concentrated on basic skills instruction. The following are the most widely replicated findings concerning the characteristics of teachers who elicit strong achievement test score gains.

Teacher Expectation/Role Definition/Sense of Efficacy   These teachers accept responsibility for teaching their students. They believe that the students are capable of learning and that they (the teachers) are capable of teaching them successfully. If students do not learn something the first time, they teach it again, and if the regular curriculum materials do not do the job, they find or make other ones. In general, they display the qualities recommended in Chapter 3.

Student Opportunity to Learn   These teachers allocate most of their available time to instruction rather than to nonacademic activities or pastimes. Their students spend many more hours each year on academic tasks than do students of teachers who are less focused on instructional goals. Furthermore, the mix of academic tasks allows their students not just to memorize but to understand key ideas, appreciate their connections, and explore their applications (Blumenfeld, 1992).

Classroom Management and Organization   These teachers organize their classrooms as effective learning environments and use group management approaches that maximize the time that students spend engaged in lessons and activities (see Chapters 4 and 5).

Curriculum Pacing   These teachers move through the curriculum rapidly but in small steps that minimize student frustration and allow continuous progress.

Active Teaching   These teachers actively instruct—demonstrating skills, explaining concepts and assignments, conducting participatory activities, and reviewing when necessary. They teach their students rather than expecting them to learn mostly from curriculum materials. However, they do not stress just facts or skills; they also emphasize concepts and understanding.

Teaching to Mastery   Following active instruction on new content, these teachers provide opportunities for students to practice and apply it. They monitor each student's progress and provide feedback and remedial instruction as needed, making sure that the students achieve mastery.

A Supportive Learning Environment   Despite their strong academic focus, these teachers maintain pleasant, friendly classrooms and are perceived as enthusiastic, supportive instructors.

An Example

Table 9.1 shows a model for fourth-grade mathematics instruction developed by Good and Grouws (1979). Its principles were suggested by correlational studies and then tested through experimental studies. Results indicated that teachers who

Table 9.1   SUMMARY OF KEY INSTRUCTIONAL BEHAVIORS

Daily Review (first 8 minutes except Mondays)

1. Review the concepts and skills associated with the homework
2. Collect and deal with homework assignments
3. Ask several mental computation exercises

Development (about 20 minutes)

1. Briefly focus on prerequisite skills and concepts
2. Focus on meaning and promoting student understanding by using lively explanations, demonstrations, process explanations, illustrations, and so on
3. Assess student comprehension using
   a. Process/product questions (active interaction)
   b. Controlled practice
4. Repeat and elaborate on the meaning portion as necessary

Seatwork (about 15 minutes)

1. Provide uninterrupted successful practice
2. Momentum—keep the ball rolling—get everyone involved, then sustain involvement
3. Alerting—let students know their work will be checked at the end of the period
4. Accountability—check the students' work

Homework Assignment

1. Assign on a regular basis at the end of each math class except Friday's
2. Should involve about 15 minutes of work to be done at home
3. Should include one or two review problems

Special Reviews

1. Weekly review/maintenance
   a. Conduct during the first 20 minute each Monday
   b. Focus on skills and concepts covered during the previous week
2. Monthly review/maintenance
   a. Conduct every fourth Monday
   b. Focus on skills and concepts covered since last monthly review

Source: Good, T., & Grouws, D. (1979). The Missouri Mathematics Effectiveness Project: An experimental study in fourth-grade classrooms. *Journal of Educational Psychology, 71,* 821–829.

implemented the model elicited greater achievement gains than control teachers who used whatever methods they had developed on their own. Good and Grouws's model is similar to traditional fourth-grade mathematics instruction in many ways, although it is more systematic. It includes time allocation guidelines to ensure that mathematics is taught for about 45 minutes each day and it calls for supplementing classroom instruction with homework assignments. There is a great deal of active instruction by the teacher. New concepts are presented in detail during the development portion of the lesson, the teacher makes sure that students know how to do an assignment before releasing them to work on it individually, and the assignment is reviewed the next day. The combination of active instruction, the opportunity to practice and receive feedback, and frequent testing helps ensure continuous progress (for more details, see Good, Grouws & Ebmeier, 1983).

Even for basic skills instruction in the elementary grades, *instructional models must be adapted to the subject matter, the students, and other contextual factors.* For example, Anderson, Evertson, and Brophy (1979, 1982) developed a model for small-group reading instruction in first grade, based on their teacher effects research. Their model is similar to the Good and Grouws model in its emphasis on active teaching, but it differs in many of its specifics because it is designed for different students and subject matter (it is a small-group rather than a whole-class model, its emphasis is on individual oral reading turns rather than on teacher-led problem solving, and it makes no mention of homework).

As another example, Sigurdson and Olson (1992) adapted the Good, Grouws, and Ebmeier (1983) active mathematics teaching model for use in eighth-grade units on geometry and on fractions, rates, and ratios. The adaptation, which achieved successful results, combined the daily lesson organization features of the active teaching model with some of the curriculum content features associated with recent efforts to teach mathematics for meaningful understanding (see Chapter 10).

These examples illustrate that although classroom research provides support for instructional principles of varying generality, it cannot be expected to identify specific instructional behaviors that are ideal for all types of students and situations. Different learning objectives (mastering well-defined knowledge or skills versus applying them to complex problem solving or using them creatively) require different instructional methods. Furthermore, other kinds of objectives (promoting the personal development of individuals or the social development of the class as a group) require still other methods. Research can inform teachers about the relationships between teacher behavior and student outcomes, but teachers must decide what outcomes they wish to promote and in what order of priority.

The volume of process-outcome studies has slowed in recent years, at least in this country. However, teacher effects research done here and elsewhere has continued to document the benefits of active instruction by the teacher (Weinert & Helmke, 1995). Throughout the rest of this chapter, we consider the principles involved in accomplishing three basic components of active teaching: presenting information, conducting recitations and discussions, and structuring activities and assignments. In the next chapter, we consider methods of assisting students' efforts to construct meaning from these experiences.

PRESENTING INFORMATION TO STUDENTS

Presenting information to the whole class is an efficient way to expose students to content. It allows the teacher to control the material taught, is easily combined with other methods, and is adjustable to fit the available time, the physical setting, and other situational constraints. Presentation of information is part of the active teaching pattern that is associated with strong achievement gains. These teacher presentations are typically short ones interspersed with questions or activities, however, not extended lectures. In this section, we offer guidelines about when and how to present information and we review research findings on clarity and enthusiasm.

When and How to Present Information

Despite its continuing popularity, educators have always been ambivalent about information presentation, especially when it is stereotyped as "the lecture method" (Henson, 1988; McLeish, 1976). The approach has been criticized as follows:

1. Lectures deny students the opportunity to practice social skills.
2. Lectures imply the usually incorrect assumption that all students need the same information.
3. Lectures often exceed students' attention spans, so that they begin to "tune out."
4. Lectures only convey information; they do not develop skills or dispositions.
5. Students can read facts on their own, so why not use class time for other activities?

These points are well taken. Most of us have known teachers whose lectures were ineffective because they were dull, vague, or simply too frequent and too long. However, most of these criticisms reflect overuse or inappropriate use of the lecture method, not problems inherent in the method itself. The lecture method also has much to recommend it, assuming that lectures are well organized, up to date, and presented appropriately. Ausubel (1963) pointed out that effective lectures provide students with information that would take hours for them to collect on their own. He and others would ask, "Why force students to search for information for hours when a lecture will allow them to get it quickly and then move on to application or problem solving?" Obviously, this point has merit. The important question is not "Should we lecture?" but "When should we lecture?" Various authors (Gage & Berliner, 1992; Henson, 1988) have suggested that *the lecture method is appropriate in the following situations:*

1. When the objective is to present information
2. When the information is not available in a readily accessible source
3. When the material must be organized in a particular way
4. When it is necessary to arouse interest in the subject
5. When it is necessary to introduce a topic before students read about it on their own or to provide instructions about a task

6. When the information is original or must be integrated from different sources

7. When the information needs to be summarized or synthesized (following discussion or inquiry)

8. When curriculum materials need updating or elaborating

9. When the teacher wants to present alternative points of view or to clarify issues in preparation for discussion

10. When the teacher wants to provide supplementary explanations of material that students may have difficulty learning on their own

These points also are well taken. Good lectures and presentations at these times do seem preferable to available alternatives. Also, many of the criticisms of the lecture approach can be met without abandoning the approach itself. For example, consider the criticism that lecturing does not allow students to learn actively or assist them to develop social skills. Teachers could adjust to this while retaining the advantage of lectures by giving short lectures (perhaps 15 minutes) to structure problems and provide students with necessary information, but then breaking the class into small problem-solving groups. Also, there is no need to view lectures merely as convenient devices for conveying information. When presented in interesting, enthusiastic ways, lectures can stimulate interest and raise questions that students will want to address in follow-up activities.

Lecturing is an *appropriate* method if used for the purposes outlined above. How *effective* it is will depend on the care and skill with which the lecture is prepared and delivered. Effective lectures (1) begin with advance organizers or previews that include general principles, outlines, or questions that establish a learning set; (2) briefly describe the objectives and alert students to new or key concepts; (3) present new information with reference to what students already know about the topic, proceeding in small steps sequenced in ways that are easy to follow; (4) elicit student responses regularly to stimulate active learning and ensure that each step is mastered before moving to the next; (5) finish with a review of main points, stressing general integrative concepts; and (6) follow up with questions or assignments that require students to encode the material in their own words and apply or extend it to new contexts (Chilcoat, 1989; Duffy et al., 1986).

Two key features of good lectures are the *clarity* of the information and the *enthusiasm* with which it is presented.

Clarity

Clarity is essential if students are to understand concepts and assignments. Mc-Caleb and White (1980) identified five aspects of clarity that observers can attend to in classrooms:

1. *Understanding.* This is a prerequisite to clarity and involves matching the new information to the learners' present knowledge. Does the teacher
   a. Determine students' existing familiarity with the information presented?

      b. Use terms that are unambiguous and within the students' experience?

2. *Structuring.* This involves organizing the material to promote a clear presentation: stating the purpose, reviewing main ideas, and providing transitions between sections. Does the teacher
      a. Establish the purpose of the lesson?
      b. Preview the organization of the lesson?
      c. Include internal summaries of the lesson?

3. *Sequencing.* This involves arranging the information in an order conducive to learning, typically by gradually increasing its difficulty or complexity. Does the teacher order the lesson in a logical way, appropriate to the content and the learners?

4. *Explaining.* When explaining principles and relating them to facts through examples, illustrations, or analogies, does the teacher
      a. Define major concepts?
      b. Give examples to illustrate these concepts?
      c. Use examples that are accurate and concrete as well as abstract?

5. *Presenting.* This refers to volume, pacing, articulation, and other speech mechanics. Does the teacher
      a. Articulate words clearly and project speech loudly enough?
      b. Pace the sections of the presentation at rates conducive to understanding?
      c. Support the verbal content with appropriate nonverbal communication and visual aids?

Others have written more extensively about some of these aspects of clarity. Ausubel's (1963) concept of advance organizers is useful in thinking about how to structure presentations. Advance organizers tell students what they will be learning before the instruction begins. For example, before describing 20 penalties that can occur during hockey games, a physical education instructor could provide a way to organize the information: "Today we are going to discuss penalties that might be called during hockey games. We will discuss the differences between minor and major penalties and describe 15 minor penalties and 5 major penalties. At the end of the period, I will show you 20 slides and ask you to name the penalty illustrated and state whether it is major or minor."

Advance organizers give students a structure within which they can relate the specifics presented by a teacher or in a text. Without such a structure, the material may seem fragmented, much like a random list of unrelated sentences. A clear explanation of the nature of the content helps students to focus on the main ideas and order their thoughts effectively. Therefore, before lecturing, teachers should see that students know what they can expect to learn from the lecture and why it is important for them to know this information. After lectures, they should summarize the main points in a few simple sentences or ask questions to elicit a summary from students. Providing a clear introduction and a strong summary can make a big difference in the degree to which students remember essential facts and concepts (Luiten, Ames, & Ackerson, 1970; Schuck, 1981).

For extended presentations, periodic internal summaries of subparts may be needed in addition to a major summary at the end. Rosenshine (1968) discussed the value of these kinds of internal summaries and in particular the "rule-example-rule" approach, in which a summary statement is given both before and after a series of examples. He also stressed the importance of "explaining links"—words and phrases such as "because," "in order to," "If . . . then," "therefore," and "consequently" that make explicit the causal linkages between phrases or sentences. These linkages might not be clear without such language. For example, consider the following sentences:

1. Chicago became the major city in the Midwest and the hub of the nation's railroad system.
2. Because of its central location, Chicago became the hub of the nation's railroad system.

The first example presents the relevant facts but does not link them explicitly, as the second example does. If asked "Why did Chicago become the hub of the railroad system?" most students taught with the second example would respond, "Because of its central location," but many students taught with the first example would respond "Because it is a big city," or in some other way that would indicate failure to appreciate the linkage between a city's geographical location and the role it plays in a nation's transportation system.

In addition to these organization factors, presentations or questions can lack clarity because of vague or confusing language. Smith and Land (1981) reviewed studies indicating that the effectiveness of presentations is reduced by the presence of *vagueness terms* and *mazes*. They identified nine categories of vagueness terms:

1. Ambiguous designation (somehow, somewhere, conditions, other)
2. Negated intensifiers (not many, not very)
3. Approximation (about, almost, kind of, pretty much, sort of)
4. "Bluffing" and recovery (actually, and so forth, anyway, as you know, basically, in other words, to make a long story short, you know)
5. Error admission (excuse me, I'm sorry, I guess, I'm not sure)
6. Indeterminate quantification (a bunch, a couple, a few, a lot, a little, some, several)
7. Multiplicity (aspects, kinds of, sort of, type of)
8. Possibility (chances are, could be, maybe, perhaps)
9. Probability (frequently, generally, often, probably, sometimes, usually)

They gave the following as a brief example indicating how vagueness terms (italicized) can distract from the intended message.

This mathematics lesson *might* enable you to understand *a little more* about *some things we usually call* number patterns. *Maybe* before we get to *probably* the main idea of the lesson, you should review *a few* prerequisite concepts.

Actually, the first concept you need to review is positive integers. *As you know,* a positive integer is any whole number greater than zero.

Mazes refer to false starts or halting speech, redundantly spoken words, or tangles of words. The mazes are italicized in the following example:

This mathematics lesson will *enab . . .* will get you to understand *number, uh,* number patterns. Before we get to the *main idea of the,* main idea of the lesson, you need to review *four conc . . .* four prerequisite concepts. A positive *number ...* integer is any whole *integer, uh,* number greater than zero.

In addition to looking for such problems in teachers' presentations, observers can study the effects of the presentations on students. The students' facial expressions, and especially their questions or responses to the teacher's questions, should indicate that they have acquired the understandings that the teacher intended to communicate. Frequent evidence of student frustration, confusion, or misunderstanding suggests problems in teacher clarity (see Cruickshank, 1985 for related information about students' perceptions of teacher clarity; see Gliessman et al., 1989, for information about a training program for increasing teachers' clarity). Teachers who do not have access to observers but still desire to assess the clarity of their presentations can do so by collecting and studying students' notes or interviewing selected students to assess the depth and connectedness of their understandings (see McCaslin & Good, 1996).

Enthusiasm

When teachers are enthusiastic about a subject, students are likely to develop enthusiasm of their own, and ultimately to achieve at higher levels (Rosenshine, 1970; Rosenshine & Furst, 1973). Young people develop interests through modeling others, including teachers. If teachers appear to enjoy learning about school subjects, students are likely to develop similar interests.

Teacher enthusiasm includes at least two major aspects. The first is conveying sincere interest in the subject. This involves modeling, and even shy teachers can demonstrate it (Cabello & Terrell, 1994). The second aspect is dynamic vigor. Enthusiastic teachers are alive in the room; they show surprise, suspense, joy, and other feelings in their voices and they make material interesting by relating it to their experiences and showing that they themselves are interested in it.

Effective Demonstrations

When learning processes and skills, students need not only verbal explanations, but also physical demonstrations. It is important for teachers to learn to demonstrate effectively, because poor demonstrations can be more confusing than helpful. You may have discovered this for yourself if you have sought out a friend or relative for driving lessons or instructions about how to cook a complicated dish. Professional instructors teach these skills to beginners with ease and efficiency, but most other people do not, even if they are able to drive or cook very well.

What's the trick? Expert instructors tailor their demonstrations to learners' needs. They demystify the process by not only showing the physical movements involved but also verbalizing the thinking that guides these movements. Their explanations emphasize the general principles involved rather than just the particular applications that apply to the example at hand. As a result, learners acquire strategies that they can use intelligently and adapt to varying situations, not just fixed routines learned by rote and applied without variation.

Expert instructors break processes down into step-by-step operations. They define each term they introduce and point to each part as they label it. They describe what they are going to do before each step and then talk through the step as they perform it. They have the learner master one step at a time rather than try to do the whole job at once. They give corrections in a patient tone so the learner can concentrate on the task and not worry about looking inept.

The same principles apply to teachers' demonstrations of new academic skills (e.g., word decoding, mathematical problem solving, research and report writing, use of laboratory equipment) and instructions for assignments. A good demonstration proceeds as follows:

1. Focus attention. Be sure that all students are attentive before beginning, and focus their attention by holding up an object or pointing to where you want them to look.
2. Give a general orientation or overview. Explain what you are going to do, so that students can get mentally set to observe the key steps.
3. If new objects or concepts are introduced, label them. If necessary, have the students repeat the labels. Students cannot follow an explanation if they do not know what some of the words mean.
4. Go through the process step by step. Begin each new step with an explanation of what you are going to do, and then describe your actions as you do them. Think out loud throughout the demonstration.
5. If necessary, perform each action slowly with exaggerated motions.
6. Have a student repeat the demonstration so you can observe and give corrective feedback. If the task is short, have the student do the whole thing and give feedback at the end. If it is longer, break it into parts and have students do one part at a time first.
7. In correcting mistakes, do *not* dwell on the mistake and the reasons for it, but instead redemonstrate the correct steps and have the students try again.

Thinking out loud at each step is crucial, especially when the task is primarily cognitive. While you demonstrate physical procedures such as pouring into a test tube, writing a number on the board, or making an incision, describe how you are filling the test tube to the 20 ml line, carrying two 10 units and adding them to the 10s column, or starting your incision at the breast bone and stopping short of the hip bones. Unless you verbalize the thinking processes that guide what you do and how you do it, some students may learn no more from watching your demonstration than they would from watching a magician perform a baffling trick.

If a demonstration is lengthy, help the students to follow it by summarizing its subparts and noting the transitions between them. If continuity is broken by student questions or discussion, reestablish the desired learning set by reminding the students of the overall structure of the presentation and of the place at which it is being resumed.

CONDUCTING RECITATIONS AND DISCUSSIONS

Teacher-led reviews, recitations, and discussions are important parts of the active teaching pattern that is associated with strong achievement gains. Furthermore, one common element in models for teaching school subjects for understanding is teacher-student discourse featuring thoughtful discussion or dialogue (Brophy, 1989). Thus, besides being able to make effective presentations, teachers need to know how to plan good sequences of questions that will help their students to develop understanding of the content and provide them with opportunities to apply it.

Teacher-student discourse relating to academic content occurs in a variety of formats. At one extreme is the *drill* or fast-paced *review* that is designed to test or reinforce students' knowledge of specifics. Here, the emphasis is on obtaining "right answers" and moving at a brisk pace. At the other extreme is *discussion* designed to stimulate students to respond diversely and at higher cognitive levels to what they have been learning. Here, the pace is slower and the emphasis is on developing understanding and pursuing implications. Higher-level questions that admit to a range of possible answers are used to engage students in critical or creative thinking. In between reviews and discussions are *recitation* activities that vary in pace and cognitive level of question. They include the questioning and response segments that occur between teacher presentation segments, as well as most activities that teachers refer to as "going over the material" or "elaborating on the text."

Educational critics often speak warmly of discussion but criticize drill and recitation as boring, unnecessarily teacher dominated, restricted to low-level objectives, and tending to make students passive and oriented toward producing right answers rather than thinking. Clearly, recitation should not be used in ways that create such problems. Many of the problems result from inappropriate use of the recitation method, however, and thus can be minimized or avoided. Like the lecture method, recitation persists as a common approach to instruction because it has certain legitimate uses and is in some respects well suited to classroom teaching (Farrar, 1986). It allows the teacher to work with the whole class at one time, provides students with opportunities to learn from one another as well as from the teacher, is an efficient way to enable students to practice and receive immediate feedback on their learning of new content, is a convenient way for teachers to check on student understanding before moving on, and is much easier to manage than individualized instruction. Thus, as with lecturing, the operative question about recitation for most teachers is not whether to use it but when and how to use it effectively.

The more effective forms of recitation are blended with information presentation in lecture/recitation lessons that develop students' understanding of a topic's most important ideas. Questions are asked not just to monitor comprehension but also to stimulate students to think about the content, connect it to their prior knowledge, and begin to explore its applications.

Thus, unless recitation activities are explicitly intended as review or preparation for tests, they ordinarily should not take the form of rapidly paced drills or attempts to elicit "right answers" to miscellaneous factual questions. Instead, such activities should be means for engaging students with the content they are learning. Questions should stimulate students to process that content actively and "make it their own" by rephrasing it in their own words and considering its meanings and implications. Questions should focus on the most important elements of the content and guide students' thinking in ways that move them systematically toward key understandings. The idea is to build an integrated network of knowledge anchored around powerful ideas, not to stimulate rote memorizing of miscellaneous information. Questions are devices for teaching, not just for testing.

We review advice about questioning techniques offered by various authors. Most of it is based not only on process-outcome research but on logical analyses of the characteristics of different types of questions and their appropriateness to different instructional goals (Carlsen, 1991; Dillon, 1988, 1990; Wilen, 1991).

Cognitive Levels of Questions

Teacher questioning has been a popular area of classroom research, partly because it is among the easiest of teacher behaviors to observe and code reliably. Many investigators have used hierarchies based on the Bloom taxonomy (Bloom et al., 1956) to classify questions according to the cognitive levels of the responses that they demand from students. *Knowledge* questions are considered low in cognitive demand; *comprehension* and *application* questions are intermediate; and *analysis, synthesis,* and *evaluation* questions are high. Other investigators have used simpler classifications such as fact versus thought questions or convergent versus divergent questions.

So far, research findings based on such classifications have been mixed and relatively uninformative about when and why different kinds of questions should be used. The research underscores the complexities involved and cautions against attempts to substitute simple formulas for careful planning of question sequences. For example, higher-order questions do tend to elicit higher-order responses from students and the frequencies of higher-order questions often correlate positively with student achievement gains. However, students often respond at a lower cognitive level than the question called for, and the frequencies of lower-order questions often correlate positively with student achievement gains as well, even gains on higher-order objectives. Thus, it is not true that thought questions are always better than fact questions, that divergent questions are always better than convergent questions, or that higher-order or complex questions are always better than lower-order or simpler questions.

Even to phrase the issue this way is to impose a false dichotomy. Varying combinations of lower-order and higher-order questions will be needed, depending on the goals that a teacher is pursuing. Guidelines need to focus on *sequences* of questions designed to help students develop connected understandings, not just on the cognitive levels of individual questions considered in isolation from one another. Sequences that begin with a higher-level question and then proceed through several lower-level follow-up questions are appropriate for purposes such as asking students to suggest possible applications of an idea and then probing for details about how these applications might work. However, sequences featuring a series of lower-level questions followed by a higher-level question would be appropriate for purposes such as calling students' attention to relevant facts and then stimulating them to integrate these facts and draw a conclusion.

Issues surrounding cognitive level of questions should take care of themselves if sequences of questions are planned to accomplish worthwhile goals that are integral parts of well-designed units of instruction. However, plans will need to be revised if the questions appear to be random test items or if the questions are all at the knowledge level when the activity is supposed to stimulate students to analyze or synthesize what they have been learning. Similarly, certain types of questions would be appropriate for arousing interest in a discussion topic, but other types would be needed to stimulate critical thinking about the topic or to see whether students have attained the intended understandings.

Questions to Avoid

Groisser (1964) identified questioning habits that often lead to underproductive responses. He described four types of questions that are particularly misused: (1) yes-no questions, (2) tugging questions, (3) guessing questions, and (4) leading questions.

Yes-No   Yes-no questions typically are asked only as warm-ups for other questions. For example, the teachers asks, "Was Hannibal a clever soldier?" After a student answers, the teacher says, "Why?" or "Explain your reason." Groisser claimed that these initial yes-no questions confuse the lesson focus and waste time, so it is better to ask the real question in the first place.

We see two additional dangers in yes-no questions or other questions that involved a *simple choice between alternatives* ("Was it Hamilton or Jackson?"). First, such questions encourage guessing, because students will be right 50 percent of the time even when they have no idea of the correct answer. When a teacher asks too many of these questions, students are apt to try to "read" the teacher for clues about which answer is correct instead of concentrating on the question itself.

Also, choice questions have *low diagnostic power*. Because of the guesswork factor, responses to these questions do not reveal much about students' understandings. Choice questions sometimes are useful for low-achieving or shy students who have a difficult time responding, because they provide a warm-up that can help these students respond better to more substantive questions that follow. Ordinarily, however, these questions should be avoided.

Tugging   Tugging questions or statements often follow a halting or incomplete response ("Well, come on." "Yes. . . ?"). They say "Tell me more" but provide no help to the student, so they may be perceived as nagging or bullying.

When students answer correctly but incompletely, teachers are more likely to elicit an improved response if they ask new, more specific questions than if they continue to ask: "What else?" "What's another reason?" and so forth. For example, a teacher might ask, "Why did the Jamestown settlers live in a fort?" A student might respond, "To protect themselves from the Indians and from animals." If the teacher wants to focus on the advantages of community living, the next question should cue the student in this direction: "What advantages did they gain from living in a group?"

Guessing   Guessing questions require students to guess or reason about a question, either because they do not have the facts ("How many business firms have offices on Wall Street?") or because the question has no correct answer ("If Columbus hadn't discovered America in 1492, what European explorer would have, and when?"). Guessing questions can be useful in capturing students' imagination and involving them in discussions. However, if such questions are overused or used inappropriately, they encourage students to guess thoughtlessly rather than to think carefully. Guessing questions are useful primarily as parts of larger strategies for helping students to think about what they are learning.

Leading   Leading questions ("Don't you agree?") and other rhetorical questions ("You want to read about the Pilgrims, don't you?") should be avoided. *Questions should be asked only if the teacher really wants a response.* Students should develop the expectation that when the teacher asks a question, something important and interesting is about to happen.

Characteristics of Good Questions

Although the complete definition of a good question depends on context, certain guidelines can be applied. Groisser (1964) indicated that good questions are (1) clear, (2) purposeful, (3) brief, (4) natural and adapted to the level of the class, (5) sequenced, and (6) thought provoking.

Clear   Questions should specify the points to which students are to respond. Vague questions can be responded to in many ways (too many), and their ambiguous nature confuses students. For example, Groisser wrote:

> If a teacher of Spanish wished to call attention to the tense of a verb in a sentence on the board and asked, "What do you see here?" the student would not know exactly what was being called for. Better to ask, "What tense is used in this clause?"

Vague questions often result in wasted time as students ask the teacher to clarify the specific attack point. Questions can also be unclear if they are asked as part of an uninterrupted series. Groisser writes of a teacher who,

> in discussing the War of 1812 asks, in one continuous statement, "Why did we go to war? As a merchant, how would you feel? How was our trade hurt by the Napoleonic War?" The teacher is trying to clarify his first question and to focus thinking on an economic cause of the war. In his attempt, he actually confuses.

This teacher should have asked a clear, straightforward question initially ("What was the cause of the War of 1812?"), waited for a response, and then probed for economic causes if the response failed to mention them.

Questions should cue students to respond along specific lines. This does not mean that the teacher cues the answer; it means that the teacher communicates the specific question to which the student is asked to respond.

Purposeful   Purposeful questions help achieve the lesson's intent. Advance planning is helpful here. Such planning should not be too rigid, because it may be worth pursuing an unanticipated teachable moment opened up by a student's question or comment. Still, it is worth remembering that teachers who improvise most of their questions ask many irrelevant and confusing questions that work against achievement of their own goals.

Brief   Questions should be brief. Long questions are often unclear. The longer the question, the more difficult it is to understand.

Natural   Questions should be phrased in natural, simple language (as opposed to pedantic, textbook language) and should be adapted to the level of the class. If students do not understand the question, they cannot engage in the kind of thinking that the teacher intended to stimulate.

We do not mean that teachers should avoid unfamiliar words. Students benefit from learning new words and from exposure to modeling of sophisticated verbal communication. However, teachers must consider students' vocabularies. When teachers introduce new words, they should clarify their meanings and engage students in using the words within application contexts.

Sequenced   If questions are intended as teaching devices and not merely as oral test items, they should be asked in carefully planned *sequences,* and the answers to each sequence should be integrated with previously discussed material before moving on. Initial questions might lead students to identify or review essential facts. Then the students might be asked to refine their understandings and apply them to authentic problems ("Now that we have identified the properties of these six types of wood, which would you use to build a canoe?").

Alternatively, the teacher might initiate a problem-solving or decision-making discussion by first posing a question or issue to be addressed, then eliciting suggested resolutions, and then engaging students in critical thinking about the trade-offs that each of the suggested resolutions offers.

The sequence and the meaningfulness of information exchange are critical here, not the cognitive level of each individual question. For example, Table 9.2 shows how a sequence of relatively low-level factual questions can lead to meaningful insights. In this sequence, the teacher helps students to understand the historical events that preceded the Boston Tea Party and to appreciate that events can be viewed from different perspectives. Key information is tied to the concept of monopoly and representative taxation, and the factual questions raised help students to *understand* the historical significance of events. For example, "What was the tea worth?"—a simple fact question—should help students to realize that in colonial times tea was quite valuable. The fact that the colonists were willing to dump the tea into the harbor rather than taking it home indicated how outraged they were.

Table 9.2   A REASONABLE QUESTIONING SEQUENCE

1. What was the Boston Tea Party?
2. What events preceded the Boston Tea Party?
3. What is a monopoly?
4. Under what conditions might a monopoly be justified?
5. Do we provide favorable circumstances for certain industries in this country that make it difficult for foreign countries to compete?
6. What did the Boston Tea Party mean to British citizens? To American citizens?
7. Who participated in the Boston Tea Party?
8. How much was the tea worth?

Similarly, the question, "Who participated in the Boston Tea Party?" is intended to develop appreciation of the wide range of citizens who participated in the demonstration.

In the unreasonable sequence shown in Table 9.3, the fact questions are often trivial and are not used to develop a thoughtful examination of what the Boston Tea Party represented. Questions about the number of ships in the harbor or how the colonists were dressed may allow the teacher to evaluate whether a student has read the book carefully, but they fail to develop important points. It is usually counterproductive to emphasize such trivial details. The questions evaluating knowledge of the Townshend Duties and Coercive Acts might have been productive if used to place the Boston Tea Party within the context of its antecedents and its subsequent effects, but in this sequence these questions merely test for knowledge of disconnected facts.

Distinctions among the cognitive levels of questions help teachers to think about the cognitive demands that they place on students, but questions need to be planned in sequences designed to develop systematic discussion of a topic. A good set of questions is good not merely because it contains a significant percentage of higher-level questions but also because it helps students to think about the topic systematically and emerge from the discussion with connected understandings.

Thought Provoking   Good questions are thought provoking. Especially in discussions, questions should arouse strong, thoughtful responses from students, such as, "I never thought of that before," or "I want to find the answer to that question." Discussion should help students to clarify their ideas and to analyze or synthesize what

Table 9.3   AN UNREASONABLE SEQUENCE

1. What was the Boston Tea Party?
2. How many ships containing tea were in the harbor?
3. How did the colonists dress when they entered the ships to destroy the tea?
4. Define Townshend Duties.
5. Define Coercive Acts.
6. Who was Thomas Hutchinson?
7. On what date did the Boston Tea Party occur?

they are learning. Fact questions often are needed to establish relevant information, but subsequent questions should stimulate students to use the information rather than just recite it and should motivate them to respond thoughtfully.

Groisser (1964) also suggested that questions should be addressed to the whole class, balanced between fact and thought questions, distributed widely, asked conversationally, and sometimes asked to allow students to respond to classmates' answers.

Calling on Students to Respond to Questions

Addressing questions to the class involves first asking the question, then allowing students time to think, and only then calling on someone to respond. This makes everyone in the class responsible for the answer. If the teacher names a student to respond before asking the question or calls on a student immediately after doing so, only the student who is named is responsible for answering. Other students are less likely to try to answer it.

Groisser (1964) noted three special situations in which a teacher might want to call on a student before asking a question: (1) drawing an inattentive student back into the lesson, (2) asking a follow-up question of a student who has just responded, and (3) calling on a shy student who may be "shocked" if called on without warning.

Groisser's point that students need time to think seems self-evident but actually raises several complicated issues. Optimal wait time varies with the question and the situation.

Wait Time   Good questioning technique allows students sufficient time to think about and respond to questions. Rowe (1974a & 1974b) reported data that at the time seemed remarkable: After asking questions, the teachers she observed waited less than one second before calling on someone to respond. Furthermore, even after calling on a student, they waited only about a second for the student to give the answer before supplying it themselves, calling on someone else, or rephrasing the question or giving clues. These findings do not seem to make sense because they suggest that the teachers minimized the value of their questions by failing to give students time to think.

Rowe followed up these observations by training teachers, to see what would happen if they extended their wait times. Surprisingly, most of the teachers found this difficult to do, and some never succeeded. However, in the classrooms of teachers who extended their wait times to three to five seconds, the following desirable changes occurred:

1. Increase in the average length of student responses
2. Increase in unsolicited but appropriate student responses
3. Decrease in failures to respond
4. Increase in speculative responses
5. Increase in student-to-student comparisons of data
6. Increase in statements that involved drawing inferences from evidence
7. Increase in student-initiated questions
8. A greater variety of contributions by students

In short, Rowe found that longer wait times led to more active participation in lessons by a larger percentage of the students, coupled with an increase in the quality of this participation. Subsequent research has verified that increasing wait time leads to longer and higher-quality student responses and participation by a greater number of students (Rowe, 1986; Swift, Gooding, & Swift, 1988; Tobin, 1983). These effects are most notable on the less able students in the class.

Subsequent research also verified Rowe's finding that many teachers experience difficulty in extending their wait times. DeTure (1979) found that even after training, no teacher attained an average wait time longer than 1.8 seconds. Why should this be? The answer lies in the pressures on teachers to maintain lesson pacing and student attention. Some teachers are reluctant to extend their wait times because they fear that they may lose student attention, or even control of the class, if they do. This illustrates one of the continuing dilemmas that require teacher decision making and adjustment to immediate situations. Longer wait times are generally preferable to shorter ones because they allow more thinking by more students, but the teacher may have to use shorter wait times when the class is restive or when time is running out and it is necessary to finish the lesson quickly.

Most teachers adjust wait times according to the type of question asked. They are likely to wait longer following higher-level questions (especially analysis and synthesis questions) than following lower-level questions (Arnold, Atwood, & Rogers, 1974). Furthermore, the causal linkages between question level and wait time seem to work in both directions. In addition to noting effects on students, some of the investigators who trained teachers to increase wait times noted that this change also led to interaction patterns in which the teachers asked fewer questions per time unit than before, but more questions at higher cognitive levels (Fagan, Hassler, & Szabo, 1981; Rice, 1977).

Thus, interactions featuring mostly lower-level questions tend to move at a quicker pace with shorter wait times than interactions featuring higher-level questions. *The appropriateness of these pacing and wait time factors depends on the objectives of the activity.* Although most studies in which teachers were trained to slow the pace and extend wait time have produced positive outcomes, these studies have focused on intermediate- and upper-grade levels and on instruction in abstract or difficult material. Anshutz (1975) reported no science achievement differences between short and long wait times for students in grades 3 and 4, and Riley (1980) reported interaction effects on science achievement in grades 1 through 5: A decrease in achievement occurred when wait time was extended from medium to long for low-level questions, whereas an increase in achievement was noted when wait time was extended for higher-level questions.

These studies show that pacing and wait time should be suited to the questions being asked and ultimately to the goals these questions are designed to accomplish. A fast pace and short wait times are appropriate for drill or review activities covering specific facts. However, if questions are intended to stimulate students to think about material and formulate original responses rather than merely to retrieve information from memory, it is important to allow time for these effects to occur. This is especially true for complex or involved questions. Students may need several seconds to merely process such questions before they can even begin to formulate responses to them. When a slow pace and thoughtful responding are desired, teachers should not only adjust their wait times but also make their goals clear to students. Unless cued, some students may not realize that they are supposed to formulate an original response rather than search their memories for something taught to them explicitly, and some may think that the teacher is looking for speed rather than quality of response.

Distributing Questions to a Range of Students   Teachers should distribute questions widely rather than allow a few students to answer most of them. Students learn more if they are actively involved in discussions than if they sit passively without participating. A few reticent students who rarely participate in discussions may still get excellent grades, but most students benefit from opportunities to practice oral communication skills, and distributing response opportunities helps keep them attentive and accountable. Also, teachers who restrict their questions primarily to a small group of active (and usually high-achieving) students are likely to communicate undesirable expectations (Good & Brophy, 1974) and generally to be less aware and less effective.

Feedback About Responses   Feedback is important both to motivate students and to let them know how they are doing. This probably seems obvious, but teachers sometimes fail to give feedback, especially to low achievers (Brophy & Good, 1974). Sometimes this is appropriate, such as when ideas are being "brainstormed" for later evaluation or the discussion involves exchanges of opinion on questions that do not admit to right and wrong answers. When an answer is either correct or incorrect, however, this information needs to be conveyed.

Unless it is understood that no response indicates correctness, teachers should give some sort of acknowledgment every time students answer such questions. Feedback need not be long or elaborate, although sometimes it has to be. Often a head nod or short comment like "Right" is all that is needed. Also, teachers do not always have to provide feedback personally. They can provide access to answer sheets that allow students to assess their own work or can arrange for students to provide feedback to one another.

Reasons for Questioning

Some types of questions suggest to students that the teacher is more interested in quizzing them than in sharing or discussing information (see Roby, 1988). Teachers who question students in harsh terms are likely to threaten them and make it difficult for them to share their thinking. In contrast, questions that present interesting challenges and invite friendly exchanges of views are likely to maximize motivation and yield productive responses.

That is what Groisser (1964) meant when he suggested that questions should be asked conversationally. He also suggested that allowing students to respond to one another is helpful:

Many teachers seize upon the first answer given and react to it at once with a comment or with another question. . . . It is more desirable, where possible, to ask a question, accept two or three answers, and then proceed. This pattern tends to produce sustaining responses, variety, and enrichment. It encourages volunteering, contributes to group cooperation, and approaches a more realistic social situation.

Such techniques model teacher interest in the exchange of information about a topic (as opposed to pushing for the right answer) and indicate that there is not always a single correct answer. Students are likely to listen more carefully to one another if they are called on to respond to one another's answers occasionally. Wright and Nuthall (1970) found that teachers who redirected questions to other students during science lessons got better achievement than those who did not.

Inquiry Approaches

Although most approaches to teaching start with presentation of information to students and only then proceed to asking them questions, inquiry approaches *begin* with questions and rely on them heavily thereafter as ways to stimulate student exploration, discovery, and critical thinking about subject matter. Here questioning is the basic method of instruction.

Collins and Stevens (1983) described an inquiry approach built around ten instructional strategies: (1) select positive and negative examples, (2) vary case studies systematically, (3) select counterexamples, (4) generate hypothetical cases, (5) form hypotheses, (6) test hypotheses, (7) consider alternative predictions, (8) entrap students, (9) trace consequences to a contradiction, and (10) question authority. Examples are selected and sequenced to create dissonance or curiosity in students and set the stage for inquiry-oriented discussion. Students are challenged to form and evaluate hypotheses rather than given rules or principles, and are prodded to consider alternative predictions whenever they jump to conclusions without adequately considering alternatives. Hypothetical cases are used to challenge students' reasoning or force them to take into account factors that they are currently ignoring. Entrapment is used to reveal the inadequacies of erroneous preconceptions. It involves using the students' own thinking to show how it leads to incorrect predictions or conclusions. Tracing consequences to a contradiction is a similar strategy. Finally, questioning authority involves training students to think for themselves rather than to rely on the teacher or the book for correct answers.

In addition to discussing these instructional strategies, Collins and Stevens (1983) presented rules for structuring and sequencing dialogues designed to achieve particular objectives. We mention their work briefly here to underscore the point that thoughtful planning is just as important for inquiry approaches to instruction as it is for more didactic methods.

Conducting Discussions

Drill and recitation occur frequently in classrooms, but true group discussion is rare. Even activities that teachers call "discussion" tend to be recitations in which teachers ask questions and students respond by reciting what they already know or are now learning. Few such activities are actual discussions in which the teacher and students share opinions in order to clarify issues, relate new knowledge to their prior experience, or attempt to answer a question or solve a problem (Alvermann, O'Brien, & Dillon, 1990; Tharp & Gallimore, 1988).

To conduct discussions, teachers must adopt a different role from the one they play in recitation activities, where they act as the primary source of information and the authority figure who determines whether answers are correct. Teachers lead discussions by establishing a focus, setting boundaries, and facilitating interaction, but in other respects, they assume a less dominant and less judgmental role. Even if a discussion begins in a question-and-answer format, it should evolve into an exchange of views in which students respond to one another as well as to the teacher and respond to statements as well as to questions.

If ideas are being collected, the teacher should record them (listing them on the board or on an overhead projector) but should not evaluate them. Once the discussion is established, the teacher may wish to participate in it periodically in order to point out connections between ideas, identify similarities or contrasts, request clarification or elaboration, invite students to respond to one another, summarize progress achieved so far, or suggest and test for possible consensus as it develops. However, the teacher does not push the group toward some previously determined conclusion (if the teacher were to do so, the activity would be a guided discovery lesson rather than a discussion).

The pace of discussions is notably slower than that of recitations, with longer periods of silence between speech. These periods provide participants with opportunities to consider what has been said and to formulate responses to it. Dillon (1988, 1990) illustrated that teachers' statements can be just as effective as questions for producing lengthy and insightful responses during discussions. He also noted that questions may impede discussions at times, especially questions perceived as attempts to test students rather than to solicit their ideas. To avoid this problem, Dillon (1979) listed six *alternatives to questioning* that teachers can use to sustain discussions.

1. *Declarative statements.* In discussing the effects of war on the domestic economy, the teacher might respond to a student's statement by saying, "When the war broke out, unemployment dropped," rather than by asking a question such as "What happens to the unemployment rate in wartime?" The statement provides information that the students have to accommodate and respond to; compared with the question, however, it invites longer and more varied responses.

2. *Declarative restatements.* Teachers can show that they have attended to and understood what students have said by occasionally summarizing. Such summarizing may be useful to the class as a whole, and reflecting students' statements to them may stimulate additional and deeper responding.

3. *Indirect questions.* When a direct question might sound challenging or rejecting, the teacher can make a statement such as, "I wonder what makes you think that" or "I was just thinking about whether that would make any difference." Such indirect questions might stimulate further thinking without generating anxiety.

4. *Imperatives.* Similarly, statements such as, "Tell us more about that" or "Perhaps you could give some examples" are less threatening than direct requests for the same information.

5. *Student questions.* Rather than asking all of the questions themselves, teachers can encourage students to ask questions in response to statements made by their classmates.

6. *Deliberate silence.* Sometimes the best response to a statement is to remain silent for several seconds to allow students to absorb the content and formulate follow-up questions or comments.

In general, if teachers expect an activity to involve genuine discussion and not merely recitation, they have to make this fact clear to students and alter their own behavior accordingly.

STRUCTURING ACTIVITIES AND ASSIGNMENTS

There are three main ways that teachers help their students to learn. First, they explain, demonstrate, model, or in other ways present information. Second, they lead the students in review, recitation, discussion, or other forms of discourse surrounding the content. Third, they involve students in activities or assignments that provide them with opportunities to practice or apply what they are learning (and in the process, provide them with coaching, task-simplification strategies, or other forms of scaffolding that may be needed to enable them to complete the activities successfully).

Only limited research is available on activities and assignments (Brophy, 1992a), even though most students spend half or more of their time in school working independently (Fisher et al., 1980). Similarly, although it is known that homework can provide a useful supplement to classroom instruction and may increase student achievement, at least in the secondary grades (Cooper, 1989, 1994; Epstein, 1988; Miller & Kelley, 1991; Olympia, Sheridan, & Jenson, 1994), little is known about how much or what kinds of homework to assign.

Process-outcome research suggests that *independent seatwork is probably overused and is not an adequate substitute either for active teacher instruction or for recitation and discussion opportunities.* This is especially the case when the seatwork emphasizes time-consuming but low-level tasks that reinforce memory for facts and mastery of subskills practiced in isolation but do not provide opportunities to think critically or creatively about what is being learned or apply it in problem-solving or decision-making situations.

So far, most research on activities has been conducted not by subject-matter specialists but by the researchers who developed principles for managing classrooms (Chapter 4) and motivating students (Chapter 6). This work suggests that activities and assignments should be varied and interesting enough to motivate student engagement, new or challenging enough to constitute meaningful learning experiences rather than pointless busywork, and yet easy enough to allow students to achieve high rates of success if they invest reasonable effort.

Student success rates, and the effectiveness of seatwork assignments generally, are enhanced when teachers *explain the work and go over practice examples with students before releasing them to work independently*. Furthermore, once students are released, the work goes more smoothly if teachers *circulate to monitor progress and provide help when needed*. If the work has been well chosen and explained, most of these "helping" interactions will be brief, and at any given time, most students will be progressing through an assignment rather than waiting for help.

Teachers should also monitor performance for completion and accuracy and provide students with timely and specific feedback. When performance is poor, teachers will need to provide not only feedback but reteaching and follow-up assignments designed to ensure that the material is understood.

Activities that provide opportunities to extend or deepen knowledge and to apply learning are important components of a well-rounded instructional program, but some activities are pointless or even counterproductive. Much of the seatwork assigned to students is just busywork or is defective in ways that make it unlikely to meet its intended objectives. This is just as true of the workbooks and other assignments provided with published curricula as it is of seatwork that teachers design themselves (Osborn, 1984). Frequently, these tasks are either too easy or too difficult for most students, poorly coordinated with what is being taught at the time, or more likely to confuse or mislead the students than to teach them target concepts. Osborn included the following among her guidelines for seatwork and workbook tasks.

1. A sufficient portion of these tasks should be related to current instruction in the rest of the unit.
2. Another portion should provide systematic and cumulative review.
3. Tasks should reflect the most important (and seatwork-appropriate) aspects of what is being taught.
4. Extra tasks should be available for students who need extra practice.
5. Instructions should be clear and easy to follow; brevity is a virtue.
6. Response modes should be as close as possible to actual reading and writing (as opposed to circling, underlining, drawing arrows from one word to another, etc.).
7. The artwork should be consistent with the prose of the task.
8. Cute, nonfunctional, space- and time-consuming tasks should be avoided.
9. Tasks should be accompanied by brief explanations of purpose.

Criteria to Consider in Selecting or Developing Activities

For teachers interested in selecting or developing their own activities and assignments, Brophy and Alleman (1991) suggested the following guidelines. First, *begin with a focus on the unit's major goals* and consider the kinds of activities that would promote progress toward those goals. With clear goals to provide guidance, teachers can make good decisions about whether to use activities suggested in the manual that accompanies a published curriculum and about what other activities may need to be included. Ideally, major goals will focus on students' understanding of the content and ability to apply it to their lives outside of school, and thus will guide teachers toward activities that are whole-application tasks that carry students through to the intended outcomes rather than just providing them with isolated practice of part skills.

Given the instructional goals, different activities might be considered: (1) essential; (2) directly relevant and useful, even if not essential; (3) directly relevant but less useful than other activities that serve the same functions more effectively; (4) tangentially relevant but not very useful because they do not promote progress toward major goals; or (5) irrelevant or inappropriate to the goals. For example, suppose that an American history course is designed to emphasize student understanding and appreciation of the development of American political values and policies. With these primary goals, a unit on the American Revolution and the founding of the new nation would emphasize the historical events and political philosophies that shaped the thinking of the writers of the Declaration of Independence and the Constitution. Essential activities for such a unit would call for research, debate, or critical thinking and decision making about the issues that developed between England and the colonies and about the ideals, principles, and compromises that went into the construction of the Constitution. Less essential, but still relevant and perhaps useful activities might include studying more about the thinking of key framers of the Constitution or about the various forms of oppression that different colonial groups had experienced. Activities that are similar in form but less useful in content would be studying the lives of Paul Revere or other revolutionary figures who are not known primarily for their contributions to American political values and policies, or studying the details of each of the economic restrictions that England imposed on the colonies. Irrelevant to the goals would be activities that focused on the details of particular Revolutionary War battles. To the extent that they were time-consuming (e.g., construction of a diorama depicting the battle of Yorktown), such activities not only would fail to deliver goal-relevant benefits but would impose costs by reducing the scope and continuity of the goals-driven aspects of the program.

Activities that are not relevant to certain programs or courses might be highly relevant to others. For example, courses in military history would be developed with very different goals than those of the course described above, so activities that developed knowledge of particular battles might be very useful or even essential to accomplishment of these goals. Thus, although generic concepts such as cognitive level of task demand are useful for examining activities, the potential pedagogical value of these activities ultimately must be assessed within the context of the major goals that a curriculum is designed to accomplish.

A second set of criteria concerns the *feasibility* and *cost-effectiveness* of a proposed activity. Is the activity feasible given its assumptions about students' prior knowledge and the time, space, and equipment that it will require? Do the benefits that the activity is expected to bring to the students justify its costs in time and trouble?

To be worthwhile in the first place, all activities considered for inclusion in an instructional program must meet these *primary criteria* of goal appropriateness, feasibility, and cost-effectiveness. Activities that do not meet these criteria should not even be considered.

In selecting from among activities that do meet these primary criteria, teachers might consider several *secondary criteria:*

1. Students are likely to find the activity interesting or enjoyable.
2. The activity provides opportunities for interaction and reflective discourse, not just solitary seatwork.
3. If the activity involves writing, students will compose prose, not just fill in blanks.
4. If the activity involves discourse, students will engage in critical or creative thinking, articulate and defend problem-solving or decision-making approaches, and so on, not just regurgitate facts and definitions.
5. The activity is targeted for students' zones of proximal development; it is not merely an occasion for exercising overlearned skills.
6. The activity focuses on application of important ideas, not incidental details or interesting but ultimately trivial information.
7. As a set, the activities offer variety and in other ways appeal to student motivation to the extent that this is consistent with curriculum goals.
8. As a set, the activities include many ties to current events or local and family examples or applications.

Structuring and Scaffolding Students' Learning

Besides being well chosen, activities need to be effectively presented, monitored, and followed up if they are to have their full impact. This means preparing the students for an activity in advance, providing guidance and feedback during the activity, and structuring postactivity reflection afterward (Brophy & Alleman, 1991).

In introducing activities, teachers need to stress their purposes in ways that will help students to engage in them with clear ideas about the goals they are trying to accomplish. Such emphasis may need to be supplemented by statements or questions that call students' attention to relevant background knowledge, modeling of strategies for responding to the task, or scaffolding that will simplify the task for the students.

Teachers can scaffold by providing any needed information or help concerning how to go about completing task requirements. If reading is part of the task, for example, teachers might summarize the main ideas, remind students about strategies for developing and monitoring their comprehension as they read (paraphrasing, summarizing, taking notes, questioning themselves to check understanding), or provide them with advance organizers that will help them to approach the material in the intended ways. If necessary, teachers might provide additional scaffolding in the form of partial outlines or skeletal notes to fill in while listening to a presentation or reading an assignment (Kiewra, 1987), study guides that call attention to key ideas and structural elements, or task organizers that help students to keep

Table 9.4   OUTLINE FOR STUDENT NOTE TAKING ON THE TOPIC OF CAREERS
IN THE BIOLOGICAL SCIENCES

I. Major career fields in the biological sciences
   A. Botanists
   B. Zoologists
   C. Entomologists
   D. Microbiologists
   E. Anatomists
   F. Physiologists
   G. Geneticists
   H. Emerging areas of "synthesis"
II. Employment opportunities
   A. Universities and colleges
   B. Federal government
   C. Private industry
      1. Hospitals
      2. Clinics
      3. Laboratories
      4. Research foundations
III. Working conditions
   A. Qualifications—necessary training
   B. Prospects of employment
   C. Income/fringe benefits
   D. Degree of mobility
IV. References for additional information
   A. History of field
   B. Training program
   C. Career opportunities

track of the steps involved and the strategies they are using to complete these steps. For example, a teacher discussing careers in science in a seventh-grade life science class might distribute the outline presented in Table 9.4 as a way to help students to take notes effectively.

Once students begin working on activities and assignments, teachers should monitor their progress and provide assistance if necessary. Besides keeping these interventions short for the classroom management reasons described in Chapter 4, teachers should ordinarily confine themselves to minimal and indirect forms of help at these times. That is, assuming that students have a general understanding of what to do and how to do it, teachers should help them past rough spots by providing relatively general and indirect hints or cues. If their assistance is too direct or extensive, teachers will end up doing tasks for students instead of providing them with scaffolding to enable them to do the tasks themselves.

Most tasks will not have their full effects unless they are followed by reflection or debriefing. Here, the teacher reviews the task with the students, provides general feedback about performance, and reinforces the main ideas as they relate to the overall goals. These debriefing and reflection activities should also include opportunities for students to ask follow-up questions, share task-related observations or experiences, compare opinions, or in other ways deepen their appreciation of what they have learned and how it relates to their lives outside school.

Homework

The same guidelines that apply to assignments done in the classroom apply as well to homework assignments, but with the additional constraint that the homework must be realistic in length and difficulty given the students' abilities to work independently. Thus, 5 to 10 minutes per subject might be appropriate for fourth graders, whereas 30 to 60 minutes might be appropriate for college-bound high school students.

Also, homework performance must be monitored and followed up. Voluntary homework may be of some use to those students who do it conscientiously, but if homework is to have instructional value for the class as a whole, it will be necessary to set up accountability systems to make sure that it is completed on time and to review it the next day. In addition, reteaching and follow-up assignments may be needed for certain students.

SUMMARY

In this chapter we began our consideration of instruction by reviewing research on relationships between teacher behavior and student achievement. Then we addressed three important components of active teaching: presenting information to students, involving them in recitations and discussions, and engaging them in learning activities and assignments. In the process, we noted that instructional methods are means, not ends. The appropriateness of such methods depends on the teacher's instructional goals, and their effectiveness depends on the quality of their implementation. Research can inform teachers about the trade-offs that different instructional methods offer, but it cannot tell teachers what their goal priorities should be.

School effects and teacher effects research have identified factors associated with gains on standardized achievement tests. School effects research points to the importance of strong academic leadership that produces consensus on goal priorities and commitment to instructional excellence, an orderly school climate, positive teacher attitudes and expectations, a focus on instructional use of the available time, careful monitoring of progress toward goals through student testing and staff evaluation programs, strong parent involvement programs, and consistent emphasis on the importance of academic achievement. Teacher effects research indicates the value of teacher role definitions that emphasize positive expectations and a sense of efficacy, time allocation policies that maximize student opportunities to learn, use of effective classroom management and organization approaches, curriculum pacing that moves students through the curriculum rapidly but in small steps that minimize frustration, active instruction by the teacher (as opposed to expecting students to learn mostly on their own from textbooks and assignments), making sure that students achieve mastery of basic objectives, and maintaining a supportive learning environment.

Lecture/presentation and drill/recitation activities are well suited to the classroom context in certain respects and have their places as parts of a comprehensive approach to instruction. However, teachers should avoid using these techniques too frequently or in ways that limit the curriculum to rote memorizing of miscellaneous items of information. These techniques are used most effectively in lecture/recitation segments of lessons in which teachers help their students to develop networks of knowledge that are built around connected sets of important ideas and are learned with their applications in mind.

Lectures and other forms of information presentation are useful for arousing students' interest in a topic, providing advance organizers and learning sets to help them appreciate the topic's significance and approach it with appropriate learning strategies, bringing together and efficiently communicating important ideas about the topic, and providing information that students will not get from their textbooks. Good presentations are delivered enthusiastically and in clear, well-organized language. Where the instruction focuses on processes or skills, students will need not only verbal explanations but physical demonstrations. Such demonstrations should focus on the general principles involved and demystify the processes by articulating the thinking that guides observable actions.

Most activities based on teacher questioning should be recitations or discussions designed to provide opportunities for students to actively think about, respond to, and apply the content being taught. The questions should address a variety of cognitive levels of response and should be clear, brief, natural, and thought provoking. Most of all, they should be selected and sequenced so as to accomplish significant instructional goals. Questions should be addressed to the class as a whole and should be followed by sufficient wait time to allow students to process what is being asked and to begin to formulate responses to it. Students' responses should receive immediate feedback or other appropriate follow-up.

Discussions do not occur as frequently as they should in most classrooms. They require teachers to switch from the role of information source and authority figure to that of discussion leader who establishes a focus for the discussion and facilitates interaction but does not dominate it unnecessarily. In addition to asking questions, teachers can stimulate contributions to the discussion by making declarative statements or restatements, offering opinions, encouraging students to ask questions or elaborate on their previous statements, or simply remaining silent and waiting for a student to take the initiative.

Learning activities and assignments also are important components of instruction, even though they can be overused (especially when they take the form of silent individual work on fill-in-the-blank worksheets and other low-level tasks). Learning activities and assignments are valuable to the extent that they promote progress toward important instructional goals and are feasible and cost-effective given the constraints that apply. The most valuable activities tend to provide opportunities for interaction and reflective discourse rather than just solitary seatwork, and to engage students in thinking critically and creatively about and applying what they are learning, not just regurgitating facts and definitions. In order to have their full impact, activities and assignments need to be structured sufficiently to enable students to engage in them with awareness of their goals, and student work needs to be monitored and scaffolded sufficiently to ensure that they accomplish those goals satisfactorily. The same principles apply to homework assignments, but with the additional constraint that the assignments must be realistic in length and difficulty given the students' abilities to work independently.

SUGGESTED ACTIVITIES AND QUESTIONS

1. Since research on teaching first began, the lecture-and-recitation approach has always been found to be used heavily, if not exclusively, in most classrooms, even though educational theorists have been critical of it. Why is this? Can you see ways to (a) avoid overuse of this approach in your own teaching and (b) make sure that you use the approach effectively when you do use it?

2. Give concrete examples of instances when lecturing might be desirable.

3. How can you make your information presentations and skill demonstrations easier for your students to follow and remember?

4. Role-play the process of introducing and ending lessons *enthusiastically* and with *clarity*. Describe the classroom situation (age of students, etc.) so that others may provide you with appropriate feedback.

5. We have stressed that questions should be asked not just to assess student learning but to promote it. What does this mean? How can questions help students to develop important understandings?

6. How should teachers' questioning and feedback strategies in recitations differ from those in discussions?

7. Plan a brief (15-minute) discussion. Write out the sequence of questions you will use to advance the discussion fruitfully, applying the criteria we suggested for effective oral questions. Role-play your discussion if possible.

8. The criteria for effective *oral* questions mostly apply to written questions as well, but there are some exceptions. Try to identify other criteria that are applicable only to written questions. In what important ways do written and oral questions differ?

9. Why should students be allowed to talk freely about opinions that differ from those of the teacher or the book?

10. What is the optimal difficulty level of an assignment?

11. Given your current or intended teaching context (grade level, subject matter, types of students), what kinds of learning activities and assignments will be most needed for enabling your students to meet your instructional goals?

12. Would regular homework assignments be appropriate for this teaching context? If so, what kinds of assignments and for what purposes?

13. Why does active teaching, in which the teacher presents content to students and structures their subsequent practice and application exercises, generally produce more learning than approaches in which students are encouraged to learn on their own?

14. Why is it impossible to give a precise definition of an *effective teacher*?

15. Interview some first- or second-year teachers and some veteran teachers (with at least eight years in service) concerning their beliefs about classroom discussions. Which group uses more discussion, and why? Are there differences in how they approach the discussion method or in the purposes for which they use it?

16. Think through your experiences with the discussion method as a student, and discuss them with peers. Can you agree on the trade-offs that the method offers students? In what ways is it a desirable learning method? In what ways is it frustrating or otherwise problematic? What does this imply about when, why, and how to use discussion in your teaching?

REFERENCES

Alvermann, D., O'Brien, D., & Dillon, D. (1990). What teachers do when they say they're having discussions of content area reading assignments: A qualitative analysis. *Reading Research Quarterly, 25,* 296–322.

Anderson, L., Evertson, C., & Brophy, J. (1979). An experimental study of effective teaching in first-grade reading groups. *Elementary School Journal, 79,* 193–223.

Anderson, L., Evertson, C., & Brophy, J. (1982). *Principles of small-group instruction in elementary reading.* Occasional Paper No. 58. East Lansing: Michigan State University, Institute for Research on Teaching.

Anshutz, R. (1975). An investigation of wait-time and questioning techniques as an instructional variable for science methods students microteaching elementary school children. (Doctoral dissertation, University of Kansas, 1973). *Dissertation Abstracts International, 35,* 5978A.

Arnold, D., Atwood, R., & Rogers, V. (1974). Question and response levels and lapse time intervals. *Journal of Experimental Education, 13,* 11–15.

Ausubel, D. (1963). *The psychology of meaningful verbal learning: An introduction to school learning.* New York: Grune & Stratton.

Beck, I., & McKeown, M. (1988). Toward meaningful accounts in history texts for young learners. *Educational Researcher, 17*(6), 31–39.

Blumenfeld, P. (1992). The task and the teacher: Enhancing student thoughtfulness in science. In J. Brophy (Ed.), *Advances in research on teaching.* Vol 3. *Planning and managing learning tasks and activities* (pp. 81–114). Greenwich, CT: JAI.

Bloom, B., Englehart, M., Furst, E., Hill, W., & Krathwohl, D. (1956). *Taxonomy of educational objectives: The classification of educational goals. Handbook I: Cognitive domain.* New York: Longmans Green.

Brophy, J. (1988). Research on teacher effects: Uses and abuses. *Elementary School Journal, 89,* 3–21.

Brophy, J. (Ed.). (1989). *Advances in research on teaching.* Vol. I. *Teaching for meaningful understanding and self-regulated learning.* Greenwich, CT: JAI.

Brophy, J. (Ed.). (1992a). *Advances in research on teaching.* Vol. 3 *Planning and managing learning tasks and activities.* Greenwich, CT: JAI Press.

Brophy, J. (1992b) The *de facto* national curriculum in U.S. elementary social studies: Critique of a representative example. *Journal of Curriculum Studies, 24,* 401–447.

Brophy, J., & Alleman, J. (1991). Activities as instructional tools: A framework for analysis and evaluation. *Educational Researcher, 20*(4), 9–23.

Brophy, J., & Good, T. (1974). *Teacher-student relationships: Causes and consequences.* New York: Holt.

Brophy, J., & Good, T. (1986). Teacher behavior and student achievement. In M. C. Wittrock (Ed.), *Handbook of research on teaching* (3rd ed.). New York: Macmillan.

Cabello, B., & Terrell, R. (1994). Making students feel like family: How teachers create warm and caring classroom climates. *Journal of Classroom Interaction, 29,* 17–23.

Carlsen, W. (1991). Questioning in classrooms: A sociolinguistic perspective. *Review of Educational Research, 61,* 157–178.

Chilcoat, G. (1989). Instructional behaviors for clearer presentations in the classroom. *Instructional Science, 18,* 289–314.

Clark, C., & Peterson, P. (1986). Teachers' thought processes. In M. C. Wittrock (Ed.), *Handbook of research on teaching* (3rd ed.). New York: Macmillan.

Collins. A., & Stevens, A. (1983). A cognitive theory of inquiry teaching. In C. Reigeluth (Ed.), *Instructional-design theories and models: An overview of their current status.* Hillsdale, NJ: Erlbaum.

Cooper, H. (1989). *Homework.* New York: Longman.

Cooper, H. (1994). *The battle over homework: An administrator's guide to setting sound and effective policies.* Thousand Oaks, CA: Corwin.

Creemers, B., & Scheerens, J. (Guest editors). (1989). Developments in school effectiveness research. *International Journal of Educational Research, 13,* 685–825.

Cruickshank, D. (1985). Applying research on teacher clarity. *Journal of Teacher Education, 36,* 44–48.

DeTure, L. (1979). Relative effects of modeling on the acquisition of wait-time by preservice elementary teachers and concomitant changes in dialogue patterns. *Journal of Research in Science Teaching, 16,* 553–562.

Dillon, J. (1979). Alternatives to questioning. *High School Journal, 62,* 217–222.

Dillon, J. (Ed.). (1988). *Questioning and teaching: A manual of practice.* London: Croom Helm.

Dillon, J. (Ed.). (1990). *The practice of questioning.* New York: Routledge.

Dreher, M., & Singer, H. (1989). Friendly texts and text-friendly teachers. *Theory into Practice, 28,* 98–104.

Duffy, G., Roehler, L., Meloth, M., & Vavrus, L. (1986). Conceptualizing instructional explanation. *Teaching and Teacher Education, 2,* 197–214.

Elliott, D., & Woodward, A. (Eds.). (1990). *Textbooks and schooling in the United States, Part I: Eighty-ninth Yearbook of the National Society for the Study of Education.* Chicago: University of Chicago Press.

Epstein, J. (1988). *Homework practices, achievements, and behaviors of elementary school students* (Report No. 26). Baltimore: Center for Research on Elementary and Middle Schools, the Johns Hopkins University.

Fagan, E., Hassler, D., & Szabo, M. (1981). Evaluation of questioning strategies in language arts instruction. *Research in the Teaching of English, 15,* 267–273.

Farrar, M. (1986). Teacher questions: The complexity of the cognitively simple. *Instructional Science, 15,* 89–107.

Fisher, C., Berliner, D., Filby, N., Marliave, R., Cahen, L., & Dishaw, M. (1980). Teaching behaviors, academic learning time, student achievement: An overview. In C. Denham & A. Lieberman (Eds.), *Time to learn.* Washington, DC: National Institute of Education.

Freiberg, H., Prokosch, N., Treister, E., & Stein, T. (1990). Turning around five at-risk elementary schools. *School Effectiveness and School Improvement, 1,* 5–25.

Gage, N., & Berliner, D. (1992). *Educational psychology* (5th ed.). Boston: Houghton Mifflin.

Gliessman, D., Pugh, R., Brown, L., Archer, A., & Snyder, S. (1989). Applying a research-based model to teacher skill training. *Journal of Educational Research, 83,* 69–81.

Good, T. (1996). Teacher effectiveness and teacher evaluation. In J. Sikula, T. Buttery, & E. Guyton (Eds.), *Handbook of research on teacher education* (2nd ed., pp. 617–665). New York: Macmillan.

Good, T., & Brophy, J. (1974). Changing teacher and student behavior: An empirical investigation. *Journal of Educational Psychology, 66,* 390–405.

Good, T., & Brophy, J. (1986). School effects. In M. C. Wittrock (Ed.), *Handbook of research on teaching* (3rd ed.). New York: Macmillan.

Good, T., & Grouws, D. (1979). The Missouri Mathematics Effectiveness Project: An experimental study in fourth-grade classrooms. *Journal of Educational Psychology, 71,* 355–362.

Good, T., Grouws, D., & Ebmeier, H. (1983). *Active mathematics teaching.* New York: Longman.

Groisser, P. (1964). *How to use the fine art of questioning.* New York: Teachers' Practical Press.

Henson, K. (1988). *Methods and strategies for teaching in secondary and middle schools.* New York: Longman.

Joyce, B., & Weil, M. (1986). *Models of teaching* (3rd ed.). Englewood Cliffs, NJ: Prentice-Hall.

Kiewra, K. (1987). Notetaking and review: The research and its implications. *Instructional Science, 16,* 233–249.

Luiten, J., Ames, W., & Ackerson, G. (1970). A meta-analysis of the effects of advance organizers on learning and retention. *American Educational Research Journal, 17,* 211–218.

McCaleb, J., & White, J. (1980). Critical dimensions in evaluating teacher clarity. *Journal of Classroom Interaction, 15,* 27–30.

McCaslin, M., & Good, T. (1996). *Listening to students.* New York: HarperCollins.

McLeish, J. (1976). Lecture method. In N. Gage (Ed.), *The psychology of teaching methods* (Part I). *(75th Yearbook of the National Society for the Study of Education).* Chicago: University of Chicago Press.

Miller, D., & Kelley, M. (1991). Interventions for improving homework performance: A critical review. *School Psychology Quarterly, 6,* 174–185.

Olympia, D., Sheridan, S., & Jenson, W. (1994). Homework: A natural means of home-school collaboration. *School Psychology Quarterly, 9,* 60-80.

Osborn, J. (1984). Workbooks that accompany basal reading programs. In G. Duffy, L. Roehler, & J. Mason (Eds.), *Comprehension instruction: Perspectives and suggestions.* New York: Longman.

Reynolds, A. (1992). What is competent beginning teaching? A review of the literature. *Review of Educational Research, 62,* 1–35.

Rice, D. (1977). The effect of question-asking instruction on preservice elementary science teachers. *Journal of Research in Science Teaching, 14,* 353–359.

Riley, J. (1980). *The effects of teachers' wait-time and cognitive questioning level on pupil science achievement.* Paper presented at the annual meeting of the National Association for Research in Science Teaching, Boston.

Roby, T. (1988). Models of discussion. In J. Dillon (Ed.), *Questioning and discussion: A multidisciplinary study* (pp. 163–191). Norwood, NJ: Ablex.

Rosenshine, B. (1968). To explain: A review of research. *Educational Leadership, 26,* 275–280.

Rosenshine, B. (1970). Enthusiastic teaching: A research review. *School Review, 78,* 499–514.

Rosenshine, B., & Furst, N. (1973). The use of direct observation to study teaching. In R. Travers (Ed.), *Second handbook of research on teaching.* Chicago: Rand McNally.

Rowe, M. (1974a). Science, silence, and sanctions. *Science and Children, 6,* 11–13.

Rowe, M. (1974b). Wait time and rewards as instructional variables, their influence on language, logic, and fate control: Part I—Wait time. *Journal of Research in Science Teaching, 11,* 81–94.

Rowe, M. (1986). Wait time: Slowing down may be a way of speeding up! *Journal of Teacher Education 37,* 43–50.

Schuck, R., (1981). The impact of set induction on student achievement and retention. *Journal of Educational Research, 74,* 227–232.

Sigurdson, S., & Olson, A. (1992). Teaching mathematics with meaning. *Journal of Mathematical Behavior, 11,* 37-57.

Smith, L., & Land, M. (1981). Low-inference verbal behaviors related to teacher clarity. *Journal of Classroom Interaction, 17,* 37–42.

Swift, J., Gooding, C., & Swift, P. (1988). Questions and wait time. In J. Dillon (Ed.), *Questioning and discussion: A multidisciplinary study* (pp. 192–212). Norwood NJ: Ablex.

Teddlie, C., & Stringfield, S. (1993). *Schools make a difference: Lessons learned from a 10-year study of school effects.* New York: Teachers College Press.

Tharp, R., & Gallimore, R. (1988). Rousing minds to life: Teaching, learning and schooling in social contexts. Cambridge, Cambridge University Press.

Tobin, K. (1983). The influence of wait-time on classroom learning. *European Journal of Science Education, 5*(1), 35–48.

Tyson-Bernstein, H. (1988). *A conspiracy of good intentions: America's textbook fiasco.* Washington, DC: Council for Basic Education.

Waxman, H., & Walberg, H. (Eds.). (1991). *Effective teaching: Current research.* Berkeley, CA: McCutchan.

Weinert, F., & Helmke, A. (1995). Learning from wise Mother Nature or Big Brother Instructor: The wrong choice as seen from an educational perspective. *Educational Psychologist, 30,* 135–142.

Wilen, W., *What research has to say to the teacher: questioning techniques for teachers,* (3rd ed.) 1991, National Education Association, Washington DC.

Wright, C., & Nuthall, G. (1970). The relationships between teacher behaviors and pupil achievement in three experimental elementary science lessons. *American Educational Research Journal, 7,* 477–492.

FORM 9.1. Teacher Lectures, Presentations, and Demonstrations

USE: When the teacher lectures, presents information, or demonstrates skills to the class.
PURPOSE: To assess the effectiveness of the presentation.
Enter a check mark for each of the following features that was included effectively in the presentation, and a 0 for each feature that was omitted or handled ineffectively. Add your comments below, emphasizing constructive suggestions for improvement.

CHECKLIST

INTRODUCTION

_____ 1. States purpose or objectives
_____ 2. Gives overview or advance organizer
_____ 3. Distributes a study guide or instructs the students concerning how they are expected to respond (what notes to take, etc.)

BODY OF PRESENTATION

_____ 4. Is well prepared; speaks fluently without hesitation or confusion
_____ 5. Projects enthusiasm for the material
_____ 6. Maintains eye contact with the students
_____ 7. Speaks at an appropriate pace (neither too fast nor too slow)
_____ 8. Speaks with appropriate voice modulation (rather than a monotone)
_____ 9. Uses appropriate expressions, movements, and gestures (rather than speaking woodenly)
_____ 10. Content is well structured and sequenced
_____ 11. New terms are clearly defined
_____ 12. Key concepts or terms are emphasized (preferably not only verbally but by holding up or pointing to examples, writing or underlining on the board or overhead projector, etc.)
_____ 13. Includes appropriate analogies or examples that are effective in enabling students to relate the new to the familiar and the abstract to the concrete
_____ 14. Where appropriate, facts are distinguished from opinions
_____ 15. Where appropriate, lengthy presentations are divided into recognizable segments, with clear transitions between segments and minisummaries concluding each segment
_____ 16. When necessary, questions the students following each major segment of a lengthy presentation (rather than waiting until the end)
_____ 17. Monitors student response; is encouraging and responsive regarding student questions and comments on the material

CONCLUSION

_____ 18. Concludes with summary or integration of the presentation
_____ 19. Invites student questions or comments
_____ 20. Follows up on the presentation by making a transition into a recitation activity, a follow-up assignment, or some other activity that will allow the students an opportunity to practice or apply the material

COMMENTS:

FORM 9.2. Questioning Techniques

USE: When teacher is asking class or group questions.
PURPOSE: To see if teacher is following principles for good questioning practices.
For each question, code the following categories:

BEHAVIOR CATEGORIES

A. TYPE OF QUESTION ASKED
    1. Academic: Factual. Seeks specific correct response
    2. Academic: Opinion. Seeks opinion on a complex issue where there
       is no clear-cut response
    3. Nonacademic: Question deals with personal, procedural, or disciplin-
       ary matters rather than curriculum

B. TYPE OF RESPONSE REQUIRED
    1. Thought question. Student must reason through to a conclusion or
       explain something at length
    2. Fact question. Student must provide fact(s) from memory
    3. Choice question. Requires only a yes-no or either-or response

C. SELECTION OF RESPONDENT
    1. Names child before asking question
    2. Calls on volunteer (after asking question)
    3. Calls on nonvolunteer (after asking question)

D. PAUSE (AFTER ASKING QUESTION)
    1. Paused a few seconds before calling on student
    2. Failed to pause before calling on student
    3. Not applicable: teacher named student before asking question

E. TONE AND MANNER IN PRESENTING QUESTION
    1. Question presented as challenge or stimulation
    2. Question presented matter-of-factly
    3. Question presented as threat or test

CODES

#	A	B	C	D	E
1.	1	2	2	1	2
2.	1	2	2	1	2
3.	1	3	2	1	2
4.	1	2	2	1	2
5.	1	2	2	1	2
6.	1	3	2	1	2
7.	1	2	2	1	2
8.	2	1	2	1	1
9.	1	2	2	1	2
10.	1	2	2	1	2
11.	1	2	2	1	2
12.	1	2	2	1	2
13.	—	—	—	—	—
14.	—	—	—	—	—
15.	—	—	—	—	—
16.	—	—	—	—	—
17.	—	—	—	—	—
18.	—	—	—	—	—
19.	—	—	—	—	—
20.	—	—	—	—	—
21.	—	—	—	—	—
22.	—	—	—	—	—
23.	—	—	—	—	—
24.	—	—	—	—	—
25.	—	—	—	—	—
26.	—	—	—	—	—
27.	—	—	—	—	—
28.	—	—	—	—	—
29.	—	—	—	—	—
30.	—	—	—	—	—
31.	—	—	—	—	—
32.	—	—	—	—	—
33.	—	—	—	—	—
34.	—	—	—	—	—
35.	—	—	—	—	—
36.	—	—	—	—	—
37.	—	—	—	—	—
38.	—	—	—	—	—
39.	—	—	—	—	—
40.	—	—	—	—	—

    Record any information relevant to the following:
Multiple Questions. Tally the number of times the teacher:
1. Repeats or rephrases question before calling on anyone __ll__

2. Asks two or more questions at the same time __0__

Sequence. Were questions integrated into an orderly sequence, or
did they seem to be random or unrelated?
    Teacher seemed to be following sequence given in manual
(led up to next history unit).
Did the students themselves pose questions? No

Was there student-student interaction? How much? None

When appropriate, did the teacher redirect questions to several students, or ask students to evaluate their own or others' responses? No

Helping Students to Construct Usable Knowledge

*T*he following is part of the transcript of a fifth-grade literature lesson recorded by Quirk and Cianciolo (1993). The teacher is asking her students to consider the importance of the setting in the book under discussion (*The Lion, the Witch, and the Wardrobe*), and in fanciful fiction in general. Note her reliance on questioning rather than didactic explanation. How would you assess her method as a way to develop understanding and appreciation of setting as an element of literature? Would you do anything differently? How might you follow up this segment after Martha makes her concluding comment?

TEACHER: How important is the setting to this story?

SUSIE: Very, very.

TEACHER: Why?

SUSIE: Because if the setting was in a different place, they wouldn't have got [sic] the wardrobe. And then they wouldn't have gone to Narnia.

TEACHER: Okay. Jessica.

JESSICA: I think they could have changed the setting a little. They had to make it into a different world, but they didn't have to make it all snow. They could have made it spring and the children always wanted it to be winter.

TEACHER: Okay. So they could have changed the seasons very easily. But you said something about it had to be Narnia.

JESSICA: It didn't have to be Narnia, but it had to be a different world.

TEACHER: A different world. Why? That's a very good point, Jessica. Why would it have to be a different world? Darrin?

DARRIN: Because it makes you like, interested because you could go through a wardrobe and walk and walk, and then you enter into a new world.

TEACHER: Okay, and what do you think Steve?

STEVEN: I think it [the setting] is very important, because if you put them [the characters] in a setting like [our town] it wouldn't be exciting. I mean, like in Narnia you have all these monsters and the witch.

TEACHER: What does it do to our imagination when we have, as Jessica suggested, another world, or another time, or another place? Barbara?

BARBARA: If it's exciting, we want to read more. You can make it the world you want it to be.

TEACHER: Absolutely, very good. Jason?

JASON: When it's another world it makes your mind wander and makes you want to get out of everything. But it also makes you think that you're actually in that world. It's kinda boring if it was just in the professor's house or something. But it's more exciting when it's in another world.

TEACHER: Why is it okay to have this other world situation in Narnia, but in *The Tales of a Fourth Grade Nothing*, it is a familiar situation. Judy Blume books are set in familiar places we can identify like [our town], or whatever. Why is it okay for those books, but I'm hearing some of you say Narnia has to be way out some place. Barbara?

BARBARA: Because Judy Blume's telling what could really happen, but here in C. S. Lewis' books it's imagination and imagination has to lead you the way or else you aren't gonna get anywhere.

TEACHER: Okay. One last comment. Martha?

MARTHA: I think that it can be different because of the titles. There wouldn't be a lion, a witch, and a wardrobe in [our town]. It has to be somewhere, where anything can happen.

TEACHING FOR UNDERSTANDING, APPRECIATION, AND APPLICATION OF KNOWLEDGE

In Chapter 9 we reviewed research that documented the connections between active teaching (presenting information, structuring discourse, monitoring work on assignments) and student gains on achievement tests. These widely replicated research findings are gratifying for several reasons. First, they reaffirm the fact that teachers make a difference, by showing that some teachers elicit more achievement gains than others do and by pointing to the classroom management and instructional behaviors associated with these gains. Also, such findings move the field beyond unsupported claims about effective practices toward scientific statements based on credible data. Finally, the findings are gratifying to most teachers because they validate principles that teachers have developed through experience.

Even as the contributions of research on school effects and teacher effects were being consolidated and applied in teacher education, research on teaching was moving on to new phases. One reason for this was increasing recognition of certain limitations in process-outcome research. First, this research focused on important but very basic aspects of teaching. The findings differentiated the least effective teachers from other teachers, but they did not address the subtler fine points that distinguish the most outstanding teachers. Second, most of this research relied on standardized tests as the measures of learning. Consequently, its assessment focused on mastery of relatively isolated knowledge items and skill components without evaluating the degree to which students had developed understanding of networks of connected content or could use this content in realistic application situations.

These concerns led to new forms of research on subject-matter teaching. The new studies focused on teaching for *understanding*, which implies that students learn not only the individual elements in a network of related content but also the connections among them, so that they can explain the content in their own words and can access and use it in appropriate application situations in and out of school (Bereiter & Scardamalia, 1987; Brophy, 1989; Bruer, 1993; Glaser, 1984; Perkins, 1992; Prawat, 1989; Resnick, 1987). Students who learn content with understanding not only learn the content itself but appreciate the reasons for learning it and retain it in a form that makes it usable when needed. Recent research on subject-matter teaching has involved exemplary teachers who know their subjects thoroughly and emphasize developing understanding when planning their instruction. The research focuses intensively on particular curriculum units or lessons, taking into account the teacher's instructional goals and assessing students' learning accordingly. The researchers find out what the teacher is trying to accomplish, record detailed information about classroom processes, and then assess learning using evaluation measures keyed to the instructional goals. Often the evaluation methods include detailed interviews or portfolios of student work in addition to or instead of more conventional short-answer tests.

Knowledge as Constructed

While deepening our understanding of the role of the teacher in stimulating student learning, recent research has also emphasized the role of the student. This reflects the influence of developmental and cognitive psychologists who hold *constructivist* views of learning and teaching (Davis, Maher, & Noddings, 1990; Duffy & Jonassen, 1992; Resnick & Klopfer, 1989; Steffe, Cobb, & von Glasersfeld, 1988; Steffe & Gale, 1995). Constructivists believe that students learn through a process of active construction that involves making connections between new information and existing networks of prior knowledge. Constructivists emphasize the importance of relating new content to the knowledge that students already possess, as well as providing opportunities for students to process and apply the new learning. They believe that before knowledge becomes truly *generative*—usable for interpreting new situations, solving problems, thinking and reasoning, and learning generally—students must elaborate and question what they are told, examine the new content in relation to more familiar content, and build new knowledge structures (Resnick & Klopfer, 1989). Otherwise, the knowledge may remain *inert*—recallable when cued by questions or test items similar to those used in practice exercises, but not applicable when it might be useful in everyday living.

Although the term *constructivist* is relatively new, many constructivist ideas can be traced to John Dewey and Jean Piaget and some go back at least as far as Socrates. Many are embodied in historically significant educational movements such as open education, inquiry learning, and discovery learning, as well as in contemporary movements such as whole-language teaching and portfolio assessment. Current constructivist approaches to teaching for understanding include a variety of theoretical rationales and suggested teaching methods, but they all involve some subset of the following key ideas.

The core idea of constructivism is that *students develop new knowledge through a process of active construction.* They do not merely passively receive or copy input from teachers or textbooks. Instead, they actively mediate it by trying to make sense of it and relate it to what they already know (or think they know) about the topic. This is precisely what we want them to do, because unless students build representations of the new learning, "making it their own" by paraphrasing it in their own words and considering its meanings and implications, the learning will be retained only as relatively meaningless and inert rote memories. However, each student builds his or her own unique representation of what was communicated, and this may or may not include a complete and accurate reconstruction of what the teacher or textbook author intended to convey. Sometimes the learning is incomplete or distorted.

Even when the basic message is reconstructed as intended, it gets connected to each learner's unique set of prior understandings. As a result, each learner constructs a unique set of meanings and implications of "the same" set of ideas, and "files" it in memory accordingly. For example, on reading a fictional or nonfictional narrative about mountain climbers who overcame potential disasters to achieve their goals successfully, one reader might remember and think about the text primarily as a story about achievement motivation, another as a story about the value of teamwork, another as a story about how shared adventure seals the bonds of friendship, and yet another as an illustration of the challenges and specialized techniques involved in mountain climbing. The students were exposed to the same narrative as constructed by its author and their reconstructions of it all include the same basic story line, but they emphasize different meanings and potential implications.

Constructivists differ in their ideas about the nature of knowledge. Empirically oriented constructivists believe that knowledge is anchored in the external environment and exists independently of learners' cognitive activities, so they speak of helping learners to construct accurate conceptions (Case, 1982; Ginsburg & Opper, 1979; Rumelhart & Norman, 1981). In contrast, radical constructivists believe that knowledge resides only in the constructions of learners. Consequently, one cannot teach precise representations of "truth," but can only negotiate shared meanings with students and provide them with opportunities to construct useful understandings by overcoming obstacles or contradictions that arise as they engage in purposeful activity (Cobb, 1986; Cobb, Yackel, & Wood, 1992; von Glasersfeld, 1984). Whatever their underlying philosophical views, however, all constructivists emphasize that teachers need to go beyond information transmission models (teachers or texts tell, students memorize) and move toward knowledge construction models of teaching and learning. These involve structuring reflective discussions of the meanings and implications of content and providing opportunities for students to use the content as they engage in inquiry, problem solving, or decision making (Brooks, 1990).

Knowledge construction models of teaching and learning have been emphasized in the curriculum and instruction guidelines released in recent years by the American Association for the Advancement of Science, the National Council of Teachers of Mathematics, the National Council for the Social Studies, the National Council of Teachers of English, the National Research Council (science education standards), and other professional organizations concerned with K–12 education in general or with the teaching of particular school subjects. In addition, organizations concerned with the education of young children have emphasized knowledge construction models in documents describing developmentally appropriate practice in preschool and primary classrooms (Bredekamp, 1987; National Association of State Boards of Education, 1988).

Knowledge Networks Structured Around Powerful Ideas

As educators, we want students not just to retain information but to develop deep understandings and reflect thoughtfully about what they are learning. We want them to become scientific inquirers, critical thinkers, systematic problem solvers, and value-based decision makers. If these lofty goals are to be accomplished, we need to teach with emphasis on higher-order thinking about and applications of what is learned. However, misuse of hierarchical schemes such as the Bloom taxonomy of cognitive objectives (Bloom et al., 1956) to guide curriculum development has implanted the notions that instructional strands are hierarchies of knowledge and that one must proceed through them in sequence, moving linearly from lower levels to higher levels. Thus, one introduces a topic by beginning at the knowledge level and staying there until a complete base of information has been developed, then moves to the comprehension level by helping students begin to translate the information into different terms and probe its connections, then moves to the application level, and so on. Movement to higher levels (analysis, synthesis, and evaluation) occurs only after mastery of lower levels has been accomplished.

Recent theory and research suggest that there is no need to impose such a rigid, linear hierarchy on teaching and learning (Brophy, 1989; Marzano et al., 1988). The argument is that, instead of viewing knowledge as composed of linear hierarchies, we should view it as composed of networks structured around key ideas. These networks include facts, concepts, and generalizations, along with related values, dispositions, procedural knowledge (implementation skills), and conditional knowledge (of when and why to access and apply parts of the network). An important implication of this conception of knowledge is that one can enter and begin to learn about a network almost anywhere, not just at the low end of a linear hierarchy. Learning can be couched within an applications context and students can be engaged in higher-order thinking about a topic right from the beginning of instruction. For example, a teacher might begin teaching about a mathematical operation by posing a problem that requires the operation for efficient solution. Or, the teacher might begin a lesson on climate and weather by asking students to speculate about why there often is wet weather on one side of a mountain range but dry weather on the other side.

Shifting from a linear to a network conception of knowledge structuring fits well with ideas about teaching subjects for understanding, appreciation, and application. Because comprehension (i.e., understanding) is near the bottom of the Bloom taxonomy, teaching for understanding is sometimes viewed as a low-level cognitive objective. However, in order to achieve understanding of a network of knowledge, students will have to engage in application, analysis, synthesis, and evaluation activities, not just in activities designed to build knowledge and comprehension. Consequently, the notion of separating cognitive levels of learning and addressing them in sequential order breaks down when one is confronted with the kinds of integrated instruction involved in teaching for meaningful understanding.

The preceding paragraphs assume that the content has been selected and organized as means to move students toward important educational goals. That is, they assume that the content is *worth* understanding, appreciating, and applying in the first place. If so, it will be structured as a series of networks of connected knowledge, not as a disconnected parade of facts and isolated skills. Furthermore, it will be taught with emphasis on the powerful ideas that anchor the networks and provide a basis for potential applications.

Many more things are worth teaching than we have time to teach in school, so breadth of topic coverage must be balanced against depth of development of each topic. This is an enduring dilemma that can only be managed in sensible ways, not a problem that can be solved once and for all. In recent decades we have drifted into addressing far too many topics and including too many trite or pointless details. Curriculum analyses in all of the subject areas suggest the need for teacher decision making about how to reduce breadth of coverage, structure the content around powerful ideas, and develop these ideas in depth.

The Role of Prior Knowledge

Construction of knowledge goes more smoothly when learners can relate new content to their existing background knowledge. New content is not first understood in some abstract way and only later related to existing knowledge; instead, it is interpreted from the beginning within contexts supplied by that existing knowledge. Collections of prior knowledge that provide contexts for meaningful interpretation of new content are usually called *schemas* (Anderson, 1984; diSibio, 1982). If new content can be related to existing schemas, activation of these schemas can help learners to develop expectations about the nature of the content, identify and pay special attention to its most important elements, and fill in gaps where information is implied rather than stated explicitly. Consider the following paragraph:

> When Mary arrived, the woman at the door greeted her and checked her name. A few minutes later, she was escorted to her chair and shown the day's menu. The attendant was helpful but brusque, almost to the point of being rude. Later, she paid the woman at the door and left.

You probably were able to interpret this rather sketchy narrative because you recognized that the events took place in a restaurant, that Mary had made reservations, and that she was seated by a hostess at a table (not merely in a chair), that the "attendant" was a waiter, and that the "woman at the door" was a cashier. You could infer all of this information, even though none of it was explicit in the text, because you possess a *"restaurant"* schema that includes such slots as "being seated," "ordering," and "paying the check" (Schank & Abelson, 1977).

Activation of relevant background knowledge can make learning of new content easier and more efficient, at least if the activated schemas are suited to the instructional goals (Adams, 1990; Anderson, 1984; Gagne & Dick, 1983). Teachers can prepare students for story reading by telling them what the story is about and asking them questions to activate schemas that they will find useful in comprehending it. Teachers also can help students to activate relevant prior knowledge by drawing analogies or suggesting examples that link the new content to familiar ideas or experiences, by taking an inventory of what students know (or think they know) about the topic before beginning instruction, or by asking questions that require students to make predictions about the content or to suggest solutions to problems based on it. The K-W-L technique described in Chapter 6 is another way to stimulate relevant prior knowledge when introducing new content.

Knowledge Restructuring and Conceptual Change

Activation of relevant schemas will facilitate learning if the schemas are accurate and support accomplishment of the instructional goals. When existing schemas are not accurate or not well suited to the goals, however, their activation will interfere with learning (Alvermann, Smith, & Readence, 1985). If the new content is filtered through schemas that are oversimplified, distorted, or otherwise invalid, students may develop misconceptions instead of the target conceptions that the teacher is trying to teach. For example, many students believe that the sun orbits the earth, because they have "seen" it do so. Sometimes this prior knowledge is so well entrenched that it causes certain students to misunderstand what the teacher or textbook is saying about cycles of day and night. Such students may emerge from a lesson having learned that areas of the earth experience daylight at times when they are exposed to the sun, yet still believing that cycles of day and night are due to orbiting of the sun around the earth instead of vice versa.

Besides adding new elements to an existing cognitive structure, active construction of knowledge may involve changing the structure through processes of *restructuring* and *conceptual change*. Sometimes the needed restructuring is relatively minor and easily accomplished, but sometimes students need to undergo more radical restructuring that involves simultaneous change in large networks of connected knowledge (Carey, 1985; Chinn & Brewer, 1993; Vosniadou & Brewer, 1987). Radical restructuring can be time-consuming and difficult to accomplish.

Mere exposure to correct conceptions will not necessarily stimulate the needed restructuring because learners may activate long-standing and firmly believed misconceptions that cause them to ignore, distort, or miss the implications of aspects of the new learning that contradict what they "know." It may be necessary to help students first to see the contradictions between what they currently believe and what the teacher is trying to teach, and then to appreciate that the target concepts are more valid, more powerful, more useful, or in some other way preferable to their existing concepts.

Knowledge as Socially Constructed

Some constructivist accounts of learning, especially those influenced heavily by the developmental psychology of Jean Piaget, depict learning as primarily a solitary activity. The focus is on the individual child who develops knowledge through exploration, discovery, and reflection on everyday life experiences. However, most constructivist accounts are variants of *social constructivism.* In addition to emphasizing that learning is a process of active construction of meaning, social constructivists emphasize that the process works best in social settings in which two or more individuals engage in sustained discourse about a topic. Such discussions help participants to advance their learning in several ways. Exposure to new input from others makes them aware of things that they did not know and leads to expansion of their cognitive structures. Exposure to ideas that contradict their own beliefs may cause them to examine those beliefs and perhaps restructure them. The need to communicate their ideas to others forces them to articulate those ideas more clearly, which sharpens their conceptions and often leads to recognition of new connections. As a result, cognitive structures become better developed (both better differentiated and better organized).

Social constructivist ideas have been influenced heavily by the writings of the Russian developmental psychologist Lev Vygotsky (1962, 1978). Vygotsky believed that children's thought (cognition) and language (speech) begin as separate functions but become intimately connected during the preschool years as children learn to use language as a mechanism for thinking. Gradually, more and more of their learning is mediated through language, especially learning of cultural knowledge that is difficult if not impossible to develop through direct experience with the physical environment. Children initially acquire much of their cultural knowledge through overt speech (conversations with others, especially parents and teachers). Then they elaborate on this knowledge and connect it to other knowledge through inner speech (thinking mediated through language, or self-talk).

Literacy, numeracy, and knowledge in the subjects taught at school are prominent examples of the kinds of cultural knowledge that Vygotsky viewed as socially constructed. He suggested that this learning proceeds most efficiently when children are consistently exposed to *teaching in the zone of proximal development.* The zone of proximal development refers to the range of knowledge and skills that students are not yet ready to learn on their own but could learn with help from teachers. The children already know things that are "below" the zone, or can learn them easily on their own without help. They cannot learn things that are "above" the zone, even with help.

Ideas about teaching within the zone of proximal development, sometimes summarized in the term *zone theory,* resemble in some ways the ideas connected with the notion of *readiness* for learning. However, readiness is passive in its implications, suggesting that teachers can do little but wait until children become ready to learn something (presumably due to maturation of needed cognitive structures) before trying to teach it to them. Zone theory assumes that children's readiness for learning something depends much more on their accumulated prior knowledge about the topic than on maturation of cognitive structures, and that advances in knowledge will be stimulated primarily through the social construction that occurs during sustained discourse, most rapidly through teaching in the zone of proximal development (Moll, 1990; Newman, Griffin, & Cole, 1989; Rogoff & Wertsch, 1984; Tharp & Gallimore, 1988; Wertsch, 1985, 1991; Wertsch & Tulviste, 1992).

Social constructivists emphasize teaching that features sustained dialogue or discussion in which participants pursue a topic in depth, exchanging views and negotiating meanings and implications as they explore its ramifications. Along with teacher-structured whole-class discussions, this includes cooperative learning that is constructed as students work in pairs or small groups (King, 1994). Key features of social constructivist approaches to teaching and learning are summarized in Table 10.1.

Table 10.1 TEACHING AND LEARNING AS TRANSMISSION OF INFORMATION VERSUS AS SOCIAL CONSTRUCTION OF KNOWLEDGE

Transmission View	Social Construction View
Knowledge as fixed body of information transmitted from teacher or text to students	Knowledge as developing interpretations coconstructed through discussion
Texts, teacher as authoritative sources of expert knowledge to which students defer	Authority for constructed knowledge resides in the arguments and evidence cited in its support by students as well as by texts or teacher; everyone has expertise to contribute
Teacher is responsible for managing students' learning by providing information and leading students through activities and assignments	Teacher and students share responsibility for initiating and guiding learning efforts
Teacher explains, checks for understanding, and judges correctness of students' responses	Teacher acts as discussion leader who poses questions, seeks clarifications, promotes dialogue, helps group recognize areas of consensus and of continuing disagreement
Students memorize or replicate what has been explained or modeled	Students strive to make sense of new input by relating it to their prior knowledge and by collaborating in dialogue with others to coconstruct shared understandings
Discourse emphasizes drill and recitation in response to convergent questions; focus is on eliciting correct answers	Discourse emphasizes reflective discussion of networks of connected knowledge; questions are more divergent but designed to develop understanding of the powerful ideas that anchor these networks; focus is on eliciting students' thinking
Activities emphasize replication of models or applications that require following step-by-step algorithms	Activities emphasize applications to authentic issues and problems that require higher-order thinking
Students work mostly alone, practicing what has been transmitted to them in order to prepare themselves to compete for rewards by reproducing it on demand	Students collaborate by acting as a learning community that constructs shared understandings through sustained dialogue

Situated Learning and Authentic Tasks

Many social constructivists believe that instruction in schools should be modeled as much as possible on the instruction that occurs in natural settings. Schooling brings people together and thus makes the social construction of knowledge possible, but it tends to teach generic knowledge and skills that have been abstracted and removed from the application settings that gave birth to them. Too often, this generic learning is forgotten or remains inert—not easily accessible when needed in out-of-school settings.

Scholars who have studied learning in home and job settings believe that it is a mistake to separate knowing from doing, or what is learned from how it is learned and used (Brown, Collins, & Duguid, 1989; Lave & Wenger, 1991; Rogoff, 1990). They believe that *cognition is situated;* that is, that knowledge is adapted to the settings, purposes, and tasks to which it is applied (and for which it was constructed in the first place). Consequently, they argue, if we want students to learn and retain knowledge in a form that makes it usable for application, we need to make it possible for them to develop the knowledge in the natural setting, using methods and tasks suited to that setting. In this view, the ideal model for schooling is the on-the-job training that occurs as experienced mentors work with novices or apprentices.

Whatever the merits of this notion, there are obvious limits to the degree to which it is feasible to shift significant portions of the school's curriculum from in-school to out-of-school settings. However, the notion of situated cognition has implications for the design of in-school instruction as well. In particular, it implies that we ought to be more conscious of potential applications when we select and plan our teaching of curriculum content, and we should emphasize those applications in presenting the content to students.

Also, as much as possible, we should allow students to learn through engagement in authentic tasks. *Authentic tasks* require using what is being learned for accomplishing the very sorts of life applications that justify the inclusion of this learning in the curriculum in the first place. If it is not possible to engage students in the actual life applications that the curriculum is supposed to prepare them for, then one can at least engage them in realistic simulations of these applications. Examples of authentic activities are listed in Table 10.2. The notion of situated cognition implies that students will need to learn such things as inquiry, critical thinking, and problem solving by engaging in them under realistic conditions. Teachers will have to work within the constraints imposed by students' current readiness and by access to settings and equipment, but they still can engage their students in inquiry into worthwhile and meaningful questions, critical thinking about significant policy issues, and discussion of potential methods of solving real problems.

Scaffolding and Transfer of Responsibility for Managing Learning from Teacher to Learner

Ideas about situated learning and about teaching in the zone of proximal development tend to cluster around the notions of scaffolding and gradual transfer of responsibility for managing learning from the teacher to the student. Instructional

Table 10.2 AUTHENTIC ACTIVITIES

K–3

Math: Apply basic four functions to problems in saving/budgeting money, sharing/dividing treats

Science: Observe and take notes on plant growth and decomposition, events occurring in the class aquarium

Social Studies: Recreate the school day in a nineteenth-century one-room schoolhouse; implement Mini-Society or other economics simulations calling for students to produce, buy, and sell goods and services

Reading: Listen to and discuss story read by teacher, read good children's literature

Writing: Correspond with pen pals, write thank-you notes to classroom visitors

4–6

Math: Develop specifications for a garden or construction project

Science: Monitor air pollution on each of the four sides of the school building, collect and analyze life forms and residues found in a nearby pond

Social Studies: Plan an extended vacation trip, with maps and itinerary; debate whether the American Revolution was justified

Reading: Read genre fiction, discuss and write reactions; learn and apply content-area reading and study skills

Writing: Poems and short essays for self-expression; journals for recording observations and insights

7–12

Math: Apply probabilities to making predictions about the relative effectiveness of alternative strategies for addressing a problem or issue, use algebra for solving compound interest problems to inform decisions about loans and investments

Science: Apply scientific principles to household engineering problems (spot removal, appliance troubleshooting), develop projects for science fairs and displays

Social Studies: Debate current policy issues, simulate legislative budget debates (e.g., acting as state legislators representing districts with different agendas)

Reading: Read and discuss youth theme novels, compare and contrast different authors who work in the same genre or different works by the same author

Writing: Compose short stories, term papers, and other research reports

---

scaffolding is a general term for the task assistance or simplification strategies that teachers might use to bridge the gap between what students are capable of doing on their own and what they are capable of doing with help. Scaffolds are forms of support provided by the teacher (or another student) to help students progress from their current abilities to the intended goal (Rosenshine & Meister, 1992). Like the scaffolds used by house painters, the support provided through scaffolding is temporary, adjustable, and removed when it is no longer needed. Examples of scaffolding include cognitive modeling (in which the teacher demonstrates task performance while articulating the thinking that guides it), prompts or cues that help students move on to the next step when they are temporarily stuck, and questions that help them to diagnose the reasons for errors and develop repair strategies.

Following Wood, Bruner, and Ross (1976), Rogoff (1990) suggested that appropriately scaffolded instruction includes the following six components:

1. Developing student interest in accomplishing the intended goal of the task
2. Demonstrating an idealized version of the act to be performed
3. Simplifying the task by reducing the number of steps required to solve a problem, so that the student can manage certain components and recognize when these are being accomplished successfully
4. Controlling frustration and risk in problem solving
5. Providing feedback that identifies the critical features of discrepancies between what the student has produced and what is required for an ideal solution to a problem
6. Motivating and directing the student's activity sufficiently to maintain continuous pursuit of the goal

Closely associated with the notion of scaffolding is the notion of *gradual transfer of responsibility for managing learning.* Early in the process, the teacher assumes most of the responsibility for structuring and managing learning activities and provides students with a great deal of information, explanation, modeling, or other input. As students develop expertise, however, they can begin to assume responsibility for regulating their own learning by asking questions and by working on increasingly complex applications with increasing degrees of autonomy. The teacher still provides coaching or other scaffolding needed to assist with challenges that students are not yet ready to handle on their own, but this assistance is reduced little by little in response to gradual increases in student readiness to engage in independent and self-regulated learning.

Tharp and Gallimore (1988) described a model of *assisted performance* that involves teaching in the zone of proximal development, scaffolding learning through responsive assistance, and transferring responsibility to the learner as expertise develops. Teacher assistance is contingent on and responsive to the learner's level of performance. The emphasis is on patience and on allowing learners to handle as much as they can on their own and to learn through their mistakes, except where mistakes might be costly or dangerous and thus must be minimized through more direct and controlling forms of instruction.

Tharp and Gallimore (1988) identified six means of providing responsive assistance:

1. Modeling, especially cognitive modeling that includes overt verbalization of strategies
2. Contingency management, especially praise of good performance
3. Providing feedback about the correctness of responses
4. Instructing—telling the student specifically what to do; to be used sparingly
5. Questioning, to stimulate the student to think and communicate about the task, especially if this will produce mental operations that might not be produced otherwise

6. Cognitive structuring—stating principles or generalizations that pull things together and make for better organized representation of the learning

Cognitive structuring may focus on the content being learned or on the learners' cognitive activities. When focused on the content, cognitive structuring provides explanations (e.g., that the expansion of gases that occurs as they are heated during chemistry experiments occurs because molecular activity increases with temperature, or that the next story in the reader is about the dangers and challenges faced by a group of mountain climbers as they work their way up a mountain). When cognitive structuring focuses on the learners' cognitive activity, it provides explanation or reminders of the strategies that students are expected to use (e.g., "So, whenever you come to a new word that you are not sure about, you first look for clues, then put the clues together with what you already know about the word to decide on a meaning, and then check to see if that meaning fits with the rest of the sentence").

Similarly, Collins, Brown, and Newman (1989; see also Collins, Brown, & Holum, 1991) have drawn on ideas about situated cognition and about learning through apprenticeship in the workplace in order to develop the *cognitive apprenticeship* model of schooling. The model includes four important aspects of traditional apprenticeship: modeling, scaffolding, fading, and coaching. The master models task performance for the apprentice, provides coaching and other forms of scaffolding as the apprentice practices portions of the task, and then fades these forms of assistance as the apprentice becomes proficient enough to accomplish tasks independently. Cognitive apprenticeship in the classroom includes these same elements, along with additional ones that are needed because of the more abstract content taught there. The modeling includes thinking out loud in order to make the teacher's cognition perceptible to students, and the teacher asks many questions designed to make student cognition perceptible to the teacher as well. Also, by emphasizing authentic tasks and contexts for learning that make sense to students, teachers attempt to build in some of the task meaningfulness and motivation that are ordinarily built into learning that is situated in the workplace. Finally, because the teacher must teach for transfer, cognitive apprenticeship exposes students to a range of tasks and encourages them to note their common elements and consider their applications to life outside of school.

The emphasis placed here on students becoming more active learners is consistent with the view of classroom management expressed in Chapters 4 and 5. There is a growing consensus that education must include problem solving, integration, and elaboration of meaning (Good, McCaslin, & Reys, 1992; McCaslin & Good, 1992). If students are to become active learners, teachers must align management and instructional goals so that students are consistently expected to engage in appropriate problem-solving behavior.

Summary and Implications

Recent research on teaching school subjects for understanding, appreciation, and application has begun to move beyond the basics implied in the term *active teaching* in order to identify the subtleties involved in the best teaching. Along with ideas drawn from educators' writings about curriculum and instruction, these studies have been informed by the writings of psychologists and cognitive scientists on thought and language, cognitive development, situated cognition, and the social construction of knowledge. Different authors emphasize different theoretical rationales and instructional methods, but most of their ideas are compatible with one another and with notions about active teaching developed from earlier research. Compatibilities are especially evident when instructional goals are taken into account and it is recognized that different goals call for somewhat different approaches to curriculum and instruction.

The notion of teaching for understanding implies helping students construct connected networks of knowledge by relating new content to existing knowledge in ways that allow them to appreciate the connections and to access the knowledge for use in appropriate application situations. Students develop new knowledge through a process of active construction in which they develop and integrate a network of associations linking the new content to preexisting knowledge and beliefs anchored in concrete experience. Thus, teaching involves inducing conceptual change, not infusing knowledge into a vacuum. To the extent that students' preexisting beliefs about a topic are accurate, they facilitate learning and provide a natural starting place for teaching. To the extent that students harbor misconceptions, however, these misconceptions will need to be corrected so that they do not persist and distort the new learning.

When the new learning is complex, the construction of meaning required to develop clear understanding of it takes time and is facilitated by the interactive discourse that occurs during lessons and activities. Clear explanations and modeling from the teacher are important, but so are opportunities to answer questions about the content, discuss or debate its meanings and implications, and apply it in problem-solving or decision-making contexts. These activities allow students to process the content actively and "make it their own" by paraphrasing it in their own words, exploring its relationships to other knowledge and to past experience, appreciating the insights it provides, and identifying its implications for personal decision making or action. The teacher provides whatever structuring and scaffolding the students need in order to accomplish the goals of learning activities successfully, but this assistance is faded as student expertise develops. Ultimately, students engage in independent and self-regulated learning.

RESEARCH ON TEACHING FOR UNDERSTANDING

Research on teaching school subjects for understanding and higher-order applications is still in its infancy, but it already has produced successful experimental programs in most subjects. Even more encouraging, analyses of these programs have identified a set of principles and practices that is common to most if not all of them (Anderson, 1989; Brophy, 1989, 1992; Prawat, 1989). These common elements, which might be considered components in a model or theory describing good subject-matter teaching, include the following:

1. The curriculum is designed to equip students with knowledge, skills, values, and dispositions that they will find useful both inside and outside of school.

2. Instructional goals emphasize developing student expertise within an application context and with emphasis on conceptual understanding of knowledge and self-regulated application of skills.

3. The curriculum balances breadth with depth by addressing limited content but developing this content sufficiently to foster conceptual understanding.

4. The content is organized around a limited set of powerful ideas (basic understandings and principles).

5. The teacher's role is not just to present information but also to scaffold and respond to students' learning efforts.

6. The students' role is not just to absorb or copy input but also to actively make sense and construct meaning.

7. Students' prior knowledge about the topic is elicited and used as a starting place for instruction, which builds on accurate prior knowledge and stimulates conceptual change if necessary.

8. Activities and assignments feature tasks that call for problem solving or critical thinking, not just memory or reproduction.

9. Higher-order thinking skills are not taught as a separate skills curriculum. Instead, they are developed in the process of teaching subject-matter knowledge within application contexts that call for students to relate what they are learning to their lives outside of school by thinking critically or creatively about it or by using it to solve problems or make decisions.

10. The teacher creates a social environment in the classroom that could be described as a learning community featuring discourse or dialogue designed to promote understanding.

Teaching for understanding requires "complete" lessons that are carried through to include higher-order applications of content, which means that the breadth of content addressed must be limited in order to allow for more in-depth teaching of the content that is included. Unfortunately, both state and district curriculum guidelines (which often feature long lists of knowledge items and subskills to be "covered") and typical curriculum packages supplied by educational publishers (which respond to these state and district guidelines by emphasizing breadth over depth of coverage) discourage in-depth teaching of *limited* content. Teachers who teach for understanding and higher-order applications of subject-matter content both (1) limit what they try to teach by focusing on what they see as most important and omitting or skimming over the rest, and (2) structure what they do teach around important ideas and elaborate it considerably beyond what is in the text.

Besides presenting information and modeling skills application, such teachers structure a great deal of discourse surrounding the content. They use questions to stimulate students to process and reflect on the content, recognize relationships among and implications of its key ideas, think critically about it, and use it in problem-solving, decision-making, or other higher-order applications. Such discourse is not mere factual review or recitation featuring rapid-fire questioning and short answers, but instead is sustained and thoughtful examination of a small number of related topics, in which students are invited to develop explanations, make predictions, debate alternative approaches to problems, or otherwise consider the implications or applications of the content. Some of the questions admit to a range of defensible answers, and some invite discussion or debate (e.g., concerning the relative merits of alternative suggestions for solving problems). In addition to asking questions and providing feedback, the teacher encourages students to explain or elaborate on their answers or to comment on classmates' answers, and also capitalizes on "teachable moment" opportunities offered by students' comments or questions (by elaborating on the original instruction, correcting misconceptions, calling attention to implications that have not been appreciated yet, and so on).

Skills are taught holistically within the context of applying the knowledge content, rather than being practiced in isolation. Thus, most practice of reading skills is embedded within lessons involving reading and interpreting extended text, most practice of writing skills is embedded within activities calling for authentic writing, and most practice of mathematics skills is embedded within problem-solving applications. Also, skills are taught as strategies adapted to particular purposes and situations, with emphasis on modeling the cognitive and metacognitive components involved and explaining the necessary conditional knowledge (of when and why the skills would be used). Thus, students receive instruction in when and how to apply skills, not just get opportunities to use them.

Activities, assignments, and evaluation methods incorporate a much greater range of tasks than the familiar workbooks and curriculum-embedded tests that focus on recognition and recall of facts, definitions, and fragmented skills. Curriculum strands or units are planned to accomplish gradual transfer of responsibility for managing learning activities from the teacher to the students in response to growing student expertise on the topic. Plans for lessons and activities are guided by the overall curriculum goals (phrased in terms of student capabilities to be developed), and evaluation efforts concentrate on assessing the progress that has been made toward accomplishing these goals.

SUBJECT-SPECIFIC EXAMPLES

In discussing what is involved in teaching school subjects for understanding, appreciation, and application, we have so far concentrated on generic aspects that cut across the various school subjects. In the following sections, we provide examples showing how these principles have been embodied in programs developed to foster such teaching in particular subjects.

Reading

We recommend the report *Becoming a Nation of Readers* (Anderson et al., 1985) for its integration of research-based principles for teaching reading for understanding and application. The report calls for teaching reading as a sense-making process of extracting meaning from texts that are read for information or enjoyment (not just to get reading practice). Thus, the emphasis is on reading and interpreting text rather than on practicing fragmented skills. Important skills such as decoding, blending, and noting main ideas are taught and practiced, but primarily within the context of application (reading for meaning). There is considerable explicit instruction and modeling of skills currently being phased in, but such skills instruction is phased out as students develop expertise. Phonics and blending, for example, receive a great deal of emphasis in the first grade but are phased out by the end of the second grade.

Activities and assignments feature more reading of extended text and less time spent with skills worksheets. Students often work cooperatively in pairs or small groups, reading to one another or discussing the meanings or implications of the text. Rather than being restricted to the somewhat artificial stories found in basal reading series, students often read genuine literature written to provide information or pleasure to the reader (children's literature, poetry, biography, nonfictional material about the physical or social world).

Most current innovations in reading instruction feature attempts to incorporate these principles. The principles apply at least as much to instruction of disadvantaged students or to remedial instruction of students having difficulty learning to read as they do instruction of other students (Knapp, 1995). They are featured prominently in the KEEP program that was developed to meet the needs of native Hawaiian children who previously had difficulty learning to read (Au et al., 1985; Au & Carroll, in press; Tharp & Gallimore, 1988), as well as in the Reading Recovery program used to tutor first graders who have failed to learn to read when taught by traditional methods (Anderson & Armbruster, 1990; Hiebert, 1994; Lyons, Pinnell, & DeFord, 1993). The principles are also embedded in several theoretically derived and empirically validated experimental programs.

Paris, Cross, and Lipson (1984) developed Informed Strategies for Learning (ISL), a program designed to increase awareness and use of effective reading strategies. The program contains 14 weekly modules that show students what is involved in using each strategy, when to use it, and what benefits can be expected from using it. Students first observe models using the strategies and then use the strategies themselves with guidance and feedback from the teacher. The strategies are explained and illustrated using metaphors familiar to the students. For example, a lesson on preassessment to discover clues to the topic, length, and difficulty of a passage uses the metaphor "Be a reading detective." Similarly, comprehension-monitoring strategies are taught using analogies to traffic signs such as "Stop—say the meaning in your own words," or "Dead end—go back and reread the parts you don't understand." ISL has been used successfully in third- and fifth-grade classes (Cross & Paris, 1988).

Hansen and Pearson (1983) improved fourth graders' reading comprehension using a program that featured strategy training and practice in answering questions. Strategy training was conducted through story introductions in which students were asked to relate their prior knowledge about situations like those depicted in the upcoming story, then predict what the protagonist would do. They wrote their prior knowledge answers on one sheet of paper and their predictions on another, then combined the two to demonstrate that reading involves combining what one knows with what is in a text. Following these preparations, students read the story and compared their predictions with what actually occurred.

The other part of the treatment involved changing the nature of the questions asked following story reading. Typically, students are asked about 80 percent factual questions and only 20 percent inferential questions. For this study, the students were asked only inferential questions concerning such issues as the characters' motives or the larger moral or meaning that the story was meant to communicate. This combination of strategy training and inferential questions improved the experimental students' reading comprehension over that of control students taught in traditional ways. The treatment was especially effective with poor readers.

Duffy, Roehler, and their colleagues (Duffy, 1993; Duffy & Roehler, 1987, 1989; Duffy, Roehler, & Herrmann, 1988; Duffy et al., 1987) have shown that poor readers in the intermediate grades learn to read with better comprehension and increased awareness of their strategies when they are provided with *explicit instruction* in these comprehension strategies. The strategies are the same ones taught typically, such as identifying the main idea in a paragraph or using the dictionary, but they are taught much more explicitly and thoroughly than usual. Teachers learn to explain the nature of each strategy in detail, tell when and why it is used, model by verbalizing the mental processes that occur when using it, point out sequential aspects and salient features of these processes, and then provide students with opportunities to use the strategy and see its effectiveness for themselves.

During the practice and application phases, teachers provide *responsive elaboration* on their original instruction. That is, they tailor their feedback to the specific misunderstandings that emerge during the reading and discussion of text (e.g., failure to use a strategy when it was applicable suggests the need to clarify when and why the strategy is useful, whereas failure to use a strategy correctly suggests the need for additional modeling). Instruction continues until students not only can use the strategy effectively to make sense of what they read but also can explain when and why the strategy should be used.

Palincsar and Brown (1984) developed a *reciprocal teaching* method for teaching four comprehension-fostering and comprehension-monitoring strategies to poor readers: summarizing, questioning, clarifying, and predicting. In reciprocal teaching, the teacher does most of the initial modeling and explaining but gradually turns over these responsibilities to the students. Eventually, students take turns acting as the teacher and leading small-group discussions of texts. To begin, the teacher notes the title and asks for predictions about the content of the passage. Then the group reads the first segment silently and the student "teacher" asks a question about it, summarizes it, and then offers a prediction or asks for clarification if appropriate. If necessary, the adult teacher provides guidance by prompting, "What questions do you think a teacher might ask here?"; instructing, "Remember, a summary is a shortened version; it doesn't include detail"; or modifying the activity, "If you are having a hard time thinking of a question, why don't you summarize first?" The adult teacher also provides feedback about the quality and specificity of questions, the logic involved in making predictions, and so on.

The following dialogue (from Palincsar & Brown, 1989) illustrates reciprocal teaching as implemented in a first-grade classroom.

TEACHER (*Reading from text*):   The pipefish change their color and movements to blend with their surroundings. For example, pipefish that live among green plants change their color to a shade of green to match the plants.

CLAIRE (*The child leading the discussion*): One question that I had about this paragraph is: "What is special about the way that the pipefish looks?"

KEITH (*Clarifying*):   Do you mean the way that it is green?

ANDY (*Elaborating*):   It's not just that it's green; it's that it's the same color as the plants around it, all around it.

CLAIRE (*Resuming*):   Yes. That's it. My summary is this part tells how the pipefish looks and that it looks like what is around it. My prediction is that this is about its enemies and how it protects itself and who its enemies are.

MONTY: They also talked about how the pipefish moves . . .

KEITH: It sways back and forth.

ANDY: Along with the other plants.

TEACHER: What do we call it when something looks like and acts like something else? The way that the walkingstick was yesterday? We clarified this word when we talked about the walkingstick.

ANGEL: Mimic.

TEACHER: That's right. We said, we would say, that the pipefish mimics the . . .

SEVERAL STUDENTS: Plants.

TEACHER: OK! Let's see if Claire's predictions come true.

Over time, as students become more familiar with reciprocal teaching activities, the dialogue becomes less routinized and the strategies are used in more flexible ways. The teacher turns over more responsibility for leading and sustaining the dialogue to the students, gradually engaging less in modeling and instruction but more in coaching students' participation in the discussion.

Reciprocal teaching has produced sizable gains in reading comprehension in several studies (Kelly, Moore, & Tuck, 1994; Palincsar & Brown, 1989; Rosenshine & Meister, 1994). It combines key elements of teaching for understanding and self-regulated learning (modeling of strategic application of skills, scaffolded instruction that gradually releases increasing responsibility to the students themselves) with provision of opportunity for students to learn cooperatively in small groups.

Strategy training in reading is not just for elementary students. It can be helpful to secondary students too if it is focused on strategies needed for accomplishing tasks encountered at their grade levels. Dimino et al. (1990) illustrated this in a study comparing two methods of improving low-achieving ninth graders' comprehension of short stories. Compared to a group taught using traditional basal instruction, students taught to analyze stories using strategies based on story grammar did significantly better on several outcome measures. These students learned to analyze stories by identifying the primary problem or conflict, the main character, the character's attempts to solve the problem or conflict, the resolution of these efforts, twists in the plot, information about the character's reactions to the depicted events, and the overall theme suggested. Andre and Anderson (1978–1979) trained high school students to generate questions about the main points of a text as they studied it. These students learned more than a group who simply read and reread the text and also a group who were directed to ask themselves questions but were not trained in strategies for doing so.

Cook and Mayer (1988) showed that training in strategies for content-area reading and text study can significantly improve learning even in college students. The students they studied initially had difficulty in sorting passages from chemistry texts into categories on the basis of their organizational structures (e.g., generalizations supported by examples or elaboration, enumeration of lists, linear sequences, classification systems, comparison and contrast passages). After training in strategies for recognizing these text structures and using this information to aid study, trained students showed considerably improved recall of highly conceptual information and ability to use what they had learned when responding to application questions.

Michael Pressley and his colleagues have analyzed and synthesized a great many studies of training students in strategies for improving reading comprehension. Pressley et al. (1989) concluded that research support is particularly strong for the following strategies: summarizing the gist of a paragraph or set of paragraphs, emphasizing the main ideas; constructing images to represent visually what the text is describing verbally; using mnemonic devices to help remember the meanings of new words; generating story grammar analyses or constructing story maps for narrative passages; generating questions to ask oneself about the meanings and implications of the text; attempting to answer any questions that have been included in the text as aids to checking for understanding; and activating relevant prior knowledge by making predictions about the text and by comparing depicted events with one's own experiences.

Pressley and his colleagues developed what they called transactional methods to teach students to become "good strategy users" through classroom discourse and provision of support and guidance as students engage in content-area reading and study (Pressley et al., 1992). They also illustrated ways in which good strategy instruction incorporates many of the methods advocated by social constructivists, even though these approaches are often viewed as quite different or even contradictory (Pressley, Harris & Marks, 1992). They argued that good strategy instruction differs from social constructivist recommendations in its emphasis on explicit statement, modeling, and explanation of strategies, but that otherwise it emphasizes classroom discourse, scaffolded and responsive assistance to students, and related constructivist notions.

Many students appear to develop efficient reading and study strategies on their own and do not need much explicit instruction or practice, but many need help from teachers. Low-achieving students in particular stand to benefit considerably from instruction and guidance in self-regulated reading and study strategies. For more information, see Dole et al. (1990), Paris, Wasik, and Turner (1991), or Pressley and Beard El-Dinary (1993).

Writing

When writing is taught for understanding and application, the instructional goals focus on teaching students to use writing for organizing and communicating their thinking to particular audiences for particular purposes, and skills are taught as strategies for accomplishing these goals. There is explicit instruction concerning when, why, and how to use the skills, and this is elaborated later during responsive feedback to students' composition efforts. Key basic skills such as printing and cursive writing are taught explicitly and practiced to mastery, but a great deal of this practice is embedded within writing activities that call for composition and communication of meaningful content. Composition activities emphasize "authentic" writing intended to be read for meaning and response, not mere copying or exercises focused on displaying skills for the teacher (Applebee, 1986; Bereiter & Scardamalia, 1987; Calkins, 1986; Florio-Ruane & Lensmire, 1989; Graves, 1983; Rosaen, 1989).

Thus, composition is taught, not as an impersonal exercise in writing a draft to conform to the formal requirements of a genre, but as communication and personal craftsmanship calling for developing and revising an outline, developing and revising successive drafts for meaning, and then polishing into final form. The emphasis is on the cognitive and metacognitive aspects of developing compositions, not just on writing mechanics and editing.

In helping students plan and work through successive drafts, teachers concentrate first on purpose, audience, and content and organization of the ideas to be communicated, and only later on the fine points of grammar and spelling. Writing is done for a variety of purposes and audiences, so that students learn to consider not just what they want to say but how their message will need to be phrased if it is to have the intended effects on the intended audience. Also, writing is used as a method of learning school subjects, through assignments calling for students to analyze, synthesize, evaluate, or in other ways use higher-order thinking to respond to what they have been learning in science, social studies, literature, or other subjects.

One experimental program that embodies many of these principles is the Cognitive Strategies in Writing program developed by Englert and Raphael (1989). In addition to providing initial explicit explanation and modeling and follow-up responsive elaboration concerning writing goals and strategies, this program offers scaffolded assistance to students' composition efforts. Students are provided with sets of questions to guide their planning, outline forms, and suggestions for recording and organizing ideas on "think sheets."

For example, a think sheet to assist students in planning their compositions asks them to respond to the following questions: Who am I writing for? Why am I writing this? What do I already know about my topic? and How do I group my ideas? To further assist planning, the think sheet contains numbered lines under the "What do I already know about my topic?" question (so that students can enter separate ideas on separate lines), as well as boxes with lines underneath them under the "How do I group my ideas?" question (so that students can enter group labels in the boxes and then list examples on the lines under the boxes). Similarly, a think sheet for organizing information for comparison and contrast writing contains boxes for identifying the dimensions on which comparisons will be made and then separately listing the ways in which the things to be compared are alike and different.

Mathematics

The National Council of Teachers of Mathematics (1989) has released guidelines for mathematics instruction that emphasize teaching for understanding and higher-order applications. Goals focus on developing students' mathematical *power*, a term that refers to their abilities to explore, conjecture, and reason logically, as well as to use a variety of mathematical models effectively to solve nonroutine problems. The notion of developing mathematical power is based on the recognition that mathematics is more than a collection of concepts and skills to be mastered; it includes methods of investigating and reasoning, means of communication, and notions of context.

An ideal program would emphasize teaching of mathematical concepts, not just mathematical operations. Both the concepts and the operations would be embedded in networks of knowledge structured around key ideas and taught within an application context right from the beginning. Compared with what is typically done now, students would spend less time working individually on computation skills sheets and more time participating in teacher-led discourse concerning the meanings and implications of mathematical concepts and their application to problem solving. Teachers would explain and model the mathematical reasoning used to address classes of problems, then stimulate students to engage in such reasoning themselves. In addition to well-structured exercises that merely require them to recognize problem types and then apply familiar formulas, students would often be exposed to the kinds of ill-structured problems that occur in real life and require us to discover and invent ways of framing and solving the problem. Often such applications can be approached in many different ways, thus providing opportunities for students to examine potential solution strategies. Teacher-led discourse surrounding such applications would involve sustained, thoughtful examination of a small number of related questions rather than fast-paced recitation of number facts. It would feature a great deal of higher-order mathematical reasoning in generating and debating ideas about how the problems might be approached.

One experimental approach that embodies many of these principles is Cognitively Guided Instruction (CGI), a program developed by Fennema, Carpenter, and Peterson (1989) for increasing primary grade teachers' effectiveness in introducing young children to mathematics. CGI places more emphasis on word problems than on computational practice. The problems emphasize applications to students' current lives, and teachers elicit and foster discussion of students' own invented strategies for solving such problems. Teachers learn that problems that can be solved through addition and subtraction fall into eight basic types and that children possess intuitive knowledge about and strategies for solving each problem type that can be used as a starting point for instruction. Problems are taken up in the order in which children naturally develop interest in them, and the students are encouraged to discover knowledge and invent strategies in addition to learning from teacher explanation and modeling. Evaluation data have revealed that students in CGI classrooms showed significant advantages in problem solving and mathematical confidence compared with students in control classrooms, with no loss in computation skills (Carpenter et al., 1989; Villasenor & Kepner, 1993).

Two other approaches to introducing mathematics in the primary grades feature similar philosophies and have achieved similar results to those described for CGI. Hiebert and Wearne (1992) provided first graders with "conceptually based" instruction on place value and on addition and subtraction, using methods reflecting the guidelines published by the National Council of Teachers of Mathematics (1989). Compared with students who were taught the same content using more traditional methods, the experimental students showed more understanding of key concepts and ability to apply the strategies they had learned. Cobb and his colleagues (Cobb et al., 1991; Wood, Cobb, & Yackel, 1990) drew on the same principles and on social constructivist ideas to develop a method of teaching mathematics to second graders that emphasized teacher-led discussion of alternative suggestions about solving problems. Compared with students taught more conventionally, the experimental students developed higher levels of conceptual understanding in mathematics as well as a preference for collaborating with others to achieve understanding rather than competing with them for rewards.

As with the CGI program, students taught using the Hiebert and Wearne program and the Cobb et al. program not only outperformed comparison students on measures of conceptual understanding and higher-order applications, but also equaled or exceeded their performance on arithmetic computations, even though the experimental programs placed much more emphasis on problem solving than on computation practice. Soled (1990) achieved similar results with seventh-grade science students and ninth-grade mathematics students. Thus, within limits at least, the gains in understanding, appreciation, and strategic application of skills that can be achieved through instruction that emphasizes authentic applications over isolated skills practice apparently can be accomplished without a corresponding reduction in skills development.

Lampert (1989) has emphasized teaching for understanding and developing mathematical power in the intermediate grades. She teaches not just skills but a language to use in describing mathematical phenomena, connects mathematical operations and relations to more familiar and concrete operations and relationships, and guides students' construction of meaning concerning mathematical symbols and operations so that it centers on key ideas drawn from the discipline. Lampert instructs actively, but with stress on processes, relationships, multiple methods, and chances for students to evaluate and discuss proposed solutions to problems. Group inquiry featuring dialogue or argument is emphasized over teacher presentations, and discussion focuses on the relative merits of alternative suggestions for approaching problems rather than on finding a "right answer."

Lampert identified five keys to her approach: (1) involving learners with phenomena that feel problematic to them, so that finding solutions *matters* to them; (2) using multiple representations of concepts to ensure that students understand their meanings; (3) emphasizing dialogue (including argument, not just discourse) as the vehicle for joint establishment of meaning; (4) diagnosing students' levels of understanding and needs for corrective explanation as the dialogue progresses, and providing the needed instruction; and (5) teaching the students to become willing and able to collaborate in solving problems and constructing new knowledge.

Constructivist approaches to instruction call for considerable teacher knowledge of subject matter and pedagogical strategies, as well as a great deal of on-the-spot decision making about how to respond to students and whether or not to pursue the issues that they raise. For case excerpts and information about how teachers plan and carry out such instruction in mathematics, see Ball (1993), Fennema et al. (1993), or Lampert (1992).

These approaches to mathematics teaching that have been developed recently in the United States have much in common with methods emphasized in Japan and China (Stigler & Stevenson, 1991). Mathematics classes in these countries consist of coherent lessons that are presented in a thoughtful, relaxed, and nonauthoritarian manner. They are oriented toward problem solving rather than rote mastery of facts and procedures (Perry, VanderStoep, & Yu, 1993). Teachers use many different types of representational materials and often rely on students as sources of information. They lead the class in discussions of problems, acting as knowledgeable guides who seek to stimulate students to produce, explain, and evaluate potential solutions rather than as prime dispensers of information and arbiters of what is correct (Fernandez, Yoshida, & Stigler, 1992; Lappan & Ferrini-Mundy, 1993; Wheatley, 1992).

Science

Blumenfeld (1992) drew on case studies of fifth- and sixth-grade science teaching to identify practices that promote student thoughtfulness in learning science. She listed the following as characteristics of the more successful teachers:

Opportunities: Topic coverage focuses on a few key ideas developed in depth; learning activities relate to these main ideas, focus on application rather than mere verification, and involve engagement in meaningful problems relating to children's experience or to real events; the products produced through these activities also relate to the main ideas and require processing at higher cognitive levels.

Instruction: Clear presentations highlight main points and critical information, take into account students' prior knowledge, and use examples, analogies, and metaphors; these presentations build connections by linking with prior knowledge, making relationships among new ideas evident, focusing on similarities and differences among ideas, and showing their application; they include scaffolding in the form of modeling of learning and of metacognitive and problem-solving strategies.

Press (use of questions and feedback): Questions focus attention on main ideas; teacher checks understanding by asking comprehension questions, asking for summarization, asking for application, focusing on content rather than procedures, adding higher-level questions to worksheets, and asking for alternative representations of content; teacher draws out student reasoning by probing, asking for justification or clarification, and elaborating on student responses; teacher uses errors to diagnose and clear up misunderstandings; teacher encourages making of connections by asking about relationships of key ideas to prior knowledge, relationships among new ideas, how an activity's procedures relate to its content, and how the results of the activity illustrate main ideas; teacher ensures widespread responding by calling on many students, using debate, and using voting or asking who agrees or disagrees with a statement.

Support: Teacher helps students to accomplish tasks by breaking down problems, simplifying procedures, modeling procedures, or providing models and examples; teacher promotes independence, self-regulation, and cooperation by encouraging students to work together, providing time for planning, asking about students' individual contributions to group work, and asking students whether they agree or disagree with their group's conclusions.

Evaluation: Teacher holds students accountable for understanding by adding questions to worksheets that focus on the meanings of key ideas; evaluation focuses on learning rather than performance, features recognition of individual contributions and improvement, and deemphasizes grades and correct answers.

A series of four articles published in 1994 in the *Elementary School Journal* described the implementation of project-based instruction in middle school science classes. The lessons learned from this work are summarized by Blumenfeld et al. (1994).

Anderson and Roth (1989) have developed an approach to teaching science that emphasizes depth over breadth and focuses on the teaching of powerful ideas in ways that encourage students not only to learn them with understanding but to recognize their value for describing, explaining, making predictions about, or gaining control over real-world systems or events. Through real-life examples and involvement of students in discussion of applications, their approach aims to make science content more meaningful to students by connecting it with their experience-based knowledge and beliefs. The focus is on producing *conceptual change,* building on accurate current knowledge and correcting misconceptions.

Students often find science harder to learn than other subjects. In part, this is because science courses typically require them to learn a great many new concepts very quickly (the average science course introduces more new vocabulary than the average foreign language course!). An additional problem, however, is that students typically enter these courses with misconceptions about the content they will be studying. For example, most middle-school science textbooks contain units on plants that emphasize their roles as food producers via the photosynthesis process. Students typically enter these courses knowing little about photosynthesis, but a great deal about food, especially food for people. They know that (1) food is something that you consume or eat, and it is taken in from the outside environment; (2) there are many different kinds of food.

These beliefs may produce distorted understandings if they lead students to assume that, like people, plants must take in food from their environment in many different forms. However, plants make their own food. Neither soil nor water nor fertilizers (despite their sometimes being called "plant food") are taken in as food or consumed for energy. Nor do plants take in any other form of food. Their only source of food is that which they manufacture themselves through the photosynthesis process. They transform light energy from the sun into chemical potential energy stored in food and available for use both by the plant and by animals. The matter that they take in during this process (carbon dioxide, water, and soil minerals) is not food because it is not a source of energy. Students must go through a process of conceptual change if they are to attain understanding of photosynthesis and the food production function of plants. They must abandon their assumptions about the metabolic similarities between plants and humans and restructure their thinking about the nature of food (focusing on the scientific definition of food as potential energy for metabolism).

Unless misconceptions are corrected, they are likely to persist and distort new learning. Unfortunately, neither curriculum writers nor teachers typically are very aware of common misconceptions that students are likely to harbor about scientific content, so that the instruction they provide not only fails to confront these misconceptions directly but often is presented in such general or imprecise terms that students can interpret the new input as consistent with their existing misconceptions (Anderson & Smith, 1987).

For example, Smith and Anderson (1984) found that less than a quarter of students had dropped misconceptions about plants as producers of food and acquired the correct scientific conceptions following a unit of instruction on photosynthesis. Analyses of the instruction documented ways in which students' misconceptions affected their interpretations of what they were learning.

One crucial experiment involved growing plants in the light and in the dark. To set the stage for an explanation of photosynthesis, students were to observe that the plants in the dark would begin to grow at first but then wilt. The scientific explanation for this is that the plants in the dark die because they cannot engage in photosynthesis without light, and photosynthesis is their only source of food once food stored in their seeds is used up. However, the students' misconceptions caused them to interpret the experiment differently. Because they assumed that plants take in water, minerals, and other "food" from the soil, they saw no connection between the experimental findings and the question of where plants get their food. They interpreted the results as showing that plants need light in order to stay green and healthy (for reasons that they were not very clear about), but they missed the point that the plants were dying of starvation because they could no longer produce food through the photosynthesis process (which requires sunlight).

None of the 14 teachers was very successful in getting students to abandon their misconceptions in favor of scientific conceptions. *Activity-driven teachers* focused on the activities to be carried out (textbook assignments, demonstrations, experiments, etc.). These teachers seemed to think that students would learn automatically if they engaged in these activities. However, the teachers often unknowingly modified or deleted crucial aspects of the program in ways that made it difficult if not impossible for the students to discover the intended concepts.

Didactic teachers presented information directly to the students and regarded the text as a repository of knowledge to be taught. They did not seem to be aware of student misconceptions and thus did not see a need to be certain that the students had interpreted the information as intended. Also, because these teachers did not question students in ways that would allow them to express their own thinking, the teachers denied themselves the opportunity to become aware of students' misconceptions.

Discovery-oriented teachers tried to avoid telling answers to their students and instead encouraged them to develop their own ideas about the results of the plant-growing experiment. These teachers did not realize that the program they were using, although described as a discovery program, calls for direct instruction concerning certain concepts, including photosynthesis. Also, rather than question students in ways that would challenge their misconceptions and lead them to consider specific theoretical issues, the teachers merely invited students to interpret their own observations in their own ways. Unfortunately, most students used their *misconceptions* as the basis for interpreting the experiments.

The teachers failed to develop understanding because they failed to surface and correct students' misconceptions. Posner et al. (1982) have suggested that four conditions must be satisfied if students are to be induced to change their understandings of key concepts: (1) Dissatisfaction with existing concepts must be induced, (2) the new concepts must be intelligible, (3) the new concepts must be initially plausible, and (4) the new concepts must appear fruitful.

Anderson and Roth (1989) have developed a conceptual-change teaching approach designed to accomplish these goals. Two general features of the approach are (1) a curricular commitment to teaching limited content for understanding rather than to covering a wide range of content superficially, and (2) recognition that teaching for conceptual change requires an array of teaching strategies used flexibly in response to students' needs. These strategies all share an important characteristic, however: They engage students in conceptual change sense-making by involving them in actively struggling with ideas rather than just witnessing the teacher's performance.

The process begins by adjusting the curriculum. In contrast to typical textbook treatments, Anderson and Roth's treatments omit much of the technical vocabulary and detail—all that can be omitted without sacrificing much explanatory power. Their materials on photosynthesis, for example, do not present the scientific formula for photosynthesis or discuss the role of chlorophyll, because these are not seen as crucial elements for developing understanding of the process. Instead, the materials are developed around the central problem of "food" for plants: What is "food" for plants and how is it similar to and different from food for people and animals? The unit begins by asking students to define food and food for plants and to respond to a problem. This provides the teacher with information about students' conceptions and makes the students more aware of these conceptions.

Next, students are given explanations about different ways of defining food, including the scientific definition of food as energy-containing matter. Then the students are asked to address questions that give them a chance to use this new definition of food to explain everyday phenomena (Is water food? Juice? Vitamin pills? Can you live on vitamin pills alone? Why or why not?).

Throughout the unit, students use this definition of food to analyze experimental observations of plants, think about similarities and differences between plants and animals, distinguish materials taken into plants from materials made by the plants during photosynthesis, and distinguish between energy-containing and non-energy-containing materials that people consume. These activities encourage students to make connections between their own ideas and scientific concepts, as well as to use their newly structured conceptions to make predictions and to develop more satisfying explanations of familiar everyday phenomena.

Anderson and Roth (1989) speak of creating learning communities in which teacher and students work together to develop and use scientific knowledge. When operating most successfully, these learning communities feature three kinds of activities. First, the teacher establishes problems that engage students in scientific thinking. Instruction begins with questions that elicit students' reasoning about the topics they will be studying. This activates prior knowledge and helps make the students aware of its limitations, provides diagnostic information to the teacher, and engages the teacher and students in dialogue about commonly understood issues. In the photosynthesis unit, for example, students are asked at the outset to (1) write down their ideas about how plants get food, (2) write down their ideas about what kind of food plants use, and (3) draw pictures on a diagram of a plant to show how they think food moves inside the plant. At the end of the unit, the students reread what they had written and describe how their ideas have changed.

A second feature is modeling and coaching through scaffolded tasks and dialogue. The teacher models by showing how scientific knowledge can be used to solve problems, then provides problem-solving opportunities. The students' initial attempts are scaffolded through simplification or clarification of tasks and through classroom dialogues in which teacher and students listen carefully and respond to one another, sometimes critically but in ways that reflect respectful attention to the speaker's ideas. In the photosynthesis unit, for example, students are asked at several points to answer sets of questions that require them to make predictions and explanations about plants. Scaffolding is provided via reminders of key ideas that need to be kept in mind or provision of chart outlines to help students make key comparisons (e.g., between food for plants and food for people).

The third feature is student work that leads to independent use of scientific knowledge and integration with scientific ideas developed in other contexts. As students develop expertise, they are encouraged to work more independently to describe, explain, make predictions about, or exert control over scientific phenomena in everyday life.

The work of Anderson and Roth (1989) is representative of recent trends in science education that place greater emphasis on eliciting students' prior knowledge (including misconceptions) when introducing topics and then developing the topics through social constructivist teaching. A great deal has been learned in recent years about the kinds of misconceptions that students develop in various areas of science (Glynn, Yeany, & Britton, 1991; Novak, 1987) and about addressing these through conceptual change teaching (Roth, 1990). For information about programs and techniques that have been used at various elementary and secondary grade levels, see Appleton (1993), Driver et al. (1994), Hand and Treagust (1991),

Minstrell (1989), Neale, Smith, and Johnson (1990), Palincsar, Anderson, and David (1993), Shapiro (1994), and White (1992).

Social Studies

Newmann (1990, 1992) has conducted research on social studies teaching that is built around his conception of higher-order thinking. He defines higher-order thinking as challenging students to interpret, analyze, or manipulate information in response to a question or problem that cannot be resolved through routine application of previously learned knowledge. In order to meet such higher-order thinking challenges successfully, students need a combination of (1) in-depth knowledge of content, (2) skills in processing information, and (3) attitudes or dispositions of reflectiveness.

Instruction is organized to offer depth on a few related topics rather than breadth in covering a great many topics, and activities encourage students to go beyond gathering information in order to participate in disciplined inquiry by scrutinizing arguments for logical consistency, distinguishing between relevant and irrelevant information and between factual claims and value judgments, using metaphor and analogy to represent problems and solutions, developing and defending positions by referring to relevant information, and making reasoned decisions. These activities both develop and reflect a set of student dispositions that together constitute *thoughtfulness:* a persistent desire that claims be supported by reasons (and that the reasons themselves be scrutinized), a tendency to be reflective by taking time to think problems through rather than acting impulsively or automatically accepting the views of others, a curiosity to explore new questions, and a flexibility to entertain alternative and original solutions to problems.

Newmann identified six key indicators of thoughtfulness observed in high school social studies classes:

1. Classroom interaction focuses on sustained examination of a few topics rather than superficial coverage of many.
2. Interactions are characterized by substantive coherence and continuity.
3. Students are given sufficient time to think before being required to answer questions.
4. The teacher presses students to clarify or justify their assertions, rather than accepting and reinforcing them indiscriminately.
5. The teacher models the characteristics of a thoughtful person (showing interest in students' ideas and their suggestions for solving problems, modeling problem-solving processes rather than just giving answers, acknowledging the difficulties involved in gaining a clear understanding of problematic topics).
6. Students generate original and unconventional ideas in the course of the interaction.

Thoughtfulness scores based on these scales distinguished classrooms that featured sustained and thoughtful teacher-student discourse not only from classrooms that featured lecture, recitation, and seatwork, but also from classrooms in which teachers emphasized discussion but did not foster much thoughtfulness (because they skipped from topic to topic too quickly or accepted students' contributions uncritically). Other noteworthy findings were that

1. Teachers with high thoughtfulness scores tended to make writing assignments that required students to draw inferences, give reasons, integrate information from a number of sources, develop an idea or theme, or generate original responses.
2. Thoughtfulness scores were unrelated to entry levels of achievement, indicating that teachers can structure thoughtful discourse with students at all ability levels.
3. High-scoring teachers were more likely to mention critical thinking and problem solving as important goals.
4. In talking about the satisfactions of teaching, high-scoring teachers tended to mention evidence of good student thinking about the content, whereas low-scoring teachers tended to talk about student interest or positive response to lessons (but without emphasizing good thinking).
5. In talking about their goals for students, high-scoring teachers were more likely to mention longer-range and farther-reaching dispositional goals in addition to more immediate knowledge and skill goals.
6. High-scoring teachers were more confident that they could influence the performance of below-average students.
7. All teachers mentioned that students are likely to resist higher-order thinking tasks, but the high-scoring teachers nevertheless emphasized these tasks.
8. All teachers felt pressure to cover more content, but high-scoring teachers experienced this primarily as external pressure and tended to resist it by favoring depth of topic development over breadth of coverage, whereas low-scoring teachers experienced it primarily as internal pressure and thus emphasized breadth.
9. Students identified high-scoring teachers' classes as more difficult and challenging, but also as more engaging and interesting.

Newmann's findings provide cause for optimism because they suggest that thoughtful, in-depth treatment that fosters higher-order thinking about social studies topics is feasible in most classrooms (not just those dominated by high achievers) and that teachers with the knowledge and determination to do so can overcome students' resistance to higher-order thinking activities and even bring the students to the point where they see such activities as more engaging and interesting than lower-order recitation and seatwork. Only limited research relevant to Newmann's work has been done at the elementary level, but Thornton and Wenger (1990) reported observing lessons that exhibited many of the characteristics of thoughtfulness described by Newmann, and Stodolsky (1988) reported that the quality of students' task engagement was higher during more cognitively complex activities than during lower-level activities.

Fraenkel (1992) drew on case studies of instruction in high school social studies classes, looking for factors associated with differences in effectiveness. Like Newmann (1990, 1992), Fraenkel found that the major factor determining the success of a class was the teacher, not student achievement levels, the subject matter, or other aspects. Impressive teachers were found in nonelite as well as in elite schools, and many of the teachers in the elite schools were not impressive.

The less effective teachers tended to present ideas ready-made rather than to ask students to develop ideas for themselves. They tended to talk *to* students rather than *with* them. They often did not seem to have a clear sense of where they were heading. They tended to engage students in busywork and to stress memorization and regurgitation of facts rather than understanding of ideas. These teachers often did not seem to like what they were doing, to like their students, or to be having much fun. Unsurprisingly, their students rarely were active learners and often were discipline problems.

In contrast, the more effective teachers often engaged students in discussions. When they did lecture, they combined lectures with use of the overhead or showing pictures, maps, or other visuals. Their questions tended to elicit discussion rather than mere recitation and they often asked students to respond to one another's comments. Students often worked in pairs or small groups while the teacher circulated and interacted with them. They were often required to function as active learners by role playing or giving presentations in class. The teachers made a point of engaging students in activities to help them understand and require them to use the ideas they were learning.

In the process, these teachers appeared to like what they were doing, like their students, and like their subjects. They had high expectations for their students, emphasized depth rather than breadth of coverage, were able to explain things clearly using examples that related to the students' lives, had good wait times and were good listeners when students talked, demonstrated patience when students did not initially understand, varied their instructional approaches and types of activities, and displayed considerable command of their subject and ability to relate it to a variety of daily-life examples.

They were highly attuned to their students. They encouraged them to take public risks by contributing their opinions to discussions and publicly discussing their mistakes or confusions. Yet they were quick to notice indicators of confusion or anxiety and to react by providing additional explanations, alternative assignments, or other scaffolding. They emphasized bringing to light students' thought processes for public examination and discussion. They established personal contacts with their students and arranged for frequent interaction among students through cooperative small-group activities.

CONCLUSIONS

Interpreting Research on Teaching: Face Up to the Complexities

Science generates and organizes knowledge. Viewed from a distance, progress in developing a field of knowledge may appear as slow and steady accumulation, akin to adding grains of sand to a pile. However, closer analysis reveals that the development of a scientific knowledge base is much like the development of a living organism. Along with growth (increase in the size of existing parts), there is development of new parts, differentiation of existing parts into subparts, and reorganization of parts into new configurations. Some of the reorganizations are major ones that bring significant changes in views on the centrality or implications of previously developed knowledge. For scientists with "up close and personal" involvement, these developments include emotionally arousing conflict that sometimes threatens cherished belief systems, not just dispassionate analysis of technical and interpretive issues.

Conflicts among scientists who generate knowledge are just the beginning of the story. People interested in applications of the knowledge have their own axes to grind, so they often approach the knowledge base looking for ammunition to support already adopted positions rather than for research-based information to inform critical thinking about issues. Some of them feel little need to inform themselves about research findings at all, having become "true believers" in some ideology. Unfortunately, education has been plagued with the latter problem. Too often, policy issues are argued on an ideological rather than a scientific basis, and policies are undertaken because they conform to a currently popular theory rather than because they have been carefully studied and validated in the schools.

The result has been an "out with the old, in with the new" approach to educational reform. Instead of a steady accumulation of knowledge and empirically grounded practice, this leads to cycles featuring swings between extremes. It also leaves teachers confused and cynical about applications of educational theory and research. This is unfortunate, because recent decades have produced a significant body of useful knowledge about teaching, much of which is summarized in this book.

To apply this knowledge base effectively, teachers need to resist temptations to look to ideologies or other oversimplifications of the complexties of the profession and instead develop rich repertoires of knowledge and skills that will enable them to make good decisions about the kinds of teaching needed in particular situations. With respect to current controversies in the field, this means avoiding overreacting to labels such as "transmission models" or "constructivist models" and seeking to develop complete and balanced instructional programs. As Dixon and Carnine (1994) put it, optimal generation and use of knowledge about teaching require emphasis on specific practices, not "broad, vague, and often emotive educational ideologies" (p. 356). Most researchers, teacher educators, and teachers understand this. However, in recent years extreme views have been directed at teacher educators and teachers by people who identify themselves as radical constructivists (primarily in mathematics and science education) or whole language theorists (primarily in reading and language arts education).

Radical constructivists have argued that there are no correct meanings, only self-chosen positions. This has led Ford, Barnes, and Canas (1994) to state that

> Granted, we are not deities and thus cannot be certain about many things. This, however, does not justify the constructivists' aversion to prespecified course content or knowledge goals. Humans invented arithmetic, but nonetheless $2 + 2 \neq 6$. Arithmetic has an agreed upon mechanism. Similarly, agreed upon correct answers are found in all fields of human endeavor. Society's technological and cultural accomplishments arise not only from the creative construing of individuals, but also from our ability to communicate

our functional but fallible knowledge from one generation to the next. It is not necessary to reinvent the world from scratch. (p. 616).

These authors went on to observe that the extreme positions taken by radical constructivists and their penchant for sloganism, as well as a tendency to homogenize and caricaturize other positions, does not lead to productive discussion. Leaders in the constructivist movement in mathematics and science education have expressed similar concerns (Cobb, 1994; Driver et al., 1994). These authors endorsed social constructivism as a general orientation toward thinking about teaching and learning, but they rejected the romantic notion that teachers need only to facilitate students' intrinsically motivated explorations. They emphasized that teachers need to provide modeling and explanations, to support students' construction of knowledge through well-chosen questions and activities, and to scaffold the students' work. They characterized romantic views of learning through social construction of knowledge as fundamental misunderstandings and misapplications of constructivist theory.

Similar problems exist with respect to the whole language movement. However, they are much more widespread and serious because some of the most ideological, evangelical, and antiscientific statements have come from some of its most visible leaders. Concern about this has led several major journals to devote entire issues or special sections to the whole language movement and its critics (see the Summer 1995 issue of the *American Educator;* the Fall 1994 issue of the *Educational Psychologist;* the November 1990 issue of the *Educational Researcher;* the November 1989 issue of the *Elementary School Journal;* the December 1991 issue of the *Journal of Educational Psychology;* the Fall 1994 issue of the *Journal of Special Education;* or the Fall 1994 issue of *Reading Research Quarterly*).

In these and other sources, critics of the whole language movement typically acknowledge that it has much to offer (especially its integration of reading and writing and its emphasis on reading genuine literature rather than artificially constructed stories). However, they also suggest that whole language advocates do not appreciate the need for students in general, and students at risk in particular, to receive systematic instruction in basic skills such as word decoding and spelling. They argue that whole language teaching ideas apply well in preschool and kindergarten before the initiation of systematic instruction in beginning reading, and that they may apply well in the intermediate and later grades after students have mastered basic skills and are focusing on comprehending and responding to what is read and on writing to organize and communicate knowledge. In the primary grades, however, students appear to need a great deal of instruction in beginning reading and writing, not just exposure to literature and writing tools.

Critics also attack whole language advocates for their zealotry in promoting extreme views. For example:

Within the constructivist perspective there exists a viewpoint that was represented at a recent conference on writing instruction where one contributor, who identified himself as a whole language advocate, suggested sincerely that we should consider "teaching" to be a dirty word—and one that we would strive never to use. According to this viewpoint, it is not necessary to teach explicitly; rather, children will come to learn all that they need to know and develop all the abilities and skills they need through interaction with and immersion in meaningful contexts and authentic learning tasks. (Harris & Graham, 1994, p. 237)

Critics also point to research findings that provide at best mixed support for the whole language advocates' claims (Stahl & Miller, 1989) or that contradict some of the movements' basic assumptions (Adams, 1990). For example, one basic assumption is that readers pay attention only to those aspects of a text that they need to process in order to get its meaning. Early studies of expert readers seemed to support this idea. However, more recent studies done with sophisticated scientific equipment that monitors minute eye movements have demonstrated beyond doubt that even the most expert readers process every letter in every word. They do so mostly automatically and with great rapidity, but they do not skip letters or words or divine meaning from processing just a few key subparts of texts.

When given the opportunity to respond to these and other research-based concerns about their views, whole language advocates have typically ignored or glossed over the issues raised, restated their own views, and claimed that the value of instructional practices should be determined by their fit with whole language principles rather than by the findings from empirical studies. This sort of arrogance and evasiveness has not helped their cause, and as they continue to proselytize with evangelical fervor despite the continued accumulation of troublesome empirical findings, critics are beginning to question their ethics along with their scientific responsibility.

As a recent case in point, the state of California recently found to its dismay that 1995 national assessment data placed the state's elementary students near the bottom of the nation in reading and language arts achievement. Scores have dropped precipitously in recent years from those displayed earlier, and in all subgroups of students (i.e., not just among immigrants learning English as a second language). This drop in achievement probably reflects the effects of multiple causes, but one important cause is that some years ago the California State Department of Education (1987) mandated a whole language approach to language arts instruction. In implementing this mandate, a great many California school districts forbade the use of basal reading series and the teaching of phonics. Influenced by the zealotry of whole language advocates, the state's educational policymakers ignored the accumulated wisdom of decades of research on beginning reading, and several hundred thousand of its students have since paid the price.

It will be unfortunate if debacles like these lead to wholesale abandonment of whole language principles and replacement with reading and language arts programs that focus too narrowly on phonics and skill sheets. It should be obvious by now that a complete and well-rounded program in any school subject will incorporate a considerable range of curricular and instructional elements and that the mixture of these elements will evolve as students proceed through the grades (Weinert & Helmke, 1995). Such programs will not result from application of a few principles rooted in ideology, but they can be constructed on the basis of grounded theory that respects the complexities of classroom teaching and is informed by the accumulated knowledge base produced through educational research.

Adapt Teaching to the Situation

Teaching well is difficult, especially if one aims high by teaching for understanding, appreciation, and application. It requires a good working knowledge of the subject (including its purposes and goals, its most powerful ideas, and the ways in which these ideas are connected and applied), of students (their likely prior knowledge about the subject, including misconceptions; what important knowledge and skills are within their current zones of proximal development), and of pedagogy (how to represent these aspects of the subject to the students and assist them in constructing new understandings). Development of this kind of expertise takes time, although researchers are beginning to learn more about it (Brophy, 1991) and about how to develop it through preservice and in-service teacher education (see Chapter 11).

The best teaching is adapted to the situation, including the instructional purposes and goals, the students, and the subject matter. For example, the techniques associated with the terms *active teaching, strategy instruction,* and *situated learning* are most relevant when the situation calls for presenting new information, modeling skills, or coaching students as they attempt to implement skills or procedures. In contrast, the techniques associated with terms such as *social constructivism* or *teaching for thoughtfulness* are most relevant when one wishes to develop understanding and appreciation of networks of knowledge through shared construction and negotiation of meanings and implications. A principle such as transferring responsibility for managing learning from the teacher to the students applies to all teaching situations, but figuring out exactly how to apply it (how much modeling, explanation, coaching, and other scaffolding to provide and how quickly to fade this support) takes experience with the content and the students. Even then, some trial and error may be required. What worked well with last year's class might not work well with this year's class.

Research findings sometimes reflect these complexities. Swing, Stoiber, and Peterson (1988) compared the effects of two contrasting interventions on fourth-grade students' mathematics achievement. In the thinking skills intervention, teachers learned how to teach the cognitive strategies of defining and describing, thinking of reasons, comparing, and summarizing. In the learning time intervention, teachers learned how to increase students' engagement and academic learning time. The researchers expected that the thinking skills intervention would produce better results than the learning time intervention, but the effects differed according to student achievement level. Higher-achieving classes did better with the thinking skills intervention, but lower-achieving classes did better with the learning time intervention. Within the classes that received the thinking skills intervention, however, lower achievers benefited more than the higher achievers. Thus, the same treatment can have different effects on different types of students.

Also, an approach that is well adapted to one situation might not work well in another. We noted earlier that the reciprocal teaching method developed by Palincsar and Brown has shown impressive results as a method of improving students' reading comprehension. However, two attempts to teach mathematical problem solving using the same basic strategies that are used in reciprocal teaching produced unsatisfactory results (Brown & Campione, 1990; Resnick, 1989). The reasons are not yet clear, but it is obvious that the reciprocal teaching method is well adapted to teaching reading comprehension but not to teaching mathematical problem solving. Similarly, the Kamehameha Early Education Project (KEEP) that had been developed for teaching native Hawaiian children had to be adjusted when it was implemented with Navajo children. Native Hawaiian children are accustomed to learning collaboratively through lively discussions and cooperative work on tasks, so the KEEP program built on these strengths by incorporating a great deal of conversational discussion of reading selections during group lessons and cooperative learning in independent activity centers. However, Navajo children tend to be less verbally interactive in groups and more independent in their patterns of task engagement, so the KEEP program elements that had been specifically incorporated for and worked well with native Hawaiian children did not work well at all with Navajo children (Tharp & Gallimore, 1988).

Rather than viewing these complexities in research findings simply as frustrations or even as failures, researchers and teachers need to appreciate them as indications of the complexities involved in adapting instruction to students and situations. Researchers are making progress in learning about these complexities and their potential implications for instruction, and they will continue to build on this knowledge base. Still, research-based information can only inform teachers about the trade-offs involved in decision alternatives; it cannot make those decisions for them. It is teachers who must decide what goals to pursue with their students and what combinations of content representations, instructional methods, and learning activities will be most helpful in assisting their students to accomplish the goals.

To cope with these complexities and keep their curriculum and instruction well matched to each successive class of students, teachers need to be reflective about their practice and prepared to engage in diagnosis and experimentation when goals are not being met. Teacher colleagues can help one another here by meeting regularly to share insights, identify and generate possible solutions to common problems, and coordinate efforts to expand students' opportunities to assume responsibility for self-regulated learning. In-service professional development programs that promote such collegial collaboration are discussed in Chapter 11.

Keep the Goals in Sight

In order to make good decisions about what to teach and how to teach it, teachers need to establish worthwhile goals and keep these goals in sight as they develop and implement their plans. This can be difficult, because as curriculum guidelines get translated into separate strands and then become segmented by grade level and by units within grades and lessons within units, the goals that are supposed to guide the entire process sometimes fade into the background, along with many of the originally recognized connections and intended life applications (Brophy & Alleman, 1993). For example, consider the following goals drawn from social studies:

District-wide goal: Prepare young people to become humane, rational, participating citizens in an increasingly interdependent world.

Program-area goal for social studies, K–12: Enable students to appreciate that people living in different cultures are likely to hold both common values and also different values that are rooted in experience and are legitimate in terms of their own cultures.

Grade-level goal for social studies, Grade 1: To understand and appreciate that the roles and values of family members may differ according to the structure of the family, its circumstances, and its cultural setting.

Unit-level goal for social studies, Grade 1: To understand that families differ in size and composition.

The last (unit-level) goal is phrased in purely descriptive, knowledge-level language, and it is trite for a unit goal even at the first-grade level. It makes no reference to the concepts concerning cultures and roles that are referred to in the higher-level goals, nor to the related values and dispositions (multicultural appreciation and citizen participation). Unless the teacher has a coherent view of the purposes and nature of social education, or unless the manual does an unusually good job of keeping the teacher aware of how particular lessons fit within the big picture, the result is likely to be a version of social studies that is long on isolated practice of facts and skills but short on integration and application of social learning.

Unfortunately, typical manuals do little or nothing to help teachers put these lower-level goals into perspective as pieces of a larger plan to move students toward major goals. Often, in fact, the curriculum materials were developed not to systematically accomplish major goals, but instead only to cover long lists of disconnected knowledge topics and isolated skills. In this case, students might learn a few obvious generalities about families (they differ in size and composition, they grow and change, and their members work and play together), but not much about variations in family roles across time and culture, the reasons for these variations, or the lifestyle trade-offs that they offer. This will not do much to advance students' knowledge of the human condition, help them put the familiar into broader perspective, or even stimulate their thinking about family as a concept.

To avoid such problems, teachers need to think through their goals, identifying the capabilities and dispositions that they want to develop in their students throughout the year as a whole and in each of their curriculum units. Then they can examine curriculum materials in the light of these goals. Taking the viewpoint of the students, they can first read the student text (i.e., not the teacher's manual, which contains more guidance and information) to see what information is included and emphasized and what information is not, noting places where additional structuring or input will be necessary to focus students' learning on important ideas. Then teachers can study the manual, assessing its suggested questions, activities, and evaluation devices to determine the degree to which they will be useful as tools for helping students accomplish their primary goals. To help their students focus on important aspects of the content, teachers may need to augment the text with additional input (or replace it with something else if necessary), skip pointless questions and activities, and substitute other questions and activities that support progress toward major goals.

Through such planning, teachers can overcome some of the limitations in materials that feature trite goals, parade-of-facts content, and parade-of-skills-exercise activities. Ideally, they can begin to teach for understanding, appreciation, and application to life outside of school by developing a limited number of important ideas in depth; organizing the content into networks structured around these important ideas; teaching the ideas with an emphasis on their connections; asking questions and making comments that produce reflective discourse that focuses on these key ideas; engaging students in activities that provide opportunities for authentic applications of what they are learning; and evaluating the learning using measures that feature authentic tasks and assess accomplishment of major goals.

SUGGESTED ACTIVITIES AND QUESTIONS

1. Teaching for understanding requires reducing breadth of content coverage so as to be able to develop the most important content in greater depth. This creates dilemmas for teachers, who are caught between their desire to focus on important topics in depth and their felt responsibilities to cover a broader range of content. Focusing on grades at which you teach or intend to teach, interview several teachers about how they respond to this dilemma.

2. Focusing on particular grades and school subjects, interview teachers to determine what they consider to be authentic activities for their students. To what extent do they use similar criteria and identify similar activities? Do they actually use these authentic activities in their teaching, or do they rely more on worksheets and other less authentic assignments? If the latter, why?

3. We discussed several aspects of teaching in this chapter; however, we did not provide a summary synthesizing this information. Show your mastery of the important aspects of the chapter by writing your own summary in a couple of typewritten pages. Compare your summary with those made by classmates and fellow teachers.

4. What are some of the advantages and disadvantages involved when students are asked to summarize material on their own?

5. Much of the research reviewed in this chapter was conducted by scholars who believe that standardized achievement tests are incomplete or even inappropriate as measures of student learning. To find out what you think about this, obtain samples of standardized achievement tests to study and discuss with peers. What do you see as their strengths and weaknesses as measures of learning outcomes? What does this imply about the strengths and weaknesses of the research reviewed in Chapter 9?

6. Some educators think that there are important differences between active teaching as described in Chapter 9 and helping students to construct usable knowledge as described in Chapter 10. Others believe that the former is subsumed within the latter and that the differences are more in underlying philosophy than in what would actually be done in the classroom. Discuss this with

peers and see whether you come to agreement on implications for classroom teaching.

7. Examine samples of K–12 textbooks that you use now or likely will use in the future. Do they present networks of connected knowledge structured around powerful ideas, or just parades of disconnected facts? What does this suggest about your use of such texts with students?

8. Learning with understanding is usually described as a process of relating new content to one's existing prior knowledge. But what if students are so unfamiliar with certain content that they possess no readily available schemas within which to assimilate it and very little useful prior knowledge to bring to bear? Is it possible to develop their understanding of such content? If so, can it be done through social constructivist methods or will it be necessary to begin by providing information through texts, teacher explanations, or other input sources? Using a realistic example from your current or future teaching, plan how you would introduce and develop a topic for which students had little or no prior knowledge.

9. How might you determine your students' zones of proximal development with respect to a particular curriculum unit or topic? What does this imply about forms of preinstructional assessment of student knowledge and thinking that you might incorporate into your teaching?

10. For each subject that you teach or plan to teach, establish a file of authentic activities and assignments that will allow your students to use what they are learning in the process of conducting inquiry, solving problems, or making decisions. Be prepared to use these activities and assignments in place of those supplied with or suggested in the manuals that accompany your curriculum materials, whenever the latter activities or assignments are not worth using.

11. How does ideal scaffolding of students' learning efforts differ from forms of teacher assistance that are less desirable?

12. Define *conceptual change teaching* in your own words. Why is more time for instruction not always effective?

13. What is the difference between teaching "main idea" as a concept and teaching about how identifying and focusing on main ideas can be a useful strategy for guiding one's efforts to learn with understanding? What does this imply about your teaching about main idea (regardless of whether you teach reading to your students)?

14. What is meant by the phrase *writing to learn*? What does this imply about the kinds of writing assignments that you should include in your teaching?

15. We suggested that there might be limits on the degree to which one could emphasize authentic applications over skills practice without experiencing reductions in skills development. What might these limits be? In the subjects that you teach, are there certain things that simply must be memorized or practiced repeatedly? If so, why?

16. The discovery-oriented teachers studied by Smith and Anderson (1984) used methods similar in many ways to those advocated by social constructivists. However, they did not get positive results. What were some crucial differences be-

tween these teachers and teachers who use social constructivist methods to teach for understanding?

17. Can you relate the goals and objectives of each of your lessons and activities to larger purposes and goals? Can you see how each lesson or activity contributes to the long-run development of knowledge, skills, values, and dispositions that school subjects are ostensibly designed to develop? Test yourself by selecting a few lessons and activities at random and seeing whether you can explain to others' satisfaction why they are needed in the curriculum. If you have trouble doing this, you may need to think through larger purposes and goals and keep them in mind as you develop your teaching plans.

18. Review and revise (as necessary) the statements you made after reading Chapter 1, when you attempted to identify teaching behaviors and characteristics that are signs of effective teaching. How much has your view of effective teaching changed?

19. You have now completed reading the substantive chapters of this book that describe effective teaching. What important aspects of teacher and student behavior have we neglected? Why do you believe these behaviors are important? What information do you need as a teacher that we have not addressed? Compare your list with others.

REFERENCES

Adams, M. (1990). *Beginning to read: Thinking and learning about print.* Cambridge: MIT Press.

Alvermann, D., Smith, L., & Readence, J. (1985). Prior knowledge activation and the comprehension of compatible and incompatible text. *Reading Research Quarterly, 20,* 420–435.

Anderson, C., & Roth, K. (1989). Teaching for meaningful and self-regulated learning of science. In J. Brophy (Ed.), *Advances in research on teaching.* Vol. 1: *Teaching for meaningful understanding and self-regulated learning.* Greenwich, CT: JAI.

Anderson, C., & Smith, E. (1987). Teaching science. In V. Richardson-Koehler (Ed.), *Educators' handbook.* New York: Longman.

Anderson, L. (1989). Implementing instructional programs to promote meaningful, self-regulated learning. In J. Brophy (Ed.), *Advances in research on teaching.* Vol. 1: *Teaching for meaningful understanding and self-regulated learning.* Greenwich, CT: JAI.

Anderson, R. (1984). Role of the reader's schema in comprehension, learning, and memory. In R. Anderson, J. Osborn, R. Tierney (Eds.), *Learning to read in American schools: Basal readers and content texts.* Hillsdale, NJ: Erlbaum.

Anderson, R., & Armbruster, B. (1990). Some maxims for learning and instruction. *Teachers College Record, 91,* 396–408.

Anderson, R., Hiebert, E., Scott, J., & Wilkinson, I. (1985). *Becoming a nation of readers: A report of the Commission on Reading.* Washington, DC: National Institute of Education.

Andre, M., & Anderson, T. (1978–1979). The development and evaluation of a self-questioning study technique. *Reading Research Quarterly, 14,* 605–623.

Applebee, A. (1986). Problems in process approaches: Toward a reconceptualization of process instruction. In A. Petrosky & D. Bartholomae (Eds.), *The teaching of writing* (Eighty-fifth Yearbook of the National Society for the Study of Education). Chicago: University of Chicago Press.

Appleton, K. (1993). Using theory to guide practice: Teaching science from a constructivist perspective. *School Science and Mathematics, 93,* 269–274.

Au, K., & Carroll, J. (in press). Improving literacy achievement through a holistic approach: The KEEP demonstration classroom project. *Elementary School Journal.*

Au, K., Tharp, R., Crowell, D., Jordan, C., Speidel, G., & Calkins, R. (1985). The role of research in the development of a successful reading program. In J. Osborn, P. Wilson, & R. Anderson (Eds.), *Reading education: Foundations for a literate America.* Lexington, MA: Lexington Books.

Ball, D. (1993). With an eye on the mathematical horizon: Dilemmas of teaching elementary school mathematics. *Elementary School Journal, 93,* 373–397.

Bereiter, C., & Scardamalia, M. (1987). An attainable version of high literacy: Approaches to teaching higher-order skills in reading and writing. *Curriculum Inquiry, 17*(1), 9–30.

Bloom, B., Englehart, M., Furst, E., Hill, W., & Krathwohl, D. (1956). *Taxonomy of educational objectives: The classification of educational goals. Handbook I: Cognitive domain.* New York: Longmans Green.

Blumenfeld, P. (1992). The task and the teacher: Enhancing student thoughtfulness in science. In J. Brophy (Ed.), *Advances in research on teaching. Vol. 3: Planning and managing learning tasks and activities* (pp. 81–114). Greenwich, CT: JAI.

Blumenfeld, P., Krajcik, J., Marx, R., & Soloway, E. (1994). Lessons learned: How collaboration helped middle grade science teachers learn project-based instruction. *Elementary School Journal, 94,* 539-551.

Bredekamp, S. (Ed.). (1987). *Developmentally appropriate practice in early childhood programs serving children from birth through age 8.* Washington, DC: National Association for the Education of Young Children.

Brooks, J. (1990). Teachers and students: Constructivists forging new connections. *Educational Leadership, 47*(5), 68–71.

Brophy, J. (Ed.). (1989). *Advances in research on teaching.* Vol. 1. Greenwich, CT: JAI.

Brophy, J. (Ed.). (1991). *Advances in research on teaching.* Vol. 2. Greenwich, CT: JAI.

Brophy, J. (1992). Probing the subtleties of subject-matter teaching. *Educational Leadership, 49*(7), 4–8.

Brophy, J., & Alleman, J. (1993). Elementary social studies should be driven by major social education goals. *Social Education, 57,* 27–32.

Brown, A., & Campione, J. (1990). Interactive learning environments and the teaching of science and mathematics. In M. Gardner, J. Greeno, F. Reif, A. Schoenfeld, A. diSessa, & E. Stage (Eds.), *Toward a scientific practice of science education* (pp. 111–139). Hillsdale, NJ: Erlbaum.

Brown, J., Collins, A., & Duguid, P. (1989). Situated cognition and the culture of learning. *Educational Researcher, 18*(1), 32–42.

Bruer, J. (1993). *Schools for thought: A science of learning in the classroom.* Cambridge: MIT Press.

California State Department of Education. (1987). *Handbook for planning an effective literature program, kindergarten through grade 12.* Sacramento: Author.

Calkins, L. (1986). *The art of teaching writing.* Exeter, NH: Heinemann.

Carey, S. (1985). *Conceptual change in childhood.* Cambridge, MA: MIT Press.

Carpenter, T., Fennema, E., Peterson, P., Chiang, C., & Loef, M. (1989). Using knowledge of children's mathematical thinking in classroom teaching: An experimental study. *American Educational Research Journal, 26,* 499–532.

Case, R. (1982). Learning, maturation, and the development of computation strategies in elementary arithmetic. In T. Carpenter, J. Moser, & T. Romberg (Eds.), *Addition and subtraction: A cognitive perspective* (pp. 156–170). Hillsdale, NJ: Erlbaum.

Chinn, C., & Brewer, W. (1993). The role of anomalous data in knowledge acquisition: A theoretical framework and implications for science instruction. *Review of Educational Research, 63,* 1–49.

Cobb, P. (1986). Making mathematics: Children's learning and the constructivist tradition. *Harvard Educational Review, 56,* 301–306.

Cobb, P. (1994). Where is the mind? Constructivist and sociocultural perspectives on mathematical development. *Educational Researcher, 23*(7), 13–20.

Cobb, P., Wood, T., Yackel, E., Nicholls, J., Wheatley, G., Trigatti, B., & Perlwitz, M. (1991). Assessment of a problem-centered second-grade mathematics project. *Journal for Research in Mathematics Education, 22,* 3–29.

Cobb, P., Yackel, E., & Wood, T. (1992). A constructivist alternative to the representational view of mind in mathematics education. *Journal for Research in Mathematics Education, 23,* 2–33.

Collins, A., Brown, J., & Holum, A. (1991). Cognitive apprenticeship: Making thinking visible. *American Educator, 15*(3), 6–11, 38–46.

Collins, A., Brown, J., & Newman, S. (1989). Cognitive apprenticeship: Teaching the craft of reading, writing, and mathematics. In L. Resnick (Ed.), *Knowing, learning, and instruction: Essays in honor of Robert Glaser.* Hillsdale, NJ: Erlbaum.

Cook, L., & Mayer, R. (1988). Teaching readers about the structure of scientific text. *Journal of Educational Psychology, 80,* 448–456.

Cross, D., & Paris, S. (1988). Developmental and instructional analyses of children's metacognition and reading comprehension. *Journal of Educational Psychology, 80,* 131–142.

Davis, R., Maher, C., & Noddings, N. (Eds.). (1990). *Constructivist views on the teaching and learning of mathematics. Journal of Research in Mathematics Education Monograph No. 4.* Reston, VA: National Council of Teachers of Mathematics.

Dimino, J., Gersten, R., Carnine, D., & Blake, G. (1990). Story grammar: An approach for promoting at-risk secondary students' comprehension of literature. *Elementary School Journal, 91,* 19–32.

diSibio, M. (1982). Memory for connected discourse: A constructivist view. *Review of Educational Research, 52,* 149–174.

Dixon, R., & Carnine, D. (1994). Ideologies, practices, and their implications for special education. *Journal of Special Education, 28,* 356–367.

Dole, J., Duffy, G., Roehler, L., & Pearson, P. (1990). Moving from the old to the new: Research on reading comprehension instruction. *Review of Educational Research, 61,* 239–264.

Driver, B., Asoko, H., Leach, J., Mortimer, E., & Scott, P. (1994). Constructing scientific knowledge in the classroom. *Educational Researcher, 23*(7), 5–12.

Duffy, G. (1993). Rethinking strategy instruction: Four teachers' development and their low-achievers' understandings. *Elementary School Journal, 93,* 231–247.

Duffy, G., & Roehler, L. (1987). Improving classroom reading instruction through the use of responsive elaboration. *Reading Teacher, 40,* 514–521.

Duffy, G., & Roehler, L. (1989). The tension between information-giving and mediation: Perspectives on instructional explanation and teacher change. In J, Brophy (Ed.), *Advances in research on teaching.* Vol. 1: *Teaching for meaningful understanding and self-regulated learning.* Greenwich, CT: JAI.

Duffy, G., Roehler, L., & Herrmann, B. (1988). Modeling mental processes helps poor readers become strategic readers. *Reading Teacher, 41,* 762–767.

Duffy, G., Roehler, L., Sivan, E., Rackliffe, G., Book, C., Meloth, M., Vavrus, L., Wesselman, R., Putnam, J., & Bassiri, D. (1987). Effects of explaining reasoning associated with using reading strategies. *Reading Research Quarterly, 22,* 347–368.

Duffy, T., & Jonassen, D. (1992). *Constructivism and the technology of instruction: A conversation.* Hillsdale, NJ: Erlbaum.

Englert, C., & Raphael, T. (1989). Developing successful writers through cognitive strategy instruction. In J. Brophy (Ed.), *Advances in research on teaching.* Vol. 1: *Teaching for meaningful understanding and self-regulated learning.* Greenwich, CT: JAI.

Fennema, E., Carpenter, T., & Peterson, P. (1989). Learning mathematics with understanding. In J. Brophy (Ed.), *Advances in research on teaching*. Vol. 1: *Teaching for meaningful understanding and self-regulated learning*. Greenwich, CT: JAI.

Fennema, E., Franke, M., Carpenter, T., & Carey, D. (1993). Using children's mathematical knowledge in instruction. *American Educational Research Journal, 30,* 555-583.

Fernandez, C., Yoshida, M., & Stigler, J. (1992). Learning mathematics from classroom instruction: On relating lessons to pupils' interpretations. *Journal of the Learning Sciences, 2,* 333–365.

Florio-Ruane, S., & Lensmire, T. (1989). The role of instruction in learning to write. In J. Brophy (Ed.), *Advances in research on teaching*. Vol. 1: *Teaching for meaningful understanding and self-regulated learning*. Greenwich, CT: JAI.

Ford, K., Barnes, W., & Canas, A. (1994). Educational babies and constructivist bathwater. *Contemporary Psychology, 39,* 616-617.

Fraenkel, J. (1992, November). *A comparison of elite and non-elite social studies classrooms*. Paper presented at the annual meeting of the National Council for the Social Studies, Detroit.

Gagne, E., & Dick, W. (1983). Instructional psychology. In M. Rosenzweig & L. Porter (Eds.), *Annual review of psychology*. Palo Alto, CA: Annual Reviews.

Ginsburg, H., & Opper, S. (1979). *Piagetian theory of intellectual development* (2nd ed.). Englewood Cliffs, NJ: Prentice-Hall.

Glaser, R. (1984). Education and thinking: The role of knowledge. *American Psychologist, 39,* 93–104.

Glynn, S., Yeany, R., & Britton, B. (Eds.). (1991). *The psychology of learning science*. Hillsdale, NJ: Erlbaum.

Good, T., McCaslin, M., & Reys, B. (1992). Investigating work groups to promote problem solving in mathematics. In J. Brophy (Ed.), *Advances in research on teaching*. Vol. 3. *Planning and managing learning tasks and activities* (pp. 115–160). Greenwich, CT: JAI.

Graves, T. (1983). *Writing: Teachers and children at work*. Exeter, NJ: Heinemann.

Hand, B., & Treagust, D. (1991). Student achievement and science curriculum development using a constructive framework. *School Science and Mathematics, 91,* 172–176.

Hansen, J., & Pearson, P. (1983). An instructional study: Improving the inferential comprehension of fourth-grade good and poor readers. *Journal of Educational Psychology, 75,* 821–829.

Harris, K., & Graham, S. (1994). Constructivism: Principles, paradigms, and integration. *Journal of Special Education, 28,* 233–247.

Hiebert, E. (1994). Reading Recovery in the United States: What difference does it make to an age cohort? *Educational Researcher, 23*(9), 15–25.

Hiebert, J., & Wearne, D. (1992). Links between teaching and learning place value with understanding in first grade. *Journal for Research in Mathematics Education, 23,* 98–122.

Kelly, M., Moore, D., & Tuck, B. (1994). Reciprocal teaching in a regular school classroom. *Journal of Educational Research, 88,* 53-60.

King, A. (1994). Guiding knowledge construction in the classroom: Effects of teaching children how to question and how to explain. *American Educational Research Journal, 31,* 338–368.

Knapp, M., (1995). *Teaching for learning in high-poverty classrooms*. New York: Teachers College Press.

Lampert, M. (1989). Choosing and using mathematical tools in classroom discourse. In J. Brophy (Ed.), *Advances in research on teaching*. Vol. 1: *Teaching for meaningful understanding and self-regulated learning*. Greenwich, CT: JAI.

Lampert, M. (1990). When the problem is not the question and the solution is not the answer: Mathematical knowing and teaching. *American Educational Research Journal, 27,* 29–63.

Lampert, M. (1992). Practices and problems in teaching authentic mathematics. In F. Oser, A. Dick, & J. Patry (Eds.), *Effective and responsible teaching: The new synthesis* (pp. 295–314). San Francisco: Jossey-Bass.

Lappan, G., & Ferrini-Mundy, J. (1993). Knowing and doing mathematics: A new vision for middle grades students. *Elementary School Journal, 93,* 625-641.

Lave, J., & Wenger, E. (1991). *Situated learning: Legitimate peripheral participation.* Cambridge: Cambridge University Press.

Lyons, C., Pinnell, G., & DeFord, D. (1993). *Partners in learning: Teachers and children in Reading Recovery.* New York: Teachers College Press.

Marzano, R., Brandt, R., Hughes, C., Jones, B., Presseisen, B., Rankin, S., & Suhor, C. (1988). *Dimensions of thinking: A framework for curriculum and instruction.* Alexandria, VA: Association for Supervision and Curriculum Development.

McCaslin, M., & Good, T. (1992). Compliant cognition: The misalliance of management and instruction goals in current school reform. *Educational Researcher, 21,* 4–17.

Minstrell, J. (1989). Teaching science for understanding. In L. Resnick & L. Klopfer (Eds.), *Toward the thinking curriculum: Current cognitive research: 1989 Yearbook of the Association for Supervision and Curriculum Development.* Alexandria, VA: Association for Supervision and Curriculum Development.

Moll, L. (Ed.). (1990). *Vygotsky and education: Instructional implications and applications of sociohistorical psychology.* Cambridge: Cambridge University Press.

National Association of State Boards of Education. (1988). *Right from the start: The report of the NASBE task force on early childhood education.* Alexandria, VA: Author.

National Council of Teachers of Mathematics. (1989). *Curriculum and evaluation standards for school mathematics.* Reston, VA: Author.

Neale, D., Smith, D., & Johnson, V. (1990). Implementing conceptual change teaching in primary science. *Elementary School Journal, 91,* 109–131.

Newman, D., Griffin, P., & Cole, M. (1989). *The construction zone: Working for cognitive change in school.* Cambridge: Cambridge University Press.

Newmann, F. (1990). Qualities of thoughtful social studies classes: An empirical profile. *Journal of Curriculum Studies, 22,* 253–275.

Newmann, F. (Ed.). (1992). *Student engagement and achievement in American secondary schools.* New York: Teachers College Press.

Novak, J. (Ed.). (1987). *Proceedings of the second international seminar on misconceptions and educational strategies in science and mathematics* (Vol. 2). Ithaca, NY: Cornell University.

Palincsar, A., Anderson, C., & David, Y. (1993). Pursuing scientific literacy in the middle grades through collaborative problem solving. *Elementary School Journal, 93,* 643-658.

Palincsar, A., & Brown, A. (1984). Reciprocal teaching of comprehension-fostering and comprehension-monitoring activities. *Cognition and Instruction, 1,* 117–175.

Palincsar, A., & Brown, A. (1989). Classroom dialogues to promote self-regulated comprehension. In J. Brophy (Ed.), *Advances in research on teaching.* Vol. 1: *Teaching for meaningful understanding and self-regulated learning.* Greenwich, CT: JAI.

Paris, S., Cross, D., & Lipson, M. (1984). Informed Strategies for Learning: A program to improve children's reading awareness and comprehension. *Journal of Educational Psychology, 76,* 1239–1252.

Paris, S., Wasik, B., & Turner, J. (1991). The development of strategic readers. In R. Barr, M. Kamil, P. Mosenthal, & P. Pearson (Eds.), *Handbook of reading research* (Vol. 2, pp. 609–640). New York: Longman.

Perkins, D. (1992). *Smart schools: From training memories to educating minds.* New York: The Free Press.

Perry, M., VanderStoep, S., & Yu, S. (1993). Asking questions in first-grade mathematics classes: Potential influences on mathematical thought. *Journal of Educational Psychology, 85,* 31-40.

Posner, G., Strike, K., Hewson, K., & Gertzog, W. (1982). Accommodation of a scientific conception: Toward a theory of conceptual change. *Science Education, 66,* 211–228.

Prawat, R. (1989). Promoting access to knowledge, strategy, and disposition in students: A research synthesis. *Review of Educational Research, 59,* 1–41.

Pressley, M., & Beard El-Dinary, P. (Guest Editors). (1993). Special issue on strategies instruction. *Elementary School Journal, 94,* 105–284.

Pressley, M., El-Dinary, P., Gaskins, I., Schuder, T., Bergman, J., Almasi, J., & Brown, R. (1992). Beyond direct explanation: Transactional instruction of reading comprehension strategies. *Elementary School Journal, 92,* 513–555.

Pressley, M., Harris, K., & Marks, M. (1992). But good strategy instructors are constructivists! *Educational Psychology Review, 4,* 3–31.

Pressley, M., Johnson, C., Symons, S., McGoldrick, J., & Kurita, J. (1989). Strategies that improve children's memory and comprehension of text. *Elementary School Journal, 90,* 3–32.

Quirk, B., & Cianciolo, P. (1993). *The study of literature in a fifth-grade classroom: One teacher's perspective* (Elementary Subjects Center Report No. 83). East Lansing: Michigan State University, Institute for Research on Teaching, Center for the Learning and Teaching of Elementary Subjects.

Resnick, L. (1987). *Education and learning to think.* Washington, DC: National Academy Press.

Resnick, L. (1989). Treating mathematics as an ill-structured discipline. In R. Charles & E. Silver (Eds.), *The teaching and assessing of mathematical problem solving.* Hillsdale, NJ: Erlbaum.

Resnick, L., & Klopfer, L. (Eds.). (1989). *Toward the thinking curriculum: Current cognitive research: 1989 Yearbook of the Association for Supervision and Curriculum Development.* Alexandria, VA: Association for Supervision and Curriculum Development.

Rogoff, B. (1990). *Apprenticeship in thinking: Cognitive development in social context.* New York: Oxford University Press.

Rogoff, B., & Wertsch, J. (Eds.). (1984). *Children's learning in the "zone of proximal development."* San Francisco: Jossey-Bass.

Rosaen, C. (1989). Writing in the content areas: Reaching its potential in the learning process. In J. Brophy (Ed.), *Advances in research on teaching.* Vol. 1: *Teaching for meaningful understanding and self-regulated learning.* Greenwich, CT: JAI.

Rosenshine, B., & Meister, C. (1992). The use of scaffolds for teaching higher-level cognitive strategies. *Educational Leadership, 49*(7), 26–33.

Rosenshine, B., & Meister, C. (1994). Reciprocal teaching: A review of the research. *Review of Educational Research, 64,* 479-530.

Roth, K. (1990). Developing meaningful conceptual understanding in science. In B. Jones & L. Idol (Eds.), *Dimensions of thinking and cognitive instruction* (pp. 139–175). Hillsdale, NJ: Erlbaum.

Rumelhart, D., & Norman, D. (1981). Analogical processes in learning. In J. Anderson (Ed.), *Cognitive skills and their acquisition* (pp. 335–359). Hillsdale, NJ: Erlbaum.

Schank, R., & Abelson, R. (1977). *Scripts, plans, goals, and understanding.* Hillsdale, NJ: Erlbaum.

Shapiro, B. (1994). "That's not true—it doesn't make sense": An approach to understanding students' views of scientific ideas. *Qualitative Studies in Education, 7,* 19–32.

Smith, E., & Anderson, L. (1984). *The Planning and Teaching Intermediate Science study: Final report.* East Lansing: Institute for Research on Teaching, Michigan State University.

Soled, S. (1990). Teaching processes to improve both higher and lower mental process achievement. *Teaching and Teacher Education, 6,* 255–265.

Stahl, S., & Miller, P. (1989). Whole language and language experience approaches for beginning reading: A quantitative research synthesis. *Review of Educational Research, 59,* 87–116.

Steffe, L., Cobb, P., & von Glasersfeld, E. (1988). *Construction of arithmetical meanings and strategies.* New York: Springer-Verlag.

Steffe, L., & Gale, J. (Eds.). (1995). *Constructivism in education.* Hillsdale, NJ: Erlbaum.

Stigler, J., & Stevenson, H. (1991). How Asian teachers polish each lesson to perfection. *American Educator, 15*(1), 12–20, 43–47.

Stodolsky, S. (1988). *The subject matters: Classroom activity in math and social studies.* Chicago: University of Chicago Press.

Swing, S., Stoiber, K., & Peterson, P. (1988). Thinking skills versus learning time: Effects of alternative classroom-based interventions on students' mathematics problem solving. *Cognition and Instruction, 5,* 123–191.

Tharp, R., & Gallimore, R. (1988). *Rousing minds to life: Teaching, learning, and schooling in social context.* Cambridge: Cambridge University Press.

Thornton, S., & Wenger, R. (1990). Geography curriculum and instruction in three fourth-grade classrooms. *Elementary School Journal, 90,* 515–531.

von Glasersfeld, E. (1984). An introduction to radical constructivism. In P. Watzlawick (Ed.), *The invented reality* (pp. 17–40). New York: Norton.

Villasenor, A., & Kepner, H. (1993). Arithmetic from a problem-solving perspective: An urban implementation. *Journal for Research in Mathematics Education, 24,* 62-69.

Vosniadou, S., & Brewer, W. (1987). Theories of knowledge restructuring in development. *Review of Educational Research, 57,* 51–67.

Vygotsky, L. (1962). *Thought and language.* Cambridge, MA: MIT Press.

Vygotsky, L. (1978). *Mind in society: The development of higher psychological processes* (Edited by M. Cole, V. John-Steiner, S. Scribner, & E. Souberman). Cambridge: Harvard University Press.

Weinert, F., & Helmke, A. (1995). Learning from wise Mother Nature or Big Brother Instructor: The wrong choice as seen from an educational perspective. *Educational Psychologist, 30,* 135–142.

Wertsch, J. (1985). *Vygotsky and the social formation of mind.* Cambridge: Harvard University Press.

Wertsch, J. (1991). *Voices of the mind: A sociocultural approach to mediated action.* Cambridge: Harvard University Press.

Wertsch, J., & Tulviste, P. (1992). L. S. Vygotsky and contemporary developmental psychology. *Developmental Psychology, 28,* 548–557.

Wheatley, G. (1992). The role of reflection in mathematics learning. *Educational Studies in Mathematics, 23,* 529–541.

White, R. (1992). Implications of recent research on learning for curriculum and assessment. *Journal of Curriculum Studies, 24,* 153–164.

Wood, D., Bruner, J., & Ross, G. (1976). The role of tutoring in problem solving. *Journal of Child Psychology and Psychiatry, 17,* 89–100.

Wood, T., Cobb, P., & Yackel, E. (1990). The contextual nature of teaching: Mathematics and reading instruction in one second-grade classroom. *Elementary School Journal, 90,* 497–513.

FORM 10.1. Teaching Content for Understanding and Application

PURPOSE: To assess the degree to which the teacher teaches content, not just for memory but for understanding and application.
USE: When you have detailed information about the curriculum, instruction, and evaluation enacted during a content unit or strand.
Enter a check mark for each of the following features that was included effectively in the content unit or strand, and a zero for each feature that was omitted or handled ineffectively. Then add detailed comments on a separate sheet, emphasizing constructive suggestions for improvement.

CHECKLIST

_____ 1. *Goals* were expressed in terms of long-term student outcomes (acquisition of knowledge, skills, values, or dispositions to be applied to life outside of school), not just in terms of short-term content mastery.

_____ 2. Limited content was taught in sufficient *depth* to allow for development of understanding.

_____ 3. The *knowledge* content was represented as *networks* of related information structured around powerful key ideas.

_____ 4. In presenting and leading discussions of the content, the teacher helped students to recognize the centrality of key ideas and to use them as bases around which to structure larger content networks.

_____ 5. In addition to providing explicit explanations, the teacher asked questions and engaged students in activities that required them to process the information actively, test and if necessary repair their understanding of it, and communicate about it.

_____ 6. *Skills* (procedural knowledge) were taught and used in the process of applying information (propositional knowledge) content rather than being taught as a separate curriculum.

_____ 7. Most skills practice was embedded within inquiry, problem solving, decision making, or other whole-task application contexts rather than being limited to isolated practice of part skills.

_____ 8. If skills needed to be taught, they were taught with emphasis on modeling their strategic use for accomplishing particular purposes, as well as explaining when and why the skills would be used.

_____ 9. Content-based *discourse* emphasized sustained and thoughtful discussion featuring critical or creative thinking about key ideas, not just fast-moving recitation over specifics.

_____ 10. *Activities and assignments* called for students to integrate or apply key ideas and engage in critical and creative thinking, problem solving, inquiry, decision making, or other higher-order applications, not just to demonstrate recall of facts and definitions.

_____ 11. In *assessing* student learning, the teacher focused on understanding and application goals, not just low-level factual memory or skills mastery goals.

FORM 10.2. Social Construction of Knowledge

USE: When a teacher engages students in reflective discussion designed to stimulate construction of knowledge.
PURPOSE: To assess the degree to which the discussion includes features that support social construction of knowledge.

Check each feature that was included in the discussion:
A. POSES A WELL-CHOSEN PROBLEM

___ 1. Problem is appropriate in familiarity, difficulty; Students have enough prior knowledge to allow them to discuss it intelligibly, but they also must engage in reasoning and higher-order thinking
___ 2. Problem is authentic, significant to the students
___ 3. Teacher requires them to predict, explain, develop justified problem-solving or decision-making strategies that call for applying the powerful ideas being developed

B. ELICITS SUGGESTIONS AND RELATED JUSTIFICATIONS

___ 1. Students act as learning community, teacher facilitates
___ 2. Poses problem, calls for ideas about how to approach it
___ 3. Lists suggestions on board or overhead
___ 4. Doesn't judge but calls for clarification, elaboration, justification

C. ELICITS ASSESSMENTS AND DISCUSSION

___ 1. Invites students to critique by offering justified arguments for or against contributed ideas
___ 2. Invites contributors to revise their thinking if they wish
___ 3. Encourages student-student interaction and debate
___ 4. If necessary, scaffolds by breaking question into separate issues or substeps, asking about a neglected aspect, listing what is given or has been agreed upon separately from what still is at issue

D. AS ISSUES GET CLARIFIED, MOVES STUDENTS TOWARD RESOLUTION(S)

___ 1. Tests for consensus when it appears to have developed; if disagreement still exists, asks about unresolved issue(s)
___ 2. If necessary, asks questions to focus attention on unwarranted assumptions, misconceptions, or complications that have not yet been recognized
___ 3. If necessary, temporarily interrupts discussion to allow students time to get more information or interact more intensively in subgroups
___ 4. When consensus is finally achieved, asks questions to help students reformulate what they have discovered about this particular case into more general principles

E. CONSTRUCTS SUMMARY OF MAIN IDEAS AND THEIR CONNECTIONS

___ 1. Invites students to summarize what has been learned
___ 2. If necessary, asks clarification and elaboration questions to make sure that the summary includes all main points and connections between them that need to be emphasized
___ 3. Follows up by having students work individually or in small groups to reconstruct the new knowledge (by writing in journals or composing reports, etc.) and perhaps to apply it to new cases

NOTES:

CHAPTER

11

Improving Classroom Teaching

INTRODUCTION

We have described a variety of instructional activities and learning opportunities that can assist students to learn productively in the classroom. Although the ideas we provide are practical and useful, they are not intended as prescriptions for how to teach. As we stress throughout the book, teachers have different needs and interests; hence, in-service programs must be tailored to participants, and teachers must adapt program content to meet their own needs (Sizer, 1992; Smylie, 1995). In this chapter we present guidelines for in-service training and self-improvement.

You need to integrate the theory, research, and concepts we have presented with your own personality and teaching style and apply them to your teaching context. This view is similar to Biddle and Anderson's (1986) perspective on the role of theories in research on teaching: "They provide a synthesis and explanation for findings to date, they suggest predictions that we might make for teaching contexts we have not yet examined, they make explicit the assumptions with which we think about events, and they provide tools we can use to think about and comprehend the confusing phenomena of teaching" (p. 246).

You must go beyond theory and research by reflecting on your own earlier experience as a student, your beliefs about what appropriate teaching is, and your actual teaching experience as well as by learning to use other teachers to gain insight into their teaching (Ball & Goodson, 1985; Biddle, Good, & Goodson, 1996; Gitlin et al., 1992). Exciting developments are occurring in teaching today—a growing citizen awareness of the importance and complexity of teaching and the willingness of some administrators to share with teachers power and responsibility for staff development (Hart, 1995; Maeroff, 1988). We discuss ways to design in-service programs to facilitate your personal growth. We begin with sections about individual programs of self-growth and informal study groups of volunteer teachers. Then we discuss staff development that occurs as part of a school system's official in-service program.

Teachers, like everyone else, are sometimes unwilling to engage in self-evaluation. Is this because teachers are not committed to their profession or are unwilling to do the extra work necessary to improve? We doubt it. Teachers seek opportunities to evaluate and improve their teaching if acceptable and useful methods are available (Good & Mulryan, 1990). However, certain obstacles minimize self-improvement in some teachers, and these must be removed if continual development is to take place. The following vignettes illustrate how colleagues can assist or hinder self-evaluation.

A Junior High Example

Janice Taylor is an ambitious social studies education major who is student-teaching at Oak Junior High. Oak students come from the same kinds of middle-class homes that Janice comes from. Still, she is sometimes apprehensive about teaching. She has not been in a junior high for several years, and although she has gained useful information in her college classes, she has never taught. Will students obey her? Can she make them enjoy schoolwork? These doubts increase as the time for her to begin teaching nears. She has been observing Ms. Woodward's class for two weeks. In another week she is to become the teacher.

Janice watches Ms. Woodward intently because she wants to learn how to get students to respond and obey. She believes Ms. Woodward is a good teacher who treats students fairly and is respected by them. However, Janice is a shy and soft-spoken person who frequently becomes nervous when she is around loud, assertive people. Consequently, she is often upset by the forceful way in which Ms. Woodward runs the class. She speaks in a booming voice and does not hesitate to give misbehaving students a tongue-lashing or send them out of the room. Her favorite tactic when students are disruptive is to yell, "I'm telling you once and for the last time, listen to your classmates when they talk!" Students typically stop after Ms. Woodward yells at them.

One week later, when Janice is teaching the class, she loudly addresses some misbehaving students in the same way, "I'm telling you once and for the last time, listen to your classmates!" Think about these two questions:

1. Why did Janice imitate Mrs. Woodward's teaching style?
2. How might Janice have taught if she had had a different cooperating teacher?

A High School Example

Jessica Tyler has taught chemistry for 15 years at Riverside High School, an affluent high school in a western state. She is respected as a teacher by both colleagues and students. Today she is meeting with Sharon Mendoza, a first-year history teacher. Ms. Tyler believes that peer teacher observation and feedback are useful. Although math teachers typically work with math teachers, and so forth, the principal encourages teachers to cross subject-matter lines on occasion to help colleagues better understand instructional issues that are not subject-specific (clarity, etc.). Today, Jessica observed Ms. Mendoza's third-period class. Now, during fifth period they are meeting to discuss the observation. Ms. Tyler begins the conversation immediately. "Sharon, it was a pleasure to observe in your class. I enjoyed it a lot. It was a good lesson. There are only a few mistakes that I'd like to talk about."

What do you think about peer observation? Should teachers observe other teachers? Would you like for classmates to observe you? What should happen during a feedback conversation? What do you think of the way Ms. Tyler began the conversation?

Obstacles to Teacher Self-Improvement

One obstacle to teacher self-improvement results from the way we were socialized. Most of us have seldom taken part in self-evaluation designed not just to uncover weaknesses but to eliminate those weaknesses. We may occasionally engage in destructive self-criticism, but we rarely link such behavior with constructive plans for improvement.

We act this way in part because our socialization (especially our experience in schools) has not helped us to develop the needed skills. For example, has a teacher ever returned an "A" paper to you with instructions to reflect on the paper and to improve it? Certainly, most of us have had to rewrite papers, but seldom "A" papers, and rarely have we been asked to rethink and incorporate new ideas of our own into such work. Indeed, school seldom allowed most of us time to *think* about what we were doing. We were too busy finishing assignments to reflect on them.

Socialization in schools tends to emphasize this idea: Do not look back, keep moving forward. Yet we must examine our past and present performances so that we can monitor progress and determine whether we are moving forward or merely traveling in circles.

A second obstacle to self-improvement is that our school experience has often emphasized analytical thinking, not synthesis. The following tenth-grade social studies dialogue represents analytical thinking:

> TEACHER: Keith, what's wrong with electing members of Congress every two years?
>
> KEITH: (*Hesitantly and in a soft tone*) Well, ah, I think that they spend too much time trying to be reelected. (*The teacher is beaming and nodding, so Keith begins to speak more confidently and loudly.*) Since they face reelection every two years, they always need money for reelection. They build their campaign chest primarily with funds from the people who financed their original candidacy, so they owe these people a double debt. It's hard for them to be their own person.
>
> TEACHER: Good answer, Keith. Alicia, what did Keith imply when he said, "be their own person"?
>
> ALICIA: Well, that the candidates' debts and their continual dependency on special interests who have given money make them cater to these groups. But even if members of Congress are strong, the two-year election procedure is bad because they continue to run, make speeches, raise money, and have little time to do their real job.

Although such discussions are important, they seldom go beyond an analysis stage that defines the problem. However, the teacher might point out the desirability of controlling campaign spending and making the sources of contributions public knowledge and then challenge students to go beyond these common solutions that *others* have suggested. For example, the teacher might "playfully" suggest that senators, even though they are elected for six-year terms, spend much time running for reelection and make most of their decisions accordingly. The teacher could also have students suggest ways in which elected representatives could be held accountable: Should they keep daily logs of how their time is spent, hold regular office hours for the public, or spend a designated number of days in the district or state they represent? Students could be encouraged to speculate on the effects of term limits that have been approved in some states.

Demands are seldom made on students for original, practical suggestions because most teachers were socialized in schools that demanded and rewarded analytical thinking. This emphasis gave most of us plenty of practice in pinpointing weaknesses but comparatively little experience in solving problems by generating constructive alternatives.

Also, most of the evaluation we experienced in schools was external and nonconstructive. The way it was handled told us where we stood, but not how we could improve. Thus, we tended to avoid evaluation. Since evaluation was so strongly associated with negative consequences, it often evoked the fear that "I'm going to be exposed" rather than the anticipation "I'm going to receive useful feedback." Consequently, evaluation may make us anxious, even when it is just self-evaluation.

Another factor that has limited teachers' ability to grow as professionals is that some teacher education programs have not assisted students in developing skills in collegiality and in learning about themselves through feedback from others. Teachers need to study models of collegial relationships and to practice giving and receiving feedback.

Given a lack of opportunity to learn ways to give and receive peer feedback, teachers might be confused about how to do this. Smylie (1992), in studying teachers' reports of their interactions with teacher leaders, concludes that teachers and teacher leaders often conceptualize the role of the teacher leader differently. Hence, often teachers perceive their needs differently from teacher leaders. Further, it is clear that teacher leaders in Smylie's sample wanted to provide more classroom support for teachers (observe, teach, offer resources), but the organizational structure in which they worked often made it impossible for them to work with teachers during the instructional day. Thus, if peer leadership programs are to work, there must be both careful goal conceptualization and appropriate structural supports (i.e., time).

EXPERIMENTING AND IMPROVING

As a teacher you are an individual with a unique pattern of strengths and weaknesses. You have to develop a style that allows you to express yourself and teach students in your own way. To do so, you may have to experiment with different methods before you find an approach that is right for you (i.e., you feel comfortable using it and your students learn and respond positively to it). If you try an approach systematically for a reasonable time and it does not work, *then discard it and develop techniques that do work for you.* There is no need to teach the way your cooperating teacher did without regard to your own feelings or to the response of your students. Similarly, there is no necessary reason that you should teach like peers or mentor teachers (a topic we will return to at the end of the chapter).

Even after identifying a satisfying style, successful teachers continue to experiment with new methods and to find new ways to stimulate student learning. They also constantly reflect on their teaching and stay abreast of new research and developments. Given the demands of preparing for class and grading papers, finding time for professional reading is often difficult. But continued reading is essential if teachers are to grow professionally and to become knowledgeable colleagues (Darling-Hammond, Bullmaster, & Cobb, 1995).

Teaching Is Difficult

Few teachers are excellent in all aspects of teaching. All teachers occasionally teach lessons that fail, say the wrong thing to students, and so forth. Although teaching is difficult, one can succeed at it by continuing to strive for improvement. Too often teachers enter the classroom with unrealistically high expectations ("I will capture the interest of every student at every moment, and every lesson I teach will be completely successful."), so that when outcomes do not match expectations, they may become depressed, blame students, or begin to justify and rationalize their behavior rather than to search for new styles of teaching. This occurs in part because they do not realize that other teachers also have difficulties.

Like everyone else, teachers tend to talk about successes, not failures. Thus, some teachers, especially new ones, may become anxious and discouraged when they have trouble because they hear nothing but the good or interesting things that other teachers are doing. They experience feelings of disappointment and ineptness when they do not achieve easy success, yet are reluctant to ask veteran teachers for help because they believe they would be admitting failure (Rosenholtz, 1989).

If you have thoughts like these, dismiss them. Teaching is challenging and exciting work, but it takes time to develop and refine teaching skills. Most experienced teachers are sympathetic to the problems of beginning teachers and are glad to help them. However, few of us like to be approached by someone who says, "Tell me what to do." It is better to approach other teachers by telling them you have a teaching problem and would like to exchange ideas with them and benefit from their experience. Experienced teachers can also learn from beginning teachers.

Identifying Good Teaching

You must decide what is good practice by studying the effects of your behavior and classroom learning opportunities on students. (Do tests reveal appropriate learning? Do lectures lead students to raise their own questions? Do students enjoy and understand cooperative group assignments?) There is no single formula specifying good teaching because no one set of teaching behaviors is clearly related to student achievement in all situations (Good, 1996; Sikula, Buttery, & Guyton, 1996) and, in any case, achievement is only one of many student outcomes that must be considered. Our advice is based on research, but we have often gone beyond the data in order to provide suggestions. To reiterate, the statements in this book are not intended to tell you how to teach but rather to provide you with a way of looking at and analyzing classroom life.

As a teacher it is useful to reflect on personal experiences (as a child, as a student, as a student teacher, etc.) in order to understand your current beliefs about instruction. Reflecting on experiences (one's own or reading stories of other teachers) can stimulate self-insight and new goals or approaches to teaching (Ball & Goodson, 1985; Gitlin et al., 1992; Russell & Munby, 1992). Finally, numerous valuable sources discuss self-evaluation (e.g., Barber, 1990) and how self-improvement and staff development can hinder or facilitate teachers' personal and professional growth depending on program goals and quality of feedback (Gitlin & Smyth, 1989).

Starting Self-Evaluation

The first step in improving teaching is to evaluate your current strengths and weaknesses. Go back through this text and list your behaviors on three pages entitled (1) *Perform Capably,* (2) *Needs Work,* and (3) *Not Sure.* Take the first list, which represents progress you have made as a teacher, and store it in your desk so you can examine it from time to time and add to it.

You may note that you already ask a variety of factual and higher-order questions and that you ask questions before calling on students. On your list for *Needs Work,* you may note a tendency not to follow through on warnings and an inconsistency as a classroom manager or decide that you want to help students to become better self-evaluators. After a few hours of thinking about strengths and weaknesses, you will have an outline of your ability as a teacher and will be ready to begin work on the list of needed improvements.

If you have trouble deciding where to start, you might have a teacher or supervisor whom you respect observe your class and make suggestions. Alternatively, you could listen to a tape-recorded session of your class. It is difficult to evaluate what occurs in classrooms because so much happens so quickly, so it may take some time to identify strengths and weaknesses.

Making Explicit Plans

To improve your teaching, you must decide what you want to do and how to determine whether your plans are working. Be specific—get beyond vague improvement notions that are like halfhearted New Year's resolutions that are never fulfilled. Goals such as "I want to teach in diverse ways" are seldom accomplished simply because they are not concrete goals that can guide planning. Resolutions are more likely to be fulfilled when they specify the desired change: "I want to increase the time I spend in small-group and project-based work by 25 percent."

Self-evaluation is possible in many teaching situations, although certain teacher behaviors are more difficult to evaluate than others and evaluation may benefit from peer or student feedback. Teachers frequently set goals for students as well as for themselves. A teacher may say, "I want all of my ninth-grade students to participate more actively during small-group lab projects." This resolution calls for evaluating the behaviors of both the teacher and the students.

If you do not know where you are going, you are unlikely to get there. By understanding the problem you are addressing, it is easier to clarify the beliefs, norms, and behaviors you are trying to improve. However, we recognize that problem identification is not always easy and that change can be complex at times. For example, teachers who want to implement small-group cooperative learning may find that they must do considerable reading and visit other classrooms in order to decide what role small-group teaching will play in their classrooms.

Action

After developing appropriate goals (or needs for knowledge from which to form goals), the next step is to choose two or three behaviors or beliefs to change or new ones to try. Do not try to change too many things at once, lest you become overwhelmed and discouraged. Consider a few issues at a time and carefully monitor your progress. For example, if you try to call on students randomly, you may have to write their names on flash cards and shuffle the stack periodically. Always calling on students who have their hands up is a difficult habit to break. You may improve classroom communication by explaining why you ask questions, thus helping students to understand their roles.

As you implement a change, assess its effectiveness. After you introduce lessons by telling students why the lessons are important, try to assess whether more students follow the directions or seem interested. Similarly, if you call on students to react to other students' responses, note whether students pay greater attention to the discussion (and whether student essays reflect more awareness of diverse opinion, etc.).

Individual Self-Study

Some questions that might be useful for self-study include the following:

What aspects of teaching do I most enjoy and what does this imply about my beliefs on what is good teaching?

How do my instructional goals match those of my peers? (As an algebra teacher, how much time do I spend on particular topics? To what extent is my curriculum relevant to male and female students and students from various races or ethnic groups? As a music teacher, do I emphasize history as much as other teachers do?)

Do my low and high achievers indicate that I have equal interest in them?

Do low- and high-achieving students have different beliefs about the value of subject matter?

Do my questions emphasize understanding or only quick, correct answers?

How long do I wait for students to respond? Is this figure different for high and low achievers?

When students work in small groups, do some students do most of the work?

Which students want to work in small groups the most? The least? Why?

What percentage of my day is spent in actual instruction?

When I teach my subject specialty (art, biology, honors English, French), how do I teach the content I am most knowledgeable about and interested in versus content I am least knowledgeable about?

What percentage of a student's day is spent learning new material versus reviewing? Why?

Do some students who need help rarely seek me out to get it? Which students initiate contact with me and which ones don't? Why?

How much time do I spend with individual students in a given day?

How much time do I spend in math, social studies, language arts? Do students' achievement gains reflect time spent?

Are undesirable gender roles or inappropriate cultural expectations being communicated?

How often do I get requests from students to tailor an assignment to their interests? Do I handle such requests appropriately?

How much time do my students spend on their homework? Do I need to work to get some students to take homework more seriously?

How do students study for exams (in groups, individually, in pairs)? Does it seem to make any difference?

How interesting do students rate my presentations? Does this interest vary as a function of gender or achievement level?

Exploring such questions would provide you with information about aspects of your classroom that you might want to change. That is, the results could lead you to ask questions such as: Can I raise the average amount of time I spend with individual low achievers during mathematics from two minutes to five minutes a day? If so, what effect will this have on their attitudes, achievement, and attention spans (when they work independently)? When I implement learning centers and peer-tutoring activities, do I have more time to work with individual students? Can I change certain routines to make the classroom more interesting for me and my students?

Classroom Example

Let us consider an example to see how a teacher could use information to improve instruction. Assume that sixth-grade teacher Joe Hernandez's students do less well in math than in all other subjects. Joe is puzzled by this. He enjoys teaching math and feels well qualified to do so. Students' attitudes measured earlier in the year were generally positive toward him and the instructional program. However, math drew the most criticism when students commented on specific subjects.

Joe decides to obtain anonymous information from students about the problems they encounter in math and about how the program might be improved. Upon doing so, he is discouraged to find that much of the information is contradictory (what some students prefer is disliked by others) or does not lead to suggestions for action (students do not believe that the math period is too long). However, one theme is evident in the comments of several students: "I often don't know what I'm supposed to do for my assignment"; "When we start a new unit, I'm always lost"; "I don't understand my work until you explain it the next day."

Subsequently, Joe notices that students engage in more neutral or aimless activity when working on math assignments than at any other time during the day. He decides that he does not spend enough time explaining how the work relates to preceding work, modeling how to do problems, and allowing students to generate and discuss examples before he has students begin work on assignments. In particular, he wants students to discuss more of their background knowledge and to think about the bridge between what they already know and the current instruction.

If students had expressed low interest, Joe might have considered peer tutoring or devising a mathematics learning center to add novelty and provide more time for him to work with individuals. However, students' self-reports ("Often I'm confused, but after a while I catch on.") match his own observations that the problem is not low motivation (boredom) but lack of understanding. Joe's plan is to increase his ratio of explanation, modeling, and student verbalization of thinking to practice work, especially at the beginning of a unit, and to see whether this strategy improves students' attitudes and achievement.

Note that Joe's plan is based on only a hypothesis, a hunch about how to proceed. It must be judged by its effects on students' performance. Plans must not become "answers" adopted without consideration of their effects on students. Joe might find that some other factor (assignments too long, feedback inadequate) is related more directly to student achievement. By evaluating the effects of his changes in classroom processes on student outcomes (achievement, attitude), eventually he will find procedures that work for his class.

Self-improvement plans might also focus on changing knowledge. Teachers could evaluate and then enhance their knowledge of particular subjects (art history, geometry) or concepts. Similarly, teachers might improve curriculum units (How can I promote more higher-order thinking about social studies topics? How can I teach fewer topics but make them more integrated and meaningful?). And, of course, teachers might focus on collegial relations (How can I find more time to discuss important issues with peers? How can we arrange to do guest lectures to extend our own knowledge?). We continue to focus our discussion on changing instruction, but you should note that the general process of change is similar across different types of outcomes.

You Are Not Alone

You may wish to begin your evaluation and operate for awhile without feedback from others. Nevertheless, all teachers who want to improve as a teacher will eventually benefit from discussing classroom teaching with other teachers.

If you have access to videotape equipment, arrange to have one or two of your typical lessons videotaped. Do not attempt to construct special units or to review old material. Teach your regularly scheduled lessons in your normal fashion. After a couple of weeks, tape some similar lessons so you can watch for signs of progress in your classroom behavior, your decision making, and in the responses of students. If your school does not have video equipment, check with your principal to see if you can get it from the central office. Central school officials are usually delighted to loan video equipment. If it is impossible to secure video equipment, cassette audio recorders are readily available and can be used to collect useful information.

You can obtain feedback from other sources too. Some people teach in teams or other situations where it is easy to arrange for another teacher to observe them. You can also request release time to work with peers or make arrangements to trade weekly visits with other teachers during free periods. Finally, you can use student teachers, student observers, or parents on occasion.

It usually is best to specify what an observer is to look for, because there is so much to see that he or she may not notice the things you would like to receive feedback about. The observer, of course, can always volunteer additional information.

Curriculum supervisors also can provide you with relevant feedback. Most supervisors are delighted when teachers make explicit observation requests. However, supervisory visits are often frustrating for the supervisor as well as for the teacher (McDaniel, 1981). Since supervisors may not know the goals of a lesson or how it fits into a unit, it is difficult for them to provide helpful feedback. Armed with a specific request, though, they can provide relevant comments about areas of interest to teachers.

Students are another source of information. Anonymously administered questionnaires can provide useful information. Teachers who have never solicited student evaluations may be dismayed at first when they see the variety of comments. Students have unique perspectives, and different students may label the same behavior as a weakness or a strength. However, feedback usually includes some comments on which most students agree.

We have found that student feedback is most useful if it is given anonymously. Also, rather than requesting global comments or ratings, it is usually better to ask for specific reactions. One method is to request three or more statements about strengths and three or more about weaknesses, which forces students to be specific and to provide a more balanced critique than do global, free-response methods.

Various standardized instruments are available for obtaining student feedback (Fraser, 1986). One especially good source (Anderson, 1983) provides extensive coverage of affective assessment, including examples of self-report measures, procedures for developing new measures, and strategies for interpreting affective data. Teachers who collect anonymous information should demonstrate to students the usefulness of this information; that is, they should call students' attention to program changes made in response to their feedback.

Informed conversations are another good way to learn from students. McCaslin and Good (1996) describe various methods for learning from students through classroom conversations. This book provides detailed advice about useful ways that teachers can gain rich insights into student perspectives from student interviews and conversations. Richards (1987) describes questions she used in attempting to motivate secondary students who did not want to learn. She provides an intriguing discussion of how she was able to increase students' motivation by increasing her understanding of the students' perspectives.

Self-Study Groups

You can often use regularly scheduled in-service time for work in self-improvement groups. This procedure is especially useful when the time is devoted to small-group work with teachers who have common problems (e.g., elementary teachers working at the same grade, secondary teachers who teach the same subject). Self-study groups can also be formed on the basis of interest (e.g., beginning teachers who want to form a support group or learn a particular skill). Small groups provide an excellent place for teachers to receive feedback and suggestions from peers.

Different goals call for different groupings. For example, to improve curriculum continuity, teachers in contiguous grades should work together. However, if the goal is to allow elementary and secondary teachers to realize that some of their assumptions about what occurs at the other level do not apply, then it is important to mix teachers from the two levels. To promote the exchange of information about teaching style or classroom climate, teachers who teach different subjects and at various grade levels are needed. Beginning teachers should sometimes meet together (where they feel free to express problems); at other times, experienced teachers should meet with beginning teachers (i.e., to offer the benefit of experience in responding to problems).

Self-improvement teams may wish to view and provide feedback about tapes of one another's teaching, especially feedback about aspects that are of special interest to the teacher taped. This procedure contrasts markedly with the typical in-service program, which provides teachers with information on issues that the consultant wishes to discuss. Many staff development programs are designed by persons outside schools to "fix" teachers' deficiencies as these persons perceive them. Too often teachers view in-service activities as unrelated to their teaching needs (Smylie, 1995; Spencer, 1984).

Some self-study group programs are created to encourage teachers to teach in one and only one way. We believe, however, that the role of self-study groups is to help teachers to develop their own styles, not to impose a style on them. The goal is self-development through professional reflection, not standardization of teaching practice (see Gitlin & Smyth, 1989; Gordon, 1992).

Participation in self-study groups usually should be voluntary. Nothing hurts a program that involves discussing and evaluating teaching more than someone who takes part solely because it is required. Consideration should be given, however, to teachers who want to assess their instructional programs and develop their own goals before joining a group. Such teachers should have a chance to join self-study groups when they are ready to do so.

Three rules should be kept in mind when in-service groups begin to function. The first rule is that group structure and feedback exist to provide teachers with information that augments their self-development. The group provides the unique perspectives of its members as well as resources that enable it to give a teacher feedback regarding specific instructional plans. Thus, teachers function as decision makers, setting their own developmental goals. The group functions as a barometer, telling how it views the teacher and suggesting alternative ways to reach the goals the teacher has set. Teachers in the group will have their own viewpoints, of course, and each will react in terms of his or her own perspective.

Each teacher lists current goals and outlines what behaviors and techniques the group should examine when they view videotapes or observe the classroom. So as not to do too much at once, the teacher initially focuses on improving a few areas, and the group restricts its comments to these. After the group has functioned for a few weeks, the "video teacher of the week" may be ready to ask the group to focus on all dimensions of teaching that were exhibited.

The second rule to follow, then, especially in the group's formative weeks, is not to overwhelm a teacher with information. Restricting discussion to a few areas will help, and it may be useful to limit the number of comments each group member makes. We can profit from only so much information at one time, particularly negative feedback.

In-service groups may benefit from a rule such as this: Each participant provides a written discussion of two or three strengths and two or three weaknesses of the presentation. This guideline limits the amount of information a teacher receives and focuses attention on a small, manageable list of "points to consider." The rule also allows the teacher to have in writing (for future review) the reactions of each participant to the lesson.

Useful feedback focuses on specific ways to improve teaching. Ensuing discussions should include alternative procedures that the teacher might use to produce more desirable student responses. Thus, the teacher should receive both realistic reactions (positive and negative) to his or her performance (on goals that are of personal value) and information about alternative behaviors to consider.

A third rule is to be honest. Self-study groups lose their effectiveness when individuals engage in either of two participatory styles: Pollyanna and Get-the-Guest. Too many teachers are unwilling to say what they feel about another teacher's behavior, perhaps because they are afraid that frankness will lead other teachers to respond in kind when they are being evaluated, or because they believe that the teacher will be hurt by an honest reaction. Yet teachers can improve only if they receive honest, objective feedback. Criticism followed by new ideas or approaches that may improve teaching is the best way the group can assist a teacher in self-development. To be sure, teachers should communicate the good things that a teacher does. We all like to know when we have done well, and it is especially important to receive acknowledgment and encouragement for improvement.

The other undesirable participant role is that of the carping critic who criticizes excessively and thoughtlessly. Perhaps such behavior is motivated by the need for self-protection ("If everybody looks bad, I'll be okay"). Perhaps such teachers are just insensitive to the needs of others. At any rate, their behavior rarely does any good, and they need to be helped to deliver criticism tactfully and to link it with positive suggestions. Those who are not willing to temper excessive criticism should not continue in the group.

Opportunities to Observe and Obtain Feedback

Supervisory Feedback   Research has established that teachers often profit from feedback about their instruction when it is supplied by knowledgeable, sensitive classroom observers. Eash and Rasher (1977) reported that classroom observation was an important component of an in-service program to help teachers cope with the greater student diversity due to desegregation, and thus to improve students' achievement. The supervisory personnel who observed classrooms needed additional training for this role, however, because observation does not automatically improve instruction. Observation is useful only when conducted by competent persons who have a framework for conducting an observation. As Hart (1995) has noted, increasingly school districts are encouraging peer teachers to mentor other teachers by observing and counseling other teachers.

Feedback from Researchers   In interviews with teachers, Good and Brophy (1974) found that teachers were unaware of much of their differential behavior toward high and low achievers, such as the percentage of time that they "stayed with" or "gave up" on students who did not immediately give a correct response. When teachers were presented with information about their behavior that both intrigued and bothered them, they wanted to change. Subsequent observation showed that they succeeded in doing so, and there were signs that students altered their behavior as a result of changed teacher behavior.

Feedback from Peers   Teachers also benefit from feedback from teacher researchers who share important information. For example, Martin and Kerman's Equal Opportunity in the Classroom project (see Martin, 1973) attempted to help teachers become aware of self-defeating treatment of low-achieving students and learn new ways to interact with these students. First, teachers were presented with detailed information about teacher behavior that might be occurring in their own classrooms. They were then trained to treat low achievers in specific ways and also to observe and be observed by fellow teachers.

Teachers' reports about the project were enthusiastic. In particular, they benefited from feedback from other teachers and from observing other teachers themselves. Watching other teachers provides a valuable way to see new techniques. Observational data illustrated that project teachers began to treat low achievers much differently, whereas control teachers did not. In addition, the attitudes of low-achieving students in project classrooms were better than those in control classes.

Researchers continue to provide evidence that feedback can improve instruction. Sparks (1986) studied 19 junior high teachers who were given workshop training on how to increase low achievers' time on task and to improve interactive teaching. The teachers were placed into one of three groups. The first group participated only in the workshops. They were trained to use a coding system (SSOI; see Stallings, 1986), examined their own teaching profiles as exhibited by the SSOI, and discussed recent research findings. The second group participated in the workshops and also received the results of two classroom observations by a peer following the workshop training. The third group of teachers participated in the workshops and received two in-classroom coaching sessions from the trainer. Results showed that teachers who received workshops plus peer observations made the most change.

Sparks (1986) listed several possible reasons why the peer observational treatment was most effective. She noted that secondary teachers rarely observe other secondary teachers instruct and that observing another teacher can generate new ideas about teaching. A second advantage of peer observation is that the teachers were also collecting and coding data as they observed. This may have helped them to analyze both their peers' and their own teaching behavior more reflectively.

Feedback from Students   Feedback from students also can be useful in changing teacher behavior, although teachers do not change their behavior simply because they receive information (Kepler, 1977). To be useful, the information must relate to goals that are important to teachers. When evaluation forms do not reflect teachers' goals or needs, teachers are likely to reject the feedback as meaningless.

When teachers are given specific and accurate information, and especially when their collection of student feedback is voluntary, they can use it to improve instruction. Pambookian (1976) reported that when a group of college teachers was informed of significant discrepancies between their own perceptions and their students' perceptions of their teaching, they changed their teaching behavior. Instructors with student ratings lower than their own ratings improved their teaching the most. As we have seen earlier, students can supply insightful information about their reaction to school events, rules, etc. If student feedback is to have optimal value, teachers must be involved in the construction of the evaluation instruments to insure that questions of personal importance are included, and instruments need to be changed occasionally to present teachers with information about different behaviors and different goals (Good, 1996).

Quality of Feedback   Quality of feedback is critically important, irrespective of its source (supervisor, researcher, peer, student). Unfortunately, little research has focused on this topic. Pajak and Glickman (1989) examined the extent to which teachers and supervisors could discriminate among three types of supervisory communication: information only, information with suggestions, and information with directives. They showed each experimental group videotapes simulating supervisory conferences that differed in the use of informational versus controlling language. The information-only treatment ended with the following message: "The only thing I notice for future improvement is that three students were not following the assignment. I went over to them and noticed that they were unclear as to what they were supposed to do. They had hardly begun the assignment by the end of the class" (p. 96). The information-with-suggestions treatment ended in the following way: "What you might do is meet with those three students before next class and ask them about the directions. During seatwork time, you could move around the classroom and look over their shoulders to see how they are doing. You can check their work while they are still doing it. You may want to make these changes" (p. 96). The information-with-directives treatment ended in the following way: "What you must do is meet with those three students before next class and ask them about the directions. During seatwork time you should move around the classroom and look over their shoulders to see how they are doing. You have to check their work while they are still doing it. I want you to make these changes" (p. 97).

Teachers in each of the three treatment conditions were asked to rate the videotaped conference in terms of supportiveness, authenticity, loyalty, trust, and productivity. Teachers gave their highest ratings to the conference in which the supervisor communicated with suggestions, followed by the conference in which the supervisor communicated information only and then by the conference in which the supervisor communicated information with directives.

Teachers saw information with directives, which implies little choice for teachers, as undesirable. This finding is consistent with Deci and Ryan's (1985) theory of information and control, which suggests that the more choice individuals are given over their activities, the more productive and satisfied they are. If the degree of choice alone was what determined the favorable perceptions, teachers would prefer information only over information with suggestions, because this procedure would allow them more choice about their subsequent behavior. In the context of professional supervision, however, teachers expect supervisors to give them suggestions for improvement. Information alone fails to provide teachers with a basis for improving their instruction, whereas information with suggestions provides teachers with a guide for reflecting on supervisors' advice (i.e., a basis for accepting, revising, or rejecting the suggestions).

These results indicate that the way information is provided —in this case, the degree of control communicated—may determine whether teachers listen to the information. Efforts to help teachers to be specific about the types of information they want from observers may help the latter to be informative without being perceived as "controlling."

Individualizing Feedback   There is growing interest in making teaching assessment and feedback more sensitive to individual teachers' needs and interests. In their book, *Marching to Different Drummers,* Guild and Garger (1985) raise issues associated with teaching styles and discuss the value of such information for teacher supervision and staff development. Guild and Garger illustrate how administrators' understanding of individual teachers' field dependence and field independence can be useful in designing supervisory conferences (see Tables 11.1 and 11.2).

We include these suggestions as a way to stimulate thinking about differential needs. Individuals are not dichotomous (most teachers demonstrate both field orientations). Hence, principals or teachers should interpret these tables as heuristical models—suggesting that teachers have different needs. In order to establish communication with an individual teacher, the emphasis should be placed on open communication, understanding of goals, and frequent feedback, not a static definition of teacher style.

Emerging conceptions of supervision are based on recognition of the fact that teachers have diverse needs and that there is not a single approach to instruction or supervision that is effective for all teachers and all situations (Good, 1996). For example, Glickman (1990) has proposed a model that calls for supervisors to understand and to use various interpersonal approaches in working with teachers,

Table 11.1   WHAT TEACHERS EXPECT FROM AN ADMINISTRATOR

Field Dependence	Field Independence
To give warmth, personal interest, support	To focus on tasks
To provide guidance, to model	To allow independence and flexibility
To seek their opinions in making decisions	To make decisions based on analysis of the problem
To like them	To be knowledgeable about curriculum and instruction
To have an open door	To maintain professional distance
To "practice what they preach"	To be professionally experienced in appropriate content areas
To use tones and body language to support words	To give messages directly and articulately

Source: Guild, P., & Garger, S. (1985). *Marching to different drummers.* Alexandria, VA: Association for Supervision and Curriculum Development.

including directive, collaborative, and nondirective approaches. These models are used depending on the particular educational situation and the developmental level of the teacher.

Gordon (1992) has discussed several shifts in thinking that have occurred concerning the supervision of teachers, including the movement from control to empowerment, a change in emphasis from sameness to diversity, and a movement away from occasional supervisor assistance to continuous collegial feedback and support. He notes that the control perspective mandated the forms of teaching that should be in place. Visions associated with direct control included "teacher-proof" curricula and supervisors who consistently tell teachers the "correct" way to teach. More recently, educational leaders have emphasized an empowerment that helps teachers to become highly skilled and reflective decision makers capable of choosing the form of instruction they will use and suggesting the type of supervisory support they need. Empowerment also implies that teachers are involved in collabora-

Table 11.2   HOW TEACHERS WANT TO BE EVALUATED

Field Dependence	Field Independence
With an emphasis on class "climate," interpersonal relationships, and quality of student-teacher interaction	With an emphasis on accuracy of content, adherence to learning objectives, and assessment of learning
With a narrative report and personal discussion	With a specific list of criteria
With consideration of student and parent comments	With consideration of academic achievement and test scores
With credit for "effort" and for trying	With evidence and facts to support comments

Source: Guild, P., & Garger, S. (1985). *Marching to different drummers.* Alexandria, VA: Association for Supervision and Curriculum Development.

tive curriculum development and instructional leadership, often shifting from external to internal accountability.

Gordon also notes the movement from occasional supervisor assistance (from a formal supervisor or principal) to continuous interactive feedback with colleagues. Concerning the application of research findings, there has been a shift in perspective from research as providing answers to research as stimulating professional inquiry (Anderson & Biddle, 1991; Brophy, 1988; Griffin, 1985a), and being applied within the context of the particular situation and curriculum values.

IMPROVING WORKPLACE CONDITIONS FOR TEACHING

Increasing Professional Opportunities for Teachers

There has been increased recognition that workplace conditions must change if teachers are to have time to work with colleagues, engage in collaborative planning activities, and become more involved in making school-wide decisions. Hart (1995) suggests the following reasons for increasing teachers' leadership in schools: (1) to enhance democratic functioning in schools, (2) to make better use of teachers' expertise in planning coherent instructional programs, (3) to assist in recruiting capable teachers by making the work more interesting (e.g., more professional autonomy and decision making, etc.), (4) to address the need for instructional and curriculum reform, and (5) to develop a more professional workplace.

Maeroff (1988) argues that raising teachers' status by increasing their competence in some aspect of teaching or inviting them to play a role in decision making leads to enhanced commitment and better teaching. These optimistic conclusions come from conversations with teachers who were participating in a program intended to raise their morale, deepen their intellectual background, allow them to make decisions, and increase their confidence and ability. The program also was designed to help teachers develop increased knowledge in various areas, improve their writing, build interdisciplinary units with other teachers, and explore new content.

Maeroff acknowledges that such large-scale programs require outside money and leverage (to get release time for teachers, etc.) and that sometimes there were problems in obtaining administrators' permission for teachers to participate in programming decisions or in securing space and time to plan, implement, and institutionalize the changes. It was also difficult to get teachers to view themselves as change agents who demand the opportunity to shape instructional philosophy and content rather than simply carrying out what is dictated to them by others. Teachers' willingness to act to reform their school environments is a key variable, especially in districts that do not have outside funding to support change or to legitimate the importance of restructuring schools and increasing teachers' professional opportunities (Smylie, 1992).

Smylie (1995) notes that an enormous literature has developed in recent years around advocacy for enhancing teacher leadership in the school and its policies. The Educational Research Information Clearinghouse has over 2100 published and unpublished papers on teacher leadership, 2500 papers on participative decision making, 1300 on lead, master, and mentor teachers, and 1600 on career ladders. Despite this intense interest, Smylie notes that very little of the literature is based on "systematic empirical investigation with identifiable questions for inquiry, specified methodologies, and collection and analysis of original data" (p. 4). Most of the papers are position statements or project descriptions with little or no explication of formal theory or of original data. Still, this literature is useful in stimulating ideas about staff development and personal growth.

Types of Professional Collaboration

There has been an increasing recognition of the need to involve teachers as colleagues in a variety of educational programs. Teachers are collaborating more often with professors in conducting classroom research (e.g., Lieberman, 1986), and the need for teacher education programs to develop skills for collegial interaction is evident (e.g., Rosenholtz, 1989). Glatthorn (1987) notes at least five ways in which teacher teams can work together: professional discussion, curriculum development, peer observation, peer coaching, and action research.

Professional Discussion   Professional dialogue facilitates reflection about teaching. In groups, teachers can discuss issues of common interest—issues specific to a particular subject (e.g., the teaching of controversy in social science, available software for teaching human physiology) or applicable to all subjects (student motivation, ability grouping, critical thinking). Thus, discussion groups do not have to focus on changing teacher or student classroom behavior; they also can emphasize general professional issues.

There are no systematic data concerning the effects of professional dialogue, but participants' reports about such opportunities are generally positive. Although there are many ways to design discussion groups, Glatthorn (1987) suggests one model based on his experience.

The first stage emphasizes external knowledge, or what can be found in the literature about a particular problem (e.g., Do experts agree on the issue—or on strategies for how to respond to such problems?). At this stage, participants should not attempt to dispute external knowledge but rather should explore and try to understand it. In the second stage, discussion centers on personal knowledge (What does my experience with the problem suggest? How does our collective sense of the problem compare with what others have said about it?). Glatthorn suggests that by active listening, sharing, and reflection, teachers learn from a healthy tension between personal and external knowledge and from attempting to integrate the two types of knowledge. The third stage explores future actions (How does the discussion inform future teaching plans? What actions might be taken as a result of increased awareness of the problem and reflection about possible actions?). Depending on the interests of the group, this stage could focus on the needs of individual teachers or on implications for the entire school.

This model is a reasonable one for exploring topics like the pros and cons of ability grouping; however, discussion groups might have to explore and adopt new models that support their inquiry, especially topics that deal with personal values. For example, if teachers are sharing insights about why they decided to become (or remain) a teacher, they might want to examine their own feelings in depth before reading literature reviews (Brookhart & Freeman, 1992) or before exploring the personal examples of how other teachers' decisions have evolved (Bullough, 1992).

One possibility for such groups would be a general discussion organized around understanding the dynamics of and improving teacher-parent communication. At one level, teachers might want to consider their own role in minimizing contact with families. As Weinstein and Mignano (1993) indicate, there are various reasons why teachers are reluctant to involve families in school activities—or even to maintain contact with parents. For example, simply calling each parent in a class of 30 and spending only 10 minutes on the phone would require that teachers spend a minimum of five hours on the telephone, assuming teachers do not have to call parents back repeatedly in order to reach them. Calling parents would be an additional demand on a workload that often does not leave teachers time to grade papers adequately, let alone design and undertake new activities. Teachers are aware of their time commitments and are sometimes reluctant to seek parental involvement because they recognize that parents also have pressing responsibilities.

Hence, teachers might profitably spend time identifying their expectations and those of parents that might reduce effective communication and develop goals and strategies for productive collaboration.

Clearly, countless topics could be used for professional discussions (computers in the classroom, dealing with diversity, enhancing bilingual programs, portfolio grading, etc.).

Curriculum Development   According to Glatthorn (1987), curriculum development involves cooperative activity in which teachers enhance the district's curriculum guides (e.g., English teachers might create a unit on local or regional dialects). Others have suggested additional ways for teachers to work on curriculum issues. Mitman et al. (1984) concluded that too little attention is given to the processes of science (conducting experiments, making and testing inferences) and too much time is spent on low-level memorization. Their work suggests that it is valuable to study curriculum materials to determine the extent to which the curriculum encourages thinking versus memorization. Teachers might profitably exchange ideas about textbooks, assignments, learning stations, learning kits, computer labs, problem sets, quizzes, tests, unit reports, and so on.

In addition to analyzing materials, teachers can also help one another by developing and sharing materials. For example, teachers might design clever ways to begin selected science units with experiments or assignments that have practical value to students. Developing such units takes time, and if teachers worked together they could have more time to develop a few themes in greater depth. In most schools, teachers working in isolation are so busy getting ready for the next day or unit that they do not have sufficient time for curriculum development.

Peer Observation   Peer observation, or peer supervision, as Glatthorn (1987) refers to it, is a process in which classroom observation is used to improve teaching (as we have discussed earlier in the chapter). The observation is data based and focuses on the teacher's own goals. Under the right conditions—teachers know what information they want, and peers are sensitive—peer feedback encourages teachers to improve their performance (see Roper & Hoffman, 1986). Moreover, the teachers who observe may gain as much as those who are observed (Sparks, 1986).

Peer Coaching   According to Glatthorn, peer coaching is similar to peer observation but involves some key differences. Peer observation suggests more choice for individual teachers with regard to what will be observed. In contrast, peer coaching is usually based on a staff development theme (often selected by district staff or administrators). That is, teachers would be given theoretical orientation to a model or set of skills, would observe the model or skills being implemented, and then would try to implement the model or skills while receiving frequent feedback.

Structure and follow-up appear to be vital to successful staff development efforts. Joyce (1981) argued that all of the following elements should be included in good staff development programs:

1. Presentation of theory or description of teaching skills or strategies
2. Modeling or demonstration of teaching skills or strategies
3. Practice in simulated and real classrooms
4. Structured and open-ended feedback about performance
5. Coaching for application—in-classroom, hands-on assistance in transferring new knowledge and skills to the classroom

Joyce (1981) estimates that fewer than 20 percent of the trainees master the skills of a training program if they do not receive feedback about their performance and if they are not coached in how to apply new skills. These conditions are often missing in staff development programs.

Action Research   Lieberman (1986) notes that action research can be used as a means for pursuing various goals, including increasing teacher reflection, collegial teacher interaction, and teacher status and efficacy; reducing the gap between doing research and implementing its results; and legitimating the professional value of practical classroom concerns.

According to McKernan (1987), action research is self-reflective problem solving that enables practitioners to better understand and solve problems in social settings. He suggests that the critical aspect of action research is that it allows practitioners to improve their performance by the direct study of their work. He notes that action research is defined differently by various persons and that some individuals define it narrowly.

We agree with McKernan that narrow definitions of how to conduct action research are self-defeating. Engaging in self-reflective inquiry independently or with peers is productive. Whether teachers collect data, compare and contrast curriculum units, or develop new tests is less important than the quality of action research—the opportunity to apply scholarship to a practical problem.

Our endorsement of the concept of action research suggests a view of teachers not only as recipients of knowledge but also as professionals who can produce knowledge for themselves and for others. Teachers are not necessarily expert researchers but are inquirers who see knowledge about curriculum and instruction as open to question (Llorens, 1994). In its best form, action research is a basis for not only curriculum reform but also professional development.

If action research is to be successful, teachers must have the time and resources to collect and organize data and to discuss implications of their findings. Although good teaching involves considerable art (e.g., timing, using an example that appeals to students' affective and aesthetic needs as well as cognitive ones), it also has a scientific basis (Good, 1996; Weinert & Helmke, 1995). As Billups and Rauth (1987) persuasively argue, if the public views teaching only as an art, with no scientific basis, it is unlikely to accept teaching as a profession. What is crucial about action research is the opportunity it provides for teachers to discuss ideas, reflect on teaching, and extend their knowledge of alternative practices. However, teachers need time if they are to engage in reflective scholarship (time to observe, make tapes, keep journals about their teaching, and discuss these ideas with colleagues—see *Prisoners of Time,* [National Education Comission on Time and Learning, 1994]).

SCHOOLS AS SOCIAL SYSTEMS

So far we have discussed the effects of professional collaboration and staff development on teachers' development. But there is also evidence that school settings influence teachers' expectations and performance.

Rosenholtz (1989) showed that the social structure of the workplace varies remarkably from school to school and that the social organization in which teaching takes place significantly affects teachers' commitment, leadership, cooperation, and the quality of both teachers' and students' school lives. She analyzed questionnaire data provided by over 1200 teachers from 78 elementary schools concerning social organizational variables within schools (e.g., teacher goal setting, teacher collaboration, etc.). Results indicated that perceptions about workplace conditions were generally similar among teachers within each school and that in schools where teachers perceived high goal consensus, they also reported high commitment, and so forth.

To understand the teacher perspective better, Rosenholtz interviewed randomly selected teachers in schools that represented particular types of social organization. These interviews revealed that individual teachers' reports were heavily influenced by the social environments in which they taught. For example, in high-consensus schools, only 8 percent of the teachers felt that "there is no time to talk," whereas in moderate- and low-consensus schools 11 and 20 percent of the teachers, respectively, felt this way. These data describing little time for teachers to talk in school are similar to findings presented in the 1989 OERI report, *What Works: Research About Teaching and Learning.* In some studies as many as 45 percent of the teachers reported *no* contact with one another during a school day, and another 32 percent reported infrequent contact with colleagues.

In comparing what high- and low-consensus teachers discussed (when they had the opportunity to talk), Rosenholtz found that only 4 percent of the high-consensus teachers mentioned that they complained about student behavioral problems when they talked with other teachers, but 54 percent reported discussing issues related to curriculum and instruction. In contrast, 28 percent of the teachers in low-consensus schools reported talking about student problems, whereas only 19 percent said they discussed curriculum and instruction.

In terms of leadership, teacher leaders in schools that had collaborative orientations were seen as helping other teachers to solve problems, but no teacher leader in schools that had isolated climates was seen as willing to help other teachers to solve problems. Among teachers who sought help, those whose comments focused on students' problems were largely relegated to dealing with problems reactively, whereas, those who focused on curriculum and instruction were able to use the skills and resources of other teachers proactively.

When asked, "Where do your new teaching ideas come from?" teachers in "learning-enriched" schools reported learning from a variety of sources. Ninety percent reported learning from other teachers, 45 percent from professional conferences, and 72 percent from their own problem solving and creativity. In the "learning-improved" schools only 32 percent of the teachers reported learning from other teachers, none from professional conferences, and only 4 percent from their own problem solving and creativity.

A key concept in Rosenholtz's theoretical position is uncertainty about how teaching can best be conducted to help students learn. A technical culture is uncertain if outcomes of work are unpredictable. Work in schools reflects an uncertain technical culture because there are few codified means for helping individual students achieve specific goals (e.g., learn problem solving or engage in complex, abstract synthesis). Thus, work in schools is seen as nonroutine, and the role of teaching is often fraught with uncertainty.

Organizational uncertainty has consequences for individual teachers, just as uncertainty affects behavior and beliefs in any social situation. When we are unable to control situations or to make positive things happen, we may question our ability or develop self-protective strategies (refuse to participate, not try) in order to avoid embarrassment. In schools where principals' or teachers' views of their job competence are sufficiently threatened, they may engage in self-defensive tactics to protect their own sense of self-worth.

Although uncertainty is endemic to teaching, it is the reaction of schools to uncertainty—the social culture in which teaching takes place—that determines whether the uncertainty becomes a disability (e.g., teachers develop routine ways to deal with situations that are not routine, deny problems, etc.) or a creative tension (teachers learn to discuss ideas and to collaborate to solve problems and to improve teaching). According to Rosenholtz, uncertainty is reduced by two conditions. First, teachers have the opportunity to obtain positive feedback about their abilities from peers and principals in a variety of ways. Second, teachers are provided with occasions to increase their technical knowledge (i.e., knowledge of teaching) and hence to gain more expertise in dealing with more situations. Rosenholtz argues that teachers' commitment to schools and to continued learning is heavily influenced by three workplace conditions: (1) task autonomy—teachers' sense that they can adapt instruction to their own contexts; (2) continuous opportunities for learning that provide them with greater mastery and control of the environment; and (3) "psychic" rewards that ensure their continuous contributions to schools (their opinions are requested, they have the opportunity to interact with peers, they receive needed information when appropriate, etc.).

THE GROWING IMPORTANCE OF STAFF DEVELOPMENT

The ideas we have presented thus far in the chapter are organized and written as informal suggestions that a group of teachers at a given school might implement. However, self-improvement programs can also be an important part of the official school district in-service program. Hart (1995) notes that staff development today is not the same as the in-service education of earlier decades, when teachers were thought to have primary responsibility for their professional development and self-renewal. There is, however, growing interest in broadening the concept of staff development and including teachers more in the decision-making process (Smylie, 1995). Today's teachers function in a complex environment of policy, law, regulation, special programs, and professional associations. Modern staff development usually involves groups of teachers working together with specialists, supervisors, administrators, parents, and university personnel. In some districts a large percentage of the discretionary budget is spent on staff development.

Despite the perceived importance of staff development, planning for it in some districts is not as systematic as it should be. In-service programs are frequently one-time events (a speaker is brought in, but little, if any, follow-up occurs), and there is too little attention to assessing program effects.

Improving the Entire School

A staff development program should first help teachers to address their individual needs. Once these needs are met, teachers can address broader school concerns through cooperative in-service programs. Ultimately, staff development should lead to the improvement of a school's entire teaching staff. Working collectively to improve is a potent determinant of the value of a staff development program. Little (1981) writes,

> First, the school as a workplace proves extraordinarily powerful. Without denying differences in individuals' skills, interests, commitment, curiosity, or persistence, the prevailing pattern of interactions and interpretations in each building demonstrably creates certain possibilities and sets certain limits. . . . We are led from a focus on professional improvement as an individual enterprise to improvement as particularly an organizational phenomenon. Some schools sustained shared expectations (norms) both for extensive collegial work and for analysis and evaluation of and experimentation with their practices; continuous improvement is a shared undertaking at schools, and these schools are the most adaptable and successful of the schools we have studied. (pp. 9, 10)

Little (1995) notes that in high schools school reform movements and general interest in enhancing teacher leadership have presented opportunity for teachers to engage in leadership issues outside of their traditional classroom responsibilities and subject-matter knowledge. As a case in point, she notes that in some schools there has been an increasing tendency to organize schools along subject specialism and to place students' and teachers' subject-matter knowledge as the front and center issue. However, in some high schools teachers are being organized in different ways in order to combat the impersonality and lack of connection that often exist in high schools. For example, in some high schools, teachers and students are organized in units or house clusters so that teachers teaching different subject matter are working with the same cohort of students. In these schools, the attempt is to try to focus more holistically on schooling and to look at learners as social beings as well as subject-matter specialists. Along these lines, some educators have developed explicit organizational strategies for enhancing the connectedness of schooling (see, for example, Sizer, 1992).

Staff Development in Effective Schools

The way in which resources in schools are used and the manner in which teachers are encouraged to interact with one another help to predict the overall effectiveness of a school (Good & Brophy, 1986; Little, 1981; Rosenholtz, 1989; Sizer, 1992). Hence, it is important to consider how best to develop the talents of the teaching staff. School and classroom processes must be considered at the same time in an attempt to identify processes and interrelationships that facilitate or hinder goals at each level. How can schools focus on high-quality instruction at the same time that individual teachers are helping students to develop their talents as effectively as possible? How can opportunities for practice, display, and reward of learning accomplishments be improved? How best can activities such as school newspapers, journals, and assemblies be used to supplement the efforts of teachers in individual classrooms (Good & Weinstein, 1986)? Although much research remains to be conducted in this area, some practical, innovative ideas have already emerged (Barth, 1990; Deal, 1985).

Teacher-Teacher Communication

Teachers must work jointly to build a favorable school environment. However, the most basic contribution that an individual teacher can make to a school is to develop an effective classroom. Only then can the teacher help other teachers understand what they are doing in their classrooms. There is no need for teachers in the same school or district to use similar styles and practices; there are many different ways to instruct effectively. Through working with peers, however, teachers can exchange ideas and improve instruction. If schools are to affect student outcomes significantly, teachers must be cognizant of how other teachers in the same school teach.

It is not uncommon to visit schools in which assignments of fifth graders are less demanding than those for third graders. Students in lower grades often have more choices of books to read, more freedom to work with other students, and more opportunities to plan work on assignments than students in higher grades. In some secondary schools, seventh graders write original essays, but ninth graders only answer questions about various works of history and English. Such discrepancies not only fail to challenge students to become progressively more independent and self-reliant but may lower older students' interest in schoolwork. Unfortunately, many teachers do not provide appropriately challenging assignments because they are unaware of what other teachers in the same school are doing.

What we are advocating here is broader than teachers simply sharing information, although the exchange of information is vital. We are also referring to a sense of community among teachers who try to develop appropriate, positive expectations for all students and to challenge students by designing tasks based on information obtained in carefully planned and coordinated discussions with other teachers, in-service training, and so on.

Teachers should have regular time built into their schedules to exchange ideas with other teachers. Table 11.3 summarizes some of the topics that teachers might discuss. Rosenholtz's (1989) work makes it clear that, in schools where little effective instruction takes place, teachers tend to communicate infrequently and to complain rather than to solve instructional problems when they do talk. In effective schools, teachers want to discuss professional concerns, including curriculum and instruction.

Table 11.3   STAGES OF INTERACTION CONTEXT

1. Nonteaching duties
   a. Clerical routines (attendance, forms)
   b. Simple management routines (lineup, etc.)
   c. Playground supervision
   d. Lunchroom supervision
2. Materials
   a. Seatwork assignments
   b. Homework assignments
   c. Laboratory assignments
   d. Daily quizzes
   e. Unit tests
3. School-level meetings
   a. Committee meetings
   b. Before- and after-school duties
   c. Extracurricular activities
   d. Ceremonies, special events
4. Preactive teaching
   a. Lesson plans
   b. Evaluation plans
5. Adult relationships
   a. Principals
   b. Other teachers
   c. Parents
   d. Secretaries
   e. Other building staff members
   f. Outside administrators
   g. Board members
   h. Representatives of teacher organizations

6. Classroom management
   a. Getting/maintaining attention
   b. Responding to student misbehavior
   c. Task management—time allocation during seatwork
   d. Interruptions
   e. Student record keeping
7. Teacher behavior
   a. Lesson introduction
   b. Quality of teacher explanations
   c. Quality of questions asked
   d. Pace of lesson
   e. Appropriateness of assigned task
8. Student learning
   a. Student-initiated questions
   b. Student explanations
   c. Student responses
   d. Student understanding
   e Student interest
9. Explanatory mechanisms
   a. Motivation theory
   b. Development theory
   c. Learning theory
   d. Instructional theory
   e. Classroom management/organization theory
   f. Research on teaching

The Principal as Facilitator

One clear mandate from the effective schools literature is that principals need to be active leaders and to support the instructional efforts of teachers. Educators have increasingly urged that principals must be more than building and budget managers (Sergiovanni, 1994).

It is nevertheless important to have realistic expectations for principals because they are busy simply running their schools, and a typical day is filled with conflicts and interruptions. If teachers are interested in additional assistance and if administrators are able and willing to play a facilitative rather than merely an evaluative role, then principals and teachers can work together to improve instruction.

Principals can arrange for teachers to observe and provide feedback to one another. They can allow teachers to use in-service time for discussion, self-study groups, or action research—not just listening to lectures. Principals can facilitate self-study efforts by soliciting funds to buy appropriate video equipment and by scheduling videotaping so that optimum use can be made of it.

Building on Teachers' Interests

When teachers find in-service training programs boring and a waste of time, it is usually because the programs are unrelated to their needs. Much time and effort are currently spent developing curricula that are more interesting to students and allow them more opportunity to pursue topics collaboratively. Perhaps corresponding emphasis should be placed on identifying ways for teachers to become more active in the development of in-service training programs that meet their needs and interests rather than subject them to a passive role. Allowing teachers to use in-service time to engage in independent self-improvement activities, either as individuals or in groups, would be valuable.

After teachers begin to work on self-improvement, they are in a position to advise the principal about the type of university consultant who would facilitate their program. Teachers who plan their own in-service training typically take the task seriously and work earnestly to develop useful programs. As a resource specialist and facilitator, the principal can aid immeasurably by supplying teachers with copies of recent books and journals that focus on classroom practice, research, and theory.

The Principal's Role

Observing Classrooms   Many principals have been trained primarily as managers rather than as instructional leaders; hence, some of them do not have the skills necessary to observe teachers and to provide them with information about their classroom behavior. Most teachers welcome ideas from principals about how to improve their work, but they rarely receive them. The average teacher is visited by a supervisor only once a year and then receives only general and vague feedback. In contrast, principals who are good supervisors frequently visit classrooms and help teachers to improve by giving feedback that is of interest and value to teachers. Such principals encourage teachers to come to them for help without branding these teachers as "weak." Principals need to develop skills for this role by reading recent books on teaching, curriculum, and supervision. Even principals who are adequate observers will gain by allowing teachers to assume more responsibility for self-evaluation and improvement of teaching.

Feedback to Individual Teachers   An interesting question for future research is how principals influence instructional behavior of teachers. It is not enough simply to observe in classrooms—principals must provide teachers with appropriate and useful information in a sensitive fashion. Many interesting issues merit exploration. How do principals communicate expectations and establish instructional priorities? If principals encourage teachers to determine their own instructional goals, how do principals become aware of each teacher's goals and how do they monitor and provide feedback about progress? Dwyer et al. (1982) provide a helpful profile that characterizes effective principals as *active*. Considering that effective principals are more visible to teachers and students in their schools, it is important to know whether or not their decisions and actions are related to student progress. For example, when and how often do principals visit particular classrooms? Do successful principals spend more time with teachers they believe to be average, or do they observe less capable teachers more closely? How specific is the feedback they provide to teachers? On what topics do conferences focus? Do effective principals discuss curriculum and instruction, or do they talk only about general issues of classroom management, resources, and human relations?

We believe that what is critical is not the frequency of teacher-principal interaction but the nature of the interaction and whether it leads to more thoughtful instruction. Table 11.4 illustrates that principals can communicate their expectations to teachers in various ways.

Stimulating Teachers' Growth   Although principals must build a school climate and an instructional program, they cannot lose sight of the need for teachers to have flexibility and to function as decision makers. Principals can help classrooms function more productively by making teaching more satisfying and stimulating—a profession rather than an occupation that requires the performance of a limited number of classroom skills.

Furthermore, it is important that principals involve teachers in discussing and planning school as well as classroom change. Schools where teachers engage in considerable job-related discussion and share in decisions about instructional programs and staff development are more effective than schools where decisions are made by rule-bound bureaucratic procedures (Barth, 1990; Schlechty & Vance, 1983). Thus, one challenge confronting principals is how to provide teachers with the time to reflect and grow.

Bruce Joyce (Brandt, 1987) points out that teachers need more than one period to prepare for five or six teaching periods and that time for planning must increase if teachers' roles expand. Joyce argues that to provide more time for teacher reflection, students must spend considerably more time working independently. However, he adds that if teachers are to have time to develop more complex lessons that stimulate student thinking, students must be prepared to accept the extra responsibility for their own learning.

Obviously, teaching students to assume more responsibility for independent study and self-evaluation also takes instructional time (Rohrkemper & Corno,

Table 11.4 PRINCIPALS' COMMUNICATION OF COMPETENCY EXPECTATIONS TO INDIVIDUAL TEACHERS

1. Classroom visitation
   a. Frequency of classroom visitation
   b. Frequency of feedback conferences
   c. Types of exchanges—social versus instructional
   d. Content focus (to the extent that interactions focus on instruction, what is the content of these interactions?)
2. Opportunity to have contact with other teachers
   a. Be visited by other teachers
   b. Visit other teachers
   c. Visit teachers in other schools
   d. Planning time with other teachers
3. Resource allocation
   a. Equipment budget
   b. Materials budget
   c. Free time/extra assignments
   d. Availability of substitutes so teachers can participate in in-service workshops
   e. Active voice in how in-service funds will be used
4. Leadership roles
   a. Principal selects teachers to represent school at district or state meeting
   b. Teacher serves as chair of committee (e.g., textbook selection)
   c. Principal solicits teachers' opinions privately and publicly
5. Curriculum teaching assignment
   a. Principal assigns teachers advanced sections
   b. Principal assigns honor students to these teachers
   c. Teacher has free period at advantageous time

1988). Thus, the best uses of independent study or other instructional approaches (computerized instruction, parent volunteers, more classroom teachers, etc.) to increase release time for teachers are not clear. However, principals who can find some extra time for teachers to plan and communicate with peers will be providing some of the necessary conditions for expanding teachers' roles—and eventually improving student learning.

TEACHER EVALUATION

The purpose of this chapter is to discuss ideas for stimulating professional growth and development of teachers. It is not our purpose to discuss the formal evaluation system that school districts impose for tenure and other accountability purposes (for more information about this topic, see Gifford & O'Conner, 1992; Good, 1996; House, 1986; and Millman & Darling-Hammond, 1990). However, we would be remiss if we did not comment on a few issues.

First, it is important to emphasize that formal evaluation systems can erode teachers' professional development programs. For example, the goals of an evaluation system may be in conflict with professional growth and development intentions. For example, evaluation systems can be in place to (a) help beginning teachers grow, or (b) identify beginning teachers who need to be dismissed from the profession. Similarly, evaluation systems can be in place to (1) identify veteran teachers who need either remediation or dismissal, or (2) provide professional growth and development for relatively inexperienced teachers, and (3) offer professional growth and development for more experienced and more capable teachers.

Traditional systems of evaluation have often prevented administrators and teachers from focusing on classroom instruction and how to improve students' learning opportunities. Good (1996) has recommended the following principles for consideration in building an evaluation system: (1) developing an environment of respect and trust; (2) promoting cooperation and collegial sharing of knowledge; (3) developing the full potential of teachers by providing important continuing opportunities for continuous learning; (4) promoting staff empowerment involvement; (5) achieving excellence in individual teacher performance and performance across the school; (6) developing leadership capabilities of all teachers; and (7) communicating effectively with parents and patrons in the broader community.

It is extremely important for school districts to assure that the accountability system does not undermine professional growth. Teachers, especially experienced teachers, consider evaluation systems which are primarily designed to identify incompetence (or minimum competence) as punitive, limiting, and inconsistent with teacher improvement and empowerment. A good evaluation system should help all teachers to reflect on their practice and to grow professionally. Ironically, new incentive plans or professional growth programs sometimes inadvertently exaggerate this problem by promoting work on activities other than classroom teaching and professional development (see Henson & Hall, 1992).

We agree with Dillon-Peterson (1986) that administrators need to trust teachers to know what is good for them and to allow teachers more opportunity for planning and evaluating in-service programs. Teachers can assume more responsibility for self-growth and self-evaluation when given appropriate training, support, and time. Although administrators have considerable responsibility for teacher evaluation, effective administrators involve teachers in this process and use their professional knowledge to good advantage.

RECENT DEVELOPMENTS IN TEACHING

Two recent developments have enriched teachers' opportunities for professional growth: (1) the attempt to differentiate teachers' career roles (master teacher programs, career ladders/school management teams, etc.), and (2) the growing involvement of teachers in beginning teacher induction programs.

The Master Teacher

There has been some interest in differentiating the work of teaching and in designating some teachers as master teachers. In part this effort is intended to attract and retain good teachers by rewarding teacher effectiveness. According to Griffin (1985b), there are two dominant ways to describe and identify a master teacher.

The first is based on a "better than" assumption: One teacher engages in essentially the same activities as another but is judged to be better at accomplishing those activities. This approach raises questions about the specification of criteria for evaluating performance, as well as about the objectivity, validity, and reliability of human judgments in a complex social situation.

A second conception of the master teacher that Griffin describes is based on a "more than" perspective. In this view, the master teacher, who may or may not engage in traditional teaching, performs specialized functions in schools and classrooms (National Education Association, 1983). For example, the master teacher may plan curriculum for a group of other teachers, monitor student progress, formulate and administer evaluation schemes, or serve as a mentor by helping beginning teachers with special instructional or curricular needs.

Griffin believes that master teacher plans may increase the professional status of teachers, but only if these plans move away from narrow definitions of good teaching and provide greater freedom for teachers to make curriculum decisions. In this view, proposals that differentiate teachers on the basis of varied role expectations have more promise than ones that assume a few teachers can perform presumably key teaching tasks better than others. This conception of effectiveness holds that mastery is supported by knowledge and skills that are accessible to all practitioners; not just the qualities of a few extraordinary teachers (see also Smylie, 1995).

Career Ladder Plans

In many districts teacher incentive or professional growth plans are called career ladder plans. As Hart (1995) notes, career ladder plans can have various notable features, including (1) increased use of teacher expertise in making curriculum decisions in the school, (2) providing teachers with a staged career, (3) providing a basis for meaningful and innovative changes in curriculum and instruction, and (4) providing teachers with increased authority and financial rewards.

Henson and Hall (1992) illustrate that plans to provide teachers with more professional status and rewards do not always translate into successful academic programs. In their study of career ladder plans, they found that plans created considerable conflict between teachers, instructional leaders, and principals. Recent teacher leadership policies have argued for more authority for teachers to participate in the decision-making structure of schools. As Hart (1995) notes, these policies come under various titles such as site-based management, participative decision making, and shared governance.

Hart (1995) writes:

> The isolation of teaching and teachers' separation from central educational decisions outside their immediate classrooms receive past and ongoing criticism. Shared decision-making plans that structure participation on the broadest possible scale address many of the egalitarian and communitarian values expressed by critics of hierarchy. They bring teachers out of their classrooms and into the arena of visible work, problem solving, and resource allocation. Buy-in and commitment from teachers are goals identified by advocates. They also believe better decisions will result, leading to school improvement and increased student learning. (p. 16)

Sometimes these models work well. However, as Hart and others have noted, these models are vulnerable to manipulation by the school principal and may create a powerful teacher group that is organized more in terms of their political ability than their expertise in curriculum and instruction. To work well, extant beliefs in the importance of teacher leadership must be constructed in ways that allow teachers and administrators to be active collaborators. Meier (1995) describes her staff-run school in the following way:

> We remained a "staff-run" school, but not a principal-less collective, as we had originally envisioned. Although formally I was still "just" a teacher, I was no longer full-time in a classroom of kids. The bottom line remained: the staff (and the parents who chose to join us) continued to be central to all decisions, big and small, the final plenary body directing the life of the school. Nothing was or has ever been "undiscussable," although we have learned not to discuss everything—at least not all the time. This has actually meant more time for discussing those issues that concern us most: how children learn, how our classes really work, what changes we ought to be making and on what basis. We have also become better observers of our own practice, better collectors of information, documenters of practice as well as users of expertise. We thus have more to bring to the collective table. Yet the complexities of school governance—by whom and how decisions are made, questions of "we" and "they"—still crop up from time to time to bedevil us. How teachers can take collective responsibility for supervising each other, for determining school rules, disciplinary consequences, and school schedules, as well as for the trickier issue of standards and evaluation, while also maintaining sufficient classroom autonomy and focus has not been resolved. We console ourselves with Winston Churchill's paean to democracy as "the worst form of government except all those other forms that have been tried from time to time." (pp. 25–26)

Beginning Teachers

The transition from preservice to in-service teaching can be traumatic as teachers move from the idealistic world of the college classroom to the reality of everyday teaching. For a variety of reasons, teachers may experience role-adjustment problems. New teachers may experience some problems because they have had only general training and are thus not ready for a specific job. For example, one may student-teach in an inner-city first-grade classroom but then be assigned to teach full time in a sixth-grade class in a suburban school district. For this reason, we recommend that teachers-in-training spend time in various types of schools.

There are other reasons why teachers may have difficulties when they start to teach, and there are some problems that teachers cannot prepare for in advance. First-year teachers are not only becoming teachers and learning to deal with students, parents, and other adults; they are also assuming new responsibilities (making new friends, paying off loans, etc.). Thus, anxiety and role conflict are expected at this time.

Goodson (1991) argues that one of the problems for beginning teachers is that they are typically asked to implement a curriculum that has been developed by others. In addition to learning to negotiate the school, a new role, and new students, now teachers must simultaneously implement an unfamiliar curriculum and also develop a teaching style that fits their particular context. Bullough (1992) expresses the potential dilemma this way: "At times the two demands are contradictory: the adopted curriculum prohibits establishing a satisfying role; and the desired role makes it difficult to implement the established curriculum" (p. 239).

Becoming a teacher affects individuals in different ways. Some teachers alter their behavior after their initial teaching experiences. Bergmann et al. (1976) found that 57 percent of beginning teachers reported that they changed their initial student-focused teaching to a more traditional instructional model. A more student-centered style can be effective, but many new teachers do not have the necessary management and curriculum skills to maintain such an approach. Moskowitz and Hayman (1974) reported that many beginning teachers ignore too much misbehavior (seemingly in the hope that, if not acknowledged, it will disappear).

Reported Problems   Veenman (1984) reviewed the problems beginning teachers reported in 83 studies. The most serious problem reported was *classroom discipline*. The next most salient problem was *motivating students*. Other frequently reported problems were dealing with individual differences among students, assessing students, and communicating with parents.

Despite the fact that many teachers report problems, most teachers enter teaching successfully. Thus, many beginning teachers will be ready to profit from teachers' advice about new curriculum or new instructional ideas (not just survival skills).

Different Needs   Beginning teachers with different skills and needs react to teaching in different ways. Glassberg (1980) found that more mature beginning teachers emphasized the need to understand individual students and to be flexible, whereas less mature novices held a more restricted view of teaching. Thus, new teachers may need different types of in-service training.

There are several models for analyzing the development level of teachers (e.g., Hunt & Joyce, 1981; Sprinthall & Thies-Sprinthall, 1983). The first explicit theory describing teacher development was proposed by Fuller (1969) and elaborated by Fuller and Bown (1975). The first stage of teaching is concern with *survival*. (Will I be liked? Can I control students? Will others think I am a good teacher?) The second stage is concern with the *teaching situation* (methods, materials, etc.), and the third stage reflects concern with *students* (their learning and needs). The early, self-centered concerns are considered less mature than later, more student-centered concerns. However, until teachers deal with early concerns (Will I survive? Can I refine my teaching skills?), they will have less ability to respond to individual students' needs.

Realistic resources, relevant experience, content knowledge, and good supervision (i.e., during student teaching) can help many new teachers at least to be past the survival stage when they enter the classroom. Teachers need to work through a variety of personal (Will anybody listen to me?) and procedural teaching concerns (how to use the computer, how to structure small-group instruction) before they can devote most of their attention to the effects of teaching (i.e., student learning).

The advice and strategies for self-growth we have provided are useful for all teachers, even those who have taught successfully for several years. However, the recommendations are especially important for beginning teachers. Unfortunately, too many teachers who experience difficulty deny their problems (at least to others) and fail to avail themselves of the experience of other teachers and supervisors. New teachers need to use discretion in deciding which teachers to approach for information; some teachers are better sources of information and are more empathic than others, and obviously student teachers and beginning teachers need to exercise tact when they ask for assistance. However, a broader, more pervasive problem is failing to obtain help.

New teachers must recognize that their questions naturally differ from those of successful, experienced teachers. Some beginning teachers believe that they should "think" like veteran teachers and hence are hesitant to ask questions. However, all teachers—experienced as well as inexperienced—should obtain knowledge about any topic of concern. Beginning teachers ask many questions about management, planning, and motivation (experienced teachers also discuss motivation and management), but in time, beginners' concerns move from general class issues to adapting instructional and motivational models to the needs of specific students.

Huling-Austin (1986) argues that induction programs can help in five areas:

1. Improve the teaching performance of beginning teachers
2. Increase the retention rate of promising beginning teachers during the induction year
3. Screen out the least promising teachers
4. Promote personal and professional well-being by fostering each teacher's professional self-esteem
5. Satisfy mandated requirements related to induction and certification

She notes, however, that it is *unreasonable* to expect induction programs to (1) overcome major problems that exist in schools, such as misplacement of teachers (teaching in an area that they have not been trained for), overcrowded classrooms, or too many classroom preparations; (2) develop into successful teachers those who enter the classroom without the necessary ability and personal characteristics to be competent professionals; and (3) substantially improve the long-range retention of teachers if changes are not made in the broader educational system as well (improved status in the eyes of society, better salaries and working conditions).

Mentor Teachers' Roles   In many districts, experienced and successful teachers are appointed to help beginning and less experienced teachers adjust to their role in the school and improve their effectiveness in promoting student learning. Mentor teachers need realize that beginning teachers' needs may be different from their own. Beginning teachers have more concerns about self and classroom management, whereas other teachers have more concerns about student learning (i.e., beginning teachers' views of teaching may be different from those of other teachers until they develop a better understanding of curriculum content and classroom procedures).

Mentors will be most helpful if they heed the advice presented earlier in this chapter: allowing beginning teachers to structure their own self-improvement plans and helping by providing appropriate feedback. Mentors must also realize that many different teaching styles can be effective.

Zeichner and Tabachnick (1985) note some advantages to loose supervision of first-year teachers. For example, some first-year teachers they observed maintained their own styles and perspectives despite a differing school philosophy (Tabachnick & Zeichner, 1984). Mentors, supervisors, and principals should offer teachers assistance, but beginning teachers (and student teachers, for that matter) should not be guided so rigidly that their independent role in adapting content and designing classroom environments is eroded.

Hart (1995) has noted that mentor plans have advantages and disadvantages depending on the quality of implementation and the particular context. For example, mentor teachers often benefit from extra income, and also from the opportunity to learn leadership skills as they exercise influence over the growth of new professionals. As Hart notes, mentor teachers have responsibilities for observing, counseling, advising, and generally assisting other teachers.

Using mentors in order to capitalize on teachers' expertise and to use it as a resource for beginning teachers is a much better approach than the "sink or swim" philosophy that was followed in too many schools until recently. Thus, under the best circumstances, mentor programs provide valuable resources for new teachers and provide rich learning opportunities for experienced teachers.

Ironically, teacher mentors are typically assigned to teachers who work in other schools and thus, mentors find little opportunity to work with new teachers during the actual school day. Hart (1995) has noted that under some circumstances, mentor teacher and career ladder plans may have negative consequences. For example, they introduce a new differential in teacher status, benefiting some teachers more than others, and in some circumstances, may establish new hierarchies and diminish collegial relationships among teachers. Like most things, the value of the experience depends on the particular people, the quality of the interactions, and the context. As Hart has noted, teacher mentors can be tormentors under certain circumstances.

Mentoring Good Planning

We illustrate the complexity of mentoring to highlight potential differences between beginning and more experienced teachers. We use the example of planning, but beginning and more experienced teachers are apt to show differences concerning many other aspects of teaching.

For many years, those writing on the topic of planning cited Ralph Tyler's (1950) work as a good example of appropriate planning for classroom instruction. Tyler's linear model consists of four steps: (1) specify objectives, (2) select learning activities, (3) organize learning activities, and (4) specify evaluation procedures. Tyler's model was accepted at face value for about 20 years before researchers examined directly the planning process that teachers used and compared what teachers actually did with their plans.

Borko and Niles (1987) discuss the implications of classroom research on planning for teachers-in-training (e.g., preservice teachers). They argue that preservice teachers can learn from research that planning typically focuses on subject matter and the selection of corresponding activities, and that teachers pay relatively little attention to objectives or evaluation. However, they note that if teachers are to use this information appropriately, they must understand *why* experienced teachers plan this way and why their plans include certain elements and exclude others. According to Borko and Niles, experienced teachers do not specify objectives because these are implied in the materials and curriculum guides. However, preservice teachers have not had as many opportunities as experienced teachers to work with these objectives and most likely will need to focus more on them.

Teachers should realize that it is natural for experienced teachers to use indirect means to determine which students have reached objectives for a particular lesson. Experienced teachers have a broader range of experience and a variety of procedures for receiving and interpreting information from students (e.g., the way they ask questions, examination of seatwork, etc.). Borko and Niles conclude that Tyler's model, which includes objectives and evaluation, may have more relevance for preservice and beginning teachers than for experienced teachers. Hence, it may be important for less experienced teachers to begin with a formal model for planning and later to adapt that model to their own classes. Mentor teachers need to expect and to accept the fact that beginning teachers may use different models from the ones other teachers use. Plans are valuable to the extent that they provide organization and direction for the teacher and students in the class; however, they can cause teachers to react rigidly to students and may impede creative responding. Simply put, plans need to be thorough but not rigid.

More generally, mentor teachers need to be sensitive to the fact that there are multiple ways to be effective in the classroom and that their role is to guide and advise, not prescribe practice.

DO LOOK BACK

Our intent here is to encourage you to look at your classroom behavior and to plan ways to make the classroom a more meaningful and exciting place. We have stressed that objective, improvement-oriented self-evaluation is difficult for many of us to engage in because we have not been trained to do it. Any significant new experience is always a challenge, and self-evaluation is no exception. Your first efforts to examine your instructional decisions will be difficult and perhaps frustrating. However, such analysis, when linked to systematic strategies for improving behavior, can lead to better teaching and the satisfaction that accompanies it.

We have included observation forms and materials to help you assess your behavior and plan new instructional strategies, but ultimately you and only you can evaluate the effects of your teaching. Do not avoid your responsibility by uncritically accepting someone else's advice or teaching philosophy.

Remember, a teaching strategy is good when two basic conditions are satisfied: (1) students understand and can apply key subject-matter concepts, and (2) students find the learning process so interesting and rewarding that they initiate efforts on their own and can progressively assume more responsibility for planning and evaluating their work.

It is up to you to identify instructional plans and decisions that meet these criteria and develop a teaching style with which you feel so comfortable that you look forward to your work. You are the teacher, and *you* must assume responsibility for establishing a learning atmosphere that is stimulating and exciting for you as well as for students. If you do not enjoy class, your students will not either!

SUMMARY

We have urged you to assess your strengths and weaknesses as a teacher by collecting objective information on your classroom decisions, behavior, task selection, and their effects on students. A good way to begin is to consider the concepts and guidelines presented throughout this book, listing those that you are using effectively, those that you need to work on or have not tried, and those for which you are uncertain about your performance. The question marks can be reduced by arranging to obtain feedback. You can collect information about some behaviors by keeping records, consulting your students, or arranging to be audiotaped or videotaped. For many behaviors, however, it will be necessary for you to arrange to be observed by someone who agrees to visit your classroom and conduct focused observation designed to obtain objective information about the behaviors of interest to you. Your choices of content and what to examine briefly or in depth can be compared in dialogue groups with those of peers.

Observational feedback is also important in providing you with information about the effects of new curriculum plans or teaching techniques that you are trying for the first time. We have offered suggestions for enlisting the help of peer teachers and principals in self-improvement efforts and, in particular, for working with other teachers in cooperative self-help groups. The group approach is likely to be especially valuable, provided that each teacher sets individual priorities and goals, focuses on a few issues at a time, and receives balanced and honest feedback. Self-help programs that follow these guidelines have been popular with teachers and have helped them to increase their awareness of and control over their classroom behavior. We have also argued that at least a part of a school district's in-service program should be organized around the needs of individual teachers and designed to promote professional satisfaction and growth.

Finally, we have discussed two current trends that contribute to the professionalization of teaching: professional development programs and beginning teacher induction programs.

SUGGESTED ACTIVITIES AND QUESTIONS

1. Read some of the literature on teachers' personal stories about their involvement in changing their educational practice (see, for example, Gitlin et al., 1992). How do teachers' personal stories or action research differ from the use of other types of research information? In general, how would you compare and

contrast the systemization of a given teacher's knowledge based on her or his experience, the integration of experience across several teachers (perhaps four or five teachers relating their common and differing experiences), and formal research? In this chapter, we have taken the position that all of these sources of knowledge are data. Do you agree or disagree?

2. Try to interview briefly three or so teachers who are relatively inexperienced (first- or second-year teachers) and a few teachers who have several years of experience (eight or more years). Compare and contrast their attitudes about in-service activities. Would one group want more responsibility for in-service activities than another? How much time are they willing to devote? What topics and strategies would the teachers like to be involved in? To what extent is experience a relevant factor in planning in-service programs?

3. The authors in this chapter argue that teachers should take progressively more responsibility for their own in-service education. How realistic is this? What percent of teachers would want to actively participate in in-service activity if it were voluntary? Would participation vary according to type of organizational setting (elementary, middle school, high school, rural, suburban, etc.)?

4. Make a list of all the books and ideas you want to explore. Do not limit your selection to materials listed in this text. Rank the three things you most want to learn, which will serve as your in-service map. Compare your notes with other teachers', and if you have similar needs and interests, share material and collectively urge the principal to design in-service programs that will satisfy these needs.

5. Make a list of the two concepts or topics you believe are the most difficult for you to teach. Arrange to see other teachers present these topics, or discuss with other teachers how they teach these concepts.

6. Make a list of your teaching strengths and weaknesses. Make specific plans to improve your two weakest areas.

7. What are the possible advantages and disadvantages of using parents or retired, capable adults as observers who supply teachers with feedback about their behavior?

8. Why is it difficult for most of us to engage in self-evaluation?

9. How can teachers initiate self-improvement programs?

10. Should new teachers seek advice from veterans? If so, under what circumstances and in what manner?

11. As a teacher, how can you help your students to develop skills and attitudes for evaluating their own work nondefensively?

12. What are some of the dangers involved in having teachers evaluate other teachers? What are the advantages of peer evaluation?

13. What are your views about master teachers? What criteria are most important for teachers to satisfy if they are to become master teachers? What percentage of teachers should be able to become master teachers—only a few, or most? Why do you feel this way?

14. Reread the narratives in Chapter 1. If these teachers were members of your self-study team, what advice would you offer? Be specific.

15. What is the role of research in defining effective teaching? Can teachers be effective in one school district and not in another? How likely is it that teachers

might vary in effectiveness because districts use different criteria for judging effectiveness?

16. We have stressed the need for you to seek evaluative comments and to analyze your behavior if you are to grow and to improve. In that spirit, we seek your comments about this book. We would like to know how useful it is to you and about any deficiencies that can be remedied in future editions. We encourage you to write us (Tom Good, College of Education, University of Arizona, Tucson, AZ 85721; Jere Brophy, College of Education, Michigan State University, East Lansing, MI 48824) with your comments (What was your general reaction to the book? Is it relevant to teachers and future teachers? What topics are omitted that you believe should be included in future editions? What advice or suggestions do you disagree with, and why? Did we communicate negative expectations or provide contradictory advice, and if so, where and how? Were some sections of the book especially helpful, and why?). We will be delighted to receive your suggestions and criticisms and will give your comments serious consideration for the next edition.

REFERENCES

Anderson, C. (1983). The causal structure of stituations: The generation of plausible causal attributions as a function of the type of event situation. *Journal of Experimental Social Psychology, 19,* 185–203.

Anderson, D., & Biddle, B. (Eds.) (1991). *Knowledge for policy.* London: Falmer.

Ball, S., & Goodson, I. (Eds.). (1985). *Teachers' lives and careers.* London: Falmer Press.

Barber, L. (1990). Self-assessment. In J. Millman & L. Darling-Hammond (Eds.), *The new handbook of teacher evaluation: Assessing elementary and secondary school teachers* (pp. 216–228). Newbury Park, CA: Sage.

Barth, R. (1990). *Improving schools from within.* San Francisco, CA: Jossey-Bass.

Bergmann, C., Bernath, L., Holmann, I., Krieger, R., Mendel, G., & Theobald, G. (1976). *Schwierigkeiten junger Lehrer in der Berufspraxis.* Giessem: Zentrum fur Lehreraus-bildung der Justus Liebig-Universitat.

Biddle, B., & Anderson, D. (1986). Theory, methods, knowledge, and research on teaching. In M. C. Wittrock (Ed.), *Handbook of research on teaching* (3rd ed., pp. 230–254). New York: Macmillan.

Biddle, B., Good, T., & Goodson, I. (1996). *The international handbook of teachers and teaching.* New York: Kluwer.

Billups, L., & Rauth, M. (1987). Teachers and research. In V. Richardson-Koehler (Ed.), *Educators' handbook: A research perspective* (pp. 167–187). White Plains, NY: Longman.

Borko, H., & Niles, J. (1987). Descriptions of teacher planning. In V. Richardson-Koehler (Ed.), *Educators' handbook: A research perspective* (pp. 167–187). White Plains, NY: Longman.

Brandt, R. (1987). On teachers coaching teachers: A conversation with Bruce Joyce. *Educational Leadership, 44,* 12–17.

Brookhart, S., & Freeman, D. (1992). Characteristics of entering teacher candidates. *Review of Educational Research, 62,* 37–60.

Brophy, J. (1988). Research on teacher effects: Uses and abuses. *Elementary School Journal, 89*(1), 3–22.

Bullough, R., Jr. (1992). Beginning teacher curriculum decision making, personal teaching metaphors, and teacher education. *Teaching and Teacher Education, 8,* 239–252.

Darling-Hammond, L., Bullmaster, M., & Cobb, V. (1995). Rethinking teacher leadership through professional development schools. *Elementary School Journal, 96,* 87–106.

Deal, T. (1985). The symbolism of effective schools. *Elementary School Journal, 85,* 601–620.

Deci, E., & Ryan, R. (1985). *Intrinsic motivation and self-determination in human behavior.* New York: Plenum.

Dillon-Peterson, B. (1986). Trusting teachers to know what is good for them. In K. Zumwalt (Ed.), *Improving teaching.* Alexandria, VA: Association for Supervision and Curriculum Development.

Dwyer, D., Lee, G., Rowan, B., & Bossert, S. (1982). *The principal's role in instructional management: Five participant observation studies of principals in action.* San Francisco: Far West Laboratory for Educational Research and Development.

Eash, M., & Rasher, S. (1977). Mandated desegregation and improved achievement: Longitudinal study. *Phi Delta Kappan, 58,* 394–397.

Fraser, B. (1986). *Classroom environment.* London: Croom Helm.

Fuller, F. (1969). Concerns of teachers: A developmental conceptualization. *American Educational Research Journal, 6,* 207–226.

Fuller, F., & Bown, O. (1975). Becoming a teacher. In K. Ryan (Ed.), *Teacher education* (Seventy-fourth yearbook of the National Society for the Study of Education). Chicago: University of Chicago Press.

Gifford, B., & O'Conner, M. (Eds.). (1992). *Cognitive approaches to assessment.* Boston: Kluwer-Nijhoff.

Gitlin, A., Bringhurst K., Burns, M., Cooley, V., Myers, B., Price, K., Russell, R., & Tiess, P. (1992). *Teachers' voices for school change: An introduction to education research.* New York: Teachers College Press.

Gitlin, A., & Smyth, J. (1989). *Teacher evaluation: Educative alternatives.* New York: Falmer.

Glassberg, S. (1980). *A view of the beginning teacher from a developmental perspective.* Paper presented at the annual meeting of the American Educational Research Association, Boston.

Glatthorn, A. (1987). Cooperative professional development: Peer-centered options for teacher growth. *Educational Leadership, 44,* 31–35.

Glickman, C. (1990). *Supervision of instruction* (2nd ed.). Needham Heights, MA: Allyn & Bacon.

Good, T. (1996). Teaching effects and teacher evaluation. In J. Sikula, T. Buttery, & E. Guiton (Eds.), *Handbook of research on teacher education* (2nd ed). New York: Macmillan.

Good, T., & Brophy, J. (1974). Changing teacher and student behavior: An empirical investigation. *Journal of Educational Psychology, 66,* 390–405.

Good, T., & Brophy, J. (1986). School effects. In M. C. Wittrock (Ed.), *Handbook of research on teaching* (3rd ed., pp. 570–604). New York: Macmillan.

Good, T., & Mulryan, C. (1990). Teacher ratings: A call for teacher control and self-evaluation. In J. Millman & L. Darling-Hammond (Eds.), *Handbook of teacher evaluation* (2nd ed.). Beverly Hills, CA: Sage.

Good, T., & Weinstein, R. (1986). Teacher expectations: A framework for exploring classrooms. In K. Zumwalt (Ed.), *Improving teaching* (pp. 63–86). Alexandria, VA: Association for Supervision and Curriculum Development.

Goodson, I. (1992) Studying teachers' lives: Problems and possibilities. In I. Goodson (Ed.). *Studying teachers' lives* (pp. 234–249). New York, Teachers College Press.

Gordon, S. (1992). Paradigms, transitions, and the new supervision. *Journal of Curriculum and Supervision, 8*(11), 62–76.

Griffin, G. (January-February, 1985a). Teacher induction: Research issues. *Journal of Teacher Education, 36,* 44.

Griffin, G. (1985b). The school as a workplace and the master teacher concept. *Elementary School Journal, 86*, 1–16.

Griffin, G. (1995). Influences of shared decision making on school and classroom activity: Conversations with five teachers. *Elementary School Journal, 96*, 29–46.

Guild, P., & Garger, S. (1985). *Marching to different drummers*. Alexandria, VA: Association for Supervision and Curriculum Development.

Hart, A. (1995). Reconceiving school leadership: Emergent views. *Elementary School Journal, 96*, 9–28.

Henson, B., & Hall, P. (1992). Linking performance evaluation and career ladder programs: Reactions of teachers and principals in one district. *Elementary School Journal, 93*(4), 323–353.

House, E. (Ed.). (1986). *New directions in educational evaluation*. London: Falmer.

Huling-Austin, L. (1986). What can and cannot reasonably be expected from teacher induction programs. *Journal of Teacher Education, 37*, 2–5.

Hunt, D., & Joyce, B. (1981). Teacher trainee personality and initial teaching style. In B. Joyce, C. Brown, & L. Peck (Eds.), *Flexibility in teaching*. New York: Longman.

Joyce, B. (1981). A memorandum for the future. In B. Dillon-Peterson (Ed.), *Staff development/organization development*. Alexandria, VA: Association for Supervision and Curriculum Development.

Kepler, K. (1977). *Descriptive feedback: Increasing teacher awareness, adopting research techniques.* Paper presented at the annual meeting of the American Educational Research Association, New York.

Lieberman, A. (1986). Collaborative research: Working with, not working on . . . *Educational Leadership, 43*, 28–33.

Little, J. (1981). *School success and staff development in urban desegregated schools: A summary of recently completed research.* Paper presented at the annual meeting of the American Educational Research Association, Los Angeles.

Little, J. (1995). Contested ground: The basis of teacher leadership in two restructuring high schools. *Elementary School Journal, 96*, 47–64.

Llorens, M. (Ed.), (1994). Action research: Are teachers finding their voice? *Elementary School Journal, 95*, 3–10.

Maeroff, G. (1988). *The empowerment of teachers*. New York: Teachers College Press.

Martin, M. (1973). *Equal opportunity in the classroom* (ESEA, Title III: Session A Report). Los Angeles: County Superintendent of Schools, Division of Compensatory and Intergroup Programs.

McCaslin, M., & Good, T. (1996). *Listening to students*. New York: HarperCollins.

McDaniel, T. (1981). The supervisor's lot: Dilemmas by the dozen. *Educational Leadership, 38*, 518–520.

McDonnell, L. (1985). Implementing low-cost school improvement strategies. *Elementary School Journal, 85*, 423–438.

McKernan, J. (1987). Action research and curriculum development. *Peabody Journal of Education, 64*, 6–19. [Special issue: Potential and practice of action research, Part I. Editors: D. Kyle & R. Hovda.]

Meier, D. (1995). *The power of their ideas: Lessons for America from a small school in Harlem.* Boston: Beacon Press,

Millman, J., & Darling-Hammond, L. (Eds.). (1990). *The new handbook of teacher evaluation: Assessing elementary and secondary school teachers*. Newbury Park, CA: Sage.

Mitman, A., Mergendoller, J., Packer, M., & Marchman, V. (1984). *Scientific literacy in seventh-grade life science: A study of perceptions and learning outcomes* (Final report). San Francisco: Far West Laboratory for Educational Research and Development.

Moskowitz, G., & Hayman, J. (1974). Interaction patterns of first-year, typical, and "best" teachers in inner-city schools. *Journal of Educational Research, 67,* 224–230.

National Education Association. (1983). *Statement by the National Education Association on excellence in education.* Paper presented to the House Budget Committee Task Force on Education and Employment, Washington, DC.

National Education Commission on Time and Learning. (1994, April). *Prisoners of time.* Washington, DC: U.S. Government Printing Office.

Pajak, E., & Glickman, C. (1989). Informational and controlling language in simulated supervising conferences. *American Educational Research Journal, 26,* 93–106.

Pambookian, H. (1976). Discrepancy between instructor and student evaluation of instruction: Effect on instruction. *Instructional Science, 5,* 63–75.

Richards, M. (1987). A teacher's action research study: The "bums" or "8H." *Peabody Journal of Education, 64,* 65–79. [Special issue: Potential and practice of action research, Part I. Editors: D. Kyle & R. Hovda.]

Rohrkemper, M., & Corno, L. (1988). Success and failure on classroom tasks: Adaptive learning and classroom teaching. *Elementary School Journal, 88,* 299–312.

Roper, S., & Hoffman, D. (1986). *Collegial support for professional improvement: The Stanford collegial evaluation program.* Eugene: University of Oregon, School Study Council.

Rosenholtz, S. (1989). *Teachers' workplace: The social organization of schools.* New York: Longman.

Russell, T., & Munby, H. (1992). *Teachers and teaching from classroom to reflection.* London: Falmer Press.

Schlechty, P., & Vance, V. (1983). Recruitment, selection, and retention: The shape of the teaching force. *Elementary School Journal, 83,* 469–487.

Sergiovanni, T. (1994). *Building community in schools.* San Francisco, CA: Jossey-Bass.

Sikula, J., & Buttery, T., & Guiton, E. (Eds). (1996). *Handbook of research on teacher education* (2nd ed). New York: Macmillan.

Sizer, T. (1992). *Horace's school: Redesigning the American high school.* Boston: Houghton Mifflin.

Smylie, M. (1992). Teachers' reports of their interactions with teacher leaders concerning classroom instruction. *Elementary School Journal, 93,* 85–98.

Smylie, M. (1995). New perspectives on teacher leadership. *Elementary School Journal, 96,* 3–8.

Sparks, G. (1986). The effectiveness of alternative training routines in changing teacher practices. *American Educational Research Journal, 23,* 217–225.

Spencer, D. (1984). The home and school lives of women teachers: Implications for staff development. *Elementary School Journal, 84,* 299–314.

Sprinthall, N., & Thies-Sprinthall, L. (1983). The teacher as an adult learner: A cognitive-developmental view. In G. A. Griffin (Ed.), *Staff development* (Eighty-second yearbook of the National Society for the Study of Education). Chicago: University of Chicago Press.

Stallings, J. (1986). Using time effectively: A self-analytic approach. In K. Zumwalt (Ed.), *Improving teaching.* Alexandria, VA: Association for Supervision and Curriculum Development.

Tabachnick, R., & Zeichner, K. (1984). The impact of the student teaching experience on the development of teacher perspectives. *Journal of Teacher Education, 35,* 28–36.

Tyler, R. (1950). *Basic principles of curriculum and instruction.* Chicago: University of Chicago Press.

Veenman, S. (1984). Perceived problems of beginning teachers. *Review of Educational Research, 54*(2), 143–178.

Weinstein, C. & Mignano, A., Jr. (1993). *Elementary classroom management: Lessons from research and practice.*

Weinert, F., & Helmke, A. (1995). Learning from wise Mother Nature or Big Brother Instructor: The wrong choice as seen from an educational perspective. *Educational Psychologist, 30,* 135–142.

Zeichner, K., & Tabachnick, R. (1985). The development of teacher perspectives: Social strategies and institutional control in the socialization of beginning teachers. *Journal of Education for Teachers, 7,* 1–25.

Zumwalt, K. (Ed.). (1986). *Improving teaching.* Alexandria, VA: Association for Supervision and Curriculum Development.

Name Index

Subject Index